D1492283

The Dictionary of

Important Ideas and Thinkers

The WITHDRAWN

WATERFORD CITY AND COUNTY

LIBRARIES

The
DICTIONARY

of

IMPORTANT IDEAS

and

THINKERS

CHRIS ROHMANN

HUTCHINSON
LONDON

Ref 103/01522268

Copyright © 2000 by Chris Rohmann

The right of Chris Rohmann to be identified as the author of this work has been asserted by him in accordance with the copyright Designs and Patents Act, 1988

All rights reserved

1 3 5 7 9 10 8 6 4 2

This book is sold subject to the condition that it shall not, by way of trade or otherwise, be lent, resold, hired out, or otherwise circulated without the publisher's prior consent in any form of binding or cover other than that in which it is published and without a similar condition including this condition being imposed on the subsequent purchaser

First published in the United Kingdom in 2001 by Hutchinson
The Random House Group Limited
20 Vauxhall Bridge Road, London, SW1V 2SA

Random House Australia (Pty) Limited
20 Alfred Street, Milsons Point, Sydney,
New South Wales 2061, Australia

Random House New Zealand Limited
18 Poland Road, Glenfield
Auckland 10, New Zealand

Random House (Pty) Limited
Endulini, 5a Jubilee Road, Parktown, 2193, South Africa

The Random House Group Limited Reg. No. 954009
www.randomhouse.co.uk

A CIP catalogue record for this book is available
from the British Library

Grateful acknowledgment is made to A. P. Watt Ltd. for permission to reprint an excerpt from "The White Man's Burden" by Rudyard Kipling. Reprinted by permission of A. P. Watt Ltd., on behalf of The National Trust for Places of Historic Interest or Natural Beauty.

Some of the quotations displayed at certain entries in this book were drawn from the following sources:

Ayer, A. J., and Jane O'Grady, eds., *A Dictionary of Philosophical Quotations* (Oxford, UK, and Cambridge, Mass.: Blackwell, 1992)—the absurd, Beauvoir, Heidegger, Kierkegaard, Marx, Spinoza.

Jones, Alison, ed., *Chambers Dictionary of Quotations* (Edinburgh and New York: Chambers, 1997)—atomism, Burke, Confucianism, Einstein, James, Mao Zedong, négritude, Ortega y Gasset, Stanton, truth.

Mackay, Alan L., *A Dictionary of Scientific Quotations* (Bristol: Institute of Physics Publishing, 1991)—Darwin, dialectical materialism, Jung.

Maggio, Rosalie, ed., *Quotations by Women* (Boston: Beacon Press, 1996)—feminism.

Rawson, Hugh, and Margaret Miner, comps., *The New International Dictionary of Quotations* (New York: Dutton, 1986)—Galileo, Locke, Plato, uncertainty principle.

Seldes, George, comp., *The Great Thinkers* (New York: Ballantine Books, 1985)—Arendt, Du Bois, Emerson, evolution, fascism, freedom, Luther, race and racism, relativism, Russell, Tocqueville.

Simpson, James B., ed., *Simpson's Contemporary Quotations* (New York: HarperCollins, 1997)—affirmative action, communism.

Tripp, Rhoda Thomas, comp., *The International Thesaurus of Quotations* (New York: Crowell, 1970)—equality, humanism, identity.

Papers used by Random House UK Limited are natural, recyclable products made from wood grown in sustainable forests. The manufacturing processes conform to the environmental regulations of the country of origin

ISBN 0 09 179373 4

Printed and bound in Great Britain by
Mackays of Chatham plc, Chatham, Kent

For Chrissie Bell,
who kept the idea alive

WATERFORD CITY AND COUNTY
WITHDRAWN
LIBRARIES

Contents

About This Dictionary   ix

Acknowledgments   xiii

How to Use the Dictionary   xvii

THE DICTIONARY OF
IMPORTANT IDEAS AND THINKERS   1

Further Reading   439

Index of Key Terms and Proper Names   442

About This Dictionary

It all began with dialectical materialism. I was aware of the term, had seen or heard it used a hundred times. But one day, finding it mentioned in a magazine article, I realized I had no idea exactly what it is and couldn't accurately define it. The brief dictionary definition didn't help much, and it didn't appear at all in my desk encyclopedia.

It occurred to me that lots of other concepts, old and new, were vaguely familiar but elusive: ideas I'd heard of or learned something about in school but now had a faded impression of, at best.

Wouldn't it be great to have a dictionary of ideas, I thought—not things or events, but those intangibles that fuel our thoughts: theories, philosophies, beliefs, ideologies, and the thinkers who have articulated them. That set me on a search through bookstores and libraries for the volume I had in mind: a compact, alphabetical guide to significant ideas and thinkers, with entries long enough to enlighten but short enough to digest, covering all fields of thought and written in ordinary English.

I couldn't find it, so I wrote it.

The book you are holding represents the fruits of what I now think of as my second college education, one pursued outside a formal institution (but with the crucial assistance of numerous scholars) and which took as long as the first one. My ambition was not only to get a grasp on a world's worth of concepts but to explain them in terms that I, a nonacademic, and others like me could understand. It was a daunting but exhilarating challenge.

Ideas, I appreciated anew, are the foundations of our culture. They inspire our thoughts and inform our beliefs. Many of them form the very basis of our identity. Some, such as those from non-Western traditions, are only now entering our awareness as our society becomes more genuinely multicultural. While the ideas of the past have shaped the social, political, and religious institutions of today's world, new concepts continually challenge our perceptions, fuel debate, and pave our way to the future.

The topics of *The Dictionary of Important Ideas and Thinkers'* 444 entries were chosen in consultation with a number of respected scholars in the various fields covered. The process, of course, was one of exclusion as much as selection from a nearly limitless field of possibility. In making our decisions on which ideas and thinkers to include in this relatively small volume, we were guided by two main criteria: their influence on human thought and their continuing relevance in today's discourse.

The fields of knowledge gathered here include philosophy, psychology, politics, history, economics, sociology, religion, science, and the arts. Entries on ideas in these areas define them and briefly explain their history, implications, and wider significance. The 111 profiles of major thinkers provide outlines of their most influential ideas rather than purely biographical sketches. Hundreds of additional, related ideas and thinkers are discussed in the text and referenced in the Index.

What is an "idea" in this book? Theoretically, the term could cover everything from a philosophical argument to a nifty new invention. I've left gadgets and other "bright ideas" out of *The Dictionary of Important Ideas and Thinkers,* while keeping my definition of an idea as broad as possible: a theoretical construct, a belief or guiding tenet, an essential concept in a field of study, an ideological proposition, an influential thought or opinion. I'm personally attracted to the theoretical and propositional—debatable, questionable, or unprovable notions—but not exclusively. Primarily descriptive terms are excluded, but general concepts, fields of theory, schools of thought, and similar broad categories are covered here.

A note about some of the things you will and won't find in this book. You will find that a majority of the entries reflect European culture, the Greek philosophical tradition, Judeo-Christian religion, etc. This simply acknowledges the way things are: despite a growing awareness of other cultures and traditions, the ideas that are our cultural currency are still predominantly those of "Western civilization."

Yet this book also reflects recent changes in our world-views. Where they have wide relevance, concepts and beliefs from Asian, African, and Middle Eastern traditions are included. You will also find more women and nonwhite thinkers than many works of this sort recognize—people whose contributions (and even access) to the history of ideas have for too long been neglected.

You will also find a somewhat greater emphasis on *contemporary* thought than might be expected in a broad survey of ideas. This is largely because modern theorists and their ideas are among those most currently discussed and most likely to be overlooked in other reference works. While the classic ideas and figures in *The Dictionary of Important Ideas and Thinkers* have had a decisive influence on modern thought, the newer concepts and contemporary thinkers will shape the future.

Although I have tried to be scrupulous about using gender-neutral terminology ("he or she," "humanity") when referring to people in general, and avoiding the discredited sexist convention of the generic masculine ("mankind," "he"), you will find exceptions. These are in cases when to imply the feminine would misrepresent a thinker's outlook, because women have been (and are) so often excluded from consideration. When Jefferson, for example, wrote that "all men are created equal," he was talking about men. The same consideration applies to almost all references to the God of Judaism, Christianity, and Islam, who is traditionally conceived as male.

You will *not* find main entries on any primarily literary figures or artists; no Shakespeare or Goethe, Michelangelo or Picasso (though all of these geniuses appear at least briefly in the book). This restriction was forced by the limited space between these covers, and I hope to be able to include these thinker-artists in a later edition.

For the same reason, you will probably not find every idea that might be of interest to you; the world of ideas is as expansive as the world itself. However, I believe you will discover here an intriguing and useful array of concepts and consequential thinkers. And, yes, you will find dialectical materialism.

Acknowledgments

It is customary for authors to thank the people "without whom this work would not have been possible." In my case, that is literally true. In writing this book, I have been more the student than the teacher; without the help of the scholarly friends and friendly scholars who helped shape its content, prepare its entries, and review its text, this book would not exist. I was also the lucky recipient of valuable suggestions and warm encouragement from many quarters, which contributed, respectively, to the quality of the work and to my ability to persevere.

I am indebted first and last to the scholars who served as academic advisors on this project, lending their judgment and insight to decisions about the book's content, the evaluation of draft entries, or both. They are:

Douglas Amy, Mount Holyoke College
Glenn Benson-Lewis, Behavioral Health Network
Anne Bernstein, Wright Institute
James T. Campen, University of Massachusetts
Joan Cocks, Mount Holyoke College
Bruce T. Dahlberg, Smith College (emeritus)
Laurin Raiken, New York University
Karen Smith, Emporia State University
Elizabeth V. Spelman, Smith College
Albert B. Stewart, Antioch College (emeritus)
Paula Treichler, University of Illinois
Stephen Wangh, New York University

The individual entries were researched and written with the participation of graduate scholars, most of them doctoral candidates at the University of Massachusetts, Amherst. These experts provided insights into their respective fields and, in many cases, first drafts of the entries themselves. Foremost among them is Shaun Coon, a brilliant young scholar who worked with me on all the entries in philosophy, ancient and modern; his breadth and depth of knowledge, his clarity, and his good humor propelled the early stages of the project.

The other scholars who actively contributed to the creation of the book are: Mark K. Anderson (physics), Carl Bromley (social and political theory), Chris Erickson (social and political theory), Lee Fearnside (art history), Rolf Flor (philosophy), Debra Barrett Glennon (women's studies), Elizabeth Harding (religion and science), Rajmund Horvath (literary theory), Jennifer Ladd (social issues), Kristina Lentz-Judd (women's studies), John M. Lund (social and political theory), Yaseen Noorani (religion), Kathleen Banks Nutter (political theory), Michaela Orizu (social issues and theory), Shelby E. Robinson (religion), Ellen Rooney (psychology and linguistics), Colleen Sellers (economics), Stephen F. Soitos (African-American studies), and Diana Wagner (religion). Peter DeSimone, Cindy Frantz, Janet Mittman, Paul Shepard, Carol Silverman, and Martha Yoder gave constructive advice on the content of the entry-term list.

I am also grateful to several people who vetted individual entries and groups of entries in their particular areas of expertise: Andrea Ayvazian, Walton G. Congdon, Sara Elinoff, Tawna Sanchez, and Millie Thayer.

For the inspiration and support (and frequent reassurance) I received from a great number of people directly and indirectly connected to the project, I am endlessly thankful. First among these wise and generous souls is my agent, Sandra Dijkstra, who thought it was a good idea in the first place and kept her faith in it. The text's four consecutive editors at Ballantine Books—Leslie Helm, Phebe Kirkham, Andrea Schulz, and Susan Randol—shepherded the book through its development, creation, completion, and revision, respectively, and their enthusiasm survived all the delays, course corrections, and changes of the guard. I am also thankful for Sue Warga's thoughtful copyediting and for Eileen Gaffney's patient attention to the book's myriad style elements.

The members of my writers' support group—Janet Kaye, B. J. Roche, Steve Simurda, Stanley Wiater, Miryam Williamson, and Allen Woods—were a priceless source of comfort and courage throughout what must have often seemed an ongoing soap opera of trials and triumphs. All are members of the National Writers Union, to which I am also indebted, in the person of Phil Mattera, for a careful review of my contracts.

To all these, and many more there isn't space to acknowledge, my profound thanks. I really couldn't have done it without you.

How to Use the Dictionary

All the entries are arranged alphabetically, dictionary-style, by headword. Subentries associated with main entries follow the main entry or are set off in boxes on a facing page. For instance, a box on the sacraments appears with CHRISTIANITY, and STRUCTURALISM has a supplementary entry on major structuralist thinkers. Within an entry, important terms are set off typographically at their first significant occurrence; main-entry terms are in SMALL CAPITALS, and other key words are in *italics*. Note that entry terms may be found in their adjectival forms, e.g., ABSTRACT (ABSTRACTION), CONSERVATIVE (CONSERVATISM). Cross-references with "see also," within or at the end of entries, point to other entries in which further aspects of the topic are discussed.

Cross-references to words in main headings and subentry headings, and to some other important names and terms, appear alphabetically between entries. For example, the cross-references for Catholicism (see ROMAN CATHOLICISM), induction (see DEDUCTION AND INDUCTION), and Herbert Marcuse (see box at CRITICAL THEORY) follow the entries for CATHARSIS, INDIVIDUALISM, and MAO ZEDONG, respectively.

If you can't find a term or topic you are looking for, consult the Index at the back of the book. It contains all the key terms and proper names found in the text, with references to the entries in which they are found.

A

a priori/a posteriori

Central terms in EPISTEMOLOGY, contrasting two kinds of knowledge according to the way the human mind apprehends it, that is, with and without recourse to experience. A priori knowledge is *prior* to, and independent of, observation or experiment; a posteriori knowledge comes only *after* direct experience.

A priori is the problematic side of this pairing. Determining what constitutes a priori knowledge depends on the assumptions one begins with. Knowledge can be said to be a priori if it is independent of a *particular* experience (e.g., I know that if I drop a stone it will fall) or if it precedes *any* experience (this is the concept of INNATE IDEAS). Similarly, some hold that certain statements in LOGIC and mathematics are a priori (or *analytic,* see below), since they depend only on the laws of their discipline; but others insist that those rules presuppose the truth of the axioms that support them.

Parallel to the a priori/a posteriori distinction is that between *analytic* and *synthetic* judgments—the difference, in effect, between statements whose truth depends purely on the meaning of their terms ("All bachelors are unmarried," "2 + 2 = 4") and those that require outside evidence to determine their truth or falsity ("All bachelors live alone," "Two of my children are girls and two are boys"). Analytic judgments are a priori because they do not depend on experience; however, since they tell us nothing new, they are of no practical use. The absolute distinction between analytic and synthetic statements has lately been questioned, especially by the American philosopher Willard van Orman Quine, who argues that since the definitions of words are changeable, imprecise, and disputed, the "synonymy" required to make a true analytic statement may be impossible to achieve.

See also DEDUCTION AND INDUCTION; KANT.

Absolute, the

The ultimate reality or principle, perfect and complete, independent and unlimited; a central concept in theology and METAPHYSICS. In the JUDAIC and CHRISTIAN traditions, the Absolute is often equated with God, the consummate spiritual power and only truly independent being. The Absolute, whether God or another cosmic force, is generally seen as the source of all things, an infinite, wholly unrestricted entity that is independent of creation but interacts with it in some manner, rather than standing wholly outside it. For example, in HINDUISM the Absolute, called *brahman*, is the eternal, abstract principle of cosmic existence and oneness, unity with which is the ultimate goal of Hindu devotions.

The most prominent example of the concept in modern Western philosophy occurs in the IDEALISM of HEGEL, for whom history was a progressive, DIALECTICAL process leading eventually to complete knowledge of the Absolute. The *absolute idealism* of late-19th-century Hegelians such as Josiah Royce and F. H. Bradley incorporated this notion, seeing the Absolute as the unifying force in human society and in our understanding of the world.

See also GOD, CONCEPTS OF; HEGEL; HINDUISM; MYSTICISM.

absolutism (absolute monarchy)

Political system in which all power is held by a monarch or other authoritarian ruler. In philosophy, the term describes any doctrine that asserts there is only one correct way of seeing or explaining things; the opposite of RELATIVISM. Absolutism also refers to any rigid adherence to a prescribed set of ideas.

Political absolutism, primarily associated with European monarchies of the 17th and 18th centuries, was characterized by autocratic, hereditary authority sanctioned by the church and the nobility. It arose with the consolidation of power and the creation of cohesive STATES in the wake of the ceaseless religious, territorial, and dynastic warfare that devastated early-17th-century Europe. The intellectual foundation of European absolutism was laid by the French lawyer Jean Bodin, who, in *Six Books of the Commonwealth* (1576), argued that only an absolute sovereign commanding absolute obedience could prevent civil turmoil. Absolute monarchy was justified by the doctrine of the *divine right of kings,* which held that the king ruled by the will of God and was answerable only to God.

The epitome of the absolute monarch was Louis XIV of France (1638–1715), who was known as the Sun King—everything revolved around him. Louis's advisor Bishop Jacques Bossuet defined royal authority as sacred, paternal, and absolute, but also subject to REASON. The latter quality gained importance in the 18th century, as the ENLIGHTENMENT spawned rulers who claimed legitimacy not from divine right but because of the benefits they conferred on their subjects. These "benevolent despots" were exemplified by Peter I and Catherine II of Russia, who attempted to modernize and westernize Russia through civil reforms, and Frederick II of Prussia, who favored the title "first servant of the state."

In practice, absolute monarchy was never absolute; it was circumscribed by local opposition to centralized power, ineffective royal bureaucracies, and the power of the clergy, the nobility, and, to some extent, popular opinion. Twentieth-century TOTALITARIANISM has been equated with absolutism, but whereas absolutism encompasses only political power, totalitarian systems seek to control all aspects of the social order as well.

See also SOVEREIGNTY; cf. REPUBLICANISM; SOCIAL CONTRACT.

abstraction

The process of culling the universal from the particular, the general from the specific. The ability to identify essential features and generalize from them is seen by some as the defining human characteristic, distinguishing human intellect from animal brain function. Abstraction is the foundation of mathematics, an important philosophical concept, and the basis of much of modern art (see box).

Mathematics abstracts the numerical and geometrical qualities of objects from the objects themselves. It began with the observation that certain objects or phenomena, though unalike in many ways, share common abstract properties. For instance, two trees and two rocks share the property of "two-ness"; lute strings and shafts of sunlight have the common property of straightness. Such correlations led to the development of the axioms that form the basis of math, such as "Two things equal to the same thing are equal to each other." Abstraction is basic to number theory and modern SET THEORY and to the notion of ARTIFICIAL INTELLIGENCE.

In philosophy, abstraction—drawing out a universal from the sum of common particulars—has played a significant, and often controversial, role. The ARISTOTELIAN concept of *categories,* by which objects and beings in the world are classified according to their distinctive properties and common features, is reflected in many philosophers' systems for organizing reality (see, e.g., HEGEL; box at KANT) and is central to LOGIC. The question of whether abstract qualities actually inhere in objects, or are merely the words we use to organize our understanding of them, provoked the medieval debate over UNIVERSALS. The philosophical penchant for abstraction has been challenged in the 20th century by perspectives that discount universals and generalized abstractions, emphasizing a world of concrete particulars (e.g., EXISTENTIALISM; PHENOMENOLOGY; RELATIVISM).

ABSTRACT ART

Abstraction in art takes two general forms: the reduction of images from the natural world into shapes suggested by, but not conventionally representational of, actual objects (for example, the smooth, ovoid head of Constantin Brancusi's sculpture *Sleeping Muse*), and the "pure" use of color, line, shadow, mass, and other traditional, formal elements of painting and sculpture to create an image whose only reference is itself. Both approaches are found in the folk and decorative arts of all cultures as well as in formal, or "fine," art. In the fine arts, abstraction is almost entirely a product of the 20th century (see also MODERNISM). Foreshadowed by movements such as post-IMPRESSIONISM, FAUVISM, EXPRESSIONISM, and CUBISM, it has become the most important current in 20th-century art, influencing representational art as well as spawning a variety of styles and movements (see below; see also CONSTRUCTIVISM; SURREALISM). The cutting edge of stylistic innovation in abstract art, at first centered in Europe, shifted largely to the United States after World War II.

In the late 20th century, the line between abstraction and representation has become increasingly blurred. Reactions to the detachment and ambiguity of pure abstraction include *neoexpressionism* and *new realism,* figurative styles that revived subjectivism and narrative, and *conceptual art,* in which the artist assembles existing materials in various media (including found objects, words, and print, film, and video images) to express a particular idea, often a comment on the nature of art itself.

Some abstract art movements
- *Neoplasticism (de Stijl)* was a rigorously abstract style containing only "plastic" elements (lines, planes, and colors), with no hint of reference to actual objects. It was developed by the Dutch painter Piet Mondrian, who specified that painting should consist pictorially only of vertical and horizontal straight lines and rectangles and chromatically only of primary colors, black, white, and gray. Mondrian called for art to be "denaturalized," purified of any relation to nature in order to express an ideal, universal harmony. His ideas, and those of his disciple Theo van Doesburg, were promulgated in the journal *De Stijl* (The Style), published 1917–28, by which name the movement was also known.

- *Geometric abstraction,* or *concrete art,* was described by van Doesburg in the 1930s as being based on simple lines and planes and having "no other reference than itself." Its major stylistic and ideological inspirations were neoplasticism and the Russian art movements CONSTRUCTIVISM and *suprematism,* the latter founded in 1913 by Casimir Malevich, who proclaimed "the supremacy of pure feeling" expressed in stark geometric shapes. The center of geometric abstraction in the prewar years was Paris, where artists' groups such as Abstraction-Création promoted the "cultivation of pure plasticity [with no] explanatory, anecdotal, literary, or naturalistic elements."
- *Abstract expressionism,* a term first applied to the Russian abstractionist Wassily Kandinsky before World War I, was revived in the 1940s to describe the work of a group of painters in New York who rejected the cool formalism of geometric abstraction in favor of personal expression, intuition, and antirationality. Borrowing the internal focus of EXPRESSIONISM, the improvisational methods of SURREALISM, and JUNG's idea of the *collective unconscious,* they strove to make the UNCONSCIOUS visible. They emphasized the act of creation itself, in which expression is achieved through the inherent qualities of color and texture in paint and canvas and the artist's own interaction with them. This approach united artists of widely differing styles, known collectively as the New York School—from Jackson Pollock, whose practice of dripping and spattering paint onto canvas was termed *"action painting"* by the critic Harold Rosenberg (a French parallel was called *"tachisme"*), to the *color-field* painting of Barnett Newman and Mark Rothko, whose paintings used large fields of solid color, to the figurative work of Willem de Kooning.
- *Post-painterly abstraction,* a term coined by the art critic Clement Greenberg in 1964, defined the generation of artists who had rejected the expressionism, without abandoning the abstraction, of abstract expressionism. This diverse group was united by its renunciation of the abstract expressionists' "painterly" attributes, such as subjectivism, spontaneity, and expressive brushwork. Their work focused solely on shapes and colors, containing no reference to the world outside the canvas and no trace of the artist. Much of it incorporated the color-field approach—both in the large, flat, *hard-edge* forms of Frank Stella and Ellsworth Kelly and in the soft expanses of saturated color painted by Helen Frankenthaler and Jules Olitsky—

and drew attention to the canvas-and-wood support as a conscious part of the artwork.

- *Op art,* an American movement of the 1960s, grew out of geometrical abstraction and drew on experiments with optical effects by European artists of the period. Its progenitor was the Hungarian-French painter Victor Vasarely. The name was an abbreviation of "optical art" (and a play on "pop art," the contemporaneous movement that employed images from advertising, comic books, and other realms of mass culture). Op art incorporated optical illusions in stark black and white or brilliant colors, especially designs that create the impression of movement as the eye runs over them. Many op artists studied the psychology and physiology of PERCEPTION to create their effects, which were sometimes called *psychedelic,* mimicking drug-induced hallucination.

- *Minimalism (minimal art)* arose in the 1960s as a reaction against the emotiveness of abstract expressionism, especially among American sculptors such as Donald Judd, Robert Morris, and Carl André. Minimal art (also called "ABC" art) is primarily concerned with an awareness of space, of the third dimension, in contrast to the two-dimensional, illusionistic space of painting. Much of it thus consists of three-dimensional structures based on elementary geometric forms and constructed from industrial materials such as plastic and steel. The work is expunged of personal meaning and the artist's role is primarily conceptual; the finished work is often produced by an artisan or a factory.

absurd, the

In philosophy, the concept that human existence is essentially incoherent and meaningless. In CHRISTIANITY, a proof of the validity of Christian doctrine that employs its very implausibilies (e.g., the notion of God becoming mortal in order to suffer for humanity): if it is too absurd to have been invented, it must be true. First enunciated by the early church father Tertullian in the maxim "Credo quia absurdum est" (I believe it because it is absurd), this idea was taken up in the 19th century by Søren KIERKEGAARD, who argued that by its very nature faith is irrational; we must either embrace it as such or seek another way to confront the ambiguity and uncertainty of human existence.

The concept of the absurd formed the basis of 20th-century EXISTENTIAL-

ISM, which sees a universe without intrinsic meaning, in which individuals must struggle to create meaning for themselves. It also influenced SURREALISM. Related to both these movements, the *theater of the absurd* reached its peak in the 1950s in the works of Samuel Beckett, Eugène Ionesco, and others—plays that forsake traditional dramatic form, logic, and character to illustrate the futility of modern life.

Adorno, Theodor W. See box at
CRITICAL THEORY

> *"Man stands face-to-face with the irrational. He feels within him his longing for happiness and for reason. The absurd is born of this confrontation between the human need and the unreasonable silence of the world."*
> —Albert Camus,
> *The Myth of Sisyphus*, 1942

advantage, comparative and absolute

Principles of economics that state the conditions under which trade with another nation is considered advantageous. The concept of absolute advantage revolutionized economics and international trade in the late 18th century, and its 19th-century successor, comparative advantage, is still the foundation of modern trade policies.

According to the theory of *absolute advantage,* formulated by Adam SMITH in *The Wealth of Nations* (1776), a country should specialize in and export the goods it can produce more cheaply and efficiently than its trading partners, and import those it cannot. This seemingly obvious idea was startling at the time because under the MERCANTILIST system the primary purpose of trade was foreign exchange—trading goods for gold—rather than an efficient exchange of commodities.

Comparative advantage, introduced by the British economist David Ricardo in his *Principles of Political Economy* (1817), takes into account not just the absolute cost of producing something for export but also the OPPORTUNITY COST of employing the country's resources to make that product instead of another. This more complex approach explains why one country may choose to import a product it can produce more efficiently than another country: because it is comparatively more advantageous to specialize in what it can produce *most* efficiently. Even if a country has an absolute advantage in all goods in comparison with another country, it is advisable to trade for the goods it is *least* efficient at producing, because it will be able to use its resources more efficiently and will therefore be better off. The theory of comparative advantage thus holds that international trade is beneficial to all countries, even those that could be utterly self-sufficient.

Adventism

Belief in the literal and imminent Second Coming of JESUS. A minority strain in American PROTESTANTISM, Adventism arose from the 19th-century revival movement in the teachings of William Miller, who became an evangelical Baptist preacher after a conversion experience. From biblical passages, Miller calculated that the Advent, or return of Christ, would occur in 1843 (later revised to 1844). When their expectations were not fulfilled, the Millerites who did not lose faith rationalized the failed prophecy in various ways (cf. COGNITIVE DISSONANCE) and eventually separated into several sects.

By far the most numerous and widespread of these sects, now numbering some five million worldwide, is the Seventh-Day Adventists. It was founded by Ellen Gould White, whose numerous visions and voluminous writings formed the faith's doctrine. A central tenet is the conviction that the deferral of the second Advent is due to CHRISTIANS' failure to observe the biblical Sabbath, that is, on the seventh day of the week instead of the first. The church also stresses the avoidance of drugs, stimulants, and meat, in the belief that the human body is a temple of the Holy Spirit and must be kept pure and treated with respect. Modern-day Adventists still expect the imminent coming of Christ and engage in tireless evangelism in anticipation of it.

See also ESCHATOLOGY; MILLENARIANISM.

aestheticism

Artistic movement of the late 19th century epitomized by the slogan "art for art's sake." Its adherents, reacting against the Victorian notion that a work of art must be uplifting, educational, or otherwise socially or morally beneficial, believed that an artwork is autonomous and self-justifying, needing no reason but itself, having no purpose but to be beautiful. Oscar Wilde's comment "All art is quite useless" reflected the rejection of utility and meaning in art in favor of exquisite style and polished artifice—the triumph of form over FUNCTION. Aesthetes further disdained the "natural," organic, and homely in both art and life, seeing art as the pursuit of perfect beauty and life as the quest of sublime experience.

The aesthetic movement originated in France and reached its zenith in England, where it was introduced by the critic Walter Pater and found its most extravagant expression in the poems and plays of Wilde and the ornate designs of Aubrey Beardsley.

Aestheticism's prime French exponent was Théophile Gautier, to whom the maxim "art for art's sake" is often attributed. He was a leader in the circle of so-called Parnassian poets, who embraced the catchphrase as their credo, and an influence on Charles Baudelaire. Baudelaire, in turn, became the central figure of the offshoot Decadents, who likened their era to the Roman Empire in decline and celebrated the decay of civilization with flamboyant behavior, drug taking, and sexual license. *Fin-de-siècle* aesthetes on both sides of the English Channel flouted conventional social norms with their dandyism, precious affectations, and contempt for bourgeois morality. In return, they became the butt of endless lampoons, most famously in Gilbert and Sullivan's operetta *Patience*, where an aesthetic poet, Bunthorne, is portrayed as a simpering fraud.

aesthetics

The study of the nature of beauty and of art; one of the five classical fields of philosophical inquiry (see also EPISTEMOLOGY; ETHICS; LOGIC; METAPHYSICS). The term, derived from the Greek for "sense perception," was coined in the mid-18th century by the German philosopher Alexander Baumgarten, but interest in what constitutes the beautiful and in the relationship between art and nature goes back at least to the ancient Greeks. Both PLATO and ARISTOTLE saw art as *imitation* and beauty as the expression of a universal quality, but Plato distinguished between ideal beauty and the (imperfectly) beautiful object, while Aristotle found beauty inherent in a harmonious work of art (see also CATHARSIS; IDEAS; UNITIES). To the Greeks the concept of "art" embraced all handcrafts, and the rules of symmetry, proportion, and unity applied equally to weaving and pottery, poetry and sculpture. Indeed, it was not until the 19th century that "art" became primarily associated with the so-called fine arts—painting and sculpture—and literature. Similarly, the idea of "artistic inspiration" is a comparatively modern notion; at least through the Middle Ages, the element of inspiration in an artwork was always seen as deriving largely from its religious function.

Immanuel KANT revolutionized aesthetics in his *Critique of Judgment* (1790). Kant saw aesthetic appreciation not simply as the perception of intrinsic beauty, but as involving a judgment—subjective, but informed. This attitude has prevailed ever since. After Kant, the primary focus of aesthetics shifted from the consideration of beauty per se to the nature of the artist, the role of art, and the relationship between the viewer and the work of art. This sort of aesthetic inquiry came into full bloom with the ROMANTIC movement, particularly in the philosophy of Friedrich Schlegel, who asserted the primary importance of the artist's free expression. Samuel Taylor Coleridge famously characterized aesthetic involvement as "that willing suspension of disbelief for the moment," in which the viewer embraces the imaginary reality presented in a work of art. Coleridge's formulation was challenged in the early 20th century by Edward Bullough's concept of *aesthetic detachment* or *psychical distance*, the idea that we can truly appreciate aesthetic qualities only if we avoid getting caught up in the work's emotional or narrative atmosphere. This approach has guided much of 20th-century criticism, which tends to see MEANING, if any, in elements of a work of art that transcend the viewer's subjective response or the artist's MIMETIC intention (see, e.g., DECONSTRUCTION; NEW CRITICISM; POSTMODERNISM).

Today the arts no longer serve primarily civic or religious functions, as they did in ancient times, nor are they necessarily considered the manifestation of a higher reality or fundamental truth, as they were by the Romantics and others. Rather, art tends to be seen as reflecting psychological, social, or political influences rather than divine inspiration or TRANSCENDENT qualities. In FREUDIAN psychology, for example, art derives from primal information in the UNCONSCIOUS; to MARXISTS, art always serves a social purpose, implicitly or explicitly supporting or undermining prevailing economic conditions.

See also AESTHETICISM; APOLLONIAN SPIRIT AND DIONYSIAN SPIRIT; CLASSICISM; FORMALISM; GESTALT; LUKÁCS; MIMESIS; SOCIALIST REALISM.

affirmative action

Policy intended to create more educational, employment, and other opportunities for victims of past or present discrimination, especially racial minorities and women. While it has been instituted in several European countries, affirmative action is primarily associated with social policy in the United States, where the term was first used in a 1965 executive order by President Lyndon Johnson requiring any contractor doing business with the federal government to take "affirmative action" to implement nondiscrimination policies. Affirmative action programs can be voluntary, statutory, or judicially imposed, and can range from actively recruiting among the target groups to giving preference to qualified members of those groups. In the 1980s and '90s there have been demands to open affirmative action to other groups, such as gays and lesbians, military veterans, and those with physical or mental disabilities.

The concept has been widely controversial. Its advocates insist that it seeks to expand access and opportunity but not to achieve a certain result; opponents charge that the policy creates quotas and gives unfair advantage to some citizens over others; supporters counter that it is a necessary remedy to the unfair advantage traditionally given to white men; the critics reply that it constitutes "reverse discrimination." Affirmative action policies and laws have frequently been challenged in American courts, often over the question of their constitutionality under the 14th Amendment's "equal protection" clause: does it require "color-blind," "gender-blind"

> *"In order to get beyond racism, we must first take account of race . . . and in order to treat some people equally, we must treat them differently."*
> —Justice Harry A. Blackmun, 1978

behavior in all circumstances, or does its very genesis (it was written to ensure fair treatment for newly freed slaves) imply that past disadvantages may be compensated for? In general, the U.S. Supreme Court has approved affirmative action programs so long as they do not impose strict quotas.

African religions

The traditional religions of sub-Saharan Africa are as diverse as its peoples, who comprise more than 3,000 distinct ethnic groups, languages, and cultural systems. Nonetheless, the indigenous religions of black Africa share certain characteristic strains of belief and practice. Central to these is a strong sense of the oneness of creation, in which the interconnections between the natural and supernatural, the physical and spiritual, the visible and invisible, the living and the dead are far more important than the differences between them. Maintaining this unity is the primary goal of religious practices.

Most African cosmologies posit a supreme being, a creator-god who made the earth and infused it with vital energy, and who determines both personal and universal destiny. Creation myths typically tell of a time when the heavens were very close to earth and humans were immortal; then, through accident or disobedience, the supreme god withdrew and death became known. An example is the story, known in many regions of central Africa, of a woman pounding yams, whose pestle repeatedly struck the overhanging floor of heaven until the god retreated to the sky. Culture heroes and demigods appearing in many African mythologies include the primeval smith, who taught humans how to make things from the earth's bounty, and the Trickster, a

MODERN AFRICAN
RELIGIOUS MOVEMENTS

Since the 19th century, nonindigenous religions, introduced by colonizers and missionaries, have steadily gained converts in African societies; a great majority of Africans now profess CHRISTIANITY or ISLAM. At the same time, defiance of colonial influences has inspired a revival of traditional religions as well as the establishment of many African-controlled PROTESTANT (and some ROMAN CATHOLIC) denominations independent of the European missionary churches. Old beliefs have often shaped the converts' understanding and practice of the new faiths, and most of the more than 7,000 new sects are *syncretic*, combining elements of old and new belief systems and modes of worship.

Separatist churches that broke away from established Christian (or in some cases, Islamic) sects include two Catholic groups, the Jamaa ("family") movement of the Congo and Zaire, which emphasizes family and community and sees the TRINITY as a "holy family," and Legio Maria, an outgrowth of the Irish Legion of Mary, which gained a large following among the Luo of Kenya in the 1970s by combining healing, exorcism, and other traditional practices with the Roman Catholic liturgy. An important Protestant separatist church is the East African Revival Movement, called Balokole ("saved ones"), an evangelical church stressing redemption through conversion and a personal apprehension of the divine.

So-called *indigenous churches* with Christian roots were founded independently of established denominations, often by charismatic leaders. One such prophet-founder was the Congolese spiritual healer Simon Kimbangu, who attracted some three million followers and in whose name the Church of Jesus Christ on Earth was established following Zairean independence. Another was the Shona evangelist who called himself John Masowe (John the Baptist) and urged his followers in Southern Rhodesia (now Zimbabwe) to form independent work cooperatives and religious communities, promising them a future paradise on earth and rejecting all the Christian sacraments but baptism (see box at CHRISTIANITY). The Harrist churches of the Ivory Coast and Ghana are founded on the teachings of William Wade Harris, a Liberian who was inspired by visions of the angel Gabriel and who practiced faith healing and denounced traditional African religion in favor of revealed Christianity.

> The colonial period also spawned *revivalist movements* that sought to revitalize ancient traditions in a modern context, often incorporating elements of Christian belief and ritual without espousing Christianity. Many of these movements saw the European occupation as a divine punishment and endeavored not only to liberate their people from foreign oppression but to purify them of the spiritual contagions that had inspired the gods' retribution.

hero-clown (often in animal form) whose fantastical adventures symbolize the emergence of order out of chaos and knowledge out of confusion.

The supreme god is represented by numerous intermediaries—lesser deities and spirits dwelling in the natural world and controlling natural forces—whose favor and assistance in preserving the cosmic order are sought through ritual, prayer, and sacrifice. African religions are focused on correcting the problems of this life, not preparing for the next; religious ritual is instrumental, not merely symbolic, seeking to control natural forces and regulate human interactions. The causes of personal and communal misfortunes are located in offenses against the gods and ancestors, including individual misdeeds and social conflicts that disturb the natural equilibrium. Rituals are thus designed not only to placate benevolent spirits and propitiate harmful ones but to repair the social fabric. Ritual practices include animal sacrifices and food offerings, feasts and dances devoted to particular divinities, rites of passage from one stage of life to another (including death), seasonal celebrations, and magical rites to summon compassionate powers and thwart WITCHCRAFT and sorcery. Many ceremonies involve *spirit possession,* in which a celebrant in a trance state becomes the physical and vocal instrument of the spirit being invoked.

The view of creation as an unbroken continuum is reflected in the role played by the ancestors, revered forebears who are not departed but are present in the souls of the living and active in the life of the community, acting as guardians and sources of wisdom. Religion is an inextricable part of everyday life, with neither established church nor professional clergy; priests, healers, SHAMANS, diviners of the future, and other mediums to the spirit world are typically elders or those recognized as having special abilities.

See also ANIMISM; GODDESS WORSHIP; SHAMANISM; WITCHCRAFT.

AFRICAN-DERIVED
RELIGIONS IN THE NEW WORLD

Many of the slaves kidnapped from West Africa and taken to the Americas in the 17th–19th centuries sought to preserve their indigenous languages, traditions, and beliefs in the new and hostile environment. Although gradual (often compulsory) conversion to CHRISTIANITY occurred, the various forms of "slave religion" that developed were *syncretic*—hybrids of African and Christian beliefs, practices, and imagery. For instance, JESUS was often regarded as the savior who would deliver the slaves from bondage, and his Second Coming was viewed in terms of the cyclical renewal of the earth. Such syntheses survive in the folk religions of the Caribbean islands and Central and South America, particularly Brazil, as well as in the Afrocentric impulses of some African-American sects.

In the new folk religions of Latin America, the God of Christian monotheism and the catalogue of ROMAN CATHOLIC saints are conflated with the African creator-deity and the pantheon of lesser gods and spirits *(orishas)*, primarily derived from Yoruban and Bantu cultures, representing natural forces or human characteristics. Rituals commonly involve dancing and drumming, singing and chanting, animal sacrifice and food offerings, spirit possessions, and divination. In Central and South America, elements of indigenous Amerindian traditions also appear.

- *Afro-Brazilian sects* include Candomble, the oldest and most African-influenced, also called Xango, after the Yoruban god Shango; Macumba, a primarily urban religion emphasizing the intercession of ancestral spirits rather than divinities (the term is also used generically to describe all the Brazilian folk cults); and Umbanda, a new, rapidly expanding, multiracial synthesis of the country's diverse African, European, and indigenous religious and cultural heritage.
- *Santería* ("the way of the saints") is centered in Cuba and practiced by some Cuban exiles in the United States (where ANIMAL RIGHTS advocates have challenged its practice of blood sacrifice). The powers and domains of Yoruban gods are attributed to Catholic counterparts; for example, Chango (Shango), god of thunder and lightning, corresponds to St. Barbara, patron saint of pyrotechnics.
- *Afro-Jamaican sects* include Pukkumina (or Pocomania, "a little madness"), a compound of PROTESTANT influences and African spirit worship stressing faith healing and possession by the spirits of departed

familial and racial ancestors; Convince, which primarily celebrates rites of passage and conceives of possession by multiple spirits, including demons; and Myal, which has strong ritual links to voodoo.

- **Voodoo** (*vodun* or *vodou*, meaning "god" or "spirit") is a Haitian composite of French Catholicism and Dahomean traditions, focused on the worship of spirits *(loa)* and ancestors. Temple rites are led by priests, both male *(hungan)* and female *(mambo)*, and include divination, faith healing, and spirit possession, in which the devotee becomes a figurative "horse" whom the spirit "rides." The practice of black magic to do evil to others and the belief in *zombies* (the bodies or spirits of dead people controlled by a god) are minor elements in the religion, embellished and sensationalized by popular mythology. In the United States, a derivation of voodoo, usually called "hoodoo," is practiced by some African-Americans, primarily in the rural South. A diffuse system of beliefs, its focus is on conjuring spirits and, in general, on preserving the African connection to natural powers.

- Other **African-American sects** likewise emphasize African or non-European heritage. In the early 20th century many black Christians responded to Marcus GARVEY's doctrine of black exceptionalism, which considered Africans the superior race, subjected to enslavement and exile for their sins against God. This renewed sense of African identity inspired the creation of several Afrocentric PROTESTANT sects, including the African Orthodox Church, founded in 1921 at Garvey's instigation. So-called Black Jews such as William S. Crowdy believed, with Garvey, that the Hebrews of the Bible were black and that Africans and their descendants represent the Lost Tribes of Israel, God's chosen people. The same sense of alienation from the European tradition has motivated the formation of BLACK MUSLIM sects, which envision a nonwhite god sanctifying a nonwhite culture, and the development of a new Christian *black theology*, which interprets the gospel in terms of deliverance from oppression. Kwanzaa, a weeklong secular African-American holiday created by Maulana Ron Karenga in 1966, blends elements from several African harvest festivals (the word means "first fruits" in Swahili) with rituals associated with Hanukkah and Christmas, and celebrates seven "principles" related to African-Americans' aspirations and sense of community.

alienation

Separation from the activity, principle, or creative force that forms one's essential self, or detachment from one's inherited social traditions; the alienated person feels isolated, powerless, and apathetic, like an alien in one's own society or a stranger in one's own skin. The concept is central to EXISTENTIALISM and MARXIST theory. (Cf. ANOMIE.)

The term was introduced into philosophy by HEGEL, who used it to describe the split between human CONSCIOUSNESS and objective material existence that inhibits our understanding of the "DIALECTICAL moment" in which historical change takes place and thus impedes the attainment of perfect knowledge, the final synthesis of subject and object. For MARX, workers in a CAPITALIST system, with no creative participation in what they produce nor ownership of the means of production, are alienated not only from the fruits of their labor but from their essential natures and each other.

The implication of Marx's analysis—that individuals' alienation is a result of economic and power relations in industrial society—has been widely influential in social theory, for example, in Max WEBER's critique of the efficiently impersonal nature of bureaucracy and Émile Durkheim's view of suicide as a failure of social integration. In the revisionist Marxism of Maurice MERLEAU-PONTY, alienation is the inability to control the MEANING of one's activity and productions. In the existentialist view, people deal with alienation either through *inauthenticity*—stagnating in thoughtless conformity or surrendering to despair in the face of a meaningless universe—or by living *authentically*, fully engaged with life. In the psychoanalytic theory of Jacques Lacan (see box at STRUCTURALISM), alienation occurs when the self is "decentered"—divorced from its ESSENCE—through socialization, which forces the individual to adopt a self-image constructed by social conventions. Many social critics have identified alienation as a symptom, or even the defining characteristic, of modern technological society, in which the individual is dehumanized and isolated by a soulless, materialistic culture (see, e.g., BAUDRILLARD; Marcuse in box at CRITICAL THEORY).

"Alienation" was used in a different sense by the German playwright Bertolt Brecht, himself a Marxist. In his *epic theater*, Brecht countered the thrust of modern REALISTIC drama, in which the audience emotionally identifies with the story. His "alienation effect" *(Verfremdungseffekt)*, created through the use of non-NATURALISTIC devices such as songs, placards, and direct address to the audience, sought to distance spectators from the imaginary reality onstage; thus freed from illusion, he believed, they would be able to more fully and critically engage the play's social and political themes.

See also EXISTENTIALISM; LUKÁCS; MARXISM.

Althusser, Louis See box at STRUCTURALISM

Anabaptism See box at PROTESTANTISM

analytic philosophy

Twentieth-century philosophical movement that stresses the analysis of statements, concepts, propositions, expressions, and logical constructs, while shunning METAPHYSICAL speculation. Its founder was Bertrand RUSSELL, who not only produced the version of symbolic, propositional LOGIC on which it relies but was the first to apply it to the problems of philosophy. As opposed to the predicate (or syllogistic) logic derived from ARISTOTLE, which considered the *qualities* of things, propositional logic emphasizes the analysis of logical propositions and seeks a "formal language" through which these propositions can be expressed most clearly. The genesis of analytic philosophy also owed much to WITTGENSTEIN's emphasis on the logical structure of language itself, and to the LOGICAL POSITIVISTS' insistence that the validity of propositions be verified logically and EMPIRICALLY. Other prominent analytic philosophers are A. J. Ayer, Willard van Orman Quine, and Saul A. Kripke.

Analytic philosophy holds that ORDINARY LANGUAGE is inexact and thus unable to express philosophical TRUTH. Indeed, analytic philosophers have generally been more concerned with analyzing logical and linguistic relations than with seeking to determine the facts of the world. Central to analytic philosophy are the logical analysis of linguistic structure and the precise definition of terms; it is thus closely related to *linguistic analysis,* the branch of philosophy that aims to clarify the meanings of words in the context of the ideas and objects they represent.

See also BEING AND BECOMING; NOMINALISM; UNIVERSALS; WITTGENSTEIN.

anarchism

Political philosophy holding that government is unnecessary and harmful and that social organization can best be achieved through voluntary cooperation among individuals and groups. From the Greek, meaning "no government," the term "anarchy" has become popularly (and inaccurately) synonymous with confusion and lawlessness, implying that government is imperative to an ordered society. Anarchists, however, see authoritarian government as the tool of the powerful, propertied CLASSES and the enemy of a just social order. The anarchist byword was coined by the founder of modern anarchism, Pierre-Joseph Proudhon, in *What Is Property?* (1840): "Property is theft."

Anarchists criticize the STATE primarily on the grounds that it serves itself and its powerful constituents at the expense of the mass of citizens, and that its legitimate functions could and should be performed at the local level. However, anarchists differ widely on the question of how a stateless society would actually work. The alternatives they envision range from INDIVIDUALISM, with every person acting as an autonomous, self-governing entity, to collectivism, in which individual interests are subordinated to the needs of the whole. Virtually all anarchist formulas place considerable faith in human nature—skepticism about which is the principal source of criticism of anarchist ideals. While anarchism is traditionally associated with radical revolutionary movements, its objections to strong government, bureaucratic power, compulsory taxation, and the like have much in common with modern LIBERTARIAN and CONSERVATIVE ideologies. (Cf. COMMUNISM; MARXISM; SOCIALISM.)

The anarchist reputation for violence—and the cartoon image of the bearded bomb thrower—developed with 19th-century Russian revolutionaries such as Mikhail Bakunin, who wished to overthrow the entire institutional, legal, and political structure of European governments and sought to initiate a general uprising with dramatic acts of terrorism. In the United States, fears of violent anarchism were often exploited by civil authorities. In the 1886 bombing in Chicago's Haymarket Square, which killed several policemen, and in the Sacco and Vanzetti case in the 1920s, anarchists were convicted of crimes on scant evidence by anxious juries.

An important related strand in anarchist history was *syndicalism* or, in its more radical manifestations, anarcho-syndicalism. Derived from militant French trade unionism, this movement declared that popular liberation could not be achieved by political means but would come about only through direct action by the working class in strikes, sit-downs, and even sabotage. Widespread in southern Europe in the late 19th and early 20th centuries, syndicalism gained little following in the United States, where it was most prominently represented by the Industrial Workers of the World labor union, whose members were called "Wobblies."

Another influential strand of anarchism developed in the early FEMINIST movement, some of whose adherents responded strongly to the anarchist critique of traditional institutions and established authority. The foremost feminist anarchist was Emma Goldman, a Lithuanian immigrant who was radicalized by the Haymarket trials and by conditions in the corset factory where she worked. She became a tireless campaigner for political and social change, a champion of workers' and women's rights, and a scandalously outspoken advocate of birth control and "free love."

Anglicanism See box at PROTESTANTISM

animal rights

The doctrine that animals are entitled to certain basic RIGHTS by virtue of being sentient, social creatures capable of emotion and pain. The concept is an implicit rejection of anthropocentrism and the "animal-machine" doctrine of DESCARTES, both of which discount the possibility that animals can have any "interests" that humans should honor. From a philosophical point of view, the animal-rights position derives partly from the ETHICS of the UTILITARIAN philosopher Jeremy Bentham, who held that although the interests of every being may differ, those interests should be equally respected, as well as from KANT's *categorical imperative* and other formulations of the GOLDEN RULE, that we should act as we would wish to be acted upon. It also rests on the conviction that animals, as CONSCIOUS beings capable of suffering, are ends in themselves, not means to human ends. These principles, most influentially asserted by the Australian philosopher Peter Singer in *Animal Liberation* (1975), lead animal-rights advocates to oppose practices that exploit and abuse animals, for example, vivisection, factory farming, and entertainments such as circuses and rodeos. Some claim that the use of animals in medical experiments and product testing constitutes a LOGICAL contradiction: we deem it acceptable to subject animals to painful experiments we would not inflict on humans because the animals are *not* like us, but we consider such procedures scientifically valid because animals *are* like us. The animal-rights doctrine is related to the environmentalist view that human intellectual superiority and technological mastery, which give us the ability to exploit the natural world, do not bestow the right to do so, but rather confer on us the responsibility to protect it.

animism

The belief that all things are inhabited by a SOUL or spirit. It can take a number of forms, including belief in a "world soul" pervading all of creation, the attribution of CONSCIOUSNESS to natural phenomena such as wind and rain, the assigning of human characteristics to animals and objects, and the belief that the soul is the animating force or vital principle in animal and plant life (see VITALISM).

Preliterate societies are typically infused with animistic beliefs; examples among traditional sub-Saharan AFRICAN RELIGIONS, for example, include the Ibo earth goddess Ala, who inhabits the earth and influences both agricultural and human fecundity, and the Mbuti sky god Tore, who lives in storms, wind, and rainbows. (See also NORTH AMERICAN NATIVE BELIEFS.) Animistic elements are found throughout the world's cultures, however. The personifications of thunder, fire, sun, and so on in the Greco-Roman pantheon were animistic in origin, and ancient animistic beliefs often survive in modern religious practice, for instance in India, where the "house spirit" is revered in many HINDU and BUDDHIST households.

The term "animism," from the Latin *anima* ("soul," from the Greek for "breath"), was coined by the English anthropologist Edward B. Tylor. In *Primitive Culture* (1871), he sought to explain the origin and evolution of religious belief in terms of the experiential world-view of prehistoric humans, which was preserved, so he thought, in preliterate tribal cultures. In Tylor's view, nature worship, combined with the veneration of dead ancestors, formed the basis of primitive polytheisms, which eventually developed and matured, losing their animistic features and culminating in monotheistic Judeo-Christian religion. This theory, which saw human history in terms of PROGRESS through successively higher stages of civilization, was highly influential for many years; it derived from and reinforced the faith in European superiority that inspired 19th-century IMPERIALISM and missionary CHRISTIANITY. It is now discounted by anthropologists, who recognize both the complexity of tribal cultures and the presence of magical and anthropomorphic elements in all religions. (See also TOTEMISM; cf. PANTHEISM.)

anomie (anomy)
Lack of moral consensus and normative controls in society, resulting from a breakdown of traditional authority; a central concept in sociology. A French term derived from the Greek for "lawlessness," anomie was introduced into social science by Émile Durkheim, who perceived a disintegration of social controls in societies undergoing major transitions. In his classic study *Suicide* (1897), Durkheim postulated that in the process of industrialization in Europe, moral controls had been outpaced by the revolution in social and economic relationships. In consequence, social organization weakened and individuals no longer felt bound by traditional constraints. This disintegra-

tion of the SOCIAL CONTRACT, he argued, leads to insecurity, ALIENATION, and, in extreme cases, suicide. Durkheim later came to regard anomie as widespread and probably permanent in modern society, where the division of labor is both inequitably allocated and isolating. The concept was modified by Robert Merton, who saw anomie as growing from the disparity between the high expectations of success in American society and the limited means of achieving it. Responses to this disjunction, Merton said, range from crime to apathy to agitation for social change.

anthropic principle

Controversial principle in cosmology, holding that any history of the universe must be compatible with the existence of humanity; thus "anthropic," from the Greek for "human." In its *weak* form, the principle states that by its nature, the universe must allow for the existence of intelligent life capable of observing it; in its *strong* form, it states that the universe must have properties that make intelligent life inevitable. The anthropic principle is considered by some cosmologists, notably Fred Hoyle, to be an argument for *design* in creation: the universe was designed in such a way as to produce life (see GOD, ARGUMENTS FOR).

The anthropic principle gained prominence in 1957, when the American physicist G. H. Dicke used it to explain the coincidences among certain dimensionless constants (ratios) that fix the relative strengths of the fundamental forces of nature. For example, the ratio of the electrical to gravitational forces between an electron and a proton—approximately equal to 10^{40}—is also the ratio of the age of the universe to the time it takes light to cross an atom, and the square root of the number of nuclear particles at the present time. If this constant were much different, life could not have arisen.

Some scientists have proposed an even stronger principle, known as the *final anthropic principle,* which states that once intelligent life (or intelligent information processing) has come into existence, it will never pass away. Since the sun will eventually die, and with it all organic terrestrial life, this principle implies that "strong ARTIFICIAL INTELLIGENCE"—intelligent, non-carbon-based, self-reproducing entities—will be developed before then.

anthroposophy

Philosophical system and spiritual movement founded by the Austrian educator and mystic Rudolf Steiner (1861–1925); also called Spiritual Science. The term is derived from the Greek words for "human" and "wisdom." Blending elements of HINDUISM, CHRISTIANITY, and THEOSOPHY, anthroposophy claims that knowledge can be gained directly from the spiritual world without the mediation of the senses. Steiner postulated four levels of human knowledge: sensory, imaginative, inspirational, and intuitive (or spiritual), each engaging a higher plane of spirituality. His distinctive applications of music, dance, and fine art (particularly color) are aimed at engaging these successive levels— notably through the practice of eurythmy, a discipline of controlled movement to music or sounds—and are thought to have curative powers. The worldwide network of Waldorf schools for gifted children was founded on Steiner's principles, as was the Camp Hill movement, which encompasses residential facilities for mentally and emotionally impaired children and adults, experimental farms, and anthroposophical research laboratories.

Apollonian spirit and Dionysian spirit

The two opposing natures, according to NIETZSCHE, that characterized the festivals of the Greek gods Apollo and Dionysus—one ruled by serenity, harmony, and intellect, the other by passion, inspiration, and ecstasy. In contrast to those who celebrated the *classical ideal* as the triumph of the Apollonian spirit (see CLASSICISM), Nietzsche argued in *The Birth of Tragedy out of the Spirit of Music* (1872) that Greek tragedy, the highest attainment of Hellenistic culture, exemplified a confluence of both principles. All art, he held, contains some mixture of these modes. Nietzsche later ascribed "the death of tragedy" in Greece to the rise of SOCRATIC reason and the resulting decline of this creative fusion. In his later work he emphasized the opposition between Socratic RATIONALISM, which he saw as dominant in European culture and institutionalized in CHRISTIANITY, and a submerged, subversive Dionysian undercurrent.

The idea of the Apollonian/Dionysian opposition is reflected in the classical-versus-ROMANTIC debate over the nature of art and the artist that, in various forms, has raged for the past two centuries: is art about the ordering of formal elements into a harmonious whole, or is it about the free expression of imagination and emotion, or both? (See, e.g., box at ABSTRACTION; AESTHETICISM; FORMALISM; IMPRESSIONISM.)

appearance versus reality

The idea that "things are not as they seem" is basic to the world-views of many philosophical systems and religious beliefs. Common to all is the notion that the everyday world is not in fact the true world, but an illusion, or at least a fragmentary plane, through which we may possibly glimpse the genuine reality it masks. The central message of most religious beliefs is that our earthly experience is only the tip of the cosmic iceberg, a limited, inferior stage on the way to a heavenly afterlife, perfect ENLIGHTENMENT, or some other ideal state.

The allegory of Plato's cave (see box at PLATO) illustrates the belief that our perceptions are merely shadows of reality. KANT's opposition of *phenomenon* ("appearance") and *noumenon* ("thing-in-itself") makes a similar distinction. Those who question or dismiss this approach (see, e.g., EXISTENTIALISM; MATERIALISM; EMPIRICISM) turn that belief on its head: they tend to see the apparent world as genuine and the "world beyond" as a delusion. It could be said that METAPHYSICS, the search for the true nature of reality, is centrally concerned with sorting out the real from the apparent.

The appearance/reality distinction can apply in the purely phenomenal world as well as in the spiritual and philosophical realms. MARXISTS, for example, hold that the surface appearances of social interactions (e.g., a free labor market) often hide the underlying reality of societal structures (the coercive economic power wielded by employers under CAPITALISM).

See also MONISM; PERCEPTION; SUBSTANCE.

Aquinas, Thomas (1225–1274)

Italian theologian and philosopher, the most important figure in SCHOLASTICISM and one of the most influential ROMAN CATHOLIC theologians. His most important works are the *Summa Contra Gentiles,* a Christian treatise addressed to Muslims, and the unfinished *Summa Theologica,* a philosophical exposition of theology.

Aquinas's great goal was the reconciliation of faith with REASON. The medieval rediscovery of ARISTOTLE by the West had challenged the reigning AUGUSTINIAN philosophy, which held that true knowledge is possible only through faith. Islamic scholars, especially IBN RUSHD (Averroës), had brought Aristotelian LOGIC to bear on theological matters, concluding that truth could be discovered by reason as well as by faith, a principle known as the "double truth" doctrine. Set forth in widely read commentaries on Aristotle's works, the double truth doctrine threatened established church teachings and provoked a theological crisis. Aquinas sought a synthesis of philosophy and revelation (a union that has been called "Aristotle's baptism"), declaring that the two are complementary, not antagonistic. He demonstrated this by applying rational analysis to theological questions, most notably in his "five ways" of understanding the existence of God, which were based on Aristotle's conception of the "unmoved mover" or "uncaused cause" (see ARISTOTLE; GOD, ARGUMENTS FOR). He insisted, however, that just as some experiences can be comprehended without the intercession of faith, some things, such as miracles, are the product of a higher reality that is not at all susceptible to reason and must be taken on faith.

As a logician, Aquinas placed limits on the power of God, who, although omnipotent, would nevertheless be incapable of thwarting the laws of logic—he could not create a circular square. As an Aristotelian, Aquinas believed that body and SOUL are inseparable, against the prevailing NEOPLATONIC notion of the soul as an eternal entity in a temporary bodily existence. Aquinas's attempt to apply reason to faith, intended to strengthen church doctrine, not only was rejected by Catholic officialdom but helped set the intellectual tone that contributed to the rise of HUMANISM and the secular attitudes of the Renaissance. Although he revolutionized philosophy, his influence in Catholic theology was dormant until the late 19th century, when Thomist philosophy was officially endorsed by the church as the basis of Catholic education.

See also JUST WAR; NATURAL LAW; NATURAL THEOLOGY; SCHOLASTICISM; TRUTH; VIRTUE.

Archimedes (c.287–212 B.C.E.)

Greek mathematician, noted for his discovery of physical and geometrical principles and his mechanical inventions. The latter included a number of war machines, including catapults, and a cylindrical screw that raised water for irrigation. He also proved the principle of the lever and invented the compound pulley, which he is said to have demonstrated by pulling a fully loaded ship onto a beach single-handedly, declaring, "Give me a place to stand, and I will move the earth."

Archimedes mechanically analyzed the equilibrium of solids and liquids, obtaining *Archimedes' principle,* which states that a body immersed in a fluid is buoyed up by a force equal to the weight of the displaced fluid. According to legend, he made the discovery while sitting in the bath and was so excited that he ran naked into the street exclaiming "Eureka!" ("I have found it"). In a similar story told by Plutarch, Archimedes was asked to determine if King Heiron's new crown was pure gold; noticing the water rising as he entered the bath, Archimedes realized that the volume of water displaced by the crown could be compared with what was displaced by an equal weight of gold—if they were different, they could not be the same material—and rushed out shouting "Eureka!" Because of their similarities, the two stories have become conflated, to the point of causing confusion over which of the two discoveries is known as Archimedes' principle.

In mathematics, Archimedes' elegant and original proofs of theorems on the areas and volumes of figures laid the foundations of differential and integral calculus. In *The Sand Reckoner* he devised ways of writing large numbers, such as the number of grains of sand required to fill the universe. Archimedes died at the hands of a Roman soldier while tracing geometrical diagrams in the sand—an incident that some have suggested is indicative of the inferiority of Roman civilization to that of classical Greece.

Arendt, Hannah (1906–1975)

German-born political philosopher, whose unorthodox analyses of modern political systems and events made her both influential and controversial. Arendt studied with and was strongly influenced by the EXISTENTIALIST philosophers Karl Jaspers and Martin HEIDEGGER. An active opponent of Nazism, she fled to Paris in 1933 and in 1941 to the United States, where she became a naturalized citizen. Arendt's writings ranged over a wide spectrum of political thought, taking novel approaches to provocative subjects such as totalitarianism, anti-Semitism, modernity, wealth, and revolution. She shared Heidegger's belief that literature and poetry can often capture the essence of things in ways "hard facts" and philosophical definitions cannot. Her philosophy falls within no particular movement or ideology; if there is a common thread in her work, it may be the insistence that politics is not a means to practical ends but an endeavor by which humans continually define and redefine themselves in the public arena, where they can be judged from a plurality of perspectives. Arendt did not seek or offer solutions to the modern social and political ills she identified and analyzed; while she believed in the individual's power to bring about change, she also cautioned that change is unpredictable and irreversible, with consequences often unintended by those who set it in motion.

Although Arendt is now recognized as one of the pivotal political theorists of the 20th century, many of her works initially aroused controversy for their unconventional assertions and conclusions. For example, in *The Origins of Totalitarianism* (1951), she pointed to the 19th-century rise of IMPERIALISM and growth of anti-Semitism as the impetus for the development of modern TOTALITARIAN states—specifically, Nazi Germany and Stalinist Russia, which

> *"The sad truth is that most evil is done by people who never make up their minds to be either good or evil."*
>
> —Hannah Arendt, *Thinking*

she essentially equated—and viewed them as systems "of a different nature" than previous oppressive regimes because they added IDEOLOGY to terror to achieve internal control and expansionist ambitions. In *Eichmann in Jerusalem* (1963), a report on the trial of Adolf Eichmann, the German officer responsible for the Nazi extermination camps, she examined "the banality of evil," claiming that Eichmann's atrocities stemmed not from calculated cruelty but from the bureaucratic mind-set, in which rules and routines overcome the capacity to reflect on one's actions.

Arendt believed firmly that meaningful action depends on careful thought. In *The Human Condition* (1958), she identified three progressively complex and thoughtful categories of activity: *labor,* which provides life's material necessities and comforts; *work,* the endeavor of artists and artisans who produce cultural objects; and *action,* the words and deeds that break with repetitive cycles to initiate a new series of events. Her unfinished trilogy, *The Life of the Mind,* of which she completed the first two parts (published in 1978), was based on another three-layered hierarchy, as indicated by its volume titles, *Thinking, Willing,* and *Judging.*

Aristotle (384–322 B.C.E.)

Greek philosopher, whose thought dominated Western philosophy and science for two millennia. A pupil of PLATO, he later founded his own school, the Lyceum, and developed much of his philosophy as a critical response to his teacher. His extant writings are treatises, probably his lecture notes, compiled after his death; the principal works include the *Organon* (on logic), the *Physics,* the *Metaphysics,* the *Nicomachean Ethics,* the *Politics,* and the *Poetics.*

Aristotle was the inventor of classical LOGIC, which also provided the foundation of his approach to scientific investigation. Aristotle's logic was founded on the *syllogism,* in which, given two premises, a certain conclusion (inference) necessarily follows, for instance: "All trees are made of wood; an oak is a tree; therefore, all oaks are made of wood." Aristotle stressed direct observation of nature and insisted that theory must follow from fact. (See also box at LOGIC.)

His cosmology posited a world composed of the four ELEMENTS—earth, air, fire, and water—surrounded by a universe composed of a fifth, superior element, *aether* (ether). He saw motion as the interaction of the moving body and its surrounding medium; terrestrial motion, he said, is discontinuous, linear, and finite, while the heavenly bodies observe a natural, circular, unending cycle. This framework of physical science lasted through the Middle Ages.

Aristotle attempted to classify everything in the universe into *categories,* the prime category being SUBSTANCE. Where Plato had seen matter as an imperfect rendering of ideal forms (see IDEAS), Aristotle postulated *hylomorphism*—form and matter uniting in the earthly sphere to form substance. For example, the "form" of the material human body is the soul; body and soul together make a living being. Aristotle further classified beings according to their common attributes and distinctive qualities; humans, for example, are animals, distinguished from other animals by the faculty of reason. (See also HIERARCHY OF BEING.)

A problem with Plato's theory of ideal (and thus presumably unchanging) forms was that natural objects grow and change. Aristotle overcame this difficulty with his concept of *potentiality.* The acorn is not an oak, but it contains the potential to become one. Form, in this sense, is the innate content of something, developed to its fullest potential either through *entelechy,* the actualization of its native potential (the mature oak tree), or through another's agency: the tree is potentially a pile of lumber, the planks are potentially a ship, and so on.

The idea of potentiality is connected to Aristotle's identification of the four CAUSES of things: *material* (matter), *formal* (form), *efficient* (action), and *final* (purpose). The efficient cause of something is the *motion* that brings it to its "final cause," what it was intended to be—the growth of an acorn into a tree or the shaping of a board into a bowsprit. Tracing efficient cause back to its source, Aristotle concluded that there must be a Prime Mover, an "uncaused cause" that is pure form and wholly actualized: God.

Aristotle's ETHICS were rooted in his identification of REASON as the prime human faculty and VIRTUE (in the SOCRATIC sense of excellence and practical wisdom) as the highest good. This led him to expound his famous principle of the Golden Mean: virtue, informed by reason, lies in the middle path between two extremes (see MEAN). Aristotle saw politics as a branch of ethics— the application of practical wisdom to society. His observation that "man is a political animal" refers to his vision of the *polis,* the system of social order, as a natural, organic entity of which other human affairs are a part. Aristotle's ideal STATE emphasized the family as the root of society and the middle CLASS as the source of equitable wealth. Although neither women nor slaves could be citizens, the polity would give everyone the opportunity to achieve the potential natural to their status.

In his AESTHETIC theory, Aristotle again disputed Plato (and Socrates), who had scorned poetry, and especially drama, as frivolous and antirational. He named tragedy—specifically, Sophocles' tragedies—as the highest form of poetry. Tragedy has the power to impart virtue through the actors' *imitation* of noble acts. It performs a valuable social function by purging negative feelings through the mechanism of CATHARSIS. (See also UNITIES.) For Aristotle, art is the imitation of the possible as well as the actual; what's more, like philosophy, it transcends the particular to embrace the universal.

See also BEING AND BECOMING; HIERARCHY OF BEING; box at LOGIC; METAPHYSICS; MIMESIS; MIND/BODY PROBLEM; VIRTUE.

artificial intelligence (AI)

The emulation of human thought processes by mechanical devices. There is a long history of machines that mimic human behavior, from moving statues in ancient Greece to modern robots that perform complex operations, but while these devices may simulate human behavior in some ways, they are not considered intelligent. Intelligence itself is ill-defined and little understood, but some suggested criteria include CONSCIOUSNESS of self, the capacity to conceive and integrate ABSTRACT concepts, and the ability to draw conclusions from incomplete data.

In the 1930s, the English mathematician Alan Turing proposed the following test for determining if a machine is intelligent. A human asks questions (via an electronic keyboard) of two hidden respondents, one human, one machine. If the questioner cannot determine from the responses whether the communication is with another person or a machine, then the machine is intelligent. To date no device has been constructed that can pass the Turing test (and some critics argue that, in any case, intelligence is a more subtle and elusive concept than could be captured by this test). However, digital computers already demonstrate many "intelligent" capabilities and promise more. Computers can translate languages, play games (including chess at a world-class level), and solve complex logical and mathematical problems. Computers known as "expert systems," which have extremely large data and memory capacities, are said to be able to "think about" the information they contain, analyzing rather than just storing and retrieving it, and thus are considered repositories of knowledge as well as data. As AI systems come to duplicate more and more human mental and behavioral characteristics, a device that can pass the Turing test becomes ever more possible.

See also ANTHROPIC PRINCIPLE; CONSCIOUSNESS; CYBERNETICS; INFORMATION THEORY.

asceticism

The principle of self-denial for the purpose of attaining a heightened state of spiritual awareness, intellectual acuity, or physical ability. The term, from Greek words meaning "hermit" and "exercise," was first applied to the austere regimen followed by soldiers and athletes, but it is primarily associated with religion; ascetic philosophies and practices are found in almost all the world's faiths. The renunciation of physical pleasures and material comforts can mean not just abstinence from pleasure but self-inflicted suffering—enduring harsh conditions, fasting, or mortifying the flesh—and sometimes entails a complete withdrawal from the outside world into a monastic life of discipline and meditation.

Asceticism is one of the two great techniques employed within religious and ethical systems to achieve a state of harmony considered impossible when one is too much involved in everyday life—the other being moderation or temperance (see MEAN). The influence of each approach tends to run in cycles within these systems, one holding sway for a time before yielding to the other. For example, attachment to the ARISTOTELIAN Golden Mean gave way during the decline of Athens to the abstemious example of the STOICS, and the ascetic rigor of the ancient HINDU religions gave way in large part to the "Middle Path" advocated by the BUDDHA. While doctrines that counsel moderation tend to seek a balance between competing worldly claims and spiritual goals, never allowing any one aim to become paramount, asceticism disdains the world, seeing it as a contaminating influence that must be purged if the spirit is to be free. It has long been part of CHRISTIAN dogma, although (as is true in most faiths) it is mitigated in practice, with ascetic strictures followed rigorously only by certain sects, cults, and members of the clergy.

See also CYNICISM; JAINISM; MYSTICISM; NEOPLATONISM.

astrology

System of divination based on the theory that the celestial bodies influence events on earth. It is founded philosophically in the belief that all of creation is interdependent and that the forces guiding the heavenly spheres also

CHINESE ASTROLOGY

The Chinese astrological system, common throughout Southeast Asia, may have initially derived from the Mesopotamian-Greek astrology that spread to India in the early CHRISTIAN era, but it developed independently to become a unique system of divination. Although it has some similarities with Western astrology, most of its symbology and interpretation of astronomical relationships is quite different. For example, where Western astrologers base their calculations on the sun's apparent course through the heavens, the traditional Chinese system emphasizes the monthly circuit of the moon through 28 "mansions." It also divides the sky into entirely different stellar constellations and stresses a planet's appearance, as viewed from the earth, as well as its position. The lunar mansions are divided into four categories corresponding to the moon's four phases and named for the four seasons. Another significant cycle is represented by 12 animal signs, which relate to the 12-year orbit of Jupiter. The animals in the Chinese zodiac are the Rat, Ox, Tiger, Rabbit (or Cat), Dragon, Snake, Horse, Sheep (or Goat), Monkey, Rooster, Dog, and Pig. Like their counterparts in the Western zodiac, each animal symbolizes particular human personality characteristics; people born in that year are said to possess those qualities and to be compatible or incompatible with those born under other signs. The emphasis in Chinese astrology is on predicting the future—in particular, as in the HINDU system, calculating the most auspicious days on which to undertake certain activities, such as business transactions, marriages, and burials.

work to shape the destinies of nations and individuals; it thus contemplates both astronomy and religion, although it has been disparaged by scientists and theologians alike. Astrological prediction is thought to have arisen around 3000 B.C.E. in Mesopotamia, where it superseded the art of reading astral omens to forecast successes and dangers; it developed much of its present form in the Greek civilizations of the first millennium B.C.E.

According to astrological principles, a person's temperament and destiny are considered to be chiefly governed by the relative positions, or aspects, of the sun, moon, planets, and stars at the moment of birth, particularly the sign of the zodiac under which she or he was born and the planet "ascendant" at the time. The zodiac, the band of sky that contains the apparent path of the sun and planets through the heavens, is divided into sectors, or "houses," of

30 degrees each, corresponding to the sun's annual movement through 12 stellar constellations. The houses are named for symbolic animals and mythological figures—Aries the ram, Taurus the bull, Gemini the twins, Cancer the crab, Leo the lion, Virgo the virgin, Libra the scales, Scorpio the scorpion, Sagittarius the archer, Capricorn the goat, Aquarius the water carrier, and Pisces the fish—each of which has characteristic attributes that are imparted to those born under its influence. Using an individual's horoscope—a map of the heavens as they appeared at the time and place of birth—the astrologer analyzes the positions and relationships of the celestial bodies and the traditional qualities associated with them to detect distinctive character traits, talents, proclivities, and liabilities.

Although the 17th-century revolution in astronomy shook many of its assumptions, especially the Ptolemaic notion of a geocentric universe in which the stars circle the earth in fixed spheres, astrology continued to be an accepted branch of science through the 18th century; both COPERNICUS and GALILEO were practicing astrologers. In the modern age, although generally condemned by religious and scientific orthodoxy (and its claim to seriousness undermined daily in frivolous newspaper "horoscopes"), astrology continues to thrive in various forms throughout the world. In India, for instance, it is relied on by many HINDU believers to determine the most auspicious times for important life events such as marriage, but it is generally rejected in BUDDHISM and SIKHISM (see also box). Many contemporary Western astrologers have linked elements of HUMANISTIC psychology to astrological practice, which they see not as fixed prediction but as an aid to personal insight. The natal chart is still thought to reveal one's core nature, but individuals, with free choice, can use that knowledge to develop the better aspects of themselves and minimize the effects of less favorable ones.

See also NEW AGE.

atomism

The theory that all matter is composed of indivisible, irreducible units; generally, any theory that sees complex structures or groupings as constituted of elementary components. HOLISTIC theories, in contrast, see the whole as more than the sum of its parts.

Deriving from the notion that all matter is formed from basic ELEMENTS, atomism offered a solution to the problems of *motion* and *change* that vexed the ancients: how to reconcile BEING with *becoming*. In the West, the theory that matter is not continuous but is composed of innumerable tiny particles—eternal, changeless, impenetrable, identical, self-moving, and indivisible—

> *"Nothing exists except atoms and empty space; everything else is opinion."*   —Democritus

was first clearly stated in the fifth century B.C.E. by the Greek philosopher Democritus, who also coined the term *atom,* meaning "uncuttable." Democritus further postulated that atoms exist and interact in empty space and that change occurs in the world through these interactions. The relative accuracy of this hypothesis is nothing less than astounding, considering that at the time it was pure conjecture and utterly counterintuitive—indeed, PLATO and ARISTOTLE condemned it as nonsense. Coincidentally and almost simultaneously, a very similar atomic theory was posed in the Indian JAINIST philosophy; the later Vaiseshika school of HINDUISM also taught an atomistic theory of physics.

In the first century B.C.E., the Roman EPICUREAN Lucretius outlined an atomistic philosophy in his poem *On the Nature of Things,* which attributed the world's variety to what he saw as atoms' inherent and unpredictable liveliness. The rediscovery of this poem in the 15th century contributed to the eventual reemergence of atomic theory to challenge the prevailing Aristotelianism of the Middle Ages, which conceived of the universe as filled with SUBSTANCE and rejected the idea of moving particles in a void.

DESCARTES and NEWTON held atomistic, or "corpuscular," theories of matter, but it was the English chemist John Dalton who revived the term "atom" and proposed that every elementary chemical is composed of identical atoms of a type unique to that element, and that what differentiates atoms is their weight. The ancient conception of atoms as the irreducible, indestructible basis of matter held firm until the atom was "split" in the 1940s, and QUANTUM physics has recently demolished the notion that reality is fundamentally solid.

Atomistic political and social theories, such as HOBBES's and MILL's, view society as composed of autonomous individuals motivated primarily by competitive self-interest (see INDIVIDUALISM). *Mental atomism* is the theory, most influentially stated by John LOCKE, that human CONSCIOUSNESS is an aggregate of discrete experiences—simple perceptions that combine, like atoms, to produce complex thought. The theory of *logical atomism,* considered and later abandoned by both WITTGENSTEIN and RUSSELL, employs the same analogy, holding that sentences or propositions are "molecular," that is, constructed from "atomic facts," or fundamental units of meaning.

See also REDUCTIONISM.

Augustine, St. (Aurelius Augustinius) (354–430)

Bishop of Hippo (now Annaba, Algeria), one of the principal founders of the theology of CHRISTIANITY. In his youthful search for spiritual and intellectual satisfaction, he first embraced Manichaeism (see DUALISM), then SKEPTICISM, then NEOPLATONISM, and finally, after a sudden conversion, Christianity. In his *Confessions,* a frank reflection on his early life, Augustine probed human nature, confessing his own frailty, for example, in the prayer "Give me chastity and continence, but not yet." For his close examination of mental faculties and his individualistic view of spirit and personality, he has been called "the first modern psychologist."

Augustine held that the highest human aspiration is truth and happiness, which can be fully achieved only by knowledge of God. In *On the Trinity* he described the soul (or mind) as composed of three faculties: memory, intellect (or understanding), and, centrally, will—a reflection of the TRINITY. His most important contribution to ROMAN CATHOLIC theology was his interpretation of the doctrine of *original sin.* He held that the sin of Adam and Eve is inherited by each human soul through the body's sexual conception; as the first sin was temptation and disobedience to God, our punishment is sexual lust, the disobedience of our body to our will; in this fallen state, unable to rule our passions, we require earthly governance and spiritual guidance, in the form of the sacraments of the church, to gain God's forgiveness. Although God has predestined certain souls for salvation, the individual must choose to accept the offer of God's grace, which can be received only through the offices of the Church.

In *The City of God,* Augustine argued that divine providence is active in history, disputed the pagan religious and philosophical systems that had dominated classical Greece and still flourished in much of the Roman Empire, and contrasted two earthly "cities," or ways of life, one ruled by the Devil, the other by God. Although the City of God has been taken as standing for the Catholic Church and the City of Man as a symbol of the decadent Roman Empire, Augustine's intention was apparently more subtle, suggesting that the church, being a worldly entity, is also subject to the Devil's influence, and that Rome—which in Augustine's time was officially Christian—contained elements of wisdom and distinction.

B

Baal Shem Tov See HASIDISM

Bacon, Francis (1561–1626)

English philosopher, author, scientist, and statesman; with DESCARTES, the thinker most closely associated with the late-Renaissance rebellion against SCHOLASTICISM and with the creation of the modern SCIENTIFIC METHOD. Most of Bacon's career was spent in politics, and his concern with practical problems reflects the opinion of the day that too much "speculation" was a sign of weakness in the pragmatic political world. His popular *Essays* (1597–1625) treated a wide variety of matters "civil and moral" in pithy aphorisms.

Bacon's lifetime project was the attempted reconstruction of philosophy, by which knowledge would become practical and hence valuable. "Knowledge itself is power," he declared. In *The Advancement of Learning* (1605), he criticized the reigning Scholastic philosophy as wholly theoretical and formal, bearing no useful relation to the real world. He felt it should be the goal of philosophy and science to understand and control nature. Bacon identified four "idols"—the errors people make in interpreting the world: those arising from the tendency to make crude or incorrect assumptions about human nature ("idols of the tribe"), from individuals' temperaments and biases ("idols of the cave"), from the undue value given to certain terms and ideas simply because they are in common currency ("idols of the marketplace"), and from unthinking acceptance of traditional philosophical attitudes ("idols of the theater"). In the latter category, he particularly criticized overreliance on DEDUCTION, which accomplishes little more than defining terms; exclusive reliance on *experience*, which tempts one to jump to unjustified general conclusions;

THE BACONIAN METHOD

The system of scientific investigation set forth by Francis Bacon in his *Novum Organum* (1620), by which general hypotheses are derived from concrete observations and then rigorously tested. A synthesis of EMPIRICISM and induction (see DEDUCTION AND INDUCTION), it became the basis of the modern SCIENTIFIC METHOD. It requires the collection and recording of data through observation and experimentation, the derivation of theoretical generalizations from comparative analysis of the data, and thorough testing of these hypotheses. Bacon himself was not an experimental scientist; he felt his role was to construct a system that others might use to gradually build up useful human knowledge of the natural world. His one important practical discovery, that heat is produced by motion, provides a good illustration of his method.

Bacon began by identifying a problem: the inability to explain the general nature of heat. He collected data on instances of heat and arranged them in three "tables of investigation"—the tables of presence, absence, and degrees—according to whether the quality of heat was present, absent, or present to a degree. Comparing the information in the tables, Bacon identified features that accompanied the presence, absence, or qualified presence of heat and developed explanatory hypotheses, which he then tested. In these experiments, Bacon discovered that the instances in which heat occurred were accompanied by motion (albeit often on a very small scale), that this quality was absent when heat was absent, and that the degree of heat was proportional to the intensity of the motion. This conclusion, that heat is produced by motion, became a general principle applicable in a variety of situations.

Bacon also originated the idea of the *crucial experiment*, which he called the "crucial instance" or "fingerpost"—a single experiment or set of experiments that would identify the correct hypothesis among several possibilities. Both DESCARTES and NEWTON also subscribed to the notion. In the 20th century, though, scientists such as Karl Popper have argued that a "crucial experiment" may disprove but cannot definitively confirm a scientific hypothesis (see VERIFIABILITY AND FALSIFIABILITY).

and what he called "superstition," in which the metaphors of theology, myth, and poetry are given the status of objective truth.

In place of these flawed approaches, Bacon proposed a method that combined inductive reasoning (see DEDUCTION AND INDUCTION) and EMPIRICAL investigation. This alloy, he argued, would lead to conclusions that are both general and constructive, thus extending human control over nature. (Bacon is thus often credited with the birth of modern, human-centered science, which seeks to tame nature, not just understand it.) The Baconian method (see box), in which hypotheses are developed from empirical observation rather than theoretical speculation, proved a milestone in the development of the scientific method. Bacon's faith in the power of his method was reflected in his UTOPIAN novel *The New Atlantis* (1626, published posthumously), in which he imagined an ideal society whose prime goal was scientific discovery, from which social order followed naturally.

Baha'i

Religion teaching the unity of God, of all religions, and of humanity. Although it is descended from ISLAM, Baha'i is considered a heresy by orthodox Muslims because it rejects the doctrine that Muhammad was the final prophet; Baha'is have at times been persecuted in Islamic countries.

Baha'i was founded in the mid-19th century in Persia (now Iran) by Mirza Husayn Ali Nuri, known as Baha'ullah (Splendor of God), who is considered the latest in a line of prophets, or "divine manifestations" of God, including Moses, ZOROASTER, the BUDDHA, JESUS, and MUHAMMAD. Baha'i grew out of Babism, a reformist Shi'ite offshoot formed by Mirza Ali Muhammad, called the Bab (Gateway) because he was considered the herald of the *mahdi*, a messianic prophet who would reveal the "hidden" Islam and initiate a new prophetic cycle. After the Bab's assassination in 1850, Baha'ullah proclaimed himself the *mahdi*, and most of the Babis became Baha'is. The faith now has some five million adherents throughout the world.

Baha'is believe that God is utterly TRANSCENDENT and therefore unknowable, but is manifested in his messengers, the prophets and founders of the great world religions. Each of these, bringing the message appropriate to his era, has progressively revealed the divine purpose. All religions and their scriptures thus represent expressions of sacred truth, and in the era inaugurated by Baha'ullah it is God's will that all of them be merged into a world religion united by common principles. The Baha'i faith is therefore comprehensively egalitarian, teaching EQUALITY between the sexes, RACES, and CLASSES, and urging all people to work toward world peace, world government, a universal language, worldwide freedom of conscience and endeavor, the end of extreme wealth and poverty, and the reconciliation of religion and science. Baha'i has no dogma, no formal program of worship, and no clergy. Adherents are expected to pray daily, to observe an annual fast and a number of other holy days in the 19-month Baha'i calendar, and to make pilgrimage at least once to the faith's headquarters in Haifa, Israel.

balance of power

A key concept in international relations, usually defined as a rough power equilibrium among STATES, achieved by maintaining military might sufficient to deter aggression by the other(s). A balance of power may be established between individual states of similar strength or through alliances, for example, when several smaller states unite to offset the power of one or two larger ones. It may be *bipolar,* between two states or alliances, or *multipolar,* among several competing centers of power or within an alliance. The term is used in other, sometimes conflicting, senses, as when a nation seen as the linchpin of an alliance, or one possessing a preponderance of military force, is said to "hold the balance of power." It can also refer to a balanced structure or situation in domestic politics.

Although balance-of-power arrangements are at least as old as the classical Greek city-states, the doctrine was first articulated in the 16th century by Francesco Guicciardini, who described in his *History of Italy* the Florentine city-state's policy of preventing any one state from dominating the Italian peninsula. The term first appeared in the 1713 Treaty of Utrecht, which attempted to restore stability among European nations after the War of the Spanish Succession. From the 16th through the 19th century, Europe was the scene of shifting alliances as emerging nation-states combined to thwart single powers or menacing blocs. In the wake of World War I, the formation of the League of Nations was in part an effort to replace the old balance-of-power status in Europe with a system of collective security.

While a balance of power is intended to promote stability, some have argued that such a policy provokes an arms race and inevitable war. In the mid-18th century, the French philosopher Montesquieu criticized contending European alliances as a "disease" that could only lead to "mutual ruination." During the Cold War the nuclear threat of mutual annihilation created a "balance of terror" between the United States and the Soviet Union (see DETERRENCE). While it made all-out war "unthinkable," it did not prevent conflict between the two superpowers but merely channeled it into economic and technological competition and "proxy wars" in smaller countries such as

Angola and Nicaragua—civil wars in which each side was supported militarily and ideologically by one of the superpowers.

See also PLURALISM; REALISM.

Baptists See box at PROTESTANTISM

Barthes, Roland See box at STRUCTURALISM

Baudrillard, Jean (1929–)

French philosopher and sociologist, considered by many the quintessential POSTMODERNIST for his skeptical analysis of contemporary CAPITALISM, consumer culture, and mass media, his critique of the MARXIST and HEGELIAN notion of PROGRESS in history, and his contention that philosophy, sociology, history, and reality have been superseded by *simulation*. His many works of social criticism include *For a Critique of the Political Economy of the Sign* (1972), *The Mirror of Production* (1973), *In the Shadow of the Silent Majorities* (1978), and *Simulacra and Simulation* (1981). Baudrillard both employs and questions the SEMIOTICS of the STRUCTURALIST Ferdinand de Saussure, who identified language as a system of conventional signs. Baudrillard notes that in the new phase of CAPITALISM represented by mass consumer society, the sign is no longer a representation of something real but "an accomplice of capital." In a culture based on consumption rather than production, the meaning of an object derives not from its use but from its acquisition. Need is no longer the result of actual scarcity but a *simulation*, a fraudulent fabrication designed to perpetuate itself through the endless acquisition of objects to satisfy inauthentic, and thus never satiated, needs. Culture is defined not by people but by *simulacra*—unreal images—and commerce becomes a means of social control; there is no more "society," just the "mass."

Baudrillard's analysis also applies to his view of the Hegelian/Marxist concept of "the end of history." In *The Illusion of the End* (1992), he notes that "the acceleration of modernity"—especially the proliferating power of technology, global communications, and the mass media—has taken us to "escape velocity," transcending historical modes of understanding and history itself. In such conditions the "defects" of history—events that do not fit our notion of how they *should* be—are "repaired" by simulations such as "docudramas" and staged news footage. Things become *hyperreal*, undiscernible from reality but artificially conforming to preconceived notions. In *The Gulf War Did Not Take Place* (1995), Baudrillard argues that the 1991 war with Iraq was a simulated event, a charade with a foregone conclusion enacted on television to satisfy both sides' need for self-justifying images. In the realm of the hyperreal, history does indeed come to an end, but not in the way envisioned by Hegel and Marx. Rather than attaining the ultimate stage of development, humankind stagnates in the present. With instant communications, everything happens in real time, and all events—the simulated past as well as the simulated present—come to be seen as taking place simultaneously. History turns back on itself and becomes spherical rather than linear, destroying all notions of past and future.

Beauvoir, Simone de (1908–1986)

French philosopher, novelist, social critic, and political activist, a leading exponent of EXISTENTIALISM and a founder of modern FEMINISM. She is best remembered for *The Second Sex* (1949), perhaps the greatest classic of feminist thought, which set the intellectual stage for virtually all the variants of feminist theory that later emerged. However, like many other French philosophers, de Beauvoir expressed her ideas primarily in works of fiction. A feminist-existentialist theme, that women must take responsibility for their own lives, runs through novels such as *She Came to Stay* (1943) and *The Mandarins* (1954) and especially her cycle of autobiographical works, from *Memoirs of a Dutiful Daughter* (1958) to *All Said and Done* (1972).

Although de Beauvoir's existentialism and that of her associate and companion, Jean-Paul SARTRE, shared a HEGELIAN, PHENOMENOLOGICAL framework, in which our beliefs and actions are seen as resulting from our social relations, hers was of a different character. Whereas in Sartre's existential outlook the world and other people were viewed largely as obstacles to be transcended, eliminated, or assimilated, de Beauvoir, in *The Ethics of Ambiguity* (1948), saw social interactions as by nature ambiguous and unpredictable. The assertion of our own authenticity and freedom, therefore, depends on recognizing the authenticity and freedom of others.

In *The Second Sex*, de Beauvoir examined women's social and intellectual marginalization, in which women are stuck in the sphere of *immanence*, defined by and limited to their biological functions, whereas men alone are TRANSCENDENT, able to create new ideas, institutions, and objects. Historically, she argued, men have defined themselves as "the subject, the ABSOLUTE," and women as "the Other," different from them and hence inferior. Men are seen as rational, intelligent, and moral, women as emotional, intuitive, and

> *"Man is defined as a human being and a woman as a female— whenever she behaves as a human being she is said to imitate the male."*
>
> —Simone de Beauvoir,
> *The Second Sex*

unprincipled; women are considered inessential and incomplete without men, while men are whole in and of themselves. Searching for the origin of this asymmetry between the sexes, de Beauvoir considered a number of "definitions" of the human female—biological, psychological, socioeconomic—and found them all inadequate. She also examined the various ideological means—religious, literary, mythological, scientific—by which the idea of women's "Otherness" has been reproduced. She concluded finally that patriarchy is a thoroughgoing, multilayered, self-perpetuating system that has comprehensively denied women the means of achieving not just EQUALITY but "transcendence." Acquiring political power and economic autonomy is necessary, but not sufficient, she maintained; the societal definitions of masculinity and femininity must change as well, to acknowledge the comprehensive natures of both sexes.

becoming See BEING AND BECOMING

behaviorism

Primarily American school of psychology, based on the study of observable, measurable behavior. The behavior of humans and animals alike is seen by behaviorists in terms of conditioned responses to environmental stimuli, and the role of "subjective" phenomena such as thought, intention, and emotion is either minimized or treated as unknowable and thus untestable.

Behaviorism was born of the attempt by psychologists influenced by LOGICAL POSITIVISM to make psychology an EMPIRICAL science. In his 1913 article "Psychology as the Behaviorist Views It," often called "the behaviorist manifesto," John B. Watson heralded "a purely objective experimental branch of natural science," free of subjective judgments, whose "goal is the prediction and control of behavior." In the "nature/nurture" debate over whether behavior and personality are determined more by innate dispositions or by environmental conditioning, behaviorists came down squarely on the "nurture" side. Indeed, Watson and others have taken the position that consciousness is an aggregate of muscular/glandular "motor" responses and that character, intelligence, talent, and other human qualities are entirely determined by learning.

The behaviorist approach derived from experiments in animal psychology, particularly those of the Russian physiologist Ivan Pavlov, whose famous observations of anticipatory salivation in dogs led to his theories of what is now called *classical conditioning.* B. F. Skinner's "radical" behaviorism, or "operationism," was based on *operant conditioning,* in which reinforcement and punishment are used to instill a learned response to a given action based on the subject's perception of its likely outcome. (See CONDITIONING.) In *Walden Two* (1948) and *Beyond Freedom and Dignity* (1971), Skinner envisioned behavior modification techniques used on a societal scale as a benevolent tool of social control.

Behaviorism was the most influential movement in American psychology from the 1920s into the 1970s. Although its authority has waned (see, e.g., CHOMSKY), it was responsible for establishing the empirical approach that still dominates psychological research, and many of its principles are widely applied. Operant conditioning, for example, has been successfully used to treat conditions ranging from overeating to autism.

See also BIOLOGICAL DETERMINISM; COGNITIVE PSYCHOLOGY; CONSCIOUSNESS; DETERMINISM; POSITIVISM; SOCIAL LEARNING THEORY; STRUCTURALISM.

being, hierarchy of See HIERARCHY OF BEING

being and becoming
A satisfactory definition of "being" would end an age-old philosophical debate. What it means to exist—to be—is the subject of the branch of metaphysics known as *ontology* (from the Greek words for "being" and "knowledge"), sometimes called "first science" or "first philosophy."

One great ontological dispute has been over whether being is a unity or a plurality. PLATO and ARISTOTLE came down on opposite sides of the question; Plato saw this world as an illusory reflection of a perfect ideal (see IDEAS), while Aristotle identified two kinds of being, divided between things that exist only potentially and those that are actualized. Those who espouse unity assert that either things exist or they don't—as Parmenides put it, "That which is, is, and that which is not, is not and can never be." Champions of multiplicity argue that even things we say do not exist must possess some variety of being—if only in our imaginations—since otherwise we could not conceive of them, but we would not grant such things the same degree of being as things we can see and touch.

Implicit, and often ignored, in this debate is the issue of *becoming,* the fact of change. If being were mutable, it could not "be." The concept of *coming-to-be* occupied thinkers before Plato (he placed being in the world of ideal forms and becoming in the material world) but has taken an increasingly important place in philosophy since HEGEL, who designated becoming as the DIALECTICAL interplay between being and nothing—an idea taken up by the EXISTENTIALISTS. A number of philosophers—notably Alfred North Whitehead in the 20th century—have identified becoming, not being, as the fundamental principle of the world. Modern ANALYTIC PHILOSOPHERS tend to see being in terms of LOGICAL and linguistic forms; to them, saying that something exists depends on the values we assign to the vocabulary we happen to use when referring to it; as the American philosopher Willard van Orman Quine stated it, "To be is to be the value of a variable."

See also ATOMISM; BERKELEY; CAUSE; HEIDEGGER; HIERARCHY OF BEING; METAPHYSICS; MONISM; NIETZSCHE.

Benjamin, Walter See box at CRITICAL THEORY

Berkeley, George (1685–1753)
Anglo-Irish philosopher and clergyman, a major figure in British EMPIRICISM. His philosophy, first set out in *A New Theory of Vision* (1709) and *The Principles of Human Knowledge* (1710), developed as a critique of his predecessor LOCKE and as an attempt to reconcile the conviction that all ideas originate in sensory experience (the central tenet of philosophical empiricism) with belief in an omnipresent God.

Taking the empiricist assumption a step further, Berkeley maintained that the objects of perception exist *only* in our experience of them. Locke had held a MATERIALIST conception of things and distinguished between their primary and secondary qualities, that is, between the qualities inherent in things and those derived from our experience of them (see box at LOCKE). Berkeley maintained that what we do not perceive does not exist and what we do perceive exists only by virtue of our perception. He called this view "immaterialism" and summed it up in the phrase "esse est percipi" ("to be is to be perceived"). In Berkeley's theory, a version of IDEALISM, the objects of our perception are "ideas" that, like all the ideas of the human mind, cannot exist outside our CONSCIOUSNESS; there is, therefore, no material world as such. Berkeley did not believe, however, that the world disappears when we close our eyes: these ideas also exist in the mind of God, who guarantees the continued existence of things that escape fallible, temporary human perception.

An omniscient, ever-vigilant God *must* exist, in fact, to preserve the stability and continuity of the universe.

To many of his contemporaries, Berkeley's notion that objects are not really material confounded common sense. Samuel Johnson, deriding the theory, is said to have kicked a stone, stubbing his toe and exclaiming, "I refute it thus."

See also PHENOMENALISM.

big bang theory

The theory that the universe originated from an infinitely dense, infinitely hot point that spontaneously exploded, creating all the matter in the universe. When the EXPANDING UNIVERSE theory was proposed, in the 1920s, one question it immediately raised was what had made it expand. The Belgian mathematician Georges Lamaître proposed that the explosion of a "cosmic egg" or "primeval atom" created the universe, which has been expanding and cooling ever since. But it was not until the late 1940s that the Russian-born American physicist George Gamow and two colleagues fully formulated the "big bang" theory. They postulated that all the chemical elements in the universe today were created in the first few minutes after the explosion, when the extreme density and temperature fused subatomic particles. They further predicted that "reverberations" of the big bang would remain today as background radiation in space.

That hypothesis was confirmed in the 1960s by the radio astronomers Robert Penzias and Arno Wilson and has been repeatedly corroborated. The "big bang," thought to have occurred between 10 and 20 billion years ago, is now the most widely accepted cosmological theory, although alternative scenarios have been offered to explain the background radiation. There is also disagreement on the eventual fate of the universe: will it continue expanding forever (the "open universe" theory), or will it eventually slow and stop, then collapse back in on itself (the "oscillating" or "pulsating" universe theory), perhaps to be born again in another big bang?

biogenesis See SPONTANEOUS GENERATION AND BIOGENESIS

biological determinism

The belief that human behavior is determined more by physiology than by environment and experience; also called *biologism* and *genetic determinism*. According to this perspective, which is the basis of the controversial interdisciplinary field of *sociobiology,* there is a direct link between genetics and behavior. Not only biological traits but social and cultural phenomena are seen as the end result of EVOLUTION through *natural selection.* An essential tenet is the idea of the "selfish gene"—that individual organisms and the species they comprise are simply vehicles for the perpetuation of genes and that behaviors that promote the reproductive ability of an individual or group will be propagated in the gene pool. In this analysis, behavioral patterns, such as the aggressive male/passive female dyad, have arisen because of their value for environmental adaptation and survival (e.g., the aggressive male is better able to hunt and fight, the passive female more readily submits to sex and therefore conception). The evolutionary accretion of these "social traits" results in the behavioral repertoire characteristic of the species.

The term "sociobiology" was first employed in the 1940s in the field of animal BEHAVIORISM, denoting the application of biological theory and methodology to the study of animal behavior and societies. It was extended and popularized by Edward O. Wilson in *Sociobiology: The New Synthesis* (1975), where he argued that the same techniques can be applied to human societies; just as animal behaviors and social structures have a genetic, or "hard-wired," basis, so do those of humankind. The field now encompasses a number of disciplines in the natural and social sciences.

Sociobiology and biological determinism have faced considerable hostility from the scientific and academic communities. Critics view the arguments for genetic determination of psychological attributes and social roles—especially those involving RACE and gender—as pseudoscientific justifications of the status quo, shaped more by personal ideologies and political trends than by scientific rigor. Many FEMINISTS, for example, regard the identification of innate "female qualities" as the patriarchal imposition of stereotypes.

black Muslims

Popular name for African-American adherents of new ISLAMIC sects, particularly the movement founded as the Lost-Found Nation of Islam. Several sects looking to Islam as an alternative to white, European CHRISTIANITY arose in the early 20th century, but it was with the Nation of Islam that the faith took root among large numbers of black Americans. The Nation of Islam was established in 1930 by Wallace Fard, called Master Wali Fard Muhammad, and led by a former GARVEYITE, Elijah Muhammad, after Fard's disappearance in 1934. Its early teachings were black supremacist and messianic, holding that blacks were the original human race and the founders of civilization, that they had been enslaved by whites (an inferior race of mutant "devils") as a test from God, and that they would soon regain their dominant position in a separate black nation after the destruction of white civilization and Christianity. Then as now, it advocated racial separatism and economic self-sufficiency, imposed a strict code of morality, dress, and diet, and proselytized extensively among the inmates of black ghettos and prisons. Many black Muslims have adopted African or Arabic names or taken the surname X, standing for their lost African names, in place of their "slave names," the surnames given their forebears by white slaveholders.

The movement grew rapidly in the late 1950s and early '60s, largely through the charismatic, often inflammatory rhetoric of Malcolm X. Since then it has suffered two ruptures. The first occurred after Malcolm, following a pilgrimage to Africa and the Middle East, disputed the doctrine of black superiority and Elijah Muhammad's moral and spiritual authority (which many believe led to Malcolm's assassination in 1965). The second, after the leader's death in 1975, split the movement into two main factions. One of these, led by Elijah Muhammad's son Wallace, has affiliated with the orthodox Sunni sect (see box at ISLAM) and abandoned separatist ideology, even accepting whites into its ranks. The other, headed by Louis Farrakhan, continues the BLACK NATIONALIST impulse of the early Nation of Islam.

black nationalism

Political ideology and movement among African-Americans that stresses African-derived cultural values, economic independence, and RACIAL unity and pride; also, NATIONALIST and pan-African sentiment among Caribbean and African blacks in response to colonialism.

In the United States, black nationalism is based on the premise that blacks are systematically oppressed by white society and must liberate themselves by rejecting the majority culture and developing autonomous social and economic institutions. Its most influential early spokesman was Marcus GARVEY, who advocated black entrepreneurship and established a short-lived "back-to-Africa" movement. Some black nationalists, Garvey included, have preached not merely racial equality but black superiority, and have made their goal a complete separation of the races, sometimes through repatriation to the African "homeland."

African nationalism, first articulated in the late 19th century by American blacks promoting the establishment of independent African STATES, sounded many of these themes. African nationalists sought an end to white, European influence in black Africa—both political, by colonial governments, and spiritual, by foreign-based missionary organizations (see IMPERIALISM; box at AFRICAN RELIGIONS). Growing out of but contesting nationalism was pan-Africanism, which envisioned a single sub-Saharan African state. Nationalism prevailed over pan-Africanism when the former colonies became independent in the 1950s and '60s and new nation-states were established within the old, often artificial colonial boundaries. The pan-African ideal, notably espoused by the Ghanaian leader Kwame Nkrumah, was acknowledged in the goals of the Organization of African Unity, founded in 1963 to promote common interests among African states, and is still debated in African societies.

The example of newly independent African nations, together with the civil rights movement of the 1960s, gave new impetus to black nationalism in the United States. Civil rights activists such as Stokely Carmichael, impatient with the rate of progress toward equality and skeptical of the goals of integration, called for "BLACK POWER." The separatist doctrine of ethnic pride and self-reliance articulated by Malcolm X, an explicit rejection of the predominantly white, CHRISTIAN American mainstream, remains fundamental to the program of the Nation of Islam (see BLACK MUSLIMS).

See also NÉGRITUDE.

black power

Militant movement in the U.S. civil rights struggle, originating in the 1960s, aimed at asserting African-American political power and reclaiming black dignity and cultural pride in opposition to the dominant white culture. The term, introduced by the singer and activist Paul Robeson in the 1950s, was popularized by Stokely Carmichael, leader of the Student Nonviolent Coordinating Committee.

Black power was a response to the perceived failure of the civil rights movement to substantially improve the circumstances of African-Americans. Its proponents rejected the ideal of integration into the broader American society sought by moderate civil rights leaders such as Martin Luther King Jr. They saw integration as leading to assimilation and the dilution of black culture; instead, they advocated cultural autonomy and encouraged independent political and economic endeavors. This view was epitomized in the BLACK MUSLIM social program articulated by Malcolm X. For some radical groups, such as the Black Panthers, black power also implied the shift from NONVIOLENCE to armed resistance.

See also BLACK NATIONALISM; GARVEY.

Bohr, Niels See box at QUANTUM THEORY

Brownmiller, Susan See box at FEMINISM

Buddha (Siddhartha Gautama) (c.563–c.483 B.C.E.)
Indian religious philosopher, founder of BUDDHISM. The epithet "Buddha" means "enlightened one" and refers—especially in the Mahayana tradition (see box at BUDDHISM)—not only to one man but to the "Buddha nature" that exists eternally in a state of perfect bliss and is from time to time incarnated in human form. Much of the Buddha's biography is legendary, elaborated in traditional accounts of his life. Born Siddhartha Gautama in what is now Nepal, he was the son of a king of the Shakya clan (and thus is sometimes called Shakyamuni, "the Shakya sage"). As a young man he is said to have been dissatisfied with his comfortable but hollow life; wandering one day, he encountered the "four signs" that transformed him—an old man, a sick person, a dead body (these three personifying the world's suffering in the form of old age, disease, and death), and a mendicant monk. These sights and the holy man's example of simplicity and serenity set him on a quest to understand and overcome the afflictions of existence. At the age of 29 he made the Great Renunciation, surrendering family and riches to become a roaming beggar. For six years he sought spiritual awakening with various HINDU teachers and practiced a rigorous ASCETICISM, but ultimately, finding the practices ineffectual and repelled by the Hindu CASTE system, he abandoned that course. He turned to contemplation and finally, after meditating for seven weeks beneath a bo tree, attained perfect ENLIGHTENMENT, or Buddhahood.

In his first sermon after his enlightenment, the Buddha introduced the principles of DHARMA, the vehicle of enlightenment, to five disciples who became the first members of his community *(sangha)*. Central to his teaching are the Four Noble Truths, which identify the causes of suffering and its cure; the Eightfold Path to enlightenment, which prescribes a moderate, "Middle Way" of life; and the idea that all things, including the self, are ephemeral (see BUDDHISM). The Buddha spent the remainder of his long life traveling, gathering a growing following of disciples and founding religious communities that admitted people of any caste and women as well as men.

Buddhism

Religious philosophy based on the life and teachings of the BUDDHA, practiced primarily in Asia. Buddhism is nontheistic; its adherents are taught to seek liberation from life's inevitable suffering by revering the processes of nature, living a virtuous life, and aspiring to oneness with the universe. While ASCETICISM is not part of Buddhist teaching per se, there is a long tradition of ascetic monasticism within Buddhism, and meditation and personal discipline are central to the spiritual practices of all Buddhists.

The three central features of the tradition—the Buddha, Buddhist practice, and the Buddhist community *(sangha)*—are called the Three Jewels, in which Buddhists consider themselves as "taking refuge." The practice of DHARMA is the way to ENLIGHTENMENT, or perfect awareness and understanding. It begins with accepting the Four Noble Truths—that life is suffering, that the cause of suffering is ignorance and craving (desire), that suffering ends when craving is overcome, and that this can be accomplished by following the Eightfold Path. The Eightfold Path, or Middle Way (see MEAN), is one of moderation, neither ascetic nor excessively worldly but concentrating on "right" behavior in eight categories: right understanding, right aspiration, right speech, right action, right livelihood, right endeavor, right mindfulness, and right contemplation.

To the Four Noble Truths is added another crucial fact of existence, that nothing is permanent, even the self. In contrast to the Hindu concept of *atman,* the permanent, transmigrating soul, the Buddha postulated *anatman,* or "no-self." In the Hindu (and JAINIST) view, the soul passes from body to body through the cycle of birth, death, and rebirth *(samsara).* To Buddhists, however, life is only a fleeting union of cosmic elements *(skandhas)* that are constantly in flux. The idea that we have a continuous IDENTITY is an illusion that impedes enlightenment; rebirth occurs because attachment to selfhood generates the repeated aggregation of *skandhas,* causing a chain of bodily existences that can be broken only by shedding the delusion of self. With enlightenment comes the final shedding of karma—the baggage of past lives—the end of the cycle of reincarnation, and the attainment of NIRVANA, a pure spiritual state free from suffering, delusion, and all attachments.

In the centuries after the Buddha's death, his teachings spread throughout India, branching into several major schools, and eventually reached every corner of the Asian continent. In the course of this dispersal Buddhism developed numerous variations of belief and practice as it was absorbed into the continent's diverse cultures (see box). It merged with the folk religions of Tibet, for instance, and in China adopted many of the emphases of TAOISM and even some of the CONFUCIAN concern with societal relationships.

See also KARMA; NONVIOLENCE; SUNYATA; TANTRISM.

BUDDHIST SCHOOLS

The BUDDHA's teachings were at first transmitted orally, resulting in varying interpretations and the establishment of 18 different Buddhist schools of thought. The Mahayana school, or "great vehicle," which arose as a liberalizing tendency about 500 years after the Buddha's death, belittled the older schools as the Hinayana, "lesser vehicle." Of the Hinayana sects, only the Theravada school remains today. Most of the other existing forms of Buddhism are strands of the Mahayana tradition. The following are several of the most important forms of Buddhism practiced in the modern world.

- *Theravada Buddhism* (Way of the Elders), the oldest extant Buddhist school, claims to perpetuate the authentic teachings of the Buddha according to the scriptures of his early followers. The state of Buddhahood can be attained only by the few and only through the rigorous devotions of a monastic life. Wisdom and discipline are the most highly prized virtues. Ritual is not central to devotional practices, but meditation is crucial. The commentaries of the scholar Buddhaghosa (fifth century B.C.E.), especially the *Visuddhimagga* (Path of Purification), are the central Theravada scriptures.

- *Mahayana Buddhism,* in contrast to the stricter Theravada tradition, is the Buddhism of ordinary people. Mahayana differs from Theravada chiefly in its belief that Buddhahood is attainable, in principle, by everyone, and in its doctrine of the *bodhisattva,* the enlightened person who elects to postpone the final attainment of NIRVANA in order to remain in the world and help others along the path. It thus stresses that compassion for those less fortunate and love for all creation are more important than wisdom. The Mahayana tradition also extended the notion of the "Buddha nature"—the inner human potential that was fully realized by the Buddha—into an object of worship. Mahayana Buddhism has given rise to a number of distinct traditions, incorporating a broad variety of rituals and devotional practices (see below).

- *Zen Buddhism* ("Ch'an" in Chinese) is an amalgam of Mahayana Buddhism with TAOISM. Zen is the way of enlightenment through meditation and simple living, avoiding abstract theorizing in favor of direct experience by an "empty" and open mind. Zen was introduced in Japan in the 12th century, where two predominant strains developed. Rinzai Zen was founded by the monk Eisai, who taught via *koans* (paradoxical riddles) and stressed spontaneous enlightenment.

Eisai's student Dogen established the more popular Soto tradition, emphasizing disciplined mental and bodily concentration in meditation. Zen schools also teach painting, calligraphy, and other arts as expressions of an uninterpreted connection with nature. The Buddha is not worshiped in Zen but is regarded as the ultimate example of human potential. Zen was popularized in the West in the 1950s through the writings of D. T. Suzuki and Alan Watts.

- *Pure Land Buddhism,* a widespread Mahayana devotional school, is the cult of a Buddha or *bodhisattva* who dwells in a heavenly "pure land." In India and China he is Amitabha (Infinite Light), in Japan Amida (Infinite Light and Life). His devotees seek to be reborn in the Pure Land, where they will attain enlightenment. The sect thus emphasizes faith, worship, and salvation through heavenly grace. It grew out of the ancient Tendai Buddhist tradition, which taught that the "Buddha nature" exists in all people.

- *Nichiren Buddhism,* also known as the Lotus Sect, is a Japanese Mahayana school also derived from the Tendai tradition. It was founded in the 12th century by the monk Nichiren, who taught that the only true Buddhist teachings were contained in the Lotus Sutra, a first-century scripture that envisions an eternal, cosmic Buddha who is repeatedly manifested in earthly Buddhas. Nichiren introduced the mantra "namu-myoho-renge-kyo" as the central act of devotion, an homage to the Lotus Sutra that, through meditative repetition, can bring salvation. Nichiren Buddhism consists of about 40 different subsects, of which the largest is Nichiren Shoshu.

- *Tibetan Buddhism,* also called Lamaism, is a Mahayana school derived primarily from Indian traditions. Tibetan Buddhism embraces the doctrine of the *bodhisattva* and the gradual road to Buddhahood, achieved through a strict monastic discipline. It consists of four main sects, the most important of which is the Gelugpa school, founded by Tsongkhapa Lozang Dragpa in the late 14th century. The Gelugpa spiritual leader is the Dalai Lama, a title meaning "ocean guru"—a teacher whose wisdom is as deep and wide as the sea. The Dalai Lama is considered the incarnation of the *bodhisattva* Avalokiteshvara, and each successive Dalai Lama is believed to be the reincarnation of the previous one. From the 17th century, the Dalai Lama was also the temporal leader of Tibet, until the country was occupied by China in 1959 and the Dalai Lama was exiled.

Buridan's ass See box at DECISION THEORY

Burke, Edmund (1729–1797)
Anglo-Irish statesman and political theorist, considered the founder of CONSERVATISM. He was a member of Parliament for nearly 30 years, most of them as a member of the WHIG faction, and was known to his contemporaries primarily as a reformer, in the literal (and conservative) sense of the term: re-form. "We must reform in order to preserve" existing institutions, he declared, not transform or replace them. To Burke, society was not the result of an intentional SOCIAL CONTRACT among people but the outcome of an organic, cumulative process of development over time. He disputed the RATIONALISM of the ENLIGHTENMENT, trusting instead in the traditional customs, unwritten rules, and habitual interactions by which society operates; these he called "prejudice," as distinct from consciously applied doctrines. The status quo, therefore—including the hierarchical social order, the monarchy, and the established church—is to be preferred over abstract political theories. The strength of the English constitution, he felt, lay in its reliance on the COMMON LAW guided by precedent. Burke also embraced the LAISSEZ-FAIRE economics of Adam SMITH, maintaining that "the laws of commerce . . . are the laws of nature, and consequently the laws of God."

Burke's most famous and influential work was his *Reflections on the Revolution in France* (1790), in which he condemned the French Revolution, even before it entered its RADICAL stage, as a dangerous experiment that could only lead to chaos and war. The revolution, he wrote, threatened the traditional order by attempting to reshape society according to idealistic notions such as "the RIGHTS of man." But Burke was not unequivocally antirevolutionary. He defended the Glorious Revolution of 1688 as a reaffirmation of traditional institutions and supported the American colonists' revolt against taxation without representation as a historically established right of free Englishmen.

> *"Those who attempt to level never equalize."*
> —Edmund Burke,
> *Reflections on the Revolution in France*

Butler, Judith See box at FEMINISM

C

cabala See KABBALAH

Calvin, John; Calvinism See PROTESTANTISM; box at PROTESTANTISM

capitalism

Economic system driven by the profit motive and characterized by wage labor and private ownership of the means of production. It is contrasted with SOCIALISM, in which the means of production and distribution are publicly owned. *Capital* is property devoted to producing goods—everything from tools and machinery to money invested in production. It is classically seen as one of the three factors of production, the others being land and labor. Central to capitalism is the idea of *private property,* the view that individuals and corporations have the legal and moral right to own property and accumulate wealth. Capitalism is also widely identified with *free enterprise,* in which production decisions are governed by MARKET forces, with minimal government control and regulation; but capitalism can also exist in a planned economy (see SOCIALISM).

The term "capitalism" was coined in the 19th century to describe the rapid industrialization and economic INDIVIDUALISM that characterized the Industrial Revolution, but the system had developed over several centuries. The origins and growth of capitalism—and the reasons it arose only in western Europe—have been attributed to numerous factors, ranging from the Protestant ethic of work and saving (see WEBER) to the decline of the feudal system, when tracts of common land became private property and peasants were forced to become wage laborers. The ideological rationale for capitalism was put forward in the late 17th century by the French economists called Physiocrats and by Adam SMITH, who argued that private ownership and LAISSEZ-FAIRE commerce would yield not only the most efficient but the most socially advantageous utilization of resources. Although the latter assertion is still argued over, few dispute capitalism's unrivaled productive capacity. The most thoroughgoing and influential critic of capitalism has been Karl MARX, who contended in *Capital* (3 vols., 1867–95) that the quest for ever greater profits leads to the exploitation and ALIENATION of workers and to the concentration of wealth in fewer and fewer hands.

No pure form of capitalism exists or ever has; government ownership and regulation play at least some role in all capitalist economies. In the late 19th and early 20th centuries, monopolies and other excesses of capitalism prompted government intervention in the United States in the form of antitrust and worker-protection laws. The Great Depression gave rise to state-sponsored WELFARE services and KEYNESIAN economic policies, which sought to preserve capitalism by tempering two of its intrinsic consequences, a permanent core of unemployment and recurrent cycles of expansion and recession.

Comparisons of capitalism and socialism commonly but erroneously equate capitalism with the free market and DEMOCRACY, and socialism with central economic planning and TOTALITARIANISM. While capitalism shares much of its ideology with classical LIBERALISM, it is not incompatible with authoritarian government. In Italy and Germany under FASCISM, Argentina under Juan Perón, and Indonesia under Sukarno and Suharto, for example, private enterprise coexisted with ruthless political control and various degrees of state ownership and central planning.

caste

The system of social stratification in Indian society, the world's strictest, most immobile, and probably oldest system of social hierarchy, sanctioned by HINDU law and enforced by tradition; by extension, any rigidly imposed CLASS structure. The word "caste" comes from the Portuguese for "clan" or "RACE." The system is based on four main hereditary divisions *(varnas)* denoting occupation, social status, and degree of ritual purity established over 2,000 years ago: Brahmans, or priests; Kshatriyas, nobles and warriors; Vaishyas, merchants and farmers; and Shudras, servants and slaves. Another group, Panchamas ("fifth division"), commonly called Untouchables or *pariahs,* are social outcasts deemed so unclean that their very shadows are considered a pollution.

There are now perhaps 3,000 subcastes (*jati*), ranked according to the degree of purity or pollution associated with their traditional occupation. Caste law designates a fixed, predestined station for each member of society; it restricts social intercourse, and forbids marriage, outside the caste and limits one's choice of profession. The structure is maintained by religious authority that regards it as the natural order of things. The Hindu concept of KARMA, for example, holds that one's present situation is determined by actions in a previous life. Despite periodic opposition (both BUDDHISM and SIKHISM were founded partly out of objection to it), the caste system has survived to the present day, although some restrictions have eased under the pressure of modern reformers. Mahatma GANDHI was particularly critical of the treatment of Untouchables, whom he called Harijan (children of God), and untouchability is now officially outlawed in India, though it still persists.

catastrophism and uniformitarianism

Opposing theories of geological and natural history, especially the formation of the earth's physical features. Catastrophists maintain that dramatic geological irregularities, such as mountains and canyons, could only have been caused by one or more extraordinary, catastrophic events in the earth's history, such as a global flood or collision with a giant meteor. Uniformitarians believe that geological processes at work today, including erosion, earthquakes, and volcanic activity, formed the earth over a very long period of time. A version of uniformitarianism, called *actualism,* holds that these forces were more active or powerful in the past and have steadily diminished. EVOLUTIONARY theory, while fundamentally uniformitarian, embraces those who believe that natural selection has proceeded in irregular leaps, possibly precipitated by environmental cataclysms (cf. PUNCTUATED EQUILIBRIUM).

Before the 19th century, most Western scientists were catastrophists, not least because the age of the earth as envisioned in the Bible—just a few thousand years—could not possibly be time enough for such changes to have occurred gradually. Uniformitarianism, assuming a much older earth, was introduced by the Scottish geologist James Hutton in the late 1700s and developed by Charles Lyell, whose writings influenced DARWIN. Modern geology is primarily uniformitarian, explaining terrestrial evolution in terms of *plate tectonics,* which sees the earth's crust as composed of a series of thin plates that are in constant, sometimes conflicting, lateral motion, resulting in earthquakes, volcanoes, ocean ridges and trenches, and continental drift. (This model has also given rise to the hypothesis that the earth originally contained a single land mass, a primal "supercontinent" called Pangaea, which gradually broke apart to become the present continents.) Catastrophic theory was partially revived in the 1980s when Luis and Walter Alvarez proposed that the massive extinction of the dinosaurs some 65 million years ago was the result of a global atmospheric disaster triggered by the impact of a huge comet or asteroid—a theory supported by the discovery of the remains of an enormous crater in Mexico.

See also CREATIONISM.

catharsis

From the Greek, meaning "purging" or "purification." ARISTOTLE, in his *Poetics,* defined tragedy as "the imitation of an action that is serious and complete in itself," presented with such artistry that it accomplishes, "through incidents arousing pity and fear, the catharsis of such emotions." This brief, cryptic reference has become one of the most famous of AESTHETIC pronouncements and the topic of one of the great literary debates.

In view of PLATO's opinion that the arts' irrational appeal has a destabilizing effect on society, Aristotle may have been arguing to the contrary, that tragedy purges the spectator of intense feelings that interfere with the exercise of reason, or that experiencing profound emotions in a theatrical context allows a pleasurable, safely contained release of strong passions. Or, as some suggest, he may have been referring not to the audience at all, but to the characters working out powerful emotions within the drama. Commentators have also proposed, variously, that the violence and sorrow depicted in tragedy are intended to "harden" the spectator to the realities of life and drive out the "soft" feelings of fear and pity; that pity for the fall of a noble character makes us fear for our own weak selves and thus inspires us to purge ourselves of destructive impulses; or that these purgative emotions restore the natural harmony disrupted by the events depicted in tragedy.

In psychology, the concept of catharsis—purging repressed feelings by bringing them to CONSCIOUSNESS—was basic to the founding of PSYCHOANALYSIS. It was first expounded in this context in the late 19th century by Josef Breuer and adopted by FREUD, who postulated that "hysterical" symptoms were the result of repressed traumatic memories, which, if recalled under hypnosis or through free association, could be purged and dispelled.

See also MENDELSSOHN.

Catholicism See ROMAN CATHOLICISM

cause

The belief that every action has a cause seems intuitively obvious to us, but it wasn't always so. The ancient Greeks, who saw the process of *becoming* (see BE-ING AND BECOMING) as the perpetual creation of order out of chaos, were interested not in the causes of actions but in the causes of *things*. ARISTOTLE divided causation into four categories: the *material cause,* the matter out of which an entity is created; the *efficient cause,* the action that produces the entity; the *formal cause,* the design that determines its form; and the *final cause,* the purpose toward which the entity strives, its function. The idea of cause as producing an effect was almost unknown before the Renaissance; Aristotle used it only in his argument for a Prime Mover as the cause of the universe.

The modern notion of cause and effect was first fully stated by Thomas HOBBES in the mid-17th century. As a thoroughgoing MATERIALIST, Hobbes saw all things as tangible and all events as mechanical. The world was defined by things in motion interacting, so everything that happens (effect) has a necessary antecedent (cause). Only God—Aristotle's "uncaused cause"—stands outside this never-ending chain. The Hobbesian version of causality has informed scientific thought up to the present: all events are explicable in terms of the interrelation of moving bodies, such that the previous movements are the cause of the later consequences.

Causality is often thought of in terms of *necessary and sufficient conditions.* In the absence of a necessary condition, a given event cannot happen; in the presence of a sufficient condition, it will always happen. Oxygen is a necessary but not sufficient condition for fire because fuel and a source of ignition are also necessary; rain is a sufficient but not necessary condition for wet grass because other liquids can also wet it. Causality usually involves multiple factors. An explanation that assigns only *one* cause to a given event—the assassination of Archduke Ferdinand in 1914 as the cause of World War I, for instance—is usually inadequate.

See also GOD, ARGUMENTS FOR; HUME; box at KANT; KARMA; TELEOLOGY.

central dogma (of biology)

The principle that genetic information passes from DNA into the molecular components of cells, but not in the opposite direction. Its articulation by the British molecular biologist Francis H. C. Crick was the final refutation of LAMARCKISM, which postulated that acquired characteristics can be inherited. The central dogma states that inheritance is purely genetic; the child of a great athlete may inherit some of the physical characteristics that contributed to that prowess—long legs, strong lungs, good hand-eye coordination—but not the skills the parent gained through training and experience. That postulate was first expounded by the 19th-century German biologist August Weismann in his *germ plasm theory,* which held that certain cells contain hereditary material that is passed on to offspring but which cannot be affected by any changes in the body's other cells. Weismann's theory was incorrect in detail, but it was influential in spurring research into genetics, and in the 1950s Crick and James D. Watson corroborated its essential insight with their discovery of the structure of DNA.

DNA (deoxyribonucleic acid), often called "the blueprint of life," is the substance in a cell that holds the biochemical information needed for the functioning of a living organism. It is structured as a double helix, two intertwining strands of molecular material whose varied configurations form *genes,* segments of DNA that constitute the biochemical "code." Most genes provide instructions for the synthesis of proteins needed for building, maintaining, or repairing cells. The transition from DNA to protein is not made directly but happens via an intermediate molecule, RNA (ribonucleic acid). One type of RNA acts as a "messenger," transcribing the genetic instructions from the DNA "template" and conveying them to the cellular machinery that manufactures proteins, where "transfer" RNA delivers the specific amino acids called for by the genetic code.

The flow of genetic information from DNA to RNA to protein is unidirectional, a kind of one-way assembly line. The principle that biochemical information passes out of but never into the genes, declared Crick, is "the central dogma of biology." While the recent discovery of retroviral enzymes capable of transcribing DNA from viral RNA has shown that some organisms may be capable of traveling the one-way route in the opposite direction, it remains true that genetic information cannot pass from the cell into the genes: all RNA is transcribed from DNA, and all protein is produced from the RNA message.

chaos theory

A collection of ideas and approaches to the study of complex systems whose behavior resists description by linear equations. Chaotic complex systems are seen as *nonlinear,* with effects out of proportion to their causes; *dynamic* (ever-changing); prone to *randomness;* and particularly sensitive to *initial conditions.* Chaos theory has been applied to the study of weather, population growth and decline, turbulent fluids, forest fires, epidemics, heart attacks, and many other phenomena.

Chaos theory was initially associated with the work of the mathematical meteorologist Edward Lorenz in the 1960s and '70s. While seeking more reliable long-range weather forecasting based on computer models, Lorenz found instead that weather patterns are inherently chaotic. His famous example is the proposition that the minute air currents generated by the flapping wings of a butterfly could set in motion forces that eventually result in a hurricane on another continent.

Concepts associated with chaos theory include *strange attractors,* in which a system exhibits random behavior that almost, but never quite, repeats itself; FRACTAL geometry, which measures irregular, nonintegral dimensions, such as the shapes of clouds and mountains; *self-similarity,* in which patterns repeat themselves, but in different scales; and *doubling,* as, for example, when a small change in the force driving a pendulum doubles its frequency. Chaos theory is anything but uncontroversial. Critics charge that it is overly speculative and mathematically unrigorous, and that its models and conclusions are unreliable. Nevertheless, chaos theory is becoming an important focus of scientific research, spurred by the growing power of computers, which permits increasingly detailed studies of chaotic systems and offers the potential for controlling possible sources of chaos, such as electric power grids.

Chomsky, Noam (1928–)

American linguist and social critic, whose theory of transformational-generative GRAMMAR revolutionized linguistics. Although his greatest influence has been in that field, Chomsky has also been a constant critic of American foreign and domestic policy, both of which he views as antidemocratic and driven by corporate interests. His varied political writings include *American Power and the New Mandarins* (1969), about the Vietnam War; *The Fateful Triangle: The United States, Israel, and the Palestinians* (1983); *Turning the Tide: U.S. Intervention in Central America and the Struggle for Peace* (1985); and *Manufacturing Consent: The Political Economy of the Mass Media* (with Edward S. Herman, 1988).

Chomsky's linguistic theory was first advanced in *Syntactic Structures* (1957) and developed over the next two decades. He is perhaps best known for introducing to linguistics the concept of *universal grammar.* He argued that the apparently effortless, accurate acquisition by young children of their native tongue is at odds with the "poverty of the stimulus"—the myriad incorrect, incomplete, and contradictory linguistic cues they receive from the language spoken around them. In contrast to the BEHAVIORIST view that children learn language through imitation, Chomsky proposed that the child must be born with an innate knowledge about how language works and, since any human infant is capable of learning any human language, that all languages must share the same fundamental structure.

Chomsky asserted that the grammar of every language—the device by which structurally correct sentences are produced—is *generative* (capable of generating an infinite variety of phrases and sentences), *transformational* (reflecting an abstract, "hidden" set of grammatical rules that are transformed into actual usage), and *universal* (sharing structural similarities with all other languages). Universal grammar guides the process of LANGUAGE ACQUISITION, limiting the possible choices about language structure and allowing the child to infer the specific grammatical structure of his or her language from among the options universal grammar makes available. (Some linguists have gone on to make the corollary assertion that the universality of language structure ultimately derives from the structure of the human brain.)

Chomsky's approach owes much to the artificial languages developed by logicians and computer scientists (see also ARTIFICIAL INTELLIGENCE) and to the STRUCTURALIST view that words are primarily arbitrary symbols, given meaning by convention and syntactical context. However, he departs from the structuralists in focusing on the similarities between linguistic structures rather than their differences. For him, the goal of linguistics is to develop a general theory of the structure of languages that can account for the specific grammars of all languages. Chomsky's influence has been enormous. Almost all of modern linguistic theory derives from or is otherwise indebted to his work. His evidence that language is a mental rather than social construct has also had a significant effect on COGNITIVE science generally and has contributed to the decline of behaviorism.

See also INNATE IDEAS; MEANING.

Christ, Jesus See JESUS

Christian democracy See box at DEMOCRACY

Christian Science
Religious philosophy and CHRISTIAN church founded on a rejection of the reality of disease and on the example of JESUS's miraculous healings in the New Testament. The Church of Christ, Scientist was founded in 1879 by Mary

Baker Eddy after a personal curative experience. Eddy believed that since all reality resides in God (the Infinite Mind), human infirmity—indeed, matter itself—is an illusion. Sin, sickness, and even death are the result of ignorance and error, a symptom of disharmony with the divine. Disease can be cured only by realigning oneself with the power of God through prayer and by living in accordance with the divine Truth. Christian Scientists accordingly refuse conventional medical treatment. In *Science and Health, with Key to the Scriptures* (1875 and later revisions), Eddy set out a system, which she claimed was scientifically valid, for regaining and maintaining harmony with the Ultimate.

The religion has no conventional clergy; worship is conducted by "readers" who recite biblical verses and related passages from *Science and Health* in accordance with an unvarying schedule prescribed by Eddy. Practitioners of Eddy's spiritual healing methods are trained and licensed by the church. The society evangelizes through a network of public reading rooms and a series of publications produced at its Boston headquarters; it also publishes a respected national newspaper, the *Christian Science Monitor.*

Christianity

Religion descended from JUDAISM and based on the teachings of JESUS Christ. It is the world's most broadly dispersed and widely practiced religion, with perhaps 1.5 billion adherents in its Eastern ORTHODOX and ROMAN CATHOLIC churches and numerous PROTESTANT denominations and sects. Founded as a small Jewish sect in the first century C.E. in Palestine, Christianity eventually spread throughout Europe. From the 17th century onward, European IMPERIALISM and religious evangelism have created Christian communities in every country in the world. The Christian Bible includes the Old Testament, the Jewish scripture that relates the legendary history of the Israelites, and the New Testament, written by followers of Jesus about his life and ministry and the early development of the new faith.

Christian belief varies widely among its various branches. Its primary unifying principle is the belief that Jesus is the Christ, or Messiah, prophesied in the Old Testament as the savior of Israel. Most Christians also consider him the son of God, incarnated in human form and sacrificed to atone for human sin and ensure the salvation of all souls. At the center of most Christian worship is the belief that he was resurrected after his crucifixion, a sign of life conquering death, of the coming of the promised kingdom of God, and of everlasting spiritual life for all believers. Jesus represents the reinstatement of the convenant between God and the children of Israel, which had been vio-

CHRISTIAN SACRAMENTS

In CHRISTIAN belief, God's grace—his favor, blessing, and divine presence—is bestowed on those destined for salvation. Rituals denoting the presence of grace, called sacraments, are performed in most Christian churches. The ROMAN CATHOLIC and Eastern ORTHODOX churches celebrate seven sacraments: baptism, confirmation (initiation into Christian belief), penance (confession and absolution of sins), the Eucharist, ordination into priestly or monastic orders, matrimony, and extreme unction (anointing the seriously ill in preparation for death). Of these, only two—baptism and the Eucharist—are considered sacraments by most PROTESTANT churches, following LUTHER's conviction that only these were instituted by JESUS.

Baptism, the ritual of wetting the body with water in imitation of Jesus's baptism by John the Baptist, represents induction into the faith and the cleansing of sins. It is practiced by nearly all Christian denominations, usually at birth, although the age at which it is performed and the degree of immersion vary.

The Holy Eucharist, or Communion, is a ritual reenactment of Jesus's Last Supper with his disciples, when he declared that the bread and wine were his body and blood. In the Catholic Mass, the bread and wine tasted by the celebrants are considered to manifest the "real presence" of Christ through the miracle of *transubstantiation,* in which they are converted into his body and blood (while retaining the physical characteristics of bread and wine). In Protestant ceremonies, the bread and wine are symbolic, indicating Christ's "near presence," or, as in the Lutheran doctrine of *consubstantiation,* are thought to be mixed with the substance of Christ.

Disagreement over the nature of the sacraments was central to the Protestant rebellion and separation from the Catholic Church and remains a chief point of divergence in post-Reformation Christendom. Roman Catholics believe that a sacrament, infused with God's presence, has divine power, whereas most Protestants hold that while sacraments are tokens of inner grace, they possess no intrinsic power.

lated by human sinfulness, faithlessness, and evil. In most Christian denominations, the concept of the TRINITY—God in three "persons," Father, Son, and Holy Spirit—incorporates into a monotheistic belief system the divinity of Jesus and the idea of the presence of God's grace in human lives.

The goal of Christian life may be distilled in Jesus's injunctions to his disciples to treat others with charity, mercy, justice, and, most important, love, and to work toward a perfect faith and obedience to God and his law. The way a Christian's life is lived is at least as important as the zeal of his or her worship. By following Jesus's teachings and example, Christians hope to bring their souls into final union with God.

Historically, Christians have divided over issues of religious authority, the role of the church, and the nature and content of worship. The Catholic Church divided into Eastern and Roman rites in the Middle Ages amid schisms that included disputes over the primacy of the Roman pontiff and the nature of the Holy Spirit; Protestant denominations (see box at PROTESTANTISM) split off from the Roman Catholic church beginning in the 16th century, when reformers such as Martin LUTHER challenged the authority of the Pope and the priesthood, and have subsequently proliferated into hundreds of sects formed around differing scriptural interpretations, liturgical rituals, and ecclesiastical structures.

See also AFRICAN RELIGIONS, boxes; AQUINAS; ASCETICISM; AUGUSTINE; CHRISTIAN SCIENCE; CREATIONISM; ESCHATOLOGY; FREEDOM; FUNDAMENTALISM; GNOSTICISM; GOD, CONCEPTS OF, ARGUMENTS FOR; GOLDEN RULE; JEHOVAH'S WITNESSES; LIBERATION THEOLOGY; LUTHER; MILLENARIANISM; MODERNISM; MORMONISM; MYSTICISM; NATURAL THEOLOGY; NEOPLATONISM; PENTECOSTALISM; PREDESTINATION; SCHOLASTICISM; SOUL AND SPIRIT; TEN COMMANDMENTS; TRINITY.

civil disobedience

The intentional, nonviolent defiance of a law, or of a government or its agents, regarded as unjust or illegitimate. Civil disobedience is often undertaken in obedience to what is perceived as a higher moral law (see NATURAL LAW). The term also implies an open, usually public act, risking and often inviting arrest, in order to arouse public awareness or to exert pressure on the civil authority. It is allied to the strategy of NONVIOLENT (or passive) resistance, in which the superior force of the government is confronted and, it is hoped, eventually won over or worn down by the superior numbers (and righteousness) of a multitude.

The term was coined by Henry David THOREAU in his essay "On the Duty of Civil Disobedience" (1849). While accepting the necessity of government (but endorsing the motto "That government is best which governs least"), Thoreau did not accept the necessity of acceding to its unjust or immoral actions. It is our duty, he argued, to take some action to expose and overturn the wrong and to preserve our own moral integrity. Thoreau himself was briefly jailed when he refused to pay a poll tax because the U.S. government permitted slavery and was seeking to extend it in the Mexican War of 1846–48.

> *"Noncooperation with evil is as much a duty as is cooperation with good."*
> —Mohandas Gandhi, 1922

The two most notable and successful heirs to Thoreau's notion were Mahatma GANDHI and Martin Luther King Jr., but the tactic of nonviolent direct action has also been employed, for example, in South Africa in defiance of apartheid laws and more recently in the United States by antiabortion protesters. Gandhi called it *satyagraha* (from the Sanskrit for "truth" and "persistence") and mobilized masses of people in a 30-year campaign of noncooperation with British rule in India. King was inspired by his CHRISTIAN faith and Gandhi's example, and under his leadership the American civil rights movement adopted a strategy of nonviolent confrontation and civil disobedience aimed at exposing the evils of southern discrimination and segregation. The tactic sought to appeal to whites' humanity by meeting violence and hatred with humility and love, and to pressure the U.S. government to intervene with federal power and federal law.

See also NONVIOLENCE.

class

Term denoting social divisions and inequalities based on occupation, economic standing, heredity, or other distinctions. Although social stratification is almost as old as human society—examples include the Indian CASTE system and the medieval European "estates" of nobility, clergy, and commoners—the word "class" was rarely applied to society before the early 19th century. The Industrial Revolution had brought about significant changes in the social order—including the rise of prosperous entrepreneurs and a large urban workforce—that began to be seen in terms of "classes" of people, defined according to their economic function and relation to the system of production.

Although they did not invent the concept (the French SOCIALIST Claude-Henri Saint-Simon was among the first thinkers to analyze social divisions in light of industrialization), the theory of class is associated primarily with MARX and Engels, who declared in *The Communist Manifesto* (1848), "The history of all hitherto existing society is the history of class struggles." They saw economic relations—specifically, ownership and nonownership of property and surplus resources—as the defining element of social structures and the source of social status and group identity. In this analysis, human societies have always divided into hostile groups; under capitalism, they are reduced to two: the *bourgeoisie,* or owning class, and the *proletariat,* or working class. (The French term *bourgeois* originally denoted, and still does in everyday usage, the middle class—merchants and professionals whose incomes and social status place them between the aristocracy of wealth or title, on the one hand, and laborers and the poor, on the other; this tripartite distinction is another common division of classes.) In MARXIST theory, under capitalism class divisions foster *class consciousness,* an awareness of common interests that are threatened by the other class, which fuels class conflict and leads ultimately to SO-CIALIST revolution.

The Marxist class analysis has often been challenged, most influentially by Max WEBER. Weber's concept of class was broader and more flexible than Marx's; for example, he emphasized divisions within classes, distinguished between the owning and commercial classes, and stressed inequality of *life chances* (e.g., access to educational and professional opportunities) as the crucial determinant of class divisions. He also argued that social position stems not only from class but from *status* and *power,* neither of them necessarily deriving from one's economic situation. The claim by revolutionary COMMUNIST states that class had been abolished was challenged by many, including Yugoslavian vice president Milovan Djilas, whose 1957 book *The New Class* charged that the system had spawned a bureaucratic oligarchy that ruled in its own interests.

The American ideal of EQUALITY, the comparative freedom of social mobility in American society, and the rising incomes of unionized labor in the postwar 20th century have prompted resistance to the use of class as a descriptive concept, even inspiring claims—despite great inequalities in wealth and income—that the United States is a classless society. There is, however, broad agreement that economic circumstance is not the sole factor in determining class divisions in modern society. RACISM, for example, may play a more decisive role, as the continued existence of a large African-American underclass attests.

See also ELITE THEORY; MARX; MARXISM.

THE LEISURE CLASS
In *The Theory of the Leisure Class* (1899), the American sociologist Thorsten Veblen described a CLASS of people whose chief characteristic is *conspicuous consumption:* owners and heirs who do not produce anything but who contribute to the economy by consuming goods, and thus provide employment for the producers of those goods. These goods are not only material—luxury vehicles and fashionable dress, for example— but also nonmaterial, such as education and the arts. Indeed, Veblen argued that the leisure enjoyed by the wealthy class creates a market for many of a culture's nonmaterial goods, without which they would not exist. Since it rests upon the economic and social status quo, the leisure class is generally hostile to PROGRESS, Veblen said. Although his critique was aimed specifically at the nouveaux riches of the United States, Veblen pointed out that a leisure class has arisen in every society with private ownership and material surplus.

classicism

Artistic style and cultural perspective based on principles associated with the art and thought of ancient Greece and Rome—harmony, order, REASON, intellect, objectivity, and formal discipline. It thus contrasts with ROMANTICISM, which emphasizes imagination, emotion, and free expression (cf. APOLLONIAN SPIRIT AND DIONYSIAN SPIRIT). Artworks in the classical style represent idealized perfection rather than real life. The Belvedere Apollo and Michelangelo's *David* are not realistic portraits but paragons embodying an ideal of beauty, sculpted according to AESTHETIC principles of proportion, balance, and unity of form. Classicism is also an IDEOLOGICAL viewpoint, reflecting the idea of ancient Greece as the fount of civilization and western European culture as its ultimate fulfillment.

A revival of interest in classical forms and standards first occurred in Europe during the Renaissance, with the rediscovery of the literature and art of antiquity and the rise of HUMANISM. Renaissance painting, sculpture, and architecture imitated Greek and Roman models and aspired to their purity of composition, while education stressed the study of classic literature and the appreciation of antique VIRTUES and "civilized" behavior.

The term *neoclassicism* refers generally to arts that emulate the classical style, and specifically to the classical revival that began in the mid-18th century and continued into the early 19th century. Inspired by the RATIONALISM of the ENLIGHTENMENT, the movement was spurred by archaeological discoveries such as the Roman ruins at Pompeii and Herculaneum. Rejecting the prevalent Rococo style, which favored lighthearted scenes and ornate decoration, neoclassical artists depicted classical subjects in idealized settings, often as allegories of "timeless" ideals such as heroism, duty, and sacrifice. An early-20th-century version of neoclassicism that developed in reaction to the lush self-expression of late Romanticism was seen, for example, in the precise, disciplined poetry of Ezra Pound and other Imagists and in the classical analogies in James Joyce's *Ulysses.*

The *classical ideal,* the conception of European civilization as the heir of Greek rationality, creativity, and VIRTUE, arose in the late 18th century. Its assumption of the superiority of the classical model—and its denial of African and Asian influences on either Greek or later European culture—had a lasting effect on European (and, later, white American) consciousness, and provided much of the rationale for IMPERIALISM and white RACISM.

See also MIMESIS.

Clausewitz, Karl von (1780–1831)

Prussian army officer and military theorist, an important figure in the REALIST school of politics, whose advocacy of "total war" and assertion that war is above all an instrument of political policy had a lasting effect on politics and military strategy. In his classic treatise *On War* (unfinished, published posthumously), Clausewitz defined war as "the continuation of politics by other means." He observed that war does not exist apart from the political motivations behind it and insisted that military leaders must always be subordinate to political leaders. International politics is a struggle between sovereign STATES with well-defined agendas, he said, each seeking to gain advantage at the expense of the others. Although he expounded the theory of *total war,* in which the military objective is total conquest and not only an enemy's armies but its populace and property are fair targets, he cautioned that in reality war is, and must be, limited by its political ends; if it is not, it risks escalating beyond necessity, as the enemy becomes increasingly demonized. Following on from the ideas of MACHIAVELLI and the example of Napoleon (against whom he fought at Waterloo), Clausewitz advocated a shift away from small, private armies to a large, conscripted "patriot" army. In his view, the danger an armed populace might pose to the state was outweighed by the necessity for a fully militarized state perpetually poised for war.

Clausewitz's ideas had a great impact on the military minds of the late 19th and early 20th centuries. His tactical theories formed the basis for the so-called *cult of the offensive* among strategists of the First World War, when waves of infantry were thrown against each other, to often disastrous and bloody effect. They also inspired the German *blitzkrieg,* the "lightning war" of air raids on civilian targets, in World War II. With the advent of nuclear weapons, which made all-out war "unthinkable" (see DETERRENCE), Clausewitz's view that war is a normal aspect of international politics fell into disfavor. However, his conception of war as essentially a strategic contest appealed to some Cold War strategists interested in GAME THEORY, who believed that political ends could both justify and control a limited nuclear war. Neo-Clausewitzians such as the French political scientist Raymond Aron have also sought to restore the legitimacy of war as a political tool.

cognitive dissonance

The psychological tension created by two simultaneous, conflicting cognitions (ideas, beliefs, opinions). The term was introduced by the American psychologist Leon Festinger in *A Theory of Cognitive Dissonance* (1957). Festinger observed that the conflict creates psychological discomfort, which motivates the person affected to try to resolve it by reestablishing *consonance* among his or her cognitions. This can be accomplished either by abandoning or modifying a previously held notion or mode of behavior, by adding other supportive cognitions to bolster one view and overwhelm the other, or simply by evading the conflict through denial or rationalization. The experience of dissonance is a subjective matter, depending not on whether two cognitions are logically inconsistent but on the individual's PERCEPTION that they are. Although not universally accepted, the theory has proved an influential approach to the understanding of attitude formation and change.

A classic example of cognitive dissonance was provided in a study by Festinger and two colleagues (*When Prophecy Fails,* 1956) of a group of religious ADVENTISTS who were convinced the world would end on a certain date. When the appointed day came and went, the believers were forced to deal with the clash between expectation and reality, either by forsaking their conviction or by somehow explaining the discrepancy; in this case, the group's leader announced that the world had been saved by their faith.

cognitive psychology

Approach to psychology that stresses the importance of cognition to human development and behavior. "Cognition" (from the Latin for "to know" or "to think") refers to the processes by which the mind acquires, represents, and uses knowledge, encompassing sensation, PERCEPTION, reasoning, learning, language comprehension and production, problem solving, and memory. The cognitive perspective stands in at least partial contrast to schools of thought emphasizing the affective (emotional), sociocultural, physiological, and BEHAVIORAL explanations of human thought and behavior.

The cognitive approach was prefigured by the researches of early GESTALT theorists and developed by the Swiss psychologist Jean PIAGET in his studies of child development. In the 1930s, the American behaviorist Edward Chase Tolman proposed that learning occurs through the formation of a "cognitive map" of learned relationships between experience and expectations. The development of cognitive psychology was catalyzed in the 1950s by the revolution in linguistics (see CHOMSKY) and by the growth of CYBERNETICS, both of which encouraged the twin metaphor of mind-as-computer and computer-as-mind—the view of cognitive operations as information processing, analogous to the workings of an electronic computer (see INFORMATION THEORY).

Cognitive psychotherapies work on the assumption that emotions and behavior arise from cognitive processes and that dysfunctions stem from an erroneous view of the world and one's relations to it. By identifying these unrealistic thought patterns, the individual can begin to change them. Cognitive methods are often, especially in short-term therapy, used in combination with behavioral techniques such as rewards and punishments, desensitization through "flooding" (intentional exposure to uncomfortable thoughts and the objects of phobias in order to overcome them), and behavioral "contracts" between client and therapist, to "unlearn" ingrained responses.

The interdisciplinary aspect of cognitive studies has grown since the 1970s, developing into what is now called *cognitive science,* an enquiry into the nature of thought, reasoning, belief, and knowledge, that encompasses linguistics, computer science, neuroscience, and philosophy as well as psychology. Another new interdisciplinary field, *cognitive ethology,* has begun to provide evidence for the long-ridiculed position that animals can think.

See also COGNITIVE DISSONANCE; CONSCIOUSNESS; PERCEPTION.

colonialism See IMPERIALISM AND COLONIALISM

common law
System of law based on precedent rather than written codes or statutes; the basis of the English legal system and those of most former British colonies, including the United States. In contrast, most European and Latin American countries, and some in Africa and Asia, operate under a system of *civil law,* de-

rived from the ancient Roman legal code and emphasizing statutory dictates over precedents set by decisions in previous cases. Common law (originally meaning the law that is common to and accepted throughout the realm) resides in the idea that legal principles are established on a case-by-case basis, over time—as Chief Justice Oliver Wendell Holmes observed in *The Common Law* (1881), not by LOGIC but by experience. In Britain, where common law has evolved since the 12th century and there is no written constitution, all law was "judge-made"—based on the interpretation of prior precedents—until the 19th century, when parliamentary statutes began to supplement case law. Even today, when most law is statutory even in common-law systems, appellate courts' review of lower-court decisions is based on precedent.

The cornerstone of common law is *stare decisis* (Latin, "to stand by settled decisions"), which states that judicial decisions must follow established precedent unless it is outmoded or unjust. This qualification allows for flexibility and growth in the law through the setting of new precedent, and is related to *equity*, the equally ancient doctrine that conforms the strict application of law to principles of "natural justice" (cf. NATURAL LAW).

In the United States, common law is influenced by the Constitution, which, on the one hand, sets inviolable principles of law and, on the other, grants some legislative and judicial autonomy to the states, which can enact different laws and interpret them in different ways, so long as they do not conflict with federal law. At first this freedom resulted in widely diverging court decisions from state to state, but uniform procedure codes have now been accepted by most states in areas such as criminal and commercial law, and much of the common law has been supplanted by statute.

communism

Theoretical economic and social system in which land and capital are collectively owned and CLASS divisions do not exist; also the name applied to the SOCIALIST system controlled by the Communist Party in the Soviet Union and other countries. The word, from the same root as "communal" and "community," implies common ownership and cooperative effort, the antithesis of CAPITALISM. Philosophers and social reformers have long envisioned perfected societies partly or entirely based on the communal model. For example, the "philosopher-kings" in PLATO's *Republic* were seen as living communally, sharing everything and owning nothing; Thomas More's fictional *Utopia* of 1516 imagined an ideal commonwealth based on common property, mutual benefit, and universal tolerance; the Diggers of 17th-century England practiced an agrarian communism that abolished private land and all social distinctions.

> *"Under Capitalism, man exploits man. Under Communism, the situation is reversed."*
>
> —Anonymous, Eastern Europe

Perfect communism was thought (by MARX, among others) to have existed in ancient tribal societies, but in the "civilized" world the communist ideal has never been realized outside small-scale religious communities and short-lived communal experiments (see UTOPIANISM).

Communism as a political ideology arose in the early 19th century. The term was at first used as a synonym for socialism—STATE or workers' control of the means of production—but later became associated with the view, expressed in Marx and Engels's *The Communist Manifesto* (1848), that capitalism could be overthrown only by violent revolution, not through gradual evolution. Marx conceived of "full communism" as the final stage of history, when the state would "wither away," collective labor would produce a permanent surplus of necessary goods, and each person would contribute according to ability and receive (from the common storehouses) according to need.

Marx's vision of full communism was never approached by the USSR, the first revolutionary Communist state, or by any of the other nations led by Communist parties. All have been, to a greater or lesser extent, examples of TOTALITARIAN state socialism, characterized by central economic planning and rewards conditioned on performance (as well as party loyalty). "Marxism-Leninism," adopted as Soviet orthodoxy under Stalin, purported to combine Marx's economic theories with Lenin's doctrine of *democratic centralism,* which called for grassroots participation and free debate of policy within the Communist Party hierarchy. In reality, Marxism-Leninism reinterpreted both men's thinking in order to justify dictatorial rule and enforce rigid party discipline. The Soviet dominion over world Communist ideology was weakened, from the 1950s onward, by the defections of China, Yugoslavia, and Albania from the Soviet orbit; by the NATIONALIST character of Communist movements in POSTCOLONIAL African and Asian countries; and by the rise of Eurocommunism, as several Communist parties in the West adopted platforms that urged democratic social and economic reforms within capitalist systems. Within the Soviet Union itself, Nikita Khrushchev's "de-Stalinization" program in the 1950s and Mikhail Gorbachev's PERESTROIKA reforms in the 1980s virtually abolished orthodox Soviet Communism.

See also DIALECTICAL MATERIALISM; GRAMSCI; LENIN; LUKÁCS; LUXEMBURG; MAO ZEDONG; MARKET; MARXISM; SOCIALIST REALISM; TROTSKY.

competition

In economics, MARKET rivalry among businesses. In natural science, the rivalry among life forms (both plants and animals) for limited resources, such as territory, water, and food; successful competition is the basis of natural selection (see EVOLUTION). The economic theory of competition spans a continuum, from *perfect competition,* in which many sellers offer the same product under the same circumstances, to *monopoly,* in which a product is available from only one source, which therefore has no competition. Both of these model circumstances are rare; more common are *atomistic* and *monopolistic* competition and *oligopoly.*

Perfect competition is the ideal state of a free-market economy, in which price is determined solely by SUPPLY AND DEMAND. Wholesale grain markets, for example, approach perfect competition, since there are many producers and their products are essentially identical. Atomistic competition occurs when many different products are offered by many different sellers, such as the vendors at a flea market, who compete for a limited supply of consumer cash. Monopolistic competition is seen when several firms sell different versions of the same *kind* of product. Monopolistic competition exists among restaurants, for instance, because although they are all vying for the business of people who want to eat out, each offers a different cuisine, ambience, price range, and so on; a restaurateur may have a local monopoly on Mexican food, but not on dining options.

An oligopoly is an industry with only a few big producers or sellers, whether one company's product is indistinguishable from the others' (e.g., oil) or is differentiated in one or more ways (e.g., automobiles). Because of their relatively small number, the members of an oligopoly are unusually interdependent, since the actions of one—say, raising or lowering prices—will quickly be duplicated by the others. Prices in an oligopoly tend to be fairly stable, therefore, and competition is generally carried on in other arenas (although both price fixing and price wars occur, as has happened, for instance, in the American airline industry). Trademarks, advertising, and other means of distinguishing similar products are important elements in both oligopolistic and monopolistic competition.

A monopoly exists when the production, distribution, or sale of a product—or all three—is controlled by a single firm. This occurred in the early years of the computer industry, when only one company, IBM, possessed the essential technology. In a monopoly situation, production and price are set at levels intended to maximize profit; the supply of a product is often artificially limited or its price unrealistically inflated, leading to an inefficient use of society's resources.

Comte, Auguste (1798–1857)

French social theorist, the chief exponent of POSITIVISM and founder of sociology (a term he coined, meaning the scientific study of society). In the tradition of the French ENLIGHTENMENT, Comte felt that the future of humanity lay in science and that SCIENTIFIC METHODS could equally be applied to social studies. His philosophy set forth many of the methodological assumptions that still guide scientific investigation, including the insistence that only hypotheses that can be confirmed through observation can be considered valid. However, he departed from the 18th-century English and French EMPIRICISTS in believing that the aim of science is not just to verify facts but to produce general theories under which all phenomena can be explained.

In the six-volume *Course of Positive Philosophy* (1830–42), Comte outlined his "Law of Three Stages." All human societies and intellectual disciplines, he said, have progressed from a *theological* or "fictitious" stage of belief in supernatural agents and monarchical ABSOLUTISM, through a METAPHYSICAL or "abstract" stage of speculative REASONING, to the *positive* or "scientific" stage, which was now dawning. As a social reformer in the era of revolution in Europe, he believed that empirical research into society's problems would not only alleviate them but would lead to the establishment of a new social order based on scientific principles. In this new era, society would be guided by dependable knowledge, ruled by leaders trained in sociology, and perfected by the application of science to social problems. Comte also foresaw a new "religion of humanity" that would reconcile the natural religious impulse with positive knowledge.

conditioning, classical and operant

Two related approaches to learning, both based on the association of certain stimuli with particular responses; the concepts that form the basis of BEHAVIORISM. In classical (or Pavlovian) conditioning, pioneered by the Russian physiologist Ivan Pavlov, an involuntary physiological response is triggered by a previously unrelated stimulus. Operant (or instrumental) conditioning, associated primarily with the American psychologist B. F. Skinner, involves developing *voluntary* behavioral responses based on the perceived outcome of a given action.

Pavlov's development of classical conditioning grew out of his studies of digestion, when he observed that dogs, who naturally salivate while eating, would begin to salivate in anticipation at the sight or smell of food, or even upon seeing the food dish or hearing the feeder's approach. This he called a "conditional reflex"—a response that generalizes from a particular stimulus to the conditions associated with it. (Through a mistranslation, "conditional" later became "conditioned.") Pavlov discovered that when an unconnected stimulus, such as a bell, was added, the dog would soon learn to associate the sound of the bell with the arrival of food and the *conditioned response*—salivation—could ultimately be elicited simply by ringing the bell.

Operant conditioning is derived from many of the same principles as classical conditioning. The primary differences are that it involves voluntary behavioral responses (operants) rather than automatic physiological reflexes and is based on the mechanisms of *reward and punishment* and *positive and negative reinforcement* (the introduction of desirable stimuli and the removal of unpleasant stimuli). The classic model of operant conditioning is the so-called Skinner box (or "operant chamber"), a controlled environment in which an animal's behavior can be influenced by the introduction or removal of stimuli. For example, a pigeon can be trained (conditioned) to peck at a certain switch if that action results in the appearance of a food pellet (reward, positive reinforcement), or if it causes the cessation of an electrical shock (negative reinforcement), or if pecking at the wrong switch generates a shock (punishment). Similarly, behaviorists say, human beings learn by developing conditioned responses to the desirable and aversive stimuli of their surroundings.

Confucianism

Chinese religious and moral philosophy, based on the teachings of K'ung Fu-tsu (551–479 B.C.E.), known in the West as Confucius. Rather than introducing fundamentally new concepts into Chinese thought, Confucius redefined many traditional ideas, creating a practical system of ETHICS and behavior out of what had been ritualized religious codes of conduct. He is said to have edited the Five Classics *(Wu Ching)* of ancient Chinese wisdom, including the *I Ching* (Book of Changes), a divination guide to which he may have added commentaries. His own parables and sayings were collected after his death in the *Analects,* which, with three further works by his later followers, comprise the Four Books *(Shih Shu)* of the Confucian canon. Though its social philosophy is at odds with the nonhierarchical system of TAOISM, Confucianism shares with that religious tradition many ideas central to Chinese thought. These include the concepts of YIN AND YANG, the forces of conflict and balance in the universe, and the idea of the Tao itself, the harmonious principle of nature.

Confucianism rests on the individual's relationship with society, the world, and heaven. Each person has a proper place in political, societal, and familial hierarchies, and within each of these structures one must venerate those above and care for those below. The Mandate of Heaven *(T'ien Ming)* commands that tradition and order be respected in order to maintain the continuity of existence and the equilibrium of the universe. This involves following ethical norms and practicing filial piety and *jen,* or humane benevolence. *Jen,* implying love, goodness, integrity, loyalty, and altruism, applies to every aspect of life and is the highest aspiration of every human being. It is achieved by following the MEAN, or "Middle Way" of balance and harmony, and by applying the Confucian version of the GOLDEN RULE, "What you do not want done to yourself, do not do to others." Right conduct is also governed by *li,* which refers both to the rules of custom, etiquette, and ritual and to the respectful, temperate attitude with which they are observed. The practice of *li* encompasses the veneration of departed ancestors, whose well-being is essential to earthly harmony.

Two strands of Confucianism developed in the third century B.C.E. One, emphasizing tradition, was founded on the teachings of Hsün Tzu, who saw human nature as basically evil, to be controlled through instruction, guidance, and ritual. The other, stressing intuition, is associated with the philosopher Mencius (Meng Tzu), who taught that humans are essentially good and that moral perfection can be attained by all, through study, discipline, and the cultivation of natural energies.

During the Sung Dynasty (960–1279), a neo-Confucian tendency developed, incorporating more elements of Taoism and BUDDHISM and likewise divided into two schools of thought. The most influential was the School of Principle *(Li Hsueh),* led by Chu Hsi (1130–1200), who revised the Confucian canon to emphasize the Four Books, which became the basis of Chinese civil-service exams until the early 20th century. He taught that everything in nature conforms to a single, universal principle or law *(li)* and that change and differences derive from variations in *ch'i,* the vital energy force. This view was later challenged by Wang Yang Ming (1472–1529), whose IDEALISTIC School of Mind *(Hsin Hsueh)* held that everything derives from, and is contained in, the mind. Confucian principles, based primarily on Chu Hsi's comprehensive synthesis of Confucian thought, governed the political and social life of China until the early 1900s. Though its authority steadily waned after the revolution of 1911–12 that ended the dynastic order, Confucianism remained an important influence in Chinese life until the COMMUNIST revolution of 1949.

> *"Man has three ways of acting wisely. First, on meditation; that is the noblest. Secondly, on imitation; that is the easiest. Thirdly, on experience; that is the bitterest."*
>
> —Confucius, *Analects*

Congregationalism See box at PROTESTANTISM

consciousness

From the Latin meaning, literally, "knowledge of things together," a concept commonly invoked but imperfectly understood and contradictorily defined. Consciousness has been variously said to be what separates humans from animals and what unites all creation; purely spiritual and purely physical; the basis of existence and nonexistent. Investigation of consciousness has traditionally been the province of philosophy and psychology, but in recent years it has also occupied researchers in neuroscience, INFORMATION THEORY, and CYBERNETICS.

John LOCKE may have been the first to make a noun from the adjective "conscious," or aware. For him, "consciousness" defined our capacity for introspection, the awareness of our own thoughts. Until FREUD's introduction of the theory of the UNCONSCIOUS, the field of psychology was founded on the investigation of consciousness—or, as William JAMES put it, of "consciousness-as-such," as opposed to mere sensory perception. James's image of the STREAM OF CONSCIOUSNESS, in which experience is a ceaseless, cumulative flow, contrasted with the Lockean theories of mental ATOMISM and associationism, in which PERCEPTION is seen as a string of separate events and consciousness arises from their interconnection, through association, into complex ideas.

Most theories of consciousness assume that it is identical to, or at least coexistent with, the waking state. Many recognize it as involving some interaction of *perception* and *contemplation,* serving as our connection both to the outside world and to our inner selves. Consciousness thus involves *awareness* on two levels: awareness of a mental or physical state ("I am tired") and the *self-consciousness* that allows us to reflect on that state ("I wish I didn't have to work so hard"). Many METAPHYSICAL views of consciousness see it as the basic fact of human existence, the quality comprising all the attributes that divide us from animals, such as imagination, desire, and belief.

Ideas about the *source* of consciousness range from the spiritual to the electromechanical. In Indian and other Eastern philosophies, consciousness is simply a property of everything that is, pervading and pervaded by all of reality. In the 20th century, the scientific study of consciousness has focused on the idea of the brain as data processor. BEHAVIORISTS assert that consciousness doesn't exist, that the brain works only through stimulus and response; "consciousness," therefore, is a social convention used to describe the ways we respond to our own actions. Modern COGNITIVE PSYCHOLOGY likewise discounts consciousness-as-such, viewing mental function largely as the processing of algorithms that determine our reaction to sensations, although it allows the validity of cognitive constructs such as MEANING.

Contemporary work in neurophysics and computer science tends to support the notion of the mind as essentially the world's most complex data processor. Researchers into ARTIFICIAL INTELLIGENCE believe that many of the activities associated with human consciousness—even future planning, awareness of self, and the creation of language and images—can be performed by a sophisticated computer. Critics, however, object that computers are not capable of true subjectivity or intentionality—at least for now.

See also ALIENATION; ANIMISM; ARTIFICIAL INTELLIGENCE; BEHAVIORISM; CLASS; DESCARTES; DIALECTICAL MATERIALISM; DOUBLE CONSCIOUSNESS; FREUD; IDEAS; IDENTITY; JUNG; LOCKE; PARAPSYCHOLOGY; PHENOMENOLOGY; SOLIPSISM; STREAM OF CONSCIOUSNESS.

consequentialism

In ETHICS, the position that the moral value of an action is determined by its consequences. The concept can be viewed from two perspectives, EPISTEMOLOGICAL, answering the question "How can I know how to do what is right?" and METAPHYSICAL, "How can I determine what right is?" In the first sense, it can be contrasted with *intuitionism,* which holds that we come to know the goodness of our actions through some innate sense; in the second, it can be contrasted with *deontology,* which identifies moral imperatives that we are obliged to follow regardless of the consequences.

UTILITARIANISM is the best-known form of consequentialism, holding that the best policy is the one that would result in "the greatest good for the greatest number." The consequentialist position is also applied in reverse; for example, Jeremy Bentham, one of the founders of utilitarianism, advocated a penal policy in which punishment was seen not as retribution for wrongdoing but as a deterrent to those who feared the consequences of criminal behavior; in turn, a lower crime rate, the consequence of deterrence, would prove a greater good for society.

A common objection to consequentialism, that many outcomes are ambiguous or have UNINTENDED CONSEQUENCES—spraying crops with pesticide increases the food supply but may also damage some people's health—has given rise to a controversial corollary. The *double effect* doctrine holds that an action is morally acceptable if its primary or intended consequences are positive, even if it may also have unanticipated or unavoidable negative effects.

The doctrine is used by some theologians, for example, to justify killing by soldiers in a JUST WAR, but it is rejected by others.

See also JAMES; PRAGMATISM.

conservation and symmetry, principles of

Fundamental principles of physics. Principles of conservation state the quantities (e.g., matter and energy) that remain constant in all physical and chemical processes; matter and energy can be neither created nor destroyed, though their form may change. Principles of symmetry state which changes we can make in a physical system without changing its structure.

The *conservation of matter* is an ancient philosophical principle, holding that there can be no creation ex nihilo: something cannot be created from nothing. The principle of *conservation of energy*, in its modern form, is summarized as the first law of THERMODYNAMICS, which states that the total amount of energy in a closed system remains constant. For example, the heat energy released by burning a cubic foot of natural gas equals the loss of stored chemical energy in that amount of gas. The principle of *conservation of momentum* (the product of mass and its velocity) states that the total momentum of an isolated physical system stays constant, even though the momentum of its parts may change. When a flying artillery shell explodes, the total momentum of its fragments equals the momentum of the shell before the explosion. EINSTEIN's special theory of RELATIVITY, which united space and time into space-time, also united mass and energy in the famous formula $E = mc^2$, which demonstrated that mass can be converted into energy. The classical laws of conservation of matter, momentum, and energy were thus unified in the conservation of *mass-energy*.

Principles of *symmetry* govern situations in which systems or objects can be moved or manipulated without altering their structure; for instance, a sphere is said to be highly symmetric because it remains a sphere when it is rotated. Physical laws also have symmetry; the laws of mechanics and electromagnetism have *reflection* (or right-hand/left-hand) symmetry—a propeller screw turning clockwise will obey the same mechanical laws as its mirror-image opposite, turning counterclockwise.

In 1918 the German mathematician Emmy Noether demonstrated a remarkable connection between conservation and symmetry: for every symmetry there is a conserved quantity. Systems that have rotational symmetry conserve angular momentum; systems that are symmetrical in space (that do not change when the entire system is moved) conserve linear momentum;

systems that are symmetrical in time (that do not depend on *when* they are observed) conserve energy; systems that have reflection symmetry are said to conserve *parity*. Much of modern physics has involved the search for additional symmetries, partly because physicists are charmed by the aesthetics of the concept but also because to understand change it is essential to know what does *not* change. In QUANTUM mechanics, symmetry principles state which changes in atoms are "allowed" or "forbidden," accounting for the wavelengths and intensities of radiation emitted and absorbed and enabling scientists to suggest "new" particles that might (or should) exist. All these developments support scientists' conviction that symmetry, with its correlate, conservation, is a basic characteristic of the natural world.

conservatism

Political and social outlook that seeks to preserve systems and institutions that have been tested by time; the opposite of RADICALISM and often of LIBERALISM. Conservatives are generally respectful of tradition, resistant to change—especially rapid or sweeping change—and skeptical of abstract IDEOLOGIES or UTOPIAN doctrines.

Although such principles are ancient, political conservatism as we know it first arose as an alarmed response to the ENLIGHTENMENT and the French Revolution. Edmund BURKE and others warned that the wholesale overthrow of established institutions would lead to chaos. The term seems to have been coined by the French ROMANTIC novelist Chateaubriand, but it joined the political lexicon when the British pro-monarchist Tory Party (see WHIGS AND TORIES) changed its name to the Conservative Party in 1832. In the wake of the Napoleonic Wars of the early 19th century, and amid the social and economic turmoil created by the Industrial Revolution and the rising middle CLASS, many Europeans sought stability in traditional institutions: absolute monarchy (see ABSOLUTISM), aristocracy, hereditary property, social hierarchy, and the established church.

Conservatism is not antithetical to change, as is often supposed, but sees useful PROGRESS as deriving from precedent and accumulated wisdom and therefore rooted in the virtues and values of the past. Conservatism tends to be nonideological—depending for guidance on settled tradition rather than abstract theory—and dubious of political doctrines based on idealistic views of human nature.

In the United States, conservatism has largely been a reaction, first to the political and economic egalitarianism of the American experiment (see EQUALITY), and then, in the 20th century, to the growth of federal power and the WELFARE state. Many contemporary *neoconservatives* are not conservative in the traditional sense, inspired as they are by activist social, economic, and religious ideologies. Furthermore, modern conservatives, in their resistance to governmental intrusion and advocacy of individual responsibility and LAISSEZ-FAIRE economics, embrace many of the doctrines of 19th-century LIBERALISM (q.v.).

See also BURKE.

constructionism See SOCIAL CONSTRUCTIONISM

constructivism

Primarily Russian art movement in the early 20th century, intended to embody the spirit of technology and revolutionary change. The term is also used in psychology, applied to a theory primarily associated with Jean PIAGET, that mental categories are not innate but are constructed during childhood development in response to interactions with our environment (cf. SOCIAL CONSTRUCTIONISM).

Constructivism in the arts, founded by the Russian sculptor Vladimir Tatlin, sought to represent the idea of mechanization as the road to PROGRESS. Artists and architects shaped industrial materials into pure, abstract forms; poets created works that emulated the "speed, economy, and capacity" of industrial production. Though some of its adherents, notably the brothers Naum Gabo and Antoine Pevsner, rejected its application to COMMUNISM, after the revolution of 1917 constructivism became largely identified with the ideal of building a new society in which art, too, is "construction." The defining constructivist work was Tatlin's unrealized design for the *Monument to the Third International* (1919–20), a steel-and-glass building with moving parts that would evoke the power of the machine as a revolutionary symbol. By the mid-1920s constructivism was being overtaken by SOCIALIST REALISM, and many artists emigrated to western Europe. There, International Constructivism influenced the austere, geometric FUNCTIONALISM of Bauhaus design in Germany and the abstract purity of De Stijl (also called neoplasticism) in the Netherlands (see box at ABSTRACTION).

Copernicus, Nicolaus (1473–1543)

Polish astronomer whose heliocentric theory—that the earth and the other planets revolve around the sun—overturned the universally accepted presumption of a geocentric universe. It also challenged assumptions about humanity's place in creation and laid the foundation for the Scientific Revolution.

A canon of the ROMAN CATHOLIC Church, Copernicus declined to assist in the revision of the Julian calendar, which was by then markedly out of step with the seasons, and instead set himself the task of revising the Ptolemaic system on which the calendar was based. According to that system, described by the second-century Egyptian astronomer Ptolemy, the sun and the stars move in circles around the earth and the planets move in *epicycles,* circles whose centers orbit the earth. In *On the Revolution of the Heavenly Spheres,* which he completed by 1530 but withheld from publication until just before his death, Copernicus laid out his theory that the earth is the center only of gravity and the moon, and that all the stars and planets revolve around the sun. According to this model, the earth revolves on its axis once a day and in a vast circle around the sun once a year, and the axis of the earth also rotates during its solar revolution.

In placing the earth in a new relation to the solar system, the Copernican theory overcame many, but not all, of the deficiencies in the Ptolemaic system. For example, it explained the apparently retrograde motion of some planets, which periodically seem to reverse direction in their movement across the sky, a phenomenon that had previously been understood in terms of epicycles. However, in order to account for all the astronomical observations since Ptolemy, Copernicus had to introduce additional circles and motions into his model, so that while it was more accurate than Ptolemy's, it was not much simpler.

Though not immediately condemned by the church, the Copernican system did not at first gain many adherents; the idea of a stationary sun and the earth hurtling through space confounded commonsense observation. The Copernican revolution was not completed until the 17th century, when the work of KEPLER and GALILEO bolstered Copernicus's hypotheses and NEWTON's law of universal gravitation provided the physical basis for the Copernican model.

creationism

The belief that the universe was created by God exactly as recounted in the biblical Book of Genesis; also the doctrine that the theory of EVOLUTION does not satisfactorily account for the existence of life on earth and that the evidence for a suddenly created and fixed, rather than an evolved and changing, universe is more compelling. Most religious creationists are FUNDAMENTALIST CHRISTIANS who believe that the Bible is the literal word of God, that the world was created in six days, and that it is no more than 8,000 years old.

Scientific creationism seeks to make the case for a suddenly created universe by refuting the scientific evidence for evolution and offering alternative explanations of scientific data. Its adherents (a small minority of the scientific community) maintain that life could not have sprung from nonliving matter;

that the multiplicity, complexity, and diversity of species could not have developed from single-celled organisms through mutation and natural selection, as required by the theory of evolution; that the earth's geological features have been formed by catastrophic changes rather than millennial processes (see CATASTROPHISM AND UNIFORMITARIANISM); and that scientists' predisposition to the evolutionary explanation biases their interpretation of biological, geological, and archaeological data. Many other scientists, while rejecting the biblical version of creation, nonetheless believe that the intricacy and variety of the cosmos imply design, and therefore a designer (see GOD, ARGUMENTS FOR).

See also FUNDAMENTALISM.

critical theory

RADICAL, multidisciplinary, neo-Marxist school of social and cultural criticism that emphasizes social transformation as well as critical analysis; more broadly, the term refers to a school of thought that challenges conventional beliefs and social arrangements. Critical theory is historically associated with the Institute for Social Research, founded in Frankfurt, Germany, in 1923 and known as the Frankfurt School. The approach is eclectic, drawing on a variety of intellectual traditions and seeking a synthesis of sociology, psychology, philosophy, and political theory. Max Horkheimer was the institute's director from 1930 to 1958 and contributed strongly to the formulation of its basic themes. The most important thinkers associated with the Frankfurt School in the years before World War II were Theodor Adorno, Walter Benjamin, Erich Fromm, and Herbert Marcuse; in the "second generation" of critical theorists that arose in the 1960s, the most prominent is Jürgen Habermas (see box). Most of the school's members fled Germany after the rise of the Nazis (Benjamin committed suicide rather than be captured by the Gestapo) and the institute was relocated in New York City until 1950.

The Frankfurt School promoted cooperative research but did not produce a unitary social theory. However, its members shared a general outlook and DIALECTICAL approach, and articulated similar themes. These included a critique of modern CAPITALISM that also rejected Soviet COMMUNISM and questioned many of the assumptions of orthodox MARXISM, including the crucial role of a revolutionary proletariat; an examination of the social and psychological basis of modern authoritarianism and RACISM; an AESTHETIC critique that probed the socially conditioned nature of form and MEANING; a reappraisal of the ENLIGHTENMENT ideal of REASON in light of the ALIENATION produced by technological-industrial society; and a repudiation of modern social science's POSITIVISM.

While challenging the scientism and DETERMINISM of traditional Marxist thought, critical theorists have also explored the parallels between capitalist DEMOCRACIES and societies under state SOCIALISM, finding both governed by comparable organizational, technological, and IDEOLOGICAL systems of domination. In the capitalist West the proletariat, far from being a revolutionary force, has been manipulated and co-opted—pacified with material goods and mass culture (cf. BAUDRILLARD). Critical theory questions social scientists' faith in EMPIRICISM, holding that "neutral" social analysis is an illusion. So-called objectivity serves to perpetuate the status quo; the point, as Marx had said, is not merely to interpret the world, but to change it. Further, any valid social science (including critical theory itself) must be critical not only of the assumptions underpinning social structures but of its own methodological and ideological biases (cf. WEBER).

See also LUKÁCS.

MAJOR FIGURES
IN CRITICAL THEORY

- *Walter Benjamin* (1892–1940), while formally associated with the Institute of Social Research for only a short time, significantly influenced its contribution to theories of AESTHETICS and mass culture. His writings, collected in *Illuminations* (1961) and other mostly posthumous publications, are an eccentric amalgam of unorthodox MARXISM, Jewish MYSTICISM, and aesthetic MODERNISM. He rejected as bourgeois the distinction between "high" and popular ("low") culture and was intrigued by the new technological media such as photography and motion pictures. In these and other new art forms, including jazz, SURREALISM, and the didactic theater of Bertolt Brecht, he saw the dissolution of traditional aesthetic modes and the potential for the liberation and democratization of art.

- *Theodor W. Adorno* (1903–1969) was, with Max Horkheimer, the main exponent of two major tenets of critical theory: the position that RATIONALISM has been perverted by POSITIVISM and EMPIRICISM, and the rejection of all dogmatic world-views. In *Dialectic of Enlightenment* (1947), Adorno and Horkheimer charged that subjecting everything to the test of scientific rationality in the name of PROGRESS has degraded the human spirit rather than liberating it. Adorno condemned all philosophies premised on an ABSOLUTE principle (including Marxism), saying they inevitably lead to repression and domination. In the United States, Adorno led a research project into the psychosocial roots of anti-Semitism that concluded, in *The Authoritarian Personality* (1950), that RACISM and FASCISM are grounded in UNCONSCIOUS predispositions to CONSERVATISM and rigidity that are awakened by exploitative conditions in advanced industrial society. Unlike Benjamin, Adorno deplored popular culture, calling it a product of the CAPITALIST "culture industry" that keeps the masses distracted and uncritical of their circumstances.

- *Erich Fromm* (1900–1980), in his PSYCHOANALYTIC theory, broke from the FREUDIAN theory of personality based in psychobiological drives. Fromm emphasized instead the dynamic, DIALECTICAL nature of character, formed by social interactions and socioeconomic conditions. In Fromm's EXISTENTIALIST view, humans occupy a unique and problematic position in the world, part of nature and subject to its laws but also transcending it by virtue of our self-awareness and REASON. Our CONSCIOUSNESS of this dichotomy produces feelings of anxiety and isolation. Fromm viewed characteristics such as greed and exploitativeness as self-defeating attempts to deal with a society perceived as hostile; he saw social conformity as symptomatic of the *social character* we develop in response to received ideas imposed by the prevailing socioeconomic system. Just as our essential nature is to act freely and imaginatively, our essential needs are for relationship, security, and identity. These can be met constructively through cooperative, productive, loving effort on behalf of human well-being.

- *Herbert Marcuse* (1898–1979) became a mentor to the American and European New Left and student protest movements of the 1960s. His Marxist social analysis condemned doctrinaire loyalty to any particular theoretical canon, not only rejecting the Soviet model but also scrutinizing the assumptions of classical Marxism. Marcuse's 1941 study of HEGEL, *Reason and Revolution,* argued that to be rational is to locate a critical stance that is independent of the assumptions that created the social "facts" being studied. In *Eros and Civilization* (1955) he used FREUDIAN terms of reference to envision an unrepressed and nonrepressive ideal society. In his most celebrated work, *One-Dimensional Man* (1964), Marcuse charged that the citizens of modern capitalist society are no longer autonomous individuals but objects manipulated by advertising and stupefied by

ready gratification. Such a society, he concluded, is not free, but enslaved by corporate power. Marcuse found some hope for a new
revolutionary consciousness in a coalition of those outside the prevailing system, including RADICAL students, dispossessed racial minorities, and women.

• *Jürgen Habermas* (1929–) is centrally concerned with reclaiming the
emancipatory power of rational discourse that he maintains has been
lost in modern society. In *Knowledge and Human Interest* (1968) he
identified three realms of scientific knowledge and argued that the
empirical-analytical sphere has eclipsed the HERMENEUTIC and *critical* domains: technology, in the service of political interests, has stifled the
human interests of free communication and intellectual emancipation that REASON was supposed to guarantee. To remedy this, Habermas proposed a theory of *universal pragmatics* that seeks to create the
conditions for an *ideal speech situation* in which everyone can engage in
free political dialogue unfettered by unequal power relations or con-
stricting IDEOLOGIES (cf. ORDINARY LANGUAGE PHILOSOPHY; SEMIOTICS). In
The Theory of Communicative Action (1981) he posited two types of rationality: the *purposive rationality* of economic and technological imperatives, which currently prevails, and *communicative rationality,* which
fosters full social communication and, once restored, would allow
DEMOCRATIC social and political processes to flourish.

cubism

Early-20th-century movement in the visual arts that challenged conventional
depictions of three-dimensional objects; one of the seminal movements in art
history, which set the stage for abstract art (see box at ABSTRACTION). Centered
mainly in France, cubism was pioneered by Pablo Picasso and Georges
Braque and named by a hostile critic, Louis Vauxcelles, after Henri Matisse's
description of Braque's images as "cubes."

Cubism was a stylistic reaction to the lush sensuality of IMPRESSIONISM and
a visual response to the hard-edged mechanism of the industrial world. Its approach was inspired by the bold use of color in the late paintings of Paul
Cézanne and by the geometric abstractions of African sculpture. It was
founded on the idea that space is visually and conceptually ambiguous and
that reality resides in the mind's perception of it. The cubist solution to the
eternal problem in painting, that of depicting volume on a flat plane, was to

see an object simultaneously from all sides, including the inside, and thus to reveal its totality and, beyond that, its ESSENCE. Picasso and Braque also introduced the use of collage in painting, adding materials such as paper, sand, wood, and cloth to a canvas, both to evoke the real world and to undermine the idea of a painting as a facsimile of reality.

The cubist period is traditionally dated from Picasso's 1907 painting *Les Demoiselles d'Avignon,* in which the figures are splintered into sharply angled planes, suggesting several different points of view. Other important cubist painters were Fernand Léger and Juan Gris. The poet Guillaume Apollinaire championed the movement and set out its theoretical principles in his 1913 essay *The Cubist Painters.*

cultural materialism

The view that the nature of a society's culture is determined by its material, particularly economic, conditions. The idea derives from the MARXIST analysis of social systems, but is not held exclusively by Marxists. The term was coined independently, in the 1960s and 1970s, by anthropologist Marvin Harris and literary critic Raymond Williams in relation to their respective fields (see Harris's *The Rise of Anthropological Theory* [1968] and *Cannibals and Kings: The Origins of Cultures* [1978] and Williams's *Marxism and Literature* [1977] and *Problems in Materialism and Culture* [1980]). Both approaches emphasize the role of material and environmental circumstances in shaping cultural expressions and the necessity of taking into account the historical context in which those expressions arose in order to fully understand them. For example, Harris argued that in human societies, the means of production (whether hunting and gathering or industrial manufacturing) determine the nature of economic structures, which in turn determine social relations and individuals' world-views, which shape artistic and other cultural expressions. In literary criticism, cultural materialists tend to see texts as either advancing or subverting the dominant IDEOLOGY rather than reflecting "universal truths." (Cf. DETERMINISM.)

cybernetics

The study of communication and control mechanisms in complex biological, electromechanical, and social systems; a multidisciplinary field closely related to SYSTEMS THEORY and INFORMATION THEORY. The science was founded (and the term introduced, from the Greek for "steersman") by the American mathematician Norbert Wiener in the late 1940s. In his view, all self-regulating systems, from mechanical servomechanisms to electronic computers to the human brain and nervous system, govern themselves according to the same principles. Wiener observed that all such systems operate via a recurrent *feedback loop,* detecting external influences and internal changes, making adjustments, and monitoring the results. To function effectively, therefore, all such systems must have effective communication among their constituent subsystems and efficient control mechanisms to regulate their operations. For example, the act of reaching for an apple involves an interactive sensorimotor cycle in which the information supplied to the eye about what the hand is doing is "fed back" by the brain to the nerves and muscles controlling the hand, whose movement gives more information to the eye, and so forth in a cycle that continues until the task is completed.

Wiener's cybernetic theory grew out of his work during World War II on antiaircraft tracking devices, which had to make continuous adjustments to the guns' trajectories to hit their moving targets. Cybernetics now embraces widely varied fields of endeavor, including communication theory, industrial automation, institutional management, statistics, PROBABILITY theory, ARTIFICIAL INTELLIGENCE, neurophysiology, COGNITIVE PSYCHOLOGY, and GESTALT psychology. The sociological theory of *cybernetic hierarchies,* proposed by Talcott Parsons, suggests that all complex systems, from individual organisms to society as a whole, operate through self-regulating, intercommunicating mechanisms.

Cynicism

Greek philosophical movement founded in the fourth century B.C.E., probably by Diogenes of Sinope, and influential through the fifth century C.E. The Cynics took their name either from their Athenian meeting place, called the Cynosarges, or from the word *kynikos* ("doglike"), referring to the free, unfettered lifestyle that gave them the nickname "dog philosophers."

Cynicism was informed by contempt for the established political and social norms and characterized by a rigorous ASCETICISM. The Cynics made a sharp distinction between "natural" and "artificial" values, exalting VIRTUE as the highest good and rejecting material possessions and social (as well as religious) conventions as tyrannies that caged the spirit. It is said that Diogenes slept in a tub and that once, when he saw a slave drinking from a cupped hand, he broke his only bowl. The Cynics scorned formal philosophy, refusing to debate their position and mocking, in words and action, all intellectual and material pretensions. Their disdain of worldly power is illustrated in the story of Diogenes' meeting with Alexander the Great. When Alexander asked the sage if there was some service he could do him, Diogenes replied, "Stand a little less between me and the sun."

Today's meaning of the word "cynic"—someone who assumes the worst about human nature—no doubt derives from the Cynics' contempt for conventional values. This was reflected in the caustic writings of Diogenes' pupil Crates and later those of Menippus, considered the originator of prose satire. The classic image of Diogenes, walking the streets with a lighted lantern in broad daylight searching for an "honest man," is thoroughly cynical.

In their lives of virtuous poverty, the Cynics paralleled the spiritual asceticism of BUDDHISM and HINDUISM and prefigured CHRISTIAN monasticism. Cynicism has also been called the first Western "back-to-nature" movement, rejecting the ostentation and hypocrisy of society for a simpler, purer life—an impulse that has repeatedly arisen in all historical epochs, down to the hippies of the 1960s.

See also STOICISM.

D

Dada

Artistic and literary movement during and after World War I that rejected traditional AESTHETIC forms and social values and instead exalted randomness, commonplace images, and outrageous eccentricity from a stance of ironic NIHILISM. It was founded in Zürich in 1915 by a group of political exiles including the painter Jean Arp and the poet Tristan Tzara, and named, according to legend, when Tzara chose the word *dada*—French for "hobbyhorse"—at random from the dictionary. The movement quickly spread to Paris, New York, and Berlin (where it was overtly political and revolutionary), attracting artists disillusioned by the war's hypocrisy and carnage and eager to test the boundaries of art and thought. Other important figures were the American Man Ray, the Frenchman Marcel Duchamp, the Spaniard Francis Picabia, and the German Max Ernst. In the interwar years Dadaists published several journals and manifestos and staged provocative exhibitions and performances.

Dadaists delighted in controversy and outrage. Flouting tradition, particularly artistic conventions and aesthetic idols, they wrote nonsense poems, experimented with automatic writing and other chance creations, constructed outlandish assemblages of found objects, created ironic photomontages of mass-media images, presented mundane "ready-made" objects as works of art, and lampooned classic models. The defining Dadaist works in the latter two categories are Duchamp's *The Fountain* (1917)—an ordinary urinal—and his *Mona Lisa* (1919) with a mustache and beard. Dada's iconoclastic, mischievous, cynical, often ABSURDIST stance was resolutely antibourgeois and even "anti-art," aimed at toppling the old, rational forms and creating a new cultural order based on spontaneity and instinct. While the movement itself faded in the 1920s, Dada was the direct precursor of SURREALISM and had a lasting influence on 20th-century art; its emphasis on chance, for example, reappeared in abstract expressionism (see box at ABSTRACTION), and its fascination with mass-market images was reflected in pop art (sometimes called neo-Dada).

Daly, Mary See box at FEMINISM

Darwin, Charles (1809–1882)
English naturalist whose theory of EVOLUTION through natural selection revolutionized biological science and had a profound impact on our conception of the world. Darwin's ideas were based in part on the data he collected on his round-the-world voyage with HMS *Beagle* in 1831–36, especially the observations he made of the variations between related species on the Galápagos Islands. By 1837 he had formulated the conclusion, which he termed "descent with modification," that species change, or "evolve," over time through the appearance of new traits that slowly modify ancestral forms until their descendants are distinctly different. To the question "How do new traits emerge?" Darwin first offered the LAMARCKIAN explanation that individuals' acquired characteristics can be inherited, but soon dismissed it and turned to the theory that new traits emerge randomly within populations, and that these "unsolicited novelties" are the target of evolutionary forces. According to this theory of natural selection, "preferred traits"—those that give an individual the best chance of survival and procreation—are propagated and become characteristics of descendent species, while harmful traits are bred out of the population.

Because his theory contradicted the religious doctrine of CREATIONISM, at that time largely unquestioned, Darwin delayed publishing his ideas for 20 years for fear of social ostracism and professional ridicule. He was motivated to act after learning that a colleague, Alfred Russel Wallace, had independently developed the same theory. The two men published a joint paper, "On the Tendency of Species to Form Varieties, and on the Perpetuation of Varieties and Species by Natural Selection," in 1858. This was followed a year later by Darwin's own book, *On the Origin of Species by Means of Natural Selection, or the Preservation of Favoured Races in the Struggle for Life.*

> *"It seems to me . . . that direct arguments against Christianity or Theism hardly have any effect on the public; and that freedom of thought will best be promoted by that gradual enlightening of human understanding which follows the progress of science. I have therefore avoided writing about religion and have confined myself to science."*
> —Charles Darwin,
>   letter to Karl Marx, 1880

Darwin's theory created a volcanic theological controversy (one that continues today), which escalated with the publication in 1871 of *The Descent of Man*, a work that explicitly placed humanity on the evolutionary chain. The theory was hailed, however, by many of his fellow scientists, though it also met with criticism on scientific grounds. The major theoretical problem Darwin faced, and which he was never able to overcome, was his inability to satisfactorily explain the origin of new traits and the mechanism of hereditary changes. Ironically, the answer, the genetic principle of inheritance, was established by Gregor Mendel in 1865 but ignored by the scientific community until the early 20th century.

See also EVOLUTION; SOCIAL DARWINISM.

Davis, Angela See box at FEMINISM

death of the author

A phrase first used by the French literary and social critic Roland Barthes (see box at STRUCTURALISM), consciously modeled on NIETZSCHE's proclamation of the "death of God." In essence, it means that authorial intention can no longer be seen as a legitimate means of determining the MEANING of a text. As Barthes observed in his 1968 essay "The Death of the Author," 20th-century literary criticism has consistently tended to seek textual meaning in areas beyond the author's intent. For example, MARXIST critics have asserted that the meaning of a text is best understood in terms of what it reveals about socioeconomic relations; FREUDIANS have claimed that it reveals aspects of the author's UNCONSCIOUS; in the STRUCTURALIST view, literary works are self-sufficient systems of "signs"; FEMINIST and multicultural criticism seeks to elucidate the societal assumptions underlying a given text; and DECONSTRUCTION maintains that the meaning of a text is too diverse and elusive to be finally determined at all, even by the author. In short, the "death of the author" is the declaration that assertions of a central, inherent meaning in a text must give way to more fluid lines of interpretation. While this notion was at first specific to literary criticism, the contention that meaning is contingent, not absolute, can be applied in many intellectual fields (cf. POSTMODERNISM).

decision theory

An approach to decision making that uses statistical analysis to project and evaluate probable outcomes in conditions of uncertainty and risk; employed in economics, political science, and other social sciences. It is usually applied to noncompetitive situations, where the outcome does not depend on the decisions of other parties (cf. GAME THEORY, which considers decision making in interaction with other players). Philosophically, it is in the LOGICAL POSITIVIST tradition, which seeks to rationalize thought in terms of mathematical LOGIC.

Decision theory typically weighs alternative courses of action against sets of relevant variables (e.g., MARKET conditions, past performance in similar situations) and assigns a value to the resulting probable outcome of each course of action. The favored statistical tool is *Bayesian inference,* named for the 18th-century English mathematician Thomas Bayes, which measures changes in PROBABILITY and expectations created by the addition of new information to past experience. A "successful" decision may be defined in terms of both *optimality* and *"satisficing"* (a neologism implying "satisfying," "sufficing," and "sacrificing"). The optimum result, the one with the maximum possible "payoff," is not necessarily the preferred one—if, for instance, it would take too much time, energy, or money to accomplish. A "satisficing" outcome

BURIDAN'S ASS

A problem in DECISION THEORY is the question of how choices are made between equivalent alternatives. It is epitomized by a story attributed, probably apocryphally, to the 14th-century French philosopher Jean Buridan. An ass is placed midway between two equally appetizing bales of hay; since there is no difference between them, the animal is incapable of choosing one over the other and, paralyzed by indecision, starves to death. This conundrum illustrates Buridan's contention that the greater good will always be chosen by the human will, but it must have a *sufficient reason* for doing so (see LEIBNIZ).

provides a satisfactory compromise given all the variables, which include the decision maker's personal predilections and tolerance of risk.

Decision theory is primarily prescriptive, not descriptive, a strategy for decision making that proposes an alternative to the common tactic of "muddling through." The latter approach, however, is seen by many social scientists as largely unavoidable, given that most decisions are based on incomplete or imperfect information and are subject to personal preferences and institutional pressures.

See also PUBLIC CHOICE; RATIONAL EXPECTATIONS; SOCIAL CHOICE.

deconstruction

A POSTSTRUCTURALIST approach to criticism primarily identified with the French philosopher Jacques Derrida. Initially associated with literary criticism, it has been taken up in many other disciplines. Indeed, Derrida himself uses the term "text" to include any subject to which critical analysis can be applied.

Deconstructing something means, literally, "taking it apart"—on the one hand, drawing out all its threads to identify its multitude of meanings, and, on the other, undoing the "constructs" of ideology or convention that have imposed MEANING on it. The process of deconstruction inevitably, and intentionally, exposes inconsistencies and contradictions. This leads to the conclusion that there is no such thing as a single meaning in a text, nor can it claim to express any absolute TRUTH. To the deconstructionist, language, truth, and meaning are elusive, equivocal, and relative. Insofar as a text outlasts its author and the particular context in which it was created, its meanings transcend those that may have been originally intended; in this sense, the reader brings as much to the work as the author.

Deconstruction derives from the tradition of HERMENEUTICS and shares its methodology of close textual scrutiny. But the aims of the two approaches are different—for deconstruction, to reveal meaning as fragmented and ambivalent, for hermeneutics, to discover fundamental meaning in a particular context. Derrida uses the term *différance*—a neologism implying both "difference" and "deferring"—to express his view of language as a system in which meaning is created via the contrast of differences between linguistic "signs" (see SEMIOTICS) but in which ultimate meaning, or "presence," is continually deferred because each sign refers only to another sign and never to what is actually signified. Language, so susceptible to interpretation and misinterpretation, is therefore an untrustworthy vehicle of "truth" and meaning. Furthermore, Derrida charges, language has habitually been used to construct world-views based on metaphor, ethnocentric assumptions, and biased "binary concepts"—rationalism/irrationalism, nature/culture, even speech/writing. Derrida identifies this condition as *logocentrism,* the assumption of basic principles (see LOGOS) relying on a fixed, unquestioned ideological "presence" or "center." This notion has been employed by some social critics to expose the ideological premises and contradictions of established institutions and power structures. FEMINISTS, for example, have seized on Derrida's description of *phallologocentrism* in the cultural heritage of Western civilization—the idea that language is a *man*-made artifact serving the interests of the patriarchal social order.

deduction and induction

The two sides of the faculty of REASON, opposed but complementary methods of arriving at sound conclusions. Each proceeds, as it were, in a different direction, as indicated by the Latin roots of the two words, meaning "leading *from*" and "leading *in.*" Deduction forms the basis of classical LOGIC, while induction is the foundation of the SCIENTIFIC METHOD.

Deductive reasoning begins with a UNIVERSAL—a general truth or hypothesis—and leads to knowledge of a *particular* instance of it. The classic form of deductive reasoning is the *syllogism,* in which a necessary conclusion is derived from two accepted premises: "If all cows are ruminants, and Bossy is a cow, it follows that Bossy chews her cud."

Induction begins with the particular (or *existent,* as it is often called today) and moves to the universal, a generalization that accounts for other examples of the same category or class. Unlike deduction, which is a purely mental process independent of experience, induction relies on observation and experimentation. In the case of Bossy, it can be demonstrated that she digests by rumination; if all the other cows we observe do likewise, we can declare, if not a certainty then a high PROBABILITY, that cud chewing is a distinguishing feature of all cows.

While a statement arrived at by deduction from accurate premises is virtually infallible, knowledge from induction is always conditional, since the universal can never be definitively proved through induction: one nonruminant cow would destroy the conclusion. The advantage of deduction is that its answers, if accurately derived, are indisputable. Induction, while less definitive, is generally more useful, since it can generate new information rather than simply exploring aspects of existing knowledge.

See also A PRIORI/A POSTERIORI; box at BACON; VERIFIABILITY AND FALSIFIABILITY.

Deism

Belief in one god, in contrast to atheism and polytheism (see GOD, CONCEPTS OF); specifically, a primarily English religious philosophy of the 17th and 18th centuries, holding that God exists but is not immanent, or active, in his creation. Challenging the established CHRISTIAN church, Deists embraced a NATURAL THEOLOGY that saw REASON and NATURAL LAW as humanity's only guide to moral rectitude and ultimate salvation. Faith, they held, is a logical consequence of our perception and evaluation of natural phenomena and is not dependent on the authority of ecclesiastical dogma or belief in the supernatural. They disputed the validity of revelation and miracles, rejected divine providence and the possibility of direct, personal communication with God, denied that the Bible is the revealed word of God, and repudiated the idea that God is involved in human affairs.

The founder of Deism was Lord Edward Herbert of Cherbury (1583–1648), whose "five pillars" of religion outlined the basic tenets adhered to by most Deists. These included belief in one creator-god, deserving of worship—the most appropriate form of which is a life of virtuous piety and repentance for our sins—who will reward virtue and punish wickedness in the afterlife. Deism was never a coherent theology, however; Deists were, above all, freethinkers, and held disparate views on many matters of faith. With its confidence in the power of reason, the virtues of tolerance, the legitimacy of natural RIGHTS, and the sovereignty of man, Deism was embraced by many leading figures of the ENLIGHTENMENT, including VOLTAIRE and other French *philosophes*. (Many of the *philosophes* were atheists, but all were united in the condemnation of religious "superstition" as the greatest impediment to human progress.) Several of the American Founding Fathers were Deists, including Washington, Franklin, and JEFFERSON.

demand See SUPPLY AND DEMAND

democracy

Form of government in which supreme power is held by the people and exercised either directly or through elected representatives; from the Greek for "people's rule." Although democracy comes in many forms and is subject to differing interpretations (see box), in the modern era the concept generally implies majority rule, minority and individual RIGHTS, equality of opportunity, equality under the law, and civil rights and liberties. The democratic ideal is rooted in the concepts of NATURAL LAW, natural rights, and human dignity and EQUALITY. "Democracy" is a broader term than "REPUBLIC," which denotes nonmonarchical government through elected representatives.

> *"It's not the voting that's democracy; it's the counting."*
> —Tom Stoppard, *Jumpers,* 1972

The idea of democracy originated in ancient Greek city-states such as Athens, in which all citizens (excluding women and slaves) had the right to participate directly in the governing body. PLATO, ARISTOTLE, and other thinkers distrusted pure democracy, however, fearing that majority rule would lead to mob rule. After the decline of the Roman Republic, democratic institutions and ideas lay dormant until the late Middle Ages, when the demise of feudalism and the rise of HUMANISM revived notions of individual potential and human rights. Although monarchy was challenged by many political thinkers of the Renaissance and ENLIGHTENMENT (see, e.g., MACHIAVELLI; LOCKE), few championed popular democracy, preferring instead some form of MIXED REGIME or ELITIST republic.

The democratic idea took root with the American and French revolutions—although the latter eventually confirmed skeptics' warnings that unbridled democracy would invite tyrannical majority rule or degenerate into dictatorship. All successful modern democracies have incorporated constitutional guarantees of individual rights and such structural safeguards as SEPARATION OF POWERS, judicial review, and other checks and balances. Universal adult suffrage is a comparatively recent phenomenon. The first country to grant the franchise to women was New Zealand, in 1893; literacy tests, aimed at excluding African-Americans and immigrants, were required by several U.S. states until the 1960s, when they were outlawed by federal civil rights acts.

See also DEWEY; EQUALITY; FEDERALISM; JACKSONIAN DEMOCRACY; JEFFERSON; LENIN; LIBERALISM; LOCKE; MIXED REGIME; PLURALISM; POPULISM; REPUBLICANISM; ROUSSEAU; SOVEREIGNTY; TOCQUEVILLE.

TEN PERSPECTIVES
ON DEMOCRACY

- *Bourgeois democracy* is the critical, often deprecating term used by MARXISTS and others to characterize representative, *liberal democracy* (see below) and to contrast it with *popular democracy* (see below). The term implies that a CAPITALIST state is not truly democratic because its political institutions place individual interests above those of the majority and owning-class interests above those of the working CLASS, with the result that real power is exercised by economic influence, not popular will.

- *Christian democracy* is a political movement in Europe (especially West Germany and Italy) and South America (e.g., Chile, Venezuela, El Salvador), which grew out of reformist responses in the early 20th century to the social conservatism of the ROMAN CATHOLIC Church. It is now primarily represented by center-right political parties that are officially secular but uphold CHRISTIAN values and appeal to a religious electorate, and that support a mixed-MARKET economy and social-WELFARE programs.

- *Consociational democracy* is the form of government, characterized by power-sharing and proportional representation, adopted in some countries that are split along ethnic, religious, or sectional lines; an alternative to majoritarian rule. A coalition government addresses common issues, autonomy is preserved in parochial (especially cultural) affairs, and minorities, whose representation in the government is proportional to or greater than their percentage of the population, also have a veto power. In the 20th century, European states such as Switzerland and the Netherlands have successfully employed the system. It has also been attempted, with mixed results, in many developing countries, for example, Colombia, Nigeria, and Malaysia.

- *Direct (or participatory) democracy* is a form of government in which the citizenry itself makes legislative decisions instead of delegating that power to elected representatives; often considered the "purest" form of democracy. The best-known examples of such governance are the democracy of ancient Athens and New England town meetings. Referendums, initiative petitions, and recall votes, in which all voters can participate, are also examples of direct democracy. (Cf. *representative democracy,* below.)

- *Directed (or guided) democracy* is the term used to describe (and defend) rule by an individual or an ELITE group in the name of a populace considered unprepared for self-government; a self-styled benevolent dictatorship seen as a transitional stage to *participatory democracy* (see above), found especially in developing countries. The term "guided democracy" is particularly associated with the authoritarian powers assumed by Indonesian president Sukarno in 1956.

- *Industrial democracy* denotes participation by workers in their firms' management decisions, particularly those concerning the terms and conditions of their own employment. Workers may be represented— often by their union delegates—on the firm's governing board, or vote directly on decisions affecting them. Giving employees a proprietary interest in their work is promoted as a way to increase morale, prevent ALIENATION, and minimize worker-management conflict.

- *Liberal democracy* is government characterized by the twin pillars of LIBERAL political thought: democratic *institutions,* on the one hand (e.g., elections, representative legislatures, checks and balances), and democratic *protections,* on the other, such as the personal freedoms guaranteed by the U.S. Bill of Rights. Liberal democracies typically maintain CAPITALIST economies and stress private property RIGHTS, prompting some critics to apply the label *bourgeois democracy* (see above). In its emphasis on individual RIGHTS over the popular will, liberal democracy contrasts somewhat with *popular democracy.*

- *Popular democracy* stresses self-rule by a free and equal people, sees government as an expression of the "people's will," and thus seeks to maximize citizen participation, both electorally and throughout society. Recognizing that the outcomes of democratic processes do not always reflect the popular will, democratic POPULISTS view mechanisms such as the electoral process and constitutional protections of individual liberties as mixed blessings—essential guarantees of popular sovereignty that are also constraints on the pure expression of the popular will. The term "people's democracy" has also been used in COMMUNIST and other TOTALITARIAN states that have abolished democratic institutions in the name of an overriding popular will.

- *Representative (or indirect) democracy* is the form of government in which legislation is enacted by representatives who are elected by the citizenry and in whose name they act. In contrast to *direct democracy*

(see above), representative democracy entails a delegation of power—
but not of SOVEREIGNTY—from the majority to a minority nominated
to act in their interest, either in response to their express wishes or
according to the representatives' own judgment. All large modern
nations with democratically elected governments are representative
democracies. (Cf. REPUBLICANISM.)

* *Social democracy* is the doctrine espoused by those who believe the
  goals of SOCIALISM—especially economic equity and social EQUALITY—
  can be achieved through democratic institutions via moderate redistribution of wealth within a mixed-MARKET economy in a WELFARE
  state. The Labour and Social Democratic parties of the United Kingdom and Germany, respectively, are the principal examples of postwar social-democratic political parties. In Britain, the centrist Social
  Democratic Party was born of a split in the Labour Party in 1981 and
  has since formed an alliance with the LIBERAL Party.

Derrida, Jacques See DECONSTRUCTION

Descartes, René (1596–1650)
French philosopher, scientist, and mathematician, whose application of
mathematical principles to philosophical problems laid the groundwork
for RATIONALISM and the SCIENTIFIC METHOD. Rejecting the SCHOLASTIC method,
which depended on the acceptance of basic assumptions, Descartes began
from the premise "Doubt everything." The Cartesian method, outlined in
his *Discourse on Method* (1637), had four primary rules: accept as true only
what is clear and insusceptible of doubt; divide every problem into as many
parts as necessary; consider each part clearly and completely, building by
accretion to knowledge of the whole; omit nothing from consideration that
might be a source of error. Largely because of this method, which stressed
how we know what we know rather than what it is possible to know, modern
philosophy is often said to have begun with Descartes. His other great contribution to scientific method was his systematization of analytic geometry,
whose fundamental principle—that mathematical equations can be used to
precisely describe the physical world—continues to have great influence.

Descartes set out to build a new foundation for philosophy, beginning
with the search for a base that was immune from doubt. As St. AUGUSTINE had

done before him, he concluded that doubt itself implies the existence of a doubting being. This conclusion led to his famous declaration "Cogito, ergo sum" ("I think, therefore I am"). The *cogito* argument led in turn to an ontological proof of the existence of God: since we can conceive of a perfect being (God), he must exist (see GOD, ARGUMENTS FOR). Descartes divided IDEAS into the INNATE (originating within the mind, particularly self-CONSCIOUSNESS and knowledge of God), the *adventitious* (coming through the senses), and the *factitious* (constructs made up of other ideas).

Descartes's philosophy of DUALISM distinguished strictly between mind and matter as two separate varieties of SUBSTANCE, that which can think and reason and that which simply occupies space. For Descartes, animals fell in the latter category, as purely mechanical objects incapable of any kind of thought. The notion of mutually exclusive classes of substance gave rise to the MIND/BODY PROBLEM: how can the two possibly interact? Descartes's answer was that they intersect in the pineal gland of the brain. He gave an equally fanciful solution to the problem of interactions between physical bodies, which, as dull matter, he considered incapable of independent motion. This was his *vortex theory,* according to which movement is imparted by God and takes place in the vortices within the subtle *ether* that pervades the universe. This idea, which Descartes devised after the cosmology of COPERNICUS was anathematized by the ROMAN CATHOLIC Church, proved very influential in the growth of modern science, since it introduced a mechanical theory of motion that prefigured NEWTON yet was also compatible with the ARISTOTELIAN physics sanctioned by the church.

See also EPISTEMOLOGY; MECHANISM; SCIENTIFIC METHOD; SPONTANEOUS GENERATION AND BIOGENESIS; SUBSTANCE.

descriptivism and prescriptivism

Two opposing ways of representing a given state of affairs. The descriptive approach seeks to impartially classify its object according to the qualities it displays; the prescriptive (or normative) approach presents its object as a standard against which similar states of affairs can be judged. This distinction is made in rhetoric, where a statement such as "That's a knife" may simply identify the object or, with different emphasis, indicate its superiority ("Now, *that's* a knife!") or insignificance ("That's a knife?"). In ETHICS, descriptivism refers to the view that moral values can be derived from purely factual statements, and prescriptivism to the view that moral principles derive from an unquestionable authority. (David HUME's famous statement of the IS/OUGHT PROBLEM disputed the former position, asserting that just because something *is* a certain way does not imply that it *ought* to be so.) Whereas ethical descriptivism does not necessarily require one to act on a moral judgment, ethical prescriptivism does, often invoking a higher authority, such as God or NATURAL LAW, as the justification of its injunctions. Prescriptivism in science treats the word "law" as imperative rather than predictive; for example, the prescriptive version of the law of gravity decrees that apples *must* fall downward, whereas the descriptive version, noting that they *do* fall, predicts that they *will* do so.

In linguistics, the term "descriptivism" was first applied to the type of analysis pioneered by the anthropologists Franz Boas and Edward Sapir in their studies of Native American languages, which sought to classify and interpret sounds and meanings without reference to other languages' linguistic conventions. Linguistic prescriptivism holds that there is an absolute standard of correct grammar and syntax that overrides common usage, often dismissing regional and dialectical variations and differences between written and spoken language. Descriptive grammar seeks to document language as it is actually used, without judging what is "correct," and its practitioners are often faulted for perpetuating "incorrect" usages such as "ain't" and for condoning sexist usages, such as "mankind" and the generic "he," by not advocating gender-neutral alternatives.

determinism

The theory, arising from a strict interpretation of causation (see CAUSE), that every state of affairs is determined by the situation preceding it and constitutes a link in an unalterable chain of events. It is distinct from PREDESTINATION—the idea that God has preordained world history and human destiny—primarily in viewing the course of events as the result of unconscious physical, social, or behavioral laws, not divine agency.

The determinist thesis has been primarily applied to physical laws—the universe conceived as a self-perpetuating mechanism driven by an endless sequence of cause and effect. It is most notably associated with the 18th-century French mathematician and physicist Pierre-Simon Laplace, who speculated that a sufficient intelligence, knowing the laws of physics and the speed and position of every particle in the universe, would be able to predict its entire future. This proposition, which was current throughout the 19th century, has been undermined by QUANTUM mechanics, RELATIVITY, and CHAOS THEORY, all of which postulate the fundamentally indeterminate nature of the universe. Similarly, determinism as a philosophical stance has been challenged by EXISTENTIALISM and PHENOMENOLOGY, which emphasize absolute FREEDOM in an ABSURD universe.

The determinist model, however, has spawned numerous theories applying the concept to the social sciences. *Cultural determinism* holds that our interpretation of the world is inescapably rooted in our particular sociocultural milieu. (The term is also used as a synonym for cultural RELATIVISM, mostly by critics who feel it seeks to explain differences between people in terms of cultural determinants, to the exclusion of other factors.) According to MARX's theory of *historical materialism,* social conditions are determined by underlying economic forces, and historical PROGRESS is determined by the inexorable DIALECTICAL process of CLASS conflict. *Technological determinism* holds that changes in technology cause, or at least propel, social changes; for example, the Industrial Revolution of the late 18th century is said to have created the urban CAPITALISM of the 19th century.

In psychology, BEHAVIORISM interprets human activity as physiological responses to environmental stimuli, determined by prior conditioning. FREUD's theory of *psychic determinism* stressed the UNCONSCIOUS causes of mental and physiological processes, diminishing the scope of individual free will. His assertion that women's nature is biologically determined and inherently inferior was assailed by critics such as Karen HORNEY, whose version of cultural determinism emphasized instead the influence of cultural conditions in psychological development.

See also CULTURAL MATERIALISM; FEMINISM; FREEDOM; HORNEY; SAPIR-WHORF HYPOTHESIS; STOICISM.

deterrence

Generally, the prevention of an unwanted action by the threat of undesirable consequences; particularly, a defense policy based on the ability to inflict unacceptable damage on an aggressor. Deterrence was the foundation of the military strategy of both superpowers during most of the Cold War, based on the policy of mutual assured destruction (MAD) as a result of massive retaliation in kind against any nuclear attack.

To succeed, deterrence must be *credible:* the party practicing it must be seen as having both the capability and the willingness to carry out the threat. It also assumes that the adversary is *rational* and will not intentionally invite disastrous consequences. What in modern deterrence theory is called the *credibility problem* arises from the question of whether a policy based on mutual destruction can be considered either credible or rational, since it depends on the willingness to risk self-annihilation.

The policy of nuclear deterrence, which the United States adopted in the 1950s after the Soviet Union acquired H-bomb technology, created a functional

BALANCE OF POWER (called a "balance of terror") between the superpowers. But the notion that nuclear war was "unthinkable" also led to acts of brinkmanship such as the Cuban missile crisis of 1962, when the United States "rattled the nuclear saber" to force the withdrawal of Soviet missiles from Cuba.

The principle of *extended deterrence* was the basis of the NATO and Warsaw Pact alliances, in which the superpowers extended the "nuclear umbrella" over their allies in Europe, using the nuclear threat to discourage attack by conventional forces. However, some critics argue that the policy aimed at preventing World War III actually encouraged U.S. and Soviet involvement in "small" conventional wars—directly, as in Vietnam and Afghanistan, and indirectly, as in Ethiopia and Nicaragua—based on the calculation that the other side would not intervene to the extent of risking a nuclear confrontation.

See also GAME THEORY; JUST WAR.

Dewey, John (1859–1952)

American philosopher and educator. Heir to the philosophy of PRAGMATISM as propounded by William JAMES and primary architect of the theory of PROGRESSIVE education, Dewey is widely considered the most influential American philosopher. A central emphasis on human *experience* is evident throughout his work—in his practical philosophy (expounded in the 1920 *Reconstruction in Philosophy* and many other works), in his support of social and political causes, in his hands-on approach to education, and in his theory of art as an integral part of life, not an "impractical" peripheral.

In Dewey's version of pragmatism, which he called *instrumentalism* or *experimentalism,* the concepts of knowledge and TRUTH are entirely dependent on their practical uses. Knowledge (see EPISTEMOLOGY) is the result of EMPIRICAL inquiry that solves the problem at hand; truth is an idea that works. He rejected the "spectator theory of knowledge" that seeks UNIVERSALS or ESSENCES in things, arguing that knowledge is based on experience. He even avoided the term "knowledge," preferring "warranted assertability"—answers that serve today's purpose but may change with tomorrow's conditions. We use the best means at hand to achieve the ends we seek, which in turn become a new set of means to attack a new set of problems. The path to warranted assertability is experimental inquiry, which Dewey felt was applicable not just to empirical science but to all areas of human concern. Defining FREEDOM as the capacity to act on one's best judgments for worthwhile purposes, he held DEMOCRACY to be the political system best suited to this endeavor.

Dewey's enormously influential theory of education, worked out at his

Laboratory School at the University of Chicago and presented in *The School and Society* (1899), *Democracy and Education* (1916), and other books, proceeded directly from his philosophical conclusions. To him, the strict, authoritarian approach to education, which emphasized rote learning and relied on a fixed curriculum, was not the best means to the desired ends of a democratic society, namely, a universally educated populace capable of the level of inquiry needed to solve society's problems. He emphasized "learning by doing," in which the student learns through direct experience in classroom activities. Schooling, he felt, should be practical but also well-rounded, preparing people for an intellectually rich and economically productive life.

See also ETHICS; quotation at EVOLUTION.

dharma (dhamma)

In BUDDHISM and HINDUISM, the basic principle of existence, both individual and cosmic. The term *dharma* (from Sanskrit; *dhamma* in Pali) encompasses custom and duty, law and culture, the cosmic order and divine law. The law of dharma is the established, harmonious, right order of the universe, which dictates proper conduct and action. The rule of life, and the way of overcoming KARMA, is to follow the path of dharma. In Hinduism, each CASTE and each stage of life has its own dharma, the appropriate worldly activity and moral standard. As one of the four goals of life, dharma moderates two of the others— *artha* (material success) and *kama* (sensual and aesthetic pleasure)—and makes possible the fourth, *moksha* (spiritual liberation). Dharma is one of the Three Jewels of Buddhism, along with the Buddhist community *(sangha)* and the BUDDHA himself. The Buddha described his teaching as "turning the wheel of dharma," instructing his disciples not only in spiritual knowledge but in right living.

dialectic

From the Greek word for "discourse," originally the method of philosophical inquiry perfected by SOCRATES, later developed as the basis of the philosophies of HEGEL and MARX. In all cases, dialectic works through *contradiction*. In the Socratic method, a problem or proposition is put to the test through rigorous questioning that whittles away common misconceptions and reveals its contradictions.

Dialectical logic is a three-stage process usually stated as *thesis, antithesis,* and *synthesis*. In this triad, a proposition is presented, countered by its opposite, and ultimately transformed through the interaction of the two into a new, superior hybrid. Hegel saw this process as the basis of historical change. He identified "dialectical moments," or stages of history, in which existing concepts and institutions develop internal conflicts that are eventually overcome in the creation of a new "moment." A commonly cited instance of the dialectic is Hegel's examination of the oppositional "master-slave" relationship. In this case the "thesis," the master's dominant position, is countered by its antithesis, the slave's subjected condition. The relationship is one of conflict, which can be overcome only by a synthesis of the two conditions: a recognition of interdependence (the slave depends on the master for food and shelter; the master needs the slave for work and, indeed, for his very IDENTITY as master) from which can grow a more equal relationship.

The Hegelian dialectic has had its most influential embodiment in the MARXIST analysis. In this view, the dominance of CAPITALISM produces internal contradictions within the economic and social system, as impersonal means of production and overconcentration of wealth lead to the exploitation and ALIENATION of the proletariat; this condition produces CLASS conflict, resulting in the eventual triumph of SOCIALISM, the control of capital by workers. Although seeing history as dialectical seems to imply a never-ending sequence of contradiction, conflict, and (temporary) resolution, both Hegel and Marx envisioned a final, perfected condition—for Hegel, an ultimate state of absolute FREEDOM; for Marx, COMMUNISM, which would arise as socialism gave way through its own internal contradictions.

See also DIALECTICAL MATERIALISM; HEGEL; LUKÁCS; MAO; MARX; PROGRESS; SARTRE; SCHOLASTICISM; SOCRATES.

dialectical materialism

The core of MARXIST theory, holding that human CONSCIOUSNESS derives from material conditions and that history progresses according to DIALECTICAL laws. MARX himself did not use the term; it was employed by his collaborator Friedrich Engels, and the concept is particularly associated with Engels's elaboration of Marxian theory. Dialectical materialism is also known as *historical materialism*, although the latter term is usually applied more generally to the Marxian theory that history is propelled by technological advances and changes in social and economic organization.

Dialectical materialism is an inversion of HEGEL's theory of dialectical IDEALISM, from which it is descended. Both Marx and Hegel believed that history advances dialectically, that is, through conflicts within the prevailing order, which are resolved through their synthesis into a new order, which in due course develops its own internal conflicts and eventual resolution, and so on (see DIALECTIC). But whereas Hegel saw human consciousness (or "spirit") as the motive force in history, creating social and material circumstances, Marx believed just the opposite: "Consciousness does not determine life; life determines consciousness," he and Engels wrote in *The German Ideology* (1845–46). Specifically, economic circumstances—the "relations of production," through which nature is transformed into material goods by human labor—determine social organization, which in turn shapes our IDEAS, relationships, and IDENTITIES. The exploitative relations that characterize CAPITALIST production, Marx contended, generate CLASS conflict between workers and owners that will inevitably produce a revolutionary upheaval in which capitalism is replaced by SOCIALISM, a synthesis that achieves workers' aspirations to control the fruits of their labor while retaining the structure of the STATE, which will ultimately "wither away" under full COMMUNISM.

> *"It is man's social being that determines his thinking. Once the correct ideas characteristic of the advanced class are grasped by the masses, these ideas turn into a material force that changes society and changes the world."*
> —Mao Zedong,
> *The Thoughts of Chairman Mao*

diminishing returns, law of

In economics, the principle that as more of one production factor (labor, CAPITAL, or land) is added to a production process in which other factors are fixed, the amount of output (product) derived from each additional amount of input will eventually begin to fall; also called the law of diminishing marginal returns because of the decreasing rate of return on each additional, or "marginal," unit of input used. The law was first applied to agricultural production, notably in the work of the English economist David Ricardo (1772–1823), who observed that as more and more labor and machinery are put to work on a given quantity of land, the rate of output (e.g., bushels of harvest per worker) at first rises, but eventually declines as the productive capacity of the land is approached. By the same token, if land is brought under cultivation one field at a time, starting with the most fertile and progressing to the most infertile, as more and more land is cultivated the rate of additional output (e.g., bushels per acre) declines. Adding inputs to a production process generally results in an initial increase in productivity because of *economies of scale*—two farmhands working together may harvest 100 bushels a day where one alone could reap only 40. The related principle of *returns to scale* evaluates the change in output that occurs if all inputs are changed by the same amount. If the inputs are doubled—twice as many workers, machines, and raw materials—the firm is said to have *constant* returns to scale if output doubles, *increasing* returns to scale if output more than doubles, and *decreasing* returns to scale if it less than doubles.

Dionysian spirit See APOLLONIAN SPIRIT AND DIONYSIAN SPIRIT

double consciousness

A concept of African-American IDENTITY introduced by W. E. B. DU BOIS in *The Souls of Black Folk* (1903). According to Du Bois, because of the effects of RACISM black Americans unavoidably perceive themselves in relation to the dominant white culture around them. Their self-PERCEPTION is filtered through two levels of CONSCIOUSNESS; they see themselves not only as human individuals but also as whites see them: different in color and culture by virtue of their African ancestry, and therefore alien and second-class. This fractured consciousness deprives African-Americans of a true sense of self, Du Bois suggested, and creates a world-view that is not only false but harmful, defeating the spirit and thwarting aspirations. Later commentators, however, have proposed that double consciousness may have positive effects as well. Bernard Bell, for example, believes that the resulting conflicts and tensions have given rise to creative as well as destructive impulses, and Nathan Huggins suggests that double consciousness allows African-Americans to see the dominant society that much more clearly and therefore enables them to transcend its assumptions.

Douglass, Frederick (1817–1895)

American abolitionist, orator, social activist, and writer, the most influential African-American of his day. An eloquent and effective agitator for the abolition of slavery before the Civil War, Douglass later took up the cause of women's suffrage, opposed capital punishment (as well as southern vigilante "lynch law"), and—anticipating Booker T. WASHINGTON—promoted vocational education for blacks.

Born into slavery as Frederick Augustus Washington Bailey, Douglass escaped in 1838 and made his way to Massachusetts. There he met the abolitionist leader William Lloyd Garrison and became an agent and spokesman for Garrison's American Anti-Slavery Society. His eloquence in oratory was such that some doubted his humble slave origins; in response, he wrote his first autobiography, *Narrative of the Life of Frederick Douglass, an American Slave* (1845). He was twice forced into temporary exile in England, once in 1845–47, when his growing fame triggered fears that he might be returned to slavery through the Fugitive Slave Laws, and again in 1859, in the wake of the armed insurrection led by the radical abolitionist John Brown, whom Douglass was accused of encouraging.

In his speeches and his newspaper, *The North Star,* Douglass increasingly called not just for an end to slavery but for racial equality and black economic opportunity—sentiments that put him at odds with some of his white abolitionist friends whose opposition to slavery did not imply full equality of the races. During the Civil War, which he saw as a crusade for black emancipation, equal RIGHTS, and a renewal of the American spirit, Douglass helped recruit black troops for the Union army. During Reconstruction, as the most prominent champion of the former slaves, he worked for passage of the 13th, 14th, and 15th Amendments to the Constitution, which guaranteed freedom and basic civil rights to blacks. He stressed the importance of racial pride, integrity, and self-help, but also advocated political activism and NONVIOLENT resistance against discrimination. He wrote two further autobiographical books, *My Bondage and My Freedom* (1855) and *The Life and Times of Frederick Douglass* (1881), an expanded revision of his first memoir.

Du Bois, William Edward Burghardt (1868–1963)

American author, educator, historian, sociologist, and political activist; an influential advocate of equality for African-Americans and the most prominent black intellectual of his time. Du Bois, the first African-American to receive a Ph.D. from Harvard University, was a founder of the National Association for the Advancement of Colored People (NAACP) and longtime editor of its journal, *The Crisis.* In his early career as a college professor in the 1890s, Du Bois believed that white RACISM was a matter of ignorance and that studying it sociologically and providing accurate information to counter the misconceptions of prejudice would solve what was known as the "Negro problem." He came to regard this approach as inadequate and became an activist, pushing for black people's access to higher education and the voting booth and agitating against enforced segregation at home and European colonialism in Africa.

> *"Back of the problem of race and color lies a greater problem which both obscures and implements it; and that is the fact that so many civilized persons are willing to live in comfort even if the price of this is poverty, ignorance and disease of the majority of their fellowmen."*
>
> —W. E. B. Du Bois, quoted in 1964

Du Bois was a prolific author of scholarly and polemical works, the most enduring of which is his 1903 collection of essays on African-American life, *The Souls of Black Folk*. Although he championed black unity, he was outspokenly critical of those engaged in the same struggle with whom he disagreed. He twice left the NAACP in disputes over policy. He criticized Marcus GARVEY's black separatism while sharing his pan-African ideals (he ended his life as a citizen of Ghana). An advocate of absolute social, political, and economic equality, he feuded for decades with Booker T. WASHINGTON over Washington's philosophy of accommodation to the white majority.

Although deeply concerned with the RIGHTS and well-being of the black masses, Du Bois lacked the popular appeal of Garvey and Washington. He believed that only the educated elite, the "talented tenth" of African-Americans, was capable of leadership and should therefore guide the rest of the race. Du Bois increasingly embraced left-wing politics, belonging briefly to the American SOCIALIST and COMMUNIST parties. In the Cold War era, as head of a campaign against nuclear weapons, he was arrested on charges of subversive activities, tried, and acquitted.

See also DOUBLE CONSCIOUSNESS.

dualism

The position that the world is composed primarily of two SUBSTANCES—usually mind and matter—or that reality exists in an apparent realm and a true one. Examples of dualistic philosophies include DESCARTES's division of the universe into the physical and the spiritual and KANT's discrimination between phenomena and noumena.

Dualism had its earliest expression in the opposition of good and evil that formed the basis of the creation myth of the ZOROASTRIAN religion, established around 1000 B.C.E. The battle between good and evil, God and Satan, appears in many religious traditions. The Manichaean sect, for instance, founded in Persia in the second century C.E., saw existence as a struggle between darkness (the evil material world) and light (the spiritual realm) and religious prophets as messengers sent to liberate the light, which was imprisoned in corrupt matter. The clash of good and evil in religious belief provides the paradigm for most dualistic philosophical systems. Dualism implies polarity and conflict, not syncretism—"Never the twain shall meet" rather than "Two heads are better than one." The two sides are usually unbalanced, with one considered superior or more "real" than the other, as well as more diverse; in Descartes's view, for instance, the realm of mind is far more complex and subtle than that of matter.

The traditional objection to dualism—that two sorts of reality of entirely different orders should not be able to communicate with or act on each other—has spawned a variety of responses. ARISTOTLE proposed that form and matter unite in substance; *occasionalism* was devised by followers of Descartes wrestling with the MIND/BODY PROBLEM (q.v.); SPINOZA dismissed dualism entirely in his theory of MONISM. Modern critics such as Jacques Derrida argue that "binary concepts" such as rational/irrational and civilized/savage reflect only the hierarchical, ethnocentric assumptions they are based on.

See also GNOSTICISM; box at HINDUISM (schools).

Durkheim, Émile See ANOMIE

E

Einstein, Albert (1879–1955)

German-born physicist, the outstanding 20th-century scientist, creator of the theories of RELATIVITY and a major contributor to QUANTUM THEORY. From his earliest work he showed great intuition for, as he put it, "scenting out" *(herauszuspuren)* fundamental inconsistencies in existing theories. He did not accept NEWTON's precept "I feign no hypotheses," asserting that scientific theories are not generalizations from experience but free creations of the mind, leading to deductions that have to survive experimental trials. This *hypothetico-deductive* approach has become an important feature of modern SCIENTIFIC METHOD.

Einstein's doctoral thesis, in 1905, established a new method for determining the size of molecules, which supported the reality of atoms, a point still in dispute at the time. Three more scientific papers published the same year laid the foundation for much of 20th-century physics. The first, on Brownian motion, ascribed the irregular movement of particles suspended in fluids to collisions with molecules of the liquid, thus helping to substantiate the *kinetic molecular theory* that matter is composed of molecules in motion. The second, containing the controversial suggestion that light is composed not of continuous waves but of particles (photons) whose energy is proportional to the frequency of the light radiation, explained the *photoelectric effect* (the emission of electrons by metal surfaces when struck by light) and established a fundamental of quantum theory. (It was for this work, not relativity, that he received the 1921 Nobel Prize for physics.)

Einstein's third 1905 paper proposed the *special theory of relativity,* which extended to all of physics the principle of mechanical relativity (that objects in uniform motion perceive movement only in relation to each other) and offered the revolutionary hypothesis that space and time are not separate dimensions but are interrelated. For the next decade, he sought to generalize the special theory to include nonuniform (accelerated) motion. In his *general theory of relativity*, published in 1916, gravity was seen not as a force between massive bodies but as the influence of those bodies on the geometry of space-time. The general theory predicted that the path of starlight passing the sun would be curved, and when this was empirically confirmed in 1919, he became world-famous. (See also RELATIVITY.)

> *"The grand aim of all science is to cover the greatest number of empirical facts by logical deduction from the smallest number of hypotheses or axioms."*
> —Albert Einstein, quoted in 1970

Einstein used his celebrity to speak his mind on social and political issues. He was a pacifist (until the outbreak of World War II), an INTERNATIONALIST, a committed ZIONIST, and, after the war, a passionate advocate of nuclear arms control. With Hitler's assumption of power in Germany, Einstein moved to the United States, later becoming an American citizen. In 1939, at the urging of several colleagues, he signed a letter to President Roosevelt expressing the opinion that an atomic bomb was feasible and the fear that Nazi Germany might be developing one, but he took no part in the U.S. atomic effort.

From the 1920s to the end of his life, Einstein searched for a unified FIELD THEORY, based on general relativity, that would explain gravitational, electromagnetic, and nuclear forces in terms of a basic underlying unity, and would supplant quantum theory, which he considered flawed because of the UNCERTAINTY PRINCIPLE. He never achieved that goal, and contemporary physicists, while accepting quantum theory as fundamental despite its inherent indeterminacy, have continued the search for a unified theory that incorporates general relativity.

See also EXPANDING UNIVERSE; QUANTUM THEORY; WAVE-PARTICLE DUALITY.

elements, the four

In ancient cosmologies, particularly Greek and Indian, the four basic, irreducible substances that constitute all matter: earth, air, fire, and water. The modern understanding of chemical elements—those substances composed of only one kind of atom—has in common with the ancient concept the basic principle of irreducibility.

In the Greek tradition, each element was distinguished by its particular motion: air and fire moved naturally upward, fire more so than air; water and earth settled, earth more so. The first Greek to base his system on all four elements was Empedocles, in the fifth century B.C.E. Previous thinkers had recognized a single element as the fundamental principle of the world. The earliest, Thales, had considered it to be water, out of which the other elements were formed—and for this attempt to capture the multiplicity of the world in a unifying principle, he is sometimes called "the first philosopher." For Anaximenes, the basic principle was air, which assumed other forms through "condensation" and "rarefaction," and for Heraclitus, whose theory stressed flux and change, it was fire (an emphasis adopted by the STOICS).

Water, air, and fire were also variously identified as fundamental in the Indian Vedic tradition. The seventh-century Hindu philosopher Shankara ranked the four elements according to their "subtlety," or susceptibility to the senses, air being the most subtle since it cannot be seen, tasted, or smelled but only felt. The ancient Chinese distinguished five elements, or phases: water, fire, earth, metal, and wood.

Before ARISTOTLE, the elements were considered immutable. He assigned them the contrasting qualities hot/cold and moist/dry—earth was dry and cold, air moist and hot, fire hot and dry, water cold and moist—and theorized that any element could change into any other with which it had a quality in common, for example, air into fire, as both are hot. The idea of mutability became the basis of alchemy, which sought to turn "base" metals such as lead into gold or silver. To the four earthly elements, Aristotle added a fifth, *aether* (ether), of which the celestial sphere was composed.

The Aristotelian view of the elements survived until the 17th century, when Robert Boyle proposed a theory of "primitive and simple, perfectly unmingled bodies," many more than four, that combine to form chemical compounds. By the early 19th century this approach had given rise to the modern classification of atomic elements.

See also ATOMISM; EUCLID; ZOROASTRIANISM.

elite theory

Theory holding that domination of social and political systems by powerful minorities is inevitable. The belief that only a select few, specially endowed or belonging to a particular group or CLASS, are fit to govern society is called *elitism*. The word "elite" has the same root as "elect" and implies both senses of that term—those designated by ballot or appointment, or elevated from the multitude by God, chance, history, or natural gifts.

Elite theory, developed in the late 19th and early 20th centuries by the Italian sociologists Gaetano Mosca and Vilfredo Pareto, arose largely as a response to the MARXIST faith in popular rule. They argued that all political and social systems, including DEMOCRACIES, are controlled by elites, be they aristocrats or clergy, generals or politicians, bureaucrats or captains of industry. Elites perpetuate themselves through force, manipulation, and legitimating IDEOLOGIES shared by the populace (which, in a democracy, include the promise that anyone may aspire to join the elite). Revolution, usually resulting from stagnation in the ruling elite, merely raises another elite in its place. In Pareto's view, a regular *circulation of elites*—typically alternation between CONSERVATIVE "lions" preserving the status quo and resourceful "foxes" responding to changing conditions—is necessary to renew executive vigor and public trust. According to the *iron law of oligarchy*, a corollary theory formulated by German political scientist Robert Michels, control of any political organization will unavoidably devolve to a small group because of factors such as the need for efficient action, the leaders' love of power, and the apathy of their followers. Classical elite theory became a justification for FASCISM, with which Pareto and Michels ultimately sympathized.

Modern elite theorists often take a more PLURALISTIC approach, seeing modern democracies as characterized not by centralized power but by competition among political, economic, and institutional elites representing a variety of interests. However, sociologist C. Wright Mills contended that the upper echelons of political, military, and industrial leadership in the United States constitute an interlocking *power elite* who protect and promote their common interests.

Emerson, Ralph Waldo (1803–1882)

American essayist, lecturer, and poet, the central figure of New England TRANSCENDENTALISM. Many of his ideas were stimulated by a visit to England in 1833, where he met the ROMANTIC poets William Wordsworth and Samuel Taylor Coleridge and the historian Thomas Carlyle, who became a lifelong friend. Emerson's volume of essays *Representative Men* (1850) reflected Carlyle's view that history is determined by the acts of great, intuitive men (see "GREAT MAN" THEORY).

In common with other Transcendentalists, Emerson rejected institutionalized religion, asserted divinity in all things, stressed communion with nature, and advocated social reform. In *Nature* (1836), the earliest and still the

"Every man is a divinity in disguise, a god playing the fool."

—Ralph Waldo Emerson, "Heroism," 1841

most important distillation of his thought, he presented a version of IDEALISM that understood the material world as merely part of a spiritual wholeness, a universal Oversoul from which individuals derive their strength and freedom. Emerson conceived a natural world governed not by mechanical laws but by an inner vitality that pervades everything and which, in turn, must be cultivated by everything that exists. Self-cultivation, indeed, was Emerson's prime goal: through the development of our character and abilities we approach oneness with the Oversoul.

Emerson's reputation as an author and lecturer grew throughout his life, his popularity enhanced by a spirited, poetic writing style. In his many lectures and two volumes of *Essays* (1841, 1844) he addressed a wide range of often controversial topics, including self-reliance and INDIVIDUALISM (of which he is considered by many the essential American exponent), the abolition of slavery, and the need for a purely American literature free of European cultural domination.

empiricism

The philosophical position that all knowledge derives from experience—from the direct observation of phenomena and from introspection. It thus contrasts partially with RATIONALISM, which identifies REASON as the source of knowledge, and rejects the notion of spontaneous or INNATE IDEAS. While empirical "purists" may claim that all ideas arise *only* from experience, others object that complex thought and shared culture cannot derive purely from personal perceptions. Thus, a "softer" version of empiricism states that while not all ideas are causally connected to sense PERCEPTION, anything we can call knowledge must be *justified* through the test of experience; this is the basis of the SCIENTIFIC METHOD (see also BACON).

Empiricism as an EPISTEMOLOGICAL explanation goes back to the ancient Greeks, but the term is primarily associated with the 17th- and 18th-century British philosophers John LOCKE, George BERKELEY, and David HUME. Though their views differed on the exact nature of reality and source of ideas, the philosophies of all three start from the premise that it is only through the senses that we have access to the world, whatever its actual form. Hume's and Berkeley's version of empiricism, which holds that our *perceptions* of phenomena constitute the only reality we can have knowledge of, is called PHENOMENALISM (by contrast, Locke believed the world is composed of real things that we truly perceive). In the 19th century, a form of empiricism known as PRAGMATISM, which stressed evaluating ideas by their practical effects, was founded by the American philosopher Charles Sanders Peirce and popularized by William JAMES, who called his philosophy "radical empiricism." The theories of POSITIVISM and LOGICAL POSITIVISM (also called logical empiricism by its adherents), in their emphasis on scientific method and belief in trial by experience, can also be considered forms of empiricism.

See also COMTE; DEWEY; KANT; MILL; NATURALISM; NOMINALISM; VERIFIABILITY AND FALSIFIABILITY.

enlightenment

The state or process of coming to the truth out of ignorance—illumination after darkness. In Eastern religion, especially BUDDHISM and HINDUISM, enlightenment is the fulfillment of the human quest for perfect understanding. In European and American history, the Enlightenment refers to the predominant intellectual mood of the 18th century, exemplified by confidence in the power of REASON. While the two concepts share the image of light overcoming darkness, they are in many ways opposites: in Eastern traditions, enlightenment involves shedding earthly knowledge and attachments in order to achieve perfect understanding of cosmic reality, whereas the Western Enlightenment was focused on rational thought and human PROGRESS.

"Enlightenment" translates the Sanskrit word *bodhi*, denoting awakening, wisdom, and awareness; *bodhi* is the root of BUDDHA, "enlightened one." The Buddhist concept of enlightenment derives from the Buddha's seven-week meditation seated under a bo tree, during which he attained progressive levels of awareness, arriving finally at perfect enlightenment, or Buddhahood. Enlightenment is seeing the world and the self as they really are, free of the veils of illusion. It is the precondition and passageway to NIRVANA. (See also SUFISM.)

The new current of thought in the period known as the Age of Enlightenment (or Age of Reason) challenged many of the assumptions that had prevailed throughout the Middle Ages. It was characterized by cosmopolitanism, secularism, distrust of traditional authority, respect for human dignity, and the conviction that reason would illuminate mankind and lead to perpetual social, political, and scientific progress. Although the term "Enlightenment" (*Aufklarung*) was first used in this context in Germany—where Immanuel KANT proposed the motto "Dare to know"—the movement had its impetus in

England (and Scotland, in the work of David HUME and Adam SMITH) and its greatest flowering in France. There it was closely associated with the *philosophes,* the foremost of whom was VOLTAIRE. The philosophes were for the most part not "philosophers" as such, but popularizers of the 17th-century doctrines that inspired them, particularly the RATIONALISM of DESCARTES and SPINOZA and the EMPIRICISM of BACON and LOCKE, as well as Locke's theory of natural RIGHTS. Much of the philosophes' agenda consisted of a repudiation of the dogmatism and authoritarianism of the ROMAN CATHOLIC Church. Many of them contributed to the *Encyclopedia* (1751–72), a monumental work edited by Denis Diderot, which was intended to be a compendium of all human knowledge, particularly the "new knowledge" promoted by the philosophes. Enlightenment thought was tremendously influential in colonial and postrevolutionary America; as envoys to Paris, Thomas JEFFERSON and Benjamin Franklin befriended many of the philosophes.

See also HUMANISM; MENDELSSOHN; NATURAL THEOLOGY; PROGRESS.

entropy

A measure of the disorder in a system; the idea that natural processes tend to move from relative order toward disorder. The term was coined, from the Greek for "transformation," by the German physicist Rudolf Julius Emmanuel Clausius in 1850 in his articulation of the second law of THERMODYNAMICS, which states, in part, that "the entropy of the universe tends to a maximum." The principle of entropy holds that the disorder in a closed system never decreases, and that as the entropy of a system increases there is less energy available for work. In a steam engine, for example, the steam produced by hot water meeting cold air is converted into mechanical energy to drive a piston; however, the water and air in the steam chamber gradually approach the same temperature: the system becomes progressively less ordered and its entropy increases. Entropy is also defined in terms of *complexity,* the number of ways the parts of a system can be arranged; the greater the number of possible arrangements, the greater the entropy. (Some INFORMATION THEORISTS take issue with this definition, arguing that the growing complexity of information distribution and consumption leads to greater social and technological organization, not less.) In the mid-19th century, the German physicist Hermann von Helmholtz and others predicted that the universe (considered a closed system) will eventually "run down," ultimately reaching maximum entropy and suffering a "heat death" when all temperature differences have disappeared. That notion, however, has been called into question by QUANTUM

THEORY, which suggests the possibility of multiple universes in which the same physical laws may not apply.

Epicureanism

School of thought established by the Greek philosopher Epicurus. The academy Epicurus founded in Athens in 306 B.C.E., called the Garden after the walled enclosure that housed it, was open not only to free men but to women and slaves as well. Although our word "epicurean" suggests a cultured hedonism, the Epicurean endorsement of pleasure seeking did not at all imply the uninhibited satisfaction of desires.

The philosophy of the early Epicureans was thoroughly MATERIALIST. It was divided into three parts: a theory of knowledge that emphasized direct experience; a physical system based on ATOMISM; and an ethics incorporating both systems, grounded in physical sensation and the natural course of atomic movement. From the idea that our bodies are composed of atoms, Epicurus drew the conclusion that our sensations are due to the perturbations of these particles, and he extracted from this the idea that one's goal should be to achieve a pleasant combination of these feelings. This did not mean, however, that we should, above all else, seek pleasure and avoid pain. The Epicureans identified the ideal human condition as *ataraxia,* or serenity of body and soul, and advocated temperance and other traditional VIRTUES as the best way to secure a pleasant life.

Epicureanism was introduced into the Roman world in the first century B.C.E., above all by Lucretius, whose philosophical poem *On the Nature of Things* embraced Epicurean atomism and esteemed mental tranquillity and devotion to TRUTH as the greatest pleasures of life. In this period, however, the hedonistic distortion of Epicurean philosophy that was later associated with Roman decadence also arose, holding that since the preferred natural states are characterized by pleasure, *all* pleasurable states must be the proper ones.

epistemology

The study of knowledge; one of the five classical fields of philosophical inquiry (see also AESTHETICS; ETHICS; LOGIC; METAPHYSICS). Epistemology asks the questions What is knowledge? How do we obtain it? How can we verify it? What are its limits? What is the relationship between the knower and the known? (Knowledge in this sense is assumed to be knowledge of what is *true,* but the nature of TRUTH itself is for the most part considered more the province of logic and metaphysics than of epistemology.)

Perhaps the most common simple definition of knowledge is *true, justified belief:* I know something if I believe it to be true and that belief is justified. But the question of what knowledge *is*, at root, is so elusive that the answers tend to be by-products of a particular world-view rather than objective attempts at definition. For PLATO, knowledge is simply the opposite of opinion; for MARX, it is a construct of economic relations; for WITTGENSTEIN, it is practical know-how within a specific social context. What's more, the question is often shouldered aside by debates about the possibility of obtaining true knowledge or by doubts of its very existence.

The answers to the question of how the mind obtains knowledge fall into three main categories. According to the first, knowledge is an inherent part of our existence in the world, for example, Plato's view that we possess an intrinsic but imperfect apprehension of the world of ideal forms (see IDEAS; INNATE IDEAS) and HEGEL's belief that knowledge is produced by our involvement in the DIALECTICAL process of history. The second asserts that our faculties of intelligence and REASON enable us to draw out the truths the world contains; this is the approach taken by ARISTOTLE, DESCARTES, and Bertrand RUSSELL, among many others. The third explanation, whose adherents include NIETZSCHE, MARX, and the PHENOMENOLOGISTS, states that we *create* what we think of as knowledge out of our experience, which is so thoroughly dependent on our psychological, historical, or social condition that it cannot be considered objective knowledge at all. A fourth area of inquiry has lately been undertaken by some neuroscientists, who postulate that knowledge is a product of the way neurons acquire and store information (cf. CONSCIOUSNESS; COGNITIVE PSYCHOLOGY; INFORMATION THEORY).

The third explanation above involves the problem of the relationship between the *object* of knowledge and the *subject,* the one who does the knowing: even if something is true, how do we *know* it's true? This question was first asked by Descartes and other RATIONALISTS of the 17th century. Descartes, in what has come to be called the "epistemological turn," raised the issue of *doubt,* separating truth from certainty. This problem still forms the main thrust of modern epistemological inquiry.

See also A PRIORI/A POSTERIORI; DEDUCTION AND INDUCTION; DEWEY; EMPIRICISM; EPICUREANISM; FOUCAULT; IDEALISM; KANT; LOCKE; OBJECTIVISM AND SUBJECTIVISM; PERCEPTION; PIAGET; POSITIVISM; RELATIVISM; SOCIAL CONSTRUCTIONISM; SKEPTICISM; SOCRATES; SOLIPSISM.

equality

The idea of political and social equality is one of the oldest in Western thought, and one of the most elusive and controversial. JEFFERSON's proposition that "all men are created equal" may (or may not) be "self-evident," but the basis of that equality and the conditions under which it may flourish have always been a matter of intense dispute. While the ancient Greeks formulated the concept in terms that have persisted to the present day, those and later egalitarian ideals condoned inconsistencies unacceptable to the modern mind. Athens boasted equality of opportunity for all its citizens, but did not include women among them and sanctioned slavery. Medieval CHRISTIANITY considered all humans equal in the eyes of God, but supported ABSOLUTIST monarchies atop a rigidly hierarchical CLASS system. HOBBES's conception of the SOCIAL CONTRACT assumed the necessity of authoritarian power to ensure equal protection from the depredations of others, and ROUSSEAU's did not tolerate individual dissent from the "general will."

"The Lord so constituted everybody that no matter what color you are you require the same amount of nourishment."
—Will Rogers, *Autobiography*, 1949

Much of the debate about the meaning and purpose of equality arises from two antithetical conceptions of it—equal *opportunity* for individuals versus equal *distribution* of resources throughout society. Does social equality exist in the equal opportunity to gain unequal amounts of power or wealth, or only under conditions in which no one is allowed to have more of either than anyone else? Classical LIBERALISM and CAPITALISM rest on the former proposition, SOCIALISM and especially COMMUNISM on the latter. The basic premise of DEMOCRACY is that ultimate power should be shared equally by the whole polity, but the conviction that the polity should include the whole population is a comparatively novel idea that was first put into practice (briefly) in the French Revolution and is still imperfectly realized.

Claims to equality are often stated in terms of RIGHTS, especially the right to equal treatment within a system of just laws. The U.S. Constitution guarantees equal protection under the law and equal rights of suffrage, for example. However, in the United States, as elsewhere, legal and social equality for women, African-Americans, and other marginalized groups has been hard-won and is still incomplete.

See also DEMOCRACY; FEMINISM; UTOPIANISM.

Erikson, Erik (1902–1994)

German-born American psychiatrist, whose theory of personality development emphasized cultural and societal demands on the evolving personality
and introduced the concept of *identity crisis*. Erikson, a protégé of Anna
Freud, daughter of the founder of PSYCHOANALYSIS, based his theory of personal psychology on Sigmund FREUD's stages of psychosexual development.
However, Erikson's *psychosocial* theory assumes a broader array of psychological and social influences on development, and his developmental stages envision growth and maturation continuing beyond childhood and throughout
the life cycle. Each of the eight stages Erikson outlined in *Childhood and Society*
(1950) is characterized by a crisis precipitated by the tension between a new
challenge and the fears and insecurities it generates. If the crisis is successfully confronted and resolved, the individual confidently proceeds to the next
stage; if not, development is retarded or distorted.

The first crisis is that of *trust versus mistrust,* as a baby's utter dependence
on caregivers is tested. In the toddler stage, the crisis of *autonomy versus shame
and doubt* is triggered by the trial-and-error process of learning to walk and
toilet training. The preschooler struggles with *initiative versus guilt* as growing
independence arouses guilty feelings over "cutting the apron strings." In
school, training in skills that ready the child for a place in society sets up a
conflict of *competence (industry) versus inferiority* as ever-increasing expectations
clash with fears of being inadequate to the task. Puberty brings on the "identity crisis," or crisis of *identity versus role confusion (diffusion)*—the crux of Erikson's schema—as the adolescent attempts to integrate childhood lessons of
socialization, develop a firm identity, and make decisions about career and
life goals. The young adult grapples with *intimacy versus isolation*: whether and
how to share oneself with an intimate partner. The midlife crisis of *generativity
versus stagnation* involves the challenge to continue leading a productive life—
through parenthood, creative work, fulfilling social relationships—instead of
settling into complacency and self-absorption. Finally, the older adult faces
the approach of death and a crisis of *integrity versus despair,* seeking wisdom
and satisfaction with life's accomplishments rather than longing and regret.

See also IDENTITY.

eschatology

In religion, doctrines concerning the end of history and the final destiny of
humanity. Although all the world's religions hold beliefs about the ultimate
fate of the world and of the human soul, the term, coined in the mid-19th
century from the Greek for "last things," is primarily applied to end-time be-

liefs in JUDAISM, CHRISTIANITY, and ISLAM. While these traditions conceive the world as having a beginning (in divine creation) and an end (in divine judgment), Eastern religious philosophies tend to envisage time as an endless cycle of unfolding, destruction, and regeneration (see ETERNAL RECURRENCE).

The Judeo-Christian concept of end-time derives from Old Testament promises of God's judgment and redemption of Israel and punishment of its enemies. Biblical prophecies refer to a Day of the Lord in which the world will feel God's wrath. Others allude to a Messiah (*mashiah*, "anointed one"), a savior appointed by God who will reunite the Jews and establish God's empire on earth. Some passages predict an apocalyptic battle—or a cataclysmic upheaval in which the earth will be devastated, then renewed—that will usher in either a UTOPIAN human society or a divine kingdom. In postbiblical periods of subjection and exile, Jews have often envisioned a divinely inspired leader who would lead them in a final battle against their enemies.

Christian eschatology revolves around the Parousia, or Second Coming of Christ. In the New Testament, particularly in the epistles of St. Paul and the Book of Revelations, the resurrection of JESUS is seen as a prelude to his return to earth, when he will establish the kingdom of God and all the dead will be resurrected to face God's judgment at the conclusion of the final battle between good and evil at Armageddon. The early Christians anticipated Christ's imminent return, as promised to his disciples. When those hopes were not fulfilled, alternative expectations of a literal Second Coming emerged, many of them focusing on the millennium (see ADVENTISM; MILLENARIANISM). Much of mainstream Christianity has come to view the Parousia as either a far-distant event or a metaphorical expression of the presence of Christ in every human soul.

In Islamic eschatology, allegorical figures from Judeo-Christian scripture appear in an end-time of destruction and chaos, when the earth will be laid waste in fire and flood by the Satanic demons Gog and Magog, ruled for a time by the Antichrist, and redeemed by the messianic "divinely guided one," the Mahdi, and ultimately by Jesus. On the day of judgment, Allah will weigh the souls of the dead and assign them to the garden of paradise or to fiery hell.

See also ZOROASTRIANISM.

essence
The defining and necessary characteristic of something, its sine qua non, without which it would not be that thing; distinguished from *existence*, the actual presence of a thing in time and space (cf. EXISTENTIALISM). It is a crucial

concept in much religious thought in which God is conceived as pure essence (see, e.g., HINDUISM; SOUL AND SPIRIT; TAOISM).

The concept of essence was central to ancient Greek thought, especially in PLATO's notion that the essence of a thing resides in its ideal form and in ARISTOTLE's concept of essential SUBSTANCE, the union of intangible form and physical matter. The approach to science that followed the reinstitution of Aristotelian thought in medieval European culture was based entirely on the idea of essence. Scientific inquiry was largely devoted to the proper classification of the world's objects and beings into their appropriate species and genera, thus defining their essential character. Even God was included in this scheme, but was granted the glory of having an essence that was identical with his existence; God could not fail to exist, therefore, because existence was his essence.

Once mathematics became the essence of science, essence itself was relegated to the realm of philosophy, and is now largely maligned. Theories that seek the essence of things instead of accounting for all their complex variety are often attacked for this *essentialism*. The term is also used in modern literary criticism, usually to disparage the position, taken by the NEW CRITICS and others, that the crucial object of study in a text is its inherent quality, not its manifold meanings or historical-cultural context (cf. DECONSTRUCTION; HISTORICISM). Similarly, some FEMINIST critics have condemned the idea that there is an essential female nature—biological or cultural—that governs women's outlook and defines women writers' approach to style and subject matter; others, however, use the term "essentialism" positively, identifying a distinctive female quality that informs women's creativity.

See also IDEAS; SARTRE.

eternal recurrence (eternal return)

The idea that time and history run in cycles and that everything that exists or happens repeats itself eternally. It is generally opposed to the idea of purpose and PROGRESS in history. In Greek philosophy, the concept derives from Heraclitus and is associated primarily with the STOICS, who believed in a "Great Year" (or "World Year") many thousands of earth years long, at the end of which the earth is consumed by a worldwide conflagration, then regenerated, in an endless cycle of destruction and renewal. (A parallel concept in the HINDU tradition is the *kalpa,* or "day of Brahma," the creator-god, in which the world is born, moves through a cycle of development and decay more than four billion years long, then dies and is reborn.) The idea of a 36,000-year Great Year, adopted by the medieval NEOPLATONISTS, was condemned by the

ROMAN CATHOLIC Church as contrary to the concept of history as the fulfillment of God's purpose; St. AUGUSTINE, for example, maintained that Christ
could be incarnated and crucified only once.

The best-known example of the concept in the modern era is NIETZSCHE's
notion that the universe, finite but eternal, contains only a certain number of
possible permutations and that when they are exhausted history repeats itself
to the letter in an "eternal return of the same." This view has long puzzled
scholars, since it seems to contradict other aspects of Nietzsche's thought,
such as the WILL TO POWER, the creative force that seeks to order a world in
constant change.

ethics

The study of moral principles and behavior and of the nature of the good;
one of the five classical fields of philosophical inquiry (see also AESTHETICS;
EPISTEMOLOGY; LOGIC; METAPHYSICS), also called *moral philosophy*. The term derives from the Greek word *ethos*, which implies both "custom" and "character."
Ethics as a discipline can be divided into *normative ethics* and *metaethics*, the
first proposing principles of right conduct, the second inquiring into the usage and foundations of concepts such as right and wrong, good and evil.
When we speak of ethics we generally mean normative ethics, but metaethics
has become steadily more important to philosophers, to such an extent that
most ethical theories of the past two centuries have had little to say about how
one ought to act, but have instead questioned the role of ethics in life, the
logical foundations of particular ethical systems, and their validity.

In most systems, ethical conduct is seen in terms of personal fulfillment
(pursuit of the good), obligation to others or to accepted principles (regard
for the right), or both. Personal fulfillment may derive from happiness or
pleasure (see, e.g., EPICUREANISM) or from the pursuit of an ideal, the good-in-
itself, or potential fully realized. Obligation commonly includes not only respect for others and for established norms, but also duty to God, whose
injunctions constitute the ultimate authority for most moral systems throughout the world.

Metaethics has its root in the thought of SOCRATES and PLATO, who in-
quired into the nature of goodness as distinct from any particular good thing.
In the Greek tradition, the central questions of ETHICS revolved around the
general problem of what constitutes a life well lived (see VIRTUE) rather than
specific issues of right and wrong. The STOICS were the first to consider ethical
decisions in terms of conforming to universal harmony and the divine will—
an approach that is also basic to the Judeo-Christian value system (see JUDAISM;

CHRISTIANITY). In the 18th century, Immanuel KANT furthered metaethics with his assertion of the *categorical imperative*, an absolute, universal ethical principle that proposed a new foundation for the legitimacy of morality. Latter-day metaethical theories often deny the ethical validity of conventional morality; for instance, both NIETZSCHE's conception of "slave morality" and the MARXIST notion of "bourgeois morality" view the dominant CLASS as imposing its values on all of society. Other theorists have found the guarantee of ethical validity in social interaction rather than in the will of God or some other abstract highest good. Examples include John DEWEY's conviction that moral questions can be resolved by careful inquiry, and Jürgen Habermas's belief that free, rational discourse can provide moral guidance for society.

See also ARISTOTLE; CONFUCIANISM; CONSEQUENTIALISM; DESCRIPTIVISM AND PRESCRIPTIVISM; EPICUREANISM; GOLDEN RULE; IS/OUGHT PROBLEM; KANT; NON-VIOLENCE; RAWLS; RELATIVISM; TEN COMMANDMENTS; TORAH; UTILITARIANISM.

ethnocentrism

The tendency to judge other cultures according to the standards of one's own, and the belief that one's own ethnic or cultural group is superior to others. The term was introduced by the American anthropologist William Graham Sumner in his book *Folkways* (1907). It is generally applied to the Eurocentric viewpoint, but most societies display ethnocentric attitudes. Not only Europeans and their American descendants, but the ancient cultures of China and Japan, for example, have traditionally viewed themselves as both the center and the culmination of social evolution, with the rest of the world ranged below this summit in descending degrees of PROGRESS and ENLIGHTENMENT.

Through the 19th century, almost all Western history writing and social science began from ethnocentric assumptions. Small-scale, non-Western societies were generally seen as "primitive," to use the commonly applied term—less complex, less advanced, and less morally developed than European or Europe-derived societies. Modern cultural anthropologists studying premodern societies have been particularly sensitive to the dangers of ethnocentrism inherent in their discipline. Cultural RELATIVISM has arisen in reaction to ethnocentrism, arguing that beliefs, values, customs, and other cultural expressions must be understood and judged within their own context rather than according to outsiders' theoretical preconceptions and classifications. In *The Authoritarian Personality* (1950), T. W. Adorno and colleagues described ethnocentric hostility toward "outgroups" as characteristic of a personality type attracted to rigid, authoritarian, CONSERVATIVE ideologies, and noted that extreme animosity toward ethnic minorities actually helps to cement a sense of "in-group" identification within the targeted groups.

Euclid (fl. c.300 B.C.E.)

Greek mathematician, whose major work, the *Elements,* has been said to have exerted a greater influence on the human mind than any other book except the Bible. He founded the great school of mathematics in Alexandria and, in the 13-volume *Elements,* both catalogued and greatly extended the mathematical knowledge of his time.

From PLATONIC universal IDEAS such as "line" and "circle," Euclid created a deductive system to describe the relationships among a wide variety of geometric figures. Euclidian geometry begins with series of *definitions, postulates,* and *axioms,* and from these deduces the proofs of geometric *theorems.* After defining *point* (that which is without extension), *line* (extension, but no breadth), and *circle* (all the points equidistant from a given point), Euclid proposed five postulates based on these definitions (e.g., it is possible to draw a straight line from any point to any point), from which he derived other geometrical figures (square, cube, etc.), and presented five commonly accepted notions, or axioms (e.g., things that are equal to the same thing are also equal to one another). From these postulates and axioms he was able to methodically demonstrate the solutions to geometrical problems and to prove theorems such as the Pythagorean relation among the sides of a right triangle (the square of the hypotenuse is equal to the sum of the squares of the other two sides). The *Elements* established a new standard of LOGICAL rigor and, especially through its dissemination by Arab scholars in the Middle Ages, ensured the dominance of the geometrical form of logical proof until the 18th century, when algebraic forms of analysis came into wide use.

Euclid's fifth postulate—that through any point one and only one line can be drawn parallel to a given line—was long a source of dispute. For centuries attempts were made to derive the fifth postulate from the other four, all without success. In the 19th century, alternative fifth postulates, consistent with the other four, produced new, non-Euclidean geometries. These were put to use, for instance, in the theory of general RELATIVITY, which demonstrates that over great distances in space Euclidian postulates concerning straight lines do not apply.

evolution

Biological theory that explains the emergence, proliferation, and transformation of species, and the development of complex life forms from simpler ones, in terms of subtle changes over long periods; generally, any theory (e.g., geological or cosmological) holding that change occurs gradually over time (cf. CATASTROPHISM; CREATIONISM). The theory of biological evolution is closely associated with Charles DARWIN, who proposed that biological change occurs through natural selection: the adaptation of organisms to competitive conditions through the inheritance of beneficial traits.

The idea that life on earth evolved slowly is an ancient one, going back at least to the Greeks and Romans. Evolution was first seriously considered in the 18th century, as scientific discourse began to be freed of theological strictures, and in the early 19th century a systematic theory began to emerge. The French biologist Jean-Baptiste LAMARCK proposed that individual organisms' advantageous adaptations to their environment can be passed on to their offspring. While ultimately shown to be incorrect, this theory introduced the concept of inheritable traits, which became central to evolutionary theory.

The principle of natural selection was first presented in 1858 in a paper by Darwin and Alfred Russel Wallace and more fully developed the following year in Darwin's *On the Origin of Species*. Darwin's model was influenced by the economic theory of his contemporary Thomas MALTHUS, who related population growth and decline to competition for scarce resources. Darwin applied that analysis to species in general: as environmental conditions on earth change, organisms must change and adapt in order to survive; survival in new circumstances requires successful competition for limited resources; those best adapted for this competition will thrive and multiply, others will die out. The survival and propagation of species depends upon the constant, spontaneous emergence of fortuitous, inheritable traits, or *variations,* within populations (Darwin called them "unsolicited novelties"). The traits that provide a competitive advantage help the individual survive to produce more offspring, and are therefore propagated with greater frequency than traits that are non-advantageous or deleterious, which eventually disappear from the population. Gradually, the new traits incorporated into the population give rise to a distinctly different species, usually as a result of different populations of a species becoming isolated from each other.

The mechanism by which traits emerge and are inherited remained the key point of dispute in evolutionary theory for many years. The genetic basis of heredity was established by the Austrian monk Gregor Mendel in his experiments on varieties of peas in the 1850s and '60s but was disregarded until 1900. Mendel's findings demonstrated the principle of inheritance through what he called "particulate factors" (genes), indivisible units of information that are passed from one generation to the next. This discovery largely validated Darwin's theory, although disagreement persisted between the Darwinian view that evolution results from the gradual accretion of minute changes over extremely long periods and the Mendelian view of evolution as a process of fits and starts in which radical changes appear within species and are either adopted or rejected in subsequent generations. By the mid-20th century a majority of the scientific community had accepted the gradualist view of evolution (cf. PUNCTU-ATED EQUILIBRIUM). With the discovery of the structure of DNA in the 1950s (see CENTRAL DOGMA), the genetic mechanism for evolution was decisively established. Evolution is now seen in terms of changes in the genetic code that occur over time within a population of organisms.

> "The Origin of Species *introduces a mode of thinking that in the end was bound to transform the logic of knowledge, and hence the treatment of morals, politics, and religion.*"
> —John Dewey,
> *The Influence of Darwin on Philosophy,* 1910

See also BIOLOGICAL DETERMINISM; DARWIN; PROCESS PHILOSOPHY/THEOLOGY; PROGRESS; SOCIAL DARWINISM.

existentialism

Philosophical position holding that in an ABSURD universe without intrinsic meaning or purpose, people have unlimited freedom of choice and must take absolute responsibility for their actions. In such a world, the individual is obliged to find meaning in his or her own existence, not in any externally imposed doctrine. The most succinct statement of the position is Jean-Paul SARTRE's maxim "Existence precedes ESSENCE"—our essential natures are developed through the choices we make in our lives. Our uncertain existence creates *anxiety,* or "existential dread," the fear of nothingness that brings us face-to-face with our boundless, terrifying freedom and responsibility. In this predicament, the individual either chooses an "authentic" life or gives in to despair.

The term "existentialism" was coined by the German philosopher Karl Jaspers as a derogatory term for Sartre, Martin HEIDEGGER, and others from whom he wanted to separate his own basically existentialist views. Indeed, few thinkers called "existentialists" have accepted the designation. The first philosopher to whom the term is now applied was Søren KIERKEGAARD, who criticized the RATIONALISM of HEGEL and claimed that religious belief must be achieved through a "leap of faith" in the face of the world's fundamental absurdity. Heidegger introduced the concept of *authenticity,* the idea that humans may choose to act authentically—intelligently and responsibly, wholeheartedly committing themselves to life and the development of their true being—or inauthentically, afraid of exercising their freedom and sinking instead into mundane conformity.

The existentialist viewpoint is ingeniously illustrated in Albert Camus's essay "The Myth of Sisyphus" (1942), in which he considers the Greek legend of the man condemned eternally to pushing a heavy stone uphill, only to see it roll back down again and have to begin the futile task anew. Every human endeavor, Camus says, is characterized by this absurdity: time erodes all achievements, death cuts short our plans. Whatever purpose, meaning, or personal fulfillment we derive from our projects lies solely in our own commitment to them; the choice we make to keep pushing the rock uphill is what overcomes the nothingness of existence.

See also ABSURD; ALIENATION; BEAUVOIR; HEIDEGGER; MERLEAU-PONTY; PHENOMENOLOGY.

expanding universe

The theory that the universe is expanding in all directions, probably as a result of the BIG BANG. It began with the discovery that the "nebulae" once thought to be gaseous clouds just beyond the Milky Way galaxy are, in fact, other galaxies, some of them at immense distances from our own. In the 1920s American astronomer Edwin Hubble observed a *redshift* in the light coming from the Andromeda nebula—that is, the light's frequency is shifted toward the red in the spectrum, indicating that its source is moving away from us. In fact, from the earth's perspective the whole universe appears to be moving away from us. Hubble hypothesized that the universe is expanding and the galaxies are expanding along with it.

According to Hubble's theory, other galaxies are receding in relation to us in proportion to their distance from us. This concept is usually illustrated with the image of a balloon with dots drawn on its surface. As the balloon is inflated, an observer sitting on any one of the dots would see every other dot moving away, and the farther away it is the faster it would seem to be moving. Thus, although it appears that we are at the *center* of a universe expanding away from us in all directions, that is not the case; all the "dots" are moving away from each other. Hubble's distance-velocity formula is used to measure the distance of a galaxy from the earth; it has also been used to estimate the age of the universe, now thought to be between 10 and 20 billion years old.

More than a decade before Hubble, an early version of EINSTEIN's general theory of RELATIVITY had predicted an expanding universe. Einstein, however, did not believe it—there was at the time no evidence for an expanding or contracting universe—so he modified his formulas by introducing an arbitrary factor, known as the "cosmological constant," (Λ), to counteract the effect predicted by his theory. He later termed this "the greatest blunder of my life."

expressionism

Artistic style, practiced especially in drama and the fine arts in the early 20th century, in which the artist expresses internal emotions, usually by distorting normal forms and perspectives. Expressionism contrasts with approaches such as IMPRESSIONISM in that the artwork is an externalization of an inner landscape (often turbulent) rather than an internalization and interpretation of external stimuli. Expressionists are united not by a coherent ideology or a consistent style but by an anguished world-view expressed in troubling images. While artists from many periods have been labeled expressionist— including El Greco in the 16th century, Picasso in the period that produced his tortured antiwar painting *Guernica* (1937), and the so-called neoexpressionists who flourished in the 1980s, including the German Georg Baselitz and the American Julian Schnabel—expressionism is primarily associated with northern and central European artists in the years before and after World War I.

Modern expressionism had roots in the stylized landscapes of German ROMANTIC painting, in the dynamic colors and expressive lines of the SYMBOLIST painters, especially Vincent van Gogh, and in the bold simplicity of African and Pacific island sculpture—all presenting imposing forms with a dramatic intensity (see also FAUVISM). The term was coined in 1901 by the painter Auguste Hervé to describe his own anti-impressionist work. The earliest, and perhaps definitive, modern expressionist was the Norwegian Edvard Munch, whose haunting woodcut *The Scream* (1893) evokes existential terror in a nightmarish landscape. German expressionism was embodied by two artists' groups called Die Brücke (The Bridge) and Der Blaue Reiter (The Blue Rider), founded in 1905 and 1911, respectively. Die Brücke, describing itself as "attracting all the elements of revolution and unrest" and exploring modern humanity's sense of ALIENATION, anxiety, and tormented spirituality, came to represent the qualities associated with expressionism as a whole. The artists of Der Blaue Reiter were more concerned with MYSTICISM and spirituality, locating the source of inspiration in the imagination rather than the emotions. The dominant figures in each group were Ernst Ludwig Kirchner and the Russian-born Wassily Kandinsky, respectively. Other important expressionist artists included Emil Nolde, Käthe Kollwitz, Max Beckmann, and Georg Grosz in Germany, Egon Schiele and Oscar Kokoschka in Austria, Georges Rouault in France, and Max Weber in the United States. (See also abstract expressionism, in box at ABSTRACTION.)

Expressionism in the theater was foreshadowed in the late 19th century in the plays of August Strindberg and Frank Wedekind, both of whom worked in a highly symbolic, emotionally charged version of NATURALISM, dramatizing emotions more than ideas or events. Expressionistic drama was often rebellious, challenging bourgeois conventions and social injustices. Stylized devices such as heightened speech, masks, and heavy symbolism were used, for example, by Eugene O'Neill in his plays of the 1920s. Stark, distorted scenery and shadowy lighting reflected the influence of expressionist painting, which also stimulated an expressionist cinema of hallucinatory images and eccentric camera angles, especially in Weimar Germany, exemplified by *The Cabinet of Dr. Caligari* (1919).

falsifiability (falsification) See VERIFIABILITY AND FALSIFIABILITY

Fanon, Frantz (1925–1961)

Psychiatrist and political philosopher, an important theoretician of mid-20th-century colonial liberation and POSTCOLONIALISM. Born in the French colony of Martinique and educated in medicine and psychiatry in France, Fanon joined the staff of a psychiatric hospital in Algeria in 1953 and soon became involved with the Front de Libération Nationale (FLN), the Algerian independence movement. After being expelled from Algeria in 1957 for his political activities, he settled in newly independent Tunisia and continued to agitate for Algerian independence, and against IMPERIALISM and RACISM in general, for the rest of his short life (he died of leukemia in his mid-thirties).

In his voluminous writings on political and social theory, Fanon systematically and passionately explored the social and political underpinnings and psychological effects of racism and colonialism, called for violent resistance to oppression, and examined the legacy of dependence in postcolonial politics. The suppression and devaluation of indigenous populations and their cultures, he argued, breeds dependency, ALIENATION, and self-hate among the colonized, whose IDENTITY comes to be shaped by the values and world-view of their white rulers (thus the title of his 1952 collection of essays, *Black Skin, White Masks*). Oppressed peoples can recover from these colonial pathologies (at least temporarily) through actively participating in the anticolonial struggle. Fanon believed that violence has a cleansing effect on a colonized people and is the only means of liberation from a system that is itself based on military occupation and coercive force. Fanon believed in the peasantry's revolutionary potential, which would best be mobilized through the leadership of nationalist intellectuals. In his last and greatest work, *The Wretched of the Earth* (1961), Fanon warned that while active struggle might topple an unjust system, sociopolitical transformation and relief from oppression could prove fleeting in the postcolonial order. As the revolution is institutionalized, the new government, in the interests of securing and maintaining power, is in danger of adopting the same anti-DEMOCRATIC procedures and oppressive structures as the system it was supposed to replace.

See also POSTCOLONIAL THEORY.

fascism

Political IDEOLOGY stressing NATIONALISM, militarism, centrally regulated private enterprise, the subordination of the individual to the STATE, and single-party TOTALITARIAN government, usually under the dictatorial rule of a charismatic leader. The term derives from the Latin *fasces,* an ancient Roman emblem of authority consisting of a bundle of rods with a protruding ax. The symbol and the name were adopted by the Italian fascist movement founded by Benito Mussolini in 1919. Nazi Germany under Adolf Hitler is also generally considered a fascist state, though Nazism is not technically synonymous with fascism. The term has also been applied, especially since World War II, to other repressive, authoritarian regimes, such as Francisco Franco's in Spain (1936–75) and Augusto Pinochet's in Chile (1973–90).

The ideological foundations of fascism are found in late-19th-century reactions against CAPITALISM and LIBERAL DEMOCRACY, on the one hand, and against MARXIST MATERIALISM, on the other. The theorists who inspired fascist doctrine represented a wide ideological spectrum, but they tended to share a belief in the nation as a sacred entity in which individual interests must yield to national goals. They included the French syndicalist Georges Sorel, who advocated violence to achieve revolutionary change and the use of national "myths" to unify the populace; Charles Maurras, leader of the French nationalist movement Action Française, who espoused a monarchical nationalism; and Giovanni Gentile, theorist of the Italian "corporate state," in which economic activity was regulated by business and workers' groups under Fascist Party control. Fascist thought was also influenced by SOCIAL DARWINISM, with its implication that the strongest are most fit to survive, and by the theory of political ELITES propounded by the Italian sociologists Vilfredo Pareto and Gaetano Mosca. In the fascist state, the individual is seen as subordinate to the community; rigid discipline and unquestioning acceptance of the state's authority become an ethic of self-sacrifice and patriotic loyalty.

Hitler and the Nazis appropriated Richard Wagner's romantic nationalism, the fiction of an Aryan "master race" (see RACE AND RACISM), and NIETZSCHE's concept of the *Übermensch*—a superior being who represents a new, higher stage of civilization—to assert Germany's divine mission to lead and dominate the world. While most fascist movements have espoused an extreme nationalism, German fascism was distinguished by racist ideals that transcended national boundaries, although pan-German sentiments helped inspire the invasions of Germany's neighbors early in the war.

> *"There is a road to freedom. Its milestones are Obedience, Endeavor, Honesty, Order, Cleanliness, Sobriety, Truthfulness, Sacrifice, and love of the Fatherland."*
> —Adolf Hitler, attributed (sign at concentration camps)

In postwar European and other industrialized countries, fascist and neo-Nazi organizations have sprung up on the fringes of the political system, often in reaction to nonwhite immigration. Capitalizing on economic insecurity and political ALIENATION in the working class, especially among young men, these groups' ideologies generally envision the replacement of the present system with an orderly, racially homogeneous, divinely sanctioned nation.

fauvism

Primarily French avant-garde movement in painting in the first years of the 20th century, an important precursor of CUBISM and ABSTRACTION and a direct influence on EXPRESSIONISM. Fauvism was characterized by the use of vivid, contrasting, unnatural colors to express intense emotion and create startling effects. Led by Henri Matisse, the loose-knit group also included Raoul Dufy, Georges Braque, Georges Rouault, André Derain, and the Dutchman Kees van Dongen, among others. The *fauves* shunned (and were shunned by) the French art establishment, exhibiting their scandalizing work at independent "salons." The group's name was coined at the first of these, in 1905, when the art critic Louis Vauxcelles saw some of their paintings displayed in a room that also contained a Renaissance-style sculpture and exclaimed, "Donatello parmi les fauves!" (Donatello among the beasts). The movement was short-lived—for most of its members, a way station en route to their more mature styles—but exerted a lasting influence on the use of color in modern art.

federalism

Form of government, usually with a written constitution, in which a division of power is established between a central government and regional authorities, which cede some powers to the national government while retaining a measure of autonomy. Unlike *confederations*, in which independent states club together for common interests but maintain full SOVEREIGNTY, federal systems give the central authority at least some direct control over citizens. As a compromise between unitary power and decentralized autonomy, federation often seeks to reconcile competing interests, for instance, between ethnic or linguistic groups, as in Switzerland and India. The possibility of supranational federalism is presented by the European Union, created in 1993 from the former European Community, which contemplates the gradual elimination of economic, monetary, and many political barriers between the member countries.

The American federation was created by the U.S. Constitution in 1789, after the original confederation of states proved weak and ineffective. In the debate over the Constitution, the case for ratification was presented in the Federalist Papers, a series of 85 essays written in 1787–88 by Alexander Hamilton, James Madison, and John Jay. The authors argued that federal power was necessary to conduct foreign policy and to act decisively in the interest of the nation as a whole. The SEPARATION OF POWERS between the executive, legislative, and judicial branches would create a system of *checks and balances* that would preserve STATES' RIGHTS and individual freedoms. That structure, as well as the greater variety of interests represented in a large national union, would also balance competing economic and political forces and help prevent the growth of powerful factions. Opposing ratification, the Anti-Federalists, who included George Mason and Patrick Henry, argued that the Constitution concentrated too much power in the central government, which would override state and local interests and eventually lose the support of the people.

In the 1790s, the Federalist Party, led by Hamilton and including Madison, Jay, John Adams, and, at least implicitly, George Washington, sought to strengthen the powers of the central government. Despite their name, these Federalists were not identical with those who had championed ratification of the Constitution. They were opposed by Thomas JEFFERSON and others, including, eventually, Madison. Federalists, supported by the urban elites of the Northeast, promoted manufacturing interests and discouraged widespread democratic participation, while Jefferson's Democratic-Republicans envisioned an agrarian, decentralized REPUBLIC sustained by a broad electorate.

The Federalists dominated the national government during the 1790s but faded during the presidencies of Jefferson (1801–09) and Madison (1809–17) and were spent by the 1820s. However, it was the Federalists' vision of mercantile CAPITALISM as the foundation of American economic prosperity that eventually prevailed, although the agrarian ideal remains embedded in the American spirit.

feminism

Social, political, and cultural movement dedicated to the achievement of equal RIGHTS and status for women in all spheres of life, or, more radically, to the establishment of a new order in which men are no longer the standard against which EQUALITY and normality are measured. Feminism is not a single IDEOLOGY but a diversity of perspectives on the origin and constitution of gender and sexuality, the historical and structural foundations of male power and women's subjugation, and the appropriate means of bringing about women's emancipation. Although the idea of women's rebellion against patriarchal society is hardly new—Aristophanes dramatized it in his antiwar satire *Lysistrata* in 411 B.C.E.—modern feminism first found expression in the late 18th century, especially in the writings of Mary WOLLSTONECRAFT. The term itself was first used a century later during the widespread suffragist movement in England and the United States that sought women's right to vote and other civil rights (see, e.g., GILMAN; STANTON).

The mid-20th-century "second wave" of feminism was spurred by two key works—Simone de BEAUVOIR's *The Second Sex* in 1949 and Betty Friedan's *The Feminine Mystique* in 1963 (see box). In Europe and the United States, the movement found inspiration in the political upheavals and civil rights struggles of the 1960s and gained impetus from the entry of more and more women into the workforce. What was for a time called the women's liberation movement had such goals as equal educational and employment opportunity, sexual and reproductive freedom, and women's full participation in public politics and the creation of cultural images. The strategy of "CONSCIOUSNESS raising," aimed at gaining a critical consciousness of women's social position through discussions of personal experience, gave rise to the slogan "The personal is political." Two central political campaigns of the women's movement in this period focused on an Equal Rights Amendment to the U.S. Constitution, which passed Congress in 1972 but failed to be ratified, and "a woman's right to choose" abortion, which was guaranteed by the Supreme Court's *Roe v. Wade* decision in 1973.

"People call me a feminist whenever I express sentiments that differentiate me from a doormat or a prostitute."
—Rebecca West, 1913

Contemporary feminist thought reflects a wide variety of philosophical and political perspectives whose influence has ebbed and flowed within the movement. While LIBERAL feminists have primarily sought the integration of women into the existing sociopolitical structure, feminists with a MARXIST-SOCIALIST orientation have seen women's oppression as part of an entrenched CLASS system dominated by economic exploitation. RADICAL feminists have focused on the political nature of heterosexual relationships, seeing them as manifestations of historical power relations, and many lesbian feminists have regarded society's presumption of heterosexual gender roles as oppressive in itself. Some feminists are separatists, insisting that men are the problem and therefore cannot be part of the solution. Ecofeminists emphasize women's connection to the earth and natural processes and argue that the exploitation of women is a symptom of humanity's ALIENATION from the natural environment. Black feminists have criticized the largely white, middle-class women's movement as racially and culturally exclusive; the novelist Alice Walker coined the term "womanism" to distinguish a separate strand of feminism influenced by RACIAL issues. So-called cultural feminists, contending that there is a distinctive, essential female quality that informs women's thought and creativity, have sought either equal status in the cultural canon for "women's ways of knowing" or the complete overthrow of men's ways—a position condemned as essentialist (see ESSENCE) by feminist SOCIAL CONSTRUCTIONISTS and others who hold that supposedly "female" qualities are constructions shaped by cultural conditioning.

Since the 1970s, standard feminist assumptions have been challenged from many sides. Such challenges have come not only from cultural CONSERVATIVES trying to uphold patriarchal traditions but from POSTSTRUCTURALISTS and POSTMODERNISTS who find the very category of "woman" suspect, and who therefore question the politics of "women's issues." In the same period, feminism has slowly become a global phenomenon. As developing countries and traditional cultures undergo political change and economic and social modernization, women have sought a corresponding abolition of gender inequities and oppressive cultural practices.

See also ANARCHISM; BEAUVOIR; BIOLOGICAL DETERMINISM; DECONSTRUCTION; ESSENCE; GILMAN; GODDESS WORSHIP; "GREAT MAN" THEORY; box at HISTORICISM; HORNEY; KRISTEVA; MILLETT; POSTCOLONIAL THEORY; POSTMODERNISM; QUEER THEORY; STANTON; box at UTOPIANISM; WOLLSTONECRAFT.

FEMINIST THEORY: 12 THINKERS

Since the 1960s the movement for women's social and political equality and personal liberation has been informed and, in many cases, transformed by works of feminist cultural, political, and literary theory. Some particularly influential books—*The Feminine Mystique, The Female Eunuch, Sexual Politics,* and others—marked turning points in the movement's outlook and strategies. These and other works of the so-called *second wave* of modern FEMINISM identified the roots of women's oppression in historical social and economic structures, critically analyzed the stereotypes of women perpetuated by male artists, authors, and scholars, and called on women to reclaim their own natures. In the *third wave,* since the 1970s, much of the dialogue within the feminist movement has concerned the differences in RACE, CLASS, and sexual orientation that divide feminists, and an increasing emphasis has been placed on issues of violence against women. The 12 women profiled here are representative of contemporary feminist theorists writing in English. See also BEAUVOIR; KRISTEVA; MILLETT.

- *Susan Brownmiller* (1935–), in her exhaustive history of rape, *Against Our Will: Men, Women, and Rape* (1975), concluded that the pervasive threat of forced submission in patriarchal culture is a political act of intimidation that keeps women fearful and compliant. In *Femininity* (1984) Brownmiller differentiated between women's biological characteristics and other "feminine traits" that are presumed to be "natural" but are culturally imposed.

- *Judith Butler* (1956–) is a leading exponent of QUEER THEORY, which questions standard conceptions of gender and IDENTITY. In *Gender Trouble: Feminism and the Subversion of Identity* (1990) and *Bodies That Matter* (1993) she argued that notions of "natural" and "normal" sexual identities are artificial constructions in the service of political agendas, whether of heterosexual patriarchy or of gay and lesbian liberation. Gender is not a biologically or psychologically intrinsic state but a "performance" in which the individual has a multitude of options not limited to binary distinctions such as male/female or heterosexual/homosexual.

- *Mary Daly* (1928–), an American theologian and linguist, denounced the CHRISTIAN church and other traditional religions as misogynist in *The Church and the Second Sex* (1968) and *Beyond God the Father* (1973). Later works, including *Gyn/Ecology* (1978) and *Pure*

Lust (1984), urged women to reclaim their essential spirituality, founded in an ecstatic life force and intimate sisterhood. In her search for a new, "gynomorphic" language that DECONSTRUCTS male-centered modes of IDENTITY and reality, Daly has generated a vocabulary of woman-centered neologisms, compiled in *Webster's First New Intergalactic Wickedary of the English Language* (1987, with Jane Caputi).

* **Angela Davis** (1944–) has earned a controversial reputation as a political activist, COMMUNIST Party member, and BLACK POWER partisan. In *Women, Race, and Class* (1981), *Women, Culture, and Politics* (1989), and other writings, Davis debunked the stereotypical images of black women as dominating matriarchs, argued that social and cultural reform cannot occur without revolutionary political change, placed black feminism in the context of African-American resistance to oppression, and challenged white, middle-class feminists to consider questions of race and class when confronting issues of gender.

* **Betty Friedan** (1921–), in her 1963 best-seller *The Feminine Mystique*, indicted the socially imposed gender roles that assume all women's greatest fulfillment lies in domesticity. This pivotal work in the modern feminist movement generated a massive response that led to the founding of the National Organization for Women (NOW), of which Friedan was the first president. In *The Second Stage* (1981) she called on men to participate in housekeeping and child rearing and warned that the "sexual politics" of militant feminists would marginalize the movement.

* **Carol Gilligan** (1936–), a psychologist, challenges the traditional view of *moral reasoning* and its development. In her *In a Different Voice* (1982), she noted that men seek autonomy and tend to see ETHICAL issues in terms of rules and rights, while women cultivate relationships and respond to others' needs in moral conflicts. Although the male "justice voice" has historically been considered a higher level of moral development than the female "care voice," neither orientation is superior, Gilligan argued. A 1981–84 study of adolescent girls, which Gilligan headed, examined girls' loss of confidence in puberty when confronted with the expectations of patriarchal society.

* **Germaine Greer** (1939–), in *The Female Eunuch* (1970), charged that women are psychologically and spiritually "castrated" by patriarchy, through CAPITALISM, nuclear families, and their own submissive self-image, and called for women to reclaim their sexuality, creativity,

and power. *Sex and Destiny* (1984) criticized the worldwide politics of population control and advocated communal living while condemning sexual permissiveness.

- **bell hooks** (1952–), an outspoken critic of CAPITALIST institutions, also faults feminists and BLACK NATIONALISTS for failing to recognize that race, gender, and class oppression are "immutably connected." The title of *Ain't I a Woman* (1981), evoking the famous speech by Sojourner Truth, is an indignant reference to white feminists' frequent analogies between "women" and "blacks." *Feminist Theory: From Margin to Center* (1984) charged that theorists writing from the white, middle-class "center" of society fail to account for those on the margins.

- **Audre Lorde** (1934–1992), a poet and essayist, sought to establish the crucial role of lesbians and women of color in feminism. Seeing diversity as a "fund of necessary polarities," she urged women not to discard or downplay racial, sexual, and cultural differences in their search for community. *I Am Your Sister* (1985) urged lesbian and heterosexual black women to unite in common cause, and the essay "Uses of the Erotic" (in *Sister Outsider,* 1984) explored the fears associated with blackness and sexual difference, suggesting that issues of sexuality can be fruitful sources of dialogue, not division.

- **Catharine MacKinnon** (1946–), a lawyer and legal theorist, analyzed the cultural and legal underpinnings of pornography and sexual harassment in *Feminism Unmodified* (1987), *Towards a Feminist Theory of the State* (1989), and other writings. Her contentions that pornography is a violation of the constitutional right to equal protection and that sexual harassment constitutes workplace discrimination under the Civil Rights Act have been influential in American jurisprudence. Antipornography ordinances she drafted with Andrea Dworkin in the early eighties were overturned by the Supreme Court, but her construction of sexual harassment law, outlined in *Sexual Harassment of Working Women* (1979), has been widely adopted by U.S. courts.

- **Juliet Mitchell** (1934–) has reexamined MARXIST and FREUDIAN theory in feminist terms; she is also a leading interpreter of Jacques Lacan (see box at STRUCTURALISM). Her essay "Women: The Longest Revolution" (1966) argued that women's social condition is not simply a consequence of economic structures but a complex of four elements—production, reproduction, socialization, and sexuality—all of which must be addressed to achieve liberation. *Psychoanalysis and Feminism* (1974) argued that when Freud stated that girls developing their gender identity perceive themselves as deficient, he was not being misogynistic, merely identifying the culture's view that the patriarchal social position is the "correct" one.

- *Sheila Rowbotham* (1943–) is a MARXIST whose studies of women in history have stressed the theoretical links between gender and class issues and the affinity of feminism with SOCIALISM. *Women, Resistance, and Revolution* (1972) maintained that women's liberation depends on, and can spearhead, societal liberation; *Hidden from History* (1973), a chronicle of women in England, presented women as agents, not merely casualties, of history; and *Woman's Consciousness, Man's World* (1973) called for a revolutionary feminist movement with a working-class majority of women who have been doubly oppressed, as women and as proletarians.

field theory

Any of a number of theories, particularly in physics but also in the social sciences, focusing on "spheres of influence"—states in which the locus of force or interaction occurs in the space between objects, not within them. The theory of electromagnetic fields, for example, proposed by Michael Faraday and consolidated by MAXWELL, explained how electrical and magnetic forces could "act at a distance" without touching the objects they affect. However, such fields were at first described as properties of a subtle *ether* that fills the universe. The ancient assumption that physical interactions cannot take place in a vacuum, and therefore fields of force are composed of some kind of matter, persisted until EINSTEIN's theories of RELATIVITY made it unnecessary.

Theories that unite two or more fields or forces, such as electromagnetism, are called *unified field theories*. Einstein spent much of his life in quest of a field theory that would unify gravitation, electromagnetism, and the nuclear forces. He maintained that QUANTUM THEORY, for all its successes, could not serve as a useful point of departure and sought instead a unified theory "that shall represent events themselves and not merely the PROBABILITY of their occurrence." Neither his nor many others' attempts throughout the 20th century have yet produced such a unified theory, although scientists continue to be drawn by the idea that all physical interactions share an underlying unity. Their efforts include the search for a Grand Unified Theory that would consolidate electromagnetism with the strong and weak nuclear forces (see STANDARD MODEL) and the quest for a "theory of everything" that would unite all forces, including gravity. The latter, its adherents believe, may be contained in *superstring theory*, developed in the 1980s, which sees matter at the fundamental level not as points but as tiny pieces of "string" existing in a multitude of dimensions of space and time.

Field theory in the physical sciences has inspired some social scientists to apply the model to explanations of personal and societal functioning; some have likewise attempted to find a unified field theory of social interactions, so far without success. The psychological field theory developed in the 1930s by Kurt Lewin combines GESTALT theory's emphasis on the whole of experience with physical field theory and mathematical topology. The individual, Lewin said, lives within a field called the *life space*, the environment as she or he perceives it, with configurations and boundaries defining the "map" of experience, needs, and goals. Borrowing terms from physics, Lewin stated that a person's motivations and choices of direction in life are influenced by positive and negative "valences," or attraction and repulsion in response to people and events, which produce "vectors" of attraction or avoidance.

formalism

Any approach to theory or practice that emphasizes form, structure, or formal rules; examples include SCHOLASTICISM and STRUCTURALISM. The term is applied particularly to the attempt to derive all of mathematics from a small number of rules of symbolic LOGIC and to formal approaches to creation and criticism in the arts.

Mathematical formalism (also called *logicism*) began in the late 19th century with the creation of SET THEORY, which claimed to provide a fundamental basis for all of mathematics. It was developed through Gottlob Frege's effort to create a logic-based "universal calculus" that would contain all arithmetical statements, and through RUSSELL and Whitehead's comprehensive attempt to cast mathematics as a branch of logic. The term "formalism" was applied to this quest by the German mathematician David Hilbert, who devised a "program" in which any mathematical statement could be analyzed according to logical properties and shown to be either true or false. Interest in formalism declined after Kurt Gödel's *incompleteness theorem* demonstrated that not all true statements can be proven. An opposing approach to mathematical formalism was *intuitionism*, associated with L. E. J. Brouwer, who argued that both mathematics and logic are more than the pure manipulation of symbols; they require thought processes as well.

In the arts, formalism refers, often deprecatingly, to an emphasis on form over content (cf. FUNCTIONALISM). It applies to an artist's artificial or overly rigorous use of formal stylistic elements or structural principles, but is principally identified with AESTHETIC theories that stress formal qualities. As a critical method, formalism is exemplified by two 20th-century movements. Russian Formalism, which flourished in the early Soviet period, defined literature as a distinct linguistic form created by devices that "estrange" the narrative, giving it an unfamiliar and fresh aspect that sets it apart from everyday experience; nothing exists in the work but its technique. While the idea of the author as an ordinary craftsman appealed to the working-class spirit of the revolution (though most of the Russian Formalists denied any interest in social content), the movement was soon overtaken by SOCIALIST REALISM. The other outstanding, and far more influential, school of critical formalism was the NEW CRITICISM of the 1940s, which approached poetry from the point of view of its linguistic structure, disregarding the author's intent or the work's effect on a reader.

Foucault, Michel (1926–1984)

French philosopher and historian, whose critique of the "discourses of power" in society profoundly influenced late-20th-century social thought and cultural criticism. He has been called both a STRUCTURALIST and a POSTSTRUCTURALIST, though he preferred to think of himself simply as "a historian of systems of thought." Foucault comprehensively challenged traditional notions of truth, power, history, and morality, asking questions more than offering answers, seeking to provoke a reconsideration of our cultural assumptions. Much of his work focused on the notion of *discourse,* the complex of credentials, protocols, jargon, and specialized knowledge that defines theory and practice within the human sciences (psychology, sociology, medicine, etc.), makes them the exclusive preserve of those privy to the discourse, and allies them with dominant IDEOLOGIES and structures of power. Like NIETZSCHE, Foucault argued that power is an attempt to impose order on a world in flux and is exerted in systems of knowledge and social institutions. TRUTH, therefore, is never absolute but always contingent, an expression of prevailing social and political norms, a product of power relations rather than a leveling influence. In the modern world, power is no longer centralized but suffuses society. "Sovereign power" wielded from above has been replaced by "disciplinary power," the power of coercion exercised through systems of control ranging from penal institutions to consumer MATERIALISM.

Foucault called a socially defining system of discourses an *episteme* (from "EPISTEMOLOGY") and identified historical moments in which fundamental shifts occur from one dominant episteme to another—a concept similar to Thomas Kuhn's notion of the PARADIGM shift. For Foucault, the prime example of such a shift in Western history occurred in the 18th-century ENLIGHTENMENT, when the cult of REASON created standards for what is "normal" according to supposedly rational principles that were in fact as arbitrary and repressive as the authorities they replaced. In *Madness and Civilization* (*Folie et déraison*, 1961), for example, Foucault maintained that the definition and treatment of "insanity" constitutes a form of social control. Once "madness" was defined as abnormal, rather than simply eccentric, its victims were separated from the "sane" population by exile or incarceration; then, in the 19th century, physicians created a science of mental disease, parallel to physical medicine, with institutionalized procedures to restore patients to sanctioned standards of normalcy. This view became pivotal for "antipsychiatrists" such as R. D. Laing, David Cooper, and Thomas Szasz. In *Discipline and Punish* (*Surveiller et punir*, 1975) Foucault took a similar view of the penal system, in which the "microphysics of power" is practiced and techniques of discipline and surveillance are developed, which are later applied in the outside world in educational and other institutions. In the unfinished *History of Sexuality* (three of a projected six volumes were published in 1976 and 1984), he contended that sexuality, too, is defined by coercive discourses. This and other works of Foucault's greatly influenced contemporary theorists of sexuality and "body politics," particularly FEMINISTS with a poststructuralist viewpoint and QUEER THEORISTS.

See also NOMINALISM.

fractals

Geometrical patterns and objects that have the same shapes at different scales; a controversial concept in modern mathematics. The repetition of similar patterns of varying size is called *self-similarity;* for example, there is a change of scale in the blood vessels of the human circulatory system, from the large arteries down to the small capillaries, but no significant change of shape. The term "fractal," derived from the same root as "fraction," was coined in 1975 by the Polish-American mathematician Benoit B. Mandelbrot for the irregular, nonintegral (i.e., non-EUCLIDIAN) patterns he found in a wide range of phenomena, especially in natural forms such as plants, clouds, and coastlines. The idea of fractals is closely related to CHAOS THEORY, which studies complex, nonlinear systems.

Fractals can be defined and constructed by an iterative process (the successive division of a given shape into similar figures of different sizes). The digital computer, which can carry out a great number of successive iterations at high speed and display the resulting fractals, has made possible the modeling of complex natural objects with computer graphics using fractal geometry. It has also inspired a great deal of computer-generated art that, in some cases, has more in common with the intricate, irregular details in Old Master paintings than with the conventional geometries of abstract modern art. While some scientists dismiss fractals as interesting but inconsequential, others assert their potential for bringing about a deeper understanding of the natural world.

A particularly elegant example of computer-generated fractals is known as the *Mandelbrot set*, based on a simple mathematical formula that selects points in the set by distinguishing between numerical progressions that result in finite or infinite numbers. In its entirety, it resembles a large, hairy disc attached to a smaller one, but at greater and greater magnifications seahorse-like paisley patterns, whorls, and other organic-looking forms emerge; and the same patterns keep appearing at progressively "deeper" levels. That fractal forms have shapes found in nature is not surprising, according to Mandelbrot, since organic development through successive cell division is also an iterative process.

free trade and protectionism

Opposing international trade policies; unrestricted import and export of goods between nations, guided by comparative ADVANTAGE and subject only to SUPPLY AND DEMAND, is called free trade; prohibitions or restrictions on imports from foreign markets is called protectionism. Most countries' trade policies fall somewhere on the spectrum between completely free exchange and absolute protectionism.

Free trade was a novel idea when Adam Smith made the case for it in *The Wealth of Nations* (1776). Against the prevailing wisdom that free-flowing commerce would threaten domestic producers, Smith argued that nations should export what they can produce most efficiently and inexpensively and import "what it will cost [them] more to make than to buy." Free trade is advocated by many economists as the most efficient, cost-effective, and mutually beneficial system for all trading nations, giving each one unfettered access to markets for the goods it specializes in and allowing imports of the goods it cannot or chooses not to produce. Others object that one country's free trade is another's economic exploitation, especially in the case of developing countries, whose fragile economies can be flooded and overwhelmed by imports from larger, more efficient producers, especially multinational corporations.

Protectionism is promoted in the interest of defending domestic industries from foreign competition, particularly when that competition is seen as unfair. In the 1980s, for example, the United States government reacted to the "dumping" of Japanese steel and semiconductors on the American market by imposing import restrictions on those goods. Agitation for protectionism often flows from the perception that domestic jobs are threatened by "cheap foreign labor." Such concerns during the Great Depression led to passage of the Smoot-Hawley Act of 1930, which set U.S. tariffs (import taxes) at an all-time high and triggered retaliatory policies by other countries. Since World War II, the world's major trading nations have attempted to keep trade relatively open through the multilateral General Agreement on Tariffs and Trade (GATT).

Governments can influence trade by imposing (or selectively lowering) tariffs and import quotas, and by granting export subsidies to domestic industries. Nations may favor some trading partners over others; for example, the U.S. Congress annually confers what is called *most-favored-nation* status on certain countries, giving them lower tariff rates. *Free-trade zones* are sometimes created between several nations that remove trade barriers among themselves but not with other countries; examples are the European Union and the zone established by the North American Free Trade Agreement (NAFTA).

See also MARKET; MERCANTILISM.

freedom

A complex and controversial concept in political, social, and religious philosophy, referring both to political independence and self-determination and to personal autonomy and self-direction. In both senses, it revolves around the question of what controls us—our individual and common will, or an external force.

In political theory, the notion is often discussed in terms of the distinction between *negative freedom,* the absence of coercion or constraint, and *positive freedom,* the ability and resources to pursue one's dreams and ambitions, to be one's own master—what Erich Fromm has called "freedom *from*" and "freedom *to,*" and which Isaiah Berlin explored in a famous essay, "Two Concepts of Liberty" (1969). The two conceptions are not mutually exclusive, and many classic discussions of freedom define the limits each one places on the

> *"If liberty means anything at all, it means the right to tell people what they do not want to hear."*
> —George Orwell, introduction to *Animal Farm,* 1945

other. Both LOCKE and MILL, for example, distinguished between liberty and license; while "liberty consists in doing as one desires," Mill said, "one must not make himself a nuisance to other people." In HOBBES's vision of the *state of nature,* no one is free from the depredations of others; the SOCIAL CONTRACT exchanges that perilous ANARCHY for security—the freedom to survive and thrive—which is best guaranteed by an authoritarian government. To ROUSSEAU and the 19th-century IDEALISTS, true freedom comes from within and exists in voluntarily doing the right thing. In the view of many MARXISTS and WELFARE theorists, genuine liberty depends on a minimum standard of material well-being, without which positive freedoms are unattainable.

Human freedom is often considered in terms of *free will,* the individual's capacity to choose his or her own destiny rather than follow the dictates of DETERMINISM, which holds that whatever happens is causally linked to what has gone before, or PREDESTINATION, in which God's will overrides the individual's. In modern thought, the idea of free will is expressed, for example, in the PSYCHOANALYTIC view of the human mind as a system of CONSCIOUS and UNCONSCIOUS processes so complex as to defy prediction, and in the EXISTENTIAL and PHENOMENOLOGICAL view that freedom is the capacity to act creatively within given historical circumstances.

The idea of free will has been most contentious in the religious context, where it seems contradicted by doctrines of divine omniscience and preordination: if our actions are prefigured in the divine plan, they cannot be free, nor can we be held accountable for them. The controversy has occupied CHRISTIAN theology for centuries and has never been entirely resolved, although a variety of resolutions have been offered. St. AUGUSTINE, for instance, found freedom and predestination to be compatible, partly because to be truly free is to know and follow the divine will. Another conclusion, shared by ISLAM and other religious traditions, is that while our ultimate destiny may be predetermined, we exercise free will in our individual actions.

See also DEMOCRACY; DEWEY; EXISTENTIALISM; HEGEL; HOBBES; INDIVIDUALISM; LIBERALISM; LIBERTARIANISM; LOCKE; MILL; RIGHTS; SOCIAL CONTRACT.

Freemasonry

The Order of Free and Accepted Masons is the world's largest fraternal society, characterized by tolerant social views and complex secret rites; open to men over 21, its more than six million members are called Freemasons or simply Masons. The order, stemming from medieval stonecutters' guilds but claiming descent from the builders of King Solomon's Temple, was established in 1717 in London and quickly spread to the Continent and colonial America. Early Freemasonry emphasized RATIONALISM, PROGRESS, cosmopolitanism, and EQUALITY.

From the beginning an organization primarily of merchants and professionals, not craftsmen, the order provided a private world of like-minded men in a pleasant social environment. Many patriots of the American Revolution, including George Washington and Benjamin Franklin, were Masons; over a dozen U.S. presidents have belonged to the order. American Freemasonry was nearly destroyed in the 1830s, following the disappearance of a disgruntled Mason who threatened to publish the society's secrets. The scandal led to a precipitous drop in membership and to the formation of the Anti-Masonic Party, the country's first major third party, which considered Freemasonry elitist, esoteric, and incompatible with REPUBLICAN ideals. The Anti-Masons found support among rural and working-class Americans resentful of the political power held by the urban gentry, many of whom were Masons. Freemasonry has also been opposed by the ROMAN CATHOLIC Church as inimical to its own spiritual authority.

Each local Masonic lodge, affiliated with one of several international "rites" or branches, is organized in an elaborate hierarchy, through which members advance by mastering the order's intricate secrets and rituals. While predominantly CHRISTIAN, the society admits members of other religions, excluding only atheists; worship is considered strictly a personal matter. God is conceived as the Great Architect of the Universe, and spiritual belief is seen as the way to achieve and maintain a moral life.

Freire, Paulo (1921–1997)

Brazilian educator, a pioneer in adult education whose "pedagogy of the oppressed" seeks political empowerment through literacy and social consciousness. Born into a middle-class family that fell into poverty during the Great Depression, Freire realized at an early age that the deprivations suffered by the poor can spawn a "culture of silence"—a passive, fatalistic acceptance of oppression and ignorance. Freire began developing his educational theories while working with the urban and rural poor of Brazil as a government official in the 1950s. Challenging the image of students as empty vessels into whom information is poured, he promoted instead a vision of education as an interactive, reflective, and dynamic process that incorporates and builds on the learners' own bases of knowledge and experience. This process, stressing dialogue and using texts directly relevant to the students' lives, not only produced remarkable increases in adult literacy, it also stimulated disenfranchised people to analyze and reevaluate their position in Brazilian society and encouraged them to seek more political influence. This alarmed many powerful Brazilians, and after the military coup of 1964 Freire was briefly jailed and then exiled for 15 years.

In *Pedagogy of the Oppressed* (1970) Freire argued that literacy is more than a skill and education more than a technique. They are tools for the development of *conscientizacao* ("conscientization," or conscious awareness) of one's place within society and its power structure, pathways to transforming one's existence by becoming an active subject rather than a passive victim. Working together, students share their common experiences and build a group identity as well as self-awareness; *conscientizacao* is developed through *praxis*, the integration of action and reflection. In the 1970s and '80s, Freire's methods were adopted and his ideas disseminated by the literacy campaigns of revolutionary movements in Nicaragua, South Africa, and elsewhere, as well as by North American grassroots adult-education programs such as the Highlander Center in Tennessee.

Freud, Sigmund (1856–1939)

Austrian physician and psychiatrist, founder of PSYCHOANALYSIS and author of the theory of the UNCONSCIOUS, who fundamentally changed our ideas about human personality and sexuality. Although his theories are still controversial (he has been hailed as a visionary genius and denounced as a fraud), many of the ideas he originated have become intrinsic to our view of our inner selves. His major work, *The Interpretation of Dreams* (1900), was followed by many others, including *Totem and Taboo* (1913), *The Ego and the Id* (1923), and *Civilization and Its Discontents* (1930).

Trained in neurology, Freud developed the beginnings of his psychoanalytic theory in the 1880s, while working on hypnosis therapy with women suffering from "hysterical" paralysis with no apparent neurological cause. He suspected that the symptoms were manifestations of disturbing memories locked in the unconscious mind—memories, he initially thought, of childhood sexual abuse. Though Freud later modified this "seduction theory" to acknowledge fantasies of incest as well as actual abuse, it was an early instance

FREUD'S STAGES OF PSYCHOSEXUAL DEVELOPMENT

In Freudian theory, the human personality develops during childhood in five stages—oral, anal, phallic, latency, and genital—called *psychosexual* because Freud associated psychological development with changes in the focus of sexual energy within the body. The first three stages are characterized by "polymorphous perversity," when the infant finds pleasure in oral, anal, and genital sensations that would be considered perversions in adults. When development has stalled in one of the stages a person is said to be *fixated*—trapped in old behavior patterns that are no longer useful.

In the *oral* stage, during the first year or two of life, pleasure is associated with nursing and focuses on the "incorporation" of nurturing things into the body via the mouth. The adult need for oral gratification, such as smoking and overeating, is a throwback to this stage.

The *anal* stage, occupying the second or third year, is associated with toilet training and its lessons in self-control. In Freudian thought, excessive punishment for "accidents" in this period can lead to an "anal retentive" personality, compulsively tidy and emotionally closed, while overindulgence results in "anal expulsive" adult behavior, disorderly and aggressive.

The *phallic* (or Oedipal) stage, from about age three to six, coincides with the discovery of pleasurable feelings in the genitals. Children at this stage see the parent of their own sex as a rival for the affections of the parent of the opposite sex. Freud called this feeling the *Oedipus complex,* after the Greek myth of the king who killed his father and married his mother. (The syndrome in girls has sometimes been called the *Electra complex,* after the Greek princess who sought to avenge her mother's murder of her father.) In the Oedipal stage, boys see their father as a threat, particularly to their newly discovered sex organs, and feel *castration anxiety,* which they finally allay by forsaking the infatuation with their mother and identifying with the father. Girls, on the other hand, feel *penis envy,* blaming the mother for their apparent deficiency. While the boy's anxiety is soon resolved, Freud theorized, the girl's lingers until she fulfills herself in childbirth. (Cf. HORNEY.)

From about age six until the onset of puberty a *latency* period prevails, in which socialization progresses and the early sexual feelings are repressed. In the *genital* stage, during adolescence, the individual matures sexually and moves out of the self-centered childhood sphere into integration with the larger society. Freud emphasized that many adults never complete (or, in some cases, even reach) the genital stage, but remain frozen in infantile, narcissistic patterns of social and sexual intercourse.

of his conviction that the seeds of adult neuroses are sown in childhood psychosexual development (see box).

In Freud's theory, the personality is structured by three elements—the *id,* the *ego,* and the *superego*—which determine behavior through their interactions, often conflicting. The id is primal and instinctive, driven by the *pleasure principle* to avoid anxiety and pain. It contains two contending instincts: the life force, including the sex drive, and the death instinct, the seat of aggression. Freud called these two instincts Eros and Thanatos, after the Greek gods of love and death; his concept of the *libido,* or sexual energy, developed over time to eventually include both the life and death impulses. The ego is the rational impulse, operating according to the *reality principle,* which modifies one's instinctive impulses into socially acceptable conduct. The ego mediates between the irrational id and the authoritarian superego, the internalized voice of socialization, conscience, and morality.

In the healthy, fully integrated adult, all three elements are in harmonious balance. However, if the id's desires clash too forcefully with the superego's strictures, the ego may censor, or *repress,* the content of that conflict, withdrawing it from memory; hidden in the unconscious, it continues to subtly influence CONSCIOUSNESS and behavior. Other defense mechanisms— unconscious devices that protect consciousness from having to deal with disturbing realities—include *regression* to an earlier, more comfortable, stage of emotional development; *denial* of a troubling emotion or fact; *reaction formation,* in which an "inappropriate" feeling is converted into its acceptable opposite, as when someone is immoderately solicitous toward a relative she or he loathes; *projection* of one's own feelings onto others, where they can be condemned without self-reproach; *displacement* of an emotion, such as anger, from its true object to a less threatening one; and *sublimation,* the displacement of a dangerous impulse into a more constructive channel, for example, the artist's creative expression of repressed emotions. *Neurosis* is the expression of unconscious anxieties in psychological or physical distress, including phobias, compulsions, obsessions, and bodily ailments.

Some early followers of Freud, who later broke with him, revised or rejected key elements in his system. Carl JUNG, for example, saw the libido as a generalized "life urge" rather than a specifically sexual force. Alfred Adler stressed the *inferiority complex,* created by the child's impotence and compensated for by aggressive drives, over Freud's emphasis on primal instincts. Karen HORNEY attributed female subordination to social forces, not "penis envy" (see box). Harry Stack Sullivan held that interpersonal relations are more important determinants of personality than "intrapsychic" events occurring solely in one's own conscious and unconscious mind.

See also AESTHETICS; CATHARSIS; DETERMINISM; box at FEMINISM; HORNEY; JUNG; OBJECT RELATIONS; PSYCHOANALYSIS; STREAM OF CONSCIOUSNESS; SURREALISM; TOTEMISM; UNCONSCIOUS.

Friedan, Betty See box at FEMINISM

Friedman, Milton See MONETARISM

Fromm, Erich See box at CRITICAL THEORY

functionalism
Separate but related approaches in the social sciences, as well as philosophy and the arts, in which function—purpose or utility—is seen as the primary organizational principle. Functionalism was introduced in the 19th century by the sociologists Herbert Spencer and Émile Durkheim, who applied a biological metaphor to society, seeing it as an interrelated organism, each of whose elements contributes to the stability and survival of the whole. The perspective was developed in the early 20th century in social anthropology by Bronislaw Malinowski, who stressed that social institutions develop not in response to historical forces but for the purpose of fulfilling basic human *needs,* and Alfred Radcliffe-Brown, whose STRUCTURALIST approach to social systems interpreted customs and beliefs in terms of their utility as mechanisms of social cohesion. This orientation, which came to be called *structural-functionalism,* dominated anthropology, especially in Britain, through midcentury. The same term was applied to the equally influential sociological theory of Talcott Parsons, who viewed society as a SYSTEM in which institutions and cultural practices act to regulate social intercourse and achieve societal goals.

Whereas in anthropology and sociology functionalism is close to, and sometimes equated with, structuralism, *functional psychology* developed in contradiction to psychological structuralism's emphasis on mental processes. A dominant movement before World War I that greatly expanded the range of psychological inquiry, functionalism held that the proper study of the mind is to discover its usefulness to the human organism, for example, in adapting to new situations and problem solving. The position was central to William JAMES's theory of CONSCIOUSNESS and to John DEWEY's philosophy of education.

In political science, functionalism refers to the view that peace can be encouraged through international cooperation based on practical solutions to common needs that transcend national boundaries. First articulated as such during World War II, that belief became the rationale behind the United Nations' international service agencies, as well as a prime focus of those seeking global political integration and the withering away of the nation-STATE.

Functionalism in the arts was epitomized by architect Louis Sullivan's maxim "Form follows function," by which he meant that purpose should be the first—but not the only—consideration in design. This principle, which also implied that beauty resides in the purity of unornamented form, was applied in a great deal of MODERNIST design in the interwar period, for example, in the geometrical austerity of Bauhaus architecture. (Cf. FORMALISM.)

See also CONSTRUCTIVISM; MODERNISM; SYSTEMS THEORY.

fundamentalism

Generally, any belief or policy that promotes a return to basic principles and founding doctrines; most commonly associated with religious movements in Christianity and Islam. Religious fundamentalism insists on the inerrancy of scripture and obedience to traditional codes.

CHRISTIAN fundamentalism arose in the United States in the early 20th century in reaction to theological LIBERALISM, especially HUMANISTIC views of the Bible as a culturally significant but not necessarily divine document. Fundamentalist doctrine centers on the conviction that the Bible is the infallible word of God and is literally true. From this belief flow certain "fundamentals" of faith, including the authenticity of miracles, the virgin birth, and the divinity of JESUS, whose sacrifice atoned for human sin, whose resurrection confirmed his divinity, and whose Second Coming is ensured (see ADVENTISM; ESCHATOLOGY). A central tenet of literal biblical interpretation is CREATIONISM, the belief that the world was created by God exactly as recounted in Genesis. Consequently, American fundamentalists have repeatedly sought, with some success, to exclude the theory of EVOLUTION from public schools and to introduce creationism into the curriculum. The most celebrated clash over this issue oc-curred in the 1925 "monkey trial" of John T. Scopes for teaching DARWINIAN evolution in defiance of a Tennessee statute, a test case in which the prosecu-tion and defense were conducted by prominent supporters of the respective ideologies, William Jennings Bryan and Clarence Darrow. In the late 20th century, fundamentalist social and political movements have adopted an ac-tivist agenda based on the restoration of traditional moral codes and social re-lations; these campaigns, asserting Old Testament authority, include advocacy of patriarchal family structures and condemnation of homosexuality and abortion.

ISLAMIC fundamentalism likewise emphasizes scriptural authority and obe-dience to social conventions. It has also gained a measure of political power, notably in Iran, where an Islamic republic was established in 1979 under the leadership of the country's Shi'ite clergy (see box at ISLAM: Sunnis and Shi'ites). Fundamentalist Muslims consider the Qur'an (Koran) and the *shari'ah*—the corpus of Islamic law derived from the Qur'an's and MUHAMMAD's teachings—to embody the indisputable will of God, and demand strict compliance with both.

See also JEHOVAH'S WITNESSES; PENTECOSTALISM.

G

Gaia hypothesis

The theory that the earth is a living, self-regulating superorganism; named after the personification of the earth in Greek mythology. The hypothesis was introduced in 1972 by the British chemist James Lovelock, who proposed that, just as our bodies are self-regulating, compensating for changes in our activity and surroundings, so the "body" of the earth regulates itself through the living organisms that control its atmosphere, oceans, and crust (cf. CYBERNETICS). The evolution of the earth's individual life forms and physical environment, therefore, is not a series of separate processes but part of the evolution of Gaia as a whole.

Support for the biochemical aspect of the theory has come from American biologist Lynn Margulis's research into bacteria and other microorganisms. Microbes—in sheer numbers and aggregate mass, the major form of life—perform countless organic processes, from digestion in animals to nitrogen-fixing in plants, and thus may be the crucial regulatory agents of the overall biosphere. In Lovelock's view, the environmental damage inflicted by human beings has unbalanced the system, which, like the body, has an impressive but ultimately limited capacity for self-correction.

Critics of the Gaia hypothesis point out that in the long term the earth has not been stable, but has been subject to massive climatic and geological changes. The testability of the theory is also questioned: is it an authentically scientific hypothesis, subject to falsification (see VERIFIABILITY AND FALSIFIABILITY), or a metaphor—part of a HOLISTIC approach to science—that may be figuratively true but is not literally true *or* false? However, even among researchers dubious of Gaia's scientific status, the conception of the earth as an interdependent system has stimulated cooperation and cross-fertilization between normally isolated disciplines, including geochemistry, evolutionary theory, atmospheric physics, and microbiology.

Galileo Galilei (1564–1642)

Italian astronomer, mathematician, and physicist, the major instigator (with KEPLER) of the Scientific Revolution of the 17th century, who made fundamental contributions to the sciences of motion and dynamics and to the confirmation of the Copernican theory of the solar system; often considered the father of mathematical physics. Writing with rhetorical passion, and in vernacular Italian instead of Latin, he conveyed to a growing public the idea that nature's mysteries are within the grasp of human understanding. Prevailing ARISTOTELIAN conceptions of physics and astronomy were challenged by Galileo's work, of which the two most famous and influential examples were his demonstrations concerning objects in motion and his support of COPERNICUS's model of a heliocentric universe. From his studies of pendulums and inclined planes, he concluded that objects fall through the air or roll downhill at a constant acceleration (at a velocity that increases by equal amounts in equal time intervals) and that this acceleration is independent of the weight of the object. He is said to have demonstrated this by dropping balls of unequal weight from the Leaning Tower of Pisa and observing that they struck the ground at the same time.

Galileo's improvements to the newly invented telescope allowed him to detect lunar mountains, the moons of Jupiter, and individual stars in the Milky Way, as well as sunspots and the phases of Venus. These observations, attesting to a universe far larger than previously supposed, with many more stars and numerous centers of motion, were consistent with Copernican theory but incompatible with the prevailing view of a compact, unchanging, earth-centered universe. His conviction that the earth is in motion led him to his theory of RELATIVITY, that objects in equal motion (such as people on a ship) act in relation to each other as if that common motion did not exist. In 1614 he was denounced as a heretic and became embroiled in the struggle with the ROMAN CATHOLIC Church that engaged him for the rest of his life. After the publication of his *Dialogue Concerning the Two Chief World Systems* (1632), a purportedly noncommittal but transparently pro-Copernican examination of the respective merits of the Ptolemaic and Copernican systems, Galileo was condemned by the Inquisition to life imprisonment (later commuted to house arrest) and compelled to retract his assertion that the earth moves around the sun. Legend has it that immediately after recanting he murmured under his breath, "But it still moves." Galileo's view that "the book

"The Bible shows the way to go to heaven, not the way the heavens go."
—Galileo

of nature is written in the language of mathematics," that there is no sharp distinction between the heavens and earth, and that science is concerned with the proximate causes of recurring phenomena, not with any ultimate purposes, has characterized science since his time.
See also COPERNICUS; RELATIVITY.

game theory

Approach to the study of decision making that models situations of competition, cooperation, and conflict in terms of the rules, strategies, risks, and variable outcomes of games. It was founded by the Hungarian-American mathematician John von Neumann and amplified in his and Oskar Morgenstern's *Theory of Games and Economic Behavior* (1944). Game theory studies the ways in which people make decisions in circumstances where the outcome depends on others' as well as one's own strategic choices and resulting "moves," and is therefore concerned with players' assumptions and expectations about each other in interactive situations. Unlike real life, game theory assumes that all the players will act rationally and, generally, that they have complete information about the projected "payoff" of any given course of action.

Games can be *two-person*—a one-on-one confrontation—or *n-person*, in which coalitions are often necessary for success. They are *cooperative* or *noncooperative* depending on whether or not the players can profit from collaboration. *Zero-sum* games are those in which one player's gain is another's loss—the net gains and losses add up to zero. In *non-zero-sum* (or *mixed-motive*) games, both sides can benefit, or benefit to differing degrees. Non-zero-sum games are most interesting to game theorists, who are concerned with applying theoretical principles to real-world sociological, economic, and political relationships in which outcomes are usually the result of bargaining and compromises, not winner-take-all victories. Game theory has been applied, for example, to the study of MARKET behavior, DETERRENCE and arms control, and legislative strategy. It has also been criticized, however, as dependent on unrealistic assumptions and artificial models (see box).

See also DECISION THEORY.

PRISONERS' DILEMMA

The most famous example of GAME THEORY is a hypothetical non-zero-sum game known as Prisoners' Dilemma. Two men, arrested on suspicion of committing a crime together, are being questioned in separate rooms. If neither confesses, they will both go free; if both confess, each will get a moderate jail sentence; but if only one confesses and implicates the other, he will receive a light sentence and his partner will get the maximum punishment. The dilemma for both of them is whether to confess and go to jail for a short time or to keep silent and risk going to jail for a long time if the other confesses. Prisoners' Dilemma contradicts the conventional view of self-interest, because here the most self-serving outcome requires trust and cooperation. However, the *dominant strategy* in this case—the one that has the "least worst" outcome no matter what the other player does—is confession. Game theory holds that in most situations players will follow the dominant strategy.

Gandhi, Mohandas Karamchand (1869–1948)

Indian spiritual and political leader, called Mahatma ("great soul"); architect of Indian independence and author of the philosophy and practice of *satyagraha,* or constructive NONVIOLENT resistance to oppression. Gandhi's thinking drew from a diversity of sources, including the Bible and the Bhagavad-Gita, as well as more recent works such as THOREAU's "Civil Disobedience" and, above all, Tolstoy's philosophy of universal love and passive resistance to evil. Gandhi lived for two decades in South Africa, where he developed his philosophy of nonviolent direct action in a series of campaigns to end discrimination against the Indian community there, and went on to lead the 30-year crusade for Indian independence from British rule.

Gandhi saw no distinction between the social and spiritual, the personal and political. He believed that all life is part of the controlling ESSENCE of the universe (see MONISM), which he called *satya* ("truth"); we are all, literally, one, and must therefore love each other as fully as we do ourselves. Central to this belief was the ancient principle of *ahimsa,* noninjury to and respect for living beings (see JAINISM). Both Gandhi's activist strategy and his religious philosophy embraced three principal concepts: *satyagraha* (a term coined by Gandhi from the Sanskrit words for "truth" and "firmness" or "persistence"); *swaraj* (self-rule), implying both national independence and personal self-control; and *swadeshi* ("one's own land"), the development of self-sufficient local economies at the village level. The *swadeshi* movement, symbolized by the act of spinning, which Gandhi himself did every day, encouraged the wearing of homespun cotton clothing *(khadi)* and the boycott of British-manufactured cloth. His advocacy of *hind swaraj,* or home rule, urged the strengthening of Indian identity in opposition to colonial culture and called for a government rooted in indigenous values and traditions.

For Gandhi, nonviolent resistance was hardly passive, but an active confrontation of "brute force" with "soul force" that not merely disrupted colonial rule but also appealed to the essential humanity of the oppressor. *Satyagraha,* a decisive factor in achieving Indian independence in 1948, was pursued over many years by a variety of means, including mass marches and demonstrations, CIVIL DISOBEDIENCE, boycotts, and hunger strikes. Gandhi himself practiced an ASCETIC way of life, encouraged community cooperation and communal living (he considered private property a violation of the oneness of humanity), and strove for tolerance between antagonistic social groups. He vainly tried to prevent the partition of India into Hindu- and Muslim-dominated STATES, and challenged the CASTE system, calling the outcast Untouchables Harijan, or "children of God."

See also CIVIL DISOBEDIENCE; NONVIOLENCE.

Garvey, Marcus (1887–1940)

Jamaican-born political thinker and activist, founder of the first important BLACK NATIONALIST movement and an influential proponent of black pride, exceptionalism, and self-sufficiency. His Universal Negro Improvement Association, founded in 1914 in Jamaica and established in New York two years later, claimed a membership of two million. Garvey's aim was to create pride in African heritage, foster black self-determination, and support black people's achievements. The black, red, and green bars of the *bendera,* the flag he designed, represent unity, struggle, and hope for the future.

Like Booker T. WASHINGTON, Garvey questioned the possibility—and desirability—of successful integration into a majority white culture that was racist and hostile to black aspirations. In his view, the road to liberation from white prejudice and domination was racial segregation and economic autonomy. Unlike Washington, however, he was no accommodationist. He believed that modern Africans and African-Americans are the descendents of the "chosen people" of biblical times, morally and spiritually superior to whites but oppressed and exiled for their sins (see RASTAFARIANISM). His "back-to-Africa" program envisioned African independence from colonialism and offered to African-Americans and West Indian blacks the prospect of repatriation in their ancestral homeland. He encouraged black entrepreneurship and commerce, and in the years following World War I, he founded several model corporations, including the Black Star Line, a steamship company intended to facilitate international trade between black-owned businesses.

Ultimately, all these endeavors failed; an attempt to settle African-Americans in Liberia miscarried, and the Black Star Line went bankrupt, in connection with which Garvey was jailed for fraud and later deported. Garvey was criticized, not only by whites but by some black intellectuals, for his simplistic view of the American RACE problem, his superficial knowledge of Africa and its varied peoples, and his anti-integrationist views (he even met with officials of the Ku Klux Klan, who also believed in racial purity and separation). At the same time, his advocacy of racial pride and self-confidence attracted an enormous following and became a keystone of the American black nationalist, BLACK POWER, and civil rights movements of the mid-20th century.

See also box at AFRICAN RELIGIONS (New World); BLACK NATIONALISM; DU BOIS.

Gestalt

Concept in science, AESTHETICS, and especially psychology, holding that the whole is greater than, and cannot be defined by, the sum of its parts; the word is German for "form" or "configuration." Gestalt psychology was founded in the early 20th century by the German psychologists Max Wertheimer, Wolfgang Köhler, and Kurt Koffka as a reaction against the prevailing theories of mental ATOMISM and associationism, which saw mental processes as a string of separate events that are connected, through association, into images and ideas. Gestalt theory maintains that PERCEPTION and other mental phenomena are based on the mind's assimilation and ordering of entire patterns and configurations, derived more from their context than from their component parts. The mind naturally seeks to make unified wholes, or "good Gestalts," to create sense and meaning out of experience; these wholes are more significant than, and often largely independent of, their constituent parts. Gestalt theory therefore regards learning, for instance, as the progressive creation and reshaping of COGNITIVE wholes, rather than the interaction of stimulus and response posited by BEHAVIORISM.

Gestalt therapy, developed by Fritz Perls in the 1930s and '40s, takes a similarly HOLISTIC approach to treatment, discounting the MIND/BODY distinction and seeking harmonious equilibrium within the whole person. In this view, anxiety, compulsions, and other neurotic behavior arise from incomplete integration of experience, particularly unmet needs. The technique is PHENOMENOLOGICAL, stressing awareness of current existence over the unearthing of early childhood events and encouraging the client to fully and spontaneously experience emotions, thoughts, and perceptions in order to integrate them into a coherent whole.

Ghost Dance See box at NORTH AMERICAN NATIVE BELIEFS

Gilligan, Carol See box at FEMINISM

Gilman, Charlotte Perkins (1860–1935)

American economist, sociologist, author, and lecturer, one of the leading FEMINIST intellectuals of her time. Largely self-educated, she developed an early interest in writing and painting, but as a young mother suffering from postpartum depression she was prescribed a "treatment" that required her to concentrate solely on domestic duties. That experience, which drove her to the brink of insanity, contributed to her later condemnations of women's supposed "place" in society and partly inspired her short story "The Yellow Wallpaper" (1892), about a housebound woman going mad. After divorcing her first husband in 1894, she began writing in earnest. Her prolific output of books, articles, and fiction continued throughout her life, much of it appearing in *The Forerunner,* a monthly magazine of social reform that she wrote, edited, and published from 1909 to 1916. She was drawn to the utopian SOCIALISM of Edward Bellamy and the British Fabian Society, as well as to "Reform DARWINISM," which held the LAMARCKIAN view that human EVOLUTION can (and should) be influenced by positive changes in social relationships. She saw reclaiming women's rights as a central precondition of a just society, but refused to call herself a "feminist," describing society as "masculinist" and herself as a HUMANIST whose goal was to close the gulf between the genders.

Gilman's influential first book, *Women and Economics* (1898), examined the economic factor in the evolution of male and female roles. While the division of social roles based on male aggressiveness and female nurturance may have been necessary for survival at one time, this was no longer the case, she argued; the institutionalization of women's economic dependence on men now prevented women (and men to some extent) from fulfilling their natural potential. Many of the distinctions between the sexes are artificial or overblown, she believed, and serve only to obscure our common humanity.

She insisted that women could never be equal or worthy partners to their husbands so long as they were confined to the home and domestic functions for which they were not necessarily suited. In *Concerning Children* (1900), Gilman advocated professional child care, and in *The Home: Its Work and Influence* (1903), she observed that as the rest of society has progressed, the home has remained a primitive institution in which a woman is imprisoned by an oppressive role that forecloses her other talents. In *Herland*, a UTOPIAN novel first serialized in *The Forerunner* in 1915, Gilman imagined a self-sufficient all-female civilization that implicitly rebukes the irrationality and brutality of patriarchal society.

global warming

Term used by scientists and environmentalists who see recent atmospheric temperature increases as the result of human industrial and agricultural activity and who believe that in the near future such increases could result in dangerous climatic changes. Since the end of the 19th century the average global atmospheric temperature has risen by about 1° Celsius, but until the 1960s this rise was considered a natural fluctuation unrelated to human activity. However, many scientists and environmentalists now maintain that the atmosphere is indeed warming more rapidly than in the past, and will continue to do so given present circumstances, primarily because of increased amounts of carbon dioxide and other gases in the atmosphere as a result of the burning of fossil fuels—oil, coal, peat, and natural gas—and the loss of green plants and trees through deforestation. As further evidence, they point to the strong correlation throughout the earth's history between carbon dioxide concentrations and atmospheric temperature and to computer models of atmospheric processes that analyze past changes and predict future warming.

Global warming results from an increase in the *greenhouse effect*. Like the glass in a greenhouse, the earth's atmosphere is transparent to sunlight but not to infrared rays. When the sun's rays strike the surface of the earth, much of the infrared light is absorbed by carbon dioxide, water vapor, and other gases, retaining that heat energy in the atmosphere and resulting in an increase in atmospheric temperature. The more of these "greenhouse gases" present in the atmosphere, the more heat is retained and the more the overall atmospheric temperature rises.

The predicted consequences of global warming, which some estimate will raise the temperature of the earth's atmosphere by up to 4° Celsius by the middle of the 21st century, include increased instability in the weather; extensive coastal flooding as polar ice caps partially melt and raise the ocean levels;

disruption to agriculture as temperatures controlling crop cycles are altered; and unforeseeable disturbances of biological processes and ecosystems. Environmentalists argue that in order to avert these calamities, worldwide action must be taken to decrease industrial and agricultural pollution, population growth, and dependence on fossil fuels.

See also GAIA HYPOTHESIS.

Gnosticism

Teachings of a group of dissident sects of the early CHRISTIAN era that believed salvation comes from acquiring the secret knowledge (Greek, *gnosis*) of the true nature of God, creation, and Christ; generally, any belief in the power of esoteric knowledge. Gnostic beliefs had their origins in a variety of pre-Christian traditions, including JUDAISM, Greek and Near Eastern philosophies (cf. ZOROASTRIANISM), and PAGAN mystery religions. A complex of cults and sects with varying beliefs and practices rather than a distinct religion, Gnosticism flourished in the second and third centuries C.E. It produced a rich mythology and a set of supplementary gospels said to have been composed by JESUS's followers. Among the most important Gnostic sects were those founded by Basilides, Valentinus, and Marcion.

Gnostic belief was markedly DUALISTIC, dividing the spiritual and the material into realms of good and evil, light and darkness. It conceived of a supreme god, an entity of pure spirit from whom descended a series of spiritual (but finite) beings called *aeons,* one of whom, a Great Mother often called Sophia (Wisdom), produced the Demiurge, the creator-god of the Old Testament. This lesser deity, either ignorant or defiant of the higher world of spirit (the Lightworld), created the material world, including humankind. The human SOUL is a spark of light from the spirit world imprisoned in flesh. Christ was an aeon who came to earth in apparent, but not actual, human form with a message that, truly understood, will redeem imprisoned souls and restore them to the Lightworld before the material world is destroyed.

Gnosticism was condemned as a heresy by the early church fathers, including Irenaeus and Tertullian, whose writings were the principal source of knowledge about the movement until the discovery of a treasury of Gnostic documents at Nag Hammadi, Egypt, in 1945. This hostility was a response not only to the Gnostic challenge to the church's scriptural authority but also, apparently, to the threat to its patriarchal order posed by the equality of women in Gnostic societies and texts; Mary Magdalene, for example, plays a leading role in the Gnostic gospels.

God, arguments for the existence of

In NATURAL THEOLOGY, primarily CHRISTIAN, a variety of arguments have developed that purport to prove the existence of God using pure REASON and the evidence of the natural world, without recourse to scriptural authority or divine revelation. The most common arguments fall into three categories—*ontological, cosmological,* and *teleological*—all in one way or another postulating God as "the necessary being." These arguments posit, respectively, that God exists because we can conceive of him; that everything that is caused must have an ultimate First Cause; and that the design apparent in creation implies a designer. They were first developed, not by people who felt any need to defend God's existence against doubt, but by theologians who sought a clearer knowledge of the divine nature; today such arguments are more often addressed to skeptics.

The *ontological* argument was first formulated by the 11th-century SCHOLASTIC St. Anselm in his concept of "a being than which none greater can be conceived." God, the perfect being, must exist, Anselm argued, because we can conceive of such a perfect being; we could not conceive of a perfect being that does not exist because perfection is inconsistent with nonexistence. Likewise, since reality is greater than our imaginations, God must exist outside our imaginations because there is nothing conceivably greater than God. DESCARTES echoed Anselm's arguments and added an elaboration of his own: our idea of God is the idea of a perfect being, and only a perfect being could be the author of that idea; our idea that God exists cannot be false because God, in allowing us to have that idea, would not be deceitful, since that would not be in the character of a perfect being.

The *cosmological* argument, derived from ARISTOTLE's theory of CAUSE, was given its most complete theological form by Thomas AQUINAS, whose famous "five ways" of understanding God were based on motion, final cause, efficient cause, the movement from possibility to actuality, and the movement from imperfection to perfection. All start from the observation that whatever happens has a cause, which in turn has a cause, apparently ad infinitum. But to assume an infinite causal regression is to assume a universe with no beginning—an impossibility; and since no ordinary being can will itself into existence, there must be a supreme being that is self-created, immutable, and eternal, the Prime Mover who is the cause of all other things.

The *teleological* argument, also known as the argument from *design,* looks at the universe and concludes that it could not work the way it does by accident but must be the manifestation of *divine purpose.* The best-known statement of the argument was given in 1802 by the English theologian William Paley, who compared God to a master watchmaker. If examining the intricate design and construction of a fine watch makes us appreciate the work of a skilled craftsman, so much the more should we recognize an intelligent design in something like the human eye, and even more so in the universe as a whole.

Two further approaches find the proof of God's existence in universal human traits. The argument from *common consent* maintains that the worldwide belief in God, found in all ages and cultures, demonstrates its validity. The *moral* postulation of God, originated by KANT, holds that our sense of what is right and wrong is innate, not learned, and that therefore a suprahuman source of that conviction must exist.

See also ANTHROPIC PRINCIPLE; DESCARTES; RATIONALISM.

God, concepts of

The idea of a divine, supernatural being or power, greater than humanity and inspiring awe and veneration, has been the most enduring—and the most varied—feature of the human religious impulse. Although diverse, the ways of conceiving of God fall into three basic categories, distinguishing between a single God (monotheism) and a pantheon (polytheism), between a personal and an impersonal God, and between God as immanent and transcendent. In most religious traditions, however, these distinctions are far from absolute.

Monotheisms, such as JUDAISM, CHRISTIANITY, and ISLAM, place divinity in a single, supreme, SOVEREIGN deity, while polytheisms contemplate a divine hierarchy, such as the gods and goddesses of Greco-Roman mythology, with varying ranks, abilities, and dominions, possessing human attributes and divine powers, and often personifying natural forces. Monotheistic and polytheistic elements mingle in many religions, including Christianity, in which most denominations conceive of God as a TRINITY and envision a hierarchy of angels, and HINDUISM, in which a complicated polytheism is overarched by the pure, unconditioned ABSOLUTE, or *brahman*. Henotheism—the exclusive worship of one god without denying the existence of others as valid for other peoples—is thought by some scholars to have characterized the Judaism of the biblical era.

The distinction between the personal and the impersonal God is even more complex and equivocal. This tension is due to the impossibility of both extremes: a wholly personal God, accessible in purely human terms, would be insufficiently divine, and an entirely impersonal deity would be difficult to comprehend. Hence, most religions conceive of God as both personal and impersonal. Christians, for instance, believe in the incarnated Son of the all-powerful Father; Hindus envisage the life, death, and rebirth of the gods in a vast cycle within the unchanging perfection of *brahman*.

The ideas of immanence and TRANSCENDENCE—God as active in nature or outside it, implicated in the world and its development or a mystery beyond human comprehension—are similar to the personal/impersonal contrast. Here, too, neither extreme is wholly embraced in practice, since we could have no understanding of a God who is either utterly separate from us and the world or so close and penetrating as to dissolve into experience. More often than not, these apparently contradictory terms coexist within one conception of God, both involved with us and above us.

See also ABSOLUTE; AFRICAN RELIGIONS; boxes at AFRICAN RELIGIONS; ANIMISM; AQUINAS; BAHA'I; BERKELEY; CHRISTIAN SCIENCE; CHRISTIANITY; CREATIONISM; DEISM; DESCARTES; ESCHATOLOGY; ESSENCE; FUNDAMENTALISM; GNOSTICISM; GOD, ARGUMENTS FOR; GODDESS WORSHIP; HASIDISM; HEGEL; HIERARCHY OF BEING; HINDUISM; IBN SINA; ISLAM; JEHOVAH'S WITNESSES; JESUS; JUDAISM; KABBALAH; LEIBNIZ; LOGOS; LUTHER; MAIMONIDES; MORMONISM; MYSTICISM; NATURAL THEOLOGY; NEOPLATONISM; NORTH AMERICAN NATIVE BELIEFS; ORTHODOX CHURCH; PAGANISM; box at PASCAL; PREDESTINATION; PROCESS PHILOSOPHY/THEOLOGY; PROTESTANTISM; ROMAN CATHOLICISM; SHINTO; SIKHISM; SPINOZA; SUFISM; THEOSOPHY; TRANSCENDENTALISM; TRINITY; ZOROASTRIANISM.

goddess worship

Worship of a female deity or sacred image, often associated with human and agricultural fertility and the natural cycles of life; an ancient spiritual tradition dating from prehistoric times and still practiced in various forms around the world. Since the Stone Age, goddess images have symbolized fecundity, nurturance, bounty, community, and the earth itself. In PANTHEISTIC agricultural societies, female deities have typically controlled the cycles of planting, growth, and harvest, birth, procreation, and death (see, e.g., AFRICAN RELIGIONS; NORTH AMERICAN NATIVE BELIEFS).

Vestiges of the prehistoric nature goddesses persisted in the Greco-Roman pantheon, where female deities governed not only the realms of generation and domesticity (e.g., GAIA/Terra, the earth, and Hestia/Vesta, goddess of the hearth) but also embodied conventionally "male" qualities (e.g., Athena/Minerva, warrior goddess of wisdom, and Artemis/Diana, patron of the hunt as well as moon goddess). The Roman Magna Mater (Great Mother) was descended from the Phrygian fertility goddess Cybele, called "mother of the gods," who in turn was a variant of the Semitic deity known variously as Astarte, Ishtar, and Ashtoreth. The ROMAN CATHOLIC cult of the Virgin Mary is thought to have derived from this tradition. Among contemporary world religions, goddess worship is by far the strongest in HINDUISM, where the goddess (devi) is venerated in several manifestations, including Parvati, Durga, and Kali, and combines gently caring and fiercely warlike aspects in her role of maternal protectress.

In modern times, goddess worship has become a topic of controversy in anthropological and religious scholarship. The idea that the earliest human societies were matriarchal, as evidenced by ancient goddess worship, was first influentially proposed by the Swiss legal historian Johann Bachofen in the mid-19th century. It was revived by Erich Neumann in his psychological study *The Great Mother* (1955), in which he drew on Stone Age artifacts and JUNG's theory of the collective unconscious to postulate an archetypal Earth Mother revered by a primeval woman-centered culture. FEMINIST scholars such as Merlin Stone, radical theologians such as Mary Daly, and neo-PAGAN theorists such as Starhawk have argued that as patriarchal society dispossessed women of their primordial power, the Great Mother was deposed by a male god, and her earth-centered, instinctive, HOLISTIC nature was suppressed by the distant, RATIONAL heavenly Father of JUDAISM, CHRISTIANITY, and ISLAM. The theory of an ancient, monotheistic matriarchy is now discredited by a majority of scholars, including feminists. However, the modern revival of the goddess has proved a touchstone for some women, especially in Judeo-Christian societies, who seek either to reform the established religions—by, for example, referring to God as both male and female—or to abandon them and create or re-create "gynocentric" forms of worship (see PAGANISM; WITCHCRAFT).

See also ANIMISM; SHINTO; TANTRISM.

Golden Rule

Ethical principle that prescribes behavior reflexively, in effect asking the rhetorical question, "How would you like it if that happened to you?" The rule demands that we consider others' interests, rights, and feelings as if they were our own. The best-known expression of it in the Western tradition is JESUS's admonitions (in Matthew 7:12 and Luke 6:31), commonly paraphrased as "Do unto others as you would have them do unto you." But the precept, stated in different ways, transcends traditions and cultures. Indeed, it has been called the universal moral injunction and the basis of all ETHICS.

The earliest articulation of the Golden Rule may be Confucius's negative statement of it: "What you do not want done to yourself, do not do to others." In CONFUCIAN philosophy, correct behavior toward others requires, for example, giving your parents the respect you expect from your own children and your friends the treatment you desire from them. Several ancient Greek philosophers, including both PLATO and ARISTOTLE, enunciated versions of the rule. In the first century B.C.E., Rabbi Hillel summed up TORAH in similar terms: "What is hateful to you, do not do to your neighbor; all the rest is commentary." The basis of KANT's ethical theory, the *categorical imperative,* is a restatement and extension of the Golden Rule: "Act as if the principle of your action were to become by your will a universal law of nature."

See also ANIMAL RIGHTS.

grammar, theories of

Grammar is the branch of linguistics that deals with the forms of words and the way they are used to create phrases and sentences. It is traditionally seen as the study of a language's structure, either *prescriptive (normative),* decreeing what constitutes correct and incorrect usage, or *descriptive,* describing language as it is actually used by native speakers. A grammar is usually a description of a natural human language, but grammars can also describe artificial symbolic languages, such as those constructed in some branches of LOGIC and computer science. In modern linguistics, the term is also used more broadly, primarily because of the work of Noam CHOMSKY, to denote the idea of a *universal grammar* reflecting inherent principles common to all languages.

During the first half of the 20th century the prevailing theory of language usage was linguistic STRUCTURALISM, pioneered by the Swiss linguist Ferdinand de Saussure. He distinguished between language as it is spoken (or written or signed), which he called *parole* (word, speech), and *langue* (language), the abstract, underlying structure of the speaker's native tongue, which she or he draws on, often subconsciously, to create speech. American structuralism, pioneered by Leonard Bloomfield in the 1920s, added a BEHAVIORISTIC approach, seeing language development and usage as a social construct, not a mental process.

Where Saussurean linguistics saw each human language as a distinct system, Chomsky's "transformational-generative" theory of grammar, introduced in the late 1950s, focused on the structural similarities of all languages. Chomsky argued that these similarities, and the ease and accuracy of LANGUAGE ACQUISITION by young children, meant that language derives from an innate, universal COGNITIVE faculty. To account for the novelty and creativity of natural language, he said, a descriptive grammar must be *generative,* that is, its finite rules must allow for the infinite number of new expressions a living language can generate. His theory of *transformational* grammar posited a "deep structure" and "surface structure" of language, in which the speaker draws on a deep, "hidden" set of grammatical rules that can be transformed in a multitude of ways into the actual forms of speech. Chomsky held that while the actual *performance* of a language may be limited, finite, and imperfect, every native speaker possesses perfect linguistic *competence*—a complete, though implicit, knowledge of his or her language; these terms roughly correspond to Saussure's *parole* and *langue.* Most theories of grammar have traditionally been theories of performance, based on how words and sentences are produced and understood; the predominant influence of Saussure's and Chomsky's theories has been to look beneath the surface of spoken language for its fundamental structure.

See also CHOMSKY; DESCRIPTIVISM AND PRESCRIPTIVISM; LANGUAGE ACQUISITION.

Gramsci, Antonio (1891–1937)

Italian political philosopher, one of the most original and influential of Western Marxist intellectuals, whose ideas have affected not only political thought but the fields of cultural studies, literary theory, and international relations. Born into rural poverty, which he escaped through a university education, Gramsci brought to his work a practical awareness of actual working-class conditions. Diverging from the historical DETERMINISM of orthodox MARXISM, he stressed *praxis*—the necessary connection of theory to practice—and a belief in the agency, ingenuity, and spontaneity of the proletariat in creating their own history. Gramsci participated in militant workers' factory councils in Turin, helped organize the insurrectionary general strike of 1920, and led the COMMUNIST faction in the Italian parliament until his arrest and imprisonment by Mussolini in 1926. He spent the rest of his life in jail, where he wrote the *Prison Notebooks,* on which his reputation rests.

Central to these writings is Gramsci's theory of *hegemony,* the idea that in modern industrial society control is exercised not by brute force but by subtle manipulation in which the dominant class gains consent to its IDEOLOGY through the norms and institutions of bourgeois society (cf. BAUDRILLARD; CRITICAL THEORY; FOUCAULT). Gramsci disputed all POSITIVISTIC and MECHANISTIC interpretations of Marxism that neglected the role of CONSCIOUSNESS and culture in determining social action. He rejected the traditional Marxist focus on society's economic "base" as determining all social action and argued that the superstructure of civil society—the ensemble of economic, cultural, and social institutions built upon that base—is the arena where social relations are formed and enacted. It was that arena, he said, in which the protracted "war of position" against bourgeois hegemony would be waged—a war led by the revolutionary SOCIALIST party and conducted on all levels of social and political power: "force and consent, authority and hegemony, violence and civilization, agitation and propaganda." Revolutionary praxis would involve the utter transformation of work, politics, and everyday life, including the evolution of counterhegemonic institutions (such as independent workers' councils) that would challenge the dominant system in all its manifestations.

"great man" theory of history

The view that the course of history has been shaped or determined by exceptional individuals. The theory was first articulated in the early 19th century by historians and philosophers seeking to understand the French Revolution and the career of Napoleon Bonaparte. It was given its fullest expression by the Scottish social critic and historian Thomas Carlyle in his essay *On Heroes, Hero-Worship, and the Heroic in History* (1841). Carlyle held that "the history of the world is but the biography of great men." Civilization was created, he said, and historical change continues to be directed, by intelligent, intuitive individuals.

HEGEL subscribed partially to a "great man" theory, but put the changes wrought by "world-historical" figures such as Alexander the Great and Napoleon in the context of the complex DIALECTICAL process of history, in which even powerful individuals play a subsidiary and often unconscious role. Leopold von Ranke (1795–1886), the founder of modern historiography, with its reliance on primary sources over received tradition, nonetheless emphasized the deeds of monarchs and statesmen as the driving force of historical narrative. This approach was typical of history writing well into the 20th century. It has now been largely supplanted by social history, which stresses influential currents of thought and the lives of ordinary people. The "great man" view has also been assailed by FEMINIST critics as symptomatic of a "world made for men by men" perspective that systematically obscures women's contributions to civilization.

Greer, Germaine See box at FEMINISM

H

Habermas, Jürgen See box at CRITICAL THEORY

Hasidism

Movement in Orthodox JUDAISM that emphasizes joyful worship, MYSTICAL experience, and close community under the absolute authority of a charismatic leader. The name comes from the *hasidim* (pious or righteous ones), those spoken of in the Bible and rabbinical literature as particularly holy and close to God. The Hasidic movement was founded in the 18th century in Eastern Europe by Israel ben Eliezer, known by the honorific Baal Shem Tov (Master of the Good Name) or the acronym Besht. He stressed communion with God not through ritual observance and scriptural study but through spontaneous prayer, ecstatic singing and dancing, and other means accessible to the uneducated masses. The Besht taught through parables, encouraged an attitude of joyous celebration in the presence of God's creation, and developed a popularized version of KABBALAH, the medieval mystical tradition, that likewise emphasized direct experience over special knowledge. The movement expanded rapidly, spawning numerous sects named after the European towns of their origin. The leadership of each Hasidic sect is vested exclusively in the *zaddik,* or "rebbe," whose authority rests on spiritual inspiration, including alleged miraculous powers, and over time has become dynastic, handed down from father to son.

During the 19th century, what had begun as a radical revolt against conventional rabbinical authority became the most CONSERVATIVE branch of Judaism, largely in reaction to liturgical and social reforms inspired by the *Haskalah,* or "Jewish ENLIGHTENMENT" (see MENDELSSOHN). This ultraorthodoxy is manifested in the retention of traditional dress and customs by contemporary Hasidim. Hasidic Jewry was nearly extinguished by the Nazi Holocaust, and today exists as a cluster of small, insular sects, mainly in Israel and in Brooklyn, New York. The American Lubavitcher rebbe Menachem Schneerson sought to increase understanding between Hasidim and non-Orthodox Jews, and since his death in 1994 he has been hailed by some of his followers as the Messiah, whose imminent return they expect. Hasidic philosophy has been most effectively expounded in the mainstream of 20th-century thought by a non-Hasid, the Austrian theologian Martin Buber, who embraced the Hasidic ideal of constructive community and personal approach to the divine in his teaching that healthy social and spiritual relations are achieved through open, constructive dialogue between "I" and "Thou," whether one is communicating with another human being or with the deity.

Hegel, Georg Wilhelm Friedrich (1770–1831)

German philosopher, one of the most influential of the 19th century, whose thinking shaped MARXISM and EXISTENTIALISM. Hegel was the first to view history—indeed, all of existence—as a DIALECTICAL process of thesis, antithesis, and synthesis, through which two contradictory forces are resolved in a higher, more RATIONAL state. In *The Phenomenology of Spirit* and other works, he saw history as the progressive development of human understanding toward perfect knowledge. Civilization advances in stages, or "historical moments," each of which is a necessary but incomplete step in the development of human CONSCIOUSNESS, REASON, and FREEDOM. Since each stage is imperfect, its flaws give rise to opposing ideas or forces, and out of the resulting conflict comes a new, higher, and temporarily more stable stage. Hegel called this synthesis "sublation" *(Aufhebung)*, a term that implies both negation and preservation—the emergence of a condition that subsumes and supersedes the original.

This analysis was revolutionary because it placed *change* at the heart of the world, challenging the generally accepted notion of "eternal verities." However, for Hegel history was not an endless cycle of change but an upward spiral that would lead inevitably to a final condition of Absolute Knowledge. Indeed, his philosophy of "absolute (or dialectical) IDEALISM" saw human history as a rational progression in which all the subjective elements of understanding are purged, leaving only a pure, objective knowledge of the ABSOLUTE—God as pure thought, mind, or spirit.

In response to KANT's "categories of the understanding," which he saw as ultimately limited, Hegel constructed an elaborate series of "categories of thought" tracing the progression of human understanding. The Absolute, he said, is approached by art AESTHETICALLY, in the beauty of material forms; it is conceived SYMBOLICALLY in religion, whose highest manifestation is CHRISTIANITY, with its central symbol of the spirit-made-flesh; but philosophy is humanity's highest attainment because it comprehends the Absolute through REASON. Hegel perceived an intricate relationship between the family, civil society, and the STATE, and conceived the state, too, as a manifestation of the Absolute, to which the individual is, paradoxically, obligated to freely submit.

Among the most influential of Hegel's dialectical analyses was his identification of *nothingness* as not merely absence but the necessary corollary of BEING, the two connected in the dynamic process of *becoming*. This positive, formative value of negation was seized on later by the existentialists, who saw humans as having to create MEANING for themselves when faced with the essential nothingness of the universe.

Hegel saw self-knowledge as a product of *desire*. More than the desire for things, people desire the recognition of other human beings, a desire that leads to conflict. In this conflict there are winners and losers, resulting in unequal relationships that Hegel analyzed in terms of master and slave (cf. NIETZSCHE). Both are oppressed by this relationship, the slave subjugated and ALIENATED, the master enslaved by his dependence on the bondsman; but the slave finds a certain freedom in creative labor while the master is imprisoned in unproductive idleness. The slave's aspirations for liberty and self-fulfillment, arising from a consciousness of his condition, provide the subversive antithesis to the thesis of enslavement. This analysis influenced modern conceptions of freedom as related to circumstance, and the idea of "the Other" as a defining element in world-views (see, e.g., BEAUVOIR; IDENTITY).

After Hegel's death, his followers divided into conservative (Old, or Right) and radical (Young, or Left) camps. The Young Hegelians included Ludwig Feuerbach, Max Stirner, and later MARX and Engels. Their faith in human agency and concern with social alienation, as well as their radical, even revolutionary, political leanings, contrasted sharply with the Old Hegelians' social and religious conservatism and emphasis on the unchanging Absolute.

See also ALIENATION; BEING AND BECOMING; DIALECTIC; "GREAT MAN" THEORY; PANTHEISM AND PANENTHEISM; STATE.

Heidegger, Martin (1889–1976)

German philosopher, an important influence on 20th-century EXISTENTIALISM. His thought was shaped by KIERKEGAARD's view that in an ABSURD world a wholehearted commitment to life is what gives it meaning, and by his teacher

Edmund Husserl, whose theory of PHENOMENOLOGY stressed the interaction of human CONSCIOUSNESS with things and events in the "lived" world. Heidegger himself called his philosophy "existential phenomenology," emphasizing human activity in the world over the workings of consciousness. His reputation was damaged by his early support of Nazism, which he later repudiated, and after World War II he lived in self-imposed exile in the Black Forest.

Beginning with his most important work, *Being and Time* (1927), Heidegger's lifelong, unfinished quest was for a "fundamental ontology," an attempt to capture the essential nature of BEING, in and of itself, without reference to some greater being, such as God. Heidegger called human existence *Dasein,* or "being-there," implying not only presence but involvement in the world. The basic aspect of *Dasein,* Heidegger said, is *care,* the fact that we, unlike animals and inanimate objects, are aware of and concerned about our place in the world and our own mortality. This awareness leads to *anxiety,* the dread of nothingness in the groundless world we have been "thrown" into, but it also reveals the range of possibilities available to us. We tend to cope with our groundless situation through *understanding*— the ability to creatively use things and to function productively in society— and *falling,* seeking to stave off anxiety by absorbing ourselves in shallow, mundane concerns. However, confronting the world's arbitrariness permits us to face life "authentically," to make a conscious, clearheaded commitment to living fully.

Much of Heidegger's later work was critical of what he felt were his earlier philosophical mistakes. He attacked his previous position as being too close to a "philosophical anthropology" that described human nature instead of approaching the nature of being. He became interested in poetry as a means of expression that could transcend some of the limitations of philosophical discourse. He concluded that modern industrial society had produced a NIHILISM in which being had ceased to have any meaning. We remain, as he put it, in the "oblivion of being."

See also ARENDT; EXISTENTIALISM; HERMENEUTICS; OBJECTIVISM AND SUBJECTIVISM; SOLIPSISM.

Heisenberg, Werner See
UNCERTAINTY PRINCIPLE

"Man is not the lord of beings. Man is the shepherd of Being."
—Martin Heidegger,
"Letter on Humanism"

hermeneutics

The study and principles of interpretation, aimed particularly at the discovery of hidden MEANINGS in written texts and, by extension, in social action and existence as a whole. At its heart, hermeneutics assumes that a text (or issue, problem, phenomenon, etc.) must be understood within its proper context; in this way, its actual meaning and the intention of its author (or participants, proponents) can be truly understood (cf. DECONSTRUCTION). The term, from the Greek for "interpretation," derives from the so-called Hermetic texts, a set of Greek writings from the second and third centuries C.E. ascribed by legend to one Hermes Trismegistus (Thrice-Great Hermes), which were said to have been written in biblical times and to have prophesied the coming of Christ. The study of these documents sought to uncover their cryptic secrets, and the term "hermeneutics" came to be applied to the study of scripture intended to reveal, through close textual analysis, its obscure meanings, that is, God's true intent.

In the early 19th century, Friedrich Schleiermacher sought to develop a universal hermeneutic method applied to textual analysis in general. Part of his purpose was to temper the emphasis on abstract knowledge derived through pure REASON, which had characterized the ENLIGHTENMENT, with an understanding of a work's specific context. Later in the century, synthesizers such as Wilhelm Dilthey began to apply hermeneutic principles to the study of society and history. Social science, Dilthey argued, cannot use the same methods as natural science (cf. POSITIVISM) but must employ understanding *(Verstehen)* and interpretation rather than pure EMPIRICISM. In the 20th century the concept was extended still further, most significantly by Martin HEIDEGGER and his student Hans-Georg Gadamer, who saw the hermeneutic endeavor as a fundamental characteristic of humanity: that we live and work not with abstract facts or "reason," but within distinct contexts, and that language itself is the medium through which we communicate (and understand) our essential being.

hierarchy of being (great chain of being)

The concept that all creation, from the lowest inanimate matter through plants and animals to humans, angels, and finally to God, forms a continuous, progressive chain. The history of this idea, whose appeal has been widespread up to the present day, was traced by Arthur O. Lovejoy in his classic 1936 study, *The Great Chain of Being*.

The notion is rooted in ARISTOTLE's system of classifying creatures according to their common attributes and distinctive qualities. These qualities are cumulative: rocks and dirt are composed of matter; so are plants, but they also have the ability to grow and reproduce; lower animals have all the qualities of plants as well as the capacity for locomotion; and so on, up to humans, who add to all of these the faculty of REASON. The progression is from matter to spirit, from potentiality to actuality, with God at the top as pure spirit and perfect actuality.

Implicit in this system is the *principle of plenitude,* the idea that everything that can be, is. Based on the theory of ideal forms in PLATO (q.v.), and most strongly stated by Plotinus, the principle posits a transcendent creative force (God, LOGOS, the One) capable of conceiving all possible things and therefore, by its nature, creating all it can conceive, arranged in orderly perfection.

The concept of a systematic, unbroken chain of BEING has been only partially disturbed by the more dynamic and disorderly theory of EVOLUTION. The biological taxonomy created by Linnaeus in the 18th century, a more detailed and observant version of the hierarchy of being, still holds sway, despite the recent emergence of the more evolutionistic discipline of cladistics.

Hinduism

Western term for the ancient religious tradition of India. More than 4,000 years old, it has more than 500 million followers; in India, about three quarters of the population are Hindus (the word originally meant "inhabitant of India"). Unlike most other world religions, Hinduism has no identifiable beginning or founder-prophet, no fixed doctrine, no single authoritative scripture, and no specific institutional organization. Hindu practices and beliefs therefore vary widely; for example, Hinduism is polytheistic, but Hindus may worship one, many, or no gods.

For Hindus, the foundation of existence, underlying all of reality and overarching all the gods, is *brahman,* the ABSOLUTE, the source and ESSENCE of all life. The ultimate goal of Hindu devotions is *moksha,* the union of one's soul *(atman)* with brahman. *Moksha* means "release" or "liberation" from *samsara* (wandering), the cycle of birth, death, and rebirth in which the soul works out its KARMA, the cumulative effect of good and evil actions in past lives. Some animals, such as cows and snakes, are regarded as also possessing *atman* and are therefore sacred and not to be harmed; the cycle of samsara can include incarnation as plants and animals as well as humans. Karma is overcome through DHARMA, the universal law and the moral path to be followed in each stage of life. In the Hindu CASTE system of social stratification, the dharma of each caste is considered to be different, prescribing distinct societal and religious roles and the proper conduct to be observed within them.

Hindu devotions are generally performed individually—though sometimes under the guidance of a *guru* (teacher)—usually taking the form of private meditation or worship before the image of a particular god. At the head of the pantheon of Hindu gods stands the Trimurti (TRINITY). Brahma, the creator-god, personification of brahman, embodies the balance between the other two: Vishnu, the preserver, and Shiva, the destroyer (who also, paradoxically, represents fertility). Vishnu is said to have taken bodily form in nine separate *avatars* ("descents," i.e., incarnations), of whom the most important are Rama and Krishna, heroic figures who, with their lovers Sita and Radha, have themselves become the objects of cult worship; worship of Vishnu and his avatars is called Vaishnavism. The female power, *shakti*, is often seen as an aspect of Shiva and manifested as the GODDESS *(devi)*; she has many aspects, some maternal, others bloodthirsty.

The most ancient Hindu scripture is the Veda ("sacred knowledge"), consisting of four collections of sacred hymns and prayers (commonly called the Vedas) and several supplementary writings, including the Upanishads, a series of MYSTICAL, METAPHYSICAL treatises that consider the nature of brahman and samsara. The respective exploits of Rama and Krishna are recounted in the epics *Ramayana* and *Mahabharata*. The most celebrated episode in the latter, the Bhagavad-Gita (Song of the Lord), is considered the greatest single statement of Hindu belief. It is a moral lesson in which a disguised Krishna declares that there are many valid paths to salvation but not all are appropriate for each person.

In the 19th and early 20th centuries, Hinduism underwent considerable modernization under the influence of reformers who sought to alter or abolish ancient practices such as religious idolatry, the caste system, and suttee (widows' suicide). Among these reformers was Ramakrishna, who proclaimed the primacy of mystical experience and the oneness of all religions. Mohandas GANDHI's struggle for Indian independence was guided by the principle of *ahimsa*—NONVIOLENCE and respect for all life—and by a vision of social equity that condemned the injustices of the caste system.

See also ABSOLUTE; ASTROLOGY; ATOMISM; CASTE; DHARMA; ELEMENTS; ENLIGHTENMENT; ETERNAL RECURRENCE; GANDHI; GOD, CONCEPTS OF; GODDESS WORSHIP; KARMA; MATERIALISM; NIRVANA; PANTHEISM AND PANENTHEISM; TANTRISM; YOGA.

HINDU SCHOOLS OF THOUGHT

Six orthodox schools of classical HINDU philosophy—called *darshanas*, or "ways of seeing"—arose between the second century B.C.E. and the fourth century C.E. They were not organized sects, but systems of thought that presented varying but often complementary approaches to devotional practice, scriptural interpretation, and cosmology.

Vaiseshika teaches that salvation depends on an understanding of the laws of nature; its legendary founder, Kanada, presented an ATOMISTIC theory of matter. *Nyaya,* originally a school of rhetoric, approaches knowledge through logical reasoning. These two schools eventually merged. *Samkhya* is a DUALISTIC philosophy, contrasting mind (or soul) with matter and holding that *moksha,* the union of the soul with the ABSOLUTE, can be achieved only when the CONSCIOUSNESS is disentangled from mundane concerns. Samkhya forms the metaphysical basis of the *Yoga darshana,* which teaches spiritual liberation through the practice of YOGA.

The *Mimamsa* and *Vedanta* schools are concerned with interpretations of the sacred Vedic literature. Mimamsa (more properly Purva Mimamsa, "early investigation") is a HERMENEUTIC discipline, concerned with correct interpretation of the injunctions contained in the older portions of the Veda and emphasizing right action (DHARMA). The Uttara Mimamsa ("later investigation") is more commonly called Vedanta, which means "end of the Veda," referring to the Upanishads. These mystical writings provide the basis for the emphasis in Vedanta on spiritual knowledge—particularly comprehension of the Absolute—as opposed to earthly deeds. In the last millennium, Vedanta has become the most influential *darshana,* seen as the culmination and consolidation of the other five. Its most important interpreter, the ninth-century philosopher Shankara, established the influential Advaita ("nondual") school of Vedanta, teaching that the individual soul *(atman)* and the Absolute *(brahman)* are identical. This MONISTIC doctrine was modified in the 12th century by Ramanuja, who claimed that *atman* and *brahman* may be united but are not identical; Ramanuja is considered the progenitor of the *bhakti* (devotional) strand of Hinduism, the one most practiced today.

MODERN HINDU
MOVEMENTS IN THE WEST

In the mid-20th century, an intense interest in Eastern spirituality arose in Europe and the United States, largely in reaction to what was seen as a materialistic, spiritually sterile Western culture. This interest, which peaked in the 1960s and '70s, focused on BUDDHISM, especially Zen (see box at BUDDHISM), and HINDUISM, including the practice of YOGA. A number of movements arose that introduced Hindu spiritual practices to Westerners, mostly young and middle-class, with or without the trappings of Hindu religious belief and devotions. They were often personality cults led by charismatic gurus, many of whom were revered as avatars, or incarnations of God. These teachers generally found far greater followings in the West than in their native India, and many of the movements fractured or faded in the wake of their founders' deaths (or, in some cases, their scandalously worldly behavior).

- *Meher Baba* (1894–1969), whose name means "Loving Father," was the first important modern guru to gain numerous disciples in the West. Born in India to ZOROASTRIAN parents and taught by a SUFI master, he developed a teaching that synthesized several religious traditions, including the Hindu and Buddhist concepts of KARMA and cyclical reincarnation *(samsara)*. He maintained a vow of silence for more than half his life and taught, through gestures and signs, that pure love is the way to ENLIGHTENMENT.

- *The International Society of Krishna Consciousness* (ISKCON) was established in the West in the mid-1960s by A. C. Bhaktivedanta Swami Prabhupada (1896–1977). His yellow-robed disciples seek enlightenment through the study of the Vedic scriptures, especially the Bhagavad-Gita, and the chanting of a mantra in praise of Krishna and Rama (because of which the movement is popularly known as Hare Krishna). They practice an austere ASCETICISM, including celibacy except for procreation within marriage.

- *Transcendental Meditation* teaches a simple meditation method, based on a personal mantra (an incantatory word or phrase) to achieve stress reduction, personal integration, and eventual enlightenment. It was brought to the West by Maharishi Mahesh Yogi (1911–) in the late 1950s and achieved worldwide popularity when the Beatles embraced it. The movement, which has established numerous educational centers, claims scientifically verifiable results that do not depend on religious faith.

- *The Divine Light Mission,* founded in India in 1960 and in the West in 1971, proclaimed a boy-guru, Maharaj Ji (1958–), as the latest avatar of God. Initiates, called "premies," are said to "receive knowledge" directly from the guru. Four special meditation techniques enable the devotees to turn inward to experience Divine Light, Divine Harmony, Divine Nectar, and ultimately the Divine Word. The movement thrived briefly, but splintered in 1974 in response to Guru Maharaj Ji's marriage and sybaritic lifestyle.
- *Bhagwan Shri Rajneesh* (1931–1990) taught a doctrine of free love, uninhibited sexuality, and impulsive action, together with a form of "dynamic meditation" aimed at releasing the earth's energy. He established lavish ashrams in India in 1974 and then, after fleeing India in 1981 to avoid legal troubles, in the United States. His followers, distinguished by their orange garments, scattered and their numbers dwindled when Rajneesh was deported from the United States in 1985 for immigration code violations.

Hippocrates (c.460–c.370 B.C.E.)

Greek physician, considered the father of medicine because he was the first of the classical healers to attribute disease to natural rather than supernatural causes. Little is known about his life, and much of what is ascribed to him in the series of treatises known as the Hippocratic Collection was most likely the product of his school of followers. These teachings formed the foundation of medical practice for 2,000 years. The Hippocratic Oath, affirming a code of medical ethics, is still taken by physicians, although it has been modified over the centuries; the original oath, for instance, forbade the practice of surgery.

The Hippocratic theory of disease was based on the concept of four essential bodily fluids—bile, phlegm, blood, and "black bile." In their correct proportions, they governed the healthy human being; illness was the result of their imbalance in the body. These four *humors* were also thought to rule human emotions and character—choleric, phlegmatic, sanguine, and melancholic, respectively—and were further associated with other natural quartets:

the four ELEMENTS, senses, seasons, ages of man, and major bodily organs (spleen, liver, heart, and brain). The ultimate value of this theory was that it oriented medicine toward a biological approach and away from superstition, although Hippocrates still attributed the spread of contagious diseases to AS-TROLOGICAL and other supernatural causes.

The Hippocratic method for the treatment of disease consisted primarily of bed rest, with occasional herbal remedies to counteract the imbalance of humors, a practice that remained a mainstay of medical practice until the 18th century (as did bloodletting and purging, which were also thought to re-store the humors to equilibrium). The Hippocratic Collection also contains guidance on public health, citing clean air and drinking water as promoting the general well-being of a populace, and on preventive medicine, emphasiz-ing moderation in both diet and lifestyle (see MEAN).

Much of the Hippocratic creed was taken up and passed on by the second-century C.E. Roman physician Galen, whose voluminous writings cata-logued and expanded the medical knowledge of antiquity. Galen is believed to have been the first to refer to a "germ" (or "seed") as a cause of illness. He expanded on Hippocratic physiology through extensive dissection and vivisec-tion. Galen's anatomical theories and descriptions were accepted orthodoxy until the Renaissance; in the 16th century Andreas Vesalius revolutionized the study of anatomy, and in the next century William Harvey accurately de-scribed the circulation of the blood. The theory of humors likewise went undisputed until the 16th century, when Paracelsus theorized that disease originates outside the body, not within it, and can be treated with chemical remedies.

historicism (historism)

A controversial term with various, sometimes ambiguous, often conflicting meanings. It generally refers to approaching something from a historical per-spective, particularly from the position that a past event, social condition, or cultural creation must be understood in terms of its historical circumstances. The term is used pejoratively as often as approvingly, most frequently to dep-recate a given viewpoint as falsely, superficially, or manipulatively dependent on a historical perspective or on supposed "laws" of history.

The term was first associated with German critics of the POSITIVIST view that history is subject to general laws. These critics, most prominently the Ger-man philosopher Wilhelm Dilthey, insisted that every historical event is unique and unrepeatable and must be understood in its own terms, and that the lessons of the past can only be grasped by overcoming our own cultural bi-

NEW HISTORICISM

The POSTSTRUCTURALIST movement in literary and art criticism known as New Historicism developed in the 1980s in reaction to NEW CRITICISM, in which MEANING is seen as deriving solely from a work's linguistic structure, and to DECONSTRUCTION's view of meaning as elusive and conditional. In common with older historicist approaches, New Historicism holds that a literary text—and by extension, any cultural artifact or event—must be studied and understood within the social and historical context of its creation. However, the New Historians fault some previous critics for seeing historical context as a fixed "background" for a literary work; instead, they insist, both history and literature represent a complex interaction of often conflicting forces. As the critic Louis Montrose has said, New Historicism is concerned with both "the historicity of texts and the textuality of history"—that is, contemporary conditions and cultural productions influence each other. New Historicism has embraced theories such as Michel FOUCAULT's contention that power relationships determine cultural *discourses* and dominant IDEOLOGIES shape the worldviews reflected in artistic works. Such ideas have inspired the reevaluation of some AESTHETIC assumptions and traditional literary canons. Some FEMINIST scholars, for instance, have argued that distinctions such as male/female sensibilities and public/private art are more conventional than natural, and have elevated previously disregarded texts, including women's diaries and magazines, as objects of serious study.

ases. The early connotations of the term also referred to analyses such as HEGEL's view of history as progressive, inexorable, and purposeful.

In the mid-20th century, "historicism" began to be employed as a term of disparagement to characterize MARXIST and other theories in which history was seen as progressing according to certain fixed principles. Critics such as Hannah ARENDT and Karl Popper argued that such approaches (which Popper labeled "historical determinism") amounted to self-serving justifications of the claims to legitimacy of Soviet COMMUNISM and other TOTALITARIAN systems. Louis Althusser, in his revisionist Marxism, likewise challenged the notion that history is moving toward a rational goal (see box at STRUCTURALISM).

In architecture, graphic design, and the fine arts, historicism refers to the practice of borrowing styles from the past, as in the Gothic Revival of the 18th century and the neo-CLASSICISM of the 19th. In literary and art criticism, New Historicism has revived some older historicist principles while rejecting others (see box).

See also RELATIVISM.

Hobbes, Thomas (1588–1679)

English philosopher and political theorist, author of the modern notion of causality and of the classic justification of the authoritarian STATE. In voluntary exile for 11 years in Europe after supporting the monarchy in the constitutional battle that led to the English Civil War, he met GALILEO, DESCARTES, and other European thinkers and wrote his most important work, *Leviathan* (1651), setting forth his political philosophy.

Hobbes held an entirely MATERIALIST view of reality, which informed his revolutionary conception of causation (see CAUSE). He discarded the ARISTOTELIAN notion of efficient, formal, and final causes, which contemplated objects and beings in terms of their form, action, and purpose, and considered only the material cause, which he defined as *motion*. In this view, the physical world is one of *cause and effect:* things in motion interacting, changing one state of affairs into another. Everything that happens has a proximate cause, and every action has an effect (e.g., a billiard ball rolls into the pocket because it has been struck by another ball).

Likewise, Hobbes saw human PERCEPTION and thought as purely material. Our thoughts derive only from sense perceptions; indeed, memory and imagination are "decaying sense," imperfectly retained images of the material world. Ideas, similarly, are "phantasms of sense." Language develops from instinctive sounds such as animals make (he called them "natural signs"), which, elaborated and invested with arbitrary conventional meanings, allow complex social interactions (cf. SEMIOTICS). Hobbes's materialism also led him to reject the existence—or at least the relevance—of the human SOUL. Only a material force can have any meaningful effect, he reasoned; the soul is by definition nonmaterial, and an "immaterial material" is self-contradictory. (Hobbes did accept that God alone—Aristotle's "uncaused cause"—stands outside the chain of cause and effect; his attitude toward religion was not atheism but indifference.)

Hobbes was suspicious of the freedom of conscience introduced by the PROTESTANT Reformation, believing it could lead to chaos. He considered all human societies artificial, in that their form is not governed by nature. The native human condition, he said, is found in the *state of nature,* in which the

only interest is self-interest and life is "solitary, poor, nasty, brutish, and short."
In order to escape the constant fear of others' depredations, humans form societies and governments through the SOCIAL CONTRACT. The form of government that can best guarantee civil security is a state with authoritarian power,
to which personal freedom is relinquished in exchange for freedom from fear
and to which utter allegiance is to be accorded.

See also CAUSE; MATERIALISM; SOCIAL CONTRACT; SOVEREIGNTY; STATE.

holism

The idea that wholes, especially organic and social SYSTEMS, are more than
the sum of their parts and must be understood comprehensively rather than
piecemeal. Holistic medicine, for example, sees the human being as a compound of body, mind, and spirit, and seeks to treat the whole person rather
than isolated symptoms; holistic sociology studies society and explains social
outcomes in terms of comprehensive structural and systemic processes;
GESTALT psychology stems from the idea that we experience the world in organized wholes rather than in discrete sensations. Holism is the opposite of
ATOMISM, which assumes that complex systems can be reduced to their constituent parts. In its view of wholes as integrated interrelationships, it is also
contrasted with MONISM, which considers the world to be composed of a single substance. The term was coined by the South African statesman Jan
Smuts in his book *Holism and Evolution* (1926), in which he proposed that the
EVOLUTION of both biological and social systems is a progression of increasingly comprehensive syntheses responding to a universal "creative principle," of which he considered the human mind and the British Empire
prime examples. Many contemporary holistic approaches, especially holistic
medicine, are derived in part from the sensibility of Eastern religion and philosophy, notably TAOISM and Zen Buddhism (see box at BUDDHISM), which
stress the interconnectedness of things and the need to allow the world's total flow, rather than individual desires or aims, to determine the paths one
follows.

See also GAIA; GESTALT; GODDESS WORSHIP; NEW AGE; WITCHCRAFT.

hooks, bell See box at FEMINISM

Horney, Karen (1885–1952)

German-born psychiatrist, who launched a FEMINIST critique of Freudian theory and founded a neo-Freudian psychoanalytic school that stressed cultural forces and interpersonal relationships over instinctive drives in personality formation and neurotic disorders. Horney was a leading figure in the European PSYCHOANALYTIC movement when she broke with FREUD over the male-centered aspects of his PSYCHODYNAMIC theory, particularly his notion of "penis envy," that girls develop feelings of inferiority because they feel their anatomy is incomplete. She accused Freud and his followers of perpetuating a paternalistic bias against women and argued that women's inferior position in society is the result of "the power struggle between the sexes," not psychological conflict.

After immigrating to the United States in 1932, Horney adapted the anthropological concept of cultural DETERMINISM, holding that the impact of one's social environment and cultural conditioning is far more influential than the primal, physiological drives on which Freud's theory was based. In *The Neurotic Personality of Our Times* (1937), she introduced one of her central concepts, *basic anxiety,* a child's feeling of being "isolated and helpless in a potentially hostile world." The attempt to overcome this instinctive anxiety and find security, she said, is expressed in three different impulses: to move toward, away from, or against other people. In a healthy person, these three tendencies are integrated; however, they can conflict, resulting in neurosis, or one of them can come to dominate, producing a submissive, detached, or aggressive personality. While the integrated personality maintains the image of an *ideal self* that acts as a guide and a goal, someone with an incomplete or conflicted self-image may distort this vision, creating an *idealized image* that falsifies and inflates one's characteristics and leads to a vicious circle of overblown expectations, inevitable frustration, and further self-deception.

See also DETERMINISM; FREUD; PSYCHOANALYSIS.

humanism

Philosophical outlook that emphasizes the intrinsic value, dignity, and rationality of human beings. Humanistic thought largely characterized the Renaissance and the ENLIGHTENMENT and contributed to the PROTESTANT Reformation and the Scientific Revolution. Now seen as an essentially atheistic viewpoint (for many religious FUNDAMENTALISTS, the evils of the modern world are summed up in the term "secular humanism"), the movement was initially kindled by the desire to expand the medieval focus of CHRISTIANITY on sin and redemption to embrace the full human experience.

European humanism had its beginnings in Italy in the 14th century with the reemergence of Greek and Latin classics that placed man, not God, at the center of creation. The classical studies of Francesco Petrarca (Petrarch) and others fostered an appreciation of these values and freed scholarship from ecclesiastical control and from the dogmatic FORMALISM of the SCHOLASTICS. Classical

> *"What the world needs is not redemption from sin but redemption from hunger and oppression; it has no need to pin its hopes upon Heaven, it has everything to hope for from this earth."*
>
> —Friedrich Durrenmatt,
> *The Marriage of
> Mr. Mississippi,* 1952

models also revolutionized the style and content of literature and art. (The branch of learning called the humanities, founded in the Renaissance, was originally concerned solely with classical studies.) With the invention of the printing press in the mid-15th century, classical texts and humanist ideas quickly spread throughout Europe. Among the most influential figures of Renaissance humanism were the Italian philosopher Pico della Mirandola, whose *Oration on the Dignity of Man* (1496) asserted the radical notion that dignity belongs not only to God; the English statesman Thomas More, whose *Utopia* (1516) reintroduced the PLATONIC ideal of a perfect human government; and the Dutch scholar Desiderius Erasmus, whose criticism of the corrupt hierarchy of the ROMAN CATHOLIC Church helped initiate the Reformation.

In the 17th and 18th centuries, Enlightenment philosophers' conviction that all problems, social, material, and spiritual, were susceptible to rational thought made religion a matter of REASON rather than faith (see, e.g., DEISM; RATIONALISM). But the role of God in human affairs was changed even more fundamentally by DARWIN's theory of EVOLUTION, which saw the origin of humanity in natural selection, not divine genesis. Modern humanism is generally nonreligious if not antireligious, seeing intelligence, creativity, and morality as human-inspired rather than God-given. In *Existentialism Is a Humanism* (1946), Jean-Paul SARTRE made the case that EXISTENTIALISM, as an examination of human freedom and possibility, is a fundamentally humanist outlook despite its bleak reputation.

Humanistic psychology, developed in the 1960s by American psychologists Abraham Maslow, Rollo May, and others, rejected the BEHAVIORIST emphasis on MECHANISM and the PSYCHOANALYTIC accent on conflict and dysfunction, focusing instead on a "third force," human potential. Uppermost in Maslow's "hierarchy of inborn needs" was *self-actualization,* the full development of one's abilities, talents, and humanitarian impulses, often associated with *peak experiences* in which the individual senses a personal wholeness and a unity with the world (cf. TRANSPERSONAL PSYCHOLOGY).

See also AQUINAS; INDIVIDUALISM; ROMANTICISM.

Hume, David (1711–1776)

Scottish philosopher, one of the foremost British thinkers of the ENLIGHTENMENT and a leading exponent of 18th-century EMPIRICISM, particularly the branch known as PHENOMENALISM. Hume's method was skeptical and critical, and his reputation rests as much on the subversive effect his ideas had on established views—such as the nature of PERCEPTION, assumptions about God, and the value of REASON—as on his ideas themselves.

The basis of Hume's philosophy was set forth in the three-volume *Treatise of Human Nature* (1739–40), whose controversial ideas and dense prose made it a failure. "It fell dead-born from the press," he later remarked. The *Inquiry Concerning Human Understanding* (1748) and *Inquiry Concerning the Principles of Morals* (1751) were less inflammatory, more accessible revisions of this work.

As an empiricist, Hume considered that all of our knowledge is the result of sense perceptions. However, like his contemporary George BERKELEY, he went further and insisted that, as far as we can know, there are *only* perceptions, which he called "impressions." We can have no direct knowledge of external objects or, for that matter, of ourselves. Our ideas about the world are purely the result of the mind's association and ordering of impressions according to "custom" or "natural beliefs"—our habitual ways of thinking. The operation of CAUSE and effect, for instance, is merely an idea derived from the impressions of a repeated series of events; we assume that what happens when one billiard ball strikes another is a cause-and-effect relation, but that conclusion is simply a way of giving coherence to our impressions.

In his *Dialogues Concerning Natural Religion* (1779), Hume applied the same skeptical analysis to theology, concluding that none of the standard arguments for the existence of God (see GOD, ARGUMENTS FOR) was sustainable. For example, the view of the deity as First Cause assumes causation. In the section "On Miracles," he argued that belief in miracles, a prerequisite of CHRISTIAN faith, requires the believer to "subvert all the principles of his understanding and . . . believe what is most contrary to custom and experience."

Hume's assault on RATIONALISM also included his famous formulation of the IS/OUGHT PROBLEM, that "is" does not imply "ought"—in other words, that moral conclusions cannot be derived from statements of fact. Morality, Hume said, comes from emotion, not REASON, which "is and ought only to be the slave of the passions." Indeed, Hume did not believe that his philosophy should govern our daily lives, which are naturally guided by the force of immediate impressions, custom, and beliefs.

See also EMPIRICISM; IS/OUGHT PROBLEM; PHENOMENALISM; SKEPTICISM.

Husserl, Edmund See PHENOMENOLOGY

Ibn Khaldun (1332–1406)

Spanish-Arab historian, politician, and jurist, born in Tunis, whose analytical approach to historiography and theory of social organization were unprecedented in his time and strikingly prescient of modern scholarship. His great work was *Kitab al-Ibar* (Universal History), a detailed chronicle of the Arabs and Berbers of North Africa. In its famous first part, the *Muqaddimah* (Introduction to History), the author gives an overview of Arab life, sets forth general principles governing political and economic life, and describes his scientific approach to history, disdaining other historians' uncritical reliance on received tradition. Ibn Khaldun connected the rise of human societies to favorable geographical and climatic conditions and to the emergence of a SOCIAL CONTRACT under which people, innately selfish and quarrelsome, agree to live together cooperatively. Social cohesion is aided by the power of religion and enforced by an authoritarian ruler. Kings and dynasties arise from the power of nomadic chieftains, and although ABSOLUTISM brings prosperity, it eventually becomes tyrannous, degenerates, and is overthrown. These dynastic cycles last three generations, or 120 years, a progression Ibn Khaldun ascribed to certain unalterable social and physical laws.

Ibn Rushd (Averroës) (1126–1198)

Spanish-Arab philosopher, scientist, and jurist, called Averroës in Latin, whose synthesis of Greek and ISLAMIC thought influenced medieval CHRISTIAN theology, particularly that of Thomas AQUINAS and other SCHOLASTICS, and whose commentaries on ARISTOTLE reintroduced the Greek philosopher's thought into European culture. He wrote extensively on jurisprudence and medicine, and was a widely respected judge and diplomat as well as an influential and controversial religious philosopher; near the end of his life he was exiled for several years, presumably because of his unorthodox philosophy.

Ibn Rushd offered a resolution of the ancient conflict between REASON and faith, holding that they are not incompatible. TRUTH, he said, may be discovered by philosophers through LOGIC, but it may also be revealed figuratively, as it is in scriptures, so that ordinary people can also understand it. Any seeming contradiction between rational inquiry and religious authority, therefore, may be resolved through figurative rather than literal interpretation of scripture. And while certain things must be taken on faith, where religion does not specify an answer reason is the only dependable path to truth. Like his predecessor IBN SINA, Ibn Rushd held an Aristotelian and NEOPLATONIC view of creation, conceiving the universe as an emanation from God, the Unmoved Mover, First CAUSE, and necessary being. The final divine emanation, or *active intellect,* is immortal, but the human body and SOUL that derive from it are not.

Ibn Rushd's attempt to harmonize religion and philosophy was understood by many ROMAN CATHOLIC churchmen as a doctrine of "double truth," implying that philosophical truth is separate from, perhaps superior to, religious revelation and that what is true in one realm may be false in the other. This interpretation, and other elements of Ibn Rushd's theology, including his belief that the universe is eternal and the individual soul is mortal, were espoused by so-called Averroists, notably Siger of Brabant, and condemned by church leaders. Aquinas, while largely following Ibn Rushd's reading of Aristotle in his own reconciliation of reason and revelation, attacked the position that philosophical truth is the independent product of reason and that reason can provide answers not discernable through faith.

Ibn Sina (Avicenna) (980–1037)

Persian philosopher and physician, known in the West as Avicenna, a Latin corruption of his Arabic name. A child prodigy who, by his own account, surpassed his teachers, Ibn Sina was a brilliant polymath who wrote on all known fields of study. His *Canons of Medicine,* a systematic synthesis of the medical and pharmacological knowledge of his time, was the standard medical textbook in Europe for five centuries after his death. Ibn Sina's religious philosophy, particularly his conception of God as First CAUSE (see GOD, ARGUMENTS FOR), influenced IBN RUSHD, as well as later medieval CHRISTIAN and JUDAIC theologians, including Thomas AQUINAS and Moses MAIMONIDES. Drawing on ARISTOTLE and Plotinus (see NEOPLATONISM), he conceived of God as the necessary being, in whom ESSENCE and existence are identical and from whom the universe emanated in ten "intelligences," the last of which, the *active intellect*, governs the earth and imbues matter with form to create life. It is the active intellect that we comprehend when we contemplate the infinite. Ibn Sina believed that some humans can achieve "illumination," or knowledge of fundamental TRUTH, through MYSTICAL apprehension of the divine. Contradicting ISLAMIC orthodoxy, Ibn Sina held that only the SOUL, not the person, is immortal, and that the universe is eternal, having no beginning or end and thus no moment of creation in time.

idealism

In philosophy, the position that IDEAS, not objects, are the basis of reality; the opposite of REALISM and MATERIALISM. The concept takes three general forms: that all of reality is a product of the mind; that we can have knowledge only of the contents of our minds; or that the material universe is an imperfect reflection of an ideal realm beyond our senses. The everyday connotation of the term relates to these meanings in the sense that an idealist is someone in pursuit of an ideal that is beyond the horizon but firmly grasped in the mind. By extension, the idealist school of international relations holds that global politics should be conducted according to an ideal standard, as opposed to the pragmatic approach of *realpolitik* (see REALISM).

Although the term itself was not used until LEIBNIZ employed it in contrast to materialism, idealism goes back at least to PLATO's notion that the world of our senses is only a "shadow" of the World of Forms, where the perfect, archetypal versions of everything we experience reside. This view was reflected in Greek art, particularly sculpture, which sought to approach an ideal standard of beauty instead of depicting real people (see AESTHETICS), and it persisted as an important emphasis in European (and Asian) art until the modern era.

The first philosopher known as an idealist was George BERKELEY, whose "immaterialism" held that objects exist only by virtue of our perception of them; they are ideas dwelling in our consciousness and in the mind of God. The "TRANSCENDENTAL idealism" of Immanuel KANT held that ideas and knowledge result from the filtering of sense perceptions by the universal *categories of the understanding* preexisting in the mind (see box at KANT), and distinguished between the experiential world of *phenomena* and the hidden world of *noumena,* things-in-themselves. HEGEL, in his "DIALECTICAL (or absolute) idealism," did not deny the substantiality of the world but saw both nature and human CONSCIOUSNESS as manifestations of an ABSOLUTE Mind or Spirit. The last influential idealist philosopher was F. H. Bradley (1846–1924), for whom the Hegelian Absolute not only constituted ultimate reality but would, when history had sufficiently evolved, resolve all contradictions in the world of APPEARANCES.

In all its forms, idealism posits "the union of the knower and the known." The object of perception and the one who perceives it are not separate and distinct entities; either the known derives solely from the knower's consciousness or both subject and object are dependent parts of some larger mind or spirit.

See also ABSOLUTE; BERKELEY; EMERSON; HEGEL; ROMANTICISM.

ideas

Abstract thoughts, generalized concepts, or transcendent ideals. PLATO used the term "idea" *(eidos)*, along with "form" and "archetype," to describe the flawless, unchanging entities that reside in the World of Forms and provide the patterns for the things we perceive in this world. Implicit in this is the concept of INNATE IDEAS—that our thoughts are apprehensions of preexisting, eternal truths. ARISTOTLE, on the other hand, believed that ideas are general abstractions from experience: "Nothing is in the intellect that was not first in the senses." This distinction can be defined as METAPHYSICAL—idea as ESSENCE, the immortal kernel that gives something its true nature—as opposed to EPISTEMOLOGICAL, the understanding we derive from our perceptions of the external world.

Both approaches raise the question of *how* we can have knowledge of ideas. A common version of the metaphysical view holds that all ideas arise in the mind of God and are apprehended by us, however imperfectly, through divine grace. DESCARTES divided ideas into the *innate* (originating within the mind, particularly CONSCIOUSNESS of self and knowledge of God), the *adventitious* (coming through the senses), and the *factitious* (constructs made up of other ideas). On the epistemological side, EMPIRICISTS such as John LOCKE rejected the notion of innate ideas, seeing the mind as a *tabula rasa,* or blank slate, to be filled in by experience. To Locke, the triumph of the human mind was that in addition to *sensation,* which we share with all animals, we are capable of *reflection.* In tandem, these two abilities constitute thought: "simple" ideas apprehended through sensation are combined, through reflection, into limitless "complex" ideas. In the 20th century, BEHAVIORISTS and others have advanced theories in which "ideas" have no place at all, seeing all mental activity as essentially physical, the product of stimulus-and-response mechanisms.

See also BERKELEY; CONSCIOUSNESS; DESCARTES; EMPIRICISM; IDEALISM; IDEOLOGY; INNATE IDEAS; LOCKE; PLATO.

identity

In philosophy, the question concerning the conditions of change under which something can be said to remain the same thing; also the proposition (known as *identity theory*) that mental events and brain events are identical. In psychology, "identity" refers to a person's continual sense of self, based on CONSCIOUSNESS and the personal attributes and external relations she or he identifies as defining.

For both PLATO and ARISTOTLE, the central ontological question was how something can undergo change—such as growth or mutilation—and yet be considered the same. Both concluded, in somewhat different terms, that beings have a fundamental form or SUBSTANCE—in the case of humans, the SOUL—which remains constant throughout physical change. This approach prevailed among Western philosophers until the rise of EMPIRICISM in the 17th century. John LOCKE, for instance, who rejected UNIVERSALS, found identity in the differing *particulars* of different types of entities, from inert objects, which possess identity only to the extent they have the same matter (a rock split in two is no longer the same rock), to humans, whose identity is guaranteed by the continuity of consciousness and memory.

HEGEL located human identity in social activity: our consciousness of self arises from our interaction with others, a process that is both competitive and collaborative. The social basis of personal identity has also come to be described in terms of "same" and "other," referring to the common links of identification within a group that are defined and bolstered by making contrasts with those who are perceived as not the same—those of a different RACE, nationality, CLASS, culture, or other group. *Identity theory* in philosophy (also called *physicalism*) holds that *mind* and *brain* are the same thing. Mental processes are purely physical (cf. MATERIALISM); likewise, there is no distinction between bodily sensations and our mental awareness of them.

The American psychologist Erik ERIKSON defined personal identity as the integration of all the self-images and identifications we have held. During adolescence the growing pressure to decide

> *"To be nobody-but-myself—in a world which is doing its best, night and day, to make you everybody else—means to fight the hardest battle which any human being can fight, and never stop fighting."*
>
> —e. e. cummings,
> quoted in 1958

"who you are" and choose an adult social and professional role from among a profusion of possibilities creates conflict and "role confusion." This typically results in an *identity crisis,* one of eight crises at life's turning points that Erikson maintained were natural and necessary.

See also BUDDHISM; DIALECTIC; FANON; box at FEMINISM; JUDAISM; box at LOGIC; OBJECT RELATIONS; QUEER THEORY; RACE AND RACISM; box at STRUCTURALISM; TRANSPERSONAL PSYCHOLOGY.

ideology

A system of IDEAS and beliefs that informs and shapes a sociopolitical worldview; often used disparagingly. The term, coined in the late 18th century and meaning literally "study of ideas," originated in the ENLIGHTENMENT conviction that ideas, like objects, could be studied scientifically. That meaning was inverted by Karl MARX, for whom "ideology" was fundamentally unscientific. In *The German Ideology* (1845–46) and other works, Marx and Friedrich Engels used the term to describe a system that purports to accurately reflect reality but actually distorts it, creating a *false consciousness* that takes APPEARANCES for actuality. In a CAPITALIST society, ideology—the dominant system of ideas and norms—becomes an oppressive tool whereby the ruling class legitimates its own values and the working class is systematically mystified and misled. To Marx, the proper study of society was the "scientific" approach of *historical materialism,* which holds that material and economic circumstances determine how one thinks, deals with the world, and decides what is important. Disciplines such as philosophy, theology, cultural criticism, and others that ignore fundamental economic and historical reality are therefore built on falsehood.

The traditional Marxian view of ideology has often been challenged by 20th-century critics, MARXISTS and non-Marxists alike, particularly for its emphasis on CLASS and economics as the sole determinants of cultural values. The sociologist Karl Mannheim, for example, held that all social groups in modern societies develop ideological systems to support their interests; but, like Marx, he distinguished between ideology, which preserves the existing system, and UTOPIAN ideas, which seek to change it. In the revisionist Marxism of Louis Althusser, ideology is a "superstructure" made up of all the cultural forces and institutions that affect an individual—political, religious, educational, etc., as well as economic—and thus is neither inherently true nor false. The Marxist *dominant ideology thesis*—that a society's prevailing ideology is a result of political and cultural domination by the ruling class—has been disputed by the sociologist Nicholas Abercrombie, among others, as overemphasizing the authoritative power of orthodox values.

The widespread use of the term has given rise to a broader popular meaning of ideology, denoting any systematic social or political theory. However, this usage still retains some of the derogatory implication of ideology as more a contrivance than a deeply rooted belief.

See also CRITICAL THEORY; DECONSTRUCTION; FOUCAULT; box at STRUCTURALISM.

imperialism and colonialism

Imperialism is the extension of power by an expansionist STATE to control another country or people, economically or politically or both. From the Latin *imperium* (command or authority), the same root as "empire," imperialism dates back to the establishment of the Persian, Chinese, Roman, and other vast empires of the ancient world. But it is most commonly associated with the two great eras of European expansionism: during the 16th–18th centuries, when the Americas and parts of Asia were colonized, and the 19th century, when most of Africa came under the domination of European powers. *Colonialism* is a variety of imperialism; the two terms largely overlap, but are often distinguished by the fact that whereas imperial expansion may result in the political integration of a conquered territory (as in the U.S. annexation of Texas and California), a colony is by definition an exploited subordinate of the "mother country." The colonial occupation of large parts of Africa was often cloaked in benign rationales that assumed the cultural and racial superiority of Europeans, who were seen as bringing civilization, PROGRESS, and CHRISTIANITY to "backward," "primitive" non-white peoples. Another justification of imperialism ascribes it to "human nature," the natural tendency of the strong to dominate their inferiors; this attitude was common in FASCIST thought.

In his classic study *Imperialism* (1902), J. A. Hobson attributed late-19th-century imperialism to CAPITALIST competition for access to natural resources and cheap labor and for control of MARKETS. V. I. Lenin extended that theme in *Imperialism, the Highest Stage of Capitalism* (1916), predicting that imperial rivalries would inevitably lead to world wars in which

"Take up the White Man's burden—
Send forth the best ye breed—
Go, bind your sons to exile
To serve your captives' need."
—Rudyard Kipling,
"The White Man's Burden,"
1899

capitalism would destroy itself. Other MARXIST thinkers, before and since, have linked imperialism to capitalism and both to violence. These theorists include Rosa LUXEMBURG, who argued that as capitalism seeks ever-wider markets it requires militaristic expansion to ensure captive markets and compete with other capitalist powers.

In the POSTCOLONIAL world, imperialism has taken subtler, some say more insidious forms—for example, in the so-called *cultural imperialism* by which Western ideas and values, consumer fashions, and popular culture infiltrate other countries through the power of mass media and economic influence. The term *neocolonialism* is used to describe the economic domination of developing countries by transnational corporations seeking, as of old, raw materials, cheap labor, and new markets. Some economists fault international organizations such as the World Bank for pressuring Third World countries into patterns of development that favor the corporate interests of the industrialized world.

See also BLACK NATIONALISM; FANON; LENIN; LUXEMBURG; MANIFEST DESTINY; NATIONALISM; NÉGRITUDE; POSTCOLONIAL THEORY; PROGRESS; RACE AND RACISM; SOCIAL DARWINISM.

impressionism

Movement in painting, especially in France, from the 1860s through the 1880s, whose practitioners were concerned with creating spontaneous works observed from nature. Impressionism was never a unified artistic school with a coherent program, but rather a result of the common passions and ambitions of a group of young, aspiring artists. Their approach embodied a rejection of both academic FORMALISM and of the ROMANTIC view of art as an expression of the artist's inner vision, and was in part an outgrowth of REALISM. The early impressionists took inspiration from Gustave Courbet's depictions of ordinary life and from the carefully observed landscapes of the Barbizon School. Their style was distinguished by fragmented brushstrokes and an intense palette of color, their objective to capture the immediate impression of the effect of light and movement in a scene.

The impressionists' repudiation of rigid academic principles caused their exclusion from the official Paris Salon exhibitions and drove them to organize independent shows. The movement's name was coined at the first of these, in 1874, derived from Claude Monet's painting *Impression—Sunrise* and from a hostile critic who dismissed the artists as "impressionists" who produced unfinished work that dwelt on subjective impressions. Other members of the group were Paul Cézanne, Edgar Degas, Camille Pissaro, Alfred Sisley, and Auguste Renoir; Edouard Manet was a major influence on the movement, although he never participated in an impressionist show.

Neoimpressionism, exemplified by Georges Seurat, sought to apply systematic color theory to the impressionist style. Applying new theories about visual and physiological responses to line, color, and luminosity, Seurat and others developed *pointillism,* in which a picture is built up from small dots of paint that resolve into recognizable forms when viewed as a whole, and *divisionism,* the separation of colors through strokes of pigment to create a sense of balance and statis. Outstanding examples of these techniques are Seurat's *Sunday Afternoon on the Island of La Grande Jatte* (1884–86) and *The Parade* (1887–88), respectively. The term *postimpressionism* is also applied to the neoimpressionists, as well to the late works of impressionists such as Cézanne, who began using color to explore geometric relationships, and to the SYMBOLIST works of Paul Gauguin and Vincent van Gogh, who sought to express emotion through pure color. Impressionism and its derivatives strongly contributed to the rise of CUBISM and ABSTRACTION in the early 20th century.

individualism

Any theory that places the value, autonomy, and benefit of the individual over that of the group, society, or nation, or that makes the individual the prime unit in a social system; the opposite of *collectivism.* Individualism is at the heart of LIBERALISM—specifically, the conviction that the primary role of government is to protect and promote the rights and endeavors of individuals—and of LAISSEZ-FAIRE economics, which holds that the optimal working of the marketplace occurs through the free operation of competitive self-interest. In social theory, individualism sees all social activity as ultimately composed of individual acts (see also ATOMISM). Individualism is also implied in the ROMANTIC belief in the uniqueness of each human being.

The origin of the idea in its modern sense can be seen in Renaissance HUMANISM, with its accent on personal dignity and accomplishment, and in the PROTESTANT Reformation, which stressed unmediated communion with God and personal responsibility for one's own salvation. The term "individualism" first appeared in 19th-century France, where it had a negative connotation, denoting an emphasis on private interests at the expense of society as a whole—a tendency Alexis de TOCQUEVILLE found alarmingly prevalent in the United States. In England, however, it was associated with middle-class liberalism and the ideals of human progress and individual freedom.

Among Americans the term became (and remains) a byword for a self-image embracing limited government, free enterprise, equality of opportunity, self-reliance, and personal freedom. Herbert Hoover, touting the American system in a 1928 presidential campaign speech, coined the phrase "rugged individualism."

See also ANARCHISM; CAPITALISM; EMERSON; LIBERALISM; LIBERTARIANISM; TOC-QUEVILLE; TRANSCENDENTALISM.

induction See DEDUCTION AND INDUCTION

information theory

The study of the transmission and processing of information; a branch of statistics and PROBABILITY theory, overlapping with CYBERNETICS and SYSTEMS THEORY, whose principles have been adopted in the social sciences, particularly economics and psychology. (In mathematics and other statistical applications, "information" is divorced from MEANING, referring only to data accurately sent and received.) Information theory was pioneered in the 1940s by Claude Shannon, an electrical engineer who was primarily concerned with the efficiency and clarity of radio, telephone, and telegraphic transmissions. He investigated the effect of such factors as interference ("noise" or distortion), channel capacity, transmission speed, ENTROPY (the randomness or disorder of the information or its source), and data redundancy on the rate of errors in transmission—that is, how they affected the *probability* of an error-free transmission—and developed principles governing the construction of *binary codes* that would minimize error and maximize efficiency. The concept of *coding* in information theory, referring to the translation of data into a stream of binary "on/off" messages representing "bits" of information (the principle of the computer chip), is similar to the view of language itself as a series of "signs" or signals with conventional connotations (see SEMIOTICS; STRUCTURALISM).

In COGNITIVE PSYCHOLOGY, information-processing theory likens the human brain to a computer, considering mental processes in terms of the input, storage, manipulation, and retrieval of data. In this perspective, incoming sense impressions are almost immediately encoded according to established patterns—either as images, SYMBOLS, concepts, and so on, or, in the *connectionist* view, as separate but interconnected "bits" of information. They are then stored in memory, where they are available for future retrieval and are able to be compared with prior information in learning and problem-solving applications.

See also ARTIFICIAL INTELLIGENCE; CONSCIOUSNESS; CYBERNETICS; ENTROPY.

innate ideas

The concept that there are certain ideas preexisting in the mind. Knowledge of innate ideas does not depend on any particular experience; they cannot be "learned" but may be hidden, waiting to be uncovered. The idea had its earliest important advocate in PLATO and his concept of *anamnesis* (recollection), in which truths are simply memories of the World of Forms, where we resided before birth. To DESCARTES, ideas were either innate (originating within the mind, especially the idea of God), adventitious (acquired from experience), or factitious (assembled from other ideas).

The first philosophers to wholeheartedly criticize the notion of innate ideas were the 17th-century EMPIRICISTS, for whom knowledge could come only through experience and was consequently molded by one's particular experiences in the world. LOCKE, for one, objected that if any ideas were innate, they would be known by everyone, everywhere. KANT likewise saw ideas as derived from experience, but shaped and ordered by the A PRIORI categories of the understanding (see box at KANT).

Although the notion of innate ideas is almost universally discounted today, a number of schools of thought grant to the human mind a "hard-wired," generative faculty. The linguistic theories of Noam CHOMSKY, for instance, are predicated on the brain's possession of a set of algorithms for the production of language, with which a young child grasps, without "learning" them, the grammatical rules that govern the specific language she or he hears others speaking.

See also IDEAS; PLATO.

internationalism

The belief in creating a wider base for political community than the nation-STATE; often contrasted with ISOLATIONISM. Its most significant formulations are derived from MARX and KANT and based, respectively, on CLASS consciousness and common humanity. Where NATIONALISM was bounded by territorial limits, Marx's internationalism sought to attain a solidarity among the working classes of Europe that transcended national allegiances. This ideal was dealt a harsh blow with the outbreak of World War I when, contrary to Marx's predictions, the working classes rushed to fight on behalf of their respective nation-states. Thereafter, Marxist internationalism tended to focus on opposition to IMPERIALISM AND COLONIALISM, and in the Soviet Union it became indistinguishable from globalism (see below).

The second major formulation of internationalism, also known as *cosmopolitanism*, derives from the attitudes embodied by ENLIGHTENMENT thinkers such as VOLTAIRE and particularly from the writings of Immanual KANT, especially *Toward Perpetual Peace* (1795). Kant proposed the possibility of a global community based on the humanity, FREEDOM, and EQUALITY of its members. In the essay "Idea for a Universal History with a Cosmopolitan Purpose," he said that the most important and difficult task for humankind is the attainment of a universally just civil society based on equality and respect, in which all people would be treated as ends in themselves rather than means to others' ends. Although Kant argued that the existence of SOVEREIGN nations leads to war—the foremost obstacle to achieving such a society—he rejected the idea of one global government, suggesting instead a confederation of like-minded states; this idea was reflected in the creation of the League of Nations and the United Nations.

Although the contemporary political policy known as *globalism* shares a supranational, nonisolationist outlook with other conceptions of internationalism, it differs from most of them in its emphasis on international power and influence rather than cooperation. The term refers primarily to the U.S. policy of global engagement aimed at expanding its political influence and economic markets, but it was also applied to the Soviet Union's efforts to extend its own sphere of influence during the Cold War. "Globalism" is also applied to the view that some problems, such as ozone depletion and GLOBAL WARMING, cannot be effectively dealt with on a local or regional scale but must be attacked globally.

is/ought problem

The question of whether it is possible to derive a moral value purely from a statement of fact. The problem derives from David HUME's observation, in his *Treatise of Human Nature* (1739–40), that philosophers tend to begin with assertions ("copulations of propositions [about what] is, and is not") that then slide into imperatives—oughts and ought-nots. In Hume's view, the facts of a case do not in themselves dictate a conclusion about the way things ought to be; that step requires the interjection of an *opinion* about the facts. (The fact that some people pay taxes on a far lower percentage of their total income than others, for example, may inform, but does not compel, the conviction that they should pay more.) Around this problem has grown a major philosophical debate: can we derive values from facts? Hume's position was that we cannot; indeed, he stated the problem as part of his argument that morality arises not from REASON but from an innate "moral sense."

The is/ought problem is also known as the *naturalistic fallacy*. The same term was used by the English philosopher G. E. Moore in his criticism of the UTILITARIANS, who, he said, tended to equate the quality of "goodness" with things they identified as "good," such as pleasure. It is fallacious, Moore reasoned, to derive moral qualities from natural qualities—an echo of Hume's insistence that one can't derive ETHICS from circumstances.

See also DESCRIPTIVISM AND PRESCRIPTIVISM.

Islam

Religion in the Judeo-Christian tradition, founded in the seventh century C.E. by MUHAMMAD, with about one billion adherents in the world today. Central to Islam is the doctrine that there is only one God (*Allah* in Arabic), who has revealed his will to humankind through numerous prophets, including Abraham, Moses, JESUS, and, finally and most important, Muhammad. The word "Islam" means "submission" to God; "Muslim" means "one who submits." There are two main divisions, the Sunnis, comprising the vast majority of Muslims, and the Shi'ites (see box). All Muslims are expected to perform five principal religious duties, often called the Five Pillars of Islam (see box).

The teachings of Islam are contained primarily in the Qur'an (Koran), said to have been revealed by God to Muhammad, and the Sunnah, the body of custom and usage based on Muhammad's precepts and his exemplary acts. The Qur'an teaches that Islam is the religion of the Hebrew prophets and the natural religion of all people. The primary focus of Islam is the relationship between the individual human being and God. Each individual must worship God and live according to his commandments in order to escape hellfire and enter heaven on the day of judgment. An almost equally important responsibility is one's obligation to the Muslim community, or *ummah*. Just as the Qur'an supersedes and perfects all previous revelations, the Muslim community supplants all previous religious communities.

Along with prescribing the proper beliefs and spiritual orientation for each individual, Islam seeks to provide an ideal order for society. The sacred law, or *shari'ah,* based on the Qur'an and the Sunnah and developed over the first three centuries of Islam, is a sophisticated body of legal theory and opinion governing everything from family life to commercial transactions. Al-

THE FIVE PILLARS OF ISLAM

All Muslim believers are required to perform five principal religious duties, known as the Five Pillars of Islam. They are:

1. The confirmation of faith, made by reciting the *shahadah,* "I witness that there is no god but the God (Allah) and that MUHAMMAD is his prophet." This attestation, made before witnesses, is the only requirement for conversion to Islam.

2. Canonical worship five times a day. The Muslim must, in a state of ritual purity, face Mecca and recite prescribed phrases while performing set cycles of standing, bowing, sitting, and prostration.

3. Fasting during the holy month of Ramadan, the ninth month in the Islamic lunar calendar. The fast entails abstaining from food and drink from dawn to sunset, and is usually accompanied by an intensification of prayer and worship. The end of Ramadan is celebrated with a major feast and holiday known as Eid al-Fitr.

4. The yearly payment of *zakaat,* a set percentage of each adult's wealth, to help the poor. Shi'ites (see box) give an additional amount to support their clergy.

5. Performance of the *hajj,* the annual pilgrimage to Mecca, at least once in one's lifetime if possible. The *hajj* commemorates the willingness of the Hebrew prophet Abraham to sacrifice his son for God, and is celebrated with the Feast of the Sacrifice *(Eid al-Adha),* the most important Muslim holiday.

though in Islamic doctrine women are considered the equal of men, they are considered to have different functions and duties, and therefore do not have complete social and legal equality in practice. The importance of community in Muslim life is evidenced by the fact that year one of the Islamic era corresponds to Muhammad's emigration (*hijrah* or hegira) to the city of Yathrib (now Medina), where he organized the first Muslim community. While many different intellectual and spiritual currents have emerged over the course of Islamic history, the dominant culture of educated Muslim ELITES has been much the same everywhere, characterized by common social and political institutions and distinctive forms of literature, art, and architecture. Likewise, the early systematization of Islamic law ensured that Muslim religious practices have remained remarkably uniform to the present day.

SUNNIS AND SHI'ITES

Islam is divided into two main sects, the Sunnis, who constitute more than four fifths of Muslims, and the Shi'a, or Shi'ites, who predominate in Iran and Iraq. The split between Sunnis and Shi'ites occurred over the legitimacy of MUHAMMAD's spiritual and political heirs, and it is primarily this question that still divides the two groups.

Shi'ites believe that Muhammad designated Ali ibn Abi Talib, his cousin and son-in-law, as his successor, and that his descendants were the rightful leaders of the Muslim community, imams ("models") chosen by God. Central to Shi'ism, therefore, is the idea of the hereditary imamate. The third imam, Husayn al-Husayn, son of Ali and grandson of Muhammad, was murdered in 680 when he refused to give his allegiance to the ruling caliph. To Shi'ites, this martyrdom remains a bloody symbol of the early Muslims' failure to follow their prophet's religion, and mourning for his death is an important aspect of Shi'ite religious feeling and ritual. Most Shi'ites are "Twelvers," who believe Ali was followed by 11 other imams, the last of whom, "hidden" since the ninth century, will return at the end of time to establish justice on earth. Members of the Ismaili sect believe that the line of imams has continued to the present day; their leader is called Aga Khan. (See also BAHA'I; FUNDAMENTALISM.)

To *Sunnis,* the unity of the Muslim community is more important than the pedigree of its leader. They believe that the Prophet died without appointing a successor and that the political leaders, or caliphs, who succeeded him represented the legitimate succession. Caliphs are chosen or confirmed by a consensus of religious scholars and there is no doctrine of divine appointment and infallibility, as there is in the Shi'ite imamate. Sunnis are also distinguished from Shi'ites in their emphasis on the rational inscrutability of God and the limited scope of human free will. (See also BLACK MUSLIMS.)

Sunnism and Shi'ism have developed their own distinct, but similar, bodies of Islamic law. There are four Sunni schools of law, the Maliki, Hanafi, Shafi'i, and Hanbali, and all Sunnis must adhere to one of them. In both the Sunni and Shi'ite systems, the most learned scholars are arbiters of legal and religious matters. The Sunni *ulama'* are not an organized body, deriving their authority from the prestige of their knowledge, but Shi'ites have a hierarchical clergy, who rise according to their degree of learning, the highest rank being ayatollah.

Beginning in the 19th century, Islamic reformers such as the Egyptian scholar and jurist Muhammad Abduh sought to modernize Islam, believing that constitutional DEMOCRACY, women's EQUALITY with men, faith justified by REASON, and other Western notions are compatible with the teachings of the Qur'an. In the 20th century these movements have been bitterly opposed by Islamic FUNDAMENTALISTS who not only hold different views of scripture but are deeply distrustful of all Western influences, which they see as degrading moral standards and reminiscent of the era of European IMPERIALISM in the Arab world.

See also box at AFRICAN RELIGIONS (modern movements); BAHA'I; BLACK MUSLIMS; ESCHATOLOGY; FUNDAMENTALISM; IBN KHALDUN; IBN RUSHD; IBN SINA; JUST WAR; MUHAMMAD; SIKHISM; SUFISM.

isolationism

American foreign policy, dominant through much of the 19th and parts of the 20th century, that sought to avoid foreign military and political alliances, especially with Europe, while welcoming commercial relations. The isolationist tendency arose from the United States' geographic separation from the Old World and from the conviction that foreign "entanglements" were either unnecessary or potentially threatening to American SOVEREIGNTY. George Washington, in his farewell address of 1796, warned the country "to steer clear of permanent alliances with any portion of the foreign world." In his first inaugural address (1801), Thomas JEFFERSON likewise advocated "peace, commerce, and honest friendship with all nations, entangling alliances with none." While the concept of isolationism embraces neutrality and nonalignment—refusing to take sides in international conflicts—it also emphasizes autonomy, the idea that even in peace a nation's sovereignty is compromised by international commitments.

During World War I isolationist sentiment was strong up to the moment of America's entry into the conflict in 1917, and forcefully reasserted itself soon after the armistice, when Congress rejected the Treaty of Versailles and the League of Nations. After the outbreak of war in Europe in 1939, isolationist feeling in the United States was focused by the America First Committee, an odd alliance of Nazi sympathizers, pro-Soviet leftists (until the German-Soviet nonaggression pact collapsed), and traditional isolationists. The committee, whose most prominent spokesman was the aviator Charles Lindbergh, dissolved after the Japanese attack on Pearl Harbor brought the United States into the war in 1941.

Isolationism has come to be epitomized by the slogan "America First."

First used by Woodrow Wilson in the early days of World War I, it was later used pejoratively—as was the term "isolationism" itself—to portray the opinions of those who opposed America's increasing INTERNATIONALISM in the aftermath of World War II. The motto has been periodically revived, for example, in the 1992 and 1996 Republican presidential primaries by the CONSERVATIVE candidate Patrick Buchanan.

J

Jacksonian democracy

POPULIST movement associated with the presidency (1829–37) of Andrew Jackson and influential until the 1850s. As a frontiersman and a hero of the War of 1812, Jackson personified an egalitarian spirit that celebrated the "common man" and sought to curb the power of the propertied ELITE. He and his followers in the Democratic Party saw the federal government as the enclave of an entrenched aristocracy and the "MARKET revolution" of entrepreneurial CAPITALISM as further enriching the wealthy few at the expense of the majority. They favored an expanded franchise, limited government, and broad-based congressional representation, and opposed the economic power of the northern banks, whose credit-driven policies squeezed small farmers and western settlers.

Jacksonian democracy sounded several themes that have echoed repeatedly in American politics: EQUALITY of opportunity, individual FREEDOM, hostility to centralized government, and suspicion of elites. However, the Jacksonians' leveling vision went only so far. Suffrage, for instance, was to be "universal" only for white males. Indeed, slavery was an issue for most Jacksonians only because it confused their egalitarian message; Jackson himself was a slaveholder. In vetoing a bill rechartering the Second Bank of the United States in 1832, Jackson may have been, as he said, resisting monopoly and aristocracy, or merely favoring bankers more friendly to his policies. Jackson was the originator of the "strong presidency," asserting federal power, brandishing the veto, and capitalizing on his personal popularity.

Traditionally seen as the first flowering of popular DEMOCRACY in American politics, the movement is now assigned a mixed legacy. It expanded the electorate and broadened political participation generally, but it also contributed to economic instability, fostered the "spoils system" of government patronage, and sharpened the North-South, urban-rural tensions that led to the Civil War.

See also WHIGS AND TORIES.

Jainism

Indian religious tradition that stresses ASCETICISM and NONVIOLENCE. The sixth-century B.C.E. sage Vardhamana, called Mahavira (Great Hero), is traditionally regarded as the last in a line of 24 founder-prophets called *tirthankaras* ("pathmakers") or *jinas* ("they who overcome," from which the word "Jain" is derived). Jainism is thought to have begun as a reaction against the hierarchical CASTE system and animal sacrifice in HINDUISM, with which it still has much in common, as it does with BUDDHIST thought as well. The religion has about 3.5 million adherents, almost all of them in India. It is divided into two main sects, which formed from a schism in the first century B.C.E. and are known by the names that at that time distinguished their attitude toward dress, Shvetambara ("clad in white") and Digambara ("clad in air," i.e., nude).

Jains believe in *samsara,* the cycle of rebirth through which KARMA is worked out, and in the eventual liberation of the soul from earthly attachments. This is achieved through self-discipline and austere living, meditation, and the three "jewels" of right living: right belief, right knowledge, and right conduct. Jain monks are further required to adhere to five vows of abstention from violence, lying, theft, attachments, and sexual pleasure. Central to Jain practice is the concept of *ahimsa* (noninjury), based on the belief that violence produces bad karma, which may result in a soul's returning to earth as an animal or insect; therefore violence must be absolutely avoided and all living creatures respected. Consequently, Jains are not only pacifistic but vegetarian, and some monastics wear nose masks and carry brooms to sweep the ground before them to avoid inhaling or treading on souls in their path. The doctrine of *ahimsa* influenced Mahatma GANDHI's philosophy of nonviolence.

See also ATOMISM; KARMA; NIRVANA.

James, William (1842–1910)

American philosopher and psychologist, one of the pioneers of psychology and popularizer of PRAGMATISM. James came from a brilliant, cosmopolitan family; his brother was the novelist Henry James. William James's own writing had a straightforward, colloquial style that made him a popular author in his own right. A man of protean interests, he aspired to be an artist, then trained as a doctor, and eventually taught at Harvard, first physiology, then psychology, then philosophy.

James's thought was thoroughly conditioned by his pragmatic philosophy. He insisted that the truth of an idea is determined by its "cash value," its potential social and intellectual usefulness or ethical consequences (see CONSEQUENTIALISM). He also viewed the world as PLURALISTIC—always eluding our attempts to fully capture its nature and thus always full of fresh possibilities—and saw this variety as the source of human creative freedom.

In his first major work, *The Principles of Psychology* (1890), James underscored the functional role of CONSCIOUSNESS, which he saw as predominantly one of selection. We experience the world in a STREAM OF CONSCIOUSNESS (a term he coined), selecting, from among the mass of sensations rushing by, a comparative few that become the objects of thought and the basis of what we identify as experience. In what is now known as the James-Lange theory of emotions (a very similar theory was independently and almost simultaneously put forward by the Danish physiologist Carl Georg Lange), James contradicted the prevailing wisdom by proposing that emotions are the result, not the cause, of physiological processes. To use James's example, if we encounter a large bear in the woods, we don't run because we are afraid, we feel afraid because we are running; that is, seeing the bear produces certain physiological responses— sweating, shaking, tingling, etc.—that we have learned to associate with fear. This theory, influential for a time, is now discredited.

> "First . . . a new theory is attacked as absurd; then it is admitted to be true, but obvious and insignificant; finally it is seen to be so important that its adversaries claim that they themselves discovered it."
>
> —William James, *Pragmatism*, 1907

In the 1897 essay "The Will to Believe," James applied his pragmatic "cash-value" approach to an attempt to reconcile religious faith and EMPIRICAL science. Belief, he said, is not and should not be contingent on empirical facts. When we are faced with choices that we experience as "forced, living, and momentous," and when those choices will decisively affect our orientation to the world, belief in something beyond our senses is entirely justified. The individual's own experience, not received doctrine, is the basis of faith. That perspective was illustrated in *The Varieties of Religious Experience* (1902), James's most popular work then and now, which described the deep religious experiences of a variety of believers, including mystics and sudden converts. James was sympathetic to both religious believers and scientific skeptics; he counted himself among the latter but also believed that there is more to reality than science can account for.

See also MONISM; PRAGMATISM; PROGRESSIVISM; STREAM OF CONSCIOUSNESS; UTILITARIANISM.

Jefferson, Thomas (1743–1826)

American statesman and political philosopher, third president of the United States (1801–09), the leading exponent of ENLIGHTENMENT thought in the revolutionary period, and the most intellectually influential of the Founding Fathers. Jefferson was a lawyer, inventor, scholar, and educator as well as a statesman; he was broadly educated and endlessly curious, and his wide-ranging interests included art and architecture, science and natural history, animal husbandry, meteorology, mechanical engineering, and the classics. His heroes were Francis BACON, Isaac NEWTON, and John LOCKE; he was also indebted to the French *philosophes,* many of whom he met and befriended as U.S. minister to France from 1785 to 1789. Jefferson's contributions to the American enterprise were many and varied. He was a member of the pre- and postrevolutionary Virginia legislature and governor of that state; author of Virginia's Statute of Religious Freedom and, as a member of the Continental Congress, of the Declaration of Independence; president of the American Philosophical Society; initiator, as U.S. president, of the Louisiana Purchase, which doubled the country's size, and of Lewis and Clark's transcontinental expedition of exploration; and, in his last years, founder of the University of Virginia.

Jefferson's philosophy was based on a belief in NATURAL LAW and a faith in the ability of citizens to govern themselves. His vision of an American REPUBLIC based on agriculture and decentralized governmental powers had much in common with ARISTOTLE's ideal *polis.* In Jefferson's "agrarian democracy," yeoman farmers represented the wellspring of civic VIRTUE; he feared the rise of urban manufacturing centers, which in his view had brought only inequality, decadence, and human misery to Europe. He advocated universal education as the foundation of participatory DEMOCRACY (although he was opposed to political participation by women) and envisioned the rise of a "natural aristocracy" of democratic leaders.

As a Virginia aristocrat himself, Jefferson owned slaves, but he considered slavery a violation of natural law and contemplated freeing his slaves, though he never did. His first draft of the Declaration of Independence (1776) condemned slavery, charging King George III with forcing the institution onto the colonies; the passage was deleted from the final draft by the Continental Congress. The document nonetheless enshrined the principle that "all men are created equal," as well as affirming the SOCIAL CONTRACT between the people and the government in which the STATE is created and legitimated by "the consent of the governed"—principles that form the cornerstone of American political philosophy.

Although raised an Anglican, Jefferson espoused DEISM, which sought to eliminate those parts of CHRISTIAN thought that were contrary to REASON. He held that the teachings of JESUS were the world's greatest doctrine but that religion had been corrupted by the clergy. He saw faith as a strictly personal matter and believed, therefore, in the absolute separation of church and state.

See also FEDERALISM; ISOLATIONISM; RADICALISM; STATES' RIGHTS.

Jehovah's Witnesses

Christian sect holding FUNDAMENTALIST, MILLENARIAN beliefs, repudiating orthodox CHRISTIANITY, and refusing allegiance to any earthly authority. It began as the International Bible Students' Association, founded in 1872 by the ADVENTIST Charles Taze Russell and advanced by Joseph Franklin Rutherford. Jehovah's Witnesses regard other Christian denominations as having fallen away from the truth of the primitive church of the apostles. They use a special translation of the Bible, interpret scripture literally, and adhere to the doctrine known as Arianism, which rejects the TRINITY, holding that JESUS is not part of God but was created by him. In keeping with Russell's prediction that the Second Coming of Christ would occur in 1914, they believe that Christ's kingdom was established on that date and that he now reigns on earth invisibly and will soon lead the forces of good against Satan in the battle of Armageddon. Claiming allegiance only to Christ's kingdom, they refuse to salute the flag, to vote, to swear oaths, to perform military service (on the additional ground that all members are ministers), or to obey any law seen as contrary to God's. Worship is conducted in Kingdom Halls and private homes, and each member "witnesses" his or her faith in door-to-door evangelism. The sect maintains a worldwide missionary movement and widely distributes its journal The Watchtower and other publications.

Jesus (c.6–4 B.C.E.–c.30 C.E.)

Jewish messianic teacher, founder of CHRISTIANITY. Jesus (the Latinization of the Hebrew name Joshua or Yeshua) is believed by his worshipers to be the Christ or Messiah prophesied in JUDAIC scripture, the "anointed one" who will establish the kingdom of God on earth (see ESCHATOLOGY). In ISLAM he is considered a prophet second only in importance to MUHAMMAD. What little is known of Jesus's life and ministry is contained in the books of the New Testament, particularly the four Gospels, which were composed at least a generation after his death. Jesus was one of many preachers in Roman-occupied Judea claiming or proclaimed to be the Messiah, offering hope of deliverance from oppression and from the spiritual corruption many Jews felt had overtaken their nation. His ministry probably lasted from one to three years, beginning with his baptism in the River Jordan by his cousin, John the Baptist, and ending with his arrest and crucifixion by the Roman authorities.

Jesus gained a reputation as a rabble-rouser by fraternizing with the poor and outcast, and as a RADICAL by breaking with religious tradition to emphasize a new order over the strict observance of the law of Moses. The true spirit of the Mosaic Law, he said, was contained and transformed within his being; salvation would come only through accepting him as the son of God. Jesus and his disciples believed that the end of the world was near and that whoever wished to share in everlasting life must immediately rededicate their lives to God.

The Gospel accounts create a portrait of Jesus as a charismatic and convincing teacher who used parables, exemplary acts, and miracles to call people to repent and recast their lives. The essence of his preaching is encapsulated in the command "Love God with your whole heart, and your neighbor as yourself." His followers were to practice selflessness and charity, shun material possessions, act with unconditional love and mercy toward others, and renounce violence. Jesus evangelized among "sinners"—non-Jews, nonobservant Jews, and social outcasts—and singled out the poor and oppressed for salvation while denouncing the rich and powerful.

Jesus's suffering and death were regarded by his disciples as the fulfillment of prophecy. Through his crucifixion, they believed, Jesus made himself the sacrifice that would "ransom" the souls of humanity forever, ensuring their salvation. Through his resurrection from the grave two days later, he revealed that he was the Christ and demonstrated the victory of life over death that his coming symbolized. Jesus made no direct claim to being the Messiah during his ministry, but after his resurrection was said to have appeared before his disciples to tell them that he would return to usher in the kingdom of God. In the century after his death, Jesus's teachings were spread throughout the Roman world by his apostles, notably St. Paul, whose evangelical epistles developed the theology of early Christianity.

See also ADVENTISM; box at AFRICAN RELIGIONS (modern movements); CHRISTIANITY; GOLDEN RULE; LIBERATION THEOLOGY; MORMONISM; ORTHODOX CHURCH; ROMAN CATHOLICISM; TRINITY.

Judaism

Religious tradition and ETHICAL system of the Jewish people, who consider themselves descended from the biblical patriarchs; the oldest of the world's major religions and the first monotheism, developing among Semitic tribes in the eastern Mediterranean region from about 1300 B.C.E. Rather than a single religious ideology, Judaism is a group of beliefs and practices grounded in a common IDENTITY, genealogy, and history. Jewish identity is conferred by birth, matrilineally, not by profession of faith; though Judaism accepts converts, it is not evangelistic. Judaism is thus a cultural continuum as well as a spiritual practice, and many Jews embrace its culture and ETHICAL teachings while ignoring or rejecting its religious observances.

The central scripture of Judaism is the Hebrew Bible, or Tanakh (the Old Testament to Christians), especially the first five books, variously called the Books of Moses, the Pentateuch, and the TORAH, which describe the creation of the world and the founding of the original nation of Israel, and contain the divine laws that are the cornerstone of Jewish belief. Supplementing the Bible is the Talmud, a collection of writings on legal, ethical, and liturgical matters as well as Jewish history and legend. It comprises the Mishnah, or "oral law" (injunctions said to have been revealed by God to Moses), and the Gemara, rabbinical interpretations and commentaries on the Mishnah. Interpretive writings on the Bible are called Midrash; Talmudic law and other rabbinical decrees comprise Halakhah, which governs religious practice, while the Haggadah (or Agadah) consists of commentary on the Bible's theological and ethical teachings. The study of Torah, Talmud, and rabbinical commentaries is considered a spiritual occupation, an important path to knowledge of God (cf. KABBALAH).

The Jewish faith is founded on a series of covenants made between God and the patriarchs, beginning with Abraham and ending with Moses, in which God promised to bless and protect the Jewish people in return for their worship and obedience to his laws (see TEN COMMANDMENTS; TORAH). For this reason, Jews have traditionally considered themselves the "chosen people," who bear special responsibilities because of God's special favor, including the responsibility to make ethical choices and to create a moral and just society. The covenant

BRANCHES OF JUDAISM

Judaism is as much an inherited IDENTITY and way of life as a religious system. The distinction is often made between practicing, or "religious," Jews and "cultural" Jews, who observe few if any of the Jewish religious rituals but embrace the historical lineage and shared culture of Judaism. Both culturally and spiritually, world Jewry is quite diverse. For example, in the Diaspora (dispersion) of the Jews from Palestine in the early CHRISTIAN era, two separate communities developed in Europe, each with its own cultural patterns and Hebraic dialect: the Arab-influenced, Ladino-speaking Sephardic branch, who inhabited Spain and Portugal until their expulsion in the 1490s (the word "Sephardi" means "Spaniard"), and the Yiddish-speaking Ashkenazi ("Germans"), descended from Roman-era Palestinians, who settled in central and eastern Europe.

Beginning in the 19th century, three distinct religious communities developed, with divergent views on the importance of tradition and the divinity of scripture. *Orthodox* Judaism upholds the traditional beliefs, including the doctrine that both the biblical and "oral" law are divinely inspired, and follows established ritual practices, including strict observance of the Sabbath and kosher dietary laws. *Reform* Judaism, which grew out of the ENLIGHTENMENT's scrutiny of religious doctrine under the light of RATIONALISM (see MENDELSSOHN), downplays Talmudic authority, conducts simplified worship in the vernacular language, and attaches more importance to ETHICAL standards than to ritual law, much of which it considers irrelevant in the modern world. *Conservative* Judaism stands between, accepting scriptural authority but allowing for adaptation to changing times and conditions. In the 20th century these secularizing tendencies have been extended by the Liberal branch of Reform Judaism and by the Reconstructionist movement, founded by Mordecai Kaplan, who saw Judaism not merely as a faith but as a "religious civilization" embracing all aspects of culture and community.

also promises Jews a home in the holy land (successively called Canaan, Israel, and Palestine), a hope fulfilled by the Israelites under Moses's leadership, kept alight during centuries of persecution and exile (the Diaspora), and rekindled in 20th-century ZIONISM. Biblical references to a Messiah (*mashiah*, "anointed one") were later interpreted as prophesying a savior who will reunite the Jews, vanquish their enemies, and establish God's kingdom on earth. These beliefs gave rise to CHRISTIANITY, which considers JESUS to be the Messiah.

Judaism has no organizational hierarchy and no official clergy, although rabbis—traditionally, religious teachers revered for their scholarship and wisdom—have customarily exercised authority in spiritual matters and have evolved into congregational pastors. Worship is conducted individually and communally, in the synagogue and the home. Synagogue services, emphasizing chanted prayers and readings from the Torah, are held on the Sabbath (literally, "seventh day") and other holy days, and daily in Orthodox and Conservative synagogues (see box). The annual High Holy Days of Rosh Hashanah, beginning the new year, and Yom Kippur, the Day of Atonement, mark a period of penitence, reflection, and renewed hope. The three most important Jewish festivals commemorate moments in the Israelites' exodus from slavery in Egypt: Passover (Pesach), marking the saving of the Jews from the Angel of Death, who "passed over" them; Shavuot (Shabuoth), the Feast of Weeks, or Pentecost, marking God's revelation of the TEN COMMANDMENTS to Moses; and Sukkot, the Feast of Tabernacles, recalling the huts in which the Israelites sheltered in the wilderness.

See also ESCHATOLOGY; GOD, CONCEPTS OF; HASIDISM; MAIMONIDES; ZIONISM.

Jung, Carl Gustav (1875–1961)

Swiss psychiatrist, whose post-Freudian theory of PSYCHOANALYSIS, called *analytic psychology*, stressed the positive influences of deep-seated drives, linked personal psychology to archetypal cultural patterns, and influenced 20th-century thought in many other fields, including history, religion, and the arts. Like FREUD, Jung accepted the centrality of the *libido* and the UNCONSCIOUS in the human personality, but differed and finally broke with him over their nature. Where Freud saw the libido as primarily a sex drive and regarded that impulse as fundamental to behavior, Jung considered the libido a more general life energy and sexuality as one of several motivating forces. And whereas they agreed on the basic distinction between CONSCIOUS and UNCONSCIOUS mental processes, Jung split the unconscious in two. Each of us, he said, possesses not only a *personal unconscious*, containing repressed material from our own experience, but a part of the *collective unconscious*, containing the "racial memory" of humanity.

This concept, the most widely influential of all Jung's ideas, reflected his philosophical, even MYSTICAL approach to psychology, in contrast to Freud's (and most other psychiatrists') biophysical viewpoint. To Jung, the collective unconscious is made up of the cumulative experience of all human (and even prehuman) generations, stored in the form of universal *archetypes*. The theory,

"We can never finally know. I simply believe that some part of the human Self or Soul is not subject to the laws of space and time."

—Carl Jung, quoted in 1975

which grew out of Jung's observation that patients frequently reported images in dreams that were not part of their own experience, was developed partly during anthropological field trips he took to Africa and the Americas in the 1920s. Many themes and SYMBOLS, he found, are common to many different cultures; these are expressed in art and religion as well as in myths, folklore, and fairy tales. Knowledge of them is not learned but sensed intuitively, retrieved from the storehouse of primordial cultural memory that is the collective unconscious. Archetypes include mythic figures, such as the Hero and the Wanderer, and what Jung called the "shadow"—the preconscious, animal-like side of human nature.

Consciousness, Jung said, is expressed in one's *persona,* the public face and social self. The *anima* represents the unconscious opposite of our "public" persona, the traits we hide even from ourselves because they clash with our conscious self-image; this applies particularly to our opposite-sex qualities, men's "feminine" side and women's "masculine" side (the *animus*). Many of Jung's other ideas also tend to fall into binary categories, including his famous division of personality types into *extrovert* and *introvert*—active and outgoing versus passive and self-absorbed. This pair and three other Jungian polarities—sensing/intuiting, feeling/thinking, and perceiving/judging—are gauged in the Myers-Briggs personality test, which is used extensively in education and industry to determine aptitude and performance potential.

See also PSYCHOANALYSIS.

just war

Doctrines, initially religious, that define the circumstances under which warfare is morally and legally justified and place constraints on the conduct of such a war. The CHRISTIAN just-war theory arose in the Middle Ages, when the ROMAN CATHOLIC Church began to move away from the pacifist NONVIOLENCE practiced by JESUS's early followers. The medieval doctrine addressed both the justification for going to war (*jus ad bellum*) and what constitutes justified conduct in wartime (*jus in bello*). Thomas AQUINAS specified three conditions for undertaking a war: it must be declared by a legitimate authority, it must have a just cause, and it must be conducted with upright, unselfish intent. Just causes include self-defense and the punishment of aggressors, heretics, and infidels. Jus in bello focuses largely on the notion of *proportionality*—that the use of violence be commensurate with the just purposes of the war—and on the protection of innocent noncombatants. Crusades against heretics and (especially) infidels, however, were considered *holy wars*, in which the rules of proportionality do not apply.

From its ecclesiastical origins, the just-war doctrine was developed by secular theorists, especially the 17th-century jurist Hugo Grotius, who set forth principles that have governed international relations ever since. Believing that wars between nation-STATES are inevitable, he sought to restrict their frequency and destructiveness, postulating a limited number of just causes and warning that unjust actions can invalidate a just cause. Since World War II, the just-war thesis has been challenged by critics who question its applicability in an age of nuclear DETERRENCE based on the threat of massive destruction and suggest that its requirements are so ambiguous as to supply justification for almost any war. The doctrine of jus in bello has given rise to the notion of *war crimes,* acts that violate limits set by international convention—especially violence against prisoners or civilians—even when committed while following orders.

The Islamic notion of *jihad* ("struggle") is often considered to be synonymous with "holy war." But while the concept includes violent campaigns against nonbelievers, to a greater degree it implies an internal struggle against the evil within the community and especially within the individual. Jihad of the sword (as opposed to jihad of the word or of the pen) is similar to the Western conception of holy war, in that its aim is the destruction of the enemies of ISLAM. It is traditionally a defensive doctrine, aimed only against those who would persecute Islam and permitting nonbelievers to abide peacefully within the Islamic state.

See also CONSEQUENTIALISM.

K

kabbalah (cabala)

Term applied to Jewish MYSTICISM generally, and in particular to the esoteric movement that developed in 12th- and 13th-century Spain and Provence, with roots in mystical cults of the first centuries C.E. In Hebrew the term means "received tradition," reflecting the belief that it continues an ancient line of thought. Kabbalah seeks to understand the relationship of God to his creation and, through meditation and the study of occult formulas, to approach him directly. Much of medieval kabbalistic practice was focused on the desire to experience the heavenly vision of the *merkavah,* God's chariot-throne, as described in the book of Ezekiel.

Kabbalah ascribes secret meanings to each element of scripture, which, correctly interpreted, are thought to disclose the "hidden" part of the oral law—the Talmudic injunctions considered to have been revealed to Moses. The most influential of the kabbalistic writings is the *Zohar* (*Sefer ha-zohar,* "Book of Splendor"), compiled in the 13th century by the Sephardic scholar Moses de León but conventionally attributed to the second-century mystic Rabbi Simeon bar Yohai. In it, creation is seen as a continuous process, accomplished through a series of emanations from the Godhead—the ten *sefirot,* or elemental attributes of God—which, with the 22 letters of the Hebrew alphabet, constitute the 32 divine principles or "paths" of creation. Kabbalistic literature also includes magical formularies and systems of numerology as well as reflections on angels, the transmigration of SOULS, and the Messiah, the divine emissary prophesied to reunite the Jewish people.

In the 16th century, following the expulsion of the Jews from Spain, the center of kabbalistic activity shifted to Palestine, where Isaac Luria became the leading figure. In Luria's cosmogony, creation occurred through the contraction of the Godhead, creating a void into which God infused particles of divine light, some of which shattered, releasing sparks of evil; the role of humanity is to restore cosmic harmony through prayer and obedience to the sacred law. This doctrine of restoration and redemption inspired the 17th-century messianic movement of the "False Messiah," Sabbatai Zevi (Zvi), and, together with the kabbalistic emphasis on direct experience of the divine, also influenced HASIDISM.

Kant, Immanuel (1724–1804)

German philosopher, whose critical philosophy undermined the status of metaphysics, revolutionized epistemology, and sought to provide a rational basis for ethics and aesthetics. His philosophical work was, in effect, an attempt to synthesize RATIONALISM and EMPIRICISM, which until then had been almost totally at odds. Kant's early field of study was science, in which he is best remembered for his formulation of what has become known as the Kant-Laplace hypothesis, that the solar system condensed from a nebular formation. Originally a thoroughgoing rationalist, Kant was, as he later wrote, "awakened from my dogmatic slumber" on encountering the empiricism of David HUME. Much of his subsequent work was an attempt to develop a logically coherent basis for natural science that took into account Hume's SKEPTICISM about the possibility of direct knowledge of things outside ourselves.

In the *Critique of Pure Reason* (1781), Kant set forth a new approach to EPISTEMOLOGY, in which he proposed to reconcile empirical and rational knowledge—specifically, the tension between experiential knowledge (*a posteriori* and *synthetic* judgments) and A PRIORI and *analytic* judgments, which are independent of experience. Like Hume, Kant maintained that we can have no direct knowledge of the material world, but he distinguished between the empirical—our sensory perceptions—and the TRANSCENDENTAL, which permits knowledge by virtue of the *categories of the understanding,* a set of preexisting (a priori) concepts that give order and form to experience (see box). He also differentiated the world of *phenomena,* which is perceived by the senses and interpreted by the mind, from the "thing-in-itself" (*Ding an sich*), belonging to the world of *noumena,* which is unavailable to us. In order for something to be the object of thought at all, Kant said, it must be thought of in terms of one or more of the categories. Thus experience is not a passive absorption of sensations, but the result of our own mental processes; the phenomenal world does not reveal itself to us but is revealed *by* us. Kant called this fundamental reversal of perspective "the second COPERNICAN revolution." Given these conclusions, Kant claimed, many METAPHYSICAL questions—such

KANT'S CATEGORIES
OF THE UNDERSTANDING

The 12 A PRIORI principles resident in the human mind by which we are able to structure and understand our perceptions. Together with our innate "intuitions" of *space* and *time,* they are the preconditions of experience and knowledge—without understanding, there is only meaningless sensation. The categories relate only to the *phenomenal* world of the senses; we can have no knowledge whatsoever of the *noumenal* world, the true nature of "things-in-themselves."

Kant divided his 12 categories into four groups of three, on the principle that we understand phenomena in terms of their *quantity,* the *qualities* we perceive in them, the *relations* between them, and the *modality* of the logical judgments we make about them. In each group, the third category is intended as a synthesis of the first two.

Quantity	*Quality*	*Relation*	*Modality*
Unity	Reality (Positive)	Substance/ Accident	Possibility/ Impossibility
Plurality	Negation (Negative)	Cause/Effect	Actuality/ Nonactuality (Existence/ Nonexistence)
Totality	Limitation	Reciprocity	Necessity/ Contingency

Quantity. We perceive objects that occupy space in terms of *unity* (one independent object, such as a stone), *plurality* (plural, independent but related objects, such as a pile of stones), and *totality* (an aggregate of objects as an identifiable entity, such as a stone wall).

Quality. Our perception of things is also related to how they affect us—the kind and degree of impression they make on us. In this sense, *reality* and *negation* refer to the distinctness of the impressions we receive, from absolute *(positive)* to nil *(negative),* and *limitation* refers to the range of possible sensation between the two extremes.

Relation. The idea of the relation between SUBSTANCE and *accident*—that there is a permanent, immutable basis to reality that underlies outward appearances—allows us to deal with things as if they were not transitory. *Cause and effect*—the relation between the agent of change and what is changed (see CAUSE)—is the basis of our perception of change in the physical world. Both of these relations are seen as *reciprocal*—complementary and interacting.

Modality. These are standard alternatives used in logic to analyze possible states of affairs according to the *law of the excluded middle,* that "everything is either A or not-A." They consider whether or not these states are *possible,* and if so, whether or not they are *actual,* and then whether they are *necessary* (logically inescapable) or *contingent* (admitting of other alternatives). (See box at LOGIC; RATIONALISM.)

---

as the existence of God and the SOUL, or the extent of free will—fall beyond the possibility of human knowledge. They are the proper object of faith, but not of REASON.

Kant presented his ETHICS in the *Critique of Practical Reason* (1788). He denied the ability of pure reason to prove any ethical imperative, but accepted "practical reason" as the proper authority for moral action, necessary to control our unruly passions and to guide our behavior. The centerpiece of Kant's ethics is the *categorical imperative* to behave according to an absolute principle of right ("Act as if the principle of your action were to become by your will a universal law of nature"), in contrast to the *hypothetical imperative,* in which behavior is determined by a desired outcome. This was a novel and extremely influential approach to ethics, grounded in neither supernatural nor dogmatic authority but in the rationality of the autonomous individual.

In the *Critique of Judgment* (1790), Kant set forth his AESTHETIC theory, in which he disputed the conventional view, which had prevailed since ancient times, that what we see in a beautiful object is its inherent quality of "beauty." Although we perceive beauty, and may discern the appearance of a design in nature, we can assume neither an attribute of "beauty" independent of the beautiful object nor the existence of a "designer." The beautiful is that which gives us "disinterested pleasure"—contemplative delight free from the active ordering of the understanding. The appreciation of art or natural splendor is a product of one's own judgment; its apparently universal nature is due to the universality of human nature and imagination.

Kant's social and political views were informed by his ethics. He believed in individual freedom—not license, but freedom to pursue moral "ends," liberated by reason from the constraints of desire and selfishness. Like most other ENLIGHTENMENT thinkers, he was cosmopolitan and republican, urging in *Toward Perpetual Peace* (1795) the worldwide spread of REPUBLICANISM as the only cure for war.

See also GOD, ARGUMENTS FOR; IDEALISM; INTERNATIONALISM; METAPHYSICS; PERCEPTION.

karma

In HINDUISM, BUDDHISM, and JAINISM, the sum of one's good and evil actions, carried over from one life to the next and determining whether that life is better or worse than the previous one; the word is Sanskrit for "action" or "deed." Karma is based on the idea that the world functions according to the law of CAUSE and effect; all actions have consequences and individuals must take full responsibility for their actions. It is because of karma that we are locked into *samsara*, the cycle of birth, death, and rebirth. In order to break free and attain spiritual liberation, one must work out the effects of previous bad karma without creating any more. This may be achieved by performing good works and following the law of DHARMA.

The Hindu concept of karma is used by some to explain and justify the CASTE system of social stratification; one's station is determined by the karma from previous lives. Karma is equally important in Buddhism, though the concept has been hard to reconcile with the Buddhist rejection of *atman*, the permanent, transmigrating self. In Jainism, karma is seen as subtle matter that attaches itself to the SOUL (*jiva*), which can change in size and shape depending on the weight of accumulated karma; in order to disperse past bad karma and prevent any more from accruing, one must submit to a life of austerity and NONVIOLENCE.

See also DHARMA; JAINISM.

Kepler, Johannes (1571–1630)

German astronomer, whose three laws of planetary motion improved and simplified COPERNICUS's heliocentric model of the solar system and provided the basis of NEWTON's law of universal gravitation. Kepler combined a remarkably fertile imagination with a dogged determination to subject his ideas to the rigorous tests of mathematics and experience. Many of his theories did not work out; Kepler embodies the truism that for every scientific hypothesis that bears fruit, many more do not. His successes, however—including his meticulous study of the orbit of Mars, which vastly enhanced the prediction of planetary positions, and his improvements to astronomical telescopes—laid much of the groundwork of modern astronomy.

While a student, Kepler became a Copernican, convinced that the sun is not only the center, but also the cause, of the orbits of the earth and other planets. Using primarily the observations of Danish astronomer Tycho Brahe, by far the most accurate at the time, he formulated three postulates, now known as Kepler's Laws, governing the motion of the planets. The first two laws were published in his *New Astronomy* (1609) and the third in *Harmony of the World* (1619). Kepler's first law, derived from his observation of the Martian orbit, states that planetary orbits are not perfectly circular but elliptical; this rule eliminated the remaining complexities of the Ptolemaic view of the solar system, introduced to account for circular orbits and surviving in the Copernican model. The second law describes the varying orbital velocity of planets—fastest when the planet is closest to the sun and slowest when it is farthest away—and posits a constant in that variation, stating that a line drawn from the sun to the planet will sweep out equal areas in equal times. The third law states that the farther a planet is from the sun, the longer its *period* (the time it takes to complete one orbit), and that the relationship between the two is the same for all the planets: the ratio between the square of a planet's orbital period and the cube of its average distance from the sun is a constant. While Kepler was certain that some quality of the sun was responsible for these laws, the explanation had to await Newton's clarification of the physical concepts of mass and force and formulation of the law of gravity.

Keynes, John Maynard (1883–1946)

British economist and statesman, pioneer of macroeconomic analysis, whose economic model is the standard in the field. His theories contradicted the long-held assumptions of LAISSEZ-FAIRE economics and increased the role of government in national economies in the mid-20th century. Keynes was not only an academic but a statesman. He was an advisor to the British Treasury during both world wars, attended the Versailles peace conference in 1919, and participated in the 1944 Bretton Woods conference, which established the International Monetary Fund.

The most influential of Keynes's six books on economic theory was *The General Theory of Employment, Interest, and Money,* published in 1936 during the Great Depression. In it he sought to preserve and strengthen CAPITALISM by

correcting MARKET failures and the inequities of unrestricted free-market COM-
PETITION while protecting individual RIGHTS, private property, and capitalism's
great productive capacity. Challenging the classical economic assumption
that unemployment is spurred by high real wages and interest rates, Keynes
said it is governed by *effective demand:* if wages are cut, consumer demand will
decrease, leading to a drop in business investment and a rise in unemployment. Arguing that investment is the driving force behind economic growth,
he attributed economic instability to an inconsistent rate of investment
caused by erratic, often irrational shifts in business confidence (he called
these "animal spirits"), which lead to a state of "fundamental uncertainty."
Keynes's proposal called for targeted government spending and TAXATION to
smooth out "boom-and-bust" business cycles—raising taxes and lowering interest rates to help cool inflationary trends, and cutting taxes and boosting
interest rates to stimulate investment and savings during economic recessions. It also called for policies that would ensure full employment at stable
prices, including the creation of jobs through public works programs.

Keynes's work transformed modern economic theory, and Keynesian
economics continue to dominate government policy in Western industrialized nations, especially Britain and the United States. Like classical economists and their modern heirs (see, e.g., MONETARISM; SUPPLY-SIDE ECONOMICS),
Keynesians believe that a continuous flow of investment into the economy increases both consumption and production. However, they do not believe this
happens purely through market forces; it must be supplemented, when necessary, by government spending, even at the cost of a temporary budget deficit.

See also box at SUPPLY AND DEMAND; cf. MONETARISM; SUPPLY-SIDE ECONOMICS.

Kierkegaard, Søren (1813–1855)

Danish philosopher and theologian, regarded as the founder of EXISTENTIAL-
ISM. His early writings addressed their topics indirectly, ironically, and pseudony-
mously, sometimes taking positions contrary to his own in order to expose
them. Kierkegaard had two philosophical goals: to save CHRISTIANITY from its
tendency to apply RATIONALISM to problems of faith and to undermine systematic philosophies such as HEGEL's.

To Kierkegaard, Hegel's view that human nature is guided by historical
necessity, and the comprehensive philosophical system he built to contain it,
were wrongheaded and futile. Ambiguity and uncertainty, he argued, are basic to the human situation; the world is fundamentally ABSURD, without intrinsic meaning. Existence is thus an intensely personal affair, a matter of choice
and individual responsibility that cannot be fully accounted for by any logical

system. Where Hegel pursued perfect objectivity, Kierkegaard embraced "subjective truth," holding that personal understanding, especially of revealed religion, is more important than rational explanation.

In *Either/Or* and *Fear and Trembling* (both 1843), he envisioned human existence in terms of three spheres, or stages, through which one may ascend through self-examination: the *aesthetic life*, dominated by worldly concerns; the *ethical life*, characterized by attention to duty; and the *religious life*, in which one fully accepts the absurdity of existence and makes a commitment to life and to God. Religious belief and obligation, he said, cannot be justified through REASON, but only by a "leap of faith," as illustrated by the biblical story of Abraham's willingness to sacrifice his son Isaac out of unflinching obedience to God. Such faith, freely chosen, is far more authentic than an unexamined conformity to dogma. Although Kierkegaard wished to defend Christianity and had studied for the Lutheran clergy, this analysis enraged the established church.

In *The Concept of Dread* (1844) and *The Sickness unto Death* (1849), respectively, Kierkegaard identified two overarching human conditions that arise from a realization of life's absurdity: *dread,* the profound anxiety we feel in the face of Nothingness, which can only be remedied by a conscious commitment to life; and *despair,* which takes hold when one is unable to make that commitment and simply gives in to the world's confusion.

> *"Without risk there is no faith. . . . If I am capable of grasping God objectively, I do not believe, but precisely because I cannot do this I must believe."*
> —Søren Kierkegaard,
> *Concluding Unscientific Postscript,* 1846

Kristeva, Julia (1941–)

Bulgarian-born French philosopher, PSYCHOANALYST, linguist, and critic; author of a unique and influential POSTSTRUCTURALIST synthesis of FREUDIAN psychology, STRUCTURALIST linguistics, MARXIST historical analysis, and HEGELIAN DIALECTICS. Kristeva's formative influences included her teachers Roland Barthes and Claude Lévi-Strauss, as well as the linguistics of Ferdinand de Saussure and the psychoanalytic theory of Jacques Lacan (see box at STRUCTURALISM). Though she has dissociated herself from political FEMINISM, Kristeva's analysis of the repression of "feminine" traits has fueled the feminist critique of patriarchal society.

In *Revolution in Poetic Language* (1974) and other works, Kristeva has proposed a theory of MEANING she calls "semanalysis." The system of signs that comprise language (see SEMIOTICS), she says, is not unified but split into two interconnected yet warring components, the *semiotic* and the *symbolic*. The semiotic, or "feminine," side is rooted in the child's preverbal, pre-Oedipal stage and is linked to the *chora*, the intuitive physical and psychic bond between mother and child. By contrast, the symbolic system, the voice of patriarchy, corresponding to the father's influence, is associated with CONSCIOUSNESS, order, and rationality. The semiotic state is native to both genders; conventional sex roles are created by historical, not biological, forces. Women have been oppressed by society's devaluation of the sensual, irrational qualities associated with the semiotic side, characteristics conventionally seen as typically female. The growing child (the "subject-in-process") absorbs both the semiotic and symbolic aspects—UNCONSCIOUS and conscious, body and intellect, instinct and REASON—but through socialization and LANGUAGE ACQUISITION the semiotic is largely repressed. It surfaces only in dreams and "poetic language," the elemental voice found in myths, rituals, and the arts (for Kristeva, this voice resonates particularly in the spontaneous, ABSTRACT images of avant-garde poetry). The semiotic realm is also the source of puns, rhyme, rhythm, and *jouissance*—playfulness and uninhibited pleasure. A DIALECTICAL tension persists within the individual; on one side is the desire to reclaim one's "feminine" aspect, on the other is the "law of the Father," which associates the female (maternal) body with blood and contamination. This tension, says Kristeva, can be resolved only by a revolutionary transformation of the dominant social discourse, which now segregates the symbolic and semiotic spheres and gives one supremacy over the other.

Kuhn, Thomas See PARADIGM

L

Lacan, Jacques See box at STRUCTURALISM

Laffer curve See box at SUPPLY-SIDE ECONOMICS

laissez-faire

Economic policy holding that the economy works best when MARKETS are able to operate without interference from the government. The idea formed the basis of economic LIBERALISM in the 18th and 19th centuries. From the French phrase *laissez faire, laissez passer*—"let things happen and proceed as they will"—the concept was developed by the 18th-century French economists known as Physiocrats, led by François Quesnay. The Physiocrats, who are credited with developing the first systematic economic theory, believed that all social (including economic) activity is guided by NATURAL LAW and guarded by natural RIGHTS, which no government can command; the workings of the market should therefore be left to follow their natural course.

Many of the Physiocrats' ideas were adopted by Adam SMITH, who argued that the cumulative buying and selling decisions of individuals acting in their own self-interest will lead to the most efficient use of resources, maximize national as well as personal wealth, and enhance social progress. Government's role, Smith said, is not to intervene directly in the marketplace, as it did under the prevailing MERCANTILIST system, but simply to guarantee free-market conditions. However, he also granted that some economic functions, such as central banking, postal service, national defense, and public works, are the province of government rather than private enterprise—an exception conceded by most free-market proponents ever since.

Laissez-faire thinking prompted many European countries, especially Britain, to amend their economic policies in the late 18th century by removing commercial controls and dropping protectionist trade laws. In the United States, laissez-faire became almost an article of faith. Virtually unrestricted economic activity resulted in giant monopolies, especially in the railroad and oil industries. Beginning in the 1880s, antitrust legislation and other worker- and consumer-protection laws ended unchecked entrepreneurship (see PROGRESSIVISM).

Today, no country operates under a pure laissez-faire system; government intervenes in CAPITALIST economies in any number of ways, from environmental and safety regulations to central-bank interest rates. The belief that unregulated enterprise will spontaneously contribute to social betterment lost influence during the Great Depression of the 1930s, and the term "laissez-faire" is rarely used in modern economics. However, its legacy is felt in continuing debates among economists about the validity of perfect COMPETITION, the efficiency and morality of market forces, and other issues, as well in *neoclassical* theories such as MONETARISM and SUPPLY-SIDE ECONOMICS.

See also SMITH; cf. KEYNES.

Lamarckism

A theory of biological EVOLUTION, now discredited, which held that an organism's response to environmental pressures results in morphological changes and that these acquired characteristics can be inherited. It was developed by the French biologist Jean-Baptiste Lamarck (1744–1829). In Lamarck's view, living things have adapted and evolved in a continual struggle toward increasing complexity. In this struggle, anatomical changes occur in individual organisms as the result of extensive use (or disuse) of an organ, limb, or other feature in response to the demands of their environment—a development that Lamarck believed occurred through an act of will. A classic example is the explanation that the giraffe's neck became elongated through stretching ever higher to eat the leaves of trees. Conversely, if a part suffers prolonged disuse, it will diminish, which would account for the vestigial wings of flightless birds such as the kiwi and the penguin. These elaborations and alterations are then passed on to the offspring, enabling them in turn to adapt more efficiently to the requirements of habitat. Lamarck termed his principle of inheritable characteristics "acquired variation."

Lamarck's theory, published in the early 1800s, did not seek to explain the origin of species—which he ultimately assigned to divine agency—but only development and variation within species. Nonetheless, his ideas greatly influenced the evolutionary theories of subsequent generations of natural scientists, including Charles DARWIN. Indeed, it was not until the late 19th century that Lamarckism began to be seriously controverted. In the 1880s, the German biologist August Weismann expounded his *germ plasm theory*, holding that certain cells contain hereditary material that is passed on to offspring but cannot be affected by any changes in the body's other cells. Weismann's theory, while incorrect in detail, was influential in spurring research into genetics. The genetic principle of inheritance was further substantiated with the rediscovery in 1900 of the work of Gregor Mendel (see EVOLUTION), which had been ignored for 35 years, and was confirmed in the 1950s with the discovery of the structure of DNA (see CENTRAL DOGMA). However, a version of Lamarckism advanced by the Soviet biologist Trofim Lysenko became official policy in the USSR for a time in the 1940s and '50s. Lysenko's theory, which denied genetic inheritance, was attractive in Stalinist Russia because it bolstered the notion that the revolutionary SOCIALIST environment was creating a superior breed of people.

language acquisition

The traditional notion that children acquire their native language simply by hearing and imitating the speech of their elders has been overtaken in the second half of the 20th century by ideas derived primarily from the theoretical linguistics of Noam CHOMSKY. Contemporary language acquisition theory seeks to resolve two major problems in the conventional view: the *poverty of the stimulus*—all the incorrect, incomplete, and contradictory usage heard by a toddler—and the *projection problem*—how a finite and limited amount of data is "projected" into a complete knowledge of grammar that can be used to create an infinite variety of sentences. An infant learning a spoken language purely by hearing everyday speech has been compared to someone trying to learn the rules and strategies of chess simply by watching it being played—a chess game, moreover, in which, unbeknownst to the observer, some of the moves are illegal (ungrammatical). It is virtually impossible to deduce the logic behind all the moves from the data available. To overcome this problem, Chomsky posited a "universal GRAMMAR," an innate COGNITIVE structure that would account for the ease and accuracy of language acquisition by very young children, although both nature and nurture also seem to play a role.

One concept that supports the Chomskian theory is the *critical period,* a window of time in early childhood during which native fluency is quickly acquired and after which children's extreme facility in acquiring a language is lost or diminished. This would indicate that the acquisition of language, like the acquisition of teeth, is a genetically determined part of the growth process. Other evidence pointing to the role of apparently innate factors in language development includes the *order of acquisition* of sounds and common *error patterns* in pronunciation and usage—developmental patterns that seem to be independent of children's individual abilities and their environment, but which are consistent with the theory of universal grammar.

See also CHOMSKY; GRAMMAR.

Leibniz, Gottfried Wilhelm von (1646–1716)

German philosopher, mathematician, historian, and statesman, regarded in his own time as a brilliant polymath and still considered one of the great LO-GICIANS. As a consummate RATIONALIST, Leibniz sought to apply mathematical principles to all fields of thought. He invented the calculus independently of NEWTON and developed what became its standard system of notation. His legal expertise and mastery of statecraft were such that he was given an audience at every court in Europe, including the Vatican, where he advanced his ideas for reconciling ROMAN CATHOLICISM and PROTESTANTISM.

In philosophy, Leibniz is best known for his optimistic natural theology, propounded in the *Theodicy* (1710), and for his theory of monads, distilled in his *Monadology* (1714). Leibniz postulated, as the basis of all physical and spiritual SUBSTANCE, an irreducible, indestructible, independent center of force he called the *monad* (meaning "unit"; cf. ATOMISM). Each monad possesses its own degree and kind of force, and a corresponding degree and kind of perception; it is also a more or less imperfect microcosm, "mirroring" the universe as a whole. Monads, self-contained and self-motivating, do not interact—they are, as Leibniz put it, "windowless"—but their activities are coordinated according to a divine "preestablished harmony," like perfectly synchronized clocks ticking in unison. Higher beings, including humans, are colonies of monads, directed by a ruling monad, or *entelechy*. The human soul, for instance, is sovereign over the monads that constitute the body.

The preestablished harmony of the universe is beyond the comprehension of humans, who cannot understand, for instance, how evil and suffering fit into the divine plan. According to Leibniz's *principle of sufficient reason*, whatever happens or exists does so only if there are sufficient grounds for it to be so, and if there are, it *must* occur. Reconciling God's benevolence and omnipotence, Leibniz concluded that since God could have created any logically consistent universe, this one—the one he chose to make—must be the best of all *possible* worlds, however imperfect. This conclusion, and Leibniz himself, were famously satirized in VOLTAIRE's *Candide* (1759) in the philosophy of the preposterously UTOPIAN Dr. Pangloss, "Everything is for the best in this best of all possible worlds."

See also MIND/BODY PROBLEM; RATIONALISM; VOLTAIRE.

leisure class See box at CLASS

Lenin, Vladimir Ilyich (1870–1924)

Russian revolutionary theorist and politician, leader of the Bolshevik revolution and founder of Soviet COMMUNISM. A convert to MARXISM during his student days, when he was exiled to Siberia for RADICAL activities, he developed a revisionist interpretation of Marxian theory and a practical approach to revolutionary organization.

Contrary to MARX's vision of revolution waged by a proletariat with a highly developed revolutionary consciousness, Lenin maintained, in *What Is to Be Done?* (1902), that a disorganized working class must be led by a "vanguard" of educated professional revolutionaries who act on behalf of the masses through a disciplined party organization. Disagreements over this policy contributed to a split between Lenin's Bolshevik ("majority") faction and the Menshevik ("minority") wing of the Russian Social Democratic Party. While Lenin and TROTSKY were initially at odds over this and other matters of theory and practice, Lenin eventually came to agree with Trotsky on two key points: that revolution could occur in a developing country such as Russia, not just in industrialized Europe, as Marx had predicted, and that a successful revolution must be "permanent"—international in scope and ongoing within each revolutionary STATE. In *Imperialism, the Highest Stage of Capitalism* (1916), Lenin saw World War I as part of the death throes of CAPITALISM, as its insatiable hunger for new markets bred IMPERIALIST rivalries and self-destructive wars between the capitalist powers.

After the February Revolution of 1917 that deposed the Russian czar, Lenin opposed the "bourgeois" provisional government, insisting that all power reside with the *soviets,* or local workers' councils. In this period he wrote the pamphlet *State and Revolution,* in which he justified the violent overthrow of the oppressive "bourgeois state" and envisioned a DEMOCRATIC workers' state, in which private enterprise would gradually give way to socialism and eventually to "full communism" when the state itself would have withered away. As head of the new Soviet state after the October Revolution, Lenin formed a government that acknowledged opposition parties; later, faced with internal crises and external threats, he instituted one-party rule under the doctrine of *democratic centralism*. That policy provided for the election of each body in the Communist Party hierarchy by the membership of the one below it, and encouraged free discussion of policy matters under consideration; however, once something was decided by the central authority it was to be accepted without question. After Lenin's death "Marxism-Leninism," the official Soviet doctrine under Stalin, purported to reflect Lenin's interpretation of Marx's thought but distorted both to justify Stalin's dictatorial rule and enforce party discipline.

See also COMMUNISM; IMPERIALISM AND COLONIALISM.

Leonardo da Vinci (1452–1519)

Italian painter, sculptor, scientist, architect, inventor, and engineer; the epitome of the "Renaissance man," whose protean interests and innovative conceptions, incorporating ideas from a wide range of disciplines, were unified by a vision of art and science as inseparable elements of the quest to understand nature and humanity. All his life Leonardo kept notebooks detailing his studies and theories, as well as the plans for his many (mostly unfinished) projects. His artistic innovations had an immediate and lasting impact, but his scientific work—much of which anticipated modern discoveries, such as the airplane—was so far ahead of its time that it was not appreciated until long after his death.

Leonardo was trained as an artist and always considered that his profession, although his output of paintings was quite small (fewer than 20 survive) and he never completed a sculptural or architectural commission. Among his contributions to painting were atmospheric (or aerial) perspective, in which a receding background becomes progressively hazier, and *sfumato*, the creation of a "smoky" effect through subtle gradations of color; both techniques are exemplified in his portrait *Mona Lisa*.

Leonardo's obsessive striving to understand the workings of the natural world—born of an insatiable curiosity as well as the desire to perfect his artistic technique—led him to the study of mechanics, anatomy, optics, hydraulics, geology, mathematics, and many other disciplines. He designed war machines (including armored vehicles, portable bridges, and artillery), planned an ideal city, and conceived of flying machines based on bird flight and other aerodynamic principles. His anatomical studies encompassed geometry as well as physiology, as illustrated by his famous drawing of the ideally proportioned man within a square and circle; he dissected cadavers to discover not just their structure but their organic functioning, an undertaking never before so precisely observed and documented. Leonardo regarded painting not as a craft but as a science, superior to the arts of music, poetry, and sculpture, that synthesized ideas from many realms to create an envisioned world based on the visible world.

Lévi-Strauss, Claude See box at STRUCTURALISM

liberalism

Political, social, and economic doctrine that in its classic construction emphasized individual FREEDOM, limited government, gradual social PROGRESS, and LAISSEZ-FAIRE commerce, and in its modern incarnation favors STATE involvement in social WELFARE and economic policy while upholding personal liberty and opportunity. The term has the same root as "liberty" and implies freedom of conscience and action. Liberalism developed in the early 19th century as the IDEOLOGY of the emerging middle class of merchants and entrepreneurs. It had its intellectual basis in the political philosophy of John LOCKE, the ENLIGHTENMENT faith in human progress and RATIONALISM, the free-MARKET economic theories of Adam SMITH, and the UTILITARIANISM of Jeremy Bentham and John Stuart MILL. Locke's REPUBLICANISM and other liberal ideals played a significant part in the founding of the American republic.

Nineteenth-century liberals advocated religious tolerance, INDIVIDUALISM, and self-reliance, sought moderate political and social reforms (in England, the franchise was extended to include all male property holders), and viewed poverty as a moral failing. Liberal policies have been historically identified in England with the Liberal Party and in the United States with the Democratic Party, both of which were formed in the 1830s (see WHIGS AND TORIES).

In the 1930s, President Franklin Roosevelt resurrected and redefined the term "liberalism" to describe his New Deal programs, calling it "a changed concept of the duty and responsibility of government toward economic life." In this interpretation of liberalism, government is seen as the guarantor of individual rights and freedoms through the regulation of economic and social policy to check the excesses of CAPITALISM and provide a "safety net" against poverty (see WELFARE).

The 20th-century brand of political liberalism is sometimes labeled "neoliberalism." That term is also applied to economic policies for developing countries that emphasize free markets and FREE TRADE, as opposed to economic planning and protection of domestic industries. In international relations, the term refers to policies that favor reliance on international institutions, rather than on the traditional tools of power politics, to address global problems (cf. REALISM).

See also DEMOCRACY and box; INDIVIDUALISM; LOCKE; MILL; cf. CONSERVATISM.

liberation theology

ROMAN CATHOLIC movement that stresses social and political action on behalf of the poor and oppressed. Originating in Latin America, it grew out of a MARXIST-influenced analysis that attributed chronic urban and rural poverty to oligarchical institutions and CAPITALIST economic exploitation, and faulted the church for condoning that system instead of taking the side of its victims. Priests such as the Brazilian Leonard Boff and the Peruvian Gustavo Gutiérrez, author of the seminal *Theology of Liberation* (1971), argued for an activist gospel based on JESUS's defense of the poor, his denunciation of the rich and powerful, and his insistence on the EQUALITY of all in God's eyes. They sought to put abstract theology into political action, recasting concepts such as salvation and the kingdom of God in temporal terms—liberation and a just society. The movement grew through the formation of *base communities,* small groups of activists who combined Bible study with social organizing to meet the basic needs of local people. The movement's popular appeal proved deeply threatening to political authorities; in 1980, one outspoken cleric, Archbishop Oscar Romero of El Salvador, was murdered in his church by government agents. The program of liberation theology was endorsed by the Latin American Episcopal Conference of bishops in 1968 and 1979 but was initially resisted by the Vatican, which mistrusted its SOCIALIST ideals and gagged some of its spokesmen. More recently the church has hesitantly embraced its principles.

Liberation theology's central message, that religious doctrine must be linked to people's actual experience, has spread beyond Catholicism and inspired other social-change movements throughout the world. For example, in Korea, *minjung* ("poor-people") theology uses indigenous folktales to teach self-liberation. In the United States, *black theology* reads the Bible in terms of African and African-American experience and preaches emancipation from RACISM and white cultural paradigms.

libertarianism

Twentieth-century social and political theory, primarily American, stressing INDIVIDUALISM, limited government, and uninhibited free-market CAPITALISM. Libertarians advance the LOCKEAN notion of the individual's inalienable right to life, liberty, and property, holding that each person has the sovereign right to live in any way he or she pleases as long as the equal right of others is not violated. Drawing on Adam SMITH's theory that economic competition free of government control creates an optimal allocation of material and social resources, they insist that the STATE, if it exists at all, should be no more than a "night watchman." In this view, government's only legitimate role is to ensure protection of individuals' rights and safety, to enforce valid contracts, and to provide for the national defense. By the same token, TAXATION of any kind is considered coercion; public services should be privatized and paid for by those who use them.

The ideological foundations of libertarianism are found primarily in 19th-century ANARCHIST thought and in classical and new classical economics, including the LAISSEZ-FAIRE philosophy of Austrian economists Ludwig von Mises and Friedrich von Hayek, who contended, in *The Road to Serfdom* (1944), that economic planning would lead to TOTALITARIANISM. Among American academics, the most prominent libertarian thinker is Robert Nozick, whose *Anarchy, State, and Utopia* (1974) affirmed the principle that government be limited to the protection of persons and property and argued that any attempt to regulate economic activity is unjust. The libertarian emphasis on rational self-interest is echoed in the works of the novelist Ayn Rand, whose philosophy of *objectivism* asserts the moral right and duty of the sovereign individual to live for him- or herself and not be subject to others' will or purposes.

See also ANARCHISM; THOREAU.

Locke, John (1632–1704)

English philosopher and political theorist, the leading figure in British EMPIRICISM, whose political theories helped lay the foundations of liberal democracy (see box at DEMOCRACY); his ideas were reflected in the American Declaration of Independence (see JEFFERSON) and the U.S. Constitution. Trained in science and medicine as well as philosophy, Locke was influenced by the thinking of the Scientific Revolution; his EPISTEMOLOGICAL theories were aimed at "removing some of the rubbish which lies in the way to knowledge."

In his *Essay Concerning Human Understanding* (1690), Locke identified experience as the source of knowledge (cf. INNATE IDEAS). The mind, he said, is at birth a *tabula rasa,* or "blank slate," on which the world of experience gradually imprints itself in a series of discrete sensations—a theory known as *mental atomism* (see ATOMISM). The mind, filled and active, organizes experience logically, through the *association of ideas,* to arrive at knowledge; through introspection one gains CONSCIOUSNESS of self. Locke's empiricism was not so

PRIMARY AND SECONDARY QUALITIES

The distinction between the qualities in objects that are, respectively, independent of and dependent on the perspective of the observer is an ancient one. It goes back at least to the Greek philosopher Democritus, and was espoused by GALILEO and NEWTON, but it is primarily associated with LOCKE, who treated it in his *Essay Concerning Human Understanding* (1690). Primary qualities, such as shape and motion, are independent of our experience of them; secondary qualities, such as color and taste, depend on our individual perceptions. Locke's important contribution to the concept was to see secondary qualities as actual attributes of the perceived object rather than mere fleeting sensations, as most previous thinkers had. While Locke was an EMPIRICIST, he was not a PHENOMENALIST; he saw a world composed of real things, of which we sense two kinds of qualities. *Primary* qualities (e.g., shape, hardness, position, number) are actually present within an object and are not easily divorced from it. *Secondary* qualities are those that have the power to produce a sensation in the observer (e.g., color, scent, taste, sound). This distinction has become not only an important point in philosophy but a familiar way of understanding the world—that is, in terms of what is independent of us and what is dependent on our interaction with it.

comprehensive as to give no role to REASON, or, for that matter, to God. He insisted that only what conforms to reason can be considered knowledge; furthermore, he affirmed the truth of divine revelation, which requires the use of reason to recognize it as the authentic word of God.

Locke's political theory was outlined in his *Two Treatises on Government* (1690), written in defense of the Glorious Revolution of 1688 that established the SOVEREIGNTY of the British parliament over the monarch. In the *Treatises* he attacked the notion of the divine right of kings (see ABSOLUTISM) and proposed a constitutional monarchy based on the SOCIAL CONTRACT. The STATE, he said, is created by the will of the people, who retain sovereignty by virtue of their God-given RIGHTS: life, liberty, and property. (Locke's definition of property is unclear, and it is debated whether it was intended to extend democracy or limit the franchise.) If the state abuses its power, it may at any time be modified or overthrown.

Locke advocated a system of *checks and balances* between the legislative and executive branches of government, called for religious tolerance (but not for ROMAN CATHOLICS, whose loyalty he saw as divided between church and state), and defined the primary duty of government as protecting property. Private property, he held, derives from individuals' improvement of God's gift of the earth to men in common, and such improvements account for almost all of the earth's value. People are therefore entitled to only as much property as they can productively use—a restriction, however, from which money was exempted.

"New opinions are always suspected, and usually opposed, without any other reason but because they are not already common."
—John Locke,
Essay Concerning Human Understanding

See also box; CONSCIOUSNESS; EMPIRICISM; IDEAS; IDENTITY; LIBERALISM; NATURAL LAW; RIGHTS; SOCIAL CONTRACT; STATE.

logic

The study of what constitutes valid reasoning; one of the five classical fields of philosophical inquiry (see also AESTHETICS; EPISTEMOLOGY; ETHICS; METAPHYSICS). Logic is essentially the search for a method by which valid and consistent reasoning can be distinguished from invalid, inconsistent reasoning.

Formal logic began with ARISTOTLE, who, although he did not use the term (which derives from the Greek word LOGOS), is considered the first to organize the laws of reasoning (see box). Aristotle arranged the world in *categories,* which yielded knowledge by identifying the common qualities of different entities. From this flowed the *syllogism,* in which, given two premises, a certain conclusion (inference) necessarily follows (see DEDUCTION AND INDUCTION). The classic Aristotelian example is "All men are mortal; Socrates is a man; therefore Socrates is mortal." Syllogistic logic is also called *predicate logic* because it works by correlating a subject (Socrates) with possible predicates (man, mortal).

After Aristotle, the basic structure of logic was fixed for the next two thousand years, with few major challenges. In the 17th century, DESCARTES and others sought to minimize, if not overturn, the dominance of syllogistic logic, which was embodied in the strict FORMALISM of the medieval SCHOLASTIC philosophers and their failure to question assumptions. EMPIRICISTS such as Francis BACON advocated experience and induction as actually *creating* knowledge over the syllogistic reiteration of what is implicit in the definition.

Since the mid-19th century, Aristotelian logic has gradually been usurped

ARISTOTLE'S LAWS OF THOUGHT

First formulated by ARISTOTLE, the tautologies that form a cornerstone of classical LOGIC. Though they were not so called by Aristotle, the three interrelated precepts are commonly known as the laws (or principles) of *identity, noncontradiction* (or contradiction), and the *excluded middle,* and conventionally expressed thus: A is A; what is A cannot be not-A; everything is either A or not-A. For example, what is true is true; what is true cannot be false; a statement is either true or false.

Even Aristotle considered the law of the excluded middle somewhat shaky—what about statements concerning future conditions, such as "We will win tomorrow's battle"? Although such statements imply an unspoken "It's my opinion that . . ." (thus conforming them to the true-false test), the excluded middle is still considered questionable by logicians. In the modern era, other logical axioms have been proposed as being equally important to the foundation of logic as the original laws of thought. These include LEIBNIZ's principle of *sufficient reason,* that nothing occurs or exists without sufficient reason for it to be that way and not another.

by what is now called *symbolic logic.* The mathematician George Boole is credited with beginning this process. In his *Laws of Thought* (1854), Boole sought to place reasoning on the same logical footing as mathematics. In what has come to be called Boolean algebra, he attacked the imprecision of language, and therefore of MEANING, by representing logical statements with algebraic symbols. His reductive method was aimed at ultimately rendering all statements as purely "true" or "false"—or, stated algebraically, 1 or 0. This binary system turned out to be quite influential: it is the basis of the logic that runs computers.

Boole's approach was given a mirror image by Gottlob Frege, who attempted to create a "universal calculus" based on the laws of logic, which would contain all mathematical (or at least all arithmetical) statements. Contradictions discovered in his system led to Kurt Gödel's *incompleteness theorem,* which demonstrated the impossibility of proving all true statements. However, thanks largely to Frege, Bertrand RUSSELL, and Alfred North Whitehead, logic today deals primarily with the analysis of propositions and connective terms, and emphasizes the attainment of clarity by means of "formal languages" with mathematical rules and precise definitions.

See also A PRIORI/A POSTERIORI; ANALYTIC PHILOSOPHY; AQUINAS; ARISTOTLE; ATOMISM; DIALECTIC; FORMALISM; box at KANT; LEIBNIZ; LOGICAL POSITIVISM; MEANING; MILL; PHENOMENALISM; RATIONALISM; REASON; RUSSELL; SET THEORY; UNIVERSALS; WITTGENSTEIN.

logical positivism

Philosophical position derived from POSITIVISM that sought to apply the principles of LOGIC, mathematics, and EMPIRICAL science to all fields of thought. It was developed in the 1920s and '30s by a group of philosophers and scientists known as the Vienna Circle, including Rudolf Carnap, Moritz Schlick, and Kurt Gödel, who were influenced by the PHENOMENALISM of Ernst Mach and WITTGENSTEIN's picture theory of language. The approach was later popularized by the English philosopher A. J. Ayer.

The logical positivists maintained that all intellectual inquiry should be held to the same standards as scientific investigation. Paramount in this conception was the principle of VERIFIABILITY, which states that for a proposition to be meaningful, it must be not only logically consistent but susceptible to empirical verification—not necessarily proven, but at least able to be tested. By this criterion, all METAPHYSICAL, religious, and ETHICAL statements were banished as unverifiable and therefore meaningless; only what can be evaluated scientifically was considered significant. The verification principle was almost immediately assailed as unverifiable itself and therefore meaningless by its own definition. But despite criticisms, logical positivism was widely influential through midcentury. In the 1930s Karl Popper proposed *falsifiability* as a more useful standard of investigation than verifiability. Only if a theory can, in principle, be *disproved*, he said, can it be considered scientific. (See VERIFIABILITY AND FALSIFIABILITY.)

See also EMPIRICISM; POSITIVISM; WITTGENSTEIN.

logos

Greek term meaning, variously, "word," "reason," "speech," "discourse," and "principle"; a central concept in ancient Greek philosophy and later religious thought. While it has been used in a variety of contexts, logos usually refers in some way to a power that brings the world into order. Thus, the words according to which the world was gathered from chaos into *cosmos* (order) constitute the logos.

Heraclitus, one of the first to use the term, associated logos, the active, creative principle, ever-moving and changing, with the ELEMENT fire. Later, in the philosophies of Anaxagoras, ARISTOTLE, and others, *nous,* the world mind or universal intelligence, replaced logos as the motivating principle. The STO-ICS revived Heraclitus's concept and added the idea of the *logos spermatikos,* the seed of creation and development that spread spontaneously throughout the universe. Here logos becomes REASON, the mind of God that not only or-ders the world but imparts rational intelligence to humankind.

With the Hellenic Jewish philosopher Philo, logos assumed the meaning of a governing plan, God's blueprint for the world. The opening verse of St. John's Gospel—"In the beginning was the Word, and the Word was with God, and the Word was God"—reflects the conception of logos as something divine in and of itself, and leads to the identification of JESUS Christ as the Word in-carnate. However, CHRISTIAN theologians continue to disagree as to whether God and the Word (logos) are synonymous, analogous, or distinct.

See also HIERARCHY OF BEING; STOICISM.

Lorde, Audre See box at FEMINISM

Lukács, Georg (1885–1971)

Hungarian political philosopher and literary critic, a controversial Marxist theorist who had a major impact on Western MARXISM, notably the Frankfurt School of CRITICAL THEORY. His life and work reveal an often contradictory tension between a principled challenge to Marxist orthodoxy and a resolute loyalty to the COMMUNIST Party as the authentic revolutionary vehicle. His HU-MANISTIC interpretation of MARX and rejection of "scientific" Marxism repeat-edly cast him out of favor with Soviet officialdom—more than once he was obliged to recant his writings—but he has also been widely criticized in the West for condoning the Stalinist terror, which he considered an unfortunate but inevitable stage in the revolution.

Lukács's most significant contributions to literary theory, *Soul and Form* (1910) and *The Theory of the Novel* (1916), were written before he became a Communist in 1918 and reflect the sociological influence of his teachers Georg Simmel and Max WEBER. His AESTHETIC, nonetheless, was thoroughly Marxist; he viewed works of art as products of the social and economic cir-cumstances within which they are created and as expressions of their creators' IDEOLOGY. A champion of literary REALISM, he condemned the "art for art's sake" stance of AESTHETICISM and the detached MODERNISM of Kafka and Joyce.

But he was just as skeptical of SOCIALIST REALISM, insisting that proletarian artists must struggle critically with social issues, not merely act as instruments of party orthodoxy.

In his major work of political theory, *History and Class Consciousness* (1923), Lukács reconnected Marxism to the HEGELIAN dialectic and repudiated the historical DETERMINISM of prevailing Marxist thought. He dismissed the POSITIVIST claim that the methods of natural science can be applied to social analysis, on the grounds that the nature of human CONSCIOUSNESS involves volition and choice. Most influentially, he revived Marx's notion of *reification,* the process within CAPITALIST society that makes people relate to commodities as if the objects were independent of the complex social processes and individuals' labor that produced them. This process turns social relations into relations with objects, or *commodity fetishism,* a symptom of the *false consciousness* that pervades bourgeois society and creates ALIENATION, the split between existence and understanding that separates people from their essential natures. It also obscures and fragments the *totality* of existence, which only dialectical analysis can capture. To Lukács, both modern society and Marxism itself were guilty of reification, the latter because the doctrine of DIALECTICAL MATERIALISM assumed that history is governed by objective, unchanging laws, not people. The DIALECTIC, he argued, works through *praxis*—the unity of theory and practice—to "demystify" the working-class consciousness that has been dazed by capitalism.

Luther, Martin (1483–1546)

German theologian, principal instigator of the PROTESTANT Reformation, on whose teachings the Lutheran Church is founded (see box at PROTESTANTISM). His theology consisted of three central doctrines: that the SOUL's salvation is justified by the grace of God through faith alone, that holy scripture is the sole authority in matters of faith, and that the individual may approach the divine without the intercession of clergy ("the priesthood of all believers"). These principles contradicted prime tenets of ROMAN CATHOLIC creed, which emphasized salvation through "good works," pastoral authority in matters of theology and worship, and especially the infallibility of the Pope. Luther, an AUGUSTINIAN monk and professor of biblical theology, launched the Reformation with his protest against a symptom of the corruption that infected the Catholic Church. His Ninety-Five Theses, which he issued in 1517 (according to legend, by nailing them to the door of his local church), condemned the practice of selling indulgences—grants of merit and remission of sin—and denied both their efficacy and the Pope's authority to grant

> *"Reason is the greatest enemy that faith has; it never comes to the aid of spiritual things, but . . . struggles against the divine Word, treating with contempt all that emanates from God."*
>
> —Martin Luther,
> *Table Talk,* 1569

them. Although he desired reform, not schism, by 1520 Luther was in open revolt against the papacy, publishing a number of sermons and treatises critical of Catholic doctrine, and was excommunicated.

In Luther's teaching, "scripture alone" reveals God's truth, and is therefore the only authoritative source of Christian doctrine and practice, and "faith alone" can bring the sinner to God's mercy. God reveals himself to humans in palpable, not abstract ways—through the incarnation of JESUS, the words of the Bible, the bread and wine of the Eucharist (see box at CHRISTIANITY). God is comprehended not through REASON but through trust in Christ's bounty, and is served not only by formal worship but in daily life. Seeking to make religious devotions accessible to all, Luther simplified the liturgy, translated the New Testament from Latin into German, composed popular hymns, and wrote the *Small Catechism* (1528), which set out his creed in elementary terms. Luther's theology, summarized in the Augsburg Confession (1530–31) but never systematically expounded in his voluminous writings, was standardized in the Formula of Concord (1577), which still guides Lutheran worship.

Luxemburg, Rosa (1871–1919)

Polish-born German MARXIST revolutionary activist and theorist, an advocate of democratic SOCIALISM and mass proletarian action, and a critic of Soviet COMMUNIST elitism and bureaucratic centralism. She was a tireless organizer and pamphleteer, and her influence stems as much from the example of her life as from the inspiration of her ideas. Her motto, "Doubt all," guaranteed that she would clash with many of the leading figures of the international Left. She was repeatedly jailed for her RADICAL activities and writings and was murdered by German soldiers after participating in an abortive workers' uprising.

Soon after moving to Germany in 1898, Luxemburg became embroiled in the so-called revisionist controversy within the German Social Democratic Party over the direction of socialism. In answer to Eduard Bernstein, who claimed that socialism could be pursued gradually through parliamentary reforms and trade-union pressure, she wrote in *Social Reform or Revolution?*

(1899) that socialism could come about only through revolution. In a bourgeois STATE, she believed, parliamentary DEMOCRACY was a fraud intended to perpetuate the status quo, and trade unions alone would not be able to overcome the basic economic factors that governed the wage system. In *Mass Strike, Party, and Trade Unions* (1906), she argued that mass agitation was the key to successful revolution, predicting that the general strike—spontaneous, independent, and worker-controlled—would be the decisive instrument of revolutionary struggle, simultaneously organizing, educating, and empowering the working CLASS.

Luxemburg's major theoretical work, *The Accumulation of Capital* (1913), viewed IMPERIALISM as the result of CAPITALISM's ravenous hunger for new MARKETS, which led it to expand relentlessly around the globe; eventually, after exhausting its capacity for growth, it would collapse. Luxemburg saw the outbreak of World War I as a symptom of imperialist competition and broke with the Social Democrats over their support of it. With Karl Liebknecht, she founded the Spartacus League (named for the Roman gladiator who led a slave rebellion in the first century B.C.E.), which became the nucleus of the postwar German Communist Party. She was imprisoned during most of the war, writing passionately and voluminously from her cell. Released during the revolution that swept Germany in the war's aftermath, she began agitating to turn the Weimar government onto a socialist path. She hailed the Russian Revolution of 1917, but, as a lifelong advocate of mass participation in decision making, objected to LENIN's centralization and bureaucratization of party control.

See also IMPERIALISM AND COLONIALISM.

M

Machiavelli, Niccolò (1469–1527)

Italian political theorist, diplomat, historian, and author, widely regarded as the first modern political thinker and the prime exponent of political REALISM. Machiavelli applied what he called a "SCIENTIFIC METHOD" to his interpretation of history and government, using experience (including his own experience as a diplomat for the Florentine city-state) to see things realistically, rather than as they "ought" to be.

He is associated above all with the ideas expressed in his treatise *The Prince*, written during an exile in 1512–13 after Florence was taken over by the Medici family, but not published until 1532. In it he advises that to be successful, a ruler must "learn how not to be good," using false appearances, violence, and immoral methods when necessary. This position inspired the term "Machiavellian," describing a politics that uses deception, manipulation, and corruption to achieve expedient ends. (His first name was the source of a nickname for the Devil, Old Nick.)

But Machiavelli was more complex than his popular stereotype. Central to his thinking was the pairing of *fortuna* and *virtù*. *Fortuna* (fortune) is the play of circumstance, the unexpected. *Virtù* is the ability to adapt to fickle fortune, to turn a bad situation to one's advantage; the term implies not only virtue but also skill, strength, and boldness. The wise prince will seek to keep his subjects satisfied and obedient—through benevolence if possible but through fear if necessary—and will ultimately be judged not by his actions but by their results. In his *Discourses on the First Ten Books of Livy*, written around the same time as *The Prince* but also published posthumously, Machiavelli espoused a REPUBLICAN form of government with a SEPARATION OF POWERS between the prince, the nobility, and the people. The aim of government, he said, is the common good, which is expressed in the people's happiness, and it is the people's verdict that vindicates a ruler's sometimes ruthless actions. In Machiavelli's cyclical view of history, every STATE will eventually decline; a durable government is one that has the *virtù* to postpone the inevitable for as long as possible. Once decay sets in, the republic must be remade under the guidance of a new prince.

Not only decline, but war, is inevitable, and delay will only benefit the enemy. The republic must therefore be aggressive and expansionist. In *On the Art of War* (1520), Machiavelli advocated conscription instead of the mercenary army common in his time. Soldiers who are fighting not for profit but for their homeland, he argued, are more reliable and more fearsome. Though he failed to organize a conscripted army in Florence, his ideas were adopted to great effect by Napoleon and CLAUSEWITZ in the 19th century.

Although he is remembered primarily for his political works, Machiavelli was a writer of wide-ranging talents. He also wrote biography, history, poetry, and several plays, of which *The Mandrake* (1524), a social and political satire, is considered the outstanding example of Italian Renaissance comedy.

See also MIXED REGIME.

MacKinnon, Catharine See box at FEMINISM

Mahayana Buddhism See box at BUDDHISM

Maimonides, Moses (Moses ben Maimon) (1135–1204)
Sephardic Jewish theologian, philosopher, and physician, the central figure in medieval JUDAISM and widely considered the foremost Judaic philosopher. He was born in Córdoba, Spain, but his family fled Muslim persecution there and eventually settled in Egypt, where he became chief rabbi of the Jewish community. Most of Maimonides' prolific scholarship, which included medical treatises as well as religious and philosophical works, was composed in Arabic and translated into Hebrew, then Latin and other languages as his reputation spread. His first major work, completed in 1168 after ten years' toil, was a series of commentaries on the Mishnah, the "oral law" of Judaism; one of the essays included his Thirteen Articles of Faith, a creed still used in the Orthodox and Conservative Jewish liturgy. The *Mishneh Torah* (Torah Reviewed), also

ten years in preparation and considered Maimonides' greatest work, is an original and thoroughgoing codification of Talmudic law, written in elegant Hebrew and illuminating the foundations of Jewish law and life.

Maimonides' most influential work outside the Jewish community was the *Guide of the Perplexed* (published 1190), which sought to reconcile the conflict between biblical revelation and ARISTOTELIAN rationality. Revealed religion, he argued, is not undermined but enhanced by knowledge of the truths of science and philosophy. (For example, he defined a miracle as a confirmation of the possible but improbable, not a proof of the impossible.) We cannot know with certainty anything positive about God, Maimonides reasoned, but only his negative attributes, what he is not—not human, not finite, not material, and so on; however, a study of his creation, the natural world, leads us to an understanding of God as the *necessary being* who is the first and final CAUSE of the universe (cf. GOD, ARGUMENTS FOR). At first this reconciliation of faith and REASON aroused intense opposition in tradition-bound Jewish and Christian circles alike; at one point ROMAN CATHOLIC clerics were incited by an outraged rabbi to burn the *Guide*. But its argument outlasted its controversy, and Maimonides had an enduring impact on European thought, inspiring Thomas AQUINAS and other medieval SCHOLASTICS, and even 17th-century RATIONALISTS such as LEIBNIZ and SPINOZA.

Malthusian population theory

Economic and social theory stating that population will always increase at a faster rate than the food supply. It was postulated by the English demographer, economist, and clergyman Thomas Malthus in *An Essay on the Principle of Population* (1798) as an explanation of the seemingly intractable destitution of the poor. He observed that while the population increases geometrically (2, 4, 8, 16, etc.), food production grows only arithmetically (2, 4, 6, 8, etc.), limited by the law of DIMINISHING RETURNS. In addition, every significant increase in income is matched by an increase in family size; as a result, the standard of living never increases. Eventual human extinction can be averted only through "checks" on population growth, which Malthus divided into two categories: passive, or "preventive" checks, including abstinence, late marriage, and "vice" (in which he included abortion and birth control); and active, or "positive" checks, including war, famine, and pestilence.

Malthus's theory was embraced by English aristocrats and CONSERVATIVE politicians whose hostility to social assistance seemed vindicated by its implication that the poor were responsible for their plight and nothing could be done about it. However, his dire predictions of widespread famine in the wake of unchecked population growth were not borne out, largely because of the geometrical increases in productivity brought about by the Industrial Revolution. The steady rise in living standards in industrialized nations during the 20th century would seem to discredit the theory, but *neo-Malthusians* maintain that it still applies in the so-called Third World, where poverty persists as traditional agricultural practices are outstripped by growing populations. They also argue that growing urban congestion, environmental pollution, and poverty threaten the standard of living in developed countries as well, and advocate a worldwide policy of *zero population growth* through birth control, to halt further increases in the birth rate.

manifest destiny

Doctrine in 19th-century U.S. history expressing the belief that the expansion of American territory and influence was ordained by divine mandate and historical inevitability. The term was coined in 1845 on the eve of the Mexican War, in which the United States annexed Texas and California, when the journalist John O'Sullivan wrote of "our manifest destiny to overspread the continent allotted by Providence for the free development of our yearly multiplying millions." These sentiments expressed a self-confident faith in the nation's God-given mission to spread American civilization, embodied in Anglo-Saxon PROTESTANTISM, free-market CAPITALISM, and DEMOCRATIC government. The image of the nation expanding across an unspoiled continent was reflected in the paintings of the Hudson River School of artists, whose ROMANTIC landscapes often portrayed human settlements against towering backdrops of natural splendor.

After the closing of the frontier in the 1890s, "manifest destiny" again became a potent catchword, as expansionists urged extending the American sphere of influence into the Caribbean and Pacific, fueling the Spanish-American War of 1898 and other IMPERIALIST adventures. The theme can be detected at some moments in more recent U.S. history, too, as when John F. Kennedy pledged America to the conquest of space, declaring, "We stand today on the edge of a new frontier."

Mao Zedong (Mao Tse-tung) (1893–1976)

Chinese revolutionary leader and theorist, chairman of the Chinese COMMUNIST Party, and founder of the People's Republic of China. Mao's thought was shaped as much by Chinese culture as by orthodox MARXISM; his aphoristic style of writing echoed that of Confucius (see CONFUCIANISM) and his

"If you want to know the taste of a pear, you must taste the pear by eating it for yourself. If you want to know the theory and methods of revolution, you must take part in revolution. All genuine knowledge originates in direct experience."
—Mao Zedong, 1937

vision of endlessly recurrent DIALECTICAL contradictions evoked the conflictive harmony of YIN AND YANG. He also abandoned a key article of classical Marxist faith, the primacy of the proletariat in the revolutionary struggle, articulating instead a theory of peasant revolution ("people's war") that bypassed the stage of industrial CAPITALISM that MARX had envisioned as a necessary precursor to SOCIALISM. This doctrine, together with Mao's successful strategy of rural guerrilla warfare (influenced by the Irish revolutionary Michael Collins, known as the father of modern guerrilla warfare), had wide influence among Third World revolutionaries.

In the first years after the establishment of the People's Republic in 1949, Chinese domestic policy followed the Soviet model, with economic priority given to developing heavy industry and the Communist Party ruling through a centralized bureaucracy. Mao later repudiated key points of Soviet dogma, however, both economic and IDEOLOGICAL, which eventually led to Sino-Soviet estrangement. He called on the people to constructively criticize the party hierarchy ("let a hundred flowers bloom") and disputed the Stalinist position that socialist society is free of errors and conflicts. On the contrary, he argued, contradiction and struggle are not only inevitable but necessary to building socialism; to deny this would be to deny Marx's law of the unity of opposites, the "fundamental law of the universe" holding that change is achieved through dialectical confrontation. In this view—similar to TROTSKY's theory of permanent revolution but without its INTERNATIONALIST dimension—ongoing criticism and self-criticism ("rectification") are essential to the full achievement of communism.

The disastrous failure of the so-called Great Leap Forward of 1958, a program of forced industrialization, weakened Mao's authority but confirmed his skepticism about such a policy in a primarily agricultural economy. The Cultural Revolution of 1966–69, which likewise ended in chaos, was instigated by Mao to rid Chinese society of all distinctions of CLASS and privilege through the purging or "reeducation" of Party bureaucrats, artists, intellectuals, and others who were not manual workers. In this period the collection of maxims known as *Quotations from Chairman Mao* or simply the "Little Red Book," printed in the hundreds of millions, was read as scripture by the zealous young workers and students known as the Red Guards, as well as by student RADICALS around the world.

See also quotation at DIALECTICAL MATERIALISM.

Marcuse, Herbert See box at CRITICAL THEORY

market

A place or system in which goods and services are bought and sold. The idea of the market is a central concept in economics, affecting all areas of modern economic theory. In a *free-market* economy, producers decide what goods, and how many, are made and distributed, in response to consumers' buying decisions. The antithesis of a free market is a *centrally planned* or *command* economy, in which government agencies determine production and control distribution. No national economy has ever been completely free or completely planned, however, even in the 19th-century golden age of CAPITALIST free enterprise or the 20th-century heyday of COMMUNISM; all real-world economies fall somewhere on a continuum between these two "pure" forms of economic organization.

The free-market system was championed by Adam SMITH as the "invisible hand" by which the self-interested actions of both consumers and producers promote an optimal economic and social outcome. In a free market, prices, quantities, and production methods are governed by the forces of SUPPLY AND DEMAND. When the price of a good is stable because the supply of it matches the demand for it, the market for that good is said to be in *equilibrium*. The invisible hand is not infallible, however; unemployment, inflation, and the adverse UNINTENDED CONSEQUENCES of economic activity (known to economists as "negative externalities") are examples of *market failure*. In these situations, government often steps in, creating subsidies, regulations, public-sector industries, taxes, and other mechanisms to correct or avoid the malfunction. Government intervention in free-market economies also typically includes antitrust laws, tax incentives to encourage certain kinds of investment, and interest-rate manipulation.

The argument for central economic planning is that unchecked market forces lead to instability in prices and employment and inequality in wages, and that market-driven production does not necessarily supply consumers' real needs. Until the 1980s, many of the Communist-bloc economies in Europe and Asia were almost entirely planned. While state SOCIALISM was able to control inflation and economic growth and guarantee full employment, bureaucratic inefficiencies created chronic shortages of agricultural and industrial goods and eventually led to free-market experiments, especially in the Soviet Union (see PERESTROIKA) and China.

Most nations have some form of *mixed-market* economy, in which government as well as private enterprise provides goods and services and most economic activity is subject to government regulation. Government participation commonly entails the provision of *public goods* such as infrastructure, defense, education, and WELFARE. In some mixed economies, including Germany, Sweden, and (until the 1980s) Britain, the public sector includes nationalized industries such as telecommunications and utilities. Under *market socialism*, worker-owned enterprises compete in a free market; this system operated, with some success, in Yugoslavia from the mid-1950s.

See also CAPITALISM; COMPETITION; FREE TRADE AND PROTECTIONISM; KEYNES; LAISSEZ-FAIRE; MONETARISM; OPPORTUNITY COST; PUBLIC CHOICE; RATIONAL EXPECTATIONS; SMITH; SOCIALISM; SUPPLY AND DEMAND.

Marx, Karl (1818–1883)

German political philosopher, economist, and social theorist, whose critique of CAPITALISM profoundly influenced SOCIALIST thought and revolutionary political movements. His early influences included the French socialist Claude-Henri Saint-Simon and the radical Young Hegelians, especially Ludwig Feuerbach, who stressed the social, MATERIALIST nature of humanity over HEGEL's spiritual IDEALISM. Marx's version of Hegel's DIALECTICAL theory (he claimed to have "turned Hegel on his head") located the cause of human ALIENATION in exploitative economic relations and viewed CLASS conflict as both its symptom and the key to its solution.

In *The German Ideology* (1845–46) and *The Communist Manifesto* (1848), both written in collaboration with Friedrich Engels, Marx developed his "scientific" theory of *historical materialism*. This theory held that social, political, and cultural institutions, prevailing IDEOLOGIES, and people's very CONSCIOUSNESS are shaped by economic relations and material conditions—in Marxian terms, the social "superstructure" is supported by an economic "base." Marx and Engels identified a series of historical stages corresponding to progressive developments in material production, beginning with primitive COMMUNISM and advancing through slavery and feudalism to capitalism, which was destined to be supplanted by socialism and finally by advanced communism. Each stage, save the first and last, has been marked by an antagonistic divide between the ruling class, which controls the mode of production, and the working class, which is exploited by it. Inevitably, this friction creates problems ("contradictions") the prevailing system cannot solve; the system becomes destabilized and is ultimately overthrown by the exploited class, who become the new masters of society (see DIALECTICAL MATERIALISM). Thus the capitalist bourgeoisie, who had superseded the feudal nobility with the rise of industrialism, would in turn be ousted by the urban proletariat.

In his major work, *Capital* (3 vols., 1867–95), Marx analyzed the mechanisms by which the working class is deprived of full humanity. Where previous social reformers had attributed social inequality to the unequal distribution of wealth, Marx rooted it in the exploitative relations of *production*. He

> *"Religion is the sigh of the oppressed creature, the heart of a heartless world, just as it is the spirit of spiritless conditions. It is the opium of the people. . . . To abolish religion as the* illusory *happiness of the people is to demand their* real *happiness."*
> —Karl Marx,
> "Toward a Critique of Hegel's *Philosophy of Right*," 1844

also contradicted classical economic theorists who had seen wage labor as a reciprocal arrangement benefiting both employer and employee. Marx noted that this view failed to take into account the employer's ownership of the means of production. While accepting the *labor theory of value* propounded by Adam SMITH and David Ricardo, which states that the value of a commodity is determined solely by the amount of labor put into it, Marx turned it into an indictment of capitalism. Under the capitalist system, he argued, workers are paid far less than the value their labor adds to the manufactured product, giving rise to *surplus value* in the form of profit. The capitalist can reinvest this surplus, producing even more profit, while the laborers' wages must be spent on the necessities of material existence. The ruthless competitiveness of capitalist enterprise obliges the employer to keep wages as low and working conditions as rigorous as possible. Trapped in this exploitative relationship, with no stake in the fruits of their labor, workers become alienated, not only from their work but from their true, creative potential. The capitalist system therefore, by its nature, breeds conflict between the working and owning classes. This conflict will inevitably spark a revolution leading to socialism, under a "dictatorship of the proletariat," and ultimately to communism, a classless society in which the STATE will "wither away" (cf. ANARCHISM).

Many of the predictions of Marx's theory failed to materialize. The first successful socialist revolution did not occur in the industrialized West but in semifeudal Russia; the revolutionary Communist states became less DEMOCRATIC than many capitalist countries; and capitalism has proved far more resourceful and resilient than Marx imagined. However, his analysis of economic relations and his vision of an egalitarian society have shaped the thinking of social reformers and political revolutionaries ever since.

See also ALIENATION; COMMUNISM; DIALECTIC; EPISTEMOLOGY; IDEOLOGY; INTERNATIONALISM; STATE.

Marxism

Tradition of critical thought and political action derived from the social and economic theories and revolutionary politics of Karl MARX and Friedrich Engels. From the late 19th century to the present, diverse interpretations and applications of Marxian theory have arisen, so Marxism cannot be easily or tidily defined. Marxist analyses, however, tend to share certain assumptions. These include the proposition that CAPITALISM is based on the exploitation of wage labor, which ALIENATES people from their true capacities and from each other; that social, political, and cultural systems are shaped by exploitative economic relations, which create and perpetuate mutually hostile CLASS divisions; and that class conflict and the system's own contradictions will lead to its overthrow and replacement by a more equal and just SOCIALIST society. As well as an economic theory and a prescription for revolutionary change, Marxism is a philosophy of history, which is seen as a DIALECTICAL process of progressive change arising from conflict (see DIALECTICAL MATERIALISM), and a philosophy of human nature, seeing people as defined by their relations within society and fulfilled by controlling the fruits of their labor. Marxist principles have thus been applied in a variety of fields (see, e.g., CULTURAL MATERIALISM; FEMINISM; STRUCTURALISM). For example, Marxist literary criticism approaches texts in terms of their ideological assumptions and historical contexts, and generally holds that a work of art always serves a social purpose, implicitly or explicitly supporting or condemning prevailing conditions (see LUKÁCS; MIMESIS; SOCIALIST REALISM; cf. POSTMODERNISM; POSTSTRUCTURALISM).

Marxists have diverged from Marx to greater and lesser degrees, and from each other in numerous ways. These include, notably, debates over an apparent contradiction in Marx's theory—the historical inevitability of proletarian revolution versus the role of human agency in bringing it about—and over the question of whether the socialist revolution must be violent or can be achieved through gradualist, DEMOCRATIC methods. During much of the 20th century, Marxist thought developed largely outside of and in opposition to

Soviet orthodoxy. TROTSKY and his followers, for instance, argued that Stalin had betrayed the Marxian principles of workers' democracy and proletarian internationalism. After the Second World War, with capitalism more vigorous than ever, European and American Marxists turned to analyzing the means—including mass media and consumer culture—through which Western workers were seen as having been co-opted and incorporated into the system. The revisionist Marxism of postwar European intellectuals including Jean-Paul SARTRE, Maurice MERLEAU-PONTY, Louis Althusser (see box at STRUCTURALISM), and members of the Frankfurt School of CRITICAL THEORY rejected much of classical Marxist analysis as overly DETERMINISTIC and DUALISTIC. The New Left that emerged in the late 1950s repudiated eastern European totalitarianism while remaining critical of capitalist hegemony in the West. After the sixties, European social democrats (see box at DEMOCRACY) and "Eurocommunists," having distanced themselves from Moscow, sought the democratization of capitalist institutions rather than their overthrow. The fall of the Soviet Union and its satellite governments was widely seen as the final repudiation of Marxism; however, since the conditions Marx and Engels identified still exist, now on a global scale, many social critics still give validity to their analysis.

See also ALIENATION; BAUDRILLARD; CLASS; COMMUNISM; CRITICAL THEORY; DIALECTIC; DIALECTICAL MATERIALISM; FEMINISM; GRAMSCI; IDEOLOGY; LENIN; LUXEMBURG; MAO ZEDONG; MERLEAU-PONTY; SARTRE; TROTSKY.

Masons See FREEMASONRY

materialism

The doctrine that matter, and only matter, exists. The general position embraces philosophical, scientific, historical, and psychological explanations of reality. In contrast to DUALISM, which makes a basic distinction between mind and matter, and IDEALISM, which sees reality as fundamentally mental or spiritual, the materialist view asserts that mind is reducible to an aspect of matter (cf. MONISM). The modern colloquial connotation of the term—an obsession with material possessions—is related to the philosophical meaning only metaphorically, inasmuch as it implies that the spirit is defined by tangible property.

The earliest expression of materialism may have come from the Charvakas, a school of materialist SKEPTICS within HINDUISM around 600 B.C.E. They regarded the world as composed of the four ELEMENTS, denied the validity of REASON, and maintained that what cannot be perceived by the senses does not exist. In the West, the concept originated with the Greek ATOMISTS, who held that all objects are formed of tiny, indivisible particles, of which the mind (or SOUL) is simply a particularly subtle congregation.

In the postclassical era, because of the influence of the PLATONIC and ARISTOTELIAN systems and the rise of CHRISTIANITY, materialism was at first an idea of little consequence. It resurfaced in the 17th century in the philosophy of Thomas HOBBES, who posited a world governed not by divine influence but by the law of CAUSE and effect, a world in which even ideas are the result of matter affecting the organs of sense. After Hobbes, materialism regained respectability, particularly in the world of science. The ENLIGHTENMENT worldview combined a thoroughly MECHANISTIC materialism with faith in the power of reason to explain it. Since then, the view of natural processes as interactions of matter has only gained ground, with scientific theories ranging from EVOLUTION to QUANTUM mechanics explaining the workings of the world in purely material terms.

The MARXIST theory of history, known as historical materialism, ties human progress to advances in technology—the means of producing material goods—and the struggle over their control. DIALECTICAL MATERIALISM, the heart of Marxist theory, stresses the influence of material (especially economic) circumstances on human needs, desires, and endeavors.

While materialism may be taken for granted in the modern world as the foundation of the natural sciences, its relevance to psychology and the study of mental processes remains a source of controversy. Researchers have tried to establish a physiological basis for cognition and emotion, but no one has yet demonstrated that mental functions can be wholly explained by mapping the neural pathways of the brain.

See also CULTURAL MATERIALISM; DIALECTICAL MATERIALISM; EPICUREANISM; HOBBES.

Maxwell, James Clerk (1831–1879)

Scottish scientist, widely regarded as the outstanding physicist of the 19th century, whose theory of electromagnetism completed and unified the theories of electricity and magnetism. Maxwell's equations describing the laws governing electric and magnetic fields are regarded as parallel in importance to NEWTON's three laws of motion. Maxwell made major contributions in several other scientific fields, including THERMODYNAMICS, mathematics, and optics. His ideas about the nature of science, including the use of quantitative analogies, continue to influence scientific thought. Early in his career he proved that the rings of Saturn could not be solid and developed methods for analyzing the behavior of planetary rings composed of gravitating particles—methods late-20th-century scientists have used to account for the detailed structure of Saturn's rings. He developed a quantitative system for classifying colors and applied it to the study of color perception and color blindness. He employed statistical methods to study the behavior of gas molecules and used his results to determine how gases diffuse, conduct heat, and exert drag.

Maxwell's electrical researches, which occupied him throughout his professional life, were summarized in his *Treatise on Electricity and Magnetism* (1873). His work built on that of his immediate precursor, Michael Faraday, who had discovered electromagnetic induction, the creation of a current in an electrical circuit by moving it through a magnetic field—the principle of the electric generator. Using creative analogies, mechanical models, and mathematical analyses, Maxwell established the interrelationship of the electrical and magnetic fields. In a set of four differential equations, he set forth the laws that are the basis of almost all electrical and magnetic phenomena. One of the predictions of Maxwell's theory was that electrical and magnetic waves travel at the speed of light; this in turn led to the conclusion that light itself is a type of electromagnetic radiation. Like Faraday and most other scientists of his day, Maxwell believed that fields of force could not operate in a vacuum; he tentatively explained electromagnetic fields as distortions in a subtle *ether* that pervades the universe, an age-old notion that persisted until EINSTEIN's principle of RELATIVITY made it superfluous.

McCarthyism
Politically motivated efforts to discredit opponents through the implication of guilt by association with individuals or organizations considered leftist or subversive. First applied to the demagogic anti-COMMUNIST crusade of Wisconsin senator Joseph R. McCarthy in the early 1950s, the term, coined by Washington *Post* political cartoonist Herblock (Herbert Block), connotes false charges of disloyalty and corrupt official investigations that play on citizens' real or irrational fears. The unsubstantiated accusations of the opportunistic, media-savvy senator, portraying a vast Communist conspiracy undermining the United States, exploited Cold War fears of expansionist international Communism. They also played on more general American anxieties in the post–World War II era, as the country moved from ISOLATION to INTERNATIONALISM and from LIBERAL to CONSERVATIVE politics, distinguished particularly by a growing distrust of big government. McCarthy was finally

discredited after charging subversion within the U.S. Army and was censured by the Senate in 1954.

Many of McCarthy's techniques, including unsupported allegations, intimidating public hearings, and the presumption of guilt by association, were initiated by the House [of Representatives] Committee on Un-American Activities (HUAC). Established in 1938 to investigate subversion on both the right and left, after the war HUAC focused on seeking to expose Communist affiliations, most prominently in Hollywood, where numerous actors, directors, and screenwriters who refused to cooperate with the committee were subsequently blacklisted from employment in the industry.

Since the "witch-hunt" era of the fifties, the stigma attached to left-wing associations has abated but not vanished in American politics. Conservative politicians have increasingly demonized the word "liberal," occasionally using the McCarthyite tactic of condemning an opponent's association with an organization regarded as liberal or RADICAL; in the 1988 presidential race, Vice President George Bush's characterization of Democratic nominee Michael Dukakis as "a card-carrying member of the American Civil Liberties Union" was criticized as smacking of McCarthyism. Conversely, some have characterized liberals' efforts to impose "politically correct" speech and behavior in academic and other institutions as "neo-McCarthyism."

mean, doctrine of the

The principle of moderation as an ideal of VIRTUE. According to ARISTOTLE, virtue is found on the middle path between the extremes of excess and deficiency—usually a little closer to the former. Courage, for example, is the "Golden Mean" between the extremes of foolhardiness and cowardice; generosity lies between prodigality and avarice; justice consists in the proper balance between surrendering one's own rights and abusing those of others.

To the ancients, virtue was more than a question of right action; it was founded in a sense of moral "excellence" that allowed one to live the good life. Aristotle identified REASON as the highest human power, the exercise of which, in the service of practical wisdom, would lead to the full realization of one's natural potential, neither aiming too high nor underachieving. Similar teachings are found in many other ethical systems. The BUDDHA prescribed the Eightfold Path to the elimination of ignorance and suffering through "right" actions based in moderation. One of the classic texts of CONFUCIAN philosophy is *The Doctrine of the Mean (Chung Yung)*, conventionally attributed to Confucius's grandson, Tsu Ssu. To follow the mean, or Middle Way, entails achieving equilibrium (centrality, *chung*) and harmony *(yung)*. Equilibrium is the state of mind when one is free of strong emotions, and harmony is the state of mind when the emotions are aroused in their proper proportions. Attaining these states is central to following the Way, or TAO.

See also ARISTOTLE; BUDDHISM; CONFUCIANISM.

meaning

For most of the history of philosophy, the meaning of a word has been presumed to be its *referent,* the object the speaker is referring to (the words "tree," *"arbre,"* and *"mti"* mean the same thing to speakers of English, French, and Swahili, respectively). This understanding of meaning accords with the tradition that sees language as basically a collection of names. Language as we ordinarily use it, however, is imprecise and ambiguous, so our referents cannot always be determined unequivocally. (The term "lady," for example, may have several quite different implications—a titled aristocrat or a well-mannered commoner, a term of respect or an impudent epithet.) One of the tasks of philosophy, therefore, has been the search for an "ideal language," uncontaminated by the ambiguity of ordinary speech, in which a word and its referent would be identical. The genesis of this approach lies in the mythic notion, shared by many cultures, that word and object were once a unity that has since been broken in two.

Sophisticated versions of the referential theory are still influential. However, within the last century, beginning with the German LOGICIAN Gottlob Frege, the locus of meaning has shifted from individual words to sentences or *propositions:* a word has meaning only in the context of the statement it is part of. In the linguistic STRUCTURALISM of Ferdinand de Saussure, for example, words are seen as arbitrary symbols with conventional connotations, which gain meaning through their interrelationships. The best-known modern versions of the propositional approach to meaning are the VERIFIABILITY theory, associated with the LOGICAL POSITIVISTS, which holds that only those statements subject to analytic or EMPIRICAL verification are meaningful (the statement "God exists" would not qualify); and the *formal semantic* theory, which holds that the meaning of a statement is identical to the conditions under which it is true (e.g., "It is raining" is meaningful only if it is, in fact, raining). The linguist Noam CHOMSKY adopts an even more rigorous posture, in which meaning derives from the syntactical structure of words in a sentence (the words "The hard rain is stopping" mean something else entirely when arranged differently: "Stopping the rain is hard").

In contrast to both the referential and propositional approaches, Ludwig WITTGENSTEIN, who initially set forth an ideal-language theory, later came to the position that meaning is a social phenomenon. The meaning of an utterance, he said, depends on how it is used in social intercourse, not on any formal qualities. This approach proved extremely influential, for example, among ORDINARY LANGUAGE philosophers, who analyze language in everyday use. At an even further remove from the classic referential theory of meaning is the HERMENEUTIC view, in which meaning can be asserted only within a broad historical and cultural context and any shift in context inevitably produces a shift in meaning (see also SOCIAL CONSTRUCTIONISM).

See also DECONSTRUCTION; EXISTENTIALISM; HERMENEUTICS; MERLEAU-PONTY; NEW CRITICISM; POSTSTRUCTURALISM; PRAGMATISM; RUSSELL; SEMIOTICS; STRUCTURALISM; WITTGENSTEIN.

mechanism

The explanation of all phenomena in terms of mechanical operations, likening biological and social as well as physical processes to the actions of a machine. In its reduction of everything to matter in motion, it is opposed to VITALISM and *dynamism*, which posit a fundamental force; in its conception of SYSTEMS (biological, astronomical, political, etc.) as combinations of working components, it is opposed to *organicism*, which compares them to a living body, an organic whole that transcends the sum of its parts (see also GESTALT; HOLISM). It is basically MATERIALIST and thoroughly non-TELEOLOGICAL, seeing no intention or purpose in living activity or physical laws.

The viewpoint is chiefly associated with DESCARTES, for whom only the human mind and SOUL set people apart from the rest of matter; even animals were nothing more than organic machines. A century later, Julien de La Mettrie, in *The Natural History of the Soul* (1745) and *Man a Machine* (1747), proposed that even human intelligence and spirituality are functions of physiological processes. In the 20th century the biomechanical model of life has become standard, supported by research in molecular biology and neurophysiology. In psychology, BEHAVIORISM gives an essentially mechanistic account of human activity, and research into ARTIFICIAL INTELLIGENCE assumes a mechanistic model of mental operations. However, few today espouse a wholly REDUCTIONIST theory of mechanism, faced with the unpredictability of human intellect and the indeterminacy inherent in QUANTUM mechanics.

See also DETERMINISM; MATERIALISM.

Mendelssohn, Moses (1729–1786)

German-Jewish philosopher, a central figure in the so-called Jewish ENLIGHT-ENMENT, or Haskalah, which attempted to reconcile JUDAISM with REASON and assimilate Jews into mainstream European society. At a time when the presence of Jews in Europe was barely tolerated, he championed civil RIGHTS, denounced Jewish separatism, and advocated freedom of conscience and the separation of church and STATE. Different religions serve different needs, he reasoned, and should be judged only by their effect on their adherents' actions. To help other Jews learn German and thus gain access to German literature and culture, Mendelssohn translated the Pentateuch, Psalms, and other books of the Bible into phonetic German, printed in Hebrew characters. In his writings he presented Judaism as a theological system based in reason (and in that respect superior to CHRISTIANITY), espoused a kind of Judaic DEISM, and postulated METAPHYSICS as a scientific discipline. In *Phädon* (1767), modeled on PLATO's dialogue *Phaedo,* he argued for the immortality of the SOUL, in *Jerusalem* (1783) for Judaism as a rational religion, in *Morgenstunden* (Morning Hours, 1785) for the rationality of belief in God's existence.

Mendelssohn formed a lifelong friendship with the playwright and critic Gotthold Ephraim Lessing, with whom he shared an AESTHETIC that viewed tragic CATHARSIS not as purgation through pity and terror but as admiration and compassion for the struggles of a fellow human being. Lessing's play *Nathan the Wise* (1779), a plea for religious tolerance, was informed by Mendelssohn's thought.

Mennonites See box at PROTESTANTISM

mercantilism

Economic philosophy that dominated European trade policy in the 17th and 18th centuries, aimed at increasing a nation's wealth and power by ensuring a favorable *balance of trade.* In this period, national wealth was measured by the amount of gold and silver in the treasury, and power was judged by the armed forces the treasury could support. Merchants and statesmen therefore promoted politics of political and economic self-reliance, in the belief that exports would increase the country's wealth and importing goods would diminish it. Exports were often encouraged through government subsidies—which meant, in effect, government control of the economy—and imports were discouraged by high tariffs.

Mercantilism was practiced above all by the great European IMPERIAL powers, including Portugal, Spain, France, and Britain. Colonies in Africa, the East Indies, and the Americas were exploited as the source of raw materials that were brought to the "mother country" to be manufactured into goods for domestic consumption and export. The British Navigation Laws of the 1650s restricted foreign ships' access to British ports and gave Britain a near-monopoly on trade with its colonies. In the 1660s and '70s, Louis XIV's finance minister, Jean-Baptiste Colbert, overhauled the French economy on mercantilist lines, establishing protective tariffs, encouraging the export trade, and extending government control over economic affairs.

Mercantilism received a wounding, virtually fatal denunciation in Adam SMITH's *The Wealth of Nations* (1776). Smith (who coined the term) criticized the mercantilist system as inefficient and detrimental to domestic consumers. He argued that FREE TRADE and specialization in production—each country making and exporting what it can produce most efficiently and importing what it cannot—benefits all parties and leads to greater wealth (see ADVANTAGE). His argument was soon accepted almost universally by trading nations. In the 20th century, protectionist policies have sometimes been termed *neo-mercantilism.* The policy known as *beggar-my-neighbor,* in which a nation attempts to improve its own economic conditions at the expense of others, through currency devaluation, protective tariffs, and other measures, also has its origins in mercantilism.

See also FREE TRADE AND PROTECTIONISM; MONETARISM; SMITH.

Merleau-Ponty, Maurice (1908–1961)

French philosopher, a leading exponent of PHENOMENOLOGY and one of the central figures in French EXISTENTIALISM. He befriended Jean-Paul SARTRE when both were members of a resistance group in occupied France, and after the war the two founded (with Simone de BEAUVOIR) and coedited the influential journal *Les temps modernes.* Like most French intellectuals of his generation, Merleau-Ponty was attracted to MARXISM and admired the Soviet Union, although he questioned the Marxist ideal of human perfectibility. He defended Stalinism in his 1947 collection of essays, *Humanism and Terror,* but gradually became disillusioned with Soviet COMMUNISM; he broke with Sartre during the Korean War, and by the mid-fifties he had largely repudiated Marxism.

Merleau-Ponty was profoundly influenced by Edmund Husserl's philosophy of phenomenology, which emphasized the interactions of human CONSCIOUSNESS with the world around us. But he departed from Husserl in several important ways, especially in rejecting a division between subject and object.

In *The Phenomenology of Perception* (1945), Merleau-Ponty proposed that to have knowledge of the world is to be a part of the world, not distinct from it. Since our consciousness and our body are inseparable, and consciousness is a product of PERCEPTION, there is no such thing as perception in itself, only perception from some perspective. Perception is a physical interrelation of subject and object, perceiver and perceived, each stimulating the other and neither wholly separate. In *The Visible and the Invisible,* which he was working on at the time of his death, Merleau-Ponty uses a deceptively mundane experience to illustrate his understanding of the world. Placing the palms of his hands together, he asks, "Am I touching or being touched?" He describes this inherent and unresolvable ambiguity, the relationship between flesh and itself, as identical to the relationship between perceiver and perceived. The perceiver, in the process of perceiving the world, is simultaneously perceived by it.

From the STRUCTURALISM of Saussure, Merleau-Ponty developed the idea that MEANING is not a given but a product of lived relationships in the world. Experience is granted meaning in contrast and correlation to other experiences, in which a binary relationship also applies: meaning always coexists with meaninglessness, sense with nonsense, REASON with unreason, each entwined with and dependent on the other.

See also ALIENATION; PHENOMENOLOGY; SOLIPSISM.

metaphysics

The study of the nature and origin of ultimate reality; one of the five classical fields of philosophical inquiry (see also AESTHETICS; EPISTEMOLOGY; ETHICS; LOGIC). The term originated when the writings of ARISTOTLE were collected and his work on "first principles" was given a title that merely denoted its place among the manuscripts, *meta ta physica,* or "after the *Physics.*" Because of this linguistic accident, metaphysics has acquired the sense of being concerned with things beyond the physical.

Aristotle's *Metaphysics* was concerned with such problems as the nature of SUBSTANCE and causation (including the "first CAUSE," or God) as well as the fundamental nature of BEING, which is the subject of the branch of metaphysics known as *ontology*. For centuries after Aristotle, these preoccupations defined the content of metaphysical inquiry, and the assumption that the search for fundamental principles was a feasible undertaking went largely unchallenged.

That challenge finally came from Immanuel KANT, who presented the view that the perceived "TRUTH" of metaphysical concepts might simply be the result of COGNITIVE structures within our minds (see box at KANT). This, on top of the Cartesian policy of doubting everything (see DESCARTES) and the EMPIRICISTS' belief in nothing beyond the evidence of the senses, undermined confidence in the validity of the metaphysical enterprise. For example, while most religious beliefs are founded on a metaphysics in which the First Principle is God, much modern theology has moved toward scientific or HUMANISTIC conceptions of deity and creation.

Since Kant, metaphysics has shifted away from the search for fundamental causes toward questions such as whether reality is basically mental or basically physical (see, e.g., IDEALISM; MATERIALISM). Indeed, over the past two centuries the term has come to be used deprecatingly, as many philosophers have sought to "overcome" metaphysics, accusing others of retaining metaphysical elements in their thought. This kind of dispute hinges on the factious problem of what is metaphysical and what is not. Some say that whatever is not scientific is metaphysical, while others maintain that science is itself one metaphysical position among others; MARXISTS see the DIALECTICAL analysis of socioeconomic structures as the only stance free of metaphysics, while others call the assumption of fundamental principles in Marxist DIALECTICAL MATERIALISM hopelessly metaphysical; and so on.

See also ABSOLUTE; APPEARANCE VERSUS REALITY; BEING AND BECOMING; CONSCIOUSNESS; IDEAS; NOMINALISM; SOUL AND SPIRIT; SUBSTANCE.

Methodism   See box at PROTESTANTISM

Mill, John Stuart   (1806–1873)

English philosopher and economist, the foremost 19th-century exponent of LIBERALISM and EMPIRICISM (which he called "experimentalism"), whose commitment to INDIVIDUALISM was balanced by the convictions of a social reformer. A child prodigy who read Greek at three, he became the preeminent English intellectual of his generation. Mill wrote on a wide variety of topics, more interested in affecting the political, social, and economic conditions of his day than in developing an integrated philosophy. In *A System of Logic* (1843), he propounded a systematic approach to experimentation and inductive reasoning (see DEDUCTION AND INDUCTION) and, defending Auguste COMTE's assertion that the scientific study of society is possible and valid, sought to place all knowledge on empirical grounds. His support of women's suffrage as a member of Parliament (1865–68) and in *On the Subjection of Women* (1869) helped foster the suffrage movement of the late 19th century.

In his most famous and influential work, *On Liberty* (1859), Mill argued that the advancement of knowledge and human happiness requires the greatest possible personal FREEDOM, limited only by the condition that one "must not make himself a nuisance to other people." He championed freedom of thought and speech and asserted the right of each person to cultivate his or her individual character, desires, and life plan rather than be molded by custom, tradition, religious dictates, or public opinion. He thus advocated social and political PLURALISM, together with the free dissemination of differing ideas, as a guard against what TOCQUEVILLE had called "the tyranny of the majority." (He also supported proportional representation for the different CLASSES, with extra votes for the better-educated.) Although he embraced the principle of COMPETITION embodied in the LAISSEZ-FAIRE economics of Adam SMITH, Mill condemned CAPITALISM as unfair to the working class and supported the ideals of SOCIALISM. In his ideal economic system, free-MARKET competition between worker-owned enterprises would predominate.

> *"If all mankind minus one were of one opinion, and only one person were of the contrary opinion, mankind would be no more justified in silencing that one person than he, if he had the power, would be justified in silencing mankind."*
>
> —John Stuart Mill,
> *On Liberty*

In *Utilitarianism* (1863), Mill both defended and revised the UTILITARIANISM of his father, James, and Jeremy Bentham. Rather than simply "the greatest happiness for the greatest number," he proposed a formulation that would take into account the *value* of that happiness, distinguishing between "higher" (mental) and "lower" (sensual) pleasures. Although Mill also denounced the then-popular "intuitionist" school of ethics, which held that there are universal moral principles that we intuitively perceive, his own version of utilitarianism has been criticized for apparently requiring an intuitive, irrational evaluation of different types of pleasure.

See also FREEDOM; box at SUPPLY AND DEMAND; UTILITARIANISM; WELFARE.

millenarianism (millennialism)

A recurrent tendency in CHRISTIANITY, the literal belief in a thousand-year reign of Christ on earth before the final day of judgment, as prophesied in the Book of Revelation (see ESCHATOLOGY); also called *chiliasm*, the two terms deriving from the words for "thousand" in Latin and Greek, respectively. It is allied to ADVENTISM, the conviction that the Second Coming of JESUS is at hand (see also JEHOVAH'S WITNESSES), and has been particularly contagious in times of great social upheaval or hardship, as well as in the years before the turning of a millennium in the Christian calendar. The decades preceding the year 1000 spawned numerous millennial cults prophesying the end of the world and seeing myriad natural and social occurrences as portents, a pattern repeated in the closing years of the 20th century.

Social scientists use the term "millenarian" to describe certain beliefs developed by native peoples under the pressure of foreign cultural (including missionary) influences. The best-known example is the so-called *cargo cults* of Papua New Guinea, which in the 1920s anticipated the return of their ancestors bearing magnificent cargoes of consumer goods, expelling the invaders, and ushering in a golden age of prosperity (see also NATIVISM; box at NORTH AMERICAN NATIVE BELIEFS).

Millett, Kate (1934–)

American writer and sculptor, a leading early theorist of contemporary FEMINISM. Her first book, *Sexual Politics* (1970), defined the terms of the RADICAL feminist critique, arguing, in a survey of cultural patterns and literary models, that sexual relationships are based on power and that they are the PARADIGM of all political relations. Patriarchy, she claimed, is not simply a social convention but a political institution, perpetuating "male supremacy as a birthright" and forcing women into subservience. The boundaries between private and public are artificial—the personal is political. Analyzing four 20th-century male authors—D. H. Lawrence, Henry Miller, Norman Mailer, and Jean Genet—she noted that throughout their work sexuality is driven by the need to dominate, even in the case of the homosexual encounters detailed by Genet, where prerogative is based not on gender but on the caste hierarchies of the gay world.

Most of Millett's subsequent works have examined her own experiences to illuminate issues of political and social control. *Flying* (1974) dealt with her personal turmoil in the wake of *Sexual Politics,* especially her sudden celebrity and the acknowledgment of her bisexuality, both of which sparked controversy within and outside the women's movement. *Sita* (1977), the journal of a lesbian relationship, also proved controversial for its recognition that intimate power struggles are not confined to heterosexuality. *The Basement* (1980), the factual account of a torture-murder overseen by a woman, explored destructive impulses usually identified with male drives for power. Millett's encouragement of a nascent Iranian feminist movement was recounted in *Going to Iran* (1982), and her periods of institutionalization in the 1970s and '80s for manic-depressive episodes informed *The Loony-Bin Trip* (1990), in which she charged that labels such as "mental illness" are social constructs designed to enforce social norms (see FOUCAULT).

mimesis

The artistic imitation of things in the world (the word is Greek for "imitation"). Mimesis is both representation and emulation: a pictorial depiction of a vase of flowers, a dramatic portrayal of the fall of a king, a musical evocation of the flight of a bumblebee. To PLATO, the world itself was merely an imitation of the ideal forms in a sphere beyond our senses, so art was therefore "the imitation of an imitation," an inferior, even fraudulent exercise. ARISTOTLE redefined art as the imitation of the possible, dealing in both form and content with "the nature of UNIVERSALS" rather than simply mirroring the sensible world.

The opposition of the Platonic and Aristotelian conceptions of mimesis is the basis of an ongoing debate over the form and function of art. On one side are those, such as some MARXISTS, who see art as an often distorted reflection of reality that distracts from an understanding of actual conditions; on the other are those, such as the ROMANTICS, for whom art transcends mundane reality to grasp a deeper truth.

Mimesis also applies to artworks that imitate other artworks. The most prominent example in the Western tradition is the CLASSICISM of the Renaissance, which emulated formal and stylistic principles supposedly embodied in Greek and Roman art.

mind/body problem

The question, in philosophy and psychology, of whether there exists a distinct mental or spiritual sphere separate from the physical and, if so, how the two interact. The relationship between spirit and matter is an age-old mystery and is basic to many religious conceptions. Its importance as a philosophical problem derives from the strict DUALISM of René DESCARTES, for whom reality consisted of two disparate types of SUBSTANCE, mind and matter. The question raised by this formulation is how two utterly dissimilar substances can interact; if I cut my finger, how does my mind know it hurts?

In response, Descartes's follower Nicolas Malebranche formulated the theory of *occasionalism,* which explained the interaction of soul and body by the mediation of God: on the occasion of the soul's intention to act, God intervenes to produce the body's action. Other early attempts to bridge the mind/body gulf without rejecting it included Henry More's doctrine of *spissitude,* a quality through which spirit controls the actions of matter, and LEIBNIZ's opinion that the spiritual and material act synchronously, matching each other's movements.

On either side of dualist views are those that dismiss the mind/body problem by asserting that either the mental or the physical doesn't really exist. In the former, MATERIALIST, category are BEHAVIORISM and COGNITIVE theories that see mental function as purely neurological. The latter viewpoint is represented by the doctrines of IDEALISM, that everything is essentially mental or spiritual, and SOLIPSISM, that one's mind is the only reality. Other theories do not see a problem, perceiving mind and body as two interdependent aspects of the same substance or ESSENCE. These "double-aspect" theories include ARISTOTLE's doctrine of *hylomorphism,* in which form and matter unite to constitute earthly substance (a view adopted by the medieval SCHOLASTICS in reflections on the nature of the body and SOUL and the sacrament of the Eucharist), and SPINOZA's concept of MONISM, that God and nature, mind and matter are all aspects of one universal substance.

See also DESCARTES; DUALISM; PHENOMENOLOGY; SOLIPSISM.

Mitchell, Juliet   See box at FEMINISM

mixed regime

Form of government (also called mixed government or mixed constitution) that seeks to combine the best features of two or more different types of authority—traditionally monarchy, aristocracy, and DEMOCRACY. The notion has its origins in ARISTOTLE's identification, in his *Politics,* of an ideal *polity* that would be an amalgam of the three possible "constitutions" of government: rule by the one, the few, and the many. Rulers must govern in the general interest, not their own, and so tyranny, oligarchy, and democracy were all unacceptable (the latter because the rabble would dominate). According to the Greco-Roman historian Polybius, the Roman Republic owed its success to a perfect balance between monarchical, aristocratic, and democratic elements, each operating within its proper sphere. Taking Rome as his model, MACHIA-VELLI advocated a REPUBLICAN mixed regime as best suited to a hierarchically organized society. In the modern world, examples of mixed government are found in constitutional monarchies such as Great Britain, in which a hereditary head of state and the aristocratic House of Lords may influence—but not override—the governance of the elected House of Commons.

modernism

Tendency in Western culture, especially the arts, to reject traditional forms and conventions in favor of innovation and experimentation, usually in response to perceived changes in society and technology. Modernism is usually identified as an artistic trend that began around the end of the 19th century and dominated cultural expression until World War II or after (assessments of the duration of its influence vary widely); but it is also associated with the Renaissance idea of *modernity,* which gained currency with the Scientific Revolution of the 17th century and ascendancy during the ENLIGHTENMENT. That perspective repudiated the authority of the past—specifically, the view that Western civilization had reached its apogee in ancient Greece and Rome—and placed confidence instead in human PROGRESS through RATIONALITY and technological advances. In this sense, modernism represents, for good or ill, the victory of REASON over inspiration, practicality over established custom, and, for some, ALIENATION over human community.

Modernism in the arts developed in reaction to 19th-century ROMANTICISM and REALISM, rejecting conventional narrative content and traditional modes of expression to depict a world seen as altogether new and constantly in flux. (In the art critic Harold Rosenberg's famous phrase, modernism created "the tradition of the new.") It was never a coherent movement, but rather an approach to creation that broke old rules to express new thoughts and reflected certain assumptions, often pessimistic, about the state of the world. Where previous forms had sought to involve the audience in their subject matter, modernism was typified by distancing, self-reflective techniques. This tendency was exemplified by STREAM OF CONSCIOUSNESS in literature, for example, James Joyce's *Ulysses* and Virginia Woolf's *Mrs. Dalloway;* by dissonance and atonality in musical composition (e.g., the works of Igor Stravinsky, Arnold Schoenberg, and Charles Ives); by movements such as CUBISM, SURREALISM, and ABSTRACTION in visual art; and by austere FUNCTIONALISM in architecture (e.g., Louis Sullivan, Frank Lloyd Wright, Ludwig Mies van der Rohe). Modernism has proved elusive of precise definition, and critics also differ widely on its stylistic, philosophical, and chronological relationship to POSTMODERNISM.

The term "Modernism" was also applied to reforming tendencies in CHRISTIANITY that sought to reconcile religious doctrine with scientific thought (particularly EVOLUTIONARY theory) and social change. Such an effort among ROMAN CATHOLIC theologians was condemned as heresy by Pope Pius X in 1907. Reaction to a parallel movement in PROTESTANTISM, in which the Bible is seen as symbolically and morally, but not literally, true, spurred a revival in FUNDAMENTALISM beginning in the 1920s in the United States.

Mohammed   See MUHAMMAD

monetarism

Economic theory that emphasizes the role of the money supply in stabilizing price levels and stimulating economic activity. It stands in opposition to KEYNES-IAN economic theory, which seeks economic equilibrium through active government monetary and fiscal policy. Monetarism is primarily associated with the so-called Chicago School of economists, whose major figure is former University of Chicago economist Milton Friedman. Monetarism is a *neoclassical* economic philosophy, sharing with other approaches such as SUPPLY-SIDE and new classical economics a suspicion of government economic policy and a faith in the workings of the free MARKET.

Where Keynesians hold that economic instability results from an unrestricted free market, monetarists believe that government meddling has at best an uncertain and at worst a deleterious effect on a complex, vigorous economic system, which is best left to the self-correcting mechanisms of LAISSEZ-FAIRE competition. A central tenet of monetarism is Friedman's restatement of the *quantity theory of money,* first espoused by the European MERCANTILISTS of the 18th century, which states that prices and output are related to the supply of money and its *velocity,* or rate of circulation; a stable rate of growth in the money supply will lead to a stable economic growth rate and a constant price level. Monetarists therefore believe that government's main, perhaps sole, function in the economy should be to supply it with money at a steady rate of growth. Friedman argues that government efforts to stimulate the economy, especially when they are financed by deficit spending, may increase economic output in the short run but will eventually trigger a "crowding-out effect," that is, government borrowing drives interest rates up and squeezes out private investment, which slows economic growth.

Monetarists gained prominence and influence in the late 1960s and '70s, when they correctly predicted that Keynesian policies could not correct the high unemployment and inflation that hit the United States and other Western industrialized nations. However, monetarist policies focusing narrowly on the money supply, adopted in the United States and Britain in the late 1970s and early '80s, proved largely ineffective.

monism

The opinion that everything is composed of, or reducible to, a single substance or principle; opposed to DUALISM and PLURALISM. The term was coined by the 18th-century RATIONALIST Christian Wolff to describe solutions to the MIND/BODY PROBLEM that asserted that reality is fundamentally one or the other, that is, that it is basically mental or spiritual (see IDEALISM; SOLIPSISM) or purely physical (see MATERIALISM). Probably the most extreme monist was the pre-Socratic philosopher Parmenides, who held that there is only BEING, seamless and eternal, and that the appearance of individual things (or anything else, for that matter, including motion) is only an illusion (see ZENO'S PARADOXES). The term is most closely associated with SPINOZA, who believed that God and nature are one and that mind and matter are a "double aspect" of a single, universal SUBSTANCE. This view, known as *neutral monism*—everything is part of the same substance, fundamentally neither physical nor mental and therefore "neutral"—was held by William JAMES (and for a time by Bertrand RUSSELL), in the sense that the physical and mental are aspects of the same reality organized in different ways.

See also NEW AGE; REDUCTIONISM; RUSSELL; SPINOZA; cf. HOLISM; PLURALISM.

Monroe Doctrine

A cornerstone of U.S. foreign policy, first enunciated as a warning against European interference in the Americas and later used as grounds for American intervention in Latin America. The doctrine, presented by President James Monroe in his annual address to Congress in December 1823, was actually formulated by Secretary of State John Quincy Adams. A response to fears of encroachment by European powers, particularly against newly independent former Spanish colonies, it placed the hemisphere off-limits to new European colonization while reciprocally pledging American nonintervention in Europe and its remaining colonies.

The doctrine reflected a long-held American conception of the New World as not only geographically but socially, economically, and politically distinct from Europe. Although it was never enforced during the 19th century and has no basis in U.S. or international law, the Monroe Doctrine was the first articulation of a foreign policy that claimed the Caribbean and Central and South America as part of an American sphere of influence. It has often been restated and extended by American presidents. In 1904 Theodore Roosevelt added the so-called Roosevelt Corollary, claiming a right, "in flagrant cases of wrongdoing or impotence, to the exercise of an international police power" in the region. During the Cold War the Monroe Doctrine was invoked to justify military action against several left-wing governments in the Caribbean and Central America.

Mormonism (Church of Jesus Christ of Latter-Day Saints)

CHRISTIAN denomination that considers itself the restoration of the primitive church, which had fallen into apostasy, and takes its authority from ongoing divine revelation. Its adherents regard themselves as heirs to the apostolic mission of Christ's original followers—"saints" of the "latter days."

The church was founded in 1833 by Joseph Smith, a farmer's son in New York State, after the publication of the *Book of Mormon,* which he claimed to have discovered and decoded with divine guidance. The book tells of two of the Lost Tribes of Israel, who traveled across the Pacific and became the first human inhabitants of the New World. They were visited by JESUS Christ in the days after his resurrection, and he prophesied to them his establishment of the New Jerusalem on this continent. One of the tribes, the ancestors of American Indians, eventually turned away from Jesus's teachings and destroyed the other, righteous, tribe. The book professes to be the history of this civilization, engraved on gold plates by one of the survivors, Mormon, and hidden by his son Moroni. The Book of Mormon is regarded by believers as holy scripture that continues and supplements the Bible.

Mormon doctrine diverges from traditional Christianity in other important ways. For example, Mormons conceive the TRINITY as three separate beings, and God the Father and Jesus his Son as having material bodies. The church's strong emphasis on marriage and large families derives in part from the belief that heaven is full of souls waiting to be born and that all humans, if married in a Mormon temple, may aspire to become gods in the afterlife.

The church is a highly structured patriarchy with temple rituals similar to those of FREEMASONRY (Smith and other early church leaders were Masons). The priesthood is open only to males, and until recently women were required to swear obedience to their husbands. The church's president is regarded as a prophet who receives direct revelation from God (the early revelations to Smith and his disciple Brigham Young comprise the Mormon scripture *Doctrine and Covenants*). Such revelations, which continue to shape church doctrine, established and later revoked the controversial practice of male polygamy—a practice that helped to quickly swell the Mormons' numbers during and after their 1846–47 trek to Utah, but also intensified the social and legal persecution that drove them from the East in the first place. Another area of controversy in Mormonism has been its teachings on RACE; Mormon scripture describes Native Americans and blacks as being "cursed" with dark skin, and until 1978 they were barred from the priesthood. The church maintains an extensive private welfare system, a worldwide missionary network, and vast storehouses of genealogical information from which members can identify their non-Mormon ancestors and arrange posthumous baptisms and marriages in the church.

Muhammad (Mohammed) (c.570–632)

Arab prophet, founder of ISLAM; his full name was Abu al-Qasim Muhammad ibn Abdullah. Born in Mecca of a poor but noble family, he became a merchant and in his mid-twenties married Khadijah, a wealthy widow whose business interests he managed; most Muslims consider her the first convert to Islam. Serious, aloof, and highly moral, Muhammad was known in his youth as al-Amin, "the honest and trustworthy." He often meditated in caves outside Mecca, and it was there, at about age 40, he received the first of the revelations from God that, transcribed as they came to him over the rest of his life, became the Qur'an (Koran), the Islamic scripture. (These writings, together with Muhammad's precepts and acts as recorded by his contemporaries, became the basis of Muslim custom and law.) Although most Arabs of his time were PAGANS, the ideas and legends of JUDAISM and CHRISTIANITY had much currency throughout Arabia and influenced Muhammad's teachings.

About 610 Muhammad started to seek converts in Mecca, preaching the oneness of God, the imminence of the day of judgment, and the necessity of leading a moral life and sharing one's wealth with the poor. These sermons angered Meccans, especially the rich nobles, whose persecution finally drove Muhammad and his followers to flee to the provincial town of Yathrib (later called Medina) in 622. The date of this migration, known as the *hijrah* (hegira), marks for Muslims the beginning of the Islamic era.

Although Muhammad had been invited to Yathrib to lead and unite its tribal factions, his task of establishing a Muslim religious brotherhood that would supersede and abolish tribal loyalty proved long and difficult. He met hostility not only from the region's Jewish tribes but from the nominally Muslim converts known as "hypocrites." He also fought a protracted war with Mecca, which finally ended with his victory in 630. Through preaching, political alliances, and war, he eventually either converted or gained the political allegiance of all the Arab tribes in the Arabian peninsula. The parts of the Qur'an revealed in the Medina period consider Muhammad the successor to the Hebrew prophets and regard Islam as supplanting all previous religions. These passages focus on the establishment of a Muslim community and teach that other religious communities, which had rejected their prophets or strayed from their teachings, had been or were in danger of being destroyed by God. The social and political community Muhammad founded, and his life as a whole, are regarded by Muslims as exemplary standards for all of humanity.

mysticism

The search for direct experience of divinity or ultimate reality. Mysticism plays a part in all major religions, though its relation to the mainstream faith varies; it is often esoteric or unorthodox. It is generally distinguished from standard worship by its emphasis on personal experience rather than scripture or prescribed ritual, and in being thought of as available only to those particularly dedicated or holy. (The word comes from the same Greek root as "mystery," referring to secret rites or knowledge.) The object of the mystical quest also varies according to different spiritual traditions' definitions of the Ultimate. In Eastern religions such as BUDDHISM and HINDUISM, the mystic's goal is the merging of the SOUL with the ABSOLUTE; but in JUDAIC, CHRISTIAN, and ISLAMIC belief, where such a notion implies PANTHEISM, mystical endeavor most often seeks true knowledge of, but not union with, the Godhead.

The mystical path commonly involves prayer, meditation, and contemplation, often aided by ASCETIC practice and in some cases involving occult formulas or ecstatic trances, aimed at shedding the material, earthbound layers of the self to become open to the light of divinity normally hidden from mortals. Reports of mystical experiences typically have common elements, including infusions of light, feelings of great joy and wonder, a sense of wholeness and utter freedom, and ineffability, the impossibility of adequately describing the experience. While the mystical vision is ultimately personal, it is usually specific to the religious culture of the individual mystic, whose experience is informed by the scriptural and devotional imagery of his or her particular religious tradition.

See also ANTHROPOSOPHY; HASIDISM; HINDUISM; JUNG; KABBALAH; NEO-PLATONISM; PENTECOSTALISM; ROMANTICISM; SUFISM; TANTRISM; TAOISM; TOTEMISM; TRANSPERSONAL PSYCHOLOGY.

N

nationalism

Ideology that seeks to unify or create a nation, usually based on a common geographic, ethnic, linguistic, cultural, religious, or historical identity. Nationalism assumes the right of self-determination, free of outside influence, and usually implies the existence of a nation-STATE with full international SOVEREIGNTY. Although the origins of nationalism are debated by historians, nascent nationalist ideas arose during the collapse of the feudal order in Europe in the late Middle Ages, when the decline of dynastic and religious authority created the need for a more broadly based political community. The popular sovereignty championed by the French Revolution, and the nation-state it founded, stimulated national unification movements, notably in Germany and Italy. European nationalism contributed to 19th-century IMPERIALISM, which in turn bred nationalist insurgencies in Europe's African, Asian, and American colonies. FASCISM is an extreme, exclusionary form of nationalism in which the nation is accorded a sacred status to which all other interests are subjugated.

Ethnic nationalism differs from so-called state nationalism in that the focus is not on the political unit but on ties of race, religion, culture, or language. One form it takes is *pan-nationalism,* which envisions people united by bonds that transcend political boundaries. Pan-Africanism, for example, seeks to blur or even erase the national borders drawn by European colonial powers in Africa and, especially in the United States, to embrace all people of African ancestry (see GARVEY). A variant of ethnic nationalism is *irredentism,* a longing for reunion with the "mother country" by a population cut off from their homeland or by a nation seeking to regain territory it considers its own. The term comes from the 19th-century slogan "Italia irredenta" (Italy unredeemed), referring to the Italian-speaking enclaves of Switzerland, France, and Austria; it has been dramatically expressed by the annexation of the German-speaking Czechoslovakian Sudetenland and Austria by Nazi Germany in the 1930s, and by the Serbian attempts (termed "ethnic cleansing") to eradicate non-Serb elements in Bosnia and Kosovo in the 1990s.

Patriotism is the personal side of nationalism, a feeling of pride, loyalty, and love for one's nation. It can also lead to a chauvinistic feeling of national superiority, sometimes expressed as *jingoism,* a belligerently militaristic outlook on the world. Nationalism has often been criticized on this and other grounds. For Karl MARX, who linked the nation-state to the rise of CAPITALISM, it was a bourgeois IDEOLOGY that would wither away under SOCIALISM. Albert EINSTEIN, who attributed both world wars to European nationalism, called it "an infantile disease . . . the measles of humanity," which he believed the human race would eventually outgrow.

See also BLACK NATIONALISM; FASCISM; INTERNATIONALISM; NÉGRITUDE.

Native American beliefs See NORTH AMERICAN NATIVE BELIEFS

nativism

Antiforeigner bias by the native-born, either by the dominant majority against a subclass of newcomers or by colonized peoples against their rulers. In philosophy and psychology, nativism is the doctrine that certain capabilities are inherent rather than acquired (cf. INNATE IDEAS). In anthropology, the term refers to social movements among native peoples that seek to counter the oppressive influence of powerful outsiders by reviving selected aspects of traditional culture. In U.S. history, the outstanding example of this sort of revivalism was the Ghost Dance religion of the Plains Indians in the late 19th century (see box at NORTH AMERICAN NATIVE BELIEFS).

Bias against immigrants has been a persistent theme in American history—an ironic reality, given the popular image of the United States as a haven for the world's poor and oppressed. Each successive wave of foreign immigration has awakened fears and prejudices among the native-born, often reflecting a concern that new arrivals from another country, race, or religion will disturb the established culture. Nativist views have frequently influenced federal immigration policy, shaping laws that impose national quotas based on ethnic prejudices or bar certain groups outright.

Nineteenth-century American nativism was founded on the perception of immigrants as not fitting an image of "real" Americans—white, PROTESTANT, and of northern European descent—and was aimed notably at ROMAN CATHOLICS from Ireland and, later, Italy. The Know-Nothing Party, born as a clandestine society and so called because of its members' secretiveness, arose on an anti-immigrant, anti-Catholic platform, reflecting an ingrained view of Catholics as superstitious and undemocratic. Later called the American Party, at its height in the 1850s the organization boasted over a million members, controlled four state governments, and elected some 100 members of Congress. During the 20th century, immigration by eastern European Jews and Spanish-speaking Latin Americans, among others, has rekindled nativist sentiments.

natural law

The ideal law, innate, universal, and unchanging, against which actual human law (positive law) is measured. Natural law is said to have its basis in "nature"— in the natural order, in the human nature common to all people, or in some other pervasive principle, such as God. This view is opposed to *legal positivism,* which holds that all law derives only from human will or agreement (see POSITIVISM). According to natural law theory, any positive law that contradicts the natural law is invalid; this is the basis of CIVIL DISOBEDIENCE.

The idea of natural law has its origin in the STOIC version of LOGOS, the universal REASON that forms, guides, and orders the world. The Romans adopted this notion, distinguishing between the *jus naturale* (natural law) and *jus gentium* (law of nations). Early CHRISTIANITY interpreted natural law as an expression of God's will, and Thomas AQUINAS, going further, conceived it as the part of the eternal law that is accessible to human reason, and therefore a proper foundation for positive law. In the 17th century the Dutch philosopher Hugo Grotius and others developed the idea of *international law,* based on moral principles that transcend local law and custom and depend solely on reason, not divine law, for their force. To John LOCKE, natural law, the law of God, gives rise to humans' *natural rights*—a concept that profoundly influenced the American founders and was eloquently expressed in the Declaration of Independence.

natural theology

Understanding of the existence and nature of God derived solely from REASON and observation, without recourse to supernatural revelation; often equated with *natural religion,* which presumes a universal religious impulse in humans and rejects miracles and divine providence. The idea, which holds that the evidence of the natural world is sufficient to prove the existence of God the creator, reached its peak among the RATIONALISTS of the ENLIGHTEN-MENT (see, e.g., HUME; LEIBNIZ; SPINOZA) and was the central tenet of DEISM. Many CHRISTIAN theologians have distinguished between natural and revealed religion, that is, between religious knowledge obtainable by reason, common sense, and observation of the natural world, and what is available only through divine disclosure. Rational explanations of God were a preoccupa-tion of the medieval SCHOLASTICS such as Thomas AQUINAS, whose "five ways" of understanding God were based on the Aristotelian theory of CAUSE.

The Enlightenment interest in natural religion was in part aimed at creat-ing a universal religion appealing to all people through rational examination. Such a religion would be all-inclusive, founded in truths accessible to all, as opposed to the existing established religions, which were seen as divisive and based on supernatural authority. It was thought that the universal existence of religious belief was due to a natural human instinct, an innate perception of God and understanding of his natural and moral law. The examination of this hypothesis by Lord Edward Herbert of Cherbury, the founder of Deism, initi-ated a search by his followers to establish proof of such a tendency in history; their inability to do so eventually contributed to the decline of Deism. In his influential *Natural Theology* (1802), William Paley sought to illustrate how God's design is displayed in natural phenomena, comparing God to the watchmaker who creates his clockwork and then lets it run by itself. Natural theology remains an influential but controversial strand in Christian thought. On the one hand, rationalist interpretations of the divine are widely ac-cepted as either complementary or alternative to revelation, and on the other, these interpretations are increasingly challenged, especially in PROTES-TANTISM, by FUNDAMENTALIST doctrines committed to scriptural purity and di-vine revelation.

See also DEISM; GOD, ARGUMENTS FOR; LEIBNIZ.

naturalism

In philosophy, the position that all of reality is natural and nothing is super-natural; in the arts, a style that emphasizes scientific accuracy in the represen-tation of human life and society. The term is also applied to the view in psychology that human thought, behavior, and emotion are determined by the same natural desires, instincts, and pain-and-pleasure responses that gov-ern all animal life; and to an approach to research in the social sciences that insists on the study of people in their "natural" social environment, as op-posed to interviews, laboratory experiments, or other artificial conditions.

Philosophical naturalism holds that only those things that are amenable to empirical investigation will produce useful knowledge. It rejects the idea of divine purpose and sees human beings as simply part of the natural world. The search for METAPHYSICAL "first principles" or for the essential qualities of things is pointless because the ultimate character of reality is unobtainable. An outgrowth of EMPIRICISM, naturalism contrasts with viewpoints such as IDE-ALISM and DUALISM, which separate the realms of matter and thought; it shares with PHENOMENOLOGY an emphasis on direct experience over mental abstractions and differs from MATERIALISM only in allowing for the possibility that reality may not be purely physical.

Naturalism in the arts, especially literature, began as an offshoot of 19th-century REALISM. Works in both genres attempted to present human life and society accurately and bluntly, rejecting the idealization and artifice of the past. Naturalism, however, sought not just realism but objective scientific accuracy, with attention to often sordid detail. The French novelist Émile Zola, widely considered the founder of naturalism, was influenced by the new DAR-WINIAN world-view and scientific optimism of his day. In "The Experimental Novel" (1880) and other essays, he likened the new novelist to a scientist conducting painstaking research into the habits and habitats of the human animal, and he adopted that approach in *Les Rougon-Macquart* (1871–93), his series of 20 novels that followed a typical Parisian family through five generations. Although many critics make a point of distinguishing between naturalism and realism, the terms have become somewhat conflated. For example, Zola has also been called a pioneer of realism, and popular 20th-century theater, film, and television drama is interchangeably described as both "realistic" and "naturalistic."

See also EXPRESSIONISM; REALISM.

négritude

African literary movement based on the assertion of a cultural and AES-THETIC sensibility unique to black Africa and its diaspora; the term is French for "blackness." It was conceived in Paris during the 1930s by ex-patriate writers from French-speaking African and Caribbean colonies, notably Aimé Césaire, of Martinique; Léopold Senghor, later the first president of Senegal; and Léon Damas, of French Guiana. Central to négritude is the notion of an antithetical divide between the European and African civilizations, the former MATERIALISTIC, founded on intellect and RATIO-NALITY, the latter rooted in emotion, intuition, and nature. In affirming autonomous African values against European IMPERIALISM, négritude became

"Unlike the classical European, the black African does not distinguish himself from an object. He does not hold it at a distance, he does not look at it, he does not examine it. . . . He touches it, he fingers it, he feels it."

—Léopold Senghor, 1960

a political stance as well as a cultural statement. It informed the IDEOLOGIES of colonial liberation movements, calling on all black people, not just artists, to embrace their traditions and to resist both political oppression and cultural assimilation. Since the 1960s, in the POSTCOLONIAL era, the perspective has become linked, especially by BLACK NATIONALISTS in the United States, to the concept of *pan-Africanism,* the worldwide cultural and spiritual unity of all people of African descent. Its continuing hold on African consciousness, embodied in its enduring legacy in African literature, has been criticized, however, by the Nigerian playwright Wole Soyinka and the West Indian poet Derek Walcott, among others, who call it essentialist (see ESSENCE), REDUCTIONIST, and NATIVIST, replacing Eurocentrism with an equally limited Afrocentrism.

See also POSTCOLONIAL THEORY.

Neoplatonism

Philosophy developed by Greek and Roman followers of PLATO, and later influential in early CHRISTIANITY. Neoplatonism is based in the Platonic theory that the world of our experience is only a shadow of the true world, which is pure and unchanging (see IDEAS). It is most strongly associated with the third-century Egyptian-Roman philosopher Plotinus, who taught that the universe emanates from an infinite, perfect One. He saw existence as a graded hierarchy from pure being down through all life forms to the basest matter (see also HIERARCHY OF BEING). From the One flows *nous* (the universal intelligence), from which in turn comes the *world soul,* source of all souls. The human SOUL strives for unity with the One by struggling against fleshly corruption.

The opposition of spirit and SUBSTANCE in Neoplatonism—a reflection of its MYSTICAL, ASCETIC inclination—was absorbed easily into the early Christian church, as exemplified by St. AUGUSTINE's City of God and City of Man. The Neoplatonist belief in the preeminence of revelation over REASON dominated

Christian thought until the reemergence of ARISTOTLE's writings in Europe in the 13th century.

The Platonic theory that animated Neoplatonism can also be seen in the notion that a work of art, such as a poem or a painting, is the imperfect embodiment of a sublime idea that transcends not only the particular work but the artist as well. This outlook, present in the Renaissance, came into full bloom with the ROMANTICS.

See also ETERNAL RECURRENCE; IBN SINA; NOMINALISM.

New Age philosophy

Eclectic constellation of beliefs and attitudes characterized by attraction to non-Western modes of thought, an emphasis on the spiritual aspect of human beings, and a concern for the well-being of the planetary environment. Rooted in a disenchantment with both authoritarian Judeo-Christian theology and antispiritual scientific POSITIVISM, the New Age movement was presaged by 19th-century alternative trends such as TRANSCENDENTALISM, THEOSOPHY, and SPIRITUALISM, and germinated in the counterculture of the 1960s, which rejected the MATERIALISM, superficiality, and hypocrisy of modern industrial society. The term "New Age" derives from the ASTROLOGICAL observation of a millennial change in zodiacal relationships, with the sun moving out of the constellation of Pisces and entering Aquarius. Where the Piscean Age was marked by RATIONALISM, scientific PROGRESS, INDIVIDUALISM, and violence, the dawning Aquarian Age, it is said, will see a major PARADIGM shift, producing a peaceful synthesis of matter and spirit, individual and community, together with a renewed recognition of humans' responsibility to steward, rather than exploit, the earth and its resources.

New Age thought is not a single, coherent philosophy but a skein of related ideas and tendencies drawing on a worldwide array of spiritual and philosophical sources. There are, however, many common threads. These include interest in Eastern religious philosophies, particularly HINDUISM, BUDDHISM, and TAOISM, as well as PAGANISM and other ancient folk traditions, for their vision of the individual as part of a cosmic whole (see also box at HINDUISM: modern movements; NORTH AMERICAN NATIVE BELIEFS; WITCHCRAFT). New Age belief tends to HOLISM, MONISM, and PANTHEISM, regarding all of reality as an organic unity governed by a divine universal principle that pervades everything (see also SPIRITUALISM). The notion of cosmic oneness is expressed in the goal of attaining *group consciousness,* which transcends both individual and mass CONSCIOUSNESS and strives for the good of all. A precondition of group consciousness is personal transformation and self-actualization—the expansion of talents, benevolent impulses, and spiritual capacities—a notion manifested in the human potential movement of the 1970s and '80s (see TRANSPERSONAL PSYCHOLOGY).

New Criticism

Anglo-American FORMALIST movement in literary criticism, related to STRUC-TURALISM, emphasizing the study of form over intention and effect. Applied to literature in general but in particular to lyric poetry, it was the dominant critical mode from the 1930s to the '60s and helped revolutionize 20th-century criticism. The term came into currency with John Crowe Ransom's *The New Criticism* (1941), in which he described—and took some issue with—the critical approach of I. A. Richards, Yvor Winters, T. S. Eliot, and others. The New Critics regarded the successful poem as a harmonious, unified totality whose unity arises from its linguistic structure. The work's pattern of images and language, far from serving as mere ornament, contains its true substance; its meaning is inseparable from its form. The critic's task, therefore, is to alert the reader to the elements of this structure and the way they fit together; it is not to state the meaning or paraphrase the content, both of which tasks are considered impossible. This approach was almost totally at odds with previous criticism, which was largely aimed at discovering the author's *intention* or describing the work's *effect* on the reader/critic. W. K. Wimsatt and Monroe C. Beardsley identified and condemned these two critical "fallacies" in their influential essays "The Intentional Fallacy" and "The Affective Fallacy" (1946, reprinted in *The Verbal Icon*, 1954). The New Critics maintained that the meaning of a work of literature lies in its own language; it cannot be revealed by researching the author's life nor by investigating the idiosyncratic thoughts and feelings the poem may inspire in the mind of a particular reader, but must be discovered in the text itself.

Cf. DECONSTRUCTION; HERMENEUTICS; box at HISTORICISM; STRUCTURALISM; POSTSTRUCTURALISM.

Newton, Isaac (1642–1727)

English physicist, mathematician, and natural philosopher, whose synthesis of terrestrial and celestial mechanics crowned the development of the mechanical world-view that dominated Western thought until the 20th century and laid the foundations of modern physics. In addition to his most famous discoveries—the three laws of motion and the law of universal gravitation—Newton made fundamental contributions to the fields of mathematics and optics. Early in his career, Newton developed differential calculus, the branch of mathematics that deals with the rates of change of continuously varying quantities, such as curves and acceleration. He later feuded with LEIBNIZ, who developed the calculus independently, over who had invented it first. Newton designed and built reflecting telescopes and discovered that white light is a composite of the rainbow spectrum of colors, which he demonstrated with a prism. Much of Newton's scientific work was built on the theories of COPERNICUS, GALILEO, and KEPLER, and he attributed his achievements to "standing on the shoulders of giants." He also devoted many years to exploring alchemy and to prophetic studies of the biblical book of Revelations. He participated in the anti-Catholic agitation against King James II that led to the so-called Glorious Revolution of 1688, and served as a WHIG member of Parliament.

Newton's major work, *Philosophiae Naturalis Principia Mathematica* (Mathematical Principles of Natural Philosophy, known as the *Principia*), published in 1687, formulated in EUCLIDIAN axiomatic form the principles governing the motion of bodies and their application to the solar system. It contained his *three laws of motion,* which state that (1) objects at rest or in motion remain in that state (the state of *inertia*) unless acted on by an outside force, such as gravity or friction; (2) an object's *acceleration* (rate of increase in velocity) is directly proportional to the force applied to it and inversely proportional to its mass; and (3) for every action there is an equal and opposite reaction. From these laws and Kepler's laws of planetary motion Newton derived his *law of universal gravitation,* which states that the attraction between two bodies—the earth and the moon, for example—is directly proportional to the product of their masses and inversely proportional to the square of the distance between them. The law of gravitation contained a revolutionary and vastly influential insight: the apple falling from a tree and the moon orbiting the earth are governed by the same laws.

The *Principia* became a model for all the quantitative sciences, setting them the challenge of identifying forces analogous to the force of gravity that would account for chemical reactions and electrical and magnetic phenomena (see MAXWELL). Popularized by VOLTAIRE and others, it became one of the most influential books of all time. Its ideas, encapsulated in the conviction that the world is governed by rational laws, extended beyond the sciences to philosophy and politics and became a major inspiration of the 18th-century ENLIGHTENMENT.

Nietzsche, Friedrich (1844–1900)

German philosopher, whose ideas had a profound and lasting influence on 19th- and 20th-century thought. Much of the popular conception of Nietzsche is misconception, based largely on the later appropriation of his notions of the *Übermensch* and the *will to power* by the Nazis. His highly idiosyncratic, aphoristic style of writing has also made him difficult to interpret. The development of Nietzsche's thought reveals a stern critique of European culture, an unorthodox (for his time) AESTHETIC, and a morality that, while hardly egalitarian, was thoroughly cosmopolitan (indeed, he broke with his friend Richard Wagner over the composer's ultra-NATIONALISM and anti-Semitism).

Nietzsche's concept of the APOLLONIAN/DIONYSIAN opposition—the forces of order and harmony versus those of inspiration and ecstasy—advanced in *The Birth of Tragedy* (1872), contained an implicit condemnation of the ethos of institutionalized CHRISTIANITY, which Nietzsche saw as elevating REASON and intellect at the expense of instinct and passion, thus deflating human potential. This theme became central to his thought, culminating, in *Beyond Good and Evil* (1886), in his division of moral systems into *master morality* and *slave morality*. Slave morality, Nietzsche held, is informed by resentment of the free activity of the master, but it also leads the oppressed to define themselves in terms of their condition and to internalize their oppression—embracing their status, endorsing duty and tradition, and resisting change.

To Nietzsche, both Christianity and DEMOCRACY were guilty of promoting slave morality, with its herd mentality and false sense of EQUALITY. These systems, he felt, sought to impose a fixed order on the world, which he saw as ever-changing, always *becoming* (see BEING AND BECOMING). In such degraded circumstances, the old verities could no longer apply: "God is dead." Nietzsche's approach to a new morality began with his concept of the WILL TO POWER—the force that imposes temporary order on a world in flux. In his view, this impulse to activity and mastery was the mainspring of human enterprise and creativity.

The will to power achieves its ideal in the figure Nietzsche called the *Übermensch*—literally "overman," but commonly translated as "superman." The *Übermensch,* as described in *Thus Spoke Zarathustra* (1883–85), embodies the creative impulse and transcends the old, destructive Judeo-Christian morality of pity (slave morality) through a *transvaluation* (or *revaluation*) *of values*. Nietzsche was never clear, however, about whether such "deep-souled" men already existed or would be a product of the future.

Nietzsche's view of circumstances as conditional and temporary is related to his approach to history, called *genealogy.* Contrary to the accepted historical method, which looked for origins and saw events as manifestations of latent predispositions, he viewed human events and institutions as the product of currently prevailing forces that come together, albeit contingently, to produce what then *appear* to be natural, inevitable systems and beliefs. The theory of genealogy has been very influential with POSTMODERN French theorists such as Gilles Deleuze and Michel FOUCAULT.

See also APOLLONIAN SPIRIT AND DIONYSIAN SPIRIT; ETERNAL RECURRENCE; WILL TO POWER.

nihilism

The philosophical position that there are no standards, that knowledge is impossible or at least worthless, that all action, all thought, all ETHICAL and META-PHYSICAL conjecture is baseless and empty. Despite its present connotations, the term (from the Latin for "nothing") was first prominently associated with a Russian intellectual and revolutionary movement of the 1860s and was popularized by Ivan Turgenev in his 1862 novel *Fathers and Sons.* These nihilists held that nothing in the established order commanded automatic respect and nothing should be taken on faith. The term was quickly appropriated by others and applied to any number of social and cultural circumstances.

Whereas Russian nihilism was related to SKEPTICISM (and embraced by AN-ARCHISTS), its expansion into western European philosophy was associated more closely with the PESSIMISM of Arthur Schopenhauer, who was among the first to raise the possibility that the world as a whole might be devoid of intrinsic meaning. In the ferment of the 19th century's iconoclastic historical, political, and scientific theories, many saw nihilism as the characteristic condition of modern Western society. The popular diagnosis of the time, that nihilistic attitudes were the result of the breakdown of CHRISTIAN morality, was opposed by NIETZSCHE; he saw Christian, or "slave," morality, which suppresses intuition and passion, as the *cause* of nihilism.

This opposition has characterized thinking about nihilism ever since. In one view, tradition has broken down and must be resuscitated. The opposite view holds that something within the very nature of Western culture precipitates its deterioration and that the tradition itself must be overcome in order to produce a more vital culture. The first view has been more influential in theological and CONSERVATIVE political circles, while the second has had a powerful effect on 20th-century philosophy, literature, and RADICAL politics, particularly in Europe.

See also DADA.

nirvana (nibbana)

In BUDDHIST thought, the ultimate religious goal, release from worldly desires and limitations. The concept is also found in HINDUISM and JAINISM, primarily in the idea of *moksha,* or union between the SOUL and the ABSOLUTE and deliverance from *samsara,* the cycle of rebirth (see KARMA). From the Sanskrit for "blowing out," nirvana (*nibbana* in Pali) implies liberation from the flames of delusion, ignorance, hatred, and greed into a detached state of tranquility and purity. Nirvana is not a place, nor a state of mind, nor nothingness—nor is it *not* those things, either; it is a transcendent, inclusive condition impossible to define or describe. The BUDDHA stated that whatever is asserted or denied about nirvana is wrong, answering the question of where one goes who has attained nirvana with another question: "Where does a flame go when it is blown out?" Provisional nirvana can be achieved in life, as the Buddha did after his ENLIGHTENMENT, and final nirvana *(parinirvana)* only after death. In Mahayana Buddhism (see box at BUDDHISM), some enlightened beings *(bodhisattvas)* are said to delay achieving final nirvana out of compassion, remaining in *samsara* to help others achieve nirvana.

nominalism

One of the two major tendencies in METAPHYSICS during the Middle Ages and a continuing influence in Western philosophy. In the debate over UNIVERSALS, nominalism—which held that reality is contained in the *particulars* of form and SUBSTANCE—opposed the position of REALISM, which in this sense refers to the belief that true reality resides on a higher, immaterial plane.

Nominalism challenged the dominant philosophical school of the period, NEOPLATONISM, which held to the AUGUSTINIAN distinction between the corrupt material world and the pure world of the divine and concluded that the only genuine reality is to be found in the spiritual world. The 11th-century French philosopher Roscelin, regarded as the founder of nominalism, disputed that position, countering that all universals are merely names imposed on groups made up of individual entities (the term derives from the Latin for "name"). The reality of the world, he argued, can therefore be understood only in terms of particulars, that is, the individual beings that inhabit it.

In the debates of the Middle Ages, the nominalist position was often attacked as heretical. Roscelin, after taking the position that the TRINITY could not be a genuine unity, was forced to recant it—the implication being that if three distinct entities comprised the Godhead, that would make CHRISTIANITY a form of polytheism. Even Roscelin's follower Peter Abelard, who shifted away from strict nominalism to *conceptualism,* which held that the names we

OCKHAM'S RAZOR

The NOMINALIST principle of economy (or "principle of parsimony") attributed to the English SCHOLASTIC philosopher William of Ockham (Occam), which seeks to obtain TRUTH by eliminating the superfluous features of a hypothesis. It is usually expressed as "Entities are not to be multiplied beyond necessity." In other words, the fewer the assumptions necessary to explain something the better, or the simplest adequate explanation is usually the most reliable. The "razor" is the means of simplification, slicing away the superfluous in order to arrive at the crux of an idea. This approach was consistent with William's nominalism, which held that reality subsists in the particular, not the UNIVERSAL; abstract concepts that cannot themselves be accounted for should be avoided when trying to explain the nature of things.

give to universals denote our mind's capacity to find classifications for things, was eventually silenced.

Nominalism was an influential current in the EMPIRICIST thought of the Scientific Revolution of the 17th century, which valued hard facts, not abstract concepts. Francis BACON, for example, said the task of science is to discover the "operations" of nature rather than its general truths. This form of nominalism survives in the principle that underlies much of modern ANALYTIC PHILOSOPHY, namely, that the foundation of reality is to be found in the actual physical objects we encounter, not in any overarching relations among them. Paradoxically, this view is now called *realism*. The term "nominalism" is rarely used by contemporary philosophers, although FOUCAULT and later WITTGENSTEIN, for example, are sometimes called "extreme nominalists" for their view of society (and language) as composed of individual phenomena that are given meaning only by convention and context.

See also PRAGMATISM; UNIVERSALS.

nonviolence

A moral belief and political tactic, often going hand in hand: the belief that human life (or all life) is sacred and must be respected in all circumstances, and the tactical use of nonviolent action to overcome a powerful oppressor. Philosophical nonviolence is virtually synonymous with *pacifism*—principled opposition to war as a means of settling disputes—and *conscientious objection,* moral or religious objection to participation in combat or war preparations.

Nonviolence is firmly rooted in religious and ETHICAL philosophy. Most Eastern religions have strong injunctions against violence. In BUDDHISM and JAINISM especially, the "no-harm" principle of *ahimsa* holds that violence harms its perpetrator as well as its object, interfering with the cycle of KARMA and bringing bad karma to the violent. Early CHRISTIANS, following JESUS's teaching of universal brotherhood, were personally nonviolent and refused to serve in the Roman army, but in the Middle Ages, Christian pacifism largely gave way to the JUST WAR doctrine, which justified warfare under certain circumstances. However, some congregations, notably Quakers and Mennonites (see box at PROTESTANTISM), adhere to unequivocal nonviolent principles. Secular philosophical grounds of nonviolence are generally HUMANIST and cosmopolitan, regarding human life as intrinsically valuable and all humanity as one.

Nonviolent resistance to an unjust system as a means of social or political change is usually undertaken against a civil or military authority with an overwhelming superiority of force. It is often based in the conviction that love and "speaking truth to power" can overcome hatred and that committing violence harms the spirit. Passive resistance can take the form of demonstrations, acts of noncooperation such as boycotts and strikes, and active obstruction such as sit-ins and other types of CIVIL DISOBEDIENCE. The two most notable instances of nonviolent liberation movements in the 20th century have been Mahatma GANDHI's campaign for Indian independence and the American civil RIGHTS crusade led by Martin Luther King Jr. Some critics have qualified these successes, arguing that such tactics are practical only in LIBERAL societies with some restraints on official power, and that they would not have availed the victims of the Holocaust.

See also CIVIL DISOBEDIENCE; GANDHI; JAINISM.

North American native beliefs

The traditional beliefs and religious practices of the native peoples of North America are as varied as the continent they alone populated until the coming of Europeans in the late 15th century. Cosmologies, world-views, and rituals were shaped by the diverse habitats and ways of life of hundreds of different tribes—from nomadic hunters to settled agricultural communities—living in what anthropologists have identified as nine distinct geographical "culture areas" that spread from the subarctic region to the desert Southwest, central Plains, and eastern woodlands. Nonetheless, these peoples have also shared

GHOST DANCE

A mystical, messianic religious movement among Native Americans of the West, the Ghost Dance is the foremost example in U.S. history of religious revivalism by native peoples in resistance to foreign encroachment (see NATIVISM). Responding to America's relentless westward expansion, the Ghost Dance movement flourished briefly in the 1870s and was revived in the late 1880s by a Paiute called Wovoka. A visionary prophecy predicted the magical disappearance of whites from the earth, the return of the buffalo (by then nearly extinct), and the harmonious union of all Indians and their ancestors in a world of abundance and eternal life. This would be accomplished through the Ghost Dance ceremony, a five-night ritual that induced hypnotic states and was to be performed every six weeks until it had worked its magic. The movement spread rapidly throughout the Plains, gaining such influence that it was actively suppressed by U.S. authorities. It declined when its promises failed to materialize, particularly after Sioux warriors wearing "ghost shirts," which they believed would make them immune from soldiers' bullets, were massacred at Wounded Knee, South Dakota, in 1890.

certain characteristics of belief and practice, perhaps owing partly to what is thought to be a common ancestry in prehistoric Asia.

Central to these commonalities is the sense that humans, spirits, animals, plants, and forces of nature inhabit essentially the same realm and are fundamentally alike, all having CONSCIOUSNESS, speech, and individual will and all contributing to the earth's well-being. Similarly, religion and daily life are not distinct spheres but part of a natural whole. Many Native American creation myths tell of a primordial struggle to bring order out of chaos, sometimes a battle in which ancestral culture heroes subdued the forces of evil (see DUALISM), often with the aid of animals and superhuman spirits, and then gave their people the arts and skills necessary for life. These themes of conflict, cooperation, and sacrifice inform much of native folklore and ritual, both of which seek to understand and maintain the cosmic order.

All the native traditions posit a supreme being or Great Spirit, conceived not as an anthropomorphic god but as the pervasive, cosmic force that either created the world and its inhabitants or infused them with life-giving energy, or both. In these ANIMISTIC cultures, myriad nature spirits are believed to inhabit the world. Medicine men and women, diviners, magicians, dancers and drummers, and other religious functionaries mediate between humans and nature, supplicating and appeasing the spirits that control the weather, the food supply, the health of the tribe, and the stability of the universe (see SHAMANISM). Departed ancestors continue to exist after death, but they occupy a separate plane, usually a perfected version of the world, and are largely detached from the living community (cf. AFRICAN RELIGIONS). Initiation rites for young men often involve a *vision quest,* in which the initiate, after purifying himself in ASCETIC ordeals, seeks a vision of his guardian spirit, who reveals to him his special strengths and responsibilities.

With the Europeans came CHRISTIANITY, and in response to its influence new religious movements arose. Some grafted Christian imagery onto traditional forms—for example, the Great Spirit as Heavenly Father or the Earth Mother as the Virgin Mary—while others revitalized old beliefs and rituals in defiance of white encroachment. Two examples are the Handsome Lake religion, founded in the early 19th century by the Seneca visionary Ganioda'yo (Handsome Lake), who recast the Iroquois religion in terms of Christian concepts and Quaker morality, and the messianic Ghost Dance religion, which swept the Plains in the late 1800s, promising a return to the pristine past (see box). Both movements initially attracted throngs of followers demoralized by the impact of white civilization. The most successful of the syncretic religions that sprang up in the wake of white conquest is the *peyote cult,* established in 1918 as the Native American Church, which combines the ancient sacramental use of the hallucinogen peyote *(mescal)* with Christian ethics and a cosmology fusing Christian and native beliefs.

O

object relations theory

Approach to psychology based on the premise that psychological development occurs primarily through relations with others. The theory was developed
in the 1930s in the British school of neo-Freudian PSYCHOANALYSIS, particularly
by Melanie Klein, Donald W. Winnicott, and W. R. D. Fairbairn. Object relations theories vary, but all proceed from the assumption that personal development depends principally on early attachments. In contrast to the emphasis
in FREUDIAN theory on instinctual inner drives, object relations theorists focus
on an infant's relationship with and perception of the *objects* of attachment
in his or her environment, particularly the primary caregiver (usually the
mother). In the first year or two of life, a child relates not to the whole person
but to an objectified *representation* of her. When the mother—who is, after all,
a real, imperfect being—is sensed as being nurturing at some times and ne-
glectful at others, the child's experience of her is split; she is seen, in effect, as
two people, one all-loving, all-kind, all-protective, the other cold and cruel.
While the maturing child learns independence and comes to understand the
complexity of relationships, the dynamic tension between autonomy and attachment remains a central issue throughout life. In adulthood, the *splitting*
reaction may recur in times of distress, for example, when an argument with a
friend or lover makes one see only that person's negative qualities. Those
whose infant experiences have been predominantly painful may never grow
out of this either/or perception of others, rejecting them at the first sign of
imperfection.

Object relations and Freudian theory also diverge in their ideas about the
development of gender identity. In Freud's view, boys instinctively identify
with their father; in object relations theory, boys and girls alike at first identify

with their mother, and male identity develops as a negative: being not female. Thus men tend to develop a strong sense of independence but often have difficulty with emotional closeness and other qualities associated with their original "female" identity; women, on the other hand, never having had to separate from the mother, often have trouble asserting independence and authority.

objectivism and subjectivism

Two opposing approaches to the question of how individuals interact with the external world. Both arise from the assumption that the object that is experienced and the subject having the experience are distinct, and that one side or the other is more fundamental to the equation (cf. IDEALISM; PHENOMENALISM). Objectivism holds that the world's inherent qualities determine the observer's experience and can be accurately perceived; subjectivism holds that one's own perspective brings more to experience than is inherent in the world and colors one's judgment of it.

For philosophers, the opposition between objectivism and subjectivism is both an EPISTEMOLOGICAL problem—the problem of whether the features of the external world are resident in it or are supplied by our minds—and, even more important, an ETHICAL one. Is something "good" because of an inherent quality of "goodness" (which is difficult if not impossible to determine) or because it is conventionally considered good (in which case there can be no absolute standards of goodness)? God is often cited as the guarantor of ethical values, but the problem remains: if God declares something good because it is good, it is beyond the range of his power; if goodness is the result of a divine edict, it is arbitrary.

Contemporary thinkers such as HEIDEGGER and WITTGENSTEIN have sought to avoid this dichotomy by recasting human experience without the gulf between subject and object, seeing the relationship between the two as more fundamental than either side in itself. Another solution is Max WEBER's doctrine of *value neutrality* (or *value-freedom*) in social science, which presumes that all investigations of social interaction contain subjective biases that must be acknowledged in order to be at least partially overcome.

See also LIBERTARIANISM.

Ockham's Razor See box at NOMINALISM

opportunity cost

The cost of giving up one option in favor of another; a fundamental concept in economics. In a world of finite resources, the concept is a valuable tool in decisions about how to use or allocate those resources. In evaluating the real cost of undertaking an activity, opportunity cost takes into account the value of what is forgone—the opportunity *not* taken—rather than simply the monetary cost of the alternative chosen. For example, the opportunity cost of manufacturing only trumpets includes the loss of a share of the trombone market; the opportunity cost of a college education includes the salary the student could be earning in a job; the opportunity cost of deciding to work overtime includes the perceived value of the leisure time given up; the opportunity cost of using plastic grocery bags instead of paper ones includes the depletion of nonrenewable petrochemical resources. In all these circumstances, the option chosen is considered to be worth more, in financial or other terms, but part of its real cost is contained in the sacrifice of the "next-best" alternative. Consumers also apply the concept when deciding *how much* of which products or services to buy. Assuming a limited amount of disposable income, the opportunity cost of buying more of one thing is the necessity of buying less of something else.

ordinary language philosophy

Philosophical movement emphasizing the analysis of language in everyday use. It was introduced in the 1950s by J. L. Austin and other Oxford University philosophers influenced by WITTGENSTEIN. Ordinary language philosophy was a reaction to the strict application of LOGIC to linguistic analysis, as practiced by the LOGICAL POSITIVISTS and Bertrand RUSSELL (see also ANALYTIC PHILOSOPHY), in which a phrase or sentence was considered meaningless if it did not meet certain analytic criteria. The purpose of philosophy, Austin argued, should not be to subject language to binding definitions or rigid logical analysis, but to study the meaning of terms in ordinary usage. He therefore proposed that language should be seen primarily in terms of *performative utterances* (or "speech acts"), statements intended to accomplish something, which are meaningful by virtue of that fact. Austin distinguished among three different kinds of performative language—*locutionary,* the simple statement ("It is raining"); *illocutionary,* the intention or implication of the statement ("Let's not go out"), and *perlocutionary,* what actually happens as a result of the statement (We're not going out).

Everyday language gives an accurate view of reality, Austin said—more accurate than arcane jargon and more likely to reveal the solutions to vexing philosophical problems. The problem of separating knowledge from belief, for instance, can be overcome by recognizing that saying "I know . . ." does not make a statement about an abstract quality of knowledge, it merely stakes a claim for the validity of what is referred to. In fact, Austin argued, only the illocutionary aspect of a statement will reveal how something is meant in actual discourse, and therefore what the real sense of the word is. The speech act and its surrounding context, not the logical implications of the words themselves, are the proper focus of study. In the United States, *speech-act theory,* concentrating on statements' illocutionary and perlocutionary qualities, has become an important discipline within linguistics as well as philosophy, notably in the work of John R. Searle.

See also MEANING.

Ortega y Gasset, José (1883–1955)

Spanish philosopher, whose work paralleled that of the French and German EXISTENTIALISTS and PHENOMENOLOGISTS, and whose HUMANISTIC critique of modern society castigated both the outmoded monarchy and the new mass culture. Ortega was one of the generation of Spanish intellectuals who came of age in the wake of the Spanish-American War, which ended Spain's imperial history. His philosophy was in large part a response to the perceived need to develop a new national identity with a fresh intellectual perspective.

In contrast to the viewpoint of his influential predecessor Miguel de Unamuno, who held that the antithetical opposition of abstract REASON and "flesh-and-blood" human existence results in a "tragic sense of life," Ortega advanced the notion of *vital reason.* Far from impeding the free flow of life, reason is life's most valuable asset. It is the means by which we negotiate an indifferent world in which we are "shipwrecked" and must constantly swim, never certain of our position, never able simply to accept the truths we are offered but always forced to test them in new circumstances. Indeed, as Ortega put it, "I am I and my circumstances"—that is, we are defined by our beliefs and desires (the internal "I") and our actions and interactions (external "circumstances"). The goal of life is to "become what you are," to merge the internal and external.

In his best-known work, *The Revolt of the Masses* (1929), Ortega denounced the rise of the "masses" as the dominant cultural force in contemporary society. Mass culture, he said, breeds mediocrity and ignorance, and popular opinion now overshadows traditional morality and intellectual judgment. Satisfied by material comforts, passive and undisciplined, the masses can be manipulated by TOTALITARIAN leaders if they are not guided by the "select minority," an intellectual and moral "nobility" whose thoughtfully directed energies bring value and order to society.

Orthodox Church

Also called the Eastern Orthodox Church, one of the three major divisions of CHRISTIANITY (with ROMAN CATHOLICISM and PROTESTANTISM), the dominant religious presence in Russia and southeastern Europe, including Greece. It is a communion of independent national churches and other *patriarchates* associated with the church's ancient seats, Alexandria, Antioch, Jerusalem, and Constantinople (now Istanbul). All recognize the ecclesiastical and liturgical authority of the Patriarch of Constantinople but, unlike the Roman Pope, he does not hold absolute power nor claim infallibility. The Orthodox Church professes to represent an unbroken historical continuity with the Christian church established by the New Testament apostles. Descended from the Greek-speaking church of the Byzantine Empire, it separated from the western church in the Middle Ages after a long series of doctrinal conflicts that included disputes over the primacy of the Roman pontiff and the nature of the Holy Spirit.

The doctrine of orthodoxy (which means "true belief") holds to the unerring authority of the dogma established by the seven General Ecumenical Councils of the early Christian church, including the incarnation of JESUS as god-in-man and the TRINITARIAN nature of God, three persons in one ESSENCE. In Orthodox belief, God is both TRANSCENDENT and immanent, ultimately unknowable but present in the world in his "energies," which constitute the active principle in our lives. The last of the councils recognized by the Orthodox churches, the Second Council of Nicaea in 787, upheld the legitimacy of religious images, or *icons,* against the claim that they violated the biblical injunction against idolatry. The veneration of icons is central to Orthodox worship; the paintings depicting Christ and the saints are seen not as objects of worship in themselves but as visual representations of spiritual reality and channels of divine blessing.

> *"The man who discovers a new scientific truth has previously had to smash to atoms almost everything he had learned, and arrives at the new truth with hands blood-stained from the slaughter of a thousand platitudes."*
>
> —José Ortega y Gasset,
> *The Revolt of the Masses*

The Orthodox liturgy, written by St. John Chrysostom in the fourth century, centers around the Eucharist, as in the Roman Mass (see box at CHRISTIANITY). However, in contrast to the Catholic emphasis on the sacraments as mediating between the believer and God, the Orthodox tradition gives greater significance to personal communion with the divine. Orthodox theology is thus more MYSTICAL in spirit, belonging as much to the layperson as to the priest. It is informed equally by scriptural authority and holy tradition. The latter includes the teachings of the church fathers—such as St. Basil's doctrine of God's ESSENCE and energies and St. Athanasius's doctrine of the Trinity—the decrees of the General Councils, the holy icons, and the sense of apostolic continuity.

P

paganism

Adherence to one of the ancient polytheistic or PANTHEISTIC pre-CHRISTIAN religions; an often pejorative term recently reclaimed by so-called *neopagans*, who assert the divinity of all things, revere the earth as the mother of life, and perform ritual observances celebrating the cycles of the seasons and of human life. The Latin term *paganus,* meaning both "peasant" and "civilian," was first used—reportedly by the second-century church father Tertullian—to distinguish the "soldiers of Christ" from nonbelievers who adhered to the antique Greco-Roman religion (although early Christianity had itself absorbed and adapted a number of pagan myths and rituals). The term came to be associated with the view of European Christians that "heathens" were not only ignorant idolaters but uncivilized barbarians.

Since the 1960s a revival of self-described "paganism" has arisen, mainly in North America and Britain, as part of the NEW AGE movement and its search for an earth-centered, all-inclusive spirituality. Neopagans draw eclectically from ancient traditions, notably the ANIMISTIC nature worship of Native American cultures (see NORTH AMERICAN NATIVE BELIEFS) and the Celtic rituals of ancient Britain commemorating the solstices, equinoxes, and other seasonal occasions. While the movement is diverse and presents no organized doctrine, neopagans tend to be *pantheistic,* finding God (and Goddess) in all of nature and within every person; *ecophile,* cherishing the purity and interconnectedness of the natural world and worshiping it as GAIA, or Mother Earth; and *experiential,* celebrating the world, the self, and community in revived and newly created rituals.

See also GODDESS WORSHIP; NEW AGE; WITCHCRAFT.

Paine, Thomas (1737–1809)

Anglo-American political theorist, whose RADICAL stance, inflammatory rhetoric, and accessible prose style made him the most successful propagandist of his day. In America during the War of Independence and in France during the French Revolution, he issued a series of widely read pamphlets advocating representative REPUBLICANISM and justifying revolution as the means to achieve that end. His egalitarian political philosophy rested on a LOCKEAN theory of natural RIGHTS in which legitimate government derives from a SOCIAL CONTRACT that involves the voluntary consent of the people, who remain SOVEREIGN.

In 1776, soon after emigrating to America from his native England, Paine published (anonymously) his most popular and influential pamphlet, *Common Sense,* which denounced the colonial government of King George III as inimical to the colonists' interests and called for Americans to form an independent republican government. It sold half a million copies and set the stage for the Declaration of Independence. During the Revolutionary War, Paine helped the patriotic cause with a series of 16 stirring pamphlets titled *The Crisis,* the first of which began with the famous words "These are the times that try men's souls."

Paine returned to England in 1787, two years before the beginning of the French Revolution. In *The Rights of Man* (1791–92), a retort to Edmund BURKE's denunciatory *Reflections on the Revolution in France,* Paine rebutted the CONSERVATIVE assertion that stability depends on adherence to tradition. He savaged the monarchical system as tyrannical and fraudulent, calling the notion of hereditary rulers "as absurd as an hereditary mathematician." For this insult to the monarchy, he was prosecuted for seditious libel and fled to France, where he became one of the few foreigners elected to the French revolutionary National Convention, although he was later imprisoned and barely escaped the guillotine after opposing the execution of Louis XVI.

> *"It is wrong to say that God made rich and poor; He made only male and female, and He gave them the whole earth for their inheritance."*
>
> —Thomas Paine,
> *Agrarian Justice*

With the publication of *The Age of Reason* (1794–95), which championed DEISM and attacked organized CHRISTIANITY; *Agrarian Justice* (1795–96), which called for land reform and progressive TAXATION and envisioned a WELFARE state; and the *Letter to Washington* (1796), haranguing America's hero-president, Paine outraged opinion and alienated friends on both sides of the Atlantic. He fell into disfavor and, after returning to America in 1802, died in obscurity.

pantheism and panentheism

Related but distinct ways of understanding the relation of God to the world. Pantheism (literally, "God in all") holds that God and nature are identical, while panentheism ("all in God") holds that God contains the world but is greater than it. Both of these views are of God as essentially *immanent*—in the world and of it—in contrast to the Judeo-Christian theological tradition, in which the Creator is seen as separate from creation (see TRANSCENDENTALISM).

While both pantheism and panentheism have been of primarily intellectual interest in Western culture, they are fundamental to ANIMISTIC and other beliefs founded on the worship of nature and hold central positions in Eastern religions. In the latter case, however, it is difficult to apply these terms precisely. HINDUISM, for instance, contains a classic pantheist doctrine, that all things are a part of the unchanging *brahman*, while also including a lower realm of deities who act on and in the world. BUDDHISM tends to the belief that all things are united, but this unity is so pure as to be devoid of quality, and therefore beyond any conventional conception of deity.

The best example of Western pantheism is in the philosophy of SPINOZA, for whom God and creation were identical, nature being a limited modification of God's presence. HEGEL presents a good instance of panentheism, holding that God, the ABSOLUTE, contains not only the world as it is, but also its contradictions; history is the gradual elimination of those contradictions in a progression to ultimate unity with the Absolute. The New England TRANSCENDENTALISTS embraced a kind of pantheism emphasizing oneness with nature, which derived in part from the ROMANTICS' semi-MYSTICAL view of unspoiled nature as the earthly manifestation of a transcendent reality.

See also ANIMISM; GOD, CONCEPTS OF; GODDESS WORSHIP; PAGANISM; SPINOZA.

Pavlov, Ivan See CONDITIONING, CLASSICAL AND OPERATIVE

paradigm

An ideal or archetypal pattern or example that provides a model to be emulated. PLATO's theory of IDEAS conceived of an ideal world of forms, separate from the earthly sphere, in which the paradigms of worldly objects resided. A *paradigm case* is an exceptionally clear or representative example of something, such as a physical or mental disorder; in philosophy, the *paradigm case argument* is used to dispute SKEPTICAL or IDEALIST assertions, for example, that the objects of PERCEPTION do not exist, as in G. E. Moore's famous illustration, "Here is a hand . . . and here is another."

From the mid-20th century, a somewhat different meaning of "paradigm" has become widely influential as a theory of scientific progress. It was first elaborated by Thomas Kuhn in his book *The Structure of Scientific Revolutions* (1962). Kuhn challenged the traditional notion of scientific knowledge as purely objective, seeing it instead as based on *dominant paradigms*—accepted theories that reflect and uphold certain established viewpoints. Kuhn gives as an example the Ptolemaic picture of the universe, with the earth at its center, circled by the sun, planets, and stars, which prevailed for centuries until it was undermined by astronomical observations and COPERNICUS's heliocentric theory of the solar system.

As a generally accepted explanation of things, the dominant paradigm provides the focal point and measuring stick for scientific investigation. But its version of reality tends to become ingrained, influencing the very choice of questions deemed worthy of study, the methods used to study those questions, and the interpretations of the results. Science conducted according to the dominant paradigm, or complementary sets of paradigms, is called by Kuhn "normal science."

Scientific progress, according to Kuhn, is not incremental but proceeds in stages via the *paradigm shift*, in which one paradigm is overtaken and replaced by another. Inevitably, any theory encounters anomalies; its strength is determined to some extent by its ability to overcome them. But when too many exceptions to the rule accumulate, competing theories gain stature. Because the reigning paradigm is supported by tradition, has had careers built upon it, and is often part of a larger world-view, it does not easily fall before the force of new evidence. A period of instability, or "revolutionary science," ensues, in which the old and new paradigms compete for acceptance. The ultimate adoption of a new paradigm promotes scientific progress by providing a platform for fresh approaches to research.

parapsychology

The study of mental events and phenomena that apparently conflict with accepted scientific laws; also called *psychic research*. Mental faculties inexplicable by orthodox theories are often gathered under the term "psi." The modern scientific study of psi is focused on *extrasensory perception* (ESP), the ability to detect things outside the range of the senses, and *psychokinesis* (PK), the mind's capacity to affect external states and objects. ESP includes telepathy, the unmediated transmission of information between minds; precognition, the intuition of a future event; and clairvoyance, the nonsensory awareness of events or objects. Examples of PK are levitation and the control of bodily processes achieved through YOGA. Phenomena such as poltergeists—unexplained noises or the spontaneous movement of objects—are called "involuntary PK." Psi also encompasses out-of-body experiences and other *altered states of consciousness;* ghosts and apparitions; SPIRITUALISM (spiritism), or communication with the spirits of the dead; and hypnosis, a trancelike state of heightened suggestibility.

Hypnosis, today the only broadly accepted aspect of psi, was pioneered in the 18th century by the Austrian physician Franz Anton Mesmer. He was able to cure some ailments through the power of suggestion after placing patients in a sleeplike trance, which he ascribed (incorrectly) to a magnetic force he called "animal magnetism." Scientific investigation of paranormal phenomena in the 19th century was motivated in part by a desire to demonstrate the immortality of the SOUL, a doctrine that had been challenged by the ascendancy of scientific MATERIALISM. Séances purporting to make contact with departed spirits were studied by scientists such as Sir William Crookes, but their endorsements of the mediums' claims were generally dismissed by their colleagues. Modern experimental parapsychology was pioneered by J. B. Rhine beginning in the 1920s. His famous experiments in ESP, involving the visualization of cards, and PK, in which subjects tried to influence the roll of dice, yielded results that exceeded the normal range of chance or PROBABILITY.

Most scientists insist that parapsychology is "pseudoscience" by definition, because it is by nature unpredictable and thus elusive of EMPIRICAL investigation; they dismiss experimental evidence as either methodologically flawed or fraudulent. However, some independent research seems to support at least some aspects of psi. Theories about the nature of psi include those based on JUNG's concepts of the *collective unconscious*—that all humans share a subliminal heritage—and *synchronicity*—that certain meaningful events are linked acausally, that is, outside normal space-time boundaries. Some recent explanations for these theories derive from QUANTUM THEORY, such as the postulation of widely distributed, interconnected *quantum systems* that link energy fields over great distances, and the hypothesis of *hidden variables* that are unmeasurable and independent of space-time.

See also SPIRITUALISM.

Pascal, Blaise (1623–1662)

French philosopher, mathematician, and physicist, a polymath of great scope and originality. Although he is remembered primarily for his religious and philosophical reflections in the *Pensées,* Pascal's contributions to theoretical and empirical science were wide-ranging and influential. He invented, at age 19, the first mechanical calculating machine (the principle was the same as that of a car's odometer). He expounded the basic principle of hydraulics (known as Pascal's law), that in fluids, pressure applied at any point is transmitted equally throughout the fluid. He experimentally confirmed the theory of atmospheric pressure—that air has weight, which changes with atmospheric conditions (the principle of the barometer) and altitude. With Pierre de Fermat, he originated PROBABILITY THEORY, the branch of mathematics dealing with the correlation between possibilities and outcomes, which he later applied in some of his theological writings.

After a MYSTICAL conversion in 1654, Pascal became an adherent of Jansenism, a ROMAN CATHOLIC movement that opposed the church's opulent ceremony and rejected the RATIONALISM of the Jesuits, stressing instead an ASCETIC piety and the AUGUSTINIAN doctrine of unconditional PREDESTINATION and grace founded in God's, not man's, will. Pascal defended the Jansenists against charges of heresy in his 18 *Provincial Letters* (1656), which were distinguished as much by their succinct, ironic style as their polemical force. However, his most enduring religious statements are those collected after his death in *Thoughts on Religion and Several Other Subjects* (1670), known as the *Pensées.*

In the *Pensées,* Pascal set out to justify CHRISTIANITY within the reigning ENLIGHTENMENT spirit of doubt. To Pascal, the human condition was painfully ambiguous. Overwhelmed by the vastness of existence and unable to comprehend its minute complexities, we are certain only of our uncertainty. "Man is a reed, the frailest in nature, but he is a thinking reed," and therefore superior to nature, which is unaware of its own existence, Pascal wrote. He divided human REASON into two varieties: the *spirit of geometry,* by which abstract, analytical judgments are made, and the *spirit of finesse,* which navigates the mundane world and grasps it intuitively. However, reason alone cannot apprehend the most fundamental truths: "The heart has its reasons, which reason knows nothing of." The only means of reconciling our confusing, contradictory existence and of overcoming the corruption of original sin is redemption through God's grace.

See also PROBABILITY.

PASCAL'S WAGER

An argument for belief in God, based on PROBABILITY THEORY, proposed by PASCAL in his *Pensées* and probably addressed to his worldly, skeptical acquaintances and their love of gambling (and perhaps to his own doubts as well). Pascal proposed that to believe in God or not constitutes a wager that he exists or does not exist. Being alive and human, we cannot avoid making a bet on one side or the other. If God exists, then to believe in him is to receive eternal life, while to deny him is to suffer damnation. If he does not exist, then to either receive or refuse him is to lose nothing. Hence, the wise gambler will choose to accept God, since to win the wager is to win all, and to lose is to lose nothing.

Pentecostalism

Movement in CHRISTIANITY that emphasizes personal experience of the divine, especially the gifts of the Holy Spirit. The name derives from the passage in the New Testament (Acts 2) describing the descent of the Holy Spirit upon JE-SUS's apostles at the Feast of Pentecost. Pentecostal worship is informal and passionate, including spirited singing, spontaneous exclamations of faith, evangelical preaching, prophesying, faith healing, ecstatic trances, and "speaking in tongues" (*glossolalia*, speaking from a trance, usually in an unintelligible language)—all attributed to the presence of the Holy Spirit. Its FUNDAMENTAL-IST theology includes belief in the literal truth of scripture and in the endless torture of the damned after the Last Judgment (see ESCHATOLOGY).

Pentecostalism grew out of the Holiness movement, a 19th-century revivalist strain within American Methodism that stressed spiritual experience over formal theology and sought to reinstate ("revive") the faith and practices of the early Christian church. Beginning in Kansas around 1900, Pentecostalism quickly spread in the early years of the century; the Los Angeles ministry of William J. Seymour, a black preacher, was particularly influential. Initially interracial, the movement eventually split into mainly segregated churches. Today, the largest predominantly white Pentecostal church is the Assemblies of God and the largest black denomination is the Church of God in Christ. After a period of decline, Pentecostalism reemerged following World War II through tent revivals and the advent of "televangelism." Since the 1960s the influence of Pentecostalism has spurred a so-called *charismatic* revival (from the Greek for "gift" or "grace") within some mainstream PROTES-TANT churches.

perception

In philosophy, most ideas about the nature of our sensory experience of things in the world are to some extent attempts to define "perception." Is perception equivalent to sensation—what you see is what you perceive—or is it a mental construct applied to the physical sensation? And if direct perception is not possible, if we see the world through a "veil of appearances," how can we say that our perceptions comprise actual knowledge of real things? The ancient Greeks tended to the notion that perception occurs via an imperfect copy of the actual thing perceived, either because a representation of the object is transported to the mind of the observer or, in PLATO's theory of *ideal forms*, because we recognize in an earthly object a flawed approximation of its ideal archetype. (Although theories of perception generally encompass all sensations, most tend to discuss it in terms of sight.)

The idea that we receive direct and accurate knowledge of the external world through our senses is called—mostly by its critics—*naive realism*. The most common objection to this conclusion is known as the argument from *illusion*, which asks what we are to make of hallucinations, optical illusions, and the like: if we can see something that is not really there, how can we be confident of the accuracy of our other perceptions? Some definitions of perception explicitly exclude illusion; the *causal* and *representative* theories, for example, hold that what we perceive is only a mental representation of an object, but that the object must be real to cause genuine perception. Other theories insist that objective knowledge of the world is impossible and *only* the mental perception can be confidently regarded as real (see IDEALISM; PHENOMENALISM).

A long-standing tradition in philosophy and psychology has distinguished between sensation and perception, that is, between the "raw data" of color, shape, sound, and other sensory stimuli, and the mind's interpretation of the data into recognizable objects of experience. Immanuel KANT is the seminal figure in this tradition, holding that our perception—and common understanding—of the world is possible because our minds impose a specific structure on our sensations according to an innate, universal pattern (see box at KANT). For other thinkers in this line, such as A. J. Ayer, perception is primarily our ability to organize sense data in order to be able to create logically consistent statements from the mass of sensory experience. Most modern psychologists understand perception as the mind's ordering of sense stimuli based on the observer's previous experiences and mental and emotional state, that is, as a composite of objective stimulus and subjective interpretation. Many COGNITIVE psychologists, for whom perception is a central interest, see it in terms of information-processing theory, likening the human brain's function to that of an electronic computer (see INFORMATION THEORY).

See also BERKELEY; COGNITIVE PSYCHOLOGY; CONSCIOUSNESS; EMPIRICISM; GESTALT; HOBBES; HUME; KANT; MERLEAU-PONTY; RUSSELL.

perestroika

Program of economic and political reform proposed by Soviet leader Mikhail Gorbachev in 1984. The term, Russian for "restructuring," was applied primarily to a series of strategies aimed at gradually introducing MARKET forces and private initiative into the Soviet economy, which had previously been dictated by state-controlled central planning. It was closely associated with Gorbachev's policy of *glasnost*—literally meaning "publicity," but implying openness and free speech—which encouraged freedom of expression and restored many civil liberties.

Perestroika stemmed from an acknowledgment that state SOCIALISM as practiced in the Soviet Union had bred industrial inefficiency, a bloated bureaucracy, and economic stagnation. However, it was an attempt to salvage the socialist system, not to scuttle it. Although ultimately judged a failure, it was the first, halting attempt to change a centrally planned production system to a market-driven one that avoided the excesses and insecurities of unbridled free-market CAPITALISM. Between 1985 and 1991, Gorbachev implemented numerous plans intended to liberalize the economy by reorganizing bureaucracies, loosening rent and price controls, encouraging foreign investment, giving industrial managers more independence and flexibility, and allowing some private enterprise. The program, which met with resistance both from entrenched bureaucrats and from reformers who wanted more drastic changes, failed in several key areas. For example, the consolidation of many smaller economic ministries into one superministry, intended to allow more production decisions to be made by the market, expanded the bureaucracy rather than shrinking it. The period of perestroika and glasnost set the stage for the breakup of the Soviet Union in the early 1990s and the establishment of a competitive DEMOCRACY in the Russian Federation, whose first president, Boris Yeltsin, initiated a rapid conversion to a fully capitalist economy—a shift no less problematic and chaotic than perestroika.

pessimism

The propensity to believe or expect the worst (the word comes from the Latin for "worst"); as a philosophical perspective, the belief that this is the worst of all possible worlds, one inherently malevolent or at best apathetic. The position is primarily associated with the 19th-century German philosopher Arthur Schopenhauer, who concluded that renouncing the world is the only way to overcome its pain. Schopenhauer attacked HEGEL's optimism and based his philosophy on a version of KANT's "phenomenon/noumenon" distinction between the world of perceptions and the independent, imperceptible reality of things. In Schopenhauer's formulation, "representations" form the surface reality of the world, beneath which is a blind, irrational "will," which creates desire and the will to live. The world is evil because it enslaves humanity to the dictates of this "will." Meaning, happiness, and goodness are all illusory. One can conquer the dictates of the will by overcoming the ego that drives it, partly through acts of compassion to others (and in this, pessimism shows its ETHICAL side), but primarily by negating it through meditative, ASCETIC practices culminating in a state similar to the NIRVANA of BUDDHISM. Indeed, Schopenhauer was the first Western philosopher to utilize the insights of Eastern philosophy. The pessimistic idea is reflected, to some extent, in the Buddhist view that human life is grounded in suffering, which can be transcended only by overcoming the ignorance and cravings that cause it.

See also NIHILISM.

phenomenalism

A version of EMPIRICISM, also related to SKEPTICISM. The theory states that we can have knowledge of only the *phenomena* we perceive, that the reality of a thing depends on our PERCEPTION of it, and that therefore we cannot be certain of the true nature of reality. Matter exists, so far as we can know for sure, only if and when we perceive it. If there is a fundamental reality beyond the world of phenomena, it is unknowable and therefore not worth speculating about. (See APPEARANCE VERSUS REALITY; IDEALISM; IDEAS; KANT).

The position is largely associated with the 18th-century British empiricists George BERKELEY and David HUME. Berkeley distinguished between "BEING" and "being perceived" and maintained that the objects of perception exist *only* in our experience of them. Hume took the position that our view of reality is no more than the conglomeration of associated ideas, the apparent coherence of which is due to the strength of our "natural beliefs" or customary ways of thinking.

The unqualified phenomenalism of the 19th-century German scientist Ernst Mach questioned the very existence of atoms on the grounds that they cannot be "perceived." Mach only grudgingly conceded the possibility of abstract thought, conceiving it as at best an organizational system for groups of sensations. Mach's ideas later contributed to the foundation of LOGICAL POSITIVISM. In the 1930s, the logical positivist A. J. Ayer applied the term "phenomenalism" to his attempt at developing a mathematically logical system of thought based on the analysis of statements about physical objects in terms of statements about sense data.

See also BERKELEY; HUME.

phenomenology

Philosophical position that emphasizes human CONSCIOUSNESS and its direct experience of the world over mental ABSTRACTIONS; a significant influence on EXISTENTIALISM. The term is primarily associated with the German philosopher Edmund Husserl. In opposition to philosophies that see reality as a construct of the mind (see IDEALISM; PHENOMENALISM), Husserl held that the phenomena of the actual "lived world" (Lebenswelt) must be the basis of philosophical reflection. Husserl proposed what he called the "phenomenological reduction," which required the "bracketing," or putting aside, of all conventional assumptions—including the question of the very existence of an object or impression—in order to examine life experiences from a fresh, unbiased perspective. (In this connection Husserl also used the Greek term "epoché," or "cessation," implying suspension of judgment.)

For phenomenologists, the *intentionality* of consciousness is central: it is the fact that our consciousness is always focused on something outside itself that allows us to appreciate experience. The mind does not create reality but interacts with it. The less cluttered the mind is by preconceptions, the richer the experience. The concept of intentionality has been the most influential aspect of the theory; among other things, it offers a solution to the MIND/BODY PROBLEM posed by DESCARTES, seeing the *relation* between subject and object as more fundamental than either of the two sides. It was also embraced by Jean-Paul SARTRE and other existentialists, for whom intentionality represented the creative human will in an ABSURD universe. Maurice MERLEAU-PONTY's version of phenomenology, which saw the world as an interacting multiplicity of intentions, led to his rejection of orthodox MARXISM as overly DUALISTIC.

Phenomenology has been widely influential in the social sciences, including sociology, psychology, and GESTALT theory. Phenomenological sociology, pioneered by Alfred Schutz, emphasizes the subjective, commonsense nature of people's perceptions of and assumptions about the life-world they inhabit. Phenomenological psychologists seek to bring what David Katz called a "disciplined naïveté" to the therapeutic relationship, observing and describing experience without prejudging it.

See also EPISTEMOLOGY; GESTALT; HEIDEGGER; MERLEAU-PONTY.

Piaget, Jean (1896–1980)

Swiss psychologist, whose theories of children's intelligence and learning patterns profoundly influenced developmental and COGNITIVE PSYCHOLOGY and educational theory. Trained in biology and zoology, Piaget maintained that his interest was in "genetic EPISTEMOLOGY," the study of the biological nature of knowledge. His theory sought to account for the development of intellectual capacity within each person and within the culture as a whole. His primary focus was on the formation of language and reasoning in children and their changing perceptions of the world around them. He suggested that learning is not based on CONDITIONING, as the BEHAVIORISTS believed, but is a progressive structuring of experience, largely through trial and error, as a child grows—a process he termed "constructivism" (cf. SOCIAL CONSTRUCTIONISM). Knowledge is the result of the *assimilation* of new information into cognitive structures and the *accommodation* that results as the growing mind's framework of knowledge and expectations—the *cognitive schema*—adjusts to accept the new material.

Piaget proposed that this process occurs in four separate stages. In the *sensorimotor stage,* during the first two years of life, children interact physically with their environment—seeing, touching, and tasting things, learning that certain actions will produce certain results, and, near the end of this stage, realizing that objects continue to exist even when they are not within grasp or sight; this recognition of *object permanence* is considered the beginning of SYMBOLIC thought. The *preoperational* stage, up to about age seven, is characterized by egocentrism, centration (the inability to see more than one feature of something at a time), and the inability to perform *operations*, that is, to grasp and manipulate mental concepts. In the *concrete operational stage,* the child overcomes these deficiencies and is able to understand logical relationships, but is still largely incapable of rational or ABSTRACT thought, performing mental operations concretely, one element at a time. The integration of abstract and hypothetico-deductive REASONING occurs during the *formal operational stage,* beginning at 11 or 12 and lasting through adolescence, when the individual gains the ability to analyze ideas and hypothetical situations.

Piaget's fundamental insight, that learning proceeds from previously assimilated learning acquired through interaction with the environment, revolutionized both child psychology and educational practice. Some of the conclusions from his exhaustive researches, however, have since been questioned and discarded; for example, toddlers do not have as self-centered a view of the world as Piaget believed. Furthermore, his system has been criticized for failing to account for novelty, the creation of new, "unlearned" knowledge within the mind's cognitive structures.

Plato (428–348 B.C.E.)

Greek philosopher, pupil of SOCRATES and founder of the Academy (later called the School of Athens), which flourished for over 900 years and is regarded as the first university. Plato's thought comes down to us in his numerous dialogues; while Socrates is the main character in almost all of them, he increasingly becomes simply Plato's mouthpiece.

In his theory of IDEAS (ideals, forms, archetypes), Plato sought to resolve a dichotomy that vexed the Greek mind, the opposition between change and BEING. He said that the world we experience, the world of change, is only an imperfect outcropping of the pristine, unchanging World of Forms. That world, not this, is the real world. In it are contained the ideal forms of everything. The beautiful rose we admire is merely a flawed approximation of the ideal rose and of the ideal standard of beauty (see AESTHETICS)—an illusion, in fact, that "participates" only partially in its ideal form. Likewise, amorous passion is a poor substitute for the highest kind of love, which consists of pure contemplation of ideal forms; hence the expression "platonic love." Moreover, since we can have knowledge only of what is real, any true knowledge we possess must be of that ideal world (see box).

Just as the forms are eternal, so are individual human souls. Experience and REASON help us recall the knowledge of the World of Forms that is inscribed on our souls but forgotten at the moment of birth. This doctrine of *anamnesis* (recollection) is illustrated in the dialogue *Meno*, in which a slave boy is able, under Socrates' guidance, to expound the basic principles of geometry, which Plato considered among the highest forms of knowledge.

Plato's ideas about both education and politics, expounded in the *Republic*, are derived from his conviction that only a select few are able to ascend from the "cave" of ignorance and achieve true knowledge. Plato's ideal society is a meritocratic aristocracy, with a ruling class culled from the ablest people of all

> *"The safest general characterization of the European philosophical tradition is that it consists of a series of footnotes to Plato."*
> —Alfred North Whitehead, *Process and Reality*, 1929

backgrounds and both sexes. Education would progress from a physical regimen in early youth to the intensive study of philosophy beginning in one's early thirties; the most qualified would be groomed for power, which they would inherit automatically at age 50. These "philosopher-kings" would live communally, sharing food, lodging, and spouses and owning no property. Naturally, since they would be guided by true knowledge, the aristocracy would govern for the benefit of all.

Soldiers would comprise a separate, intermediary class above the lower orders of merchants, farmers, and artisans, who would own property, but within strict limits: there would be no slaves, and anyone whose wealth grew more than fourfold would be compelled to give the rest to the state. In Plato's construct, when each citizen is performing the task he or she is best suited for, society will embody the four cardinal VIRTUES: wisdom (the philosopher-king), courage (the soldier), temperance (the commoner), and justice (the state itself).

Within this system, the arts were at best peripheral and at worst dangerous. As beauty was a pale reflection of the ideal, art (for Plato, primarily poetry) was merely MIMESIS, an imitation of that reflection—an imitation of an imitation. The philosopher, therefore, has the only viable grasp on truth and should be responsible for overseeing the work of the artist, lest it charm the populace with seductive but false reflections.

PLATO'S CAVE

PLATO's theory of knowledge is exemplified by the allegory of the cave described by Socrates in book 7 of the *Republic*. We are asked to imagine a group of people chained from birth inside a cave. All they can see is the wall in front of them and the flickering shadows cast upon it. To these people the shadows are reality, even though they are merely illusions, or, to be more precise, imperfect copies of the real objects that exist outside the cave.

Our world is like this cave: We humans are shackled by our ignorance of the true nature of reality, which for Plato consists in his *ideal forms*. If we wish to see the world aright, we must struggle out of the cave into the sunlight. It will at first dazzle and blind us, but if we persevere, we will begin to see the real world instead of shadows. Only the philosopher, who is carefully educated as well as thoughtful and persistent, will be able to attain anything close to this true knowledge; the rest will be content to stay in the cave and watch the shadows dance.

See also AESTHETICS; ARISTOTLE; BEING AND BECOMING; HIERARCHY OF BEING; IDEAS; INNATE IDEAS; NEOPLATONISM; SOCRATES.

pluralism

In politics, the view that power in modern LIBERAL DEMOCRACIES is, and should be, held not only by government but by a diversity of autonomous institutions and associations representing various interests. In philosophy, the view that reality is composed of multiple entities and is not reducible to a single or dual principle; thus, the opposite of MONISM and DUALISM. In literary criticism, the view that there is no single valid critical method, but that various approaches are appropriate in different contexts.

Political pluralism has been praised as a harmonious mean between collectivism, which subordinates the individual to the whole, and INDIVIDU-ALISM, which depreciates society. The United States, with its FEDERAL system of government, its ethnic diversity, and its people's propensity to form organizations, has been called the perfect ground for pluralism. Modern democratic pluralism is founded on the belief that open competition among differing groups not only results in an overall BALANCE OF POWER, in which both majority and minority interests are represented, but also contributes to social equilibrium in which cultural diversity can flower. Critics charge that pluralistic competition (or even cooperation) is an unrealizable ideal because the equation is unbalanced by the inherent power of the STATE and the economic power of modern corporations. (See also ELITE THEORY.)

Popper, Karl See VERIFIABILITY AND FALSIFIABILITY

populism

Any political position that professes to represent the common people or the people as a whole may be called populist. The term specifically applies to mass agrarian reform movements in Russia and the United States in the late 19th century. The Russian populists, or *narodniki*, primarily students and intellectuals (and including many women), espoused an agrarian SOCIALISM based on the village commune. Though unsuccessful in mobilizing the peasantry, they played an important role in the resistance to czarist rule that culminated in the revolution of 1917.

The populist movement in the United States, initially a reaction to the collapse of agricultural prices after the Civil War, culminated in 1891 when a number of farmer and labor organizations combined to form the People's (or Populist) Party. The Populist platform called for the free coinage of silver and printing of paper currency in order to raise farm prices, the redistribution of wealth through an income TAX, an eight-hour workday, and nationalization of the railroads to lower freight prices. Above all, Populists championed the RIGHTS of labor, both agricultural and industrial, against the power of monopoly CAPITALISM. Although they looked to the government to secure a "moral economy" that rewarded hard work and honest relations, Populists also pressed for more direct DEMOCRACY, advocating for such voter rights as referendums, initiative petitions, and recall votes. The party faded after the 1896 defeat of the Democratic-Populist candidate William Jennings Bryan, but in the early decades of the 20th century much of the populist program was incorporated in legislation inspired by the PROGRESSIVE movement.

See also DEMOCRACY and box; JACKSONIAN DEMOCRACY.

positivism

Philosophical position holding that the only genuine knowledge is what can be obtained using the methods of science. It is therefore allied to EMPIRICISM and MATERIALISM and opposed to METAPHYSICS and theology. The term was coined in the early 19th century by the French SOCIALIST Claude-Henri Saint-Simon, and the concept was developed and popularized by his student Auguste COMTE. Both men felt that a scientific attitude was indispensable to the establishment of a harmonious society, but Comte went further. He not only asserted the methodology of science as the only valid path to reliable knowledge but maintained that scientific principles, applied to social and political questions, would bring about a new, higher stage of human advancement.

Positivism is basic to sociology, the field Comte is often credited as founding, which rests on the assumption that human behavior, like the behavior of physical forces and chemical reactions, is objectively measurable. Although modern sociology is not strictly empirical, early sociologists concentrated on observable social phenomena, avoiding analysis of intention and other nonquantifiable factors. In his classic study *Suicide* (1897) the French sociologist Émile Durkheim analyzed suicide rates statistically to reveal suicide as a social as well as personal phenomenon. The notion that the only dependable truths about humans are those that can be objectively appraised is also found in certain approaches within the other social sciences, notably BEHAVIORISM.

Legal positivism is the theory, developed in the 19th century primarily by the UTILITARIAN philosopher Jeremy Bentham and the legal theorist John Austin, that seeks to establish principles of law independent of value judgments. The validity of such principles derives not from their moral force but from an objective (even if arbitrary) criterion, such as Bentham's "greatest good for the greatest number" or Austin's "command of the sovereign," that is, the prerogative of lawful authority. Twentieth-century contributions to the theory, notably those of Herbert L. A. Hart and Hans Kelsen, similarly appeal to a societally recognized authority or a basic, grounding norm as the objective basis of law.

The term *scientism* is sometimes used synonymously with positivism, denoting the position that only scientific knowledge is reliable. It is also used in a derogatory sense, to condemn oversimplified or naive confidence in scientific methods and the drawing of unjustified parallels between natural and social science.

See also COMTE; LOGICAL POSITIVISM; NATURAL LAW.

postcolonial theory

Movement in social and literary criticism that presents responses to the effects of European IMPERIALISM on colonized peoples. Postcolonialism offers a "counternarrative," related by and on behalf of formerly colonized peoples, to the ETHNOCENTRIC assumptions of Western culture. The term "postcolonial" thus implies not only "after the colonial era" but also a critical approach that arises from, and contests the premises of, colonialism (cf. POSTMODERNISM; POSTSTRUCTURALISM).

The progenitor of postcolonialism is generally considered to be the Franco-Algerian revolutionary theorist Frantz FANON. His articulation of the colonized person's predicament—dependent on the colonizer, defined as "the Other," and thus unable to form a valid sense of personal IDENTITY— became the starting point for postcolonial discourse. The heritage of the NÉGRITUDE movement of the 1930s and '40s, which asserted the value and uniqueness of African civilization, has also been influential. In the postcolonial era, the seminal work was *Orientalism* (1978), by the Palestinian-born scholar Edward Said, who argued that the West's view of Middle Eastern and Asian civilizations, developed in the 19th century and purporting to be rooted in objective research, instead rested on and perpetuated Eurocentric and RACIST myths. Such misconceptions—above all that these societies were less advanced than the West—provided the IDEOLOGICAL foundation for the subjugation of indigenous populations.

Many of the issues addressed in postcolonial criticism are those of language, such as the effect on the postcolonial CONSCIOUSNESS of European ways of thought embedded in the imperialists' mother tongues. The same issues arise for contemporary postcolonial authors writing in European languages—for example, Salman Rushdie, from India, and Wole Soyinka, from Nigeria, both of whom write in English about their native cultures. Others, notably the Kenyan author Ngugi Wa Thiong'o, have rejected the colonial language and write only in their native vernacular.

Postcolonial theory has been embraced by FEMINIST critics who see in the structures and assumptions of colonialism many of the mechanisms of patriarchy—the identification of woman as "Other," different from, inferior to, and dependent on the dominant group. The Indian-born critic Gayatri Chakravorty Spivak, for instance, has considered the position of "subalterns"— subordinate CLASSES of all kinds—and the conditions under which they may (or may not) be able to represent and articulate their own position rather than depending on others to speak for them.

See also FANON.

postmodernism

Artistic and critical tendency characterized by eclecticism, RELATIVISM, and SKEPTICISM, the rejection of intrinsic MEANING and reality, the repudiation of PROGRESS and cultural cohesion, and an ironic embrace of ambiguity; or, as both Richard RORTY and Jean-François Lyotard have succinctly summarized it, by suspicion of *metanarrative*. For many, this stance is the distinctive attribute of late-20th-century culture, giving this era the epithet "the postmodern age."

Postmodernism grew out of MODERNISM in the second half of the 20th century, continuing some of its trends, such as stylistic experimentation, while disdaining others, such as concern with purity of form. Above all, postmodernism questions the idea of metanarrative, or *grand narrative*—the attempt to explain all of human endeavor in terms of a single theory or principle (e.g., MARXISM, FREUDIAN psychology, STRUCTURALISM). Such theories comprehensively account for human history and behavior, but in terms that in some respects are mutually incompatible. The postmodern solution to this contradiction is that there is no final narrative to which everything is reducible, but a variety of perspectives on the world, none of which can be privileged. This attitude stems in part from the conviction that contemporary society is so hopelessly fractured—by the commercialization and trivialization of culture, among other things—that no coherent understanding of it is possible.

The postmodern position has created arguments within certain fields, for

example FEMINISM and multiculturalism, between those who see it as supporting their claim to equal status with the prevailing Western narrative and those
who contend that its indiscriminate inclusiveness forecloses any grounds for
political action. Indeed, Jürgen Habermas (see box at CRITICAL THEORY) and
others maintain that postmodernism is essentially CONSERVATIVE, since it offers
no resistance to the status quo. Other influential analysts of postmodernism
include Lyotard, whose book *The Postmodern Condition* (1979) argued that traditional, inclusive, "narrative" modes of knowledge have been usurped by scientific discourses that sacrifice ends to means, and Jean BAUDRILLARD, who has
been called "the high priest of postmodernism," a mantle he declines, calling
it a regressive, degenerate cultural phase.

In the arts, postmodernism ("pomo" for short) is distinguished by eclecticism and anachronism, in which works may reflect and comment on a wide
range of stylistic expressions and cultural-historical viewpoints. There is often a
tacit embrace of normlessless and cultural chaos, as well as a conscious attempt
to break down distinctions between "high art" and popular culture, for instance, in *performance art,* which often involves a provocative mingling of musical, literary, and visual sources. The artist's self-conscious display of technique
and artifice puts self-reference at the center of creation and presentation.

See also BAUDRILLARD; FEMINISM; POSTSTRUCTURALISM.

poststructuralism

Intellectual movement arising from and contesting STRUCTURALISM. Poststructuralism departs from structuralism primarily in denying that social systems—
including language and literature—have static, underlying structures that
determine their meaning, and concentrates instead on the fragmented, multifaceted, contradictory nature of things. Frequently, but inaccurately, seen as
synonymous with POSTMODERNISM, poststructuralism can nevertheless be
viewed as a variety of the postmodern attitude. DECONSTRUCTION, in which a
text is seen as composed of a multitude of meanings, is perhaps the prime
poststructuralist theoretical position. Its foremost exponent, Jacques Derrida, rejected structuralism's "logocentric" approach, arguing that language
can never convey absolute meaning and therefore interpretation can never
be definitive.

Poststructuralism was born in the political ferment of the 1960s and '70s.
In particular, the spontaneous popular rebellions of 1968 in Europe—the student uprising in France and the "Prague Spring"—prompted a reconsideration of the notion that history and society could be understood in terms of
invariant structures and calculable trends, which was not only the structuralist

position but that of the other dominant European intellectual movement, MARXISM. Instead of looking for overarching patterns, poststructuralists tend to investigate the marginal and discontinuous aspects of a social system, literary text, or other phenomenon. They are particularly interested in what has been left out, covered up, or glossed over, seeking to demonstrate how traditions and meanings are formed by our actions, independent of our intentions. Michel FOUCAULT, for instance, investigated the role of the arbitrary and nonrational in the historical development of apparently neutral institutions (e.g., the penal system and the medical profession), which are presumed to be the natural outcome of RATIONAL thought but actually reflect shifts in power relationships within society and changes in society's view of what is "normal."

See also DECONSTRUCTION; FEMINISM; FOUCAULT; box at HISTORICISM; QUEER THEORY.

pragmatism

Primarily American philosophical movement of the late 19th and early 20th centuries. A form of EMPIRICISM (and related to UTILITARIANISM), pragmatism disparaged abstract metaphysical speculation in favor of judging ideas through experience, experimentation, and their practical effects. The term was introduced in 1878 by Charles Sanders Peirce, who proposed that ideas should be evaluated pragmatically, that is, in terms of their *consequences,* and that these consequences alone constituted their meaning. (Later, feeling that his theory had been improperly altered by others, Peirce abandoned his original term in favor of "pragmaticism," which he correctly assumed would be "ugly enough" to discourage co-optation.)

Peirce's friend William JAMES popularized pragmatism, broadening Peirce's theory of MEANING to include a theory of TRUTH and, implicitly, of action. He stated that the truth of a proposition is determined by its UTILITY—its "cash value." In turn, John DEWEY reformulated pragmatism into his philosophy of *instrumentalism,* in which he stressed Peirce's emphasis on empirical inquiry and defined an idea's value in terms of its "warranted assertibility." In this view, the search for knowledge is not a quest for abstract truth but for solutions to practical problems. Some recent thinkers, such as Willard van Orman Quine and Richard RORTY, are considered "neopragmatists" because of their view that scientific and philosophical inquiry should be connected to real-world experience and practical consequences.

See also CONSEQUENTIALISM; DEWEY; JAMES; RORTY; SEMIOTICS, TRUTH; UTILITARIANISM.

predestination

Theological doctrine holding that the course of the world, and particularly human salvation or damnation, has been predetermined by God; a key element in Calvinist theology. It stands in contrast to DETERMINISM, which sees physical and historical events as resulting from oblivious, universal laws rather than divine agency. (The ancient idea of *fate* bridges these two concepts, seeing human destinies as part of the world's natural progression but preordained by the gods.)

The concept of predestination arises from the assumption of divine omniscience and omnipotence: God has foreknowledge of all events in eternity, and his power brings them to pass. The notion, introduced into CHRISTIAN teaching by St. Paul, was condemned by Pelagius and his followers in the fourth century as inconsistent with the notion of *free will* (see FREEDOM). In reply, St. AUGUSTINE argued that the two are not incompatible, because truly free will is in harmony with God's will; concupiscence, our bodies disobeying our wills, is a manifestation of the *original sin* of Adam and Eve, which can be overcome only by heavenly grace. This doctrine, in various forms, has informed the Christian view of predestination, especially in Calvinist teachings (see box at PROTESTANTISM). While all humans are tainted with original sin, Calvin said, a select few have been chosen for salvation. It is not possible to earn God's favor, but a life of VIRTUE may be seen as an outward token of inner grace (see also PURITANISM).

Presbyterianism See box at PROTESTANTISM

prescriptivism See DESCRIPTIVISM AND PRESCRIPTIVISM

Prisoners' Dilemma See box at GAME THEORY

probability

Branch of mathematics that deals with the relationship between possibilities and outcomes. Although the question of probability is ancient—it was often discussed in terms of the impossibility of certainty or the vagaries of chance—it was first studied statistically in the 17th century by Blaise PASCAL and Pierre Fermat, reportedly in response to a request by one of Pascal's gaming friends to quantify his chances of winning or losing at dice (see also box at PASCAL). It was formalized as a mathematical discipline in the early 19th century by Pierre-Simon Laplace, who defined probability as the ratio of favorable outcomes to all equally possible outcomes. An important tool in modern probability theory is Bayesian inference (named for the 18th-century English mathematician Thomas Bayes), a statistical procedure used in decision making that takes into account *contingent probabilities,* the effect of new information added to prior knowledge (see DECISION THEORY).

Probability theory may be applied to the description of random events, such as the frequency of a seven turning up when throwing dice, or to the forecasting of unknown outcomes with random variables, such as the likely result of a horse race or the possibility of death at a given age, as listed in actuarial tables. In the former case, the probability of all possible outcomes is known in advance and can be stated precisely: there are 36 possible combinations in a throw of two dice, six of which add up to seven, so the odds of throwing a seven are six to one against. In the latter case, probabilities are estimated, based on participants' *expectations* of the outcome (pari-mutuel odds are determined by the ratio between the amount bet on a particular horse and the total amount bet on the race) or on past experience, as expressed in mortality statistics: since the probability of death increases with age, so does a life insurance premium.

See also DECISION THEORY; INFORMATION THEORY; QUANTUM THEORY; PASCAL.

process philosophy/theology
School of thought holding that reality is a constantly unfolding and advancing process of change. The view stands in contrast to philosophies that posit a basic, unalterable SUBSTANCE as the foundation of the world, and to the idea of the ABSOLUTE, an abstract and distant God or cosmic spirit. The development of process philosophy was inspired by the theory of EVOLUTION—that life is not fixed creation but an ever-evolving process—and is founded in the notion that all being has both mental and material aspects. Its foremost advocate was the English philosopher Alfred North Whitehead, who saw the world as a continuously creative process in which all things—including events in the world—strive to exceed their limitations. This includes God, who is not distinct from the world and its inhabitants but is in a constant reciprocal relationship with us: our actions are his impulses.

The American theologian Charles Hartshorne embraced and extended Whitehead's panentheistic conception of God as including the world and intimately active in it (see PANTHEISM AND PANENTHEISM). He construed God's nature as *dipolar,* both absolute and relative, encompassing some attributes that prior theologies had recognized only in part: eternal, temporal, CONSCIOUS, world-knowing, and world-inclusive. Hartshorne's process theology has become an influential current of modern CHRISTIAN thought, especially among theologians seeking to reconcile science and faith.

progress

The belief that the course of history is one of continuous human progress is ancient and widespread, but not universal. The Greek myth of a Golden Age of serene perfection persists, as that term continues to be applied to any previous era seen in hindsight as nobler, more brilliant, or less troubled than our own. The notion of progress (the term comes from the Latin for "move forward") is also distinctly Western. Eastern philosophies may stress the individual's striving for perfection (see, e.g., BUDDHISM; HINDUISM; KARMA) but tend to see human history as cyclical (see ETERNAL RECURRENCE).

The modern idea of progress has antecedents in ancient Greek thought but is generally seen as a product of the ENLIGHTENMENT. Its first important exponent was the Marquis de Condorcet, whose *Sketch for a Historical Picture of the Progress of the Human Mind* (1794) traced the development of civilization through nine epochs and predicted an imminent tenth stage in which humanity would achieve perfection through REASON and science. HEGEL saw history as a progression of "DIALECTICAL moments" in which old forms and ideas are steadily overcome by new ones, leading ultimately to a state of ABSOLUTE knowledge. MARX adapted Hegel's dialectical view of history to his own theory of social progress through CLASS conflict.

The theory of EVOLUTION, which revolutionized 19th-century thought, mirrored and fortified the image of steady and irreversible human progress. Herbert Spencer's conception of the evolutionary scale as tending to ever-increasing complexity likewise bolstered the idea of civilization as an inevitable progression, not accidental but necessary (see SOCIAL DARWINISM). This viewpoint helped foster the conviction that cultures different from our own are at a less advanced stage on the same developmental continuum, as expressed in such value-laden terms as "backward" and "primitive," and provided much of the IDEOLOGY of IMPERIALISM.

See also COMTE; ENLIGHTENMENT; HEGEL; PARADIGM; RATIONALISM.

progressivism

Generally, the belief that PROGRESS is the natural and inevitable thrust of history. In U.S. history, a loose-knit and vaguely defined reform movement of the late 19th and early 20th centuries. In this period, Americans who called themselves progressives spanned the political spectrum and differed as much as they agreed; but most shared a desire to reform the political process, curb the excesses of CAPITALISM, and create a more inclusive, equitable, and moral society. Today, "progressive" is primarily used by LIBERAL and leftist organizations to distinguish their ideas and programs from those of CONSERVATIVES.

In reaction to 19th-century formalism, which held that society develops according to fixed principles, progressive philosophers such as John DEWEY and William JAMES stressed practical problem solving and argued that people could shape their environments to build a better society. Dewey's progressive theories became a blueprint for the modern American education system. Much of the progressive spirit was religious, embracing both a sense of CHRISTIAN charity and a desire to preserve Anglo-Saxon PROTESTANT morality in an age of mass immigration from southern and eastern Europe. (The agitation for prohibition of alcohol, which many progressives joined, reflected both impulses.) The progressive mood was also embodied by muckraking journalists such as Lincoln Steffens and Upton Sinclair, and by social-WELFARE campaigners such as Jane Addams.

Progressive policies during the presidencies of Theodore Roosevelt (1901–9) and Woodrow Wilson (1913–21) resulted in far-reaching federal antitrust, consumer protection, wilderness conservation, and currency reform legislation. Four amendments to the U.S. Constitution resulted from progressive-supported campaigns: the 16th and 17th (ratified 1913), establishing the federal income tax and providing for direct election of U.S. senators, and the 19th and 20th (1920), instituting Prohibition and giving the vote to women.

Three independent presidential campaigns have been conducted under the name Progressive Party: by Theodore Roosevelt in 1912, Sen. Robert M. La Follette in 1924, and Henry A. Wallace in 1948. Roosevelt outpolled the incumbent president, William Howard Taft, but split the Republican vote, giving the election to Woodrow Wilson; both La Follette and Wallace finished far behind the major party candidates.

See also DEWEY; POPULISM.

protectionism See FREE TRADE AND PROTECTIONISM

Protestantism

One of the three main divisions of CHRISTIANITY (with the ROMAN CATHOLIC and ORTHODOX churches), with some half-billion adherents in numerous denominations throughout the world. "Protestantism" has become an umbrella term covering most of the Christian churches and sects that were established during the Reformation of the 16th century or split off later. While Protestant churches represent a wide variety of beliefs and practices, three main doctrines, originating with Martin LUTHER, characterize Protestant faith: salvation justified by the grace of God through faith alone, the supremacy of holy scripture in matters of faith, and access to the divine without the intercession of clergy. These doctrines set the early reformers at odds with the Catholic Church, which emphasized salvation through "good works," the infallible authority of the Pope, and pastoral mediation between God and the faithful. The term "Protestant" thus implies both a protest against the authority of the church of Rome and a protestation of personal faith. Most Protestant denominations profess the historical Christian creeds, or confessions of faith, and the TRINITARIAN image of God. Of the seven Christian sacraments celebrated by the Roman and Orthodox churches, most Protestant churches recognize only two, baptism and communion (see box at CHRISTIANITY).

The Protestant Reformation arose in northern Europe in opposition to what was seen as temporal and spiritual corruption within the Catholic Church. The early reformers sought above all to restore the purity of Christian worship and the religious authority of the Bible. The three most influential were Luther, who condemned the church's emphasis on earning salvation, particularly the practice of selling indulgences for the expiation of sins; the Swiss theologian Huldreich Zwingli, who urged more sweeping reforms than Luther, including the destruction of graven images and the promulgation of the Bible and the liturgy in the vernacular; and John Calvin, who emphasized the sovereignty of God in all things and the PREDESTINED, unmerited salvation of a depraved humanity.

The Reformation's rejection of pontifical authority led to a proliferation of sects with divergent views on the role of the church and the program of worship (see box). Churches differ in their acceptance of or emphasis on various aspects of liturgy, doctrine, and principle—including, for example, the ordination of women—as well as in their ecclesiastical structures. The various organizational forms include *episcopalian* (governance by a hierarchy of bishops), *presbyterian* (governance by a system of church councils and courts), and *congregational* (self-governance by local congregations).

See also ADVENTISM; boxes at AFRICAN RELIGIONS; CHRISTIANITY and box; LUTHER; MODERNISM; PENTECOSTALISM; PREDESTINATION; PURITANISM; TEN COMMANDMENTS; TRINITY; WEBER.

PROTESTANT DENOMINATIONS

Protestant churches vary widely in theology, liturgy, doctrine, and structure. Most were founded as a result of disagreements between the early Protestant reformers or in the wake of schisms within established denominations. During the 16th-century Reformation, four main strands of thought and practice arose.

- **Lutheranism,** founded on the teachings of Martin LUTHER and initially established in Germany and Scandinavia, constitutes the world's largest Protestant denomination. The Lutheran creed, set forth in the Augsburg Confession of 1531 and clarified in the Formula of Concord of 1577, emphasizes scriptural authority, salvation by divine grace through faith alone, and "the priesthood of all believers." The Lutheran liturgy retains many elements of the Roman Mass. In the 17th century, orthodox Lutheranism, preoccupied with doctrinal dogmatism, was challenged by Pietism, a reform movement stressing good works, a holy life, and Bible study in small groups.

- **Calvinism,** based on the theology of John Calvin and developed by his followers in the 16th and 17th centuries, stands in partial contrast to Lutheranism and, originally, in stern opposition to HUMANISM. It forms the foundation of Reformed and Presbyterian churches, contributed to Baptist and Congregationalist doctrine, and defined the faith of the PURITANS in England and New England and the Huguenots in France. Calvinism emphasizes the sovereignty of God, not man, in the world; the depravity of humankind as a result of original sin and the necessity of Christ for reconciliation with God; the participation of the laity in church governance; divine PREDESTINATION of souls for salvation or damnation; and the principle (which Max WEBER called "the Protestant ethic") that hard work, thrift, temperance, and self-reliance are tokens of divine grace as well as self-justifying virtues. In the 20th century, Calvinist thought experienced a revival in the work of the Swiss theologian Karl Barth, whose *crisis theology* saw humans as sinfully self-absorbed and conceived of God as "wholly other," knowable only through revelation, not REASON. (See also PREDESTINATION; PURITANISM; cf. NATURAL THEOLOGY.)

• **Anabaptists,** or "rebaptizers," a number of radical sects that arose in opposition to both the old Catholic and new Protestant orders, claimed to revive the form and mission of the New Testament church. They repudiated infant baptism, baptizing only on profession of faith; asserted strict biblical authority and church discipline; refused civil authority, insisting on the separation of church and STATE; and in many cases espoused pacifist NONVIOLENCE. They were precursors of both Baptists and Quakers (see below). Many members of Anabaptist sects, fleeing persecution, settled in the United States, among them Mennonites and Amish. The former, named for their leader, Menno Simons, are pacifist and socially PROGRESSIVE; the latter, a CONSERVATIVE Mennonite offshoot established in the late 17th century by Jakob Amman, are most conspicuously represented by the Old Order branch, who shun the modern world and retain the dress, technology, and social conventions of their founding era.

• **Anglicanism,** the form of worship represented by the Church of England and the Episcopal Church in America, was formalized during the reign of Queen Elizabeth I after the break of the English church from Rome under her father, Henry VIII. Maintaining continuity with Catholicism but absorbing influences from Reformation Protestantism, it stands between and rather apart from both traditions. For example, the episcopal structure and much of the liturgy of pre-Reformation English Catholicism are preserved, but scriptural authority is upheld and individual interpretation allowed. Anglican worship centers on the Book of Common Prayer, composed by Thomas Cranmer and others in the mid-16th century. The Anglican tradition of theological diversity and freedom of thought is exemplified in the coexistence of churches that emphasize their Catholic heritage and those with a Calvinist, evangelical tendency.

Most of the present-day Protestant churches are descended from these four Reformation tendencies. Several historically important denominations that arose in Britain and colonial America continue to influence American life and character.

- *Baptists* adhere to the doctrine of full-immersion baptism on profession of faith, and thus constitute a "gathered church" of adult believers. Baptists also traditionally uphold the separation of church and state, religious freedom, individual scriptural interpretation, and the autonomy of local congregations. The movement began with John Smyth and other PURITAN separatists of the late 16th century and is now concentrated in the United States. Divisions over racial and other issues have divided American Baptist churches on North/South and black/white lines since before the Civil War; southern and African-American Baptist churches tend to evangelism and revivalism more than their white northern counterparts.

- *Reformed and Presbyterian churches* are founded on Calvinist theological principles and presbyterian government. The church is governed at the congregational, regional, and national levels by a hierarchical system of councils or "courts" composed of clergy and elected lay elders. Presbyterianism was established in Britain in the mid-16th century by the Scottish theologian John Knox, patterned on the Reformed church established on the Continent by Calvin. The Reformed creed has been developed over centuries in a series of *confessions* clarifying theology and liturgy; the most important to Anglo-American Presbyterians is the Westminster Confession of the 1640s. In the United States, Presbyterian and Reformed churches have undergone repeated divisions and mergers.

- *Congregationalism* is based on the principle of the independence of local congregations from civil or ecclesiastical authority. Springing from the 17th-century English separatist movement led by Robert Browne and aimed at cleansing the Christian church, Congregationalism took root in PURITAN New England. It is a "gathered church" of convinced believers, with a strong missionary tradition. In the 20th century most Congregational churches have merged with other denominations.

- *Methodism,* founded by John Wesley in the 18th century as an evangelical reform movement within Anglicanism, emphasizes redemption through repentance and salvation through faith. The name is said to derive from Wesley's methodical approach to Bible study and Christian living. It was spread in England and America by revival meetings and circuit-riding preachers, traditions that are still followed in some churches. Methodism splintered in the 19th century over doctrinal and social issues, including RACE; several of the new churches that formed were African-American, of which the largest is the African Methodist Episcopal (A.M.E.) Church. (See also PENTECOSTALISM.)

- *Quakers* (Religious Society of Friends) stress individual worship and freedom of conscience, seeking the "inner light" that represents "the Christ within" oneself and others. Established in England by George Fox and in colonial America by William Penn in the 17th century, the Society abjures all formal creeds and has no organized clergy. Quakers do not worship in consecrated churches but traditionally gather in "meetinghouses" to pray or meditate silently, speaking if moved to. Historically, Quakers have been pacifist and active in social reform movements, emphasizing classless equality, simple living, and Christian fellowship. (See also NONVIOLENCE.)

- *Unitarianism* denies the TRINITARIAN doctrine that God exists in three persons, as well as most other supernatural Christian dogma, including original sin and the divinity of Christ, and thus stands at some remove from mainstream Christianity. Its stance derives from Arianism, the early Christian heresy holding that JESUS was not part of God but was created by him, and Socianism, the Reformation-era teachings of Lelio and Fausto Sozzini, who saw Jesus as human, not divine, and his life as exemplary but not redemptive. Established in New England in the late 16th century, Unitarianism is distinguished by tolerance and inclusiveness and by a LIBERAL social perspective. In the 1960s the Unitarian Church merged with the Universalist Church in the United States. Religious universalism, rejecting the doctrines of divine grace and PREDESTINATION, holds that all souls will be redeemed.

psychoanalysis

Form of PSYCHODYNAMIC therapy and approach to personal psychology developed by Sigmund FREUD, dubbed "the talking cure" by one of his patients. The method is based in the idea that adult neuroses are manifestations of traumas hidden in the UNCONSCIOUS, and that by recovering and analyzing this material its unhealthy hold on the psyche can be broken. Traditional

Freudian analysis, usually a protracted process, assumes that the inner self is locked in a struggle over conflicting messages from the ego, id, and superego, particularly over issues of sexuality governed by the libido (see FREUD). Psychoanalytic theory is said to have originated with Freud's discovery of the *Oedipus complex*, the young child's fantasies of sex with a parent; adult dysfunctions are prompted by repressed guilt feelings about these desires (see box at FREUD). Psychoanalysts assume that the reality represented by unconscious fears and desires, not conscious impressions or objective reality, is the most important determinant of a patient's behavior and self-image. They also believe that humans' capacity for psychic conflict is balanced by an aptitude for "creative synthesis," which allows adaptation and healing.

Psychoanalysis depends on two main techniques, *free association* and *transference*. Patients are encouraged to talk freely, without censorship, about their thoughts, fantasies, and dreams (which Freud saw as symbolic representations of unconscious thoughts and wishes). By progressively associating these ideas and images, they are able to recall long-buried hurts and shed the defense mechanisms that compensated for them. During this process, the patient often transfers (displaces) deep-seated emotions, originally inspired by parents or other loved ones and authority figures, onto the analyst—a "safer" target. Analysis of these feelings, now brought to light, can lead to an understanding of their cause and a diminution of their power over the patient.

Post-Freudian analytic schools have reinterpreted or departed from key elements in Freud's theory, while retaining other central premises. Three of his students were important early psychoanalytic revisionists. Carl JUNG extended the concept of *libido* to include not just sexual instincts but all creative drives, and divided the unconscious in two, positing not just a personal unconscious but a "collective unconscious" containing the *archetypes* common to all people. Otto Rank attributed adult neuroses to the trauma one suffers at birth. Alfred Adler proposed that the key human drive is the effort to compensate for feelings of inferiority derived from one's helplessness as an infant. Adler and others, including Karen HORNEY, Melanie Klein, Harry Stack Sullivan, and Erich Fromm (see box at CRITICAL THEORY), stressed early interpersonal relations over interior events as determinants of adult behavior (see OBJECT RELATIONS THEORY).

See also CATHARSIS; ERIKSON; box at FEMINISM; FREUD; HORNEY; JUNG; KRISTEVA; PSYCHODYNAMIC THEORY; STREAM OF CONSCIOUSNESS; box at STRUCTURALISM; SYMBOLISM; UNCONSCIOUS.

psychodynamic theory

General approach to psychology that emphasizes motivations and the interactions of emotional processes in behavior and personality development. FREUD's was the first psychodynamic theory, departing from previous psychological concepts, which focused on CONSCIOUS mental processes, to delve into the dynamic interrelations of UNCONSCIOUS forces. Dynamic psychology also differs from other modern psychological perspectives, such as BEHAVIORISM and COGNITIVE PSYCHOLOGY, primarily in its subjectivity. Psychodynamic therapy depends on the interpretation of dreams, fantasies, SYMBOLS, cultural myths, and the patient's own PERCEPTIONS; it is thus not amenable to EMPIRICAL testing, a circumstance that has inspired some critics to dub PSYCHOANALYSIS and other psychodynamic therapies "pseudoscience." While the field of dynamic psychology includes a wide variety of theories and approaches, most of them share certain fundamental assumptions. These include an emphasis on early childhood development, occurring in certain fixed stages (see, e.g., ERIKSON; box at FREUD; PIAGET), as the prime determinant of adult behavior and dysfunctions, and on the role of unconscious processes in that development. (See also HORNEY; OBJECT RELATIONS THEORY; SOCIAL LEARNING THEORY.)

public choice

Theory that seeks to apply certain economic principles to "nonmarket" decision making, specifically in politics; related to, and sometimes confused with, SOCIAL CHOICE theory. Founded by the economists James Buchanan and Gordon Tullock, public choice theory proceeds from the assumption that individual decision makers, like individual consumers, act largely in their own rational self-interest (cf. DECISION THEORY). It seeks to understand the behavior of organizations, bureaucracies, and other institutions by analyzing the actions of decision makers in terms of their individual preferences, incentives, and motivations. For example, the theory holds that the votes of members of Congress tend to be based not on a detached analysis of the public interest, or even solely on IDEOLOGICAL principles, but on their sense of what will improve their voter appeal and fund-raising potential in the next election; likewise, bank regulators' decisions about dealing with a financial institution in trouble are swayed by their assessment of the potential rewards or penalties they will receive from their own agency as a result of their actions. Public choice theory concludes that government in a PLURALISTIC society does not "work" as well as the free-market economy because whereas self-interest underlies the workings of both government and the MARKET, only in the latter is that acknowledged openly; in public institutions, decisions that ideally require cooperation are often undermined by the private interests of individuals.

punctuated equilibrium

Theory of evolutionary change proposed in 1972 by the paleontologists Niles Eldridge and Stephen J. Gould, who proposed that the EVOLUTION of a species occurs through long periods of stability, or *stasis*, punctuated by periods of comparatively rapid *speciation*, morphological transformation resulting in the emergence of new species. This theory contradicted the prevailing DARWINIAN theory of *phyletic gradualism*, in which evolution results from the steady, cumulative effects of environmental selection on individual organisms within a species population over time.

The punctuated equilibrium model was inspired by Ernst Mayr's allopatric (meaning "other place") theory of speciation, published in 1954, which suggests that when a small population within a species becomes geographically isolated, increased environmental pressures on a smaller gene pool can speed up the process of adaptation and natural selection. Eldridge and Gould postulated that such *massive speciation events* occasionally occur in all species populations in response to changing circumstances. They argued that their conclusion is supported by (and explains) the fossil record, which shows vast periods of time in which no observable change occurred in a species, followed by the "sudden" appearance of a new species—that is, over thousands rather than millions of years. The theory of punctuated equilibrium does not rule out gradual adaptations within species, but contends that speciation occurs in isolated bursts, not as a slow process of accretion.

See also CATASTROPHISM AND UNIFORMITARIANISM; EVOLUTION.

Puritanism

Movement of extreme Calvinist PROTESTANTS who, in the 16th and 17th centuries, sought to "purify" religion and society by reforming the Church of England. More broadly, any movement that purports to cleanse and perfect a corrupt system, accompanied by the prescription of a more rigorous morality, may be called puritan; many revolutionary and separatist movements have had an initial puritan phase.

English Puritans denounced the doctrinal, structural, and liturgical vestiges of ROMAN CATHOLICISM in the Anglican church (see box at PROTES-

TANTISM). They affirmed LUTHER's idea of the "priesthood of all believers," emphasized simplicity of worship, and opposed the church's hierarchical organization. Some dissenters separated from the established church and founded new sects. Puritans were persecuted during the reigns of James I (1603–25) and Charles I (1625–49) and took the side of the antiroyalist forces in the English Civil War (1642–48), gaining temporary political ascendancy during the rule of the Puritan Oliver Cromwell (1653–59). A migration of Puritan separatists to New England in the 1620s and '30s established the Massachusetts Bay Colony as a "holy commonwealth," free from Anglican authority but every bit as ecclesiastically rigid and doctrinally intolerant as the mother church.

Puritans believed in John Calvin's vision of a wrathful God, in the utter depravity of humanity as a result of *original sin,* and in the doctrine of *election*—that salvation and damnation are PREDESTINED by God, who bestows his grace on the "elect" regardless of their own will—although life was, nevertheless, to be spent in seeking to please God. The "Puritan ethic" demanded a life devoted to religious introspection and hard work, which nourished the community of "saints" and implanted moral values such as industry, thrift, temperance, self-discipline, self-reliance, simplicity, and humility. Such qualities, together with the sect's opposition to many public entertainments and any nonreligious Sabbath activity, gave Puritans the reputation for prudish rigidity the word still evokes.

New England Puritanism had a lasting effect on the development of the American mind and spirit, notably in its emphasis on the work ethic and self-reliance and in the idea of a community of the elect with a special mission in the world. From the latter derived the 19th-century doctrine of MANIFEST DESTINY and the abiding image of the United States as the "city on a hill," shining as a beacon of liberty.

Quakers See box at PROTESTANTISM

qualities, primary and secondary See box at LOCKE

quantum electrodynamics (QED)
Theory in modern physics that describes the interactions of electromagnetic radiation (photons) and charged particles (such as electrons and positrons). Since these electromagnetic forces are responsible for nearly all atomic and molecular interactions, QED has become the fundamental theory underlying chemistry and atomic physics, as well as classical electrodynamics (see MAXWELL).

QED was born out of the revolution in physics in the 1920s that established QUANTUM THEORY, particularly in the work of P. A. M. Dirac, Werner Heisenberg, and Wolfgang Pauli in describing the photon, the fundamental quantum unit of an electromagnetic field. Another keystone of QED was Dirac's prediction, in 1928, of the existence of the positron, the "antimatter" counterpart to the electron. Some of the basic equations in QED initially yielded infinite results, which are compensated for by a delicate process known as "renormalization." Thus corrected, the quantitative agreement between theoretical predictions and experimental results in QED is unparalleled in physics.

See also STANDARD MODEL.

quantum theory (quantum mechanics)
Branch of physics dealing with the behavior of matter at the ATOMIC and subatomic level; together with RELATIVITY, it forms the theoretical foundation of
modern physics. Quantum theory is based on the observation that at the
subatomic level matter and energy confound the "classical" laws of mechanics and thermodynamics (see MAXWELL; NEWTON). In particular, quantum
theory notes that elementary particles also have wavelike properties and that
their interactions can be predicted and calculated only to a certain degree of
PROBABILITY.

Quantum theory was founded on German physicist Max Planck's hypothesis, in 1900, that energy, like matter, is composed of tiny particles. He
named this fundamental unit of energy the *quantum* (from the Latin for
"how much"). Planck suggested that a quantum's energy is proportional to
the frequency of its radiation; this relation (usually represented as h and
known as Planck's constant) has become essential to many of the basic
equations of modern physics. Albert EINSTEIN used Planck's theory to explain certain properties of light, proposing that light (electromagnetic radiation), which had been thought of as a wave, comes in quanta, called
photons. Experiments in the 1920s, showing that photons have momentum
and that electrons can be diffracted, demonstrated that both light and subatomic matter have wavelike *and* particlelike properties (see WAVE-PARTICLE
DUALITY).

The prototype that initiated the development of quantum mechanics was
Danish physicist Niels Bohr's model of the hydrogen atom, proposed in 1913,
which successfully linked Ernest Rutherford's picture of the nuclear atom
with Planck's quantum and Einstein's photon (see box). Another cornerstone
of quantum theory is Wolfgang Pauli's *exclusion principle,* which states that no
two electrons can be in the same *quantum state,* or configuration, in an atom.
This principle, according to which the complexity of an atom's orbital system
increases as the number of electrons increases (and from which the periodic
table of the ELEMENTS can be independently derived), has become central to
the understanding of atomic physics and chemistry.

Perhaps the greatest difference between "classical" mechanics and quantum mechanics is that the former is DETERMINISTIC—Newton's laws, in principle, allow the exact prediction of the outcome of any movement in the
macroscopic world—whereas quantum mechanics is inherently uncertain
and PROBABILISTIC. The central examples of this are wave-particle duality and
the Heisenberg UNCERTAINTY PRINCIPLE, which holds that we cannot know both
the position and momentum of a particle with perfect accuracy: the act of

observing a submicroscopic particle disturbs it. These ambiguities have led to searches for "hidden variables"—formulas that might overcome the indeterminacy of quantum theory. But indeterminism seems to be an intrinsic feature of the submolecular world. In the 1960s John S. Bell proposed a set of standards that quantum mechanics must satisfy if it is indeed a localized, deterministic theory, and demonstrated that it meets none of the criteria.

See also CONSERVATION AND SYMMETRY; EINSTEIN; FIELD THEORY; QUANTUM ELECTRODYNAMICS; STANDARD MODEL; UNCERTAINTY PRINCIPLE.

BOHR'S MODEL OF THE HYDROGEN ATOM

A cornerstone of QUANTUM THEORY. In 1911 the New Zealand–born physicist Ernest Rutherford proved the existence of the nuclear atom: a positively charged nucleus orbited by one or more negatively charged electrons. However, the atomic structure predicted by classical electrodynamic theory would be inherently unstable: an orbiting electron would simply emit energy and then spiral into the nucleus. The Danish physicist Niels Bohr, attempting to solve the puzzle of why gases can emit and absorb only certain wavelengths of light and why those wavelengths are different for each gas, revolutionized atomic theory by offering a solution that also explained the stability of the atom.

Taking hydrogen, the atom with the simplest atomic structure, Bohr postulated that its single electron can occupy only a limited set of possible orbits, or "orbitals," each of which has a specific energy (or quantum) state. The electron can instantaneously "hop" from one orbit to another, in what is known as a *quantum jump* or *quantum leap*. If it descends from a higher orbit to a lower one, it gives off light in the form of a quantum of radiation of a fixed size and wavelength, and the energy radiated is exactly equal to the difference in energy between the two states. Likewise, when the electron is struck by a photon of the right wavelength it jumps to a higher orbit that corresponds to the amount of energy received from the photon. Thus the total energy remains the same, the atom remains stable, and the particular spectrum of light associated with the gas is explained. Bohr's model provided an early and influential confirmation of the inherent quantum-mechanical nature of matter at submicroscopic levels.

queer theory

Political stance and intellectual movement that not only challenges the "identity politics" pursued by many FEMINIST and gay-rights activists but questions the validity of gender IDENTITY itself. Queer theory is both an outgrowth and critique of the gay and lesbian liberation movement of the 1970s and '80s, which sought to legitimate homosexual identity and end the stigmatization of sexual orientations outside the heterosexual norm. The term "queer," long an abusive epithet applied to homosexuals, implying not only difference but abnormality and perversion, was reclaimed in the 1980s by activist groups such as Queer Nation and ACT-UP (AIDS Coalition to Unleash Power) as a flag of defiance and a mark of deviance from *everything* considered "normal." These dissidents included under the "queer" banner not just homosexuality and bisexuality but deviant "straight" sexualities and "transgendered" categories such as hermaphrodism and surgical transsexuality.

Following the POSTSTRUCTURALIST emphasis on the multifaceted and contradictory, the uncertain and provisional, queer theorists deny the existence of an ESSENTIAL sexual identity, believing that gender and sexuality are SOCIAL CONSTRUCTIONS, not "natural" states, and are thus inherently ambiguous. They repudiate binary constructions such as gay/straight, masculine/feminine, and normal/abnormal as opposites defined by the dominant power structure. Indeed, queer theory consciously evades definition, fearing that once pigeonholed it would become one of the categories of "normalcy" it seeks to defy.

Queer theory is heavily indebted to FOUCAULT's insistence that sexuality and sexual identity are shaped by coercive power relations in society. It also reflects ideas such as Jacques Lacan's psychoanalytic view of the "decentered" self, a fragmented identity fashioned from a multitude of overlapping self-images, and Louis Althusser's MARXIST theory of identity as resulting from the influence of economic and political IDEOLOGIES (see box at STRUCTURALISM). The most influential queer theorist has been Judith Butler (see box at FEMINISM), for whom gender is a "performance" (whether intentional, unconscious, or compelled) rather than an identity. To illustrate the artificiality of gender attributes, she uses the example of *drag*—an imitation by a man of conventional notions of femininity. Criticisms of queer theory include the objection that the utter DECONSTRUCTION of commonsense categories such as "man" and "woman" makes ordinary discourse meaningless—an objection countered with the argument that what is considered "common sense" is a socially imposed construct.

R

race and racism

"Race" is a categorization of human groups based on certain physiological characteristics and common ancestry, now widely recognized as a primarily social construct with no demonstrable genetic basis. Racism (or racialism) is individual and institutional bias against an individual or group identified in terms of the racial construct. The word "race" was originally used, beginning in the 16th century, to refer to any general category in nature (e.g., the "race" of fishes), ancestral line (the race of Abraham), or historical identity (the English race). The division of humanity into distinct "races" according to supposedly scientific criteria did not begin in earnest until the 19th century, when anthropologists classified human populations according to certain physiological traits, including skin color, hair texture, bone structure, and cranial capacity. The standard classification was formulated by Johann Friedrich Blumenbach, who identified five races, assigning a geographical locus and characteristic skin color to each: Caucasian (white), Mongolian (yellow), Ethiopian (black), American (red), and Malayan (brown).

The racial hypothesis quickly spawned the notion that the races were not only physiologically but psychologically and morally divergent. This, in turn, led to the assumption that racial divisions were hierarchical, with white Europeans placing themselves at the top as the cultural descendants of the consummate Greco-Roman civilization (see CLASSICISM; cf. GARVEY). Nourished by the BIOLOGICAL DETERMINISM implied in the popular theory of SOCIAL DARWINISM, the idea of racial superiority was used as an authorization for, among other things, European IMPERIALISM AND COLONIALISM, which were regarded as the natural destiny of the superior race. An influential architect of racist philosophy was Joseph Arthur de Gobineau, whose *Essay on the Inequality of Hu-*

man Races (1853–55) postulated a pure Nordic race, which he called Aryan, and attributed the decline of civilizations to the "mixed blood" of interracial mingling. Taken up by pan-German NATIONALISTS, who overlaid it with a virulent anti-Semitism, the Aryan myth eventually became a cornerstone of Nazi IDEOLOGY (see FASCISM).

> *"Segregation is the offspring of an illicit intercourse between injustice and immorality."*
>
> —Martin Luther King Jr., attributed

Modern science has largely debunked the biological basis of race, showing, for example, that there is just as much genetic diversity within racial groups as between them. Although scientists now regard race as a conventional attribution but not a scientifically valid classification—indeed, the term "ethnicity" is increasingly favored over "race"—it remains a common focus of individual or group IDENTITY; for some, particularly members of socially disadvantaged groups, it is a point of pride.

Race has been a constant theme in the history of the United States and remains the most painful and divisive American issue. Assumptions of white supremacy supported the institution of slavery and contributed to the doctrine of MANIFEST DESTINY, which sanctified the genocide of Native Americans. Post–Civil War African-American political movements have responded to prejudice and discrimination in varying ways, from accommodation with white dominance, to campaigns for civil RIGHTS and integration, to calls for separatism and self-reliance (see, e.g., BLACK MUSLIMS; BLACK NATIONALISM; BLACK POWER; DU BOIS; GARVEY; NONVIOLENCE; WASHINGTON).

See also box at CRITICAL THEORY; DOUBLE CONSCIOUSNESS; DOUGLASS; FANON; box at FEMINISM; LIBERATION THEOLOGY; MORMONISM; NATIVISM; POSTCOLONIAL THEORY; RASTAFARIANISM; SOCIAL DARWINISM.

radicalism

Approach to political theory and action that emphasizes basic principles and seeks fundamental changes in the status quo. The word "radical" derives from the Latin for "root" and thus implies a connection to foundational sources of legitimacy and TRUTH. Although radicalism is generally associated with left-wing politics, the term can be applied to any extreme FUNDAMENTALIST doctrine, for example, the unconditional INDIVIDUALISM and anti-FEDERALISM of late-20th-century American CONSERVATIVES known as the radical Right.

Anglo-American political radicalism can be traced to the Levellers, a faction in the English Civil War of the 1640s, who championed popular SOVEREIGNTY and the natural RIGHTS of the "freeborn Englishman." An even more radical group of the period, called Diggers or "True Levellers," advocated social EQUALITY and common ownership of land. British radicalism revived in the 1790s, inspired by the American and French revolutions. Polemicists including Mary WOLLSTONECRAFT, William Godwin, and, above all, Thomas PAINE defended the egalitarian objectives of the French Revolution (cf. BURKE). Politicians such as WHIG leader Charles Fox, who is said to have coined the term "radical" in a political context, pushed for parliamentary reform, expansion of the franchise, and religious tolerance—goals that became integral to 19th-century LIBERALISM.

In the United States, the REPUBLICAN ideals espoused by LOCKE and JEFFERSON and proclaimed in the Declaration of Independence—individual liberty, social equity, and civic VIRTUE—informed radical movements for a century after the American Revolution. Agitation for the abolition of slavery and for women's suffrage declared the precedence of basic human rights over established custom, and a growing labor movement demanded a living wage and "dignity for the workingman." Through the 20th century, European and American radicalism has been primarily identified with struggles by or in the name of the working CLASS to defeat the power of CAPITALISM. While political parties and labor unions with SOCIALIST or COMMUNIST ties have been a major force in Europe, especially after World War II, left-wing radicalism has been effectively marginalized in U.S. politics, and American labor has largely sought to share, not limit or expropriate, the fruits of capitalism. Student protests in the United States and Europe in the late 1960s mounted a radical but largely non-MARXIST challenge to the entrenched authority of political establishments. Jefferson's insistence on the continuing right of revolution against tyranny, which was often quoted by the student radicals, has also been invoked by radical separatist movements representing widely contrasting IDEOLOGIES, from the Black Panthers (see BLACK POWER) to the white-supremacist Aryan Nation (see FASCISM).

Rastafarianism

Religious-political movement based on a pan-African, messianic belief in the deliverance of black people from white oppression in an African homeland. The movement arose among poor, disaffected young men in Jamaica in the 1930s, taking its original inspiration from Marcus GARVEY's back-to-Africa movement and his prophecy that a "black king" would soon be crowned in

Africa who would be the savior of his people. Biblical references to Ethiopia led some of Garvey's followers to look to that country as the promised land. When Ras (Prince) Tafari Makonnen, who claimed descent from Solomon and Sheba, was made emperor of Ethiopia in 1930 under the title Haile Selassie (Power of the Trinity), they hailed him as the Messiah and adopted his name.

Initially Rastafarianism (or Ras Tafari) promoted an IDEOLOGY that combined a kind of black ZIONISM with a mirror image of white RACISM. This credo taught that the Jews of the Bible were black and that Africans and their descendants are the biblical "chosen people," that Africans were exiled from their homeland into slavery because of their sins, and that whites are a morally and spiritually inferior race. The expansion of the movement beyond Jamaica, especially in the United States from the 1950s on, was facilitated by the appeal of its distinctive music, reggae, which spread the message of black strength, pride, and hope. Many Rastafarians smoke *ganja* (marijuana) as a sacrament; they typically wear their hair in dreadlocks and dress in the colors of the *bendera*, the "African" flag of black, red, and green designed by Garvey.

Since Haile Selassie's death in 1975, the movement's messianic impulse has waned and much of its racist ideology has tempered. Most contemporary Rastafarians adhere to a stringent moral code that teaches the EQUALITY of all people without distinction by RACE or CLASS, rejects hatred, vice, and worldly indulgence, follows biblical dietary laws, and forbids shaving, piercing, tatooing, and other "desecrations" of the body. Rastafarianism is not an organized religion and has no formal creed; however, it is nominally CHRISTIAN, while repudiating elements attributed to European culture, such as the King James Version of the Bible.

rationalism

Philosophical position that REASON is a more dependable path to knowledge than experience or observation. In this sense, it is the opposite of EMPIRICISM; however, since the ENLIGHTENMENT the two approaches have also become allied in the view that valid knowledge, especially scientific knowledge, derives from sense experience informed by rational thought, rather than from nonrational sources such as personal intuition or supernatural revelation (see SCIENTIFIC METHOD).

Although the rationalist outlook can be traced back to ancient Greek philosophy and was embodied in the medieval SCHOLASTIC conviction that reason and faith are compatible, the term is primarily associated with the so-called

Continental Rationalists of the 17th century, the most important of whom were DESCARTES, SPINOZA, and LEIBNIZ. These rationalists embraced the tools of mathematical LOGIC as the only trustworthy method of obtaining TRUTH. The viewpoint is exemplified in Leibniz's distinction between the truths of fact, which are *contingent* (that is, subject to empirical disproof and therefore potentially unreliable) and the truths of reason, which are *necessary* (that is, logically inescapable). (See also A PRIORI/A POSTERIORI.)

The central thrust of rationalist thought was that through reason knowledge can be set on a secure foundation—a base that is both required, if knowledge is to progress, and inevitable, if a properly mathematical method is employed. However, most rationalists grounded their theories in the existence of God, so the "necessity" of the truths of reason stemmed ultimately from God's own necessity and perfection. Indeed, the rationalists held that the existence of God can be deduced using the tools of reason; faith is not a prerequisite (see GOD, ARGUMENTS FOR).

Thinkers of the 18th-century ENLIGHTENMENT sought to overthrow traditional intellectual and social assumptions—especially religious and other "superstitions"—with new rational and scientific modes of thought. In the 19th century, rationalism became largely associated with the IDEALISM of HEGEL, for whom reason operated not just in the human intellect but in the rational, inevitable progress of history. Strict rationalism, holding that truth can be obtained through reason alone, is no longer given much validity; the role of empirical observation in gaining knowledge is now generally accepted. The complementarity of rationalism and empiricism is reflected, for instance, in the philosophy of Alfred North Whitehead, who held that knowledge requires thought *and* experience.

See also DEISM; DESCARTES; ENLIGHTENMENT; KANT; LEIBNIZ; NATURAL THEOLOGY; REASON; SPINOZA.

rational expectations

Economic theory stating that people use all available information to forecast future conditions and base their decisions on this forecast; in other words, their actions—investing, saving, spending, etc.—are based on their rational expectations of the economic future. The theory was first proposed by the American economist John Muth in 1961 and has become one of the foundations of new classical economics, a school of thought that distrusts government's ability to effectively manage the economy and favors a freer rein for the private sector.

According to rational expectations theory, economic forecasts are at least partly self-fulfilling; for example, expectations that a stock's price will rise leads investors to purchase that stock, which boosts its price. In the area of economic policy, rational expectations theorists assume that citizens, businesses, and government all have access to the same information, so governmental efforts to manipulate economic conditions may be counterproductive as the marketplace adjusts to the same expectations. For these and other reasons, the theory assumes that outcomes do not, generally, vary significantly from expectations.

Some economists criticize rational expectations theory for its assumption that all decisions are fully informed and that behavior is always rational; indeed, they argue, what is "rational" cannot be objectively defined or measured. In contrast, the theory of *adaptive expectations* (also called *error learning*) states that people rely on past experience more than future expectations. Their decisions are largely adaptations to the difference between previous expectations and their actual outcomes; for example, an investor who lost money in a stock-market downturn may be less willing to reinvest, even in a bull market.

See also DECISION THEORY.

Rawls, John (1921–)

American philosopher, often credited with revitalizing the fields of political philosophy and normative ETHICS with his treatise *A Theory of Justice* (1972). Rawls's theory, which revives the idea of the SOCIAL CONTRACT and continues the tradition of KANT's categorical imperative, proposes an alternative to UTILITARIANISM, the prevailing approach to ethics for most of the 20th century.

Seeing a just society not simply as one that guarantees "the greatest good for the greatest number," in which actions are judged by their consequences, Rawls takes self-interest and personal aspirations into account. He postulates an agreement made by parties isolated behind a hypothetical "veil of ignorance" of their own attributes, social position, and moral convictions. In such a situation, rather than trying to maximize their own advantage, since they don't know what that would be, they will seek to minimize their potential disadvantage. From this "original position," says Rawls, two principles inevitably follow: first, each person must have the maximum amount of individual liberty compatible with others' FREEDOM to enjoy the same liberties; and second, any social and economic inequalities must offer the greatest possible benefit to the least advantaged and must derive from occupations and official positions to which there is equal opportunity of access. The first of the two principles must be met before the second can even be considered. In Rawls's estimation, the institutional structure that best fulfills these principles is a constitutional DEMOCRACY with a free-MARKET economy, although some forms of democratic SOCIALISM could also satisfy them.

Rawls's theory of justice has been called the most influential contemporary contribution to political philosophy and has been credited with revitalizing the discipline, but it has also had its critics. Some question the inevitability of his two principles, others fault the "veil of ignorance" hypothesis on the grounds that no valid decision can be made without a context to inform it. The theory's most notable critic is Robert Nozick, who has denounced it as advocating a redistribution of wealth and property; in *Anarchy, State, and Utopia* (1974) he countered Rawls's conception with a LIBERTARIAN theory of social equity based preeminently on individual RIGHTS.

realism

In philosophy and science, a sometimes contradictory series of beliefs about what constitutes ultimate reality; in the arts, a broad term generally used in contrast to idealization or ABSTRACTION; in politics, an approach that emphasizes pragmatism over principle.

The implication of "realism" today—that there is an objective world of which we can have objective knowledge—is virtually the opposite of its initial meaning in philosophy. In the medieval debate over UNIVERSALS, the belief that the real is to be found only in a universal, immaterial entity was pitted against the NOMINALIST view that reality resides in form and SUBSTANCE; the *former* conviction was called "realism." It became the basis of IDEALISM, the position that mind, not matter, is the basis of reality. Modern philosophical realism arose in opposition to idealism, in the view of EMPIRICISTS that material objects are real and that their reality is independent of our perceptions or actions (see also MATERIALISM; NATURALISM). This is still the predominant meaning of the term, although the familiar distinction of APPEARANCE VERSUS REALITY, implying an authentic reality that transcends mere appearances, continues to evoke the PLATONIC universals.

The same contrast applies in the arts. "Realism" generally denotes the attempt to present the world as it *appears* to the everyday senses. But an artist's vision of *true* reality may well be expressed in "unrealistic" forms, and even "realistic" works are governed by certain stylistic conventions that make them to some extent artificial. The 19th-century European realist movements in literature and fine art—exemplified, for instance, by the novelist Honoré de Balzac and the painter Gustave Courbet—sought to depict the ordinary lives of ordinary people without exaggeration or idealization.

Realistic drama in this period, launched by Henrik Ibsen, eschewed the artificial structure of the "well-made play" in favor of psychological character development in everyday situations. This approach required acting that imitated ordinary speech and gesture instead of the prevailing declamatory style. The realistic acting method developed by the Russian director Constantin Stanislavski in the late 1800s, known in its American version simply as "the Method," has become the dominant style in 20th-century theater and film. Critics often point out that realism is not the same as NATURALISM, but the precise distinctions have become blurred. (See also SOCIALIST REALISM).

The politics of realism, or *realpolitik,* assumes that self-interest is a more powerful motive than common interest, especially in international relations. This approach, associated above all with MACHIAVELLI, stresses the importance of seeing things as they are rather than as one would like them to be. (Here, too, though in a different sense, "realism" is opposed to "idealism.") The term *realpolitik* was first applied to the tough-minded, often ruthless policies with which Otto von Bismarck unified Germany in the 19th century. Since World War II, realism has emerged as a distinct school of thought in political science. Its adherents tend to assume that power struggles are intrinsic in human nature, or at least in the anarchic real world, and that structural restraints such as BALANCE OF POWER arrangements are the only effective checks on conflict.

reason

The power of the intellect to comprehend, reflect, abstract, analyze, and draw conclusions. It is classically considered the defining characteristic of human beings, setting us apart from the remainder of the animal world (although this distinction has lost some of its force as animals' capacity for thought has been recognized as considerably greater than once supposed). Reason is related to and often equated with LOGIC, which is more properly seen as a formalization of the means by which the faculty of reason operates.

The idea of reason has always been circumscribed by the notion that while we may be uniquely rational, we are rational *animals* nonetheless, and our reason is clouded by our passions and material nature; only God is capable of pure and incorruptible reasoning. Through the Middle Ages, reason was seen as a divine gift, the point of intersection between the heavenly and mundane spheres. With the Renaissance, however, this attitude began to give way to the modern view that reason is distinctly human and must be investigated according to its place in human existence. Francis BACON, for instance, applied the exercise of reason to the solution of practical problems, and René

DESCARTES sought to "doubt everything" in order to arrive at meaningful conclusions. (See RATIONALISM.)

The interest in reason as the focal point of human value reached its apex in the ENLIGHTENMENT of the 18th century, a period known as the Age of Reason for its confidence in the power of human knowledge to overcome injustice and other social ills, which were blamed on "superstition" and arbitrary political authority. Even during this period, however, the status of reason as the fundamental human faculty began to be questioned; as David HUME claimed, "Reason is and ought only to be the slave of the passions." In the past two centuries the idea of reason has been assimilated into EMPIRICAL science, in the doctrine that knowledge derives from observation interpreted by rational thought, and has been marginalized and absorbed by more complex models of human psychology (see, e.g., CONSCIOUSNESS; GESTALT; PSYCHOANALYSIS; TRANSPERSONAL PSYCHOLOGY; UNCONSCIOUS).

See also AQUINAS; ARISTOTLE; DEDUCTION AND INDUCTION; ENLIGHTENMENT; KANT; LOGIC; LOGOS; PASCAL; ROMAN CATHOLICISM; SCHOLASTICISM.

reductionism

Term used in the philosophy of science and other fields, sometimes disparagingly, to characterize several separate but related positions: that the principles of one theory or system can be explained in terms of another, more inclusive or fundamental; that complex systems can be fully understood in terms of their constituent parts; or, alternatively, that all systems (including the universe and reality itself) are reducible to a unitary principle. Examples of the first version include the conviction that biology can be reduced to chemistry and physics, or that psychology can be reduced to physiology; the second is the theory of ATOMISM and the third is MONISM. The reductionist perspective has been particularly controversial in the sciences, especially in the debate over *emergent properties*, the characteristics of a substance or system that cannot be entirely accounted for by its material components—for example, water (a compound of two combustible elements) and CONSCIOUSNESS in the human brain. (Cf. HOLISM; MATERIALISM; MECHANISM; PLURALISM; VITALISM.)

relativism

Philosophical doctrine that no truths or values are absolute, but are related to our own personal, cultural, or historical perspective; the opposite of philosophical ABSOLUTISM. EPISTEMOLOGICAL relativism is most commonly associated with a dictum of the SOPHIST philosopher Protagoras, "Man is the measure of all things," that is, we judge things more by our own individual perceptions and prejudices than by their objective qualities. ETHICAL relativism holds that value judgments arise not from universal principles but from particular situations. This position invites the conclusion that no position can be declared morally superior to any other, which in turn produces the objection that relativism taken to this extreme leads to moral chaos.

Cultural relativism is the view that customs, values, artistic expressions, and beliefs must be understood—and judged—on their own terms, as products of a particular culture, not according to outsiders' theoretical preconceptions and classifications. This influential concept, an outgrowth of 19th-century HISTORICISM, was developed by the American anthropologist Franz Boas, who stressed the need to study a society through close examination of its unique characteristics. This approach is basic to *multiculturalism*, which holds that the dominance of the Western cultural perspective, based on European civilization and Judeo-Christian religion, must be overcome to make room for expressions from a diversity of cultural and ethnic backgrounds. Cultural relativism has also been disparaged in some quarters as not only nonjudgmental but noncritical, providing little basis for meaningful evaluation or cross-cultural analysis. (See also SAPIR-WHORF HYPOTHESIS.)

> *"Each man calls barbarism whatever is not his own practice; for indeed it seems we have no other test of truth and reason than the example and pattern of the opinions and customs of the country we live in."*
>
> —Michel de Montaigne, *Essays*, 1588

relativity

Theories in physics stating that there is no absolute, but only relative, motion and that gravity results from the effect of matter on the four-dimensional geometry of space and time. The physical principle of relativity was first explicitly stated by GALILEO in his *Dialogue Concerning the Two Chief World Systems* (1632), where he declared that motion "exists relative to things that lack it" and that objects in equal motion (e.g., people aboard a ship on the ocean) act in relation to each other as if that common motion did not exist. Galileo was led to this principle from his conviction, following COPERNICUS, that the earth itself is in motion. Galilean relativity states that there is no *mechanical* way to distinguish between rest and uniform motion (motion at constant speed in a straight line).

In 1905, Albert EINSTEIN, in his *special theory of relativity,* applied this principle to all of physics. Beginning with the presumption that the speed of light and the laws of physics are the same for all observers regardless of their relative (unaccelerated) motion, he concluded that two observers in relative motion to each other will have differing perceptions of the positions of events and the time intervals between them. For example, the explosions of two distant stars may seem to occur simultaneously to one observer and consecutively to another, depending on their relative motion. Nothing in the universe is at rest, except in relation to something else. Einstein saw space and time as intimately interconnected; instead of three-dimensional space existing in time, he proposed a four-dimensional *space-time:* occurrences in the universe cannot be described in terms of space or time alone but only in terms of both at once.

The special theory also found that mass and energy are equivalent: the mass of a body is a measure of its energy content. Summarized in the formula $E = mc^2$ (energy equals mass times the speed of light squared), this conclusion, which showed that mass can be converted into energy, united the classical laws of the CONSERVATION of matter and energy into the conservation of *mass-energy.* It also laid the foundation for understanding nuclear reactions, in which a tiny decrease in mass results in a large release of energy—the principle behind atomic power plants and thermonuclear weapons. The theory further stated that time dilates with velocity, giving rise to the so-called *twin paradox,* which predicts that a man taking a long space trip at or near the speed of light will age more slowly than his earthbound brother.

Einstein's *general theory of relativity,* published in 1916, extended the special theory to encompass accelerated motion. Elaborating on his *equivalence principle*—the observation that someone in a sealed compartment cannot tell whether she or he is at rest in a gravitational field or accelerating upward in a gravity-free zone—Einstein postulated that gravity is a property of space-time rather than a force exerted by large bodies. Space-time is distorted, or curved, in the vicinity of massive bodies, such as the sun or the earth; objects in the region of these bodies follow curved *geodesics* rather than EUCLIDIAN straight lines, producing the "pull" a body experiences in a gravitational field, such as the curving path of a passing asteroid or the elliptical orbits of the planets and their moons. In physicist John Wheeler's succinct summary, "Mass tells space how to curve; space tells mass how to move."

The general theory of relativity has passed every experimental trial to date, from the observation of the bending of starlight by our sun in 1919 to more recent tests using radar, lasers, atomic clocks, and observations of quasars. All modern theories of cosmology make use of general relativity, which predicted both an EXPANDING UNIVERSE and the existence of *black holes*—regions where the gravitational field is so strong that even light cannot escape.

See also CONSERVATION AND SYMMETRY; EINSTEIN; EXPANDING UNIVERSE; FIELD THEORY; QUANTUM THEORY; STANDARD MODEL.

republicanism

Political philosophy that favors government in which power is vested in the citizenry and exercised by elected representatives subject to a code of laws; the opposite of monarchy (see ABSOLUTISM). The term comes from the Latin *res publica*, meaning "the people's business" but also implying "the common good." The term is often used as a synonym for DEMOCRACY, but there are differences. A republic is a more specific form of government than a democracy, in which authority may be exercised directly by the citizenry and which may be nominally headed by a hereditary sovereign (by definition, there are no monarchical republics). The duties of legislators in a democracy and a republic are traditionally seen as divergent, the former expected to carry out the will of their constituents, the latter to exercise their own judgment on behalf of the whole society. The republican ideal also stresses consensus and civic VIRTUE—the citizen's responsibility to subordinate private interest to the commonweal.

The republican idea goes back at least to PLATO, whose *Republic* envisioned an ideal state in which an enlightened meritocracy ruled for the benefit of all. The revival of interest in republicanism by Renaissance theorists such as MACHIAVELLI was based on an idealized view of the Roman Republic, which was seen as animated by a sense of civic virtue and public obligation, and whose decline was attributed to the corruption of greed and luxury. James Harrington's UTOPIAN *Commonwealth of Oceana* (1656), written just after the failure of the short-lived English Commonwealth, described a decentralized republic in which political participation was based on the ownership of property, such ownership was widespread, and rule was given to those with the greatest talent for it. This vision, as well as the SOCIAL CONTRACT theory of LOCKE and ROUSSEAU, influenced the founders of the American republic. In the 20th century, COMMUNIST "people's republics" and other one-party states have justified their legitimacy—and their use of the term "republic"—by invoking the idea of the *popular will* (cf. ROUSSEAU's *general will*), a transcendent consensus dutifully implemented by its representatives, the party leadership.

rights

Liberties, considerations, benefits, and other advantages to which a person or group is automatically entitled by virtue of citizenship or other qualifications, which may simply be the fact of being human. Broadly, the distinction is made between *natural rights* (or *human rights*), shared by all people, and *civil rights,* guaranteed by governments to their citizens. Civil rights are sometimes equated with *civil liberties* and sometimes contrasted; in the latter case, civil rights refers to government's positive obligation to implement the SOCIAL CONTRACT with its citizens and civil liberties refers to limitations on government's power to interfere with individuals' FREEDOMS.

Although the proposition that human beings have "certain inalienable rights" was proclaimed as "self-evident" by Thomas JEFFERSON in the Declaration of Independence, the concept was then comparatively novel. Until the Renaissance, participation in the polity was thought of primarily in terms of *duties* to the STATE or the monarch, not rights. The most notable precursor of this shift in outlook was the Magna Carta of 1215, which gave the English nobility and other "freemen" certain rights of property and personal safety against arbitrary royal authority and remains the cornerstone of the United Kingdom's constitutional monarchy.

The concept of political rights that belong to every citizen was first fully expressed by John LOCKE in his *Two Treatises on Government* (1690). He asserted that NATURAL LAW, which applies equally to all people by virtue of their common humanity, particularly their capacity of REASON, implies a set of *natural rights* that are available to all. To Locke, people's innate, inalienable rights were life, liberty, and the right to own and improve property, and the main function of government was to secure these rights for its citizens. The American Bill of Rights and the French revolutionary Declaration of the Rights of Man and of the Citizen reflect Lockean principles, enumerating basic rights such as free speech, assembly, and press, the right to the privacy of one's person and property, freedom of conscience and religion, and protection from arbitrary laws or governmental powers.

In the United States, as elsewhere, not all the civil rights on which the REPUBLIC was founded have applied in practice to all Americans. Social-action campaigns to extend legal rights and protections to various classes of citizens have arisen repeatedly throughout U.S. history. Of these movements, the most tumultuous have been those waged by and on behalf of industrial workers, for the right to join unions, bargain collectively with employers, and strike; women, for the right to vote and for a place in society equal to men; and African-Americans, first for emancipation from slavery, then for freedom from social and institutional discrimination.

Rights have historically been associated with citizenship and seen as applying within individual nations. But the theory of natural rights inhering in all people equally gives rise to the concept of *human rights* that transcend national boundaries and which all governments should respect. This doctrine is embodied in the United Nations' Universal Declaration of Human Rights, which goes beyond the rights taken for granted in most LIBERAL societies to specify the right of freedom from torture and political oppression, the right of free movement and emigration, the right to practice one's culture, and the right to education and an adequate standard of living.

See also ANIMAL RIGHTS; DEMOCRACY; EQUALITY; FEMINISM; NATURAL LAW; PAINE; POPULISM; STATES' RIGHTS.

Roman Catholicism

CHRISTIAN church, the largest denominational division in that faith, claiming more than half the world's Christians; its seat is the Vatican, an independent city within Rome. Roman Catholics differ from PROTESTANTS and ORTHODOX Christians primarily in their allegiance to the Pope, or Bishop of Rome. While most of its structural and doctrinal features are found, to one extent or another, in various Christian churches, Roman Catholicism is particularly characterized by its episcopalian organization, its sacramental form of worship, and its veneration of saints. The word "catholic" means "universal" and implies continuity with the original, undivided Christian church founded by the Apostle Peter, of whom the Pope is considered the divinely ordained apostolic successor. Although the Orthodox, Anglican, and Episcopal churches consider themselves catholic in the general sense, the term has become associated primarily with Roman Catholicism.

The church is organized as an episcopacy, a hierarchical system with a ranked priesthood in which the Pope holds supreme authority as the infallible "vicar of Christ." Catholic dogma derives from biblical scripture and scholarly tradition—stemming particularly from the early church fathers such as St. AUGUSTINE and the medieval SCHOLASTICS, especially Thomas AQUINAS— as interpreted by church counsels and confirmed by the Pope.

Catholicism is strongly TRINITARIAN (and patriarchal), seeing God as

VATICAN II

Reversing the centuries-old Catholic doctrine that declared the church immune and apart from changes in the world, Pope John XXIII sought to renew the church, to conform doctrine to modern circumstances, and to promote Christian and human unity. The Second Vatican Council, convened in 1961 and meeting every autumn for four years, approved the most extensive revision of Catholic thought and practice in history. (The First Vatican Council, in 1869–70, had confirmed the doctrine of papal infallibility.) The documents issued by the council, representing the deliberations of some 2,000 bishops, stated that the church must be aware of current events and help to find solutions to world problems (cf. LIBERATION THEOLOGY); acknowledged that Christianity does not have exclusive access to God's truth and urged ecumenical dialogue with other faiths; condemned anti-Semitism and upheld the right of religious freedom; moderated the power of the clergy over the laity, declaring, "Authority is for service, not domination"; and demanded that the liturgy be performed in the vernacular instead of Latin so all the faithful could understand it. The pronouncements of Vatican II stirred controversy and resistance from Catholic traditionalists, and are still being assimilated.

expressed in the Father, his incarnated Son, and the Holy Spirit that pervades the Christian community. Despite his active presence in the world, God is not directly approachable, and so acts on his people through various intermediaries, chiefly the sacraments administered by the priesthood (see box at CHRISTIANITY). Central to these is the liturgy, or Mass, which draws the faithful together in the presence of the Holy Spirit. The Catholic Church celebrates seven sacraments, the most powerful of which is the Eucharist, or Communion, a ritual reenactment of the Last Supper of bread and wine, which Catholics believe is *transubstantiated* into JESUS's true body and blood. The veneration of saints—people whose piety and earthly works have guaranteed them a place in heaven—is widespread in both Catholic and Orthodox custom. Saints are often invoked in prayer, especially in their roles as "patrons" of individuals, endeavors, and localities. Mary, the mother of Jesus, is especially revered; the doctrine of *immaculate conception,* holding that she was conceived and born free of sin, is unique to Catholicism (see also GODDESS WORSHIP).

Both RATIONALISM and MYSTICISM have substantial traditions within

Catholicism. The faculty of REASON, considered a gift of God, enables us to reconcile our earthly experiences with faith, seeing them as demonstrations (if not proofs) of the divine will. The rational and intellectual tendency in Catholicism is exemplified by the Society of Jesus, or Jesuits, a male religious order devoted to scholarship and the advancement of education. Catholic monasticism embraces numerous contemplative orders, whose members seek communion with God through liturgy, meditation, and above all prayer, often accompanied by ASCETIC practices.

See also boxes at AFRICAN RELIGIONS; AQUINAS; AUGUSTINE; LIBERATION THEOLOGY; LUTHER; MODERNISM; PROTESTANTISM; TEN COMMANDMENTS; TRINITY.

Romanticism

Artistic and philosophical movement that flourished in Europe from the late 18th to the mid-19th century and emphasized INDIVIDUALISM, imagination, free expression of feeling, communion with nature, and the idea of the creative artist as visionary genius; the antithesis of CLASSICISM and, in practice, a rebellion against the era's prevailing artistic mode, *neoclassicism*. The concept of Romanticism is somewhat elusive, largely because of a historical lack of consensus on its definition. The term derives from the medieval *romance*, a literary form marked by fanciful idealizations.

The Romantic movement was both an outgrowth of the HUMANISTIC spirit of the ENLIGHTENMENT and a reaction against its reliance on EMPIRICISM and REASON. Jean-Jacques ROUSSEAU, who held an idealized view of the natural world and encouraged the expression of inner passions, was a seminal influence on the Romantic outlook. A central theme of Romanticism was its cult of the creative genius. The artist was seen as possessing ultimate insight into fundamental reality and revealing it, through impassioned self-expression, in a work of art that embodies, however imperfectly, a sublime ideal that transcends the ordinary world. Nature, wild and unspoiled, often became a metaphor for that ideal.

Among the most influential manifestations of Romanticism in the arts were the expansive narratives of Victor Hugo (who is often considered the exemplary Romantic), the turbulent verse dramas of Johann Wolfgang von Goethe (see STURM UND DRANG), the mystical poetry and prints of William Blake, the sensuous canvases of Théodore Géricault and Eugène Delacroix, and the impassioned compositions of Ludwig van Beethoven. Romanticism in music was especially associated with the virtuoso composer-performer, epitomized by Franz Liszt. Romantic verse is identified above all with the English poets William Wordsworth, Samuel Taylor Coleridge, and the youthful trio of Lord Byron, Percy Bysshe Shelley, and John Keats, who personified the Romantic image of the tragic, incandescent genius who blazes brilliantly and dies young.

In philosophy, German IDEALISM embraced Romantic notions of personal AESTHETICS and transcendent reality, particularly in the ideas of Friedrich Schlegel, Johann Gottlieb Fichte, KANT, and HEGEL. By the mid-19th century, the Romantic emphasis on the value of each individual person had inspired social-reform movements and encouraged the development of the human-centered social sciences of psychology and sociology. For much of the century, the Romantic style coexisted with REALISM in the arts, which emphasized unadorned depictions of everyday life. By the 1870s, though, it was being overtaken by its own offshoots, such as SYMBOLISM.

See also AESTHETICS; ROUSSEAU.

Rorty, Richard (1931–)

American neo-PRAGMATIC philosopher, whose *antifoundationalism* and *anti-essentialism* have challenged mainstream traditions of Western thought. His ideas are most extensively outlined in *Philosophy and the Mirror of Nature* (1979) and *Contingency, Irony, and Solidarity* (1989). For Rorty, philosophy is not a RATIONAL foundation from which the ESSENCE of reality can be perceived, but simply another voice in an unending social conversation about the nature of knowledge, TRUTH, and IDENTITY. Critical of the "linguistic turn" taken by philosophy since WITTGENSTEIN, Rorty disputes the idea of seeking truth in logical correspondences between language and the objective world (see ANALYTIC PHILOSOPHY). Indeed, he dismisses the very notion of OBJECTIVISM—that an objective reality exists, independent of our knowledge of it and discoverable by individuals under the right EMPIRICAL, LOGICAL, or spiritual conditions—and replaces it with *intersubjectivity,* a product of interactions among people, which create a kind of collective consciousness that changes over time.

In Rorty's view, we come to know the world through what he calls our "final vocabularies"—the terms in which we define our cultural and personal identities—which result from the ongoing process of social interplay. These vocabularies are contingent and transient, determined by the historical moment and the conditions that have shaped it. The metaphors that inform these final vocabularies are developed by those Rorty calls "strong poets"— individuals who become cultural touchstones, creating perspectives and ways of expressing them that open up new directions in the social conversation; 20th-century examples include EINSTEIN, FREUD, Martin Luther King Jr., and even the Beatles. Rorty rejects traditional distinctions between "hard" (natural) and "soft" (human) sciences, noting that both are the domain of strong poets. New metaphors are constantly emerging, and any social structure that does not allow for them is doomed to institutional stagnation. The ideal perspective on the world, Rorty feels, is an awareness of the contingent, inter-subjective nature of one's knowledge that makes one less susceptible to dogmatism, more open to new ideas, and more likely to find common cause with others.

See also POSTMODERNISM; PRAGMATISM.

Rousseau, Jean-Jacques (1712–1778)

French philosopher and political theorist, one of the founders of the modern DEMOCRATIC tradition, an apostle of popular SOVEREIGNTY and free will (see FREEDOM) whose ideas influenced the French Revolution and 19th-century ROMANTICISM.

In his *Discourse on the Sciences and the Arts* (1750) and *Discourse on the Origin of Inequality* (1755), Rousseau rejected the ENLIGHTENMENT view of human history as continuous PROGRESS. He said that science and the arts have corrupted humanity, distancing us from the natural virtues that make us truly human. The primitive *state of nature*, in which the individual was a "noble savage"—isolated, self-sufficient, and self-governing—was morally superior to civilization. Contrary to almost all prior opinion, Rousseau held that laws must be solely the creation of the people, not handed down by God, dictated by a monarch, or fashioned by REASON. In Rousseau's ideal society, envisioned in *The Social Contract* (1762), the civil order would be a product of what he called the *general will,* a quasi-mystical concept implying the civic responsibility and VIRTUE toward which one naturally inclines when considering the good of all instead of one's private or *particular will.* As a direct expression of popular sovereignty, the general will would rule out the possibility of dissent; those who resisted it would be "forced to be free." As many commentators have noted, this insistence leads, paradoxically, to a position very close to TOTALITARIANISM, for such an arrangement plays into the hands of those who would consolidate power in the name of "the people's will."

Rousseau believed in the ultimate *perfectibility of man* on earth. In his novel *Émile* (1762) he outlined a new system of education, one that proved exceptionally influential. The regimen, more permissive than prevailing methods and similar to the sort of education advocated by PLATO in the *Republic,* aimed at encouraging self-expression rather than rote learning, in order to produce a well-rounded, self-reliant, free-thinking (male) citizen. His final work, the *Confessions* (1764–70, published posthumously), was modeled on St. AUGUSTINE's *Confessions* but came to a diametrically opposite conclusion—that human beings are not born of and in original sin but are born good and are corrupted by society. In the *Confessions* and the semiautobiographical novel *Julie, or The New Héloïse* (1760), Rousseau encouraged impassioned personal expression, even sentimentality, instead of cold reason. In this, he is seen as an intellectual progenitor of Romanticism and an influential figure in the development of the field of psychology.

See also SOCIAL CONTRACT.

Rowbotham, Sheila   See box at FEMINISM

Russell, Bertrand   (1872–1970)

English philosopher, author, and social activist, considered the founder of ANALYTIC PHILOSOPHY. Although born into an aristocratic (but impoverished) family, Russell was a lifelong political RADICAL. During World War I he was fired from his teaching position at Cambridge University and imprisoned for his SOCIALIST and pacifist views. Thereafter he earned most of his living from lecturing and writing popular books on philosophy and other topics, including *A History of Western Philosophy* (1946), and simplified statements of his philosophical positions, such as *Why I Am Not a Christian* (1927, published 1945). He modified his pacifism during World War II but in the 1950s became an outspoken figure in the protest movement against nuclear weapons and was again briefly jailed.

> *"Three passions, simple but overwhelmingly strong, have governed my life: the longing for love, the search for knowledge, and unbearable pity for the suffering of mankind."*
>
> —Bertrand Russell,
> *Autobiography,* 1967

Russell's major philosophical work was *Principia Mathematica* (3 vols., 1910–13), written with his teacher Alfred North Whitehead; much of Russell's later philosophical writing expanded and refined the ideas in that book. Following on from the work of Gottlob Frege and Giuseppe Peano, Russell aimed to cast mathematics as a branch of LOGIC. Numbers, he said, can be defined logically, without reference to anything numeric, by seeing them in terms of *classes* (see SET THEORY)—

RUSSELL'S THEORY OF TYPES

In his analysis of classes, RUSSELL noted a problem in classes that referred to themselves. Classes—of objects, concepts, etc., may or may not be members of themselves; the class of enumerable things is an enumerable thing, but the class of baseballs is not a baseball. However, attempting to define a class consisting of all classes that are not members of themselves leads to what is known as *Russell's paradox:* such a class would be both a member of itself and not a member of itself. Russell's solution was the *theory of types,* which distinguishes between types, or orders, of classes. A statement is meaningless, Russell said, if it is self-referential (e.g., "a bird is a bird"). In order to be meaningful, it must refer to something of a different type (on a different level) than itself. The class of all classes that are not members of themselves, and the classes it contains, are thus seen as belonging to different hierarchical orders. The class, therefore, is no longer describing itself and the paradox vanishes.

groups of objects possessing a common property; for example, "five" can be defined as the characteristic shared by all of those classes having five members. Logical propositions can be analyzed similarly, in terms of classes whose members are defined by the same proposition. Russell rejected the traditional predicate (or syllogistic) logic as too suggestive of METAPHYSICS and demonstrated that propositional logic, which deals primarily with relations and quantities, rather than qualities, is more inclusive. His *theory of definite descriptions* held that the subjects of sentences or propositions do not necessarily name definite objects, but only describe states of affairs that may or may not be true, such as Russell's classic example, "The present king of France is bald." To overcome the difficulty encountered in such statements— logically constructed, apparently reasonable, but nonsensical (since there is no king of France at present)—he adopted Frege's concept of *quantifiers,* which eliminate the qualities (such as existence or nonexistence) that attach themselves to the subjects of propositions. Only statements that express actual relationships can be considered meaningful; thus, the statement about the French king can be rendered thus: "There is no x such that x is the present king of France and that x is bald."

In Russell's theory of logical ATOMISM, the universe of discourse is constructed from simple (elementary) particulars possessing simple qualities

(UNIVERSALS) and standing in simple relations. Sentences and propositions are "molecular," constructed from these "atomic facts" or fundamental units of meaning. Although Russell later abandoned this particular notion, it is related to his central EPISTEMOLOGICAL concept, the *percept*, a kind of unit of PERCEPTION. A percept is the specific appearance of a quality in a particular space and time, and is not wholly determined by either the subject or the object of perception; what is basic is the relation between object and subject. This, in turn, accords with another principle that Russell held briefly and then rejected, that of "neutral MONISM," which holds that there is one fundamental principle of existence that is both mental and material.

S

sacraments See box at CHRISTIANITY

Sapir-Whorf hypothesis

Theory in linguistics that the language we speak structures the way we perceive and think about the external world. Also called *linguistic relativism* or *linguistic relativity,* the idea incorporates the concept of DETERMINISM as well as RELATIVISM, holding that our apprehension of the world is determined by the way our language expresses it and that differences between cultures are shaped by their unique linguistic traits. The hypothesis is named for the American linguistic anthropologists Edward Sapir and Benjamin Lee Whorf. Their studies of American Indian and Eskimo languages revealed structures and vocabularies quite different from European languages and seemingly parallel to differences in COGNITIVE and cultural outlooks. For example, they linked the absence of conventional Indo-European past, present, and future tense markers in Hopi to a cultural perception of time not as a dimension but as a condition of unchanging, certain, or uncertain knowledge. The best-known, though now somewhat discredited, example contrasts the dozens of words for "snow" in Aleut with the Aztecs' use of a single word to cover almost all snow- and ice-related conditions. Sapir and Whorf concluded that language not only expresses but helps to create a people's conceptual framework—in effect, our words *are* our concepts—and that these linguistic differences shape and reinforce cultural differences. Critics have objected that this theory, in its extreme form, implies that speakers of two unrelated languages cannot communicate satisfactorily, which is clearly not the case; despite the loss of subtleties and the fact that one language may need a phrase to render what another can express in a single word, adequate translation is possible. Nevertheless, it seems plausible to claim that any given linguistic structure facilitates the perception and expression of some concepts more than others.

Sartre, Jean-Paul (1905–1980)

French philosopher, novelist, playwright, and critic, the most influential figure associated with EXISTENTIALISM, especially the atheistic, INDIVIDUALISTIC version with which the term has become synonymous. His thought reflects the PHENOMENOLOGY of Edmund Husserl and Martin HEIDEGGER, the DIALECTICAL analyses of HEGEL and MARX, and the collaboration of his longtime companion, Simone de BEAUVOIR. Sartre's philosophical preoccupations are revealed not only in his formal essays but in novels such as *Nausea* (1938), which upends the classical conception of the world as a calculable, intelligible place, and in plays such as *The Flies* (1942) and *No Exit* (1944), in which conscious choice and personal responsibility are seen as the only salvation in this irrational world.

In his major philosophical work, *Being and Nothingness* (1943), Sartre emphasized the unlimited and terrifying freedom of human consciousness. We are "condemned to be free," having been "thrown" into an ABSURD world without intrinsic rules or structure; with neither God nor any fixed system for guidance, we are fully responsible for our own actions. Sartre captured this condition in the phrase "existence precedes essence": we are given only existence and must fashion our own essential nature for ourselves. Making free choices, unfettered by conventional morality, constitutes *authenticity;* actions controlled by external demands—for example, adopting social roles dictated by others' expectations—constitute *bad faith,* a betrayal of the free search for self.

Human CONSCIOUSNESS (the *pour-soi,* or "for-itself") is restless, active, and open to experience, but without inherent content; we seek and strive, pursuing "projects" that both occupy and define us. In contrast, the world of things (the *en-soi,* or "in-itself") may be inert and contingent, but it is also self-contained and complete, each object containing its own essence. Our interactions with the external world—to possess, use, consume, or control it—and our similar relations with other people are attempts to capture the "in-itself," to find an essence and become complete. However, the *en-soi* may become an excessive influence; someone absorbed in the mundane world, avoiding personal responsibility and active choice, is like an object, unconscious and powerless, living in bad faith.

After World War II, Sartre grew increasingly interested in politics and social theory and moved closer to MARXISM. In the monumental *Critique of Dialectical Reason* (1960), he attempted a synthesis of Marxism and existentialism, which was repudiated by Marxists and existentialists alike. He criticized the Marxist dialectical interpretation of history as limited, mechanistic, and insufficiently mindful of the individual's freedom of action. He said that authenticity is achieved through revolutionary *praxis*—practice informed by theory—in which proletarian "ensembles" take action, violent if necessary, for social and political change. But he also warned, with an eye to the Soviet Union, that any revolution is bound to ossify into intractable institutions, eventually requiring another upheaval.

See also BEAUVOIR; HUMANISM; EXISTENTIALISM.

Saussure, Ferdinand de See box at STRUCTURALISM

Say's Law See box at SUPPLY AND DEMAND

Scholasticism

A manner of thinking and, perhaps more important, a method of teaching, which dominated CHRISTIAN learning from the 11th to the 15th century. Its central figure was St. Thomas AQUINAS. The Scholastics, or Schoolmen, from whom the movement takes it name, were scholars in the early European universities. Much of the teaching was done via the formal method of the *scholastica disputatio,* a rigorous form of the DIALECTIC in which a question was put forth, negated on the strength of canonical evidence, then followed by a positive statement that was also backed by scriptural and dogmatic evidence. This method became the foundation of university education and eventually, in revised form, of virtually all schooling up to the 20th century.

Scholastics were united not by common philosophical or theological tenets but by the approach to learning embodied in the formal disputation and by the general position that REASON and faith are compatible, by virtue of their common source in the mind of God. (However, in any apparent contradiction between the two, revelation, as the specific word of God, was considered superior.) Scholastics put great store in the "authorities" of the past—the great classical philosophers and the early church fathers. Supreme among the former was ARISTOTLE (called simply "the Philosopher"), and among the latter it was St. AUGUSTINE.

The Scholastic method led to an increasing reliance on FORMALISM—the emphasis on form over content—which was later seen as a major weakness in the method. Prominent thinkers in the Scholastic tradition include Albertus Magnus, Aquinas's teacher; John Duns Scotus, who differed from Aquinas in believing that knowledge can be obtained directly through the senses and that theology can yield scientific truth; and William of Ockham, St. Anselm, and Peter Abelard, leading contributors to the debate that preoccupied the Scholastics, the dispute over particulars and UNIVERSALS (q.v.).

See also AQUINAS.

Schopenhauer, Joseph   See PESSIMISM

scientific method

Method of investigation based on induction from empirical evidence (see DEDUCTION AND INDUCTION) and the experimental verification of theoretical hypotheses; it claims that any valid knowledge must be supported by testing and confirmation, and aims to achieve objective results relatively free of guesswork and the influence of personal or cultural biases. The principles of the scientific method, developed during the Scientific Revolution of the 16th and 17th centuries, still form the basis of most research in the natural and social sciences.

The system was a product of 17th-century philosophical RATIONALISM and EMPIRICISM and of the work of scientists such as the astronomer GALILEO and the physician William Harvey, who employed direct observation and meticulous documentation instead of more speculative modes of inquiry. DESCARTES's precept "Doubt everything" and his application of mathematical principles to philosophical problems provided much of the foundation for its later development and contributed to the notion that empirical methods can arrive at fundamental TRUTH. Around the same time, Francis BACON outlined what became the structural basis of the scientific method in his *Novum Organum* (1620). According to the Baconian method, a synthesis of empiricism and induction, data derived from precise observations and careful experimentation are recorded, compared, and analyzed to produce working hypotheses, which are then thoroughly tested (see box at BACON).

Whereas scientists of Descartes's and Bacon's day approached a problem by collecting and analyzing every discernable piece of relevant information on a given topic, modern researchers tend to select a specific aspect of a phenomenon and design an experiment to investigate it. Twentieth-century science has affected the traditional assumptions of the scientific method in two important ways. The *hypothetico-deductive* approach of Albert EINSTEIN, for whom theories were not generalizations from experience but creative ideas that produce deductions subject to experimental trials, has abolished the notion that hypotheses may be derived only from observation, and the indeterminacy inherent in QUANTUM mechanics has further disturbed the ideal of perfect objectivity.

See also BACON; EMPIRICISM; MACHIAVELLI; POSITIVISM; RATIONALISM.

Scientology

Psychoreligious movement, blending elements of FREUDIAN theory and Eastern spiritual traditions, founded by author L. Ron Hubbard and established as the Church of Scientology in the mid-1950s. Its doctrine is based on the psychological theory Hubbard expounded in *Dianetics: The New Science of Mental Health* (1950), which became part of a theology of human perfectibility. During its first two decades, Scientology was regularly the subject of controversy, criticism, and official scrutiny over the validity of its religious status, recruitment methods, and schedule of fees for members' spiritual guidance.

According to the theory of dianetics, expressed in a distinctive terminology, the mind operates on two levels, the *analytical* and the *reactive*, corresponding to CONSCIOUSNESS and the UNCONSCIOUS. Traumatic and harmful experiences in this and previous lives are stored as repressed memories, or *engrams,* which subconsciously retard our happiness, achievement, and spiritual growth. These damaging influences can be brought to consciousness and removed through "auditing" with the aid of a counselor and a biofeedback device called an E-meter; when all engrams have been eliminated, the patient is "clear."

Scientology's theology is PANTHEISTIC, positing a unity of creation; it denies the existence of evil or sin, heaven or hell, and recognizes JESUS, the BUDDHA, and other religious figures as great teachers but not gods or even perfected beings. It holds that humans live in a fallen state, having once been godlike, purely spiritual beings known as Thetans but now trapped in MEST (matter, energy, space, time), unaware of our former perfection or true faculties. Beyond being "clear," the Scientologist aspires to liberate the Thetan that dwells within each person and to be released from the cycle of reincarnation (cf. KARMA).

semiotics

The study of communication through signs as they relate to the creation and transmission of meaning; it is characteristic of, but not limited to, STRUC-TURALIST theory. Semiotics (from the Greek for "interpretation of signs") is primarily identified with linguistic theory but has also been applied to literary and mass-media criticism, social science (particularly anthropology and sociology), and cultural studies generally. Signs emerge from the relationship between *signifiers*—words, gestures, signals, images, artifacts, etc.—and the objects, ideas, or intentions that are *signified.* Signifiers are meaningless in themselves but become meaningful signs through their associations, oppositions, interactions, and combinations in linguistic and social practice. Although the semiotic idea of indirect relationships between indications and implications is old (physicians in ancient Greece used the term to discuss symptoms of illness), semiotics as a formal branch of inquiry was born in the late 19th century.

The approach was first suggested by the American PRAGMATIC philosopher Charles Sanders Peirce, who identified three types of sign. An *icon* relates to its object through similarity (e.g., a painting or photograph); an *index* is created or affected by what it indicates (e.g., a high-tide mark); a *symbol* is an arbitrary sign whose meaning is a matter of convention and agreement (e.g., the Republican Party elephant). The specialized vocabulary of semiotics was introduced largely by the Swiss linguist Ferdinand de Saussure (see box at STRUCTURALISM), who distinguished not only between the signifier and the signified but also between *parole,* or language in use, and *langue,* its abstract, underlying structure. He also differentiated between the *synchronic* and *diachronic* study of a system—its state at any one moment versus its changes over time. The field of semiotics is divided into three areas of inquiry. *Semantics* explores the relationship between signs and what they represent; *pragmatics* investigates the dependence of a sign's meaning on its function and context; *syntactics* examines the relationships among signs themselves within an abstract system independent of real-world applications.

The extension of semiotics to both literary and cultural criticism is exemplified by the French structuralist Roland Barthes. He saw a text as a self-contained system of signs whose meaning arises from their interrelations, not from any outside factors such as authorial intent or historical context. In popular culture—from sports and advertising to food and fashion—he found the interplay of words, symbols, and images creating systems of meaning that repeat the structure of language and echo the social functions of mythology.

See also box at CRITICAL THEORY; KRISTEVA; STRUCTURALISM.

separation of powers

Principle and practice of government, most fully developed in the United States, in which power is divided among several autonomous branches to prevent its concentration in any one person or body. The concept in its modern form derives primarily from Montesquieu, who insisted, in *The Spirit of the Laws* (1748), that the separation of the executive, legislative, and judicial functions is a prerequisite of liberty. Montesquieu's analysis profoundly influenced the founders of the American REPUBLIC. James Madison was primarily responsible for the incorporation of the principle in the U.S. Constitution, warning in the FEDERALIST Papers (no. 47) that "the accumulation of all powers legislative, executive and judiciary in the same hands . . . may justly be pronounced the very definition of tyranny."

To be workable, the separation of powers cannot be absolute; the branches of government must act harmoniously. In the U.S. system, the three branches of the federal government are interrelated, their functions overlapping somewhat and each branch exerting some influence over the others through a series of *checks and balances* adapted from the English parliamentary system. Examples include judicial review of legislative and executive actions (a right established not by the Constitution but by the Supreme Court's 1803 decision in *Marbury v. Madison*), the congressional power of impeachment, the Senate's duty to "advise and consent" to certain presidential appointments, and the president's right to veto legislation and Congress's ability to override that veto.

See also DEMOCRACY; FEDERALISM.

set theory

System within mathematics and symbolic LOGIC that deals with things in terms of their membership in collectivities, called *sets* or *classes;* these "things" can be concrete or abstract (objects, numbers, points, ideas, phenomena, etc.). While the idea of the set—a group of objects—is a fundamental (and primitive) mathematical concept, formal set theory was first developed in the late 19th century by the German mathematician Georg Cantor, who claimed it could serve as the basis of all mathematics. He also proposed the controversial notion that *infinite,* or *transfinite,* sets (e.g., all even numbers) have the same mathematical significance as numbers and finite sets. Gottlob Frege, and then Bertrand RUSSELL and Alfred North Whitehead, sought to demonstrate that all statements, both numerical and logical, can be expressed in terms of sets. Modern set theory is governed by a series of axioms, developed by Ernst Zemelo and Abraham Fraenkl, which define the properties of sets, the possible types of sets, and the conditions under which one set may be constructed from another.

Sets are defined in terms of their *members*—for example, the whole numbers 1–10, all even numbers, or all blue automobiles—and their *properties,* such as their *cardinality* (the number of members contained in, or defined by, the set). Pairs or groups of sets are defined by the relationships between them: *equal* sets have the same members, *equivalent* sets have the same number of members; *overlapping* sets have some members in common, *disjoint* sets have none in common; and so forth. Sets may have *subsets;* for example, the set of all numbers contains the subset of all even numbers, which in turn contains the subset of all even numbers below 100. (One problem with Cantor's initial theory of infinite sets was that the set of all numbers and its subset, all even numbers, are both infinite.)

The idea of sets is useful in organizing and visualizing mathematical and logical *operations,* such as arithmetic and *mapping* (assigning corresponding elements within and between sets), and in creating a manageable conceptual framework for complex processes. In the 1960s set theory became the basis of the so-called new math, which was founded on teaching the principles of deductive logic and ABSTRACTION instead of rote memorization; the approach was abandoned or modified when it failed to equip students with basic arithmetical skills.

See also RUSSELL.

shamanism

The practice of healing, divination, control of spirits, and out-of-body travel by specially trained and inspired adepts. The term is specific to certain Eurasian and East Asian cultures (the word "shaman" comes from the language of the Siberian Tungus people) but is generally applied to such practices found in nearly all tribal societies, including those of Oceania, sub-Saharan Africa, and the Americas. The shaman's role is primarily that of mediator between the world of the living and the spirit world, protecting the community from disease, famine, natural disasters, evil spirits, and other ills.

The shaman communicates with spirits, often through possession by them, in an ecstatic trance, which is sometimes achieved with hypnotic drugs. Shamanic rituals typically involve dancing, chanting, drumming, or other spiritual catalysts. Since sickness is seen in most ANIMISTIC cultures as the absence of the SOUL from the body, the shaman's task is to seek out and return a sick person's soul, if necessary by rescuing it from the demons who have stolen it. The shaman also escorts the souls of the dead down to the other world and sometimes ascends to the heavens during trance. (Shamans' narratives of these journeys often create and embellish much of a community's mythology.) A shaman may inherit the office or be elected by a spiritual visitation; in both cases, thorough training and a complex initiation are required. The shaman may be male or female; in Korea, for instance, where shamanism is at the core of folk religion, most shamans are women.

See also AFRICAN RELIGIONS; NORTH AMERICAN NATIVE BELIEFS.

Shi'ism See box at ISLAM

Shinto

The indigenous religion of Japan, derived from ancient folk religions and incorporating elements of BUDDHISM and CONFUCIANISM. Shinto has no formal theology, doctrine, congregational worship, or scripture. Its foundational mythology is related in two texts written in the early eighth century, the Kojiki and the Nihongi (Nihon Shoki), that ascribe divine origins to the Japanese land and its line of emperors, who are said to be descended from the sun goddess, Amaterasu-Omikami. The name "Shinto," from the Chinese *shin tao,* or "way of the divine powers" (Japanese *kami-no-michi*), was coined around the same time, to distinguish the native tradition from Buddhism, recently introduced from Korea.

Shinto belief revolves around the *kami,* the creative and protective nature divinities associated with the earth (especially certain sacred spots), as well as the emperors, who were also considered divinities, or "manifest kami," and particularly powerful humans. The kami bestow life, the objective of which is to realize the divine purpose in purity of spirit and devotion to family, community, and the nation. Shinto thus stresses this life rather than the next, although it reveres ancestral spirits and envisions an underworld where the dead reside. Prayers and ceremonial rituals, performed in the home and in shrines presided over by the hereditary priesthood, focus on purification from spiritual pollution and on supplications of the kami for benevolence and protection.

Following the Meiji Restoration of 1868, which reestablished the dominion of the emperor after five centuries of rule by feudal *shoguns,* Shinto became the state religion, a compulsory expression of patriotism and veneration of the emperor. After the emperor renounced his divinity in 1946, State Shinto was disestablished and replaced by the semiofficial Shrine (*Jinja*) Shinto. In addition to the established religion, numerous sects, collectively known as Sectarian (*Kyoha*) Shinto, have arisen, especially during the Meiji period and following World War II; these stress various aspects of the tradition, including nature worship, purification, faith healing, and Confucian thought.

Sikhism

Religion combining elements of HINDUISM and ISLAM, centered in the Punjab region of India. It was founded in the late 15th century by Guru Nanak, who sought to reconcile the warring Muslims and Hindus in northern India through a fusion of the two faiths, declaring that there is only one path, "the path of God." Like Islam (and Hindu Brahmanism), Sikhism is monotheistic, conceiving of a single creator-god; like Hinduism (and BUDDHISM), it embraces the doctrines of KARMA (the good and evil effects of past lives), *samsara* (the cycle of reincarnation), and DHARMA (the path to ENLIGHTENMENT through right behavior). Sikhism teaches that God is TRANSCENDENT and formless, neither appearing in human form (*avatars*) nor able to be represented in graven images. Nanak considered elaborate devotional rituals an obstacle to knowledge of the divine, which should instead be approached through prayer and meditation, especially by repetition of the divine name, Sat Nam, and through service to family, community, and God. He also rejected the Hindu CASTE system and preached human equality.

Nanak was the first in a dynasty of ten gurus revered by Sikhs (the word means "disciples"); the last of these, Gobind Singh (1675–1708), declared the line at an end and vested the status of guru in the Sikh scripture, the Adi Granth (or Guru Granth Sahib), which contains the lessons of Nanak and other gurus. Gobind Singh also founded the main Sikh order, the Khalsa ("pure"), initially as a militant fighting force to resist persecution and secure a Sikh STATE. The Khalsa's male initiates take the surname Singh, meaning "lion" (women take Kaur, "princess"), and wear the Five K's: *kes,* unshorn hair and beard; *kangha,* a comb holding the topknot of hair under a turban; *kach,* short pants; *kara,* an iron bracelet worn as an amulet; and *kirpan,* a ceremonial dagger.

Sikh life and worship are centered on community and family; the *gurdwala,* or temple, is not only a devotional center but a gathering place where communal meals are taken. There is no formal clergy and no prescribed order of worship, which usually consists of readings from the Granth; daily prayer is a private matter, as is the believer's relation to God. Most of the world's 18 million Sikhs live in the Punjab, but communities exist in many other countries, including the United States, where in the 1970s Yogi Bhajan established the Sikh Dharma organization, often called by the name of its educational wing, the Healthy-Happy-Holy Organization (3HO).

skepticism

Philosophical doctrine that knowledge is impossible, or at least doubtful; the word comes from the Greek for "consideration" or "doubt." Skepticism takes two main forms: the belief that no position is certain (including, as is frequently noted, this position) and the view that TRUTH exists but that certain knowledge of it may be beyond our grasp.

Ancient Greek skeptics such as Pyrrho and the SOPHISTS denied the possibility of knowing anything for certain, since contradictory arguments can be marshaled against any conceivable position. Pyrrho's solution was the suspension of judgment *(epoché)* and the pursuit of *ataraxia,* or serene noncommittal. The Greco-Roman philosopher Sextus Empiricus, a Pyrrhonist, summarized the early skeptics' arguments in a set of "tropes" that challenged the ARISTOTELIAN assumption that truth can be discovered through the exercise of LOGIC.

The moderate skepticism of DESCARTES took the position that while there is knowable truth, nothing can be assumed until it is proven. HUME, however, returned to an extreme skepticism, asserting that knowledge is nothing more than custom and mental habit. Both these approaches contributed to the modern tendency in EPISTEMOLOGY that primarily seeks to discover the means of avoiding error in the search for knowledge.

Skinner, B. F.   See BEHAVIORISM; CONDITIONING

Smith, Adam   (1723–1790)

Scottish philosopher, often called the father of economics, whose theories founded the classical school of economics and are still basic to much of modern economic thought. Although today he is remembered primarily as an economist, Smith was trained as a moral philosopher. His first book, *The Theory of Moral Sentiments* (1759), was an essay on ETHICS, but it also set out many of the themes he developed in his major economic work, *The Wealth of Nations,* including the idea that self-interest and altruism are not incompatible.

On a sojourn in France in the 1760s Smith met François Quesnay, founder and leader of the school of economists known as Physiocrats. The Physiocrats' social and economic theories impressed and influenced Smith, especially their belief in a LAISSEZ-FAIRE economic system and a social order governed by NATURAL LAW.

An Inquiry into the Nature and Causes of the Wealth of Nations, published in 1776 after 12 years in the writing, was not only the first systematic treatise on economics but proved to be one of the most influential books of all time, providing a theoretical foundation for CAPITALISM and LIBERALISM. While not all its ideas were original, its comprehensive synthesis of them was unprecedented, offering a theoretical approach to economics tied to pragmatic suggestions for governmental economic policy. In it, Smith argued for FREE TRADE, competitive MARKETS, and industrial organization based on the *division of labor.* Dividing the steps of the manufacturing process into separate tasks, he said, increases efficiency and output, as each worker is able to specialize in one skill. Specialization, however, also increases the need for an exchange market in which workers can buy the goods they are unable to produce themselves. In a free market, the producer, driven by self-interest, strives to provide the most desirable goods at the most competitive prices, and is thereby "led by an invisible hand to promote an end which was no part of his intention," that is, the consumer's interest and the good of society at large. This self-regulating system also leads to the optimal allocation of society's scarce resources.

"To found a great empire for the sole purpose of raising up a people of customers, may at first sight appear a project fit only for a nation of shopkeepers. It is, however, a project altogether unfit for a nation of shopkeepers; but extremely fit for a nation that is governed by shopkeepers."
—Adam Smith,
The Wealth of Nations

Contrary to the prevailing MERCANTILIST policies of his time, which measured national wealth in terms of a country's gold reserves and viewed international trade as simply depleting them, Smith argued that a nation's wealth is determined by its supply of capital—the goods and equipment used to produce things—and is increased by free trade. A country that produces the goods it can grow or manufacture most efficiently, and imports the rest, can give its own consumers a greater freedom of choice, thus increasing the national standard of living. Smith's trade

theories effectively put an end to mercantilism, although protectionist policies have periodically resurfaced in most trading nations (see FREE TRADE
AND PROTECTIONISM).

See also ADVANTAGE; LAISSEZ-FAIRE; MERCANTILISM; TAXATION; UNINTENDED
CONSEQUENCES; WELFARE.

social choice

Theory that considers decisions made by groups of people, particularly the
relationship between individual preferences and the aggregate decisions
they produce; also called *rational choice*. It was founded in the 1950s by the
economist Kenneth Arrow, initially as a critique of WELFARE economics and
specifically the *social welfare function*, which expressed the overall well-being
of society as a function of the individual preferences of all its members. Arrow's *impossibility theorem*, which he applied most notably to voting behavior,
states that the outcome of a group (or mass) decision is not necessarily consistent with the individual choices that make it up. Arrow demonstrated that
it is not possible to formulate a rational system based on free choice that can
translate individual preferences into social preferences without violating
one or more of a small group of necessary conditions. These include the
principle of *transitivity*, which requires that if A is preferred to B, and B is
preferred to C, then A must be preferred to C. Take the example of three
voters ranking three candidates in order of preference: voter number 1
ranks them A, B, C, voter 2 ranks them B, C, A, and voter 3 ranks them C, A,
B; although a majority (two out of three) prefers A over B and B over C, a
majority (again by two to one) also prefers C over A. In light of Arrow's insight, social-choice theorists use a variety of analytical and statistical techniques to study how decisions are made and how decision-making processes
can be improved in governmental bodies and other institutions representing
diverse interests.

See also PUBLIC CHOICE.

social constructionism

Theory of knowledge holding that reality is not objective but is constructed
differently by different people, largely through social interactions, according
to cultural biases and historical conditions. In psychology, it forms part of
SOCIAL LEARNING THEORY, which emphasizes the role of our interactions with
others. Social constructionism is also called *social constructivism*, especially in
political science; it is thus often confused or conflated with CONSTRUCTIVISM,

a related psychological theory associated primarily with Jean PIAGET, which assumes an objective reality that we apprehend through the construction of COGNITIVE patterns in response to environmental influences. Both viewpoints have roots in KANT's notion that the mind does not have direct access to objective reality and must organize experience according to certain categories of knowledge (see box at KANT) and in DARWIN's theory that EVOLUTION proceeds through progressive adaptation to prevailing conditions.

Social constructionism was pioneered in the 1920s by the Soviet psychologist Lev Vygotsky, who located the mind not within the individual but in the individual-in-social-interaction. He saw the learning process not as the passive reception of a preexisting, objective reality but as a process of creation in which the child structures experience through interplay with his or her social environment. In the constructionist view, our understanding of the world is not an interpretation of what is, but a summary of attitudes formed by social interchanges within the present historical context. Likewise, TRUTH and MEANING are seen as culturally determined constructions, not absolutes (cf. STRUCTURALISM). This position is indebted to theories such as Thomas Kuhn's, that PARADIGMS of scientific knowledge reflect established, conventional viewpoints, and Michel FOUCAULT's, that knowledge is intimately tied to power relationships in society.

Social constructionism has become a highly influential perspective throughout the social sciences. It is important in modern educational theory as a model of social learning, for example. In the sociology of knowledge it is taken as a basic principle that an individual's view of the world is formed by society, as argued in Peter L. Berger and Thomas Luckmann's *The Social Construction of Reality* (1966). In political theory, the social constructionist position can be seen, for instance, in the view that DEMOCRACY and PLURALISM are superior to other forms of political organization not through any inherent VIRTUE but because an open society is better equipped to deal with a contingent and uncertain world than less flexible systems anchored in fixed IDEOLOGIES.

social contract

Theory of government holding that society is created by the common will of individuals, who see greater advantage in association than in isolation, and that legitimate political authority therefore rests on the consent of the governed. The concept goes back at least to medieval SCHOLASTICS such as

William of Ockham, who argued that the state's power derives from the people's will, but it rests primarily on ideas developed in Thomas HOBBES's *Leviathan* (1651), John LOCKE's *Two Treatises on Government* (1690), and Jean-Jacques ROUSSEAU's *Social Contract* (1762).

Arising in opposition to the theory of the divine right of kings (see ABSOLUTISM), social contract theory located the origin of society not in the will of God but in a primeval *state of nature,* a condition of unfettered freedom but chronic insecurity. Hobbes viewed the human condition as a "war of everyone against everyone" and life in the state of nature as "solitary, poor, nasty, brutish, and short." He saw the social contract, therefore, as inspired by fear, and a sovereign with absolute, irrevocable power as the best guarantee against regression into the state of nature.

Locke believed that people join in the social contract not simply out of fear but in accordance with REASON, and not only for personal protection but for mutual benefit. Hence, any tyranny that arises can and should be opposed; a society should be able to revoke and rewrite its social contract to remedy an abuse of power. This was Locke's most important contribution to the concept, contradicting prior opinion that a social contract, once established, cannot be broken. Locke's ideas were highly influential, notably to JEFFERSON and other founders of the American REPUBLIC.

Rousseau found the unkempt freedom of the state of nature in many ways superior to the strictures and corruption of civilization. In his view, one enters into the social contract grudgingly, exchanging one's natural RIGHTS for civil protections. Ideally, the STATE is legitimated by the *general will,* which is the expression of the overall welfare of the people; as such, it embodies the individual's best interest and may therefore override individual or even majority interests.

The term "social contract" has also been applied in the modern era to legislated or implicit compacts between governments and citizens, such as the economic "safety net" guaranteed by WELFARE and government-sponsored health-care and retirement programs. The agreement between British trade unions and the Labour government in the mid-1970s, which called for pro-labor policies in exchange for wage restraint, was known as the Social Contract.

See also HOBBES; IBN KHALDUN; JEFFERSON; LOCKE; RAWLS; ROUSSEAU; SOVEREIGNTY.

social Darwinism

Social theory that applies principles of biological EVOLUTION to human society. While the term refers to Charles DARWIN's theory of natural selection, the idea was first enunciated in the 1850s by the English philosopher and sociologist Herbert Spencer, whose initial statements of it predated Darwin's *Origin of Species* and whose theoretical orientation was LAMARCKIAN. Spencer saw human PROGRESS as a matter of successful competition resulting in "the survival of the fittest"; the stronger and superior survive, while the weaker perish or are ruled by the strong, a process that leads to the continuous improvement of societies.

Social Darwinism was a popular viewpoint in the late 19th and early 20th centuries, appealing particularly to CONSERVATIVE sympathies, since it tended to vindicate the status quo. It was widely used to justify IMPERIALIST expansion and to explain social stratification, economic disparities, and racial inequality as natural and unavoidable: the dominance of one nation, CLASS, or RACE over another simply demonstrated who was most fit to rule. Prominent Spencerian thinkers of the time included the English political theorist Walter Bagehot, whose *Physics and Politics* (1872) correlated natural and social science, and the American sociologist William Graham Sumner, who contended that the evolutionary imperative makes social reforms ineffectual and unnecessary.

Related to and partly inspired by social Darwinism was *eugenics,* the theory that the human gene pool can (and should) be improved through selective breeding. Proceeding from the notion that certain individuals and ethnic groups are genetically superior to others, eugenicists held that desirable traits, such as intelligence and even morals, can be increased in the population by promoting procreation among the "fittest" (which usually meant those of Anglo-Saxon stock) and discouraging or preventing it among the "unfit." The movement was particularly influential in the United States, Britain, and Germany in the years between the world wars. It was responsible for U.S. laws restricting immigration from southern and eastern Europe, forbidding miscegenation, and requiring the sterilization of criminals and "mental defectives."

By the mid-20th century, social Darwinism and its offshoots had fallen into disfavor, as scientific developments undercut many of its biological assumptions and its prominence in FASCIST ideology underscored its elitism. The term is now most commonly used as a pejorative, for example, by critics of sociobiology, which holds that human behavior is more genetically than socially determined (see BIOLOGICAL DETERMINISM; cf. SOCIAL CONSTRUCTIONISM).

social democracy See box at DEMOCRACY

social learning theory

Orientation in psychology that combines BEHAVIORIST and COGNITIVE models to explain how people learn. It was developed, beginning in the 1940s, by a number of American psychologists, notably John Dollard, Neal Miller, Julian Rotter, and Albert Bandura. While approaches differ, in general social learning theorists propose that we learn primarily through interaction with others—largely by observation and imitation—and that behavior is developed not only through stimulus-and-response CONDITIONING but by our attempts to understand and adapt to complex social relationships. According to this perspective, children learn most of their behavior from *modeling*—what they see grown-ups doing. If adult models act aggressively, for example, a child will tend to imitate that behavior. Similarly, says Bandura, much of gender identity is not inherent but reflects the learning of socially determined conduct. The imitation of observed behavior is not pure mimicry, however, but is mediated by cognitive processes, which organize experience in relation to beliefs and expectations based on previous experiences. Behavior therapies based on this perspective often make use of constructive modeling by the therapist to overcome a patient's fears and negative expectations.

See also SOCIAL CONSTRUCTIONISM.

socialism

Economic system in which the means of production and distribution are controlled by the government or the workers and decisions on the allocation of resources are made centrally or collectively. It is contrasted with CAPITALISM, which operates on the principles of private ownership, profit, and competition within a free MARKET. Like capitalism, socialism is also a social IDEOLOGY, a view of human nature and of the way the world *should* work. "Socialism" is an umbrella term for a variety of theories sharing the general view that people are basically cooperative, not competitive, and that systems of control based on private property, wealth, and CLASS are harmful to the common welfare. It is thus applied to systems as disparate as Soviet COMMUNISM and the capitalist WELFARE state.

Historically, socialists have differed over several basic questions of theory and practice. These include whether existing institutions can gradually evolve into socialism or must be swept away in a violent revolution (see, e.g., LUXEMBURG); whether socialism must be imposed from above (e.g., by an educated

ELITE) or can be built "from the bottom up" by an autonomous mass movement (see LENIN; GRAMSCI); whether central economic planning, decentralized decision making, or even limited free enterprise is most desirable; and whether socialism is compatible with political PLURALISM or must be implemented by an ideologically dedicated one-party system.

The term "socialism" came into common use in the early 19th century as the converse of INDIVIDUALISM, the acquisitive self-interest espoused by Adam SMITH and other supporters of capitalist enterprise. Modern socialist thought originated with Karl MARX, who conceived of socialism as the postcapitalist stage of history, in which government control of the means of production, under a "dictatorship of the proletariat," would eventually be replaced by communism—a perfect society, classless and stateless. In the late 19th and early 20th centuries, European socialist organizations and political parties were dominated by gradualists such as the German theorist Karl Kautsky. After the Russian Revolution of 1917, however, the Soviet Union became the model of socialism for many, and its example the template for revolutionary struggle.

> *"No business is so essentially the public's business as the industry and commerce on which the people's livelihood depends, and to entrust it to private persons to be managed for private profit is a folly similar . . . to that of surrendering the functions of political government to kings and nobles to be conducted for their personal glorification."*
> —Edward Bellamy,
> *Looking Backward,* 1888

Following World War II most Western socialists, repudiating TOTALITARIAN Stalinism and conceding the durability of capitalism, sought to reform rather than abolish capitalist institutions. Socialist and Social Democratic political parties advocated—and in Europe largely effected—the nationalization of key industries and the establishment of comprehensive state-sponsored social-welfare programs. However, in the African, Asian, and Latin American countries of the so-called Third World, many of them only recently freed from IMPERIALIST domination, socialist and communist ideals continued to inspire revolutionary movements— movements that were victorious in several countries, including China, Cuba, Vietnam, and Angola.

Most industrialized nations, particularly in Europe, now have some form of *mixed-market* economy, in which private enterprise is balanced by limited public ownership and extensive government regulation and social planning. This model, most successfully realized in Scandinavia, where living standards are higher than in most of Europe and the United States, is seen by some as the ideal marriage of capitalism and socialism, combining the former's competitive incentives with the latter's social fairness while avoiding exploitative labor relations and the bureaucratic rigidity of central planning. The similar notion of *market socialism*, social ownership of the means of production within a regulated free-market economy, was adopted in Yugoslavia in the 1950s with mixed success.

See also COMMUNISM; CRITICAL THEORY; box at DEMOCRACY; DIALECTICAL MATERIALISM; FEMINISM; GRAMSCI; LUKÁCS; LUXEMBURG; MAO; MARX; MARXISM; TROTSKY; UTOPIANISM; WELFARE.

Socialist Realism

Official doctrine of the USSR and other COMMUNIST countries that imposed on artists the duty to create optimistic, uplifting works in the service of "SOCIALIST consciousness." Inspired primarily by the works of Maxim Gorky, it was enacted as official Soviet policy in 1934 on Stalin's orders. Originating in the MARXIST idea that the political awareness of the masses needs to be nurtured by didactic works of art, Socialist Realism condemned artistic self-expression, and especially avant-garde MODERNISM, as "bourgeois" and "decadent."

An acceptable artwork endorsed the assumption that the Communist Party represented the correct point of view and that the society in which it was conceived was the best of all possible options. Literary, musical, and pictorial works depicted "typical" figures—the worker, the soldier, the peasant—often in situations calling for heroic actions, particularly self-sacrifice on behalf of the revolution. These strictures produced, for the most part, simplistic propaganda pieces. A notable exception was the Nobel Prize–winning novelist Mikhail Sholokhov, whose depictions of Soviet life managed to achieve both official sanction and artistic legitimacy. Many other creative artists, including the composers Sergei Prokofiev and Dmitri Shostakovitch, the poet Anna Akhmatova, and the novelists Boris Pasternak and Aleksandr Solzhenitsyn, were either subjected to constraints or systematically censored.

See also LUKÁCS.

Socrates (c.470–399 B.C.E.)

Greek philosopher, mentor of PLATO, tried and executed by the Athenian state on charges of denying the gods and corrupting youth. As he left no writings, his thought comes down to us through Plato's dialogues. Although Socrates is the central figure in the dialogues, only the first few—including the *Apology, Crito,* and *Phaedo,* dealing with his trial and imprisonment—are considered to truly represent Socrates' own ideas; in the later dialogues Socrates becomes the voice of Plato.

Socrates' approach to philosophy was characterized above all by his concentration on the human sphere as his subject matter and by his use of *irony.* According to a famous story, when the Delphic oracle proclaimed Socrates the wisest of men, he responded that his only wisdom was the knowledge that he was ignorant. The Socratic method, a form of the DIALECTIC, was based on this premise. He called himself a "midwife" assisting at the birth of others' ideas, but the term was, if not disingenuous, certainly ironic. In the dialogues, Socrates draws out his debating partners with questions that are purported to arise from his own ignorance but which generally serve to expose the ignorance of others. However, Socrates' purpose was not to humiliate but simply to point out that many conventional ideas are based on unquestioned assumptions and to illustrate that there are no easy answers. In the dialogues, Socratic irony works on several levels. First, the "ignorant" man, Socrates, is seen as the more attuned to the complexity of the problem; next, Socrates' pupils realize that his avowed ignorance is at least partially a debating posture; but the greatest irony is that Socrates really does consider himself ignorant, knowing only that TRUTH is at best elusive.

To Socrates, knowledge and VIRTUE were identical. When one has knowledge one acts wisely and thus virtuously; evil acts are committed only from ignorance. The highest state is *arete,* or excellence, a moral knowledge that sees clearly the best course of action in any situation. The way to *arete* is self-knowledge: as Socrates says in the *Apology,* "The unexamined life is not worth living." Socrates' supposed impiety was based on his perception that the gods of mythology no longer provided the basis of a viable ethic; instead, a morality based on knowledge was necessary. According to Plato, Socrates claimed to be guided by a *daemon* that sat inside his ear, compelling him to pursue his stubborn search for truth and to continue his reckless debunking of venerable beliefs. It was this compulsion that not only brought down the wrath of the Athenian nobility but led Socrates to reject exile and choose death.

See also DIALECTIC; PLATO.

solipsism

From the Latin meaning "the self alone," the position that nothing exists but one's own CONSCIOUSNESS, or that the mind cannot have knowledge of anything but itself. A theory is said to be solipsistic if it makes subjective experience the basis of knowledge. The solipsistic argument states that since our awareness is in the mind, what we are aware of may also be only in the mind, or at least cannot be proven otherwise. Though this position has regularly been dismissed as absurd, it has been difficult to dispel according to its own logic. In practice, however, almost all theories that tend to solipsism posit some external entity, such as God, to validate the existence of the world. (See IDEALISM; PHENOMENALISM; cf. MATERIALISM; OBJECTIVISM.)

While solipsism itself is not a widely held position, a related question known as "the problem of other minds" has had broad influence. It can be seen as the social side of the Cartesian dilemma, of which the MIND/BODY PROBLEM is the psychological side: since I can have immediate knowledge only of what is in my own mind (see DESCARTES), I cannot rationally determine that anyone other than myself has a mind. I can assume it by analogy—for instance, because others' behavior is similar to mine—but I cannot know for sure. A great deal of modern social theory has arisen, at least implicitly, from responses to this problem. For example, HEIDEGGER and WITTGENSTEIN both held, in effect, that MEANING exists only in the realm of social practice, which makes the self/other dichotomy illusory. Another answer, derived from HEGEL's observation that the desire for recognition is central in human relations, and most fully embodied in the work of the French thinkers Maurice MERLEAU-PONTY and Jacques Lacan (see box at STRUCTURALISM), is that our sense of self comes only through our interaction with others (see also SOCIAL CONSTRUCTIONISM).

Sophists

Itinerant teachers who thrived in Athens in the fifth and early fourth centuries B.C.E. From the term "Sophist" come the words "sophistry," or specious argument, and "sophisticated," with its connotation of clever glibness; but the Greek word *sophistes* denoted merely the master of a craft, a clever adept, or a wise man.

The Sophists were the first philosophers to teach for pay, a practice that earned them the scorn of SOCRATES, who believed it was one's duty to freely impart knowledge. They taught whatever was wanted by their patrons, from grammar and linguistic analysis to mathematics to techniques for success in public life. But they were, above all, rhetoricians, skilled in rational argument, and it was their reputed willingness to argue either side of a proposition with equal force that spawned their enduring reputation for deceptive reasoning.

In their thought, Sophists were more interested in human nature, politics, and society than in the search for the nature of ultimate reality, which occupied their predecessors and contemporaries, including PLATO. There was no uniform Sophist philosophy, but they tended to RELATIVISM and EMPIRICISM, in contrast to those who saw life governed by an intrinsic ideal (see IDEAS; IDEALISM). They also believed, and undertook to prove, that civic VIRTUE could be taught, with the radical implication that almost anyone could participate in politics and public life.

Foremost among the Sophists was Protagoras, best known for his dictum "Man is the measure of all things"—that is, the qualities of things are determined as much or more by our PERCEPTIONS of them as by anything innate in them. He illustrated this with the parable of the wind. One person feels a wind to be warm, another feels it to be cold; since it cannot be both hot and cold at once, they cannot both be feeling the same wind, unless, of course, these qualities are only subjective.

The view that has been distilled in the phrase "might makes right" is credited to the Sophists Thrasymachus and Callicles. They appear in Plato's *Republic* and *Gorgias*, respectively, where they argue that "justice" is established by whoever is strong enough to enforce it; self-interest is therefore the only rational course and compulsion the only reason for obedience to authority.

See also SKEPTICISM.

soul and spirit

Religious and METAPHYSICAL concepts, often equated, relating to the essential, immaterial portion of human (and, in some cultures, other living) beings. A common distinction between soul and spirit sees the former as the immortal ESSENCE of a person, surviving the body's death, and the latter as the animating principle, the spark that distinguishes life from nonlife (the Latin root, *spiritus*, means "breath"). Both soul and (more frequently) spirit are understood as the seat of CONSCIOUSNESS and the self. Spirit is the more inclusive and expansive term; soul is usually conceived as personal (and therefore envisioned as internal) and spirit as universal and TRANSCENDENT. However, in many traditions, the individual human soul is considered part of a universal or world soul. The belief that spirit infuses all creation is a common one; it is found, for instance, in both ANIMISM, which finds spirits in all things, and CHRISTIANITY, in which the TRINITARIAN God dwells within his people in the form of the Holy Spirit. *Spirits* are immaterial beings that occupy the earth, either parts of the universal spirit that inhabit living and nonliving things (with good or evil intent) or the disembodied souls of ancestors that haunt the living world (the English word "ghost" is related to the German *Geist,* or "spirit").

In most religious traditions, the soul is seen as the particle of the divine spirit humans are inbued with, superior to and separable from the body. Ancient Greek thought, exemplified by PLATO, considered the soul preexistent and immortal, a concept that was adapted to Christian doctrine, especially by St. AUGUSTINE. The soul is also the element of the human being that strives for union with the divine. In JUDAIC, Christian, and ISLAMIC tradition, at the Last Judgment the souls (and resurrected bodies) of the faithful will be united with God, while those of the wicked will be cast into hell (see ESCHATOLOGY). The spiritual goal of HINDUISM and BUDDHISM is ENLIGHTENMENT and NIRVANA, the release of the soul *(atman)* from human imperfection and its union with the ABSOLUTE.

Both terms have acquired secular connotations as well. "Soul," implying deep emotional fervor and sensitivity, has been adopted as a self-descriptive term by African-Americans, especially in reference to black music. "Spirit" (and sometimes "soul") embodies the idea of a culturally defining characteristic, as in "national spirit" or *Zeitgeist* (spirit of the age). This is at least in part the legacy of HEGEL, who made spirit the focus of his DIALECTIC, the gradual progression of knowledge to the final attainment of Absolute Spirit. The use of the term to signify cultural achievement is also illustrated in Wilhelm Dilthey's distinction between *Geisteswissenschaften* (the human sciences, or "sciences of the spirit") and *Naturwissenschaften* (natural sciences). The Greek word for the soul, *psyche,* providing the root for "psychology," has come to be associated with the mind and specifically with the idea that the workings of the mind cannot be entirely reduced to neurological impulses.

See also ABSOLUTE; AFRICAN RELIGIONS; ANIMISM; ARISTOTLE; AUGUSTINE; BUDDHISM; CHRISTIANITY; DUALISM; GNOSTICISM; HEGEL; HINDUISM; IBN RUSHD; IBN SINA; IDEALISM; IDENTITY; JAINISM; KARMA; LUTHER; MIND/BODY PROBLEM; MONISM; NEOPLATONISM; NORTH AMERICAN NATIVE BELIEFS; PAGANISM; PENTECOSTALISM; PLATO; box at PROTESTANTISM; SCIENTOLOGY; SHAMANISM; SHINTO; SPIRITUALISM; THEOSOPHY; TOTEMISM; TRINITY; VITALISM; WITCHCRAFT; ZOROASTRIANISM.

sovereignty

A central concept in political theory, denoting ultimate jurisdiction within a given political system, usually a national STATE, and autonomy in relation to other states; a sovereign entity thus recognizes no authority higher than itself. The idea of sovereignty (meaning, literally, "supremacy") was initially associated with the doctrine of ABSOLUTISM. In his *Six Books of the Commonwealth* (1576), Jean Bodin defined sovereignty as the absolute power to make laws and vested that power in the monarch, whose supreme authority over his subjects was limited only by the laws of God. In the 17th century, Thomas HOBBES, Hugo Grotius, and others introduced the concept of the *sovereign state*, Hobbes observing that a ruler's sovereignty in his own domain requires the recognition of that authority by other sovereigns. This formulation gave rise to the modern norms of noninterference in the affairs of other states.

Hobbes and other SOCIAL CONTRACT theorists also advanced the idea of *popular sovereignty*, in which ultimate authority resides not with the government but with the people who consent to be governed. This idea came to fruition in the French Revolution, when Louis XIV's declaration "L'état, c'est moi" ("I am the state") was refuted by the proclamation of the sovereignty of the people. The legitimacy of the state is now often tied to popular sovereignty as expressed in a DEMOCRACY or a REPUBLIC. Another use of the term "popular sovereignty," current in the pre–Civil War United States, referred to the right of each new state entering the union to decide for itself whether or not it would permit slavery within its borders.

The concept of sovereignty is central to almost all relations between modern states. It is codified in the charters of most international organizations as a guarantee that international commitments will not override states' rights to self-determination and nonintervention. However, the notion that the sovereign state, self-defining and self-sufficient, is a fixed and timeless political principle has been increasingly questioned in an age of growing global interdependence.

See also LOCKE; NATIONALISM; RADICALISM; ROUSSEAU; STATE.

Spinoza, Baruch (1632–1677)

Dutch philosopher, a rationalist and PANTHEIST whose unorthodox thought caused his expulsion from the Jewish community and exile from Amsterdam. He lived and wrote in obscurity, earning his living as a lens grinder. Although his work was ignored for a century after his death, he is now considered one of the most original and influential of modern philosophers.

Adopting the geometrically oriented RATIONALISM of DESCARTES while rejecting his DUALISM, Spinoza created a theory that was pure MONISM. In his major work, the *Ethics*, he envisioned the world as being the expression of a single SUBSTANCE, which he identified as *Deus sive natura*, "God or nature," in which God and all that is are one. (This particular view of creation, which led one commentator to call Spinoza "the God-intoxicated man," had a profound influence on the ROMANTICS and other poets of nature.) Although unitary, substance/God/nature has an infinity of attributes, of which we are able to perceive only two, mind and matter (thought and "extension"), the *double aspect* of universal substance. All individual things—objects, creatures, ideas—are transient modifications, or *modes,* of substance. This being so, Spinoza concluded, there can be no personal immortality. Death is the passing away of a transient mode; only substance is eternal.

> *"Love is nothing else but pleasure accompanied by the idea of an external cause: hate is nothing else but pain accompanied by the idea of an external cause."*
>
> —Baruch Spinoza, *Ethics*

Spinoza denied both divine providence and free will, holding that everything is determined by the universal, indifferent laws of nature. Indeed, he was the first to expound what has become known as *overdetermination,* in which all of the forces acting in a given sphere control the outcome of an event. He maintained that every mode—every being—possesses *conatus* (loosely, "effort"), a striving for self-preservation. Life is a constant struggle with other individuals and with our own passions. *Conatus* is expressed in *power*—the power to persist and create. To Spinoza, social and political systems are extensions of individual power, and as such deserve and require the individual's participation and support. He saw DEMOCRACY as the best expression of human interests but felt that it would remain an impractical ideal until the mass of humanity achieved the level of education and civic responsibility necessary to sustain democratic institutions.

Spinoza's rationalism was thoroughgoing. He saw the Bible as nonsense if taken literally—he dismissed the miracles as misunderstandings, which enraged the Catholic Church as well as the rabbis—but considered it an incomparable guide to ETHICS. He distinguished four progressive levels of human knowledge: knowledge derived from hearsay, from practical experience, from hypotheses based on observation, and finally from deductive LOGIC. This last, highest level, the perfect apprehension of analytic TRUTH, he described as the perception of a thing *sub specie aeternitatis,* "under the aspect of eternity."

See also MONISM; RATIONALISM.

spirit See SOUL AND SPIRIT

spiritualism

Belief in the existence of spirits that survive the death of the body and can communicate with the living; it is a version of *spiritism,* the ancient and widespread belief that the spirits of ancestors permeate the world of the living and can affect earthly events. The term is also used in philosophy for the view, similar to IDEALISM and opposed to POSITIVISM, that nature is composed not of matter but of spirit, sometimes called the *World Soul,* the pervasive, immaterial principle that creates and orders the universe (see LOGOS; SOUL AND SPIRIT).

Spiritualism as an organized movement dates from 1848, when Kate Fox and her sisters purportedly contacted the spirit of a man who had been murdered in their house in New York State. At a time when unquestioning faith in orthodox religion was losing ground in the face of scientific PROGRESS and social upheavals, this sensational event ignited a spiritualist craze. The ground had been prepared by other contemporary influences, notably the religious doctrine of Emmanuel Swedenborg, who had delivered messages from the dead while in a trance. The Fox sisters and other mediums—intermediaries between the living and dead—held séances in which departed spirits were consulted by those wishing to renew contact with deceased relatives, gain knowledge of the future, or reassure themselves of the possibility of life after death. The movement declared itself both ancient, descended from prehistoric SHAMANISM, and scientific, verified by the evidence of the senses, not faith (cf. PARAPSYCHOLOGY).

In the early 20th century several organized spiritualist churches were formed, the first and still most widespread of which is the Universal Church of the Master. This type of spiritualism is essentially CHRISTIAN, though often denying JESUS's divinity and other orthodox tenets. It also denies the existence of the Devil, although much of the criticism of spiritualism has come from Christian authorities who denounce it as either diabolical or fraudulent. Spiritualists maintain that contact with the spirit world brings the individual into communion with the TRANSCENDENT "creative intelligence" of the universe—an emphasis reflected in the new strands of spiritualism that have arisen in the NEW AGE movement, where communication with spirits is called "channeling," and in Wicca, the revived cult of WITCHCRAFT.

spontaneous generation and biogenesis

Opposing explanations of how living things originate. The ancient belief in *abiogenesis,* holding that living organisms are spontaneously generated from nonliving organic or inorganic matter (for instance, maggots from rotting meat), was generally accepted until the 17th century, and the theory of *biogenesis*—that life arises through the procreation of organisms from pre-existing like organisms—was not definitively proved until the 19th century. The ARISTOTELIAN theory of VITALISM held that life originated through the infusion of a preexisting life force or "vital principle" into inanimate matter. This view persisted, with variations, through the Renaissance. The 16th-century Swiss alchemist and physician Paracelsus proposed that certain substances derive from the *mysterium,* or generative matrix, of quite different substances, for example, frogs from mud and grain from water in the soil; likewise, the mice that infest granaries are generated by the *mysterium* of the grain. DESCARTES suggested that warm, putrefying matter could yield the necessary combination of organic materials to "quicken," producing a living organism.

By the mid-17th century, scientific theory and experimentation were beginning to cast doubt on the possibility of spontaneous generation. In 1660, the Italian physician Francesco Redi showed that maggots appeared in rotting meat only when flies had access to it. Abiogenesis was progressively discredited by further experiments over the next two centuries, capped by Louis Pasteur's demonstration in the early 1860s that microorganisms grew in nutritive solutions only if they were introduced from the external environment.

The question of whether life forms can arise spontaneously from the biomolecules that comprise them returned to the scientific forum in the 1940s, when scientists began in earnest to probe the circumstances under which life first appeared on earth. The currently predominant theory is that the gradual accretion, over millions of years, of stable, self-perpetuating biochemical compounds eventually culminated in the first microorganisms. Some theorists argue from statistics and PROBABILITY that life could have arisen by this process only once; others suggest that life, in its simplest form, may have appeared many times before a dominant life form arose and survived.

standard model

Set of theories in modern physics describing three of the four *fundamental forces* that account for all physical interactions in the universe. These forces, in order of diminishing strength, are the *strong nuclear force,* which binds protons and neutrons together in atomic nuclei; *electromagnetism,* the interaction of charged particles, which, among other things, keeps solid objects solid and produces light; and the *weak nuclear force,* which governs radioactive decay. The fourth, and weakest, force is *gravity,* the interaction of atomic particles and other bodies caused by their mass; this force is not accounted for in the standard model. Electromagnetism and gravity operate at both microscopic and macroscopic (even interstellar) scales, the strong and weak force only at the subatomic level. The theories that comprise the standard model are so called because they give the most complete experimentally confirmed explanation of the behavior of subatomic particles to date.

The standard model assumes the existence of *quarks,* indivisible subatomic particles considered, with *leptons* (electrons, muons, neutrinos, and other elementary particles), to be the fundamental building blocks of matter. Quarks are so small that they are unable to exist as free particles and thus are detectable only by theoretical inference. Their elusiveness is reflected in the whimsical terminology that describes them (the word "quark" itself comes from James Joyce's dreamlike novel *Finnegans Wake*). The six varieties, or "flavors," of quarks are called up, down, top, bottom, strange, and charm, and each flavor comes in three "colors." Quarks combine in groups of three to create protons, neutrons, and other particles.

The theory of *quantum chromodynamics,* modeled on the success of QUANTUM ELECTRODYNAMICS, describes the strong nuclear force; *electroweak* theory describes, and posits a close relationship between, the electromagnetic and weak nuclear forces. Numerous attempts to develop a Grand Unified Theory that would unite all three forces as aspects of the same force have so far been unsuccessful, as have efforts to establish a unified theory that would include gravity. *Superstring* theory, which seeks to explain subatomic forces in terms that embrace both relativity and QUANTUM THEORY, is thought by some to hold the best promise of uniting all four forces in a "theory of everything." (See also FIELD THEORY.)

Stanton, Elizabeth Cady (1815–1902)

American social reformer, one of the founders of the FEMINIST movement. Born into a privileged middle-class family, she received an elite private-school education but, being female, was unable to attend college, a disadvantage she bitterly resented. Two early experiences particularly informed her views and her later activism. In her father's law practice, she observed the extent to which women lacked basic legal rights, especially in marriage; and in London, where her husband, Henry Brewster Stanton, was a delegate to the 1840 World Anti-Slavery Convention, she saw the abolitionist Lucretia Mott, also a delegate, denied a seat because of her gender.

In 1848, Elizabeth Stanton and Lucretia Mott organized the first women's RIGHTS convention, in the village of Seneca Falls, New York, where Stanton lived.

The convention narrowly approved a controversial resolution demanding the vote for women and issued a Declaration of Sentiments, written by Stanton and modeled on the Declaration of Independence, which catalogued the injustices suffered by women, including the denial of equal educational and employment opportunities and property rights. The success of the Seneca Falls convention placed Stanton among

> *"The true Republic: men, their rights and nothing more; women, their rights and nothing less."*
> —Susan B. Anthony,
> masthead of
> *Revolution,* 1868–70

the foremost feminist intellectuals and activists of her day. In 1851 she met the social reformer Susan B. Anthony, and the two formed a lifelong partnership dedicated to the cause of women's rights, Anthony the activist and organizer, Stanton the writer and theorist. They published a feminist newspaper, *Revolution,* founded the National Woman Suffrage Association, and compiled, with Matilda Joslyn Gage, the first three volumes of the six-volume *History of Woman Suffrage* (1881–1922). Stanton was also the first woman to address the New York State Legislature, where she lobbied for laws giving married women rights to property and child custody, and was the initiator of the constitutional amendment guaranteeing women's suffrage, which was first introduced in Congress in 1878 and finally ratified in 1920.

Stanton believed that she and her cause had to demand more than they expected to get; what at first seems outrageous, she reasoned, eventually will appear reasonable. Parts of her agenda, however, were controversial even among her colleagues and supporters. She urged the reform of restrictive divorce laws, encouraged women to leave abusive marriages, endorsed birth control, and advocated "self-sovereignty"—self-reliance and personal autonomy. She was also critical of organized religion and Judeo-Christian moral conventions, and in *The Woman's Bible* (1895–98) she postulated an androgynous God and denounced oppression justified by religious tradition and authority.

state

The political community claiming SOVEREIGNTY and exercising authority over a given territory and population. The idea of the state—its foundation, function, and legitimacy—has occupied political philosophers since the first city-states arose in ancient Greece. After the Middle Ages, the notion of the state as representing a distinct ethnic, cultural, or linguistic community gave rise to the *nation-state* in place of the feudal principality (see NATIONALISM). Classically considered as encompassing all of society, the state has increasingly been defined as synonymous with government—the entity that, in Max WEBER's definition, has "a monopoly on the legitimate use of force within its territory." The term "statism" refers to the concentration of political (and sometimes economic and legal) power in a centralized government and the primacy of that authority over individual RIGHTS domestically; the term is also used in reference to the state's autonomy in international relations.

Where PLATO envisioned an ideal REPUBLIC founded in RATIONAL knowledge and ruled by paternalistic "philosopher-kings," ARISTOTLE saw the state as an elementary feature of human existence, a diverse association of people united by habit, law, and education for the purpose of developing moral excellence. This view of the state as a natural condition was contradicted by Thomas HOBBES, who saw the "state of nature" as anarchic and perilous and the state as the result of a SOCIAL CONTRACT in which individuals agree to give up their natural freedom in exchange for security. For Hobbes, the temporal and moral power of the state is absolute and the allegiance of the citizen total. Hobbes's pessimistic, authoritarian outlook was contradicted by other social-contract theorists, notably John LOCKE, whose idea that the state is subject to the will of the people, who can amend or overthrow it at will, affected 18th-century LIBERAL politics in general and the American founders in particular.

In the 19th century, two opposing and influential views of the state arose. In HEGEL's complex formulation, the ideal state is an ETHICAL entity that unites and transcends the individual and social relationships that comprise it. The state under the rule of law—that is, the DEMOCRATIC, CHRISTIAN state— values the individual while avoiding anarchy; it is the source of morality and the culmination of the development of the human spirit. Karl MARX, on the other hand, saw the contemporary state not as the expression of a transcendent impulse but as an apparatus of CLASS oppression, created for the defense of property and perpetuated through false IDEOLOGY and, ultimately, by force.

Non-Marxist thinkers, too, have questioned theories that present the state as a rational entity. In the late 20th century, for example, environmentalists and cultural critics such as Jean BAUDRILLARD have argued that territorial integrity is meaningless in the world of Chernobyl and a depleted ozone layer.

states' rights

Doctrine that the American union is rooted in the consent of the states, which possess RIGHTS and powers that cannot be infringed by the national government. The idea that the United States is a free association of SOVEREIGN states, asserted in the Articles of Confederation of 1781, was moderated with the adoption of the U.S. Constitution and the Bill of Rights, in which the Tenth Amendment stipulates that "the powers not delegated to the United States by the Constitution, nor prohibited by it to the States, are reserved to the States respectively, or to the people."

The question of a strong or weak central government is a deep current in American politics, and conflicts have regularly erupted over the rights of the states as against the federal government. In a dispute with the FEDERALISTS over the constitutionality of the Alien and Sedition Acts of 1798, resolutions in the legislatures of Kentucky and Missouri—drafted by Thomas JEFFERSON and James Madison, respectively—sought to establish the principle that federal laws could be nullified within individual states. The nullification controversy next came to a head in 1832 when South Carolina, spurred by Sen. John C. Calhoun, attempted to nullify a protective tariff seen as favoring the industrial North. Such issues of state powers, as much as the slavery question, led to the secession of the Confederacy in 1861.

Since the mid-19th century, when the Supreme Court's Dred Scott decision affirmed that states had the right even to determine that slaves were not citizens, the question of states' rights has revolved repeatedly around the denial of equal treatment to African-Americans. In 1948, southern Democrats, angered over a strong civil rights plank in the Democratic Party platform, bolted and formed the States' Rights (Dixiecrat) Party, nominating Sen. Strom Thurmond of South Carolina for president and insisting that segregation was a prerogative of state and local authorities. The same impetus bolstered resistance to school desegregation orders in the 1950s and drove the presidential candidacy of Alabama's George Wallace in 1968. In the late 20th century, support for states' rights has been strongest in the West, where land developers and industries exploiting natural resources such as timber and mining have opposed restrictive federal environmental regulations.

Stoicism

Greco-Roman school of philosophy founded in Athens in the late fourth century B.C.E. by Zeno of Citium. It was influential for 500 years and was at one time the dominant intellectual position in the Roman Empire. The name derives from the Greek *stóa*, or portico, where the first Stoics met.

Early Stoicism was an outgrowth of CYNIC philosophy, with which it shared an emphasis on VIRTUE as the only good and an indifference to material possessions and social pretensions. The Stoics, however, tempered the Cynics' harsh ASCETICISM and did not share their disdain for REASON and intellectual inquiry. Zeno's follower Chrysippus may have been the first to divide philosophy into the three disciplines of physics, LOGIC, and ETHICS, all of which informed the Stoic world-view.

The Stoics saw the cosmos as composed primarily of the ELEMENT fire, the "active principle" that gives birth to the world and periodically consumes it; this cosmic cycle is called the World Year, a cycle of ETERNAL RECURRENCE many millennia in length, each one exactly reproducing the last. The DETERMINISM of this view—that life is bounded by Fate—produced the Stoic principle of *apatheia:* immunity from feeling, indifference to pain or pleasure through acceptance of the world's predestined course. *Apatheia* had none of the negative connotations of its modern derivative, "apathy," but was seen by the Stoics as the only right way of life, an acquiescence to the implacable flow of the universe (cf. BUDDHISM).

To the Stoics, the universe was animated by the LOGOS, the RATIONAL principle. Through reason we gain knowledge—the basis of virtue and just action—by which we may aspire to live in harmony with Nature and to understand the divine will. While the early Stoics stressed the virtuous individual, their heirs in the Roman Empire of the first and second centuries C.E.—including Seneca, the Greek-born slave-philosopher Epictetus, and the emperor Marcus Aurelius—held that civic *duty* was the better part of virtue. This conviction, together with the Stoics' faith in a universal reason, led to a conception of NATURAL LAW *(jus naturale)* distinct from and transcending the *jus gentium* (law of nations), which became codified in the Roman law, the basis of most modern legal systems.

See also ETERNAL RECURRENCE; LOGOS.

stream of consciousness

Psychological term and literary technique denoting the unstructured flow of thoughts and emotions. The term was coined by William JAMES in *The Principles of Psychology* (1890) to describe his view of mental experience as a succession of events and perceptions that flow like a stream through our CONSCIOUSNESS and from which we select the relative few that capture our awareness. Related to this notion is FREUD's therapeutic technique of *free association,* in which the patient in PSYCHOANALYSIS is encouraged to relate every thought as it occurs, without organizing or censoring.

In literature, stream of consciousness depicts the random flow of thoughts and feelings within the mind of a character, revealing to the reader the actual flow of consciousness. In many cases it is used ironically, as the inner self is shown to be governed less by REASON than by an all-but-chaotic sequence of memories and sensations, ordered not by purpose or will but by arbitrary and elusive patterns of thought. The technique is thought to have first appeared in Edouard Dujardin's 1888 novella *Les Lauriers sont coupé* (translated as *We'll to the Woods No More*), and the earliest sustained use of it is sometimes credited to the English novelist Dorothy Richardson in her epic cycle *Pilgrimage*, the first volume of which was published in 1915. Classic examples of stream of consciousness occur in James Joyce's *Ulysses* (1922), Marcel Proust's *Remembrance of Things Past* (1913–27), Virginia Woolf's *Mrs. Dalloway* (1925), and William Faulkner's *The Sound and the Fury* (1929). It was a hallmark of Beat Generation prose and poetry of the 1950s and '60s and remains a staple of literary technique.

structuralism

An approach to understanding human culture holding that individual phenomena can be understood only within the context of the overall structures they are part of (social, political, economic, textual, mathematical, etc.), and that these structures represent universal sets of relations that derive meaning from their "binary oppositions"—their contrasts and interactions within a specific context; by extension, any approach that studies the basic structures underlying external phenomena. One of the most influential intellectual movements of the 20th century, structuralism flourished from midcentury into the 1970s. Associated principally with French thinkers, the structuralist perspective has been applied to many disciplines and remains an important influence in critical thought. It is related to SEMIOTICS, which studies the relationship of signs (words, gestures, images, etc.) to the meanings they convey.

Structuralism developed from the work of the Swiss linguist Ferdinand de Saussure (see box), who saw language as a system within which words act as arbitrary signs, meaningless in themselves but given meaning through their interactions within the overall structure of a language. The school of American linguistic structuralism represented by Leonard Bloomfield took a BEHAVIORIST approach to the study of language development and usage, stressing form and structure over MEANING. Structuralism was extended into the social sciences by the social anthropologist Claude Lévi-Strauss (see box), for whom human society reflects underlying, often unconscious, systems of relations that govern social behavior. That approach also became an important tendency in sociology, in which social structure is seen as guiding, if not overriding, individual agency. The MARXIST critique of society is sometimes called structuralist because it identifies underlying economic relations as the determining factors of social organization.

Structuralist literary criticism, identified primarily with Roman Jakobson and Roland Barthes (see box), derives by analogy from linguistic structuralism, seeing a text as a system of signs whose meaning is derived from the pattern of their interactions rather than from any external reference. This approach is in opposition to critical positions that seek to determine an author's intent or to clarify the relationship of a work of art to the reality it purports to reflect; it is also opposed by POSTSTRUCTURALIST approaches such as DECONSTRUCTION, which deny the existence of invariant patterns and definite meanings (cf. POSTMODERNISM). Structuralist theory has also been applied to PSYCHOANALYSIS, most prominently by Jacques Lacan (see box), as well as other fields.

See also CHOMSKY; FORMALISM; FOUCAULT; FUNCTIONALISM; GRAMMAR; NEW CRITICISM; SEMIOTICS; SYSTEMS THEORY.

MAJOR FIGURES IN STRUCTURALISM

- *Ferdinand de Saussure* (1857–1913) developed structural linguistics around the distinction he saw between the external characteristics of language as it is spoken and written, which he called *parole* (French for "word" or "speech"), and its abstract, underlying structure, or *langue* (language). In his *Course in General Linguistics* (published 1916), he described language as a system of arbitrary *signs,* which are composed of *signifiers* (words, signals, etc.) in relationship to what is *signified* (the conventional connotations assigned to signifiers). Linguistic signs have no inherent meaning in themselves, but gain meaning through the contrast of their differences—the meaning of "you," for example, is a composite of "not I," "not he," "not we," and so on. These oppositions are governed by the structure of language. Language grows and changes because while *langue* is fixed, *parole* is adaptable to an infinite variety of expression.

- *Claude Lévi-Strauss* (1908–), in his studies of tribal cultures, proposed that the essence of human society is the constant interplay of means of communication. These exchanges, including myths and rituals, maintain the multilayered structures of relationship (e.g., kinship systems) on which society is founded. Human activities and customs, Lévi-Strauss contended, are grounded in universal COGNITIVE structures—mental systems of classification that operate according to *binary oppositions* (e.g., raw/cooked, marriageable/unmarriageable) and are common to all humans. The world's social systems, therefore, have similar underlying structures, although they may give rise to widely diverse customs. The anthropologist's job is to discover the "meaning" of a given society by sorting out the basic "rules" governing cultural practices from their myriad, often contradictory, expressions in that society.

- *Louis Althusser* (1918–1990) developed a controversial revision of MARXISM holding that individuals are not autonomous actors in society but act as structural elements within complex social systems. The elements of an individual's IDENTITY—social role, personal beliefs, etc.—are formed not from within but by economic and political forces and what Althusser called "ideological state apparatuses"— religious institutions, educational systems, and other cultural influences. In contrast to classical Marxist analysis, which saw the primary structural factor in society as the subordination of the political/cultural superstructure to the economic base, Althusser argued that social forms are an example of *overdetermination,* in which numerous forces are at work—political, economic, cultural, IDEOLOGICAL—no one of which solely determines the others. Althusser's influence was considerable in the 1970s but waned after he was imprisoned for murdering his wife.

- *Roland Barthes* (1915–1980), social and literary critic, is perhaps the central figure in the French school of structuralism that took Lévi-Strauss's lead. Barthes applied Saussure's concept of language and Lévi-Strauss's analysis of myth and ritual to a wide range of popular culture, including fashion, food, advertising, and even professional wrestling. In all these he saw systems of MEANING created by the interplay of words, symbols, images, and other communicative devices. In the "garment system," for instance, personal clothing choices constitute statements of difference and affinity that locate the individual's sense of identity within the social system. Barthes approached literature, too, with the aim of obtaining meaning from the self-contained system of "signs" within a text, without reference to anything beyond it, such as its historical context or the author's purported intent. From this stance he proclaimed "the DEATH OF THE AUTHOR"—the end of authorial intention as the prime focus of criticism.

- *Jacques Lacan* (1901–1981) incorporated elements of structural linguistics into PSYCHOANALYSIS through his notion of the UNCONSCIOUS, which, he said, "is structured like a language." It is the subliminal repository of emotionally charged memories (analogous to Saussure's *langue*) that underlie and affect the events of CONSCIOUSNESS *(parole);* unable or unwilling to express all things, it censors many. The analyst's role is to uncover and interpret the subconscious system that is imperfectly (neurotically) expressed in the patient's speech and behavior. Furthermore, the self is not a unified, autonomous entity but is "decentered," the sum of a variety of self-images constructed by linguistic and social conventions; "I" is merely a sign that is defined in relation to other signs. The true self is ALIENATED through socialization, which begins in young children at the same stage as LANGUAGE ACQUISITION. Lacan's positioning of the self in a social context has had wide influence, for instance, in some FEMINIST theories that see gender identity as a socially imposed construct rather than purely innate.

Sturm und Drang

German artistic movement of the 1770s, mainly literary, that rejected CLASSICISM and embraced impulse, instinct, and emotion. The name, meaning "storm and stress," comes from the title of a 1777 play by Friedrich Maximilian Klinger. It implies both personal crisis and the disorder of a materialistic world in which the artist struggles to find a spiritual anchor. The short-lived movement, an early form of ROMANTICISM, was a reaction against the era's philosophical RATIONALISM, social turmoil, and literary artifice. It was embodied by the young dramatic poets Johann Wolfgang Goethe, Johann Gottfried Herder, and Friedrich von Schiller, who saw art as inspired by nature and intuitive genius. They were influenced by ROUSSEAU's natural philosophy and Shakespeare's epic dramas, and their work in this period was loosely constructed, melodramatic, and nationalistic. Goethe's novel *The Sorrows of Young Werther* (1774) epitomized the passionate subjectivity of the style and created a prototype of the Romantic hero.

subjectivism See OBJECTIVISM AND SUBJECTIVISM

substance

In philosophy, the basic, underlying ESSENCE of a thing that gives it existence; a fundamental concept in METAPHYSICS. From the Latin *substare,* "to stand under," substance is the substratum of reality. In most conceptions, substance can be both physical (material) and spiritual (mental). It has no qualities or properties itself, but is what qualities and properties inhere in; it is the independent, irreducible basis of something, which remains unchanged despite any outward changes. Substance is contrasted with *accident,* the external form and appearance of a thing.

The idea of substance was a consistent theme in philosophy from the ancient Greeks to the 19th century. For ARISTOTLE, substance was the prime category of reality, the basis of all things, the answer to the question of how something can change and still be considered the same thing. In his DUALISTIC philosophy, DESCARTES divided creation into two kinds of substance: the *res cogitans* ("thinking substance"), beings capable of reason, that is, humans, angels, and God, and the *res extensa* ("extended substance"), the world's physical entities, named for their sole characteristic, that they occupy space, are "extended" in it (see also MIND/BODY PROBLEM). SPINOZA accepted Descartes's distinction between mind and matter but considered them twin expressions of a single, universal substance (see MONISM). LOCKE saw substance as the unknowable substrate of reality, the essence that EMPIRICAL investigation cannot penetrate.

The idea of substance was most forcefully questioned by the 18th-century PHENOMENALISTS, who denied the reality of anything but our own perceptions. It is largely ignored by contemporary philosophers; ANALYTIC PHILOSOPHY, for example, avoids direct consideration of the classic problem of reality, preferring to analyze the language we use to describe it.

See also ARISTOTLE; DESCARTES; box at KANT; MONISM; SPINOZA.

Sufism

The MYSTICAL tendency within ISLAM, pertaining to a wide variety of practices, doctrines, and sects. Despite its diversity, Sufism is broadly characterized by renunciation of the self, fervent devotional practices, and the conviction that love of God is the ultimate truth of human existence and the means to the highest states of awareness and ENLIGHTENMENT. Sufism developed in the first few centuries of Islam in reaction to the legalistic emphasis in orthodox Islam and to the worldly luxury of the early elites. The term *Sufi,* meaning "wool-wearer," may derive from the ASCETIC practices of early Sufis, many of whom wore rough woolen garments. Some Sufi practices and doctrines have been considered blasphemous by Muslims who take the observance of Islamic law to be the most important religious duty and therefore place obedience to God above love of God. While some Sufis have regarded Islamic law as an empty ritual, the majority have always held that the observance of Islamic law follows naturally from a genuine love of God.

For most Sufis, the key to approaching God lies in relinquishing the consciousness of self, the principal source of suffering and delusion. Union with, or at least proximity to, God can be achieved by means of self-denial and intense devotional practices. These may take the form of prayer and meditation, recitation of the 99 names of God, or ecstatic trances such as those achieved in the whirling dance of the mendicant sects of *dervishes* or *fakirs.* Progress along the Sufi path, always guided by a master *(murshid* or *pir),* proceeds through progressive stages of repentance and renunciation to ultimate enlightenment. The *waliy,* or saint, attaining the highest stage, is considered second only to a prophet in access to the divine will and knowledge. In the 11th and 12th centuries numerous Sufi orders formed around charismatic leaders, of which about 100 are extant today. In the 20th century, Sufism has come under attack from Muslim modernists who deplore the authority that some Sufi "masters"—whom they see as ignorant, superstitious, and sometimes corrupt—exert over their uneducated followers.

Sunnism See box at ISLAM

sunyata

A central concept in BUDDHISM, usually translated as "emptiness." The Sanskrit term *sunyata* (or *shunyata; sunnata* in Pali) has many related meanings, and the varied interpretations of the concept have often been the focus of debate among Buddhist scholars. On one level, sunyata can refer to the impermanent, illusory nature of worldly existence, or to the emptiness of conventional thinking that clings to illusions caused by confusing APPEARANCES with reality. In another, more important, sense, it suggests the pure emptiness of the ENLIGHTENED mind, free of worldly passions and the sense of self, and thus open to a true understanding of existence as it really is. On a still deeper level, sunyata is the fundamental nature of reality, neither something nor nothing, but a perfect void in which things neither exist nor don't exist.

The concept of sunyata is particularly important in Mahayana Buddhism (see box at BUDDHISM). It was basic to the teaching of the Indian monk Nagarjuna, who founded the Madhyamika (Middle Path) school, which taught *sunyatavada* ("the way of emptiness"). Nagarjuna argued against all philosophical attempts to define reality, stressing the BUDDHA's rejection of all METAPHYSICAL speculation as "attachment" that impedes enlightenment. Instead, Nagarjuna proposed a synthesis between mundane and ultimate reality, particularly the seemingly antithetical concepts of self *(atman)* and no-self *(anatman)* (see BUDDHISM). His doctrine of "two truths" held that when viewed from an earthly perspective, material objects and personal identity serve a useful purpose, but when considered in cosmic terms everything is empty; thus we can recognize that reality is an illusion while leading productive lives within that illusion.

supply and demand

Central concepts in microeconomics, supply and demand are key factors in determining the price of goods in a free MARKET. Both reflect the relationship between price and quantity in the sale of goods; supply refers to the amount of a good a producer is willing to sell at a given price, and demand refers to the amount of the good a consumer is willing to buy at a given price. The "law" of supply and demand has two general provisions: (1) the higher the price, the greater quantity a producer will be prepared to supply, and the lower the price, the more of it the consumer will demand; (2) when supply exceeds demand, producers will lower prices to spur sales, and when demand exceeds supply, consumers will pay more for the scarce commodity. Economists plot these price/quantity relationships graphically, creating supply and demand curves that indicate how much of a given product will be produced and purchased at a given price. The intersection of the two curves is called *market equilibrium*—the ideal state in which consumers are willing to buy something at the same price and in the same quantity as the producers are willing to supply it.

Supply and demand are influenced by other factors besides price, however, and this affects actual conditions in the marketplace. Demand for a good can be altered by fluctuations in consumers' income or preferences, by shifts in the number of consumers in a given market category, by the

SAY'S LAW

A famous and controversial corollary to the law of SUPPLY AND DEMAND, named after the French economist Jean-Baptiste Say but also held by other "classical" economists of the early 19th century, including John Stuart MILL. Popularly summarized as "Supply creates its own demand," this theory of markets holds that since businesses produce income for their employees and owners, who spend it on products made by other firms, production itself creates a marketplace in which consumer demands are satisfied. The perfect correlation between production and wages is translated into a perfect correlation between goods and purchases, resulting in a market in perfect equilibrium and a full-production, full-employment economy.

This view was seen by KEYNES and others as valid, perhaps, in barter economies, but not in monetary economies, where money may be saved or invested as well as spent. Keynes pointed to the recurring recessions in market economies, and especially to the Great Depression, as a refutation of Say's Law. Others, including Joseph A. Schumpeter, have argued that overall supply/demand equilibrium is always maintained over time—a position echoed by SUPPLY-SIDE economists.

price of substitutes and complementary goods (some apple lovers may simply switch to pears if apple prices rise), and by many other factors, including the manipulation of consumer desires through advertising. Supply is affected by, for example, the cost of labor and materials, the manufacturer's production capacity, and the number of sellers of the product.

supply-side economics

The theory that economic growth is driven by the *aggregate supply* of productive factors (labor and CAPITAL) and services and is stimulated by lower TAXATION rates. It disputes the *demand-side* approach of KEYNESIAN economists, who see growth as tied to the aggregate demand for finished goods and services, stimulated when necessary by government incentives. Supply-siders argue that the higher taxes required to pay for government economic initiatives have the effect of depressing production, investment, and private savings and can actually diminish tax revenues (see box). As tax rates rise, taking an ever-greater proportion of income, they reason, people will respond by decreasing

THE LAFFER CURVE

The graphic representation of a principal tenet of SUPPLY-SIDE ECONOM-ICS, that there is an optimal, revenue-maximizing tax rate above which tax revenues actually decline. It is a 20th-century version of Adam SMITH's theory that economic behavior—working, saving, spending, and investing—is influenced by the level of taxation. The Laffer curve was developed by American economists Arthur Laffer and Jude Wanniski in 1974 and was first drawn, according to legend, on a napkin in a Washington, D.C., restaurant. The curve plots tax rates against revenues on a semicircular graph line that resembles a pot belly. As the "belly" (tax rate) grows, revenues increase; but when the tax rate gets too high, people are discouraged from making the extra effort to generate more wealth to spend, save, or invest and are more inclined to use legal loopholes or false claims to avoid paying taxes, so the "belly" of tax revenue begins to diminish. The Laffer curve was used to justify large tax cuts in the early 1980s, when President Reagan's economic advisors were convinced that tax rates had passed the optimal level. But tax revenues fell rather than increasing, and this failure to achieve the predicted outcome contributed to a perception of the Laffer curve as simplistic and unreliable.

their productive effort and thus decreasing the tax base available to the government. By contrast, lowering personal and corporate taxes increases take-home pay and net profits, which provides incentives for individuals to work harder and corporations to invest more; this increase in the aggregate supply of productive factors spurs economic growth. The same logic applies to taxes on interest, dividends, and capital gains, which create disincentives to save or invest by reducing the return on investment. According to a corollary hypothesis, the so-called *trickle-down theory*, the greater spending and investing power unleashed by tax cuts for those at the top of the economic ladder eventually "trickles down," in the form of increased employment, to benefit all of society.

Supply-side economics became influential in the mid-1970s, especially in the United States and Britain, and was adopted in the 1980s in the administrations of Ronald Reagan (1981–89) and Margaret Thatcher (1979–90), both of whom also sought to reduce governmental influence throughout society. Tax reductions in the United States under this policy, called

"Reaganomics," stimulated an economic boom, but critics claimed that this reflected not supply-side but demand-side effects: output rose in response to increased consumer spending as the tax cuts generated higher disposable incomes.

See also MONETARISM.

surrealism

Movement in art and literature, flourishing in Europe and the United States between the world wars, that rejected the phenomenal world and located reality in the subconscious. The movement, founded and led by the poet André Breton and named after a word coined by Guillaume Apollinaire in 1917, was a direct descendant of DADA and its fascination with chance. In his *Surrealist Manifesto* of 1924 and subsequent pronouncements, Breton defined surrealism as "pure psychic automatism" whose goal was to merge REASON and unreason, CONSCIOUSNESS and the UNCONSCIOUS, into "an absolute reality—a super-reality." He urged freedom from conventional morality and the liberation of the artist's inexhaustible imagination. Surrealist poets such as Paul Éluard used automatic writing, free association, and other techniques to create irrational but subconsciously resonant imagery. The movement drew inspiration from FREUD's writings—particularly his theory that the surreal landscape of dreams symbolically manifests unconscious thoughts and desires—and from the idea that only the imagination holds the key to meaning and reality.

Although founded primarily as a literary movement, surrealism is identified above all with its dreamlike paintings. Two styles of surrealist art emerged. The paintings of Salvador Dalí, René Magritte, and Giorgio de Chirico, for example, presented fantastic, hallucinatory scenes in a hard-edged, realistic manner. Other artists, including Joan Miró and Max Ernst, created works based on spontaneity and chance, using ABSTRACT images or techniques such as *frottage* (rubbing over an object placed under paper) and *assemblage* (juxtaposing unrelated objects). Dalí collaborated with the Spanish director Luis Buñuel on two silent films, *Un Chien Andalou* (1928) and *L'Age d'Or* (1930), which employed eerie, illogical juxtapositions of images. Other European artists associated with surrealism (many of whom were also Dadaists) included Jean Arp, Marc Chagall, Paul Klee, Francis Picabia, Alberto Giacometti, Pablo Picasso, Marcel Duchamp, and André Masson; the last two spent parts of their careers in the United States, where they joined an American surrealist movement that included Man Ray and the sculptor Joseph Cornell.

See also box at ABSTRACTION; DADA.

sustainable development

Concept in international development that seeks to balance the needs of the present with the future viability of natural resources and planetary ecology. The idea was first given prominence in the environmental debate by the 1987 World Commission on Environment and Development, led by Norwegian prime minister Gro Harlem Brundtland. The commission's report, *Our Common Future,* articulated a growing concern about environmental degradation and the depletion of natural resources, an emerging crisis caused by industrial, technological, and economic activity, fed by overconsumption in the industrialized world and exacerbated by rapid economic growth in developing countries. The commission called for a global commitment to "sustainable development," defined as economic and social activity that meets the present needs of the world's population "without compromising the ability of future generations to meet their own needs."

Seeking to avoid what they see as a looming social and environmental disaster, advocates of sustainable development urge measures including conservation and recycling, population control, and the development of alternative, renewable energy sources. The idea has triggered debates among ecologists, economists, and politicians over the planet's "carrying capacity," its adaptive and restorative potential, and the very definitions of the terms "development" and "sustainability." Some economists contend that current growth and consumption rates can be maintained indefinitely, as human ingenuity creates synthetic replacements for depleted resources. Others, such as Paul Hawken, argue that technology cannot compensate for the degradation of intricate natural phenomena such as weather systems and photosynthesis. Sustainability, they maintain, can be achieved only by shifting our present economic priorities away from constant material growth and toward an accommodation with the complex biophysical laws governing the global ecosystem.

symbolism

In art, literature, and ritual, the use of an image or action to represent something else, usually a tangible emblem of something ABSTRACT or a mundane object evoking a higher realm; also the name given to a European, mainly French, literary and artistic movement of the late 19th and early 20th centuries that rejected the representation of concrete reality in favor of the symbolic expression of ideas. Symbols can be based on conventional correlations (such as the rose standing for courtly love in medieval romances), physical or other similarities between the symbol and its referent (the red rose as a symbol of blood), or personal associations (Yeats's profuse rose imagery, representing death, ideal perfection, Ireland, and more). In linguistics, all words are considered arbitrary symbols, or *signs,* that are connected to what they refer to through usage and custom (see SEMIOTICS). In PSYCHOANALYSIS, symbols, particularly images in dreams, are seen as manifestations of repressed, subconscious desires and fears. Much religious imagery and ritual is symbolic; for instance, the contents of the feast table and the ceremony performed at the Jewish Passover seder are symbolic of events surrounding the Israelites' deliverance from Egypt. The didactic tradition of symbolism—the symbol guiding the reader or celebrant to a specific meaning—was broken by the ROMANTICS, who sought personal and emotional rather than conventional, intellectual connections.

The symbolist movement in literature, an outgrowth of Romanticism, sought to "clothe the idea in sensuous form," according to an 1886 manifesto. Its central figure was Charles Baudelaire, whose volume of poetry *Les Fleurs du mal* (The Flowers of Evil, 1857) is considered its founding work. In the sonnet "Correspondences," Baudelaire invoked philosopher-mystic Emmanuel Swedenborg's theory that every person exists simultaneously on the natural and spiritual planes and every word has both a natural and spiritual meaning. The symbolists also employed *synesthesia,* a free-associative method in which one sensory experience represents another; for example, in Arthur Rimbaud's "Sonnet of Vowels" (c.1870), vowel sounds correspond to colors. Other prominent symbolist poets included Paul Valéry, Paul Verlaine, and Stéphane Mallarmé. In its emphasis on personal vision and its rejection of poetic conventions, the movement had a profound effect on the development of modern verse.

Symbolism in the fine arts took two forms. Painters such as Gustave Moreau, Odilon Redon, and Pierre Puvis de Chavannes created dreamlike allegorical canvases on themes drawn largely from biblical and classical subjects. Others, notably Paul Gauguin and Vincent van Gogh in their later works, abandoned the careful visual effects of IMPRESSION-ISM for direct expression of emotion through the lavish use of pure color, an approach that contributed to the rise of abstract art (see box at ABSTRACTION).

See also EXPRESSIONISM; KRISTEVA; SURREALISM; TOTEMISM; UNCONSCIOUS.

symmetry See CONSERVATION AND SYMMETRY

systems theory

Approach to the study of organization and function in terms of purposive, self-sustaining systems, applied primarily in the social sciences, particularly sociology and psychology; also called *general systems theory*. In this context, a *system* is defined as an interrelated, interactive grouping, structured such that a change in one part of the group affects some or all of the others. According to this model, a wide variety of biological, mechanical, conceptual, and social arrangements may be considered systems, from ponds, computers, and languages to families, societies, and the earth itself (see GAIA HYPOTHESIS). Systems are self-regulating, adjusting to internal and external changes in an attempt to maintain equilibrium (see CYBERNETICS). A system may be *closed*—relatively self-contained and independent of its surroundings, such as a steam-heating system or the solar system—or *open,* requiring input from the environment and responding to its changes. All biological and most social systems are open.

The theory considers systems from both the STRUCTURAL and FUNCTIONAL points of view: how they are organized, internally and in relation to their environment, and how they work (or don't work—systems theory can be not only descriptive but prescriptive, concerned with correcting dysfunctions). Talcott Parsons's sociological theory of *structural-functionalism* viewed society as a system in which structural elements, such as institutions and cultural patterns, act to regulate social intercourse and achieve societal goals.

Psychological systems theory was pioneered by the Austrian-Canadian biologist Ludwig von Bertalanffy, whose 1968 book *General Systems Theory* described systems as composed of a *suprasystem* containing numerous *subsystems,* each with its own organization and goals, and therefore competing as well as cooperating. Family therapists who use this model see the family as an interactive system in which each member's behavior affects the whole; they therefore attempt to improve familial communication and relationships to make the system "run" better.

T

tantrism

MYSTICAL traditions within BUDDHISM and HINDUISM stressing the union of mind and body and the interaction of cosmic male and female forces. Tantric practice is based on ancient texts known as *tantras*, which detail spiritual practices and rituals, and depends on the guidance of a guru, or spiritual teacher. The Hindu tantras contrast Shakti, the active female energy in the universe (sometimes represented by Kali or another goddess), with the passive male quality embodied in the god Shiva, whose power depends on Shakti. The goal of tantrism is the union of these two forces, which is achieved through a variety of meditational, devotional, and YOGIC exercises. Tantric Buddhism—also called Vajrayana, the Diamond Vehicle or Thunderbolt Vehicle—arose within the Mahayana tradition (see box at BUDDHISM) and became prevalent in Tibet. It deemphasizes the future goal of NIRVANA in favor of attaining spiritual power and knowledge in the earthly present. Both the Hindu and Buddhist tantric traditions have "right-hand" and "left-hand" forms, the former adhering to orthodox religious practice, the latter incorporating unconventional, even taboo, practices. These include partaking of meat and intoxicating drinks and engaging in ritual sexual intercourse. Tantric practices seek to release *kundalini*, the "serpent power," or subtle psychosexual energy, and connect it with all the body's energy points *(chakras)*, achievement of which brings spiritual liberation.

Taoism (Daoism)

Chinese philosophical and religious system, based on the search for harmony with the forces of the universe. Like CONFUCIANISM, the other great indigenous

Chinese philosophy (with which it shares many concepts), Taoism is essentially nontheistic; although it includes sects that worship gods and spirits, Taoism stresses spiritual liberation through inner reflection and observation of the natural world. Its major departures from Confucianism are its nonhierarchical, classless social philosophy (cf. CLASS) and its emphasis on *wu-wei* ("nonaction" or "nondoing")—spontaneous, unforced existence in accordance with natural impulses—in contrast to the conscious endeavor of Confucian practice.

The legendary founder of Taoism was Lao Tzu, a sage of the sixth century B.C.E. He is traditionally considered the author of one of the two central texts of Taoism, the *Tao Te Ching* (Way of Power), though it was probably compiled two or three centuries later. The mystical aspects of Taoism bred popular cults whose adherents practiced divination (using the *I Ching*, or Book of Changes), magic, faith healing, and exorcism and sought physical immortality by means ranging from physical and mental hygiene to alchemy.

Both the *Tao Te Ching* and the *Chuang Tzu*, named after its traditional author, seek to approach the mysterious, indefinable Tao, or "way," the fundamental principle of the cosmos. They are composed of proverbs and parables, respectively (the latter often involving Confucius), that stress the necessity of breaking away from attachments to seek the placid core of reality, "empty" of artificial concerns. Central to Taoist thinking is the concept of YIN AND YANG, the polar forces of the universe that create unity and balance out of conflict and form the essence of everything. All living things are animated and regulated by *ch'i* (or *qi*), the vital cosmic energy, which must be nourished and cared for in order to ensure proper physical, spiritual, and mental balance. Through meditation, hygienic and dietary habits, and mental and physical discipline, one seeks to align one's ch'i with the Tao. (The best-known application of the concept of ch'i in the West is acupuncture, in which analgesia and, in some cases, re-

> *"Thirty spokes join at the hub of a wheel, but it is the hole that makes it useful;*
> *We fashion clay into a pitcher, but its use comes from the void within;*
> *The doors and windows we make in a house function because of their emptiness;*
> *Thus we gain benefit from what is and usefulness from what is not."*
> —Lao Tzu, *Tao Te Ching*

mission of disease is produced by inserting fine needles into the skin at points on the bodily "meridians" along which ch'i is considered to flow.)

See also HOLISM; YIN AND YANG.

taxation, theories of

Most modern theories of taxation are based on the four general principles expounded by Adam SMITH in *The Wealth of Nations* (1776)—that taxes should be fair (proportional to the ability to pay or the benefit received), predictable and noncapricious, convenient to pay, and efficient to collect. Taxes, levied on the income, expenditures, and property of individuals and corporations, are used to finance government programs and services. Taxes are described as *progressive* or *regressive* according to whether those with higher incomes pay a larger or smaller fraction of their incomes in taxes than those with lower incomes.

Most tax theories are based on either the *benefit* principle, which states that certain goods and services should be paid for by those who benefit from them—for example, the federal highway system is supported by gasoline and road-use taxes—or the *ability-to-pay* principle, holding that taxes should be imposed according to individuals' economic circumstances, their relative ability to pay (see also UTILITY). The ability-to-pay principle underlies progressive taxation mechanisms, such as the U.S. federal income tax, with a portion of everyone's income exempted from taxation altogether and higher incomes taxed at higher rates.

The most common regressive taxes are the *sales tax* on retail goods and *payroll taxes* such as the U.S. Social Security tax. The former is regressive because those with higher incomes spend a lower percentage of their income on goods, the latter because it applies only to labor income, not dividends, capital gains, and the like, and is applied only up to a certain maximum level of income. A variation on the sales tax is the *value-added tax* (VAT), popular especially in Europe. VAT, a tax on the "value added" to a product at every stage of production—that is, the difference between the selling price and the cost of the materials used—is charged to producers and generally passed on to consumers in the price of the product.

Since the late 1970s, SUPPLY-SIDE and other *neoclassical* economists have urged across-the-board tax reductions, especially in income, estate, and capital gains taxes, arguing that high tax rates discourage individual initiative and economic growth. In the 1990s, the idea of a *flat tax*, which would apply a single tax rate to people of all incomes, gained popularity. The flat tax claims both equity and efficiency, as it would eliminate most of the loopholes used by taxpayers to decrease their taxable income and would greatly simplify tax returns. A *consumption tax,* proposed as an alternative to the federal income tax, would tax spending rather than income by exempting all savings from taxation and thereby, in its adherents' view, encouraging thrift and enterprise. Critics, however, charge that both plans, as currently proposed, would be considerably less progressive than the present system, the flat tax because it would dramatically lower the tax rate for high incomes, the consumption tax because those with lower incomes must spend a greater portion of their earnings.

See also KEYNES; LIBERTARIANISM; MARKET; SUPPLY-SIDE ECONOMICS.

teleology

The explanation of phenomena in terms of their goals or purposes; the view that the universe exists, or events occur, in order to achieve a particular end (the word comes from the Greek *telos,* meaning "end" or "purpose"). Teleological analysis was introduced by ARISTOTLE, whose four CAUSES of things culminate in their *final cause;* things grow and change in order to become what they were intended to be, according to their inherent natures: the acorn an oak, the child an adult. The notion of purpose in nature is also evident in the JUDAIC, CHRISTIAN, and ISLAMIC conceptions of the universe as a whole: God's creation of the heavens and the earth was the genesis of a plan that will be fulfilled at the end of time (see ESCHATOLOGY). The so-called teleological proof of God's existence (see GOD, ARGUMENTS FOR) concludes that such a complex and intricately designed universe must have a designer manifesting a divine purpose. The term "teleological" is also applied to the position in ETHICS that the moral value of an action depends on its CONSEQUENCES; the foremost philosophical school based on this view is UTILITARIANISM.

Ten Commandments (Decalogue)

The ten religious and moral dictates said to have been given by God to Moses on stone tablets on Mount Sinai; the basis of JUDAIC religious and ETHICAL law and a ruling element of CHRISTIAN belief. In giving the Commandments to the people of Israel, God renewed his covenant with them, promising his special favor in return for their worship and obedience.

The Ten Commandments are enunciated in two passages in the Hebrew Bible (Old Testament), Exodus 20 and Deuteronomy 5, in substantially similar form. The first part of the edict contains religious injunctions: to recognize the God who delivered the children of Israel out of bondage; to worship no other gods and no sacred images; to forbear from taking the Lord's name in vain; and to observe the Sabbath as a holy day. The latter part, introduced by the injunction to honor one's parents, is a list of prohibitions governing relations with other people: one must not kill, commit adultery, steal, bear false witness, or covet another's wife or property.

Although conventions differ on the numbering of the Ten Commandments, their content is the same in all Jewish and Christian traditions. However, in Christianity two of the Commandments have been reinterpreted. Following the prohibition against idolatry, Judaism and most PROTESTANT denominations keep no religious statues or paintings in their places of worship; but depictions of JESUS and the saints play a major role in ROMAN CATHOLIC and ORTHODOX worship and are justified on the grounds that the image is venerated not in itself but for the divinity it represents. Most Christians observe a holy day not on the Sabbath (literally, "seventh day"), but on Sunday, called the Lord's Day, in commemoration of Christ's resurrection (but see ADVENTISM).

theosophy

Broadly, any philosophical or theological system aimed at developing a direct experience of the divine; the term, from the Greek for "knowledge of God," is particularly associated with the Theosophical Society, founded in 1875. The theosophical outlook has generally been identified with attempts to merge Eastern MYSTICISM and Christian ETHICS, but theosophical strands are also found in TAOISM and the Jewish KABBALAH, for example.

The Theosophical Society was founded by Mme. Helena Petrovna Blavatsky and Col. Henry Steele Olcott in New York City and quickly developed a large worldwide following. Mme. Blavatsky professed occult powers, claimed to have been instructed by Eastern religious sages who had achieved a highly spiritual plane, and declared herself a "World Teacher." Her idiosyncratic philosophy incorporated many elements of Eastern thought, especially HINDUISM and BUDDHISM, including the concepts of KARMA, reincarnation, and NIRVANA. She taught that all religions are essentially one, all seeking knowledge of the universal spirit; that both humanity and the universe are evolving, through seven stages, toward union with the divine spirit; and that one's goal in life is to seek that union through meditation and spiritual development, which is overseen by a secret order of Tibetan masters. Four years after its founding, the Theosophical Society moved its headquarters to India, where, in 1907, a Blavatsky disciple, the English FEMINIST and social reformer Annie

Besant, became its leader. Her protégé, Jiddu Krishnamurti, was proclaimed the new World Teacher in 1911 but later repudiated theosophy.

See also ANTHROPOSOPHY.

Theravada Buddhism See box at BUDDHISM

thermodynamics, laws of

Scientific laws, developed by experimentation in the 19th century, describing the relationship between heat (a form of energy) and work (mechanical energy). The laws of thermodynamics are more general and of broader relevance than most laws of nature, applying to the whole of the physical sciences. Thermodynamics (from the Greek words for "heat" and "power") relates the flow of heat into a system (e.g., a steam engine or a refrigerator) to the work performed by the system and to the change in the internal energy of the system as it is converted from one state into another (e.g., from fuel into heat and from heat into work).

The *first law* of thermodynamics states that energy is *conserved*: it changes form but is neither created nor destroyed (see CONSERVATION AND SYMMETRY). The law stipulates that in any isolated system (such as an engine), the work done cannot exceed the amount of heat energy consumed. This is sometimes stated in terms of the impossibility of a perpetual-motion machine, one that works without any net addition of energy.

The *second law* of thermodynamics puts limits on the efficiency with which heat can be converted into work. Heat will spontaneously flow from a warmer body to a colder one, but not in the other direction; therefore, in order for heat to be converted to work it must be transferred from a warmer to a colder reservoir (for example, when hot water meets cold air in a steam engine). The transfer cools the hot reservoir as it warms the cold one, and the more the temperatures even out, the less efficiently the system operates; when *equilibrium* is achieved, no more work is possible. Efficiency could be 100 percent only if the cold reservoir of a system were at absolute zero; but the *third law* of thermodynamics states that absolute zero is unattainable.

The second law is also stated in terms of ENTROPY, which is a measure of the disorder in a system. The total entropy of an isolated system never decreases; the direction of natural processes is always toward greater disorder. When heat flows from a hotter body to a cooler one, the entropy increases as the temperatures even out, that is, the "ordering" of the system into hot and cold breaks down. As the entropy increases there is less energy available for work.

Thoreau, Henry David (1817–1862)

American philosopher, author, and naturalist, who held an essentially LIBERTARIAN outlook and practiced the ideals of INDIVIDUALISM, self-reliance, and communion with nature promoted by the New England TRANSCENDENTALISTS. He was a friend and disciple of Ralph Waldo EMERSON, in whose home he lived for several years. Thoreau is best remembered for his two-year sojourn (1845–47) in a rustic cabin at Walden Pond near Concord, Massachusetts, portrayed in *Walden, or Life in the Woods* (1854), and for his conscientious objection to war taxes, which he justified in the influential essay "On the Duty of CIVIL DISOBEDIENCE" (1849). Most of his writings were published posthumously, many of them drawn from his copious journals.

In *Walden*, Thoreau joined the eye of a naturalist to the soul of a poet. His stated reason for retreating to a solitary life in the woods was to learn how to "live deliberately," to mold a way of life wholly independent of the cares of economy and politics. His watchword for the experiment was "Simplify, simplify," and when he ended it after two years it was to see if he could live as simply and thriftily among others as he had on his own. He examined the plant and animal life in the woods around Walden not from the standpoint of a scientist, which he considered dry and one-sided, but from the position of one who is "truly awake." Rather than seeking an ideal perspective on his surroundings, he sought as many perspectives as possible, trying to comprehend their ESSENTIAL qualities. Through his careful observation of nature, Thoreau sought to truly participate in it, holding that nature and God are but two manifestations of one encompassing reality, a reality hindered and narrowed by an overreliance on the practical concerns of the world.

See also CIVIL DISOBEDIENCE; TRANSCENDENTALISM.

Tocqueville, Alexis de (1805–1859)

French statesman, political theorist, and historian. Born into an aristocratic family, Tocqueville studied law and in 1831–32 visited the United States to study the American penal system on behalf of the French government. His travels resulted in the classic *Democracy in America* (2 vols., 1835, 1840), the first objective description of American political institutions and a penetrating analysis of the American character. He perceived in Europe, too, an

"In the United States the majority undertakes to supply a multitude of ready-made opinions for the use of individuals, who are thus relieved from the necessity of forming opinions of their own."

—Alexis de Tocqueville,
Democracy in America

irresistible tendency toward DEMOCRACY and social EQUALITY that would inevitably topple the prevailing aristocratic institutions, but he feared that such a tendency would diminish rather than enhance individual FREEDOM.

Tocqueville saw the United States in the heyday of JACKSONIAN DEMOCRACY, with its egalitarian spirit and POPULIST politics. The American preoccupation with equality, he wrote, helped give the young country a vigor and sense of possibility largely absent in Europe. But it also fostered INDIVIDUALISM, which, in Tocqueville's view, undermined social responsibility by exalting private interests and personal gain and distorted the political process by giving equal weight to all opinions, however ill-informed.

Tocqueville also noted a paradox in American democracy, a strong conformist impulse running alongside the celebration of the individual. In the United States, intellectual authority resided not in tradition but in public opinion, which created a "tyranny of the majority"—the assumption that, since everyone's opinion carries equal weight, the majority opinion must be the correct one. Such a political culture, Tocqueville feared, could lead to "a new type of despotism," one imposed not by coercion but by the manipulation of impulsive public opinion and sustained by the apathy of a populace absorbed with personal, material goals.

While Tocqueville recognized these tendencies in the United States, he also saw the American tradition of decentralized self-government, dating from the colonial period, as a powerful counterbalance. The threat, he felt, was much greater in Europe, where, for instance, the absence of democratic experience and the reliance on centralized authority had led to disaster in postrevolutionary France. The solution was to be found in encouraging strong local government and widespread education for political participation.

See also INDIVIDUALISM.

Torah

The central idea and object of JUDAISM, embracing the revealed word of God, the scripture containing that revelation, and the totality of Jewish beliefs and practices. The term *torah* (often translated as "law" but more accurately as "teaching") has several different but intimately related meanings. At one level it refers to the Pentateuch, the first five books of the Hebrew Bible, and to the parchment scroll inscribed with the text of the Pentateuch that is kept in every synagogue and read as an important part of worship. By extension, Torah is sometimes taken to designate the whole of the Hebrew Bible (Old Testament). In its largest sense, Torah refers to the divine revelation itself— God's instruction and guidance for humankind's salvation, considered to have been given to Moses on Mount Sinai, which is the basis of all Jewish teaching and study.

A further distinction is made between the "written" law transcribed in the Pentateuch and the "oral" law, rabbinical injunctions concerning civil law and ritual practices, developed over several centuries and codified around 200 C.E. This compilation, called the Mishnah, and the commentaries on it, the Gemara, comprise the Talmud, the authoritative compendium of Jewish law and custom. All the oral (i.e., nonscriptural) traditions and principles of Judaism are considered by Orthodox Jews to be part of God's revelation to Moses and therefore part of Torah. To study and be guided by Torah is to live according to God's will. Torah, then, is both the foundation and the superstructure of Jewish life—theological and liturgical, moral and ETHICAL, personal and communal, social and legal—and is therefore regarded as synonymous with Judaism itself.

See also GOLDEN RULE; JUDAISM; MAIMONIDES; TEN COMMANDMENTS.

Tories See WHIGS AND TORIES

totalitarianism

Political system in which the activities of civil society are entirely subordinated to regulation by the STATE. Like most forms of authoritarianism, totalitarian regimes are rigidly hierarchical, with virtually absolute power flowing from the top down; however, they differ from other authoritarian forms in the degree to which the public sphere controls the private and in their tendency to legitimate themselves through NATIONALIST, ELITIST, UTOPIAN, or other IDEOLOGIES. Political power is held by a single party, which is often under the control of a charismatic dictator and enforced by a comprehensive apparatus of surveillance and coercion operated by a paramilitary police force. The state also controls all mass media and most other avenues of artistic and political expression. Though rooted in earlier forms of ABSOLUTISM, totalitarianism is a phenomenon of the 20th century. It has been most clearly expressed in COMMUNIST and FASCIST regimes such as the Soviet Union and Nazi Germany;

more recent examples include Burma (Myanmar) under Ne Win and Iraq under Saddam Hussein.

Where traditional monarchies and other authoritarian systems concentrate power in the public sphere while leaving private society relatively untouched, totalitarianism erases the public/private distinction, rendering all activity public and therefore subject to regulation and surveillance by the state. The state sustains itself and maintains social cohesion by sharply distinguishing between insiders and outsiders, identifying the latter—whether domestic or external—as enemies who must be neutralized or eliminated. External enemies become the justification for an aggressive foreign policy, while internal enemies (political opponents, outcast social groups, etc.) become scapegoats and the targets of purges. Totalitarian ideologies typically envision a new social order that will replace the decadent systems of the past and cultivate a superior strain of humanity. In this sense, the interests of the people, the party, and the ruler are said to be identical; civil duties, not civil RIGHTS, are paramount. Economic as well as political power is usually centralized, and economic efficiency is almost always outweighed by political imperatives. Some social critics have seen totalitarian trends in modern CAPITALIST DEMOCRACIES, as corporate and political power become increasingly synonymous and dissent is effectively marginalized or co-opted.

See also ARENDT; FASCISM; ROUSSEAU.

totemism

The belief that an animal, plant, or natural phenomenon has a spiritual and symbolic relationship to a human group, and the mystical and ritualistic practices surrounding that belief. The word "totem," derived from the Ojibwa word *ototeman* ("sibling"), was first used by the 18th-century trader John Long, who identified it with the Ojibwa *manitou*, or guardian spirit. The best-documented examples of totemism have been found among the aboriginal peoples of Australia and in some Native American cultures. Within these communities, the formation of clans, or extended families, is based on a mystical affiliation to a particular animal, plant, or (in some cases) nonliving phenomenon such as rain or wind. Each member of the clan—not all of whom may be blood relatives—is considered to be related to the totemic object and, through it, to each other. The (usually) sacred nature of the totemic object gives rise to rituals of veneration, including taboos against killing or eating a totemic animal.

In the 19th and early 20th centuries, the nature of totemism was examined by numerous anthropologists and other social scientists, many of whose theories are now seen as striking examples of European ETHNOCENTRISM. John Ferguson McLennan, James G. Frazer, and others considered totemism a stage of EVOLUTION through which all preliterate societies had passed. Émile Durkheim, in *The Elementary Forms of Religious Life* (1912), considered it the most primitive cultural condition and the primal religion. In *Totem and Taboo* (1913), Sigmund FREUD related totemism to "primal Oedipal guilt" stemming from competition for sexual access to the females of the tribe, in which sons murder their fathers and, in remorse, revere the totem as a symbolic representation of the slain patron; this, he said, was also the origin of exogamy, the taboo against marriage within one's group.

The STRUCTURALIST Claude Lévi-Strauss called the concept of totemism as constructed by anthropologists an "illusion." He described it as a symbolic system that allows the bridging of the natural and social worlds and as an example of the general human tendency to categorize experience—in this case, the classification of human groups by contrasting them in the same way animals are contrasted by species.

See also ANIMISM.

transcendentalism

Philosophical belief in a reality that transcends everyday experience or knowledge that transcends REASON; also the philosophical and social tenets of the New England Transcendentalist movement, which flourished in the 1840s and '50s. The division between the world of the senses and a higher, purer, or more authentic realm is central to many philosophies (see, e.g., IDEALISM; KANT; NEOPLATONISM; PLATO; REALISM) and most world religions. The distinction is also made between *transcendent,* beyond nature, and *immanent,* particularly in reference to God, as either beyond nature or active in it. In the 20th century, modes of analysis that seem to proceed from universal assumptions or overly detached perspectives have been criticized as "transcendental" by some, such as MARXISTS, who claim to be engaging in "immanent" analysis grounded in concrete assessments of a situation.

The New England Transcendentalists were a loose-knit group of writers and intellectual social activists, including Ralph Waldo EMERSON, Henry David THOREAU, and the FEMINIST social reformer and critic Margaret Fuller, who founded and edited the group's journal, *The Dial.* Transcendentalism, which developed as a reaction against both Calvinist hellfire and Unitarian RATIONALISM (see box at PROTESTANTISM) and was strongly influenced by European ROMANTICISM, can be seen more as an attitude toward life and how one should live than as a systematic philosophy. Transcendalists tended to DEISM and

PANTHEISM, believing in the overall unity of existence. (Ironically, considering the name they went by, they saw God as immanent in nature, not transcendent; in this case, the term denoted a mystical, universal oneness that transcends the commonplace.) They valued intuition over reason and espoused an INDIVIDUALISM that stressed fulfillment through self-improvement, self-expression, social responsibility, and communion with nature. Most were active social reformers, agitating above all for the abolition of slavery. The short-lived UTOPIAN community Brook Farm, in West Roxbury, Massachusetts, was founded by Transcendentalists as an experiment in communal self-reliance and natural harmony.

See also EMERSON; IDEALISM; KANT; THOREAU.

transpersonal psychology

Cross-cultural, interdisciplinary theoretical and therapeutic approach that seeks to bridge Western RATIONALISM and Eastern MYSTICAL traditions and to understand human nature in terms that transcend the individual self. It originated in the late 1960s as an outgrowth of the HUMANISTIC psychology of Abraham Maslow and the human potential movement, both of which stressed subjective experience, self-actualization, and "transpersonal" motivations such as love and altruism. The perspective is also indebted to JUNG's notion of the *collective unconscious*, the common store of archetypal ideas, modes of thought, and "racial memory" shared by all humans.

Transpersonal psychology is founded in the belief that not all psychic experience can be explained by orthodox psychology, which has little room, for example, for the *altered states of consciousness* induced by mystical experiences or psychotropic drugs and little interest in *paranormal* experiences and abilities (see PARAPSYCHOLOGY). It therefore goes beyond traditional avenues of research to study worldwide religious, philosophical, and spiritual belief systems, seeking universal correlations among them and incorporating practices generally dismissed in Western thought, such as meditation and YOGA. Just as CONSCIOUSNESS is considered to have a wider variety of states than is conventionally supposed, IDENTITY is regarded in transpersonal psychology as a sense of self that potentially extends beyond the ego to embrace the wider universe of humanity and creation. Transpersonal psychotherapies use this viewpoint in treatment; Robert Assagioli's *psychosynthesis*, for example, aims to integrate an individual's personal identity with the "transpersonal self," which transcends ego boundaries.

Trinity, trinitarianism

The CHRISTIAN belief that God exists in "three persons in one SUBSTANCE"—Father, Son, and Holy Spirit. The concept retains the monotheistic God of JUDAISM while incorporating the divinity of JESUS, who is considered the son of God, and the presence of God's spirit in the fellowship of Christian worshipers. While the idea of the Trinity is nowhere explicitly stated in the New Testament, it derives from Jesus's final injunction to his apostles, in Matthew 28:19, to baptize others into the faith "in the name of the Father, the Son, and the Holy Spirit." The trinitarian concept was developed by the early church fathers during the Christological debates in the second, third, and fourth centuries over the human or divine nature of Christ. It has been a recurrently controversial element of Christian dogma. In the 11th century it contributed to the split between the western (ROMAN CATHOLIC) and eastern (ORTHODOX) branches of Christendom, the former declaring, in the so-called Filioque clause of the Nicene Creed, that the Holy Spirit "proceeds" from both the Father and the Son, the latter insisting on the procession of the Holy Spirit from the Father through the Son. Some PROTESTANT denominations deemphasize the Trinity, though still incorporating the idea of the Holy Spirit as a force working in the lives of their congregants and community. Unitarians (see box at PROTESTANTISM) are so called because they reject the Trinity (and the divinity of Jesus) altogether and believe in a unitary deity.

See also box at AFRICAN RELIGIONS (modern movements); AUGUSTINE; MORMONISM; NOMINALISM; ORTHODOX CHURCH; ROMAN CATHOLICISM.

Trotsky, Leon (1879–1940)

Russian revolutionary theorist and strategist. A charismatic orator and inspired organizer, Trotsky was a major architect of the 1917 Bolshevik revolution and later led the left-wing opposition to Stalinism. After Lenin's death in 1924 he vied unsuccessfully with Joseph Stalin for the party leadership and was subsequently marginalized, eventually exiled, and ultimately assassinated on Stalin's orders.

Contradicting the received MARXIST wisdom that the first SOCIALIST revolution would have to occur in the industrialized West, Trotsky argued that fertile revolutionary ground also lay in underdeveloped countries such as Russia, in which pockets of rapid industrialization had created restless, politically precocious proletariats. In *Results and Prospects*, written during his imprisonment following the defeat of the 1905 uprising, he expounded his theory of *permanent revolution*. In a largely backward country without fully developed CAPITALISM, a LIBERAL tradition, or a dynamic middle class, he contended, the bourgeois revolution envisioned by MARX as preliminary to socialism would be passed over by a proletarian revolt directly against the owning class. Fearing that an isolated Russian revolution would be defeated by the European powers and Russia's own material and cultural backwardness, Trotsky further insisted in his theory that revolution must be international if capitalism was to be comprehensively destroyed, and ongoing within each country if full COMMUNISM was to be achieved.

The idea of permanent revolution was anathema to Stalin, who, in the face of the Soviet Union's growing international isolation, promoted the theory of "socialism in one country." The task, he said, was to build socialism at home by constructing an industrial and military capacity that could defend the revolution and make the Soviet Union a respected world power. Trotsky denounced Stalin's position as utterly anti-Marxist and symptomatic of a "Bonapartist bureaucratic clique" that sought to emulate the West rather than achieve worldwide socialism. After World War II, with Stalin's power and prestige at their apogee, Trotskyism became a recessive current in socialist thought, most often espoused by small, militant groups. But in the post-Soviet era he has enjoyed a growing reputation, particularly for his distinctive interpretation of Marxism, his principled defiance of Stalinism, and his voluminous writings, including prescient critiques of Nazism and the Holocaust and his three-volume *History of the Russian Revolution* (1931–33).

truth

The question of truth—what it is and how we can recognize it—is among the oldest and most controversial in philosophy. Truth is also an important concept in mathematics. Historically, in both fields, truth has generally been assumed to be an absolute quality, elusive of definition or proof, perhaps, but invariable—although the ancient Greek SOPHISTS' philosophy of RELATIVISM, holding that subjective judgments are "the measure of all things," including truth, has long influenced the debate. The Euclidian idea that all mathematical axioms are statements of self-evident truths was challenged in the 19th century by the development of geometries that did not assume EUCLID's postulate concerning parallel lines. It was further undermined by 20th-century mathematics, for example, SET THEORY, according to which what is true in one sphere may not be true in another, and Kurt Gödel's *incompleteness theorem*, which states that not all true statements can be proven.

Most philosophical definitions of truth have been based on the notion of "correct description," although there is wide disagreement over what constitutes "correct." Three major theories of truth have been proposed. The most intuitive approach is the *correspondence theory*, which was defined by Thomas AQUINAS as "the correlation of thought and object," that is, our idea of something is true if it corresponds to the actuality of that thing. An objection to this theory, that our subjective perceptions may not accurately capture reality, is addressed by the *coherence theory*, according to which something can be said to be true if it is consistent with the other elements in a coherent conceptual system. This theory is exemplified by Kant's *categories of the understanding* (see box at KANT) and in the 20th century by the ideas of the American philosopher Brand Blanshard. Seeking to mediate between the two is the *pragmatic theory* of truth, associated with American PRAGMATISM, which judges the truth of something by its practical consequences: an idea is true if its implementation achieves an intended satisfactory result.

> *"We all know that art is not truth. Art is a lie that makes us realize truth."*
> —Pablo Picasso, quoted in 1972

Other theories of truth in 20th-century philosophy have tended to be versions of, or responses to, the three theories above. In the *semantic theory* of Alfred Tarski, saying something is true or false is seen as a statement about a statement, not about the state of the external world, and is thus part of a "metalanguage" that does not necessarily refer to external reality (cf. SEMIOTICS). In his *redundancy theory*, Frank P. Ramsey claimed that to say something is true ("It is true that the sun is shining") is the same as making the simple assertion ("The sun is shining") and therefore redundant. The *performative theory* of P. F. Strawson views assertions of truth not as statements that describe a state of affairs but as statements that perform an action, namely, the act of endorsing a certain statement (see also ORDINARY LANGUAGE PHILOSOPHY).

U

uncertainty principle (indeterminacy principle)

A fundamental tenet of QUANTUM THEORY, postulated by the German physicist Werner Heisenberg, which states that we cannot simultaneously know the precise position and momentum of a subatomic particle. Furthermore, the more precisely one of these variables is measured, the more uncertain the measurement of the other variable becomes.

This seemingly paradoxical state of affairs arises from the extremely small size of the particles being measured. In order to locate a particle or measure its movement, we have to observe it. But since "observing" the submicroscopic world requires, in effect, bouncing subatomic particles off each other and noting the results, the very act of observation affects the particle being observed. Observing a particle's position requires high-energy radiation, while calculating its momentum demands a minimum of radiation interference; the more precisely one variable is measured, the more imprecise the other becomes.

When Heisenberg introduced the uncertainty principle in 1927, it was at first disputed as a violation of the law of CAUSE and effect. Albert EINSTEIN, protesting that "God does not play dice," attempted unsuccessfully to reconcile it with classical mechanical theory. The idea of indeterminacy changed physics fundamentally: the universe was no longer fully predictable. However, since nature's inherent uncertainty occurs at the subatomic level, we do not experi-

> *"God not only plays dice, He also sometimes throws the dice where they cannot be seen."*
> —Stephen W. Hawking, 1975

ence it directly. This conforms to the *correspondence principle* enunciated by Niels Bohr, which states that where quantum effects are negligible, behavior in subatomic systems should approximately correspond to that predicted by classical mechanics.

unconscious, the

Hypothetical region of the mind, the part of mental function that is neither autonomic nor conscious; in PSYCHOANALYTIC theory, the repository of repressed impulses and memories. The aim of much psychotherapy is to uncover and exorcise repressed traumas that affect behavior and temperament.

The idea that the mind contains more than we are aware of is not new. It is implied in PLATO's doctrine of *anamnesis*, that all learning is the recollection of knowledge of the World of Forms that we forget at the moment of birth. The modern idea of the unconscious was originated by the German IDEALIST Friedrich Wilhelm Joseph Schelling, whose notion that conscious experience is only a partial expression of an unconscious realm greatly influenced the ROMANTICS. But it was given its most profound and lasting interpretation by Sigmund FREUD, who made it the cornerstone of his theory.

If CONSCIOUSNESS is thought of as rational, systematic, analytical, in search of MEANING, the unconscious is said to be illogical, oblivious of space and time, and indifferent to contradiction and ambiguity. The unconscious is distinguished from *subconscious* mental processes—involuntary physical operations such as the impulses for heartbeat and breathing—and from *preconscious* processes, through which deep-seated memories and thoughts are brought into awareness, sometimes in the form of intuitions or "brainstorms." The unconscious is the abode of memories, desires, fears, and thoughts our conscious minds have locked away—repressed—as too shocking, painful, or socially unacceptable to be brought into the open. However, the inmates of this mental prison make themselves known through small ruptures and major eruptions in our internal equilibrium and external behavior. The expression of unconscious material can range from dreams, where it is revealed SYMBOLICALLY, to full-blown neuroses, in which it is manifested in psychological or physical ailments.

See also CONSCIOUSNESS; DETERMINISM; FREUD; JUNG; PSYCHOANALYSIS; SURREALISM.

uniformitarianism See CATASTROPHISM AND UNIFORMITARIANISM

Unitarianism   See box at PROTESTANTISM

unintended consequences

Unanticipated or coincidental side effects, either positive or negative, of private, corporate, or governmental actions. The classic example of beneficial unintended consequences is Adam SMITH's view of the free MARKET, in which the profit-minded entrepreneur strives to produce the most desirable goods at the most competitive price and is thereby "led by an invisible hand" to promote not only his or her own advantage but the consumer's as well. Unintended consequences are more commonly associated with negative effects, though, such as TAX evasion and smoking-related lung cancer.

Unintended consequences of economic transactions are called *externalities,* also "spillover" or "neighborhood" effects—costs or benefits to third parties who are not involved in the transaction. Externalities are often seen in terms of the *social costs* of production or consumption that are not reflected in their monetary costs. Air pollution is a negative externality of the coal-burning "smokestack industries"—a coincidental and unavoidable by-product of their operation. Its cost is borne by people who contract respiratory diseases, farmers whose fields are harmed by acid rain, and others, not by the industry itself nor by its customers, unless government intervenes, imposing regulations, fines, or taxes on the factories to control and compensate for these indirect effects of their operations.

The sociologist Robert K. Merton spent a lifetime studying the "unanticipated consequences of social action." He identified several basic reasons why people's actions may have unintended collateral effects. One of these is "imperious immediacy of interest," in which the focus on a particular goal makes someone blind to potential side effects. Another is *self-defeating and self-fulfilling prophecies,* in which people's expectations influence outcomes, for example, when predictions that a concert will be sold out result in empty seats because people assume tickets are not available, or when rising prices stabilize in anticipation of lower inflation, thus lowering the inflation rate.

unities, the three

The prescription that drama—or tragedy, at least—must adhere to the unities of action, time, and place is traditionally, but imprecisely, attributed to ARISTOTLE. In his *Poetics,* Aristotle did describe tragedy (as opposed to epic poetry) as "the imitation of one action," a brief, coherent whole that would suffer from the removal of any of its parts. He also recommended, but did not insist, that the drama should take place within the span of a single day and, in one allusion, suggested that the geographic range of a tragedy should be narrower than that of an epic.

The "three unities" were first described as such in 1570 by the Italian dramatist Lodovico Castelvetro, whose translation (and liberal interpretation) of the *Poetics* revived Aristotelian notions of AESTHETICS and contributed to the neoclassical movement of the late Renaissance (see CLASSICISM). According to Castelvetro's reading, a drama must have a unified plot that unfolds within a 24-hour period in a single locale, or at least a single city. In 1630, the French tragedian Jean Mairet propounded Castelvetro's version of the unities, describing them as immutable laws dictated by Aristotle. These rules governed European, especially French, drama for over a century. Their influence was such that the violation of the unities in Pierre Corneille's *Le Cid* (1637) caused an uproar in the literary world. However, in England they were routinely disregarded by Shakespeare and other Elizabethan and Jacobean dramatists in works whose narrative, temporal, and geographic scope recalled Greek epic more than Greek tragedy.

universals

In philosophy, qualities or attributes shared by a number of *particulars* (specific instances or objects). The notion of universals is rooted in PLATO's theory of IDEAS, that every individual thing has an ideal model. It is also indebted to the ARISTOTELIAN conception that the reality of material objects is contained in their intrinsic *properties*.

The question of the nature (or even the existence) of universals was the subject of a major philosophical debate in the Middle Ages. On opposite sides of the dispute were REALISTS, such as St. Anselm, for whom universals constituted the only true reality, and NOMINALISTS, such as William of Ockham, who denied the reality of universals altogether. Between the two extremes stood *conceptualists* such as Peter Abelard, who accepted the idea of universals but saw them as primarily constructs of the mind. On this continuum, stated broadly, the realist would hold that the abstract quality of "horseness" has a reality that is independent of the existence of actual horses; the conceptualist would identify the idea of a horse as the mind's generalization from its experience of particular horses; and the nominalist would claim that "horse" is merely the name used to impose a classification on a group of beings and has nothing to do with their actual reality.

Modern ANALYTIC PHILOSOPHY gives attention to the relation between universals and particulars in its concentration on the relations and paradoxes in *classes*, that is, in categorized groups of things. This interest falls loosely into the conceptualist mold, in that these problems are generally considered to be of EPISTEMOLOGICAL rather than METAPHYSICAL importance. Since analytic philosophy attempts for the most part to dispense with metaphysical speculation, the relation of universal to particular is examined primarily for the way LOGIC allows or disallows membership within a class; the question of a universal's ability to describe reality as a whole is downplayed or even shunned. Thus, an analytic philosopher would dispense with the idea of "horseness" altogether and consider instead whether the statement "There are no flying horses" can be logically, rather than empirically, validated.

See also ABSTRACTION; DEDUCTION AND INDUCTION; NOMINALISM; REALISM.

utilitarianism

Ethical position holding that the morally superior position is the one that would result in the greatest pleasure (or happiness) and least pain for those to whom it would apply; generally expressed as "the greatest good for the greatest number." The term was coined in 1781 by Jeremy Bentham and is primarily associated with him and with James Mill, although the concepts of "general good" and "least harm" are found in many systems of ETHICS. A form of CONSEQUENTIALISM, utilitarianism replaces appeals from supernatural injunctions or reasoned arguments with the simple requirement that the moral worth of an act be judged by its consequences—in this case, its social utility.

The goals of utilitarianism were almost immediately assailed as unquantifiable: How can happiness or utility be measured? How can the outcome of an action be confidently predicted? Which is preferable—more bliss for many and more agony for some, or a better balance of both for all? In his "evolutionary utilitarianism," Herbert Spencer tried to blunt this thorn by focusing on the cumulative effects of moral ideas, for instance altruism, over the whole history of societies. John Stuart MILL, James's son, sought to quantify utilitarianism by distinguishing between "higher" and "lower" grades of happiness and between those capable of appreciating them: "It is better to be Socrates dissatisfied than a pig satisfied."

In the 20th century, utilitarianism has split into two camps. *Act utilitarians* would judge each individual act according to its good or bad effects, while *rule utilitarians* advocate general rules of moral conduct that promote the general good.

See also ANIMAL RIGHTS; CONSEQUENTIALISM; MILL; POSITIVISM; PRAGMATISM.

utility

The subjective pleasure or satisfaction a consumer derives from using a product or service, so called because of its original meaning in classical economics, referring to the utility, or usefulness, of a commodity. The theory originated in the early 19th century with Jeremy Bentham and others and was developed later by academic economists known as *marginalists*. According to the approach known as *cardinal utility*, consumer satisfaction can be numerically represented in terms of "utils," or units of satisfaction. In principle, the more someone consumes, the more utility she or he derives; but as total utility increases, *marginal utility*—the satisfaction derived from each additional consumption of a commodity—decreases. For example, if one piece of pie provides five utils of eating pleasure, the second piece might deliver only three and the third just one (or none). *Ordinal utility* gauges consumer satisfaction comparatively rather than absolutely, according to how consumers rank their preferences for different goods, services, or activities. Utility theory is used in industry, for example, to determine overtime hours and wage scales, by balancing the utility of the extra wage against the value a worker puts on leisure time; the worker will accept the combination of overtime and time off that has the highest total utility.

The theory of *decreasing marginal utility* is used to predict which desired product, and how much of it, a consumer will choose to buy more of, given limited buying power. It was also used as an argument in favor of establishing a progressive income TAX, on the principle that the higher one's income is, the less each extra increment of earnings is required for necessities—the marginal utility of each additional dollar decreases—and the more able and willing the taxpayer is to pay a higher tax rate on that "less valuable" portion of income.

utopianism

The envisioning of a perfected society, which necessarily entails the rejection of many of the features of the present one. The term (a play on the Greek words for "no place" and "good place") was coined by Thomas More, whose *Utopia* (1516) describes an ideal commonwealth where all property is held in common, individual interests yield to the common good, and education and tolerance are universal—the antithesis of the injustices and inequalities in More's England. The book inaugurated a long tradition of social criticism in the form of fiction (see box)—a genre that reached a wider audience than polemical tracts and, being cloaked as fantasy, avoided political censure. While utopianism has never been a unified school of thought, most utopian

LITERARY UTOPIAS
AND DYSTOPIAS

Following the models provided by PLATO's *Republic* and Thomas More's *Utopia*, many authors have imagined societies whose perfection disparages current social and political conditions, manifests a faith in human PROGRESS, or both. Utopian works typically envision either a society of the future or an imaginary land geographically isolated from the infection of the outside world. Two influential products of the Renaissance confidence in REASON and human perfectibility were Francis BACON's *New Atlantis* (1626), in which the ideal society flows naturally from rational scientific investigation, and Tommasso Campanella's *City of the Sun* (1623), a commonwealth modeled on Plato's ideal REPUBLIC. Nineteenth-century industrialism and CLASS conflict inspired Samuel Butler's *Erewhon* (1872), which satirically describes a land in which the customs and laws are the opposite of the unjust conditions in England, and Edward Bellamy's *Looking Backward, 2000–1887* (1888), a view of Boston at the millennium as an economic utopia based on state SOCIALISM (a departure from previous COMMUNISTIC utopias). Shangri-La, a name that has become synonymous with the utopian idyll, was given by James Hilton in his novel *Lost Horizon* (1933) to a Himalayan valley where kindness and wisdom rule. FEMINIST utopias include Charlotte Perkins GILMAN's *Herland* (1915), depicting an all-female society sheltered from and implicitly rebuking the brutality of World War I, and Marge Piercy's *Woman on the Edge of Time* (1976), which contrasts the brutal present-day metropolis with a future decentralized communal society.

Utopian visionaries' faith in RATIONALISM, science, and human perfectibility has inspired parodies and satirical *dystopias* (from the Greek for "bad places"). In VOLTAIRE's *Candide* (1759), for instance, the title character discovers and then abandons the utopian El Dorado because its unremitting perfection is so boring, and he ultimately acknowledges that although this is not "the best of all possible worlds," we must make of it what we can. Twentieth-century dystopian novels, often intended as warnings of where contemporary trends may lead if unchecked, include Yevgeny Zamyatin's bitter satire of the Soviet system, *We* (1920); Aldous Huxley's sardonic imagining of a technological future, *Brave New World* (1932); George Orwell's nightmarish critique of TOTALITARIANISM, *1984* (1949); and Margaret Atwood's feminist vision of a FUNDAMENTALIST theocracy, *The Handmaid's Tale* (1986). The genre of science fiction has bred myriad future worlds, utopian—including H. G. Wells's *A Modern Utopia* (1905) and Arthur C. Clarke's *Childhood's End* (1953)—and dystopian, such as Ray Bradbury's *Fahrenheit 451* (1967) and Ursula Le Guin's *The Lathe of Heaven* (1971).

visions share certain common features, including communal ownership, egalitarian principles, and an immutable set of just and rational laws. One of the earliest utopias was described in PLATO's *Republic*, a meritocratic aristocracy ruled by a community of "philosopher-kings." Utopian elements can be seen in the philosophies of ROUSSEAU, HEGEL, and MARX, all of which assert the perfectibility of human nature.

Utopian communities have periodically flowered, especially in the United States, where they reflect the idea of America as a land of new beginnings and counter the country's strong tradition of INDIVIDUALISM. Many of the early communitarian societies, such as those established by Mennonites in the 1600s and by Shakers in the 1700s, had a religious basis—they were attempts to manifest the laws of heaven on earth. Nineteenth-century secular communities were inspired in part by the writings and example of two European SOCIALISTS, Robert Owen, who had founded a workers' cooperative in Scotland and in 1825 organized a model community at New Harmony, Indiana, and the Frenchman Charles Fourier, whose vision of universal harmony achieved through cooperative "phalanxes" of workers was adopted at the TRANSCENDENTALISTS' Brook Farm community and elsewhere. Most of these communal experiments shared the same qualities as their fictional equivalents—common labor, wealth, and status—and were short-lived.

V

Veblen, Thorsten See box at CLASS

verifiability and falsifiability, principles of

Two criteria for judging the scientific value of a given proposition, according to the extent to which it is subject to proof (verification) or disproof (falsification). According to both principles, only things that can be addressed in these terms are the valid object of scientific research; META-PHYSICS, religion, ETHICS, and other matters of opinion and belief are considered scientifically meaningless, since they are outside the scope of EMPIRICAL investigation.

The principle of verifiability was at the core of LOGICAL POSITIVISM, the early-20th-century movement that sought to apply the precepts of LOGIC and empirical science to all fields of thought. It states that a theory that is not at least capable of empirical verification—for instance, the existence of God—is by definition meaningless. However, verifiability was vulnerable to the charge that the principle was itself unverifiable. In *The Logic of Scientific Discovery* (1934), the Austrian-British philosopher of science Karl Popper also attacked it, but from another angle. He argued that universal propositions, such as the law of gravity, can *never* be definitively verified. Cumulative evidence and repeated experimental results merely increase the *probability* that a proposition is sound. We accept the theory of gravity not because it is possible to prove that an apple will never fall upward, but because it hasn't happened so far. Popper therefore proposed *falsifiability* as a more useful criterion than verifiability. Only if a theory can, in principle, be *disproved* can it be considered scientifically meaningful, and it is the unsuccessful efforts to disprove it that give it ever more validity.

See also LOGICAL POSITIVISM; MEANING; SCIENTIFIC METHOD.

Vinci, Leonardo da   See LEONARDO DA VINCI

virtue

From the Latin for "manliness"; the ancient Greek equivalent was *arete*, or "excellence." Among the Greeks and Romans, as well as early Christians, virtue was generally seen as that part of character that allowed one to live a good life—indeed, without which the good life was impossible. While today we tend to focus our ethical concerns on whether or not a given action is right, to the ancients the central questions of ETHICS involved the full sense of how one should live.

To SOCRATES, *arete* meant above all the proper knowledge of one's circumstances; one who knew the correct course of action in a particular situation would be incapable of doing otherwise. PLATO identified the four virtues (later called the "cardinal" virtues) as wisdom, courage, temperance, and justice. ARISTOTLE made a distinction between the Socratic/Platonic *intellectual* (dianoetic) virtues and *moral* virtues, or, as he also put it, between the abstract wisdom *(sophia)* that contemplates universal principles and the practical wisdom *(phronesis)* that directs good conduct. The key to achieving Aristotle's moral virtues was to observe the mean between extremes.

In the first century C.E., St. Paul promulgated what came to be known as the three "theological" virtues—faith, hope, and charity (love). This addition to the Platonic list of virtues shifted the focus from earthly living to the hereafter. Medieval Christian thinkers such as Thomas AQUINAS referred to the "seven virtues," cardinal and theological, all of them founded on God's grace.

Not only the nature of virtue but its origin has occupied the minds of philosophers. Most have said that virtue is one of three things: a native aspect of the character of the virtuous, inherent in their soul; something acquired through habit and learning; or a divine gift. Advocates of the "native aspect" view include KANT, who held that we are endowed with a "practical reason" that allows us to guide our lives in a virtuous manner, and, in the 20th century, G. E. Moore, whose *ethical intuitionism* assumed an intuitive apprehension of the good. The "habit and learning" approach has been embraced, for example, by UTILITARIANS such as Herbert Spencer, who maintained that social EVOLUTION includes the adoption of beneficial moral codes, and by MATERIALISTS such as HOBBES and MARX, who viewed ethical systems as man-made creations.

See also CYNICISM; MEAN; STOICISM.

vitalism

The theory that living beings cannot be reduced to the principles of chemistry and physics, that there is a categorical distinction between living and nonliving things; also the related belief in a universal animating force, a "vital principle" or *élan vital*, capable of transforming inert matter into living matter. The idea originated with the ancient Greeks, especially ARISTOTLE, whose theory of *hylomorphism* postulated an infinite, omnipresent soul that predates all forms of life, engendering and sustaining it by infusing inert matter with vitality.

After the works of Aristotle were rediscovered by the West in the Middle Ages, the notion of the SOUL as a vital principle merged with the CHRISTIAN doctrine of the individual soul. The conviction that life is the result of an animating force was not seriously questioned until the 19th century, when technological advances allowed scientists to demonstrate that matter, whether organic or inorganic, is composed of the same chemical ELEMENTS. The idea that the action of a vital impulse on inorganic compounds is responsible for the formation of organic substances was disproved when the German chemist Friedrich Wöhler synthesized the organic compound urea in 1828. While Wöhler's work and that of his colleague Justus von Liebig established the exclusive role of physicochemical forces in organic synthesis, belief in the existence of a vital principle in living organisms did not begin to recede until the end of the 19th century.

Contemporary scientific thought holds exclusively to the doctrine of MECHANISM, in which organisms are seen as purely the result of the workings of physical and chemical laws. (However, psychophysiology has yet to demonstrate that human CONSCIOUSNESS can be entirely reduced to neurological impulses.) Some philosophical theories of vitalism survived into the 20th century; these include the ideas of Henri Bergson, for whom EVOLUTION was driven by a divine "creative urge" rather than natural selection, and those of Hans Driesch, who proposed that the Aristotelian principle of *entelechy*—the actualization of a being's natural potential—works as a controlling force in living things.

See also SPONTANEOUS GENERATION AND BIOGENESIS.

Voltaire (François-Marie Arouet) (1694–1778)
French philosopher and social critic, the major figure in the circle of EN-
LIGHTENMENT writers known as *philosophes*, who, in a parochial and corrupt
French society, championed REASON, cosmopolitanism, justice, and human
dignity. He was a prolific and popular writer, the author of numerous essays, stories, plays, poems, and pamphlets that castigated, often satirically,
the "relics" of the medieval social order, particularly the clergy and the
aristocracy.

Voltaire was primarily known by his contemporaries for his scathing wit,
which, when aimed at the French nobility, earned him two imprisonments in
the Bastille and exile for a time in England. He was greatly impressed by
English society, institutions, and thought, particularly the scientific RATIONAL-
ISM of BACON and the natural-RIGHTS theory of LOCKE. He admired the English
constitutional monarchy, was drawn to the PLATONIC idea of the philosopher-
king, and supported the "benevolent despotism" of rulers, such as Frederick II
of Prussia, who considered themselves the guardians of their subjects' welfare.
But Voltaire was above all a champion of social, political, and religious tolerance; the saying "I disapprove of what you say, but I will defend to the death
your right to say it" is attributed to him.

The most frequent target of Voltaire's scorn was organized religion,
which he considered the abode of "superstition," particularly as embodied in
the ROMAN CATHOLIC Church. Contrary to the atheism of most of the *philosophes*,
he professed himself a DEIST, believing in an impersonal God and rejecting as
superstitious nonsense any doctrine not subject to reason. Voltaire is best
known for his short novel *Candide* (1759), a satire of LEIBNIZ's optimistic conviction that this is "the best of all possible worlds." The book was inspired by
the devastating Lisbon earthquake of 1755, which to Voltaire demonstrated
the folly of belief in a benevolent deity.

Although guided by a spirit of SKEPTICISM, Voltaire believed strongly in
PROGRESS, the amelioration of the human condition through the unfettered
application of reason. How ordinary people live, and what matters to them,
are what is most important to the course of the world, he felt. In his historical
studies, such as the *Essay on General History and on the Customs and Spirit of Nations* (1756), he therefore emphasized the culture and economic conditions
of a people rather than individual personages and events; this approach
helped lay the foundations of the modern historical method (cf. "GREAT MAN"
THEORY).

W

Washington, Booker Taliaferro (1856–1915)

American educator, advocate of occupational education for blacks and accommodation with white authority. Washington's educational philosophy of hard work and self-elevation was largely shaped by his own life experience, as detailed in his autobiography, *Up from Slavery* (1901). Born a slave on a Virginia plantation, he taught himself to read and write, and by the age of 26 had become the founding president of the Tuskegee Institute (now Tuskegee University), an industrial, agricultural, and teacher-training school for blacks. Washington believed that for African-Americans, the ideal of racial equality and political rights was secondary to achieving economic self-reliance and moral dignity. He founded a number of schools, newspapers, and black-advancement organizations to promote those goals.

In his famous "Atlanta Compromise" speech of 1895, Washington accepted racial segregation, tacitly conceded white superiority, and appealed to whites and blacks to work together to improve conditions in the South. Widely regarded as the primary spokesman of the black race, he was admired by many Americans, black and white. His educational program received the support of philanthropists such as Andrew Carnegie and John D. Rockefeller, and he was invited by President Theodore Roosevelt to dine at the White House—the first African-American so honored.

However, some black intellectuals, such as W. E. B. Du Bois, saw his policy as wrongheaded and shortsighted, sacrificing civil and political rights for appeasement and temporary economic achievements. The founding of the National Association for the Advancement of Colored People (NAACP) was in part a response to Washington's policy of accommodation. He was also condemned for abusing his influential position, using his "Tuskegee Machine" to silence or sabotage those opposed to his philosophy. Nevertheless, in the volatile era of Jim Crow and "lynch law," his pragmatic policy achieved some measure of reconciliation between black aspirations and white supremacy. Later in life, with living conditions for most southern blacks worsening and their social and political rights eroded even further, Washington became more outspokenly critical of racial segregation and white domination. While his philosophy of accommodation to RACISM did not long prevail among black activists, the idea of black pride expressed in self-improvement and economic independence remains his lasting legacy.

"In all things that are purely social we can be as separate as the five fingers, yet one as the hand in all things essential to mutual progress."

—Booker T. Washington,
"Atlanta Compromise"
speech, 1895

wave-particle duality

A key principle in QUANTUM THEORY, based on the observation that both matter at the subatomic level and light (more generally, "electromagnetic radiation"—see MAXWELL) display properties of both waves and particles, that neither can be classified as simply a wave or a particle. The concept was proposed in 1923 by the French physicist Louis-Victor de Broglie, in response to the problem posed by EINSTEIN's explanation of the *photoelectric effect*, in which electrons are ejected from certain metal surfaces when struck by light. In 1905, Einstein theorized that light comes in discrete packets (later called *photons*), which "kick" free electrons off the electrode, generating the spark.

But the idea that light, which had long been known to behave like a wave, could also behave like a particle was inconsistent with the rest of physics. How could light behave like both a wave and a particle when matter behaves only like a particle? De Broglie suggested that this was not the case: subatomic particles also have wavelike properties. De Broglie's hypothesis was soon confirmed experimentally, showing that electrons (and subsequently other particles) behave in certain situations like waves and in others like particles. This concept, asserting nature's fundamental duality, has become a bedrock of modern physics.

Weber, Max (1864–1920)

German sociologist and political economist, one of the founders of modern sociology, a scholar whose studies of CAPITALISM, comparative religion, CLASS, and social SYSTEMS, together with his contributions to social science methodology, have continuing influence. In Weber's view, the trend in Western civilization has been toward *rationalization*, guided by a belief in PROGRESS through REASON, which has forged a path of development in social, political, and economic organization that diverges from most other cultures.

This view was most strikingly expressed in Weber's most celebrated and controversial work, *The Protestant Ethic and the Spirit of Capitalism* (1904–05). In it, Weber attributed the rise and growth of capitalism—a distinctly Western phenomenon that has comparatively recently been "exported" worldwide—partly to the work ethic imbedded in PROTESTANT, particularly Calvinist, theology (see box at PROTESTANTISM). Attributes such as industry, thrift, temperance, and self-reliance were considered not only VIRTUES in themselves but evidence of God's grace. Thus the accumulation of wealth, together with limited enjoyment of it, became a CHRISTIAN duty.

This thesis—in part a rebuttal of MARX's economic DETERMINISM, which attributed the rise of capitalism to relentless economic and historical forces, and in part Weber's attempt to understand his own passion for work—was only one component of his larger analysis of modern Western RATIONALISM and the resulting systems of authority and social organization. He identified three types of authority: *traditional*, with legitimacy deriving from custom and hereditary rule; *charismatic*, stemming from the inspirational force of religion or a dynamic, often dictatorial, leader; and *bureaucratic* (or *legal*), in which personal command is replaced by legislative and corporate rules and regulations. A bureaucracy, where power flows from the office and is not dependent on the individual officeholder, greatly enlarges the range and adaptability of administration and social control.

Weber sought to create a sound methodology for sociology based in *value-freedom*, the avoidance of value judgments that bias research; the construction of *ideal types*, or generalized concepts, against which actual systems and phenomena can be analyzed; and what he called *Verstehen*— German for "understanding," but also implying the interpretation of social actions in terms of their subjective meaning to both the "actors" and the researcher. While he insisted on rigorous methodology, Weber rejected the POSITIVIST faith that social science could duplicate the methods and achieve the EMPIRICISM of natural science. Social reality, created by people's actions and the meanings they attach to them, is too complex and unpredictable to be adequately explained, or even completely understood.

See also CLASS; STATE.

welfare

The question of social welfare is a central theme in modern social, economic, and political discourse, particularly the question of where responsibility for it primarily resides—with the STATE or with individuals and the private sector. The ideological debate between SOCIALISM and CAPITALISM is conducted at least partly in this arena, each system claiming to best promote the material well-being of society as a whole. But the argument rages even within free-MARKET systems, embracing issues such as the proper role of government, the self-reliance and social obligations of the individual, the redistribution of wealth, and the purpose and degree of TAXATION. In all modern industrial states, government plays at least some role in social welfare, a role that ranges from the provision of an economic "safety net" for impoverished citizens in the form of cash grants and subsidized services (the familiar meaning of the term "welfare"), to social security and unemployment insurance, support of the arts and public education, and universal health care. The field of *welfare economics*, pioneered by the Italian economist and sociologist Vilfredo Pareto, studies the conditions under which economic activity leads to optimal social welfare.

In the late 18th century, Adam SMITH declared that not only national economies but overall social welfare were enhanced by the free-enterprise system; at the same time, Thomas PAINE and other RADICALS argued for the state's obligation to provide for the public welfare. The LIBERAL philosophy of John Stuart MILL held that economic INDIVIDUALISM implies a public responsibility for the relief of those prosperity has passed by. The first modern *welfare state* was instituted by German chancellor Otto von Bismarck in the late 19th century. Before the Great Depression, social welfare programs were far more extensive in Europe than in the United States, where wide-ranging federal assistance programs were first created by the New Deal legislation of the 1930s. After World War II, even more comprehensive welfare systems were established in Europe, especially Great Britain, where the Labour government of Clement Attlee instituted a network of social services that sustained virtually the entire population "from the cradle to the grave." Beginning in the 1970s, most Western countries experienced a contraction in state welfare services. This trend, initiated by an economic recession that increased the number of people requiring assistance at the same time tax revenues were declining, was furthered by the arguments of CONSERVATIVE politicians and economists that government welfare is a wasteful, inefficient, and unfair use of public resources (see, e.g., SUPPLY-SIDE ECONOMICS). Most theorists, however, accept the need for some system of social assistance, whether publicly or privately supported, as an unavoidable side effect of capitalism, which depends on a permanent, underlying rate of unemployment in order to maintain an affordable labor market.

See also SOCIAL CHOICE; SOCIAL CONTRACT.

Whigs and Tories

Parliamentary factions in Great Britain in the 17th–19th centuries; in the United States, the Whig Party was active in the 1830s–50s. Whigs were generally associated with the doctrines of LIBERALISM, Tories with CONSERVATISM.

The British factions arose on either side of the controversy over allowing the Duke of York (later James II), who was a ROMAN CATHOLIC, to succeed to the English throne in the 1680s—the Tories for, the Whigs against. The names were originally defamatory. "Tory" comes from the Irish *tóraidhe,* or "outlaw," "Whig" probably from the Scottish *whiggamor,* meaning "cattle drover," a term of disparagement for 17th-century Presbyterians. The Whigs advocated a constitutional monarchy and were the primary supporters of the Glorious Revolution of 1688, which established the preeminence of Parliament. During the 18th century, Whigs represented mercantile interests and promoted political and social reforms, while the Tories stood for aristocracy and tradition. The Whigs generally supported American independence, the Tories opposed it; in the colonies, loyalists were called Tories by scornful revolutionaries. In the 1830s the Tories became the Conservative Party and the Whigs joined the RADICALS to form the Liberal Party. The term "Whig" has since disappeared, but British Conservatives are still known as Tories.

The American Whig Party was formed in 1834 out of the National Republican party and other factions to present a united front against the "tyranny" of President Andrew Jackson, whom they saw as annexing monarchical powers to his office. Led by Daniel Webster and Henry Clay, the Whigs generally espoused pro-business, pro-establishment economic policies, opposed the POPULISM of JACKSONIAN DEMOCRACY, and tried to shift the balance of political power from the executive to the Congress. They elected two presidential candidates, William Henry Harrison in 1840 and Zachary Taylor in 1848. The party dissolved in the early 1850s, mainly in dissention between "Conscience Whigs" and "Cotton Whigs" over the slavery issue and between "higher-law" and "lower-law" Whigs over the primacy of the Constitution.

See also BURKE; CONSERVATISM; RADICALISM.

Wiener, Norbert see CYBERNETICS

will to power

Term used by the philosopher Friedrich NIETZSCHE and the psychologist Alfred Adler in their respective theories. For Nietzsche, the will to power (*Wille zur Macht*) was the relentlessly active principle that orders the universe. It has two inextricable sides: activity and mastery. The idea was formed in opposition to those, such as SPINOZA and Schopenhauer, for whom the will to *live* was central. The survival instinct, Nietzsche said, presumes simply persevering in a static world; the will to power presumes a world constantly in flux—always *becoming*—on which we impose order, albeit only conditionally and temporarily. The impulse to activity and mastery—action and control—is the central motivating force for human energies and the fount of creativity.

In the Individual Psychology of Alfred Adler, introduced in 1912, the will to power is a neurotic impulse, not a creative one. For Adler, psychopathology arises from feelings of inferiority engendered in childhood (he was known as "the father of the inferiority complex"). Overcompensating for these feelings can produce a "will to power"—an exaggerated sense of self-worth and a desire to dominate (or manipulate) others. This unrealistic sense of self and others produces a "guiding fiction" that dictates the individual's life choices and, when it inevitably clashes with reality, creates anxiety and a further cycle of overcompensation.

witchcraft

Ancient spiritual practice, engaged in primarily but not exclusively by women, conventionally associated with malevolent supernatural power; lately reinvented as a neo-PAGAN religion of nature worship. In many ANIMISTIC tribal societies, especially African ones, witchcraft (as opposed to *sorcery*, which can be learned) is considered an innate, often hereditary power to manipulate the natural world and control its spirits through spells, incantations, and other occult practices. Personal misfortune is often attributed to the influence of witches, and the job of a "witch doctor" is to identify and expose them. (See also AFRICAN RELIGIONS.)

In medieval CHRISTIANITY, the magical arts employed by ancient cultures for healing, divination, the propitiation of nature, and the defeat of adversaries were condemned as the work of Satan. The existence of supernatural witchcraft was widely believed and feared, giving rise to the popular image of witches as evil purveyors of harmful spells, or "black magic." The persecution of supposed witches by the ROMAN CATHOLIC Inquisition in Europe and by the PURITAN clergy in colonial America frequently targeted eccentric or independent women, often elderly or poor, who defied social roles and conventions. Some modern writers, notably the anthropologist Margaret Murray in *The Witch-Cult of Western Europe* (1921), have argued that these witch-hunts were aimed at stamping out a widespread "old religion" practiced since pre-Christian times, in which women were powerful and in tune with nature, and thus threatening to the RATIONAL, patriarchal Christian order.

While most scholars discount the notion that such a cult ever formally existed, it has provided a potent mythology for the recently emerged witchcraft religion known as Wicca. A strand within neopaganism closely related to the new GODDESS religions, Wicca (an Old English word for "witch" or "wizard") emphasizes inner spirituality and natural harmony rather than supernatural powers (although some Wiccans practice SPIRITUALISM). There is an accent on HOLISTIC healing, an affinity with the generative forces of the earth, and a reverence for the natural cycles of life, the seasons, and especially the moon, whose monthly phases of waxing, fullness, and waning symbolize the stages of a woman's life—the young maiden, the mature mother, and the wise and wizened "crone." One of its most influential exponents is Starhawk, a self-described witch and author of several books on Wicca, including *The Spiral Dance: A Rebirth of the Ancient Religion of the Great Goddess* (1979).

Wittgenstein, Ludwig Josef Johann (1889–1951)

Austrian philosopher, who influenced LOGICAL POSITIVISM and ANALYTIC PHILOSOPHY. While a frontline soldier in World War I—during which time he underwent a MYSTICAL experience—he wrote the first of his two seminal works, the *Tractatus Logico-Philosophicus* (published 1921). In it, he stated that LOGIC (which he had studied under Bertrand RUSSELL) is necessary, but not sufficient, to describe reality, and developed the *picture theory of language* to illustrate that idea.

When we use words (or mathematics) to describe something, we create, in effect, a picture of what we want to describe. But this picture, like a photograph or a painting, is an imperfect and incomplete rendering of what we are trying to explain. The reason for this, Wittgenstein said, is because language, like a picture, is a logical structure, and that structure both shapes and limits what is said; it represents but can never fully express the reality it depicts. Attempting to capture in words the whole meaning of anything other than empirical facts, therefore, is "nonsense," Wittgenstein concluded: "Whereof we cannot speak, thereof we must be silent." This distinction was eagerly em-

braced by the Vienna Circle of logical positivists, who sought to banish META-
PHYSICAL speculation from philosophical discourse.

In his *Philosophical Investigations* (published 1958), which summarizes his
mature thought, Wittgenstein emphasized the *practical* nature of language.
Language takes its MEANING not from its structure but from its context in social practice. Words are not immutable pieces of a picture puzzle but tools to
be used as needed; they acquire meaning through their interplay in *language
games*. In this view, language and meaning are necessarily public phenomena,
created through conversation and discourse; by extension, there can be no
"private languages." This conclusion challenged the Cartesian DUALISM that
distinguishes between inner thought and external reality (see DESCARTES;
MIND/BODY PROBLEM). We should seek to rediscover language, Wittgenstein
held, as something that happens between us rather than within us.

See also OBJECTIVISM AND SUBJECTIVISM.

Wollstonecraft, Mary (1759–1797)

English author and social critic, whose writings urging EQUALITY of the sexes
are considered the first important statements of FEMINISM. A self-taught child
of genteel poverty, as a young woman she held a series of traditionally female
occupations, including governess and lady's companion. In these jobs, she
wrote, she saw the wasted potential of women of her class and began to advocate equal opportunity for women. After the failure of a school she and her
sisters had established for the informal education of novice teachers, Wollstonecraft began to write in order to maintain her economic independence.
Her 1787 pamphlet *Thoughts on the Education of Daughters* brought her into the
circle of RADICALS that met in the home of her publisher and included the
poet and artist William Blake, the American revolutionary Thomas PAINE, and
the political theorist William Godwin, whom she eventually married (she died
shortly after giving birth to their daughter, who became the novelist Mary
Shelley). Her scandalous reputation as a freethinking, sexually liberated
woman was further fueled by a liaison that resulted in the birth of an illegitimate child and ended with a suicide attempt.

Wollstonecraft's visit to France to observe the 1789 revolution at first
hand prompted her treatise *A Vindication of the Rights of Man* (1790), written
as a rebuttal of Edmund BURKE's critical *Reflections on the Revolution in France*.
The egalitarian principles of the French Revolution also inspired her major
work, *A Vindication of the Rights of Woman* (1792). In it, she argued that a society cannot be truly free unless all its citizens are considered equal, regardless
of gender or CLASS, and asserted that the primary barrier to women's equality

was lack of education. She repudiated the belief that God had created men to be superior to women, blaming women's subordination on cultural prejudices that would have them be delicate and foolish rather than strong and clever. Women should associate with men in "rational fellowship," she said, not "slavish obedience," and should have equal educational and professional opportunities. Wollstonecraft's argument was greeted largely by outrage and ridicule in her own day; it was not until her rediscovery by the 20th-century women's movement that she was remembered as more than an unorthodox freethinker and polemicist.

Y

yin and yang

The complementary, polar forces of the universe, whose tension and conflict resolve in balance, order, and change; a central concept in CONFUCIANISM and TAOISM. Yin is the female power, associated with darkness, cold, the earth, and passivity; yang is the male power, associated with light, heat, the heavens, and action. In traditional Chinese thought, neither force has supremacy over the other, but their power is cyclical, each one alternately dominant and recessive, and ultimately complementary. Their interaction accounts for the changing seasons, the harmony of nature, and the progression of change through the resolution of opposites. The terms, originally referring to the contrast between shaded and sunny spots in nature, came to represent the idea that all of creation is governed by binary forces, conflicting but interdependent. Yin and yang are conventionally symbolized by two curved, reciprocal shapes in contrasting shades, forming a circle.

yoga

Philosophical system in Indian religious tradition and one of the six orthodox schools of HINDU thought, directed at divine knowledge and liberation through physical, mental, and spiritual discipline. The term (Sanskrit for "union" or "yoke") implies the attainment of oneness with the ABSOLUTE by means of disciplined practice. The *Yoga Sutras*, attributed to the sage Patanjali (second century B.C.E.), define the goal of yoga as "cessation of the mental whirlwind." Yoga is based on the DUALISTIC Samkhya philosophy of Hinduism, which holds that mind (or SOUL) and matter are separate entities and that union with the divine can be achieved only when CONSCIOUSNESS is liberated from its mundane entanglements.

The practice of yoga involves a variety of exercises and techniques, which Patanjali divided into eight stages, comprising *raja* (royal) yoga. *Yama* (restraint) and *niyama* (discipline) entail abstinence from immoral behavior, physical and mental purification, and religious devotions; *asana* (posture), *pranayama* (breath control), and *pratyahara* (sensory detachment) prepare the physical body for the three progressively rarefied meditative states: *dharana* (meditation), *dhyana* (contemplation), and *samadhi* (absorption). Yogic systems are many and varied, stressing different parts of the royal path; among the best known are *hatha* yoga (physical discipline), *bhakti* yoga (devotion), *jnana* yoga (knowledge and intellect), *karma* yoga (works), and *kundalini* yoga (awakening of subtle energies through TANTRIC practice).

Z

Zen Buddhism See box at BUDDHISM

Zeno's paradoxes

Parmenides, founder of the Eleatic School of Greek philosophy in the fifth century B.C.E., saw existence as a unitary whole—timeless, unmoving, immutable. To the Eleatics, BEING and thought were identical, and only the unchanging laws of thought could reveal the truth; sensory experience, being contradictory and changeable, was therefore illusion. To counter the objections of common sense and experience, Parmenides' disciple Zeno constructed a series of paradoxes designed to prove the indivisibility of space and the impossibility of motion. He did this with imaginary demonstrations that led to LOGICAL contradictions and absurdities. His paradoxes are considered to have had a formative influence on SOCRATES' use of the DIALECTIC.

Zeno's most famous paradox is the one about the swift-footed hero Achilles in a race with a tortoise, who starts with a good-sized lead. By the time Achilles reaches his opponent's starting point, the tortoise has moved slightly forward. In the time it takes Achilles to close that distance, the tortoise has gained a little more ground. Although the distance between them grows ever smaller, Achilles must always cross the space separating them at any given moment, by which time the tortoise will have advanced a little. Therefore Achilles will always be fractions behind the tortoise's place and can never quite catch up.

In an even more paralyzing version, Zeno points out that in order to go from point A to point B, one has to first cover half that distance. And of course, in order to reach that halfway point one must cross half *that* space as well, and so on, ad infinitum. In order to even begin the journey, the traveler has to cross an infinite number of points, a task that cannot be accomplished in any finite period of time. Therefore, taking even the first step must be impossible.

Finally, Zeno describes an arrow in flight, an apparently unarguable example of motion. But since it cannot be in two places at once, the arrow must occupy a single set of points in space at any given moment in its flight. At that moment, therefore, it is at rest; by extension, it is at rest at *every* moment of its flight and is never truly moving at all.

Zionism

The ancient aspiration of the Jewish people for the restoration of their homeland in the biblical land of Israel, and the modern political movement to establish a Jewish STATE there. Zion, the hill in Jerusalem where King David established his city, has been an allegorical synonym for the Holy Land since ancient times. Zionism reflects a strong current in Jewish history and culture: the repeated exile of the Jews from Israel in biblical and historical times and their persistent faith in the covenant with God that promises their eventual return. This expectation has often been linked to the prophesied coming of the Messiah, who will redeem the Jews and establish God's kingdom.

The modern Zionist movement was founded in the 1890s by the Austrian journalist Theodor Herzl, who organized the World Zionist Organization and worked to create a Jewish state, seeing it as the only solution to anti-Semitism. Largely through the efforts of Chaim Weizmann (who would become the first president of Israel), the British government's Balfour Declaration of 1917 expressed sympathy with Zionist ideals, and the post–World War I British mandate in Palestine promoted the establishment of a Jewish state. Zionist ambitions, propelled by accelerating immigration into Palestine (known as "making *aliya*," the "ascent") and given new urgency by the devastation of European Jewry in the Holocaust, culminated in the founding of the state of Israel in 1948.

From the beginning, Zionism was not a homogeneous or uncontested movement. Even within JUDAISM there was considerable opposition to Zionism, ranging from Orthodox objections that the restoration of Israel could come about only through divine intervention, to liberal Jews' confidence that anti-Semitism would diminish in modern PLURALISTIC societies. Within Zionism itself there has been considerable diversity in ideology and purpose. At one end of the spectrum are religious Jews who see the creation of Israel as the fulfillment of the biblical covenant, and at the other have been social (often

SOCIALIST) visionaries for whom it was an opportunity to build an ideal society. This latter group of Zionists created the *kibbutz* movement, which founded Israeli agriculture on a collective model. The Zionist idea continues to stir dispute in contemporary Israel, which is officially secular but where some Orthodox groups believe it should be a religious state ruled by Jewish law; these are opposed by others who insist that such a nation would betray its mission as a haven for all Jews, even nonreligious ones.

On the other side of the Zionist equation are the Palestinians, for whom Israel is also ancestral land and who have been dispossessed and marginalized by the Israeli state. The Palestinian predicament illustrates the difficulties inherent in NATIONALIST solutions to ethnic persecutions.

Zoroastrianism

Monotheistic religion, originating in Persia, many of whose key concepts parallel and are thought to have influenced elements of ancient Greek philosophy (particularly DUALISM) and the theologies of JUDAISM, CHRISTIANITY, and ISLAM. It was founded by the priest and philosopher Zarathushtra (or Zarathustra; Zoroaster in its Greek form), who was traditionally considered to have lived c.600 B.C.E. but is now thought to have lived c.1000 B.C.E. or a few centuries earlier. Zoroastrianism was the official religion of Persia for a millennium but was nearly extinguished after the ascendancy of Islam in the seventh century C.E. and now survives mainly in India, among the descendants of immigrants called Parsis (the name means "Persians").

Zarathushtra rejected the PANTHEISTIC worship of his day, proclaiming only one god, Ahura Mazda ("Wise Lord"), the essence of TRUTH and justice, who created the world and its inhabitants. He and his warrior-angels *(ahuras)* are opposed by Angra Manyu (or Ahriman, "Evil Spirit"), the creator of malevolence and destruction, and his legions of demons *(daevas)*. The world is a battleground on which the forces of good and evil struggle for supremacy. Zarathushtra taught that the world would soon end in a great holocaust from which only the good would emerge. Later Zoroastrian cosmology revised that estimate, dividing the history of the world into four 3,000-year periods, the last of which began with the birth of Zarathushtra. In this period, three saviors will successively appear. The last of these will oversee the ultimate battle, the defeat of Angra Manyu, and the final judgment, when the dead will be resurrected and rewarded in heaven or punished in hell (cf. ESCHATOLOGY). Humans are given free will to choose good or evil, and that choice either weakens or strengthens Angra Manyu. Choosing good entails preserving and perpetuating life, that is, following a useful occupation and raising a family.

The main Zoroastrian scripture is the Avesta, which includes 17 hymns, the Gathas, attributed to Zarathushtra. These form the core of the liturgy for the *yasna*, the purification ceremony performed daily by two priests; its focus is a reverence for fire, considered the crucial ELEMENT and associated with life and truth. To avoid defiling the elements of the "good creation," fire, water, and earth, the dead are not burned or buried but exposed in "towers of silence" to birds of prey.

Further Reading

A book like *A World of Ideas* cannot hope to fully explore the enormous breadth and depth of ideas in our cultural sphere. The books listed below, all of them generally available in bookstores or libraries, cover in greater detail many of the concepts touched on here. Some are surveys of important fields of thought, others are readable reference books that concentrate on particular areas of interest.

Appiah, Kwame Anthony, and Henry Louis Gates Jr. *The Dictionary of Global Culture.* New York: Knopf, 1997. A handbook of multiculturalism: brief outlines of concepts and thinkers from around the world.

Breit, William, and Roger L. Ransom. *The Academic Scribblers: American Economists in Collision.* 3rd ed. Princeton: Princeton University Press, 1998. A kind of companion and sequel to Heilbroner's *The Worldly Philosophers* (see below), covering 20th-century economic theories.

Casti, John L. *Paradigms Lost: Images of Man in the Mirror of Science.* New York: Morrow, 1989. An overview of present-day understandings of the great scientific questions, including the origin of life, human behavior, language and thinking, and the nature of observed reality.

Cooper, David E. *World Philosophies: An Historical Introduction.* Oxford, UK, and Cambridge, Mass.: Blackwell, 1996. A world history of thought, from the ancients to the postmoderns.

Eagleton, Terry. *Literary Theory.* 2d ed. Minneapolis: University of Minnesota Press, 1996. An introduction to the recent trends in literary criticism, including poststructuralism, deconstruction, historicism, and Marxist theory.

Eldridge, Niles. *The Pattern of Evolution.* New York: Freeman, 1998. A chronicle of the emergence and development of life on earth, by the theorist of punctuated equilibrium.

Eliade, Mircea, and Ioan P. Couliano. *The Eliade Guide to World Religions.* San Francisco: HarperSanFrancisco, 1991. Some three dozen short chapters focusing on world religions of the past and present, with historical and geographical variants.

Ferris, Timothy. *Coming of Age in the Milky Way.* New York: William Morrow, 1988. A survey of scientific thought and humanity's changing view of cosmology.

Fischer-Schreiber, Ingrid, et al., eds. *The Encyclopedia of Eastern Philosophy and Religion: Buddhism, Hinduism, Taoism, Zen.* Boston: Shambhala, 1989. Outlines of the four great Eastern traditions, in dictionary form.

Fritzsch, Harald. *An Equation That Changed the World: Newton, Einstein, and the Theory of Relativity.* Chicago: University of Chicago Press, 1994. Classical mechanics meets space-time in this fanciful dialogue between the two giants of physics.

Gamow, George. *The Great Physicists from Galileo to Einstein.* 1961. Reprint, New York: Dover, 1988. Despite its title, not biography but a history of physical theory from the Greek atomists to the subatomic age, by the great scientist and popularizer.

Goodin, Robert E., and Philip Pettit, eds. *A Companion to Contemporary Political Philosophy.* Oxford, UK, and Cambridge, Mass.: Blackwell, 1993. Longish articles on forty central themes in social and political theory.

Gregory, Richard L., ed. *The Oxford Companion to the Mind.* Oxford and New York: Oxford University Press, 1987. A dictionary-style handbook of topics in psychology, parapsychology, neuroscience, and other brain-related fields.

Heilbroner, Robert L. *The Worldly Philosophers: The Lives, Times, and Ideas of the Great Economic Thinkers.* 6th ed. New York: Simon & Schuster, 1986. The development of economic theory, from Smith to Keynes.

Hunter, Sam, and John Jacobus. *Modern Art: Painting, Sculpture, Architecture.* New York: Abrams, 1992. A fully illustrated survey of all the important movements, from 19th-century impressionism to late-20th-century postmodern schools.

Jones, Roger S. *Physics for the Rest of Us: Ten Basic Ideas of 20th-Century Physics That Everyone Should Know, and How They Have Shaped Our Culture and Consciousness.* Chicago: Contemporary Books, 1992. The scientific, philosophic, and cosmological dimensions of relativity, quantum mechanics, and other aspects of modern physics.

Kuper, Adam, and Jessica Kuper, eds. *The Social Science Encyclopedia.* 2nd ed. London and New York: Routledge, 1996. An exhaustive overview of the social sciences—sociology, psychology, anthropology, economics, and more, in dictionary form.

Levinson, David. *Religion: A Cross-Cultural Encyclopedia.* Santa Barbara, Denver, and Oxford: ABC-Clio, 1996. An alphabetical survey of twenty world religions with comparative articles on worldwide beliefs and practices.

Miller, David, ed. *The Blackwell Encyclopedia of Political Thought*. Oxford, UK, and Cambridge, Mass.: Blackwell, 1991. Short to medium-length articles on many influential concepts and thinkers.

Read, Herbert. *A Concise History of Modern Painting*. New York: Thames & Hudson, 1974. The classic study of modernism in art, from the impressionists to the abstract expressionists.

Smith, Huston. *The World's Religions: Our Great Wisdom Traditions*. San Francisco: HarperSanFrancisco, 1991. Updated edition of the celebrated *Religions of Man,* from Hinduism to Christianity and including primal religions.

Strauss, Leo, and Joseph Cropsey, eds. *History of Political Philosophy*. Chicago: Rand McNally, 1963. A classic collection of in-depth intellectual biographies of thirty-two great philosophers, from Plato to Dewey.

Tarnas, Richard. *The Passion of the Western Mind: Understanding the Ideas That Have Shaped Our World View.* New York: Harmony, 1991. An accessible review of Western philosophy from the Greeks to the moderns.

Tavris, Carol, and Carole Wade. *Psychology in Perspective,* 2nd ed. New York: Addison Wesley Longman, 1997. An introduction to psychological theory and practice through five common approaches: the biological, learning, cognitive, sociocultural, and psychodynamic perspectives.

Tong, Rosemarie Putnam. *Feminist Thought: A More Comprehensive Introduction*. 2nd ed. Boulder, Colo.: Westview Press, 1998. Second edition of Tong's 1989 "comprehensive introduction," with coverage of liberal, radical, Marxist-socialist, psychoanalytic, existentialist, postmodern, and other strands of contemporary feminism.

Turner, Roland, ed. *Thinkers of the Twentieth Century*. 2nd ed. Chicago and London: St. James, 1987. Intellectual profiles of some 450 modern thinkers in all fields.

Weiner, Philip P. *Dictionary of the History of Ideas: Studies of Selected Pivotal Ideas.* 5 vols. and index. New York: Scribners, 1973. A classic set of encyclopedia-length discussions of three hundred key themes in human thought, from abstraction to zeitgeist.

Williams, Raymond. *Keywords: A Vocabulary of Culture and Society*. Rev. ed. New York: Oxford University Press, 1983. Short essays on the etymology, evolving meanings, and implications of 150 key terms in political and social thought.

Index of Key Terms and Proper Names

Headwords of main entries are in SMALL CAPITALS.

A PRIORI / A POSTERIORI

A. C. Bhaktivedanta Swami Prabhupada.
See box at HINDUISM: modern
movements

ABC art. See box at ABSTRACTION

Abduh, Muhammad. See ISLAM

Abelard, Peter. See NOMINALISM;
SCHOLASTICISM; UNIVERSALS

Abercrombie, Nicholas. See IDEOLOGY

ability-to-pay principle. See TAXATION

abiogenesis. See SPONTANEOUS
GENERATION AND BIOGENESIS

abolitionist movement. See DOUGLASS;
EMERSON; RADICALISM; STANTON;
TRANSCENDENTALISM; WHIGS AND
TORIES

abortion. See FEMINISM; FUNDAMENTALISM;
MALTHUSIAN POPULATION THEORY

Abraham. See JUDAISM

ABSOLUTE, THE

ABSOLUTISM

abstract art. See box at ABSTRACTION; see
also CUBISM; DADA; FAUVISM; SYMBOLISM

abstract expressionism. See box at
ABSTRACTION

ABSTRACTION

Abstraction-Création. See box at
ABSTRACTION

ABSURD, THE

acceleration. See GALILEO; NEWTON;
RELATIVITY

accident. See KANT; SUBSTANCE

accommodationism. See DU BOIS;
GARVEY; RACE AND RACISM;
WASHINGTON

Achilles. See ZENO'S PARADOXES

acquired variation. See LAMARCKISM

action painting. See box at ABSTRACTION

active intellect. See IBN RUSHD; IBN SINA

actualism. See CATASTROPHISM AND
UNIFORMITARIANISM

Adams, John. See FEDERALISM

Adams, John Quincy. See MONROE
DOCTRINE

adaptive expectations. See RATIONAL
EXPECTATIONS

Addams, Jane. See PROGRESSIVISM

Adi Granth. See SIKHISM

Adler, Alfred. See WILL TO POWER; see also
FREUD; PSYCHOANALYSIS

Adorno, Theodor W. See box at CRITICAL
THEORY; ETHNOCENTRISM

Advaita Vedanta. See box at HINDUISM (schools)
ADVANTAGE
ADVENTISM
aeons. See GNOSTICISM
AESTHETICISM
AESTHETICS
aether (see ether)
affective fallacy. See NEW CRITICISM
AFFIRMATIVE ACTION
African Methodist Episcopal Church. See box at PROTESTANTISM
African Orthodox Church. See box at AFRICAN RELIGIONS (New World)
AFRICAN RELIGIONS
African religious movements, modern. See box at AFRICAN RELIGIONS
African-derived religions in the New World. See box at AFRICAN RELIGIONS
Afrocentrism. See box at AFRICAN RELIGIONS (New World); NÉGRITUDE
Age of Reason. See ENLIGHTENMENT; PAINE; REASON
Aggadah. See JUDAISM
ahimsa. See JAINISM; see also GANDHI; NONVIOLENCE
Ahriman. See ZOROASTRIANISM
Ahura Mazda. See ZOROASTRIANISM
ahuras. See ZOROASTRIANISM
Akhmatova, Anna. See SOCIALIST REALISM
Ala. See ANIMISM
Albertus Magnus. See SCHOLASTICISM
alchemy. See ELEMENTS; NEWTON; SPONTANEOUS GENERATION AND BIOGENESIS; TAOISM
Alexander the Great. See ARISTOTLE; CYNICISM; "GREAT MAN" THEORY
Ali ibn Abi Talib. See box at ISLAM (Sunnis and Shi'ites)
ALIENATION
aliya. See ZIONISM
Allah. See ISLAM; see also ESCHATOLOGY; MUHAMMAD
allopatric speciation. See PUNCTUATED EQUILIBRIUM
altered states of consciousness. See PARAPSYCHOLOGY; TRANSPERSONAL PSYCHOLOGY

Althusser, Louis. See box at STRUCTURALISM; see also HISTORICISM; IDEOLOGY; QUEER THEORY
Alvarez, Luis. See CATASTROPHISM AND UNIFORMITARIANISM
Alvarez, Walter. See CATASTROPHISM AND UNIFORMITARIANISM
Amaterasu-Omikami. See SHINTO
A.M.E. Church. See box at PROTESTANTISM
American Indians (see Native Americans)
Amida. See box at BUDDHISM
Amish. See box at PROTESTANTISM
Amitabha. See box at BUDDHISM
Amman, Jakob. See box at PROTESTANTISM
Anabaptism. See box at PROTESTANTISM
anal-retentive/anal-expulsive personality. See box at FREUD
ANALYTIC PHILOSOPHY
analytic psychology. See JUNG
analytic and synthetic statements. See A PRIORI / A POSTERIORI; KANT
anamnesis. See INNATE IDEAS; PLATO; UNCONSCIOUS
ANARCHISM
anatman. See BUDDHISM; SUNYATA
Anaxagoras. See LOGOS
Anaximenes. See ELEMENTS
ancestors, veneration of. See AFRICAN RELIGIONS; box at AFRICAN RELIGIONS (New World); ANIMISM; CONFUCIANISM; MILLENARIANISM; MORMONISM; NORTH AMERICAN NATIVE BELIEFS; box at NORTH AMERICAN NATIVE BELIEFS; SOUL AND SPIRIT; SPIRITUALISM
André, Carl. See box at ABSTRACTION
angels. See box at AFRICAN RELIGIONS (modern movements); HIERARCHY OF BEING; GOD, CONCEPTS OF; JUDAISM; KABBALAH; SUBSTANCE; ZOROASTRIANISM
Anglicanism. See box at PROTESTANTISM
Angra Manyu. See ZOROASTRIANISM
anima/animus. See JUNG; ANIMISM
animal magnetism. See PARAPSYCHOLOGY
ANIMAL RIGHTS
animal spirits. See KEYNES
ANIMISM

ANOMIE

Anselm, St. See GOD, ARGUMENTS FOR; SCHOLASTICISM; UNIVERSALS

Anthony, Susan B. See STANTON

ANTHROPIC PRINCIPLE

anthropocentrism. See ANIMAL RIGHTS

ANTHROPOSOPHY

Antichrist. See ESCHATOLOGY

antiessentialism. See RORTY

Antifederalists. See FEDERALISM

antifoundationalism. see RORTY

Anti-Masons. See FREEMASONRY

antimatter. See QUANTUM ELECTRODYNAMICS

anti-Semitism. See ARENDT; box at CRITICAL THEORY; RACE AND RACISM; box at ROMAN CATHOLICISM; ZIONISM

anxiety. See box at CRITICAL THEORY; EXISTENTIALISM; EXPRESSIONISM; FREUD; box at FREUD; GESTALT; HEIDEGGER; HORNEY; KIERKEGAARD; WILL TO POWER

apartheid. See CIVIL DISOBEDIENCE

apatheia. See STOICISM

Apollinaire, Guillaume. See CUBISM; SURREALISM

APOLLONIAN SPIRIT AND DIONYSIAN SPIRIT

APPEARANCE VERSUS REALITY

AQUINAS, THOMAS

archetypes. See IDEAS; JUNG; PLATO

ARCHIMEDES

ARENDT, HANNAH

arete. See SOCRATES; VIRTUE

Arianism. See box at PROTESTANTISM; JEHOVAH'S WITNESSES

aristocracy. See CLASS; CONSERVATISM; JEFFERSON; MIXED REGIME; PLATO; VOLTAIRE; WHIGS AND TORIES

ARISTOTLE

"Aristotle's baptism." See AQUINAS

Aristotle's laws of thought. See box at LOGIC

Armageddon. See ESCHATOLOGY; JEHOVAH'S WITNESSES

arms control. See DETERRENCE; GAME THEORY

Aron, Raymond. See CLAUSEWITZ

Arp, Jean. See SURREALISM

Arrow, Kenneth. See SOCIAL CHOICE

Artemis. See GODDESS WORSHIP

artha. See DHARMA

ARTIFICIAL INTELLIGENCE

Articles of Faith, Thirteen. See MAIMONIDES

Aryans. See FASCISM; RACE AND RACISM

asana. See YOGA

ASCETICISM

Ashkenazi. See box at JUDAISM

Ashtoreth. See GODDESS WORSHIP

assemblage. See DADA; SURREALISM

Assemblies of God. See PENTECOSTALISM

association of ideas. See CONSCIOUSNESS; LOCKE

associationism. See CONSCIOUSNESS; GESTALT

Astarte. See GODDESS WORSHIP

ASTROLOGY

astrology, Chinese. See box at ASTROLOGY

ataraxia. See EPICUREANISM; SKEPTICISM

Athanasius, St. See ORTHODOX CHURCH

Athena. See GODDESS WORSHIP

atman. See HINDUISM; see also KARMA; SOUL AND SPIRIT; SUNYATA

ATOMISM

Attlee, Clement. See WELFARE

Atwood, Margaret. See box at UTOPIANISM

Augsburg Confession. See LUTHER; box at PROTESTANTISM

AUGUSTINE, ST.

Austin, J. L. See ORDINARY LANGUAGE PHILOSOPHY

Austin, John. See POSITIVISM

authenticity. See ALIENATION; EXISTENTIALISM; HEIDEGGER; KIERKEGAARD; SARTRE

authorial intention. See DEATH OF THE AUTHOR; DECONSTRUCTION; HERMENEUTICS; NEW CRITICISM; box at STRUCTURALISM

authoritarianism. See ABSOLUTISM; CAPITALISM; CRITICAL THEORY; box at CRITICAL THEORY; DEWEY; FASCISM; HOBBES; IBN KHALDUN; TOTALITARIANISM

automatic writing. See DADA

automatism. See SURREALISM

Avalokiteshvara. See box at BUDDHISM

avatars. See HINDUISM; box at HINDUISM
    (modern movements)
Averroës. See IBN RUSHD
Avesta. See ZOROASTRIANISM
Avicenna. See IBN SINA
Ayer, Alfred J. See ANALYTIC PHILOSOPHY;
    LOGICAL POSITIVISM; PERCEPTION;
    PHENOMENALISM

Baal Shem Tov. See HASIDISM
Bab, Babism. See BAHA'I
back-to-Africa movement. See GARVEY;
    DU BOIS; RASTAFARIANISM
BACON, FRANCIS
Baconian method. See box at BACON
bad faith. See SARTRE
Bagehot, Walter. See SOCIAL DARWINISM
BAHA'I
Baha'ullah. See BAHA'I
Bakunin, Mikhail. See ANARCHISM
BALANCE OF POWER
balance of terror. See BALANCE OF POWER
balance of trade. See MERCANTILISM
Balfour Declaration. See ZIONISM
Balokole. See box at AFRICAN RELIGIONS
    (modern movements)
Balzac, Honoré de. See REALISM
Bandura, Albert. See SOCIAL LEARNING
    THEORY
baptism. See box at CHRISTIANITY; see also
    box at AFRICAN RELIGIONS (modern
    movements); MORMONISM; box at
    PROTESTANTISM
Baptists. See box at PROTESTANTISM
Barbizon School. See IMPRESSIONISM
Barth, Karl. See box at PROTESTANTISM
Barthes, Roland. See box at
    STRUCTURALISM; see also DEATH OF THE
    AUTHOR; KRISTEVA; SEMIOTICS
base and superstructure, socioeconomic.
    See GRAMSCI; MARX; box at
    STRUCTURALISM
base communities. See LIBERATION
    THEOLOGY
Baselitz, Georg. See EXPRESSIONISM
Basil, St. See ORTHODOX CHURCH
Baudelaire, Charles. See AESTHETICISM;
    SYMBOLISM

BAUDRILLARD, JEAN
Bauhaus. See CONSTRUCTIVISM;
    FUNCTIONALISM
Baumgarten, Alexander. See AESTHETICS
Bayes, Thomas; Bayesian inference. See
    DECISION THEORY; PROBABILITY
Beardsley, Aubrey. See AESTHETICISM
Beardsley, Monroe C. See NEW CRITICISM
BEAUVOIR, SIMONE DE
Beckett, Samuel. See ABSURD
Beckmann, Max. See EXPRESSIONISM
becoming. See BEING AND BECOMING; see
    also ATOMISM; CAUSE; HEGEL;
    NIETZSCHE; WILL TO POWER
Beethoven, Ludwig van. See
    ROMANTICISM
beggar-my-neighbor. See MERCANTILISM
BEHAVIORISM
BEING AND BECOMING
being, hierarchy of. See HIERARCHY OF
    BEING
Bell, Bernard. See DOUBLE CONSCIOUSNESS
Bell, John S. See QUANTUM THEORY
Bellamy, Edward. See GILMAN; quotation
    at SOCIALISM; box at UTOPIANISM
bendera. See GARVEY; RASTAFARIANISM
benefit principle. See TAXATION
Benjamin, Walter. See box at CRITICAL
    THEORY
Bentham, Jeremy. See ANIMAL RIGHTS;
    CONSEQUENTIALISM; LIBERALISM; MILL;
    POSITIVISM; UTILITARIANISM; UTILITY
Berger, Peter L. See SOCIAL
    CONSTRUCTIONISM
Bergson, Henri. See VITALISM
BERKELEY, GEORGE
Berlin, Isaiah. See FREEDOM
Bernstein, Eduard. See LUXEMBURG
Bertalanffy, Ludwig von. See SYSTEMS
    THEORY
Besant, Annie. See THEOSOPHY
best of all possible worlds. See LEIBNIZ;
    VOLTAIRE
Bhagavad-Gita. See HINDUISM
Bhagwan Shri Rajneesh. See box at
    HINDUISM (modern movements)
bhakti. See box at HINDUISM (schools);
    YOGA

Bible. See CHRISTIANITY; CREATIONISM;
DEISM; ESCHATOLOGY; FUNDAMENTALISM;
GNOSTICISM; JEHOVAH'S WITNESSES;
JESUS; JUDAISM; LIBERATION THEOLOGY;
LUTHER; MENDELSSOHN; MODERNISM;
MORMONISM; ORTHODOX CHURCH;
PENTECOSTALISM; PROTESTANTISM; box
at PROTESTANTISM; RASTAFARIANISM;
SPINOZA; STANTON; TEN
COMMANDMENTS; TORAH; TRINITY

BIG BANG THEORY

Bill of Rights. See box at DEMOCRACY;
RIGHTS; STATES' RIGHTS

binary oppositions/constructions. See
DECONSTRUCTION; DUALISM; box at
FEMINISM; INFORMATION THEORY; JUNG;
LOGIC; MERLEAU-PONTY; QUEER THEORY;
STRUCTURALISM; box at STRUCTURALISM;
YIN AND YANG

biogenesis. See SPONTANEOUS GENERATION
AND BIOGENESIS

BIOLOGICAL DETERMINISM

biologism. See BIOLOGICAL DETERMINISM

birth control. See ANARCHISM;
MALTHUSIAN POPULATION THEORY

Bismarck, Otto von. See REALISM; WELFARE

black holes. See RELATIVITY

black magic. See box at AFRICAN
RELIGIONS (New World)

BLACK MUSLIMS

BLACK NATIONALISM

BLACK POWER

black theology. See box at AFRICAN
RELIGIONS (New World); LIBERATION
THEOLOGY

Black Jews. See box at AFRICAN RELIGIONS
(New World)

Black Panthers. See BLACK POWER;
RADICALISM

Blackmun, Harry A. See quotation at
AFFIRMATIVE ACTION

blacklisting. See MCCARTHYISM

Blake, William. See ROMANTICISM;
WOLLSTONECRAFT

Blanshard, Brand. See TRUTH

Blaue Reiter, Der. See EXPRESSIONISM

Blavatsky, Helena Petrovna. See
THEOSOPHY

Block, Herbert. See MCCARTHYISM

Bloomfield, Leonard. See GRAMMAR;
STRUCTURALISM

Blumenbach, Johann Friedrich. See RACE
AND RACISM

Boas, Franz. See DESCRIPTIVISM AND
PRESCRIPTIVISM; RELATIVISM

bodhi. See ENLIGHTENMENT

bodhisattva. See box at BUDDHISM;
NIRVANA

Bodin, Jean. See ABSOLUTISM; SOVEREIGNTY

Boff, Leonard. See LIBERATION THEOLOGY

Bohr, Niels. See QUANTUM THEORY; box
at QUANTUM THEORY; UNCERTAINTY
PRINCIPLE

Bolsheviks. See LENIN; TROTSKY

Boole, George. See LOGIC

Bossuet, Jacques. See ABSOLUTISM

bourgeoisie. See CLASS

Boyle, Robert. See ELEMENTS

bracketing. See PHENOMENOLOGY

Bradbury, Ray. See box at UTOPIANISM

Bradley, F. H. See ABSOLUTE; IDEALISM

Brahe, Tycho. See KEPLER

Brahma. See HINDUISM; ETERNAL
RECURRENCE

brahman. See HINDUISM; see also
ABSOLUTE; GOD, CONCEPTS OF;
PANTHEISM AND PANENTHEISM

Brahmanism. See SIKHISM

Brahmans. See CASTE

Brancusi, Constantin. See box at
ABSTRACTION

Braque, Georges. See CUBISM; FAUVISM

Brecht, Bertolt. See ALIENATION; box at
CRITICAL THEORY

Breton, André. See SURREALISM

Breuer, Josef. See CATHARSIS

brinkmanship. See DETERRENCE

Broglie, Louis Victor de. See WAVE-
PARTICLE DUALITY

Brook Farm. See TRANSCENDENTALISM

Brouwer, L. E. J. See FORMALISM

Brown, John. See DOUGLASS

Browne, Robert. See box at
PROTESTANTISM

Brownmiller, Susan. See box at FEMINISM

Brücke, Die. See EXPRESSIONISM

Brundtland, Gro Harlem. See
SUSTAINABLE DEVELOPMENT
Bryan, William Jennings. See
FUNDAMENTALISM; POPULISM
Buber, Martin. See HASIDISM
Buchanan, James. See PUBLIC CHOICE
Buchanan, Patrick. See ISOLATIONISM
BUDDHA
Buddha nature. See BUDDHA; box at
BUDDHISM
Buddhaghosa. See box at BUDDHISM
BUDDHISM
Buddhist schools. See box at BUDDHISM
Bullough, Edward. See AESTHETICS
Buñuel, Luis. See SURREALISM
bureaucracy. See WEBER; see also ARENDT;
CLASS; PERESTROIKA
Buridan's ass. See box at DECISION
THEORY
BURKE, EDMUND
Bush, George. See McCARTHYISM
Butler, Judith. See box at FEMINISM; see
also QUEER THEORY
Butler, Samuel. See box at UTOPIANISM
Byron, Lord. See ROMANTICISM

cabala. See KABBALAH
calculus. See NEWTON; see also LEIBNIZ
Calhoun, John C. See STATES' RIGHTS
Callicles. See SOPHISTS
Calvin, John. See PROTESTANTISM; box at
PROTESTANTISM
Calvinism. See box at PROTESTANTISM;
PURITANISM
Camp Hill movement. See
ANTHROPOSOPHY
Campanella, Tommasso. See box at
UTOPIANISM
Camus, Albert. See EXISTENTIALISM; see
also quotation at ABSURD
Candomble. See box at AFRICAN
RELIGIONS (New World)
Cantor, Georg. See SET THEORY
capital. See CAPITALISM; see also
COMMUNISM; DIMINISHING RETURNS;
LUXEMBURG; MARX; SMITH; SUPPLY-SIDE
ECONOMICS
CAPITALISM

cardinality. See SET THEORY
cargo cults. See MILLENARIANISM
Carlyle, Thomas. See EMERSON; "GREAT
MAN" THEORY
Carmichael, Stokely. See BLACK
NATIONALISM; BLACK POWER
Carnap, Rudolf. See LOGICAL POSITIVISM;
SEMIOTICS
Carnegie, Andrew. See WASHINGTON
CASTE
Castelvetro, Lodovico. See UNITIES
castration anxiety. See box at FREUD
CATASTROPHISM AND UNIFORMITARIANISM
categorical imperative. See KANT; see also
ANIMAL RIGHTS; ETHICS; GOLDEN RULE;
RAWLS
categories, Aristotelian. See ARISTOTLE;
CAUSE; LOGIC
categories of the understanding. See
KANT; box at KANT
CATHARSIS
Catherine the Great. See ABSOLUTISM
Catholicism. See ROMAN CATHOLICISM
CAUSE
cause and effect. See CAUSE; see also
DETERMINISM; HOBBES; HUME; KARMA;
UNCERTAINTY PRINCIPLE
CENTRAL DOGMA
central economic planning. See
CAPITALISM; MARKET; PERESTROIKA;
SOCIALISM
centration. See PIAGET
Césaire, Aimé. See NÉGRITUDE
Cézanne, Paul. See CUBISM; IMPRESSIONISM
ch'i. See CONFUCIANISM; TAOISM
Chagall, Marc. See SURREALISM
chain of being. See HIERARCHY OF BEING
chance. See PROBABILITY
change. See ARISTOTLE; ATOMISM; BEING
AND BECOMING; CAUSE; CONFUCIANISM;
DIALECTIC; HEGEL; PLATO; YIN AND
YANG
channeling. See SPIRITUALISM
CHAOS THEORY
charismatic movement. See
PENTECOSTALISM
charity. See CHRISTIANITY; JESUS; VIRTUE
Charles I. See PURITANISM

Charvakas. See MATERIALISM

Chateaubriand, François Auguste René de. See CONSERVATISM

checks and balances. See DEMOCRACY; FEDERALISM; LOCKE; SEPARATION OF POWERS

Chicago School. See MONETARISM

chiliasm. See MILLENARIANISM

Chinese astrology. See box at ASTROLOGY

Chirico, Giorgio de. See SURREALISM

CHOMSKY, NOAM

chora. See KRISTEVA

"chosen people." See box at AFRICAN RELIGIONS (New World); GARVEY; JUDAISM; RASTAFARIANISM

Christ. See JESUS

Christian democracy. See box at DEMOCRACY

Christian sacraments. See box at CHRISTIANITY

CHRISTIAN SCIENCE

CHRISTIANITY

chronopolitics. See STATE

Chrysippus. See STOICISM

Chrysostom, St. John. See ORTHODOX CHURCH

Chu Hsi. See CONFUCIANISM

Chuang Tzu. See TAOISM

Church of Christ, Scientist. See CHRISTIAN SCIENCE

Church of England. See box at PROTESTANTISM

Church of God in Christ. See PENTECOSTALISM

Church of Jesus Christ of Latter-Day Saints. See MORMONISM

Church of Jesus Christ on Earth. See box at AFRICAN RELIGIONS (modern movements)

CIVIL DISOBEDIENCE

civil law. See COMMON LAW

civil liberties. See RIGHTS

civil rights. See RIGHTS; see also BLACK NATIONALISM; BLACK POWER; DEMOCRACY; DOUGLASS; FEMINISM; box at FEMINISM; GARVEY; MENDELSSOHN; RACE AND RACISM

cladistics. See HIERARCHY OF BEING

clairvoyance. See PARAPSYCHOLOGY

Clark, William. See JEFFERSON

Clarke, Arthur C. See box at UTOPIANISM

CLASS

classes. See RUSSELL; box at RUSSELL; SET THEORY; UNIVERSALS

classical economics. See SMITH; see also KEYNES; MARX; box at SUPPLY AND DEMAND; UTILITY

classical ideal. See APOLLONIAN SPIRIT AND DIONYSIAN SPIRIT; CLASSICISM

CLASSICISM

CLAUSEWITZ, KARL

Clausius, Rudolf Julius Emmanuel. See ENTROPY

Clay, Henry. See WHIGS AND TORIES

coding. See INFORMATION THEORY

COGNITIVE DISSONANCE

cognitive ethology. See COGNITIVE PSYCHOLOGY

COGNITIVE PSYCHOLOGY

cognitive schema. See PIAGET

cognitive science. See COGNITIVE PSYCHOLOGY

coherence theory. See TRUTH

Colbert, Jean-Baptiste. See MERCANTILISM

Cold War. See BALANCE OF POWER; CLAUSEWITZ; DETERRENCE; INTERNATIONALISM; McCARTHYISM; MONROE DOCTRINE

Coleridge, Samuel Taylor. See AESTHETICS; EMERSON; ROMANTICISM

collective unconscious. See JUNG; see also box at ABSTRACTION; GODDESS WORSHIP; PARAPSYCHOLOGY; PSYCHOANALYSIS; TRANSPERSONAL PSYCHOLOGY

collectivism. See ANARCHISM; INDIVIDUALISM; PLURALISM

colonialism. See IMPERIALISM AND COLONIALISM

color-field painting. See box at ABSTRACTION

command economy. See MARKET

Commandments, Ten. See TEN COMMANDMENTS

commodity fetishism. See LUKÁCS

common consent, argument from. See GOD, ARGUMENTS FOR

COMMON LAW

communication theory. See CYBERNETICS

Communion. See box at CHRISTIANITY; see also LUTHER; MIND/BODY PROBLEM; ORTHODOX CHURCH; ROMAN CATHOLICISM

COMMUNISM

communitarianism. See UTOPIANISM

community. See AFRICAN RELIGIONS; boxes at AFRICAN RELIGIONS; BUDDHISM; COMMUNISM; FASCISM; box at FEMINISM; GANDHI; GODDESS WORSHIP; HASIDISM; INTERNATIONALISM; ISLAM; box at JUDAISM; MUHAMMAD; NATIONALISM; NEW AGE; PAGANISM; SHAMANISM; SHINTO; SIKHISM; TRANSCENDENTALISM; UTOPIANISM

comparative advantage. See ADVANTAGE

COMPETITION

complexes. See FREUD; box at FREUD; WILL TO POWER

complexity. See ARTIFICIAL INTELLIGENCE; ATOMISM; CYBERNETICS; ENTROPY; EVOLUTION; FRACTALS; IDEAS; LAMARCKISM; PROGRESS; SET THEORY

COMTE, AUGUSTE

conatus. See SPINOZA

conceptual art. See box at ABSTRACTION

conceptualism. See NOMINALISM; UNIVERSALS

concrete art. See box at ABSTRACTION

conditioned response. See CONDITIONING

CONDITIONING, CLASSICAL AND OPERANT

conditions, necessary and sufficient. See CAUSE

Condorcet, Marquis de. See PROGRESS

confederation, confederacy. See FEDERALISM; INTERNATIONALISM; STATES' RIGHTS

conformism. See ALIENATION; box at CRITICAL THEORY; EXISTENTIALISM; KIERKEGAARD; TOCQUEVILLE

CONFUCIANISM

Confucius. See CONFUCIANISM; see also MAO; TAOISM

Congregationalism. See box at PROTESTANTISM

conjuring. See box at AFRICAN RELIGIONS (New World)

connectionism. See INFORMATION THEORY

conscientious objection. See NONVIOLENCE; THOREAU

conscientizacao. See FREIRE

CONSCIOUSNESS

consciousness raising. See FEMINISM

CONSEQUENTIALISM

CONSERVATION AND SYMMETRY, PRINCIPLES OF

conservation of energy. See CONSERVATION AND SYMMETRY; see also THERMODYNAMICS

CONSERVATISM

Conservative Judaism. See box at JUDAISM

conspicuous consumption. See box at CLASS

constitution, political. See BURKE; COMMON LAW; DEMOCRACY; EQUALITY; FEDERALISM; LOCKE; MIXED REGIME; RIGHTS; SEPARATION OF POWERS; STATES' RIGHTS; WHIGS AND TORIES

constitutional monarchy. See LOCKE; MIXED REGIME; VOLTAIRE; WHIGS AND TORIES

constructionism. See SOCIAL CONSTRUCTIONISM

CONSTRUCTIVISM

consubstantiation. See box at CHRISTIANITY

consumption. See UTILITY; see also KEYNES; MARKET; SUPPLY AND DEMAND; TAXATION; UNINTENDED CONSEQUENCES

contemplation. See BUDDHISM; CONSCIOUSNESS; MYSTICISM; YOGA

continental drift. See CATASTROPHISM AND UNIFORMITARIANISM

contingent probabilities. See PROBABILITY

contradictions of capitalism. See DIALECTIC; MARX

control theory. See CYBERNETICS

Convince. See box at AFRICAN RELIGIONS (New World)
Cooper, David. See FOUCAULT
COPERNICUS, NICOLAUS
Corneille, Pierre. See UNITIES
Cornell, Joseph. See SURREALISM
corporate state. See FASCISM
correct description. See TRUTH
correspondence principle. See UNCERTAINTY PRINCIPLE
cosmology. See AFRICAN RELIGIONS; ANTHROPIC PRINCIPLE; ARISTOTLE; BIG BANG; CREATIONISM; DESCARTES; ELEMENTS; EVOLUTION; EXPANDING UNIVERSE; GOD, ARGUMENTS FOR; box at HINDUISM (schools); NORTH AMERICAN NATIVE BELIEFS; RELATIVITY; ZOROASTRIANISM
cosmopolitanism. See INTERNATIONALISM; see also ENLIGHTENMENT; FREEMASONRY; KANT; NONVIOLENCE; VOLTAIRE
Courbet, Gustave. See IMPRESSIONISM; REALISM
covenant, divine. See JUDAISM; TEN COMMANDMENTS; ZIONISM
Cranmer, Thomas. See box at PROTESTANTISM
Crates. See CYNICISM
creation. See AFRICAN RELIGIONS; ANTHROPIC PRINCIPLE; BIG BANG; CREATIONISM; DUALISM; GNOSTICISM; GOD, CONCEPTS OF; GOD, ARGUMENTS FOR; JUDAISM; KABBALAH; LOGOS; NEOPLATONISM; NORTH AMERICAN NATIVE BELIEFS; TELEOLOGY
CREATIONISM
Crick, Harry Compton. See CENTRAL DOGMA
crisis theology. See box at PROTESTANTISM
critical period. See LANGUAGE ACQUISITION
CRITICAL THEORY
Cromwell, Oliver. See PURITANISM
crowding-out effect. See MONETARISM
crucial experiment. See box at BACON
CUBISM
cult of the offensive. See CLAUSEWITZ
cultural imperialism. See IMPERIALISM

CULTURAL MATERIALISM
cultural relativism. See RELATIVISM; see also DETERMINISM; ETHNOCENTRISM
culture, mass/popular. See BAUDRILLARD; CRITICAL THEORY; ORTEGA Y GASSET; POSTMODERNISM; box at STRUCTURALISM
cummings, e. e. See quotation at IDENTITY
Cybele. See GODDESS WORSHIP
CYBERNETICS
CYNICISM

DADA
daevas. See ZOROASTRIANISM
Dalai Lama. See box at BUDDHISM
Dalí, Salvador. See SURREALISM
Dalton, John. See ATOMISM
Daly, Mary. See box at FEMINISM; GODDESS WORSHIP
Damas, Léon. See NÉGRITUDE
darshana. See box at HINDUISM (schools)
DARWIN, CHARLES
Dasein. See HEIDEGGER
David. See ZIONISM
Davis, Angela. See box at FEMINISM
de Kooning, Willem. See box at ABSTRACTION
DEATH OF THE AUTHOR
Decalogue. See TEN COMMANDMENTS
DECISION THEORY
Declaration of Independence. See JEFFERSON; LOCKE; PAINE; NATURAL LAW; RADICALISM; STANTON
Declaration of Sentiments. See STANTON
Declaration of the Rights of Man and of the Citizen. See RIGHTS
DECONSTRUCTION
DEDUCTION AND INDUCTION
defense mechanisms. See FREUD; PSYCHOANALYSIS
definite descriptions, theory of. See RUSSELL
Degas, Edgar. See IMPRESSIONISM
DEISM
Delacroix, Eugène. See ROMANTICISM

Deleuze, Gilles. See NIETZSCHE
demand. See SUPPLY AND DEMAND; see also
    KEYNES
Demiurge. See GNOSTICISM
DEMOCRACY
democratic centralism. See COMMUNISM;
    LENIN
Democritus. See ATOMISM; box at LOCKE
demons. See box at AFRICAN RELIGIONS
    (New World); ESCHATOLOGY;
    SHAMANISM; ZOROASTRIANISM
deontology. See CONSEQUENTIALISM
Derain, André. See FAUVISM
Derrida, Jacques. See DECONSTRUCTION;
    see also DUALISM; POSTSTRUCTURALISM
DESCARTES, RENÉ
DESCRIPTIVISM AND PRESCRIPTIVISM
DETERMINISM
DETERRENCE
development, sustainable. See
    SUSTAINABLE DEVELOPMENT
Devi. See GODDESS WORSHIP; HINDUISM
devils; the Devil (see demons; Satan)
DEWEY, JOHN
dharana. See YOGA
DHARMA
dhyana. See YOGA
DIALECTIC
DIALECTICAL MATERIALISM
dianetics. See SCIENTOLOGY
diaspora. See JUDAISM; NÉGRITUDE
Dicke, G. H. See ANTHROPIC PRINCIPLE
Diderot, Denis. See ENLIGHTENMENT
Digambara. See JAINISM
Diggers. See COMMUNISM; RADICALISM
Dilthey, Wilhelm. See HERMENEUTICS;
    HISTORICISM; SOUL AND SPIRIT
DIMINISHING RETURNS, LAW OF
Diogenes. See CYNICISM
Dionysian spirit. See APOLLONIAN SPIRIT
    AND DIONYSIAN SPIRIT
Dirac, Paul Adrien Maurice. See
    QUANTUM ELECTRODYNAMICS
discourse. See FOUCAULT; see also box at
    CRITICAL THEORY; DIALECTIC; ETHICS
divination. See box at AFRICAN RELIGIONS
    (New World); ASTROLOGY; box at

ASTROLOGY; CONFUCIANISM; SHAMANISM;
    TAOISM; WITCHCRAFT
divine right of kings. See ABSOLUTISM
Divine Light Mission. See box at
    HINDUISM (modern movements)
division of labor. See ANOMIE; SMITH
divisionism. See IMPRESSIONISM
Dixiecrats. See STATES' RIGHTS
Djilas, Milovan. See CLASS
DNA. See CENTRAL DOGMA
Doesburg, Theo van. See box at
    ABSTRACTION
Dogen. See box at BUDDHISM
Dollard, John. See SOCIAL LEARNING
    THEORY
dominant ideology thesis. See IDEOLOGY
dominant strategy. See box at GAME
    THEORY
Dongen, Kees van. See FAUVISM
double aspect theory. See MIND/BODY
    PROBLEM; MONISM; SPINOZA
DOUBLE CONSCIOUSNESS
double effect doctrine. See
    CONSEQUENTIALISM
double truth doctrine. See AQUINAS; IBN
    RUSHD
doubt. See DESCARTES; ENLIGHTENMENT;
    EPISTEMOLOGY
DOUGLASS, FREDERICK
dreams. See FREUD; JUNG; KRISTEVA;
    PSYCHOANALYSIS; SURREALISM;
    SYMBOLISM; UNCONSCIOUS
Driesch, Hans. See VITALISM
DU BOIS, W. E. B.
DUALISM
Duchamp, Marcel. See DADA; SURREALISM
Dufy, Raoul. See FAUVISM
Dujardin, Edouard. See STREAM OF
    CONSCIOUSNESS
Dukakis, Michael. See MCCARTHYISM
Duns Scotus, John. See SCHOLASTICISM
Durga. See GODDESS WORSHIP
Durkheim, Émile. See ANOMIE; see also
    ALIENATION; FUNCTIONALISM; POSITIVISM;
    TOTEMISM
Durrenmatt, Friedrich. See quotation at
    HUMANISM

Dworkin, Andrea. See box at FEMINISM
dynamism. See MECHANISM
dystopia. See UTOPIANISM

Earth Mother. See GODDESS WORSHIP;
    NORTH AMERICAN NATIVE BELIEFS;
    PAGANISM
Eastern Orthodox Church. See
    ORTHODOX CHURCH
ecology. See FEMINISM; GAIA; GLOBAL
    WARMING; SUSTAINABLE DEVELOPMENT
economies of scale. See DIMINISHING
    RETURNS
economy, principle of. See box at
    NOMINALISM
ecumenism. See box at ROMAN
    CATHOLICISM
Eddy, Mary Baker. See CHRISTIAN SCIENCE
educational theory. See AQUINAS; DEWEY;
    FREIRE; PIAGET; PLATO; ROUSSEAU;
    SCHOLASTICISM; SOCIAL
    CONSTRUCTIONISM; WASHINGTON;
    WOLLSTONECRAFT
effective demand. See KEYNES
egalitariansim. See EQUALITY
ego. See FREUD; PSYCHOANALYSIS; see also
    PESSIMISM; PIAGET; TRANSPERSONAL
    PSYCHOLOGY
egocentrism. See PIAGET
Eichmann, Adolf. See ARENDT
Eightfold Path. See BUDDHA; BUDDHISM;
    MEAN
EINSTEIN, ALBERT
Eisai. See box at BUDDHISM
élan vital. See VITALISM
Eldridge, Niles. See PUNCTUATED
    EQUILIBRIUM
Eleatic School. See ZENO'S PARADOXES
Electra complex. See box at FREUD
electromagnetism. See MAXWELL;
    STANDARD MODEL
electroweak theory. See STANDARD MODEL
ELEMENTS, THE FOUR
Eliot, T. S. See NEW CRITICISM
ELITE THEORY
Elizabeth I. See box at PROTESTANTISM
Éluard, Paul. See SURREALISM
emergent properties. See REDUCTIONISM

emergent traits. See EVOLUTION
EMERSON, RALPH WALDO
Empedocles. See ELEMENTS
EMPIRICISM
emptiness. See SUNYATA
en-soi, pour-soi. See SARTRE
Engels, Friedrich. See DIALECTICAL
    MATERIALISM; MARXISM; see also CLASS;
    COMMUNISM; HEGEL; IDEOLOGY; MARX
ENLIGHTENMENT
entelechy. See ARISTOTLE; LEIBNIZ; VITALISM
ENTROPY
environment, environmentalism. See
    SUSTAINABLE DEVELOPMENT; GAIA;
    GLOBAL WARMING; see also ANIMAL
    RIGHTS; STATE; STATES' RIGHTS
epic theater. See ALIENATION
Epictetus. See STOICISM
EPICUREANISM
Epicurus. See EPICUREANISM
Episcopalianism. See box at
    PROTESTANTISM
episteme. See FOUCAULT
EPISTEMOLOGY
epoché. See PHENOMENOLOGY; SKEPTICISM
EQUALITY
equilibrium (economics). See MARKET;
    MONETARISM; SUPPLY AND DEMAND; box
    at SUPPLY AND DEMAND
equilibrium (physics). See ARCHIMEDES;
    ENTROPY; THERMODYNAMICS
equity. See COMMON LAW
equivalence principle. See RELATIVITY
Erasmus, Desiderius. See HUMANISM
ERIKSON, ERIK
Ernst, Max. See DADA; SURREALISM
Eros. See FREUD
ESCHATOLOGY
ESP. See PARAPSYCHOLOGY
ESSENCE
essentialism. See ESSENCE; FEMINISM;
    NÉGRITUDE; QUEER THEORY; RORTY
ETERNAL RECURRENCE
ether. See ARISTOTLE; DESCARTES;
    ELEMENTS; FIELD THEORY
ETHICS
ethnic cleansing. See NATIONALISM
ETHNOCENTRISM

Eucharist. See box at CHRISTIANITY; see also LUTHER; ORTHODOX CHURCH; ROMAN CATHOLICISM
EUCLID
eugenics. See SOCIAL DARWINISM
Eurocentrism. See ETHNOCENTRISM; POSTCOLONIAL THEORY
Eurocommunism. See COMMUNISM; MARXISM
eurythmy. See ANTHROPOSOPHY
evangelism. See ADVENTISM; box at AFRICAN RELIGIONS (modern movements); CHRISTIANITY; CHRISTIAN SCIENCE; JEHOVAH'S WITNESSES; JESUS; PENTECOSTALISM; box at PROTESTANTISM
evil. See box at PROTESTANTISM; ARENDT; CHRISTIANITY; CONFUCIANISM; DUALISM; ESCHATOLOGY; ETHICS; GANDHI; GNOSTICISM; JUST WAR; KABBALAH; KARMA; LEIBNIZ; NIETZSCHE; NORTH AMERICAN NATIVE BELIEFS; PESSIMISM; SHAMANISM; SOCRATES; WITCHCRAFT; ZOROASTRIANISM
EVOLUTION
excluded middle, law of. See box at LOGIC; see also KANT; LOGIC
exclusion principle. See QUANTUM THEORY
existent. See DEDUCTION AND INDUCTION
EXISTENTIALISM
EXPANDING UNIVERSE
expansionism. See ARENDT; IMPERIALISM AND COLONIALISM; MACHIAVELLI; MANIFEST DESTINY
experience. See A PRIORI/A POSTERIORI; BERKELEY, GEORGE; COGNITIVE PSYCHOLOGY; CONSCIOUSNESS; DEDUCTION AND INDUCTION; DEWEY; EMPIRICISM; EPICUREANISM; EPISTEMOLOGY; FIELD THEORY; GESTALT; HUMANISM; JUNG; KABBALAH; KANT; LOCKE; MERLEAU-PONTY; MYSTICISM; NATURALISM; OBJECTIVISM AND SUBJECTIVISM; PERCEPTION; PHENOMENALISM; PHENOMENOLOGY; PIAGET; SOCIAL CONSTRUCTIONISM; SOCIAL LEARNING THEORY; SOLIPSISM;

STREAM OF CONSCIOUSNESS; THEOSOPHY; TRANSPERSONAL PSYCHOLOGY
experimentalism. See DEWEY; MILL
EXPRESSIONISM
externalities. See UNINTENDED CONSEQUENCES
extrasensory perception. See PARAPSYCHOLOGY
extroversion and introversion. See JUNG

Fairbairn, W. R. D. See OBJECT RELATIONS THEORY
faith. See AQUINAS; DEISM; FUNDAMENTALISM; IBN RUSHD; box at ISLAM (Five Pillars); JAMES; JEFFERSON; KIERKEGAARD; LUTHER; MAIMONIDES; PROTESTANTISM; RATIONALISM; SCHOLASTICISM; VIRTUE
faith healing. See box at AFRICAN RELIGIONS (New World); CHRISTIAN SCIENCE; PENTECOSTALISM; SHINTO; TAOISM
fallacies, intentional and affective. See NEW CRITICISM
false consciousness. See IDEOLOGY; LUKÁCS
falsifiability (falsification). See VERIFIABILITY AND FALSIFIABILITY
FANON, FRANTZ
Faraday, Michael. See FIELD THEORY; MAXWELL
Fard, Wallace. See BLACK MUSLIMS
Farrakhan, Louis. See BLACK MUSLIMS
FASCISM
fate. See PREDESTINATION; STOICISM
Faulkner, William. See STREAM OF CONSCIOUSNESS
FAUVISM
FEDERALISM
feedback. See CYBERNETICS
FEMINISM
Fermat, Pierre de. See PASCAL; PROBABILITY
Festinger, Leon. See COGNITIVE DISSONANCE
Feuerbach, Ludwig. See ALIENATION; HEGEL; MARX

Fichte, Johann Gottlieb. See
    ROMANTICISM
FIELD THEORY
Filioque clause. See TRINITY
final cause. See ARISTOTLE; CAUSE; GOD,
    ARGUMENTS FOR; MAIMONIDES; TELEOLOGY
final vocabularies. See RORTY
fire. See ELEMENTS; LOGOS; STOICISM;
    ZOROASTRIANISM
first cause. See GOD, ARGUMENTS FOR; see
    also ARISTOTLE; HUME; IBN RUSHD; IBN
    SINA; METAPHYSICS
first principles. See METAPHYSICS;
    NATURALISM
Five Pillars of Islam. See box at ISLAM
fixation. See box at FREUD
flat tax. See TAXATION
force. See ARCHIMEDES; CHAOS THEORY;
    EINSTEIN; FIELD THEORY; KEPLER;
    MAXWELL; MECHANISM; QUANTUM
    ELECTRODYNAMICS; RELATIVITY;
    STANDARD MODEL
forces, fundamental. See STANDARD
    MODEL; see also FIELD THEORY
formal language. See LOGIC
FORMALISM
forms. See ARISTOTLE; IDEAS; PERCEPTION;
    PLATO
Formula of Concord. See LUTHER; box at
    PROTESTANTISM
FOUCAULT, MICHEL
Four Noble Truths. See BUDDHA;
    BUDDHISM
Fourier, Charles. See UTOPIANISM
Fox, Charles. See RADICALISM
Fox, George. See box at PROTESTANTISM
Fox, Kate. See SPIRITUALISM
FRACTALS
Fraenkl, Abraham. See SET THEORY
Franco, Francisco. See FASCISM
Frankenthaler, Helen. See box at
    ABSTRACTION
Frankfurt School. See CRITICAL THEORY
Franklin, Benjamin. See DEISM;
    ENLIGHTENMENT; FREEMASONRY
Frazer, James G. See TOTEMISM
Frederick the Great. See ABSOLUTISM;
    VOLTAIRE

free association. See CATHARSIS;
    PSYCHOANALYSIS; STREAM OF
    CONSCIOUSNESS; SURREALISM; SYMBOLISM
free enterprise. See CAPITALISM;
    INDIVIDUALISM; MARKET; SOCIALISM
free market. See MARKET; see also
    CAPITALISM; COMPETITION; KEYNES;
    LAISSEZ-FAIRE; LIBERALISM;
    LIBERTARIANISM; MANIFEST DESTINY;
    MILL; MONETARISM; PERESTROIKA; PUBLIC
    CHOICE; RAWLS; SMITH; SOCIALISM;
    SUPPLY AND DEMAND; UNINTENDED
    CONSEQUENCES
free silver. See POPULISM
FREE TRADE AND PROTECTIONISM
free will. See FREEDOM; see also
    DETERMINISM; box at ISLAM (Sunnis
    and Shi'ites); KANT; PREDESTINATION;
    ROUSSEAU; ZOROASTRIANISM
FREEDOM
freedom of conscience/thought/
    expression. See FREEDOM; see also
    BAHA'I; EXISTENTIALISM; HOBBES;
    LIBERALISM; MENDELSSOHN; MILL;
    PERESTROIKA; box at PROTESTANTISM;
    RIGHTS
FREEMASONRY
Frege, Gottlob. See FORMALISM; LOGIC;
    MEANING; RUSSELL; SET THEORY
FREIRE, PAULO
Freud, Anna. See ERIKSON
FREUD, SIGMUND
Friedan, Betty. See box at FEMINISM
Friedman, Milton. See MONETARISM
Friends (Quakers). See box at
    PROTESTANTISM
Fromm, Erich. See box at CRITICAL
    THEORY; FREEDOM; PSYCHOANALYSIS
Fuller, Margaret. See TRANSCENDENTALISM
functional psychology. See
    FUNCTIONALISM
FUNCTIONALISM
fundamental uncertainty. See KEYNES
FUNDAMENTALISM

Gabo, Naum. See CONSTRUCTIVISM
Gadamer, Hans-Georg. See
    HERMENEUTICS

Gage, Matilda Joslyn. See STANTON
GAIA HYPOTHESIS
Galen. See HIPPOCRATES
GALILEO GALILEI
GAME THEORY
Gamow, George. See BIG BANG
GANDHI, MOHANDAS. See quotation at
  CIVIL DISOBEDIENCE
Ganioda'yo. See NORTH AMERICAN NATIVE
  BELIEFS
Garrison, William Lloyd. See DOUGLASS
GARVEY, MARCUS
Gathas. See ZOROASTRIANISM
Gauguin, Paul. See SYMBOLISM
Gautier, Théophile. See AESTHETICISM
gays and lesbians (see homosexuality)
Gemara. See TORAH; JUDAISM
gender. See FEMINISM; box at FEMINISM;
  QUEER THEORY; see also AFFIRMATIVE
  ACTION; BIOLOGICAL DETERMINISM;
  DESCRIPTIVISM AND PRESCRIPTIVISM;
  GILMAN; KRISTEVA; MILLETT; OBJECT
  RELATIONS; SOCIAL LEARNING THEORY;
  box at STRUCTURALISM
genealogy. See NIETZSCHE
general will. See ROUSSEAU; see also
  EQUALITY; REPUBLICANISM; SOCIAL
  CONTRACT
genetics. See BIOLOGICAL DETERMINISM;
  CENTRAL DOGMA; EVOLUTION;
  LAMARCKISM; PIAGET; RACE AND RACISM;
  SOCIAL DARWINISM
genital stage. See box at FREUD
Gentile, Giovanni. See FASCISM
geometric abstraction. See box at
  ABSTRACTION
Georges Rouault. See FAUVISM
Géricault, Théodore. See ROMANTICISM
germ plasm theory. See LAMARCKISM
GESTALT
Ghost Dance. See box at NORTH
  AMERICAN NATIVE BELIEFS
Giacometti, Alberto. See SURREALISM
Gilbert, W. S. See AESTHETICISM
Gilligan, Carol. See box at FEMINISM
GILMAN, CHARLOTTE PERKINS
glasnost. See PERESTROIKA
GLOBAL WARMING

globalism. See INTERNATIONALISM
glossolalia. See PENTECOSTALISM
GNOSTICISM
Gobind Singh. See SIKHISM
Gobineau, Joseph Arthur de. See RACE
  AND RACISM
GOD, ARGUMENTS FOR THE EXISTENCE OF
GOD, CONCEPTS OF
GODDESS WORSHIP
Gödel, Kurt. See FORMALISM; LOGIC;
  LOGICAL POSITIVISM; TRUTH
Godwin, William. See WOLLSTONECRAFT;
  RADICALISM
Goethe, Johann Wolfgang von. See
  ROMANTICISM; STURM UND DRANG
Gog. See ESCHATOLOGY
Gogh, Vincent van. See EXPRESSIONISM;
  SYMBOLISM
golden age. See MILLENARIANISM; PROGRESS
Golden Mean. See MEAN
GOLDEN RULE
Goldman, Emma. See ANARCHISM
good and evil. See DUALISM; ESCHATOLOGY;
  ETHICS; GNOSTICISM; KARMA; NIETZSCHE;
  ZOROASTRIANISM
Gorbachev, Mikhail. See PERESTROIKA
Gorgias. See SOPHISTS
Gorky, Maxim. See SOCIALIST REALISM
Gould, Stephen J. See PUNCTUATED
  EQUILIBRIUM
grace. See CHRISTIANITY; box at
  CHRISTIANITY; IDEAS; LUTHER; PASCAL;
  PREDESTINATION; PROTESTANTISM; box at
  PROTESTANTISM; PURITANISM; VIRTUE
GRAMMAR, THEORIES OF
GRAMSCI, ANTONIO
grand narrative. See POSTMODERNISM
Grand Unified Theory. See FIELD THEORY;
  STANDARD MODEL
Granth. See SIKHISM
gravity. See NEWTON; RELATIVITY; see also
  ANTHROPIC PRINCIPLE; COPERNICUS;
  DESCRIPTIVISM AND PRESCRIPTIVISM;
  EINSTEIN; FIELD THEORY; STANDARD
  MODEL; VERIFIABILITY AND FALSIFIABILITY
great chain of being. See HIERARCHY OF
  BEING
"GREAT MAN" THEORY OF HISTORY

Great Mother. See GNOSTICISM; GODDESS WORSHIP

Great Spirit. See NORTH AMERICAN NATIVE BELIEFS

Great Year. See ETERNAL RECURRENCE

Greco, El. See EXPRESSIONISM

Greenberg, Clement. See box at ABSTRACTION

Greer, Germaine. See box at FEMINISM

Gris, Juan. See CUBISM

Grosz, Georg. See EXPRESSIONISM

Grotius, Hugo. See JUST WAR; NATURAL LAW; SOVEREIGNTY

Guicciardini, Francesco. See BALANCE OF POWER

guru. See HINDUISM; box at HINDUISM (modern movements); SIKHISM; TANTRISM

Guru Granth Sahib. See SIKHISM

Gutiérrez, Gustavo. See LIBERATION THEOLOGY

Habermas, Jürgen. See box at CRITICAL THEORY; see also ETHICS; POSTMODERNISM

Haile Selassie. See RASTAFARIANISM

hajj. See box at ISLAM (Five Pillars)

Halakhah. See JUDAISM

Hamilton, Alexander. See FEDERALISM

Handsome Lake. See NORTH AMERICAN NATIVE BELIEFS

hard-edge painting. See box at ABSTRACTION

Harijan. See CASTE; GANDHI

Harrington, James. See REPUBLICANISM

Harris, Marvin. See CULTURAL MATERIALISM

Harris, William Wade. See box at AFRICAN RELIGIONS (modern movements)

Harrison, William Henry. See WHIGS AND TORIES

Hart, Herbert L. A. See POSITIVISM

Hartshorne, Charles. See PROCESS PHILOSOPHY/THEOLOGY

Harvey, William. See HIPPOCRATES; SCIENTIFIC METHOD

HASIDISM

Haskalah. See HASIDISM; MENDELSSOHN

Hawken, Paul. See SUSTAINABLE DEVELOPMENT

Hawking, Stephen W. See quotation at UNCERTAINTY PRINCIPLE

Hayek, Friedrich von. See LIBERTARIANISM

Healthy-Happy-Holy Organization. See SIKHISM

heaven, paradise. See AFRICAN RELIGIONS; box at BUDDHISM; CONFUCIANISM; ESCHATOLOGY; ISLAM; KABBALAH; MORMONISM; ROMAN CATHOLICISM; SOUL AND SPIRIT; ZOROASTRIANISM

hedonism. See EPICUREANISM

HEGEL, GEORG WILHELM FRIEDRICH

hegemony. See GRAMSCI

HEIDEGGER, MARTIN

Heisenberg, Werner. See UNCERTAINTY PRINCIPLE; see also QUANTUM THEORY

hell. See ESCHATOLOGY; ISLAM; SOUL AND SPIRIT

Helmholtz, Hermann von. See ENTROPY

Henry, Patrick. See FEDERALISM

Henry VIII. See box at PROTESTANTISM

Heraclitus. See ELEMENTS; ETERNAL RECURRENCE; LOGOS

Herbert, Edward, Baron of Cherbury. See DEISM; NATURAL THEOLOGY

Herder, Johann Gottfried. See STURM UND DRANG

heresy. See BAHA'I; GNOSTICISM; MODERNISM; PASCAL; box at PROTESTANTISM

HERMENEUTICS

Hervé, Auguste. See EXPRESSIONISM

Herzl, Theodor. See ZIONISM

Hestia. See GODDESS WORSHIP

heterosexuality. See FEMINISM; box at FEMINISM; MILLETT; QUEER THEORY

hidden variables. See QUANTUM THEORY; see also HIERARCHY OF BEING; PARAPSYCHOLOGY

HIERARCHY OF BEING

hijra. See ISLAM; MUHAMMAD

Hilbert, David. See FORMALISM

Hillel. See GOLDEN RULE

Hilton, James. See box at UTOPIANISM

Hindu movements in the West. See box at HINDUISM

Hindu schools of thought. See box at HINDUISM

HINDUISM

HIPPOCRATES

historical materialism. See DIALECTICAL MATERIALISM; see also DETERMINISM; IDEOLOGY; MARX; MATERIALISM

HISTORICISM (historism)

Hitler, Adolf. See FASCISM

HOBBES, THOMAS

Hobson, J. A. See IMPERIALISM

Holiness movement. See PENTECOSTALISM

HOLISM

Holmes, Oliver Wendell. See COMMON LAW

Holocaust. See HASIDISM; NONVIOLENCE; TROTSKY; ZIONISM

holy war. See JUST WAR

Holy Spirit. See TRINITY; see also ADVENTISM; CHRISTIANITY; ORTHODOX CHURCH; PENTECOSTALISM; ROMAN CATHOLICISM; SOUL AND SPIRIT

homosexuality. See QUEER THEORY; see also AFFIRMATIVE ACTION; FEMINISM; box at FEMINISM; FUNDAMENTALISM; MILLETT

hoodoo. See box at AFRICAN RELIGIONS (New World)

hooks, bell. See box at FEMINISM

Hoover, Herbert. See INDIVIDUALISM

hope. See VIRTUE

Horkheimer, Max. See CRITICAL THEORY

HORNEY, KAREN

horoscope. See ASTROLOGY

Hoyle, Fred. See ANTHROPIC PRINCIPLE

Hsün Tzu. See CONFUCIANISM

Hubbard, L. Ron. See SCIENTOLOGY

Hubble, Edwin. See EXPANDING UNIVERSE

Hudson River School. See MANIFEST DESTINY

Huggins, Nathan. See DOUBLE CONSCIOUSNESS

Hugo, Victor. See ROMANTICISM

Huguenots. See box at PROTESTANTISM

human potential movement. See HUMANISM; NEW AGE; TRANSPERSONAL PSYCHOLOGY

human rights. See RIGHTS

HUMANISM

humanistic psychology. See HUMANISM; TRANSPERSONAL PSYCHOLOGY

HUME, DAVID

humors. See HIPPOCRATES

Husayn al-Husayn. See box at ISLAM (Sunnis and Shi'ites)

Hussein, Saddam. See TOTALITARIANISM

Husserl, Edmund. See PHENOMENOLOGY; see also HEIDEGGER; MERLEAU-PONTY; SARTRE

Hutton, James. See CATASTROPHISM AND UNIFORMITARIANISM

Huxley, Aldous. See box at UTOPIANISM

hylomorphism. See ARISTOTLE; MIND/BODY PROBLEM; VITALISM

hyperreality. See BAUDRILLARD

hypnosis. See CATHARSIS; FREUD; PARAPSYCHOLOGY

hypothesis, scientific. See BACON; box at BACON; COMTE; DEDUCTION AND INDUCTION; EINSTEIN; KEPLER; box at NOMINALISM; SCIENTIFIC METHOD; SPINOZA

I Ching. See CONFUCIANISM; TAOISM

IBN KHALDUN

IBN RUSHD

IBN SINA

Ibsen, Henrik. See REALISM

icons. See ORTHODOX CHURCH; SEMIOTICS

id. See FREUD; PSYCHOANALYSIS

ideal self. See HORNEY

ideal speech situation. See box at CRITICAL THEORY

ideal types. See WEBER

IDEALISM

idealized image. See HORNEY

IDEAS

IDENTITY

identity crisis. See ERIKSON

identity, law of. See box at LOGIC

ideological state apparatuses. See box at STRUCTURALISM

IDEOLOGY

illusion, argument from. See PERCEPTION

Imagism. See CLASSICISM

imitation. See AESTHETICS; ARISTOTLE; CATHARSIS; CHOMSKY; MIMESIS; PLATO; QUEER THEORY; SOCIAL LEARNING THEORY; UNITIES

immaculate conception. See ROMAN CATHOLICISM

immanence. See TRANSCENDENTALISM; see also GOD, CONCEPTS OF; ORTHODOX CHURCH; PANTHEISM AND PANENTHEISM

immaterialism. See BERKELEY

imperative, categorical and hypothetical. See KANT

IMPERIALISM

impossibility theorem. See SOCIAL CHOICE

IMPRESSIONISM

in-itself/for-itself. See SARTRE

incompleteness theorem. See FORMALISM; LOGIC; TRUTH

indeterminacy, indeterminism. See QUANTUM THEORY; UNCERTAINTY PRINCIPLE

Indians, American. See NORTH AMERICAN NATIVE BELIEFS

INDIVIDUALISM

induction. See DEDUCTION AND INDUCTION; see also BACON; LOGIC; MILL; SCIENTIFIC METHOD

inertia. See NEWTON

inferiority complex. See FREUD; WILL TO POWER

INFORMATION THEORY

INNATE IDEAS

Institute for Social Research. See CRITICAL THEORY

intelligence. See ANTHROPIC PRINCIPLE; ARTIFICIAL INTELLIGENCE; BEHAVIORISM; CHOMSKY; CONSCIOUSNESS; EPISTEMOLOGY; MECHANISM; PIAGET

intentional fallacy. See NEW CRITICISM

intentionality. See PHENOMENOLOGY

INTERNATIONALISM

intersubjectivity. See RORTY

introversion. See JUNG

intuition. See box at ABSTRACTION; CONFUCIANISM; box at KANT; NÉGRITUDE; PARAPSYCHOLOGY; RATIONALISM; TRANSCENDENTALISM; UNCONSCIOUS

intuitionism (mathematical). See FORMALISM

intuitionism (philosophical). See CONSEQUENTIALISM; MILL; VIRTUE

invisible hand. See SMITH; see also MARKET; UNINTENDED CONSEQUENCES

Ionesco, Eugène. See ABSURD

iron law of oligarchy. See ELITE THEORY

IS/OUGHT PROBLEM

Ishtar. See GODDESS WORSHIP

ISLAM

ISOLATIONISM

Ives, Charles. See MODERNISM

Jackson, Andrew. See JACKSONIAN DEMOCRACY; see also WHIGS AND TORIES

JACKSONIAN DEMOCRACY

JAINISM

Jakobson, Roman. See STRUCTURALISM

Jamaa. See box at AFRICAN RELIGIONS (modern movements)

James I. See PURITANISM

James II. See WHIGS AND TORIES

JAMES, WILLIAM

James-Lange theory of emotions. See JAMES

Jansenism. See PASCAL

Jaspers, Karl. See ARENDT; EXISTENTIALISM

Jay, John. See FEDERALISM

JEFFERSON, THOMAS

JEHOVAH'S WITNESSES

jen. See CONFUCIANISM

Jesuits. See PASCAL; ROMAN CATHOLICISM

JESUS

Jews. See JUDAISM

jihad. See JUST WAR

jina. See JAINISM

jnana. See YOGA

John Masowe. See box at AFRICAN RELIGIONS (modern movements)

John the Baptist. See box at CHRISTIANITY; JESUS

John XXIII. See box at ROMAN CATHOLICISM

Johnson, Lyndon Baines. See AFFIRMATIVE ACTION

Johnson, Samuel. See BERKELEY

jouissance. See KRISTEVA

Joyce, James. See CLASSICISM; MODERNISM;

STANDARD MODEL; STREAM OF
CONSCIOUSNESS
JUDAISM
Judaism, branches. See box at JUDAISM
Judd, Donald. See box at ABSTRACTION
judgment, day of. See ESCHATOLOGY; see
also ISLAM; MILLENARIANISM;
MUHAMMAD; PENTECOSTALISM; SOUL
AND SPIRIT; ZOROASTRIANISM
JUNG, CARL GUSTAV
jus ad bellum, jus in bello. See JUST WAR
jus naturale, jus gentium. See NATURAL
LAW; STOICISM
JUST WAR
justice. See CHRISTIANITY; COMMON LAW;
box at FEMINISM; MEAN; PLATO; RAWLS;
SOPHISTS; VIRTUE; VOLTAIRE;
ZOROASTRIANISM

K'ung Fu-tsu. See CONFUCIANISM
KABBALAH
Kali. See GODDESS WORSHIP; TANTRISM
kalpa. See ETERNAL RECURRENCE
kama. See DHARMA
kami. See SHINTO
Kanada. See box at HINDUISM
(schools)
Kandinsky, Wassily. See box at
ABSTRACTION; EXPRESSIONISM
KANT, IMMANUEL
Kant-Laplace hypothesis. See KANT
Kaplan, Mordecai. See box at JUDAISM
KARMA
Katz, David. See PHENOMENOLOGY
Kautsky, Karl. See SOCIALISM
Keats, John. See ROMANTICISM
Kelly, Ellsworth. See box at ABSTRACTION
Kelsen, Hans. See POSITIVISM
Kennedy, John F. See MANIFEST DESTINY
KEPLER, JOHANNES
KEYNES, JOHN MAYNARD
Khadijah. See MUHAMMAD
Khalsa. See SIKHISM
Khrushchev, Nikita. See COMMUNISM
kibbutz movement. See ZIONISM
KIERKEGAARD, SØREN
Kimbangu, Simon. See box at AFRICAN
RELIGIONS (modern movements)

King, Martin Luther, Jr. See BLACK POWER;
CIVIL DISOBEDIENCE; NONVIOLENCE;
RORTY; see also quotation at RACE AND
RACISM
Kipling, Rudyard. See quotation at
IMPERIALISM
Kirchner, Ernst Ludwig. See
EXPRESSIONISM
Klee, Paul. See SURREALISM
Klein, Melanie. See OBJECT RELATIONS
THEORY; PSYCHOANALYSIS
Klinger, Friedrich Maximilian. See STURM
UND DRANG
Know-Nothings. See NATIVISM
knowledge. See EPISTEMOLOGY
Knox, John. See box at PROTESTANTISM
Koffka, Kurt. See GESTALT
Köhler, Wolfgang. See GESTALT
Kojiki. See SHINTO
Kokoschka, Oscar. See EXPRESSIONISM
Kollwitz, Käthe. See EXPRESSIONISM
Koran (see Qur'an)
Kripke, Saul A. See ANALYTIC PHILOSOPHY
Krishna. See HINDUISM; box at HINDUISM
(modern movements)
Krishna Consciousness. See box at
HINDUISM (modern movements)
Krishnamurti, Jiddu. See THEOSOPHY
KRISTEVA, JULIA
Kuhn, Thomas. See PARADIGM; see also
FOUCAULT; SOCIAL CONSTRUCTIONISM
kundalini. See YOGA
Kwanzaa. See box at AFRICAN RELIGIONS
(New World)

La Follette, Robert M. See PROGRESSIVISM.
La Mettrie, Julien de. See MECHANISM
labor theory of value. See MARX
Lacan, Jacques. See box at
STRUCTURALISM; see also ALIENATION;
KRISTEVA; QUEER THEORY; SOLIPSISM
Laffer, Arthur; Laffer curve. See box at
SUPPLY-SIDE ECONOMICS
Laing, R. D. See FOUCAULT
LAISSEZ-FAIRE
Lamaism. See box at BUDDHISM
Lamarck, Jean-Baptiste. See LAMARCKISM;
see also DARWIN; EVOLUTION

LAMARCKISM

Lange, Carl Georg. See JAMES

LANGUAGE ACQUISITION

language games. See WITTGENSTEIN

langue and parole. See box at
STRUCTURALISM; see also GRAMMAR;
SEMIOTICS

Lao Tzu. See TAOISM

Laplace, Pierre-Simon. See DETERMINISM;
KANT; PROBABILITY

Last Supper. See box at CHRISTIANITY

latency period. See box at FREUD

law, natural. See NATURAL LAW

laws of thought. See LOGIC; box at LOGIC;
ZENO'S PARADOXES

Le Guin, Ursula. See box at UTOPIANISM

learning theory. See BEHAVIORISM;
CHOMSKY; COGNITIVE PSYCHOLOGY;
CONDITIONING; DEWEY; FREIRE; GESTALT;
INFORMATION THEORY; LANGUAGE
ACQUISITION; PIAGET; SOCIAL
CONSTRUCTIONISM; SOCIAL LEARNING
THEORY

Lebenswelt. See PHENOMENOLOGY

legal positivism. See NATURAL LAW

Léger, Fernand. See CUBISM

Legio Maria. See box at AFRICAN
RELIGIONS (modern movements)

LEIBNIZ, GOTTFRIED WILHELM VON

leisure class. See box at CLASS

Lemaître, Georges. See BIG BANG

LENIN, VLADIMIR ILYICH

LEONARDO DA VINCI

leptons. See STANDARD MODEL

lesbianism (see homosexuality)

Lessing, Gotthold Ephraim. See
MENDELSSOHN

Levellers. See RADICALISM

Lévi-Strauss, Claude. See box at
STRUCTURALISM; see also KRISTEVA;
STRUCTURALISM; TOTEMISM

Lewin, Kurt. See FIELD THEORY

Lewis, Meriwether. See JEFFERSON

li. See CONFUCIANISM

Liberal Judaism. See box at JUDAISM

LIBERALISM

LIBERATION THEOLOGY

LIBERTARIANISM

liberty. See FREEDOM

libido. See FREUD; JUNG; PSYCHOANALYSIS

Liebig, Justus von. See VITALISM

Liebknecht, Karl. See LUXEMBURG

life chances. See CLASS

Lightworld. See GNOSTICISM

Lindbergh, Charles. See ISOLATIONISM

linguistic analysis. See ANALYTIC
PHILOSOPHY; ORDINARY LANGUAGE
PHILOSOPHY

linguistic relativism. See SAPIR-WHORF
HYPOTHESIS

linguistics. See ANALYTIC PHILOSOPHY;
CHOMSKY; COGNITIVE PSYCHOLOGY;
DECONSTRUCTION; DESCRIPTIVISM
AND PRESCRIPTIVISM; GRAMMAR; box at
HISTORICISM; NEW CRITICISM; SAPIR-
WHORF HYPOTHESIS; SEMIOTICS;
STRUCTURALISM; box at
STRUCTURALISM; SYMBOLISM

Linnaeus. See HIERARCHY OF BEING

Liszt, Franz. See ROMANTICISM

loa. See box at AFRICAN RELIGIONS (New
World)

LOCKE, JOHN

LOGIC

logical atomism. See ATOMISM; RUSSELL

logical empiricism. See EMPIRICISM;
LOGICAL POSITIVISM

LOGICAL POSITIVISM

logicism. See FORMALISM

logocentrism. See DECONSTRUCTION

LOGOS

Long, John. See TOTEMISM

Lorde, Audre. See box at FEMINISM

Lorenz, Edward. See CHAOS THEORY

Louis XIV. See ABSOLUTISM; MERCANTILISM;
SOVEREIGNTY

Louis XVI. See PAINE

Lovelock, James. See GAIA

Luckmann, Thomas. See SOCIAL
CONSTRUCTIONISM

Lucretius. See ATOMISM; EPICUREANISM

LUKÁCS, GEORG

Luria, Isaac. See KABBALAH

LUTHER, MARTIN

Lutheranism. See box at PROTESTANTISM

LUXEMBURG, ROSA

Lyell, Charles. See CATASTROPHISM AND
UNIFORMITARIANISM
Lyotard, Jean-François. See
POSTMODERNISM
Lysenko, Trofim. See LAMARCKISM

Mach, Ernst. See LOGICAL POSITIVISM;
PHENOMENALISM
MACHIAVELLI, NICCOLÒ
MacKinnon, Catharine. See box at
FEMINISM
Macumba. See box at AFRICAN RELIGIONS
(New World)
Madhyamika school. See SUNYATA
Madison, James. See FEDERALISM;
SEPARATION OF POWERS; STATES' RIGHTS
magic. See AFRICAN RELIGIONS; box at
AFRICAN RELIGIONS (New World);
ANIMISM; KABBALAH; NORTH AMERICAN
NATIVE BELIEFS; box at NORTH AMERICAN
NATIVE BELIEFS; TAOISM; WITCHCRAFT
Magna Carta. See RIGHTS
Magna Mater. See GODDESS WORSHIP
Magog. See ESCHATOLOGY
Magritte, René. See SURREALISM
Mahabharata. See HINDUISM
Maharaj Ji. See box at HINDUISM
(modern movements)
Maharishi Mahesh Yogi. See box at
HINDUISM (modern movements)
Mahavira. See JAINISM.
Mahayana Buddhism. See box at
BUDDHISM; see also BUDDHA; NIRVANA;
SUNYATA; TANTRISM
mahdi. See BAHA'I
MAIMONIDES, MOSES
Mairet, Jean. See UNITIES
Malcolm X. See BLACK MUSLIMS; BLACK
NATIONALISM; BLACK POWER
Malebranche, Nicolas. See MIND/BODY
PROBLEM
Malevich, Casimir. See box at ABSTRACTION
Malinowski, Bronislaw. See
FUNCTIONALISM
Mallarmé, Stéphane. See SYMBOLISM
Malthus, Thomas. See MALTHUSIAN
POPULATION THEORY
MALTHUSIAN POPULATION THEORY

Man Ray. See DADA; SURREALISM
Mandate of Heaven. See CONFUCIANISM
Mandelbrot, Benoit B. See FRACTALS
Manet, Edouard. See IMPRESSIONISM
Manichaeism. See AUGUSTINE; DUALISM
MANIFEST DESTINY
manitou. See TOTEMISM
Mannheim, Karl. See IDEOLOGY
mantra. See box at BUDDHISM; box at
HINDUISM (modern movements)
MAO ZEDONG
mapping. See SET THEORY
Marcus Aurelius. See STOICISM
Marcuse, Herbert. See box at CRITICAL
THEORY
marginality. See DIMINISHING RETURNS;
UTILITY
Margulis, Lynn. See GAIA
MARKET
market socialism. See MARKET; SOCIALISM
MARX, KARL
MARXISM
Marxism-Leninism. See COMMUNISM
Mary. See GODDESS WORSHIP; NORTH
AMERICAN NATIVE BELIEFS; ROMAN
CATHOLICISM
Mary Magdalene. See GNOSTICISM
Maslow, Abraham. See HUMANISM;
TRANSPERSONAL PSYCHOLOGY
Mason, George. See FEDERALISM
Masons. See FREEMASONRY
Mass. See box at CHRISTIANITY; ROMAN
CATHOLICISM
Masson, André. See SURREALISM
master race. See FASCISM
MATERIALISM
Matisse, Henri. See CUBISM; FAUVISM
matriarchy. See box at FEMINISM; GODDESS
WORSHIP
Maurras, Charles. See FASCISM
MAXWELL, JAMES CLERK
May, Rollo. See HUMANISM
Mayr, Ernst. See PUNCTUATED EQUILIBRIUM
McCarthy, Joseph R. See MCCARTHYISM
MCCARTHYISM
McLennan, John Ferguson. See
TOTEMISM
MEAN, DOCTRINE OF THE

MEANING

MECHANISM

meditation. See ASCETICISM; BUDDHISM;
box at BUDDHISM; ENLIGHTENMENT;
HINDUISM; box at HINDUISM (modern
movements); JAINISM; KABBALAH;
MUHAMMAD; MYSTICISM; PESSIMISM; box
at PROTESTANTISM; ROMAN
CATHOLICISM; SIKHISM; SUFISM;
TANTRISM; TAOISM; THEOSOPHY;
TRANSPERSONAL PSYCHOLOGY; YOGA

mediums. See AFRICAN RELIGIONS;
SPIRITUALISM

Meher Baba. See box at HINDUISM
(modern movements)

memory. See COGNITIVE PSYCHOLOGY;
FREUD; HOBBES; IDENTITY; INFORMATION
THEORY; JUNG; SCIENTOLOGY;
TRANSPERSONAL PSYCHOLOGY

Mencius. See CONFUCIANISM

Mendel, Gregor. See EVOLUTION;
LAMARCKISM

MENDELSSOHN, MOSES

Meng Tzu. See CONFUCIANISM

Menippus. See CYNICISM

Mennonites. See box at PROTESTANTISM;
see also NONVIOLENCE; UTOPIANISM

Mensheviks. See LENIN

MERCANTILISM

MERLEAU-PONTY, MAURICE

Merton, Robert K. See ANOMIE;
UNINTENDED CONSEQUENCES

messiah, messianism. See BAHA'I; BLACK
MUSLIMS; CHRISTIANITY; ESCHATOLOGY;
HASIDISM; JESUS; JUDAISM; KABBALAH;
box at NORTH AMERICAN NATIVE
BELIEFS; RASTAFARIANISM; ZIONISM

MEST. See SCIENTOLOGY

metanarrative. See POSTMODERNISM

METAPHYSICS

Methodism. See box at PROTESTANTISM;
see also PENTECOSTALISM

Michelangelo Buonaroti. See CLASSICISM

Michels, Robert. See ELITE THEORY

Middle Way. See BUDDHA; BUDDHISM; MEAN

Midrash. See JUDAISM.

Mies van der Rohe, Ludwig. See
MODERNISM

Mill, James. See UTILITARIANISM

MILL, JOHN STUART

MILLENARIANISM (millennialism)

Miller, Neal. See SOCIAL LEARNING THEORY

Miller, William. See ADVENTISM

MILLETT, KATE

Mills, C. Wright. See ELITE THEORY

Mimamsa. See box at HINDUISM (schools)

MIMESIS

mind. See COGNITIVE PSYCHOLOGY;
CONFUCIANISM; CONSCIOUSNESS;
DESCARTES; DUALISM; EPISTEMOLOGY;
FREUD; GESTALT; HUME; IDEALISM;
IDEAS; INNATE IDEAS; KANT; box at KANT;
LOCKE; MATERIALISM; PERCEPTION;
PIAGET; PSYCHOANALYSIS; SOCIAL
CONSTRUCTIONISM; SOLIPSISM; STREAM OF
CONSCIOUSNESS; UNCONSCIOUS;
UNIVERSALS

MIND/BODY PROBLEM

minimalism. See box at ABSTRACTION

minjung theology. See LIBERATION
THEOLOGY

miracles. See AQUINAS; box at
CHRISTIANITY; DEISM; FUNDAMENTALISM;
HUME; JESUS; MAIMONIDES; NATURAL
THEOLOGY; SPINOZA

Miró, Joan. See SURREALISM

Mises, Ludwig von. See LIBERTARIANISM

Mishnah. See JUDAISM; MAIMONIDES;
TORAH

Mitchell, Juliet. See box at FEMINISM

mixed-market economy. See MARKET;
SOCIALISM

MIXED REGIME

modeling. See SOCIAL LEARNING THEORY

MODERNISM

Mohammed. See MUHAMMAD

moksha. See DHARMA; HINDUISM; NIRVANA

monad. See LEIBNIZ

monarchy. See ABSOLUTISM; see also
CONSERVATISM; "GREAT MAN" THEORY;
HOBBES; LOCKE; MIXED REGIME; PAINE;
REPUBLICANISM; VOLTAIRE; WHIGS AND
TORIES

monasticism. See ASCETICISM; BUDDHISM;
box at BUDDHISM; box at CHRISTIANITY;
CYNICISM; JAINISM; ROMAN CATHOLICISM

Mondrian, Piet. See box at ABSTRACTION
Monet, Claude. See IMPRESSIONISM
MONETARISM
MONISM
monopoly. See COMPETITION
monotheism. See GOD, CONCEPTS OF; see
    also CHRISTIANITY; DEISM; ISLAM;
    JUDAISM; TRINITY
Monroe, James. See MONROE DOCTRINE
MONROE DOCTRINE
Montaigne, Michel de. See quotation at
    RELATIVISM
Montesquieu, Charles-Louis Secondat,
    baron de. See BALANCE OF POWER;
    SEPARATION OF POWERS
Moore, G. E. See IS/OUGHT PROBLEM;
    PARADIGM; VIRTUE
moral philosophy. See ETHICS
moral reasoning. See box at FEMINISM
More, Henry. See MIND/BODY PROBLEM
More, Thomas. See COMMUNISM;
    HUMANISM; UTOPIANISM
Moreau, Gustave. See SYMBOLISM
Morgenstern, Oskar. See GAME THEORY
MORMONISM
Moroni. See MORMONISM
Morris, Robert. See box at ABSTRACTION
Mosca, Gaetano. See ELITE THEORY; see
    also FASCISM
Moses. See JUDAISM; KABBALAH; TEN
    COMMANDMENTS; TORAH
Moses de León. See KABBALAH
most-favored-nation status. See FREE TRADE
Mott, Lucretia Coffin. See STANTON
MUHAMMAD
Muhammad, Elijah. See BLACK MUSLIMS
Muhammad, Wallace D. See BLACK MUSLIMS
multiculturalism. See DEATH OF THE
    AUTHOR; RELATIVISM; POSTMODERNISM
multiple universes. See ENTROPY
Munch, Edvard. See EXPRESSIONISM
Murray, Margaret. See WITCHCRAFT
Muslims. See ISLAM; boxes at ISLAM; see
    also BLACK MUSLIMS; FUNDAMENTALISM;
    MUHAMMAD; SUFISM
Mussolini, Benito. See FASCISM; GRAMSCI
mutual assured destruction. See
    DETERRENCE

Myal. See box at AFRICAN RELIGIONS (New
    World)
Myers-Briggs test. See JUNG
mysterium. See SPONTANEOUS GENERATION
    AND BIOGENESIS
MYSTICISM

Nagarjuna. See SUNYATA
naive realism. See PERCEPTION
Napoleon Bonaparte. See CLAUSEWITZ;
    "GREAT MAN" THEORY; MACHIAVELLI
narodniki. See POPULISM
Nation of Islam. See BLACK MUSLIMS
nation-state. See NATIONALISM; STATE
NATIONALISM
Native American Church. See NORTH
    AMERICAN NATIVE BELIEFS
Native Americans. See NORTH AMERICAN
    NATIVE BELIEFS; see also DESCRIPTIVISM
    AND PRESCRIPTIVISM; MORMONISM;
    NATIVISM; PAGANISM; RACE AND RACISM;
    SAPIR-WHORF HYPOTHESIS; TOTEMISM
NATIVISM
NATURAL LAW
natural religion. See NATURAL THEOLOGY
natural rights. See RIGHTS; see also DEISM;
    DEMOCRACY; ENLIGHTENMENT; LAISSEZ-
    FAIRE; NATURAL LAW; PAINE; RADICALISM;
    SOCIAL CONTRACT
natural selection. See EVOLUTION; see also
    BIOLOGICAL DETERMINISM; DARWIN;
    LAMARCKISM
NATURAL THEOLOGY
NATURALISM
naturalistic fallacy. See IS/OUGHT
    PROBLEM
nature, state of. See SOCIAL CONTRACT; see
    also FREEDOM; HOBBES; ROUSSEAU
nature versus nurture. See BEHAVIORISM;
    LANGUAGE ACQUISITION
nature worship. See AFRICAN RELIGIONS;
    ANIMISM; NORTH AMERICAN NATIVE
    BELIEFS; PAGANISM; ROMANTICISM;
    SHINTO; TRANSCENDENTALISM;
    WITCHCRAFT
Nazism. See ARENDT; FASCISM;
    NATIONALISM; NIETZSCHE; RACE AND
    RACISM; TOTALITARIANISM

Ne Win. See TOTALITARIANISM

necessary being. See GOD, ARGUMENTS FOR; IBN RUSHD; IBN SINA; MAIMONIDES

negative income tax. See TAXATION

NÉGRITUDE

neoclassical economics (see new classical economics)

neoclassicism. See CLASSICISM

neocolonialism. See IMPERIALISM

neoconservatism. See CONSERVATISM

neoexpressionism. See box at ABSTRACTION; EXPRESSIONISM

neoimpressionism. See IMPRESSIONISM

neoplasticism. See box at ABSTRACTION; CONSTRUCTIVISM

NEOPLATONISM

neopragmatism. See RORTY

Neumann, John von. See GAME THEORY

neuroscience. See COGNITIVE PSYCHOLOGY; CONSCIOUSNESS; EPISTEMOLOGY

neurosis. See FREUD; GESTALT; HORNEY; PSYCHOANALYSIS; UNCONSCIOUS

neutral monism. See MONISM; RUSSELL

new classical economics. See LIBERTARIANISM; MONETARISM; RATIONAL EXPECTATIONS; TAXATION

new math. See SET THEORY

new realism. See box at ABSTRACTION

NEW AGE PHILOSOPHY

NEW CRITICISM

New Historicism. See box at HISTORICISM

New Left. See box at CRITICAL THEORY; MARXISM

New Testament (see Bible)

New York School. See box at ABSTRACTION

Newman, Barnett. See box at ABSTRACTION

NEWTON, ISAAC

Ngugi Wa Thiong'o. See POSTCOLONIAL THEORY

nibbana. See NIRVANA

Nicene Creed. See TRINITY

Nichiren Buddhism. See box at BUDDHISM

NIETZSCHE, FRIEDRICH

NIHILISM

Nihongi. See SHINTO

Ninety-Five Theses. See LUTHER

NIRVANA

niyama. See YOGA

Nkrumah, Kwame. See BLACK NATIONALISM

noble savage. See ROUSSEAU

Noether, Emmy. See CONSERVATION AND SYMMETRY

Nolde, Emil. See EXPRESSIONISM

NOMINALISM

noncontradiction, law of. See box at LOGIC

NONVIOLENCE

NORTH AMERICAN NATIVE BELIEFS

nothingness. See BEING AND BECOMING; EXISTENTIALISM; HEGEL; KIERKEGAARD; NIHILISM; NIRVANA; SARTRE; SUNYATA

noumenon. See APPEARANCE VERSUS REALITY; PESSIMISM; KANT

nous. See LOGOS; NEOPLATONISM

Nozick, Robert. See LIBERTARIANISM; RAWLS

nuclear forces. See STANDARD MODEL

nullification controversy. See STATES' RIGHTS

Nyaya. See box at HINDUISM (schools)

object (see subject and object)

object permanence. See PIAGET

OBJECT RELATIONS THEORY

OBJECTIVISM AND SUBJECTIVISM

occasionalism. See DUALISM; MIND/BODY PROBLEM

occult. See KABBALAH; MYSTICISM; THEOSOPHY; WITCHCRAFT

Ockham, William of (see William of Ockham)

Ockham's Razor. See box at NOMINALISM

Oedipus complex. See box at FREUD; PSYCHOANALYSIS

Olcott, Henry Steele. See THEOSOPHY

Old Testament (see Bible)

oligarchy. See CLASS; ELITE THEORY; MIXED REGIME

oligopoly. See COMPETITION

Olitsky, Jules. See box at ABSTRACTION

O'Neill, Eugene. See EXPRESSIONISM

ontology. See BEING AND BECOMING; DESCARTES; GOD, ARGUMENTS FOR; HEIDEGGER; IDENTITY; METAPHYSICS

op art. See box at ABSTRACTION

open universe theory. See BIG BANG THEORY

operational thinking. See PIAGET

operationism. See BEHAVIORISM

operations. See PIAGET; SET THEORY

OPPORTUNITY COST

optimality. See DECISION THEORY

oral law. See JUDAISM; KABBALAH; MAIMONIDES; TORAH

ORDINARY LANGUAGE PHILOSOPHY

organicism. See MECHANISM

original sin. See AUGUSTINE; PASCAL; PREDESTINATION; box at PROTESTANTISM; PURITANISM; ROUSSEAU

orishas. See box at AFRICAN RELIGIONS (New World)

ORTEGA Y GASSET, JOSÉ

ORTHODOX CHURCH

Orthodox Judaism. See box at JUDAISM; see also HASIDISM; TORAH; ZIONISM

Orwell, George. See quotation at FREEDOM; box at UTOPIANISM

oscillating (pulsating) universe theory. See BIG BANG THEORY

O'Sullivan, John Louis. See MANIFEST DESTINY

other minds, problem of. See SOLIPSISM

Other, the. See BEAUVOIR; HEGEL; IDENTITY; POSTCOLONIAL THEORY

Oversoul. See EMERSON

overdetermination. See SPINOZA; box at STRUCTURALISM

Owen, Robert. See UTOPIANISM

pacifism. See NONVIOLENCE; see also EINSTEIN; JAINISM; JUST WAR; box at PROTESTANTISM; RUSSELL

PAGANISM

PAINE, THOMAS

Paley, William. See GOD, ARGUMENTS FOR; NATURAL THEOLOGY

pan-Africanism. See BLACK NATIONALISM; DU BOIS; GARVEY; NATIONALISM; NÉGRITUDE; RASTAFARIANISM

Panchamas. See CASTE

panentheism. See PANTHEISM AND PANENTHEISM; see also PROCESS PHILOSOPHY/THEOLOGY

Pangaea. See CATASTROPHISM AND UNIFORMITARIANISM

PANTHEISM AND PANENTHEISM

Paracelsus. See SPONTANEOUS GENERATION AND BIOGENESIS

PARADIGM

paradise (see heaven)

paradoxes. See box at BUDDHISM; RELATIVITY; box at RUSSELL; ZENO'S PARADOXES

parallelism. See MIND/BODY PROBLEM

paranormal. See TRANSPERSONAL PSYCHOLOGY

PARAPSYCHOLOGY

Pareto, Vilfredo. See ELITE THEORY; see also FASCISM; WELFARE

parinirvana. See NIRVANA

parity. See CONSERVATION AND SYMMETRY

Parmenides. See BEING AND BECOMING; ZENO'S PARADOXES

parole. See box at STRUCTURALISM; see also GRAMMAR; SEMIOTICS

Parousia. See ESCHATOLOGY

parsimony, principle of. See box at NOMINALISM

Parsons, Talcott. See CYBERNETICS; FUNCTIONALISM; SYSTEMS THEORY

particulars. See IDENTITY; NOMINALISM; UNIVERSALS

Parvati. See GODDESS WORSHIP

PASCAL, BLAISE

Pascal's wager. See box at PASCAL

passive resistance. See NONVIOLENCE

Pasternak, Boris. See SOCIALIST REALISM

Pasteur, Louis. See SPONTANEOUS GENERATION AND BIOGENESIS

Patanjali. See YOGA

Pater, Walter. See AESTHETICISM

patriarchs. See JUDAISM; ORTHODOX CHURCH

patriarchy. See BEAUVOIR; BIOLOGICAL DETERMINISM; DECONSTRUCTION; FEMINISM; box at FEMINISM; FUNDAMENTALISM; GILMAN; GNOSTICISM; GODDESS WORSHIP; KRISTEVA; MILLETT; MORMONISM; POSTCOLONIAL THEORY; ROMAN CATHOLICISM.

Paul, St. See ESCHATOLOGY; JESUS; PRESDESTINATION; VIRTUE

Pauli, Wolfgang. See QUANTUM THEORY; QUANTUM ELECTRODYNAMICS

Pavlov, Ivan. See BEHAVIORISM; CONDITIONING

peak experiences. See HUMANISM

Peano, Giuseppe. See RUSSELL

pedagogy of the oppressed. See FREIRE

Peirce, Charles Sanders. See PRAGMATISM; see also EMPIRICISM; SEMIOTICS

penis envy. See box at FREUD; HORNEY

Penn, William. See box at PROTESTANTISM

Pentateuch. See TORAH

PENTECOSTALISM

Penzias, Robert. See BIG BANG THEORY

percept. See RUSSELL

PERCEPTION

PERESTROIKA

perfectibility, human. See MERLEAU-PONTY; ROUSSEAU; SCIENTOLOGY; UTOPIANISM; box at UTOPIANISM

performance art. See POSTMODERNISM

performative. See ORDINARY LANGUAGE PHILOSOPHY; TRUTH

Perls, Fritz. See GESTALT

permanent revolution. See TROTSKY; see also MAO; LENIN

Perón, Juan. See CAPITALISM

persona. See JUNG

personality. See box at ASTROLOGY; BEHAVIORISM; box at CRITICAL THEORY; ERIKSON; FREUD; box at FREUD; HORNEY; JUNG; PSYCHODYNAMIC THEORY

PESSIMISM

Peter the Great. See ABSOLUTISM

Peter, St. See ROMAN CATHOLICISM

Petrarca, Francesco (Petrarch). See HUMANISM

Pevsner, Antoine. See CONSTRUCTIVISM

peyotism. See NORTH AMERICAN NATIVE BELIEFS

phallologocentrism. See DECONSTRUCTION

PHENOMENALISM

PHENOMENOLOGY

phenomenon. See APPEARANCE VERSUS REALITY; IDEALISM; KANT; PHENOMENALISM

Philo. See LOGOS

philosopher-king. See PLATO; VOLTAIRE

philosophes. See ENLIGHTENMENT; VOLTAIRE

photoelectric effect. See EINSTEIN; WAVE-PARTICLE DUALITY

phyletic gradualism. See PUNCTUATED EQUILIBRIUM

physicalism. See IDENTITY

Physiocrats. See CAPITALISM; LAISSEZ-FAIRE; SMITH

PIAGET, JEAN

Picabia, Francis. See DADA; SURREALISM

Picasso, Pablo. See CUBISM; EXPRESSIONISM; SURREALISM; see also quotation at TRUTH

Pico della Mirandola, Giovanni. See HUMANISM

picture theory of language. See WITTGENSTEIN

Piercy, Marge. See box at UTOPIANISM

Pietism. See box at PROTESTANTISM

Pinochet, Augusto. See FASCISM

Pissaro, Camille. See IMPRESSIONISM

Pius X. See MODERNISM

Planck, Max. See QUANTUM THEORY

plate tectonics. See CATASTROPHISM AND UNIFORMITARIANISM

PLATO

Plato's cave. See box at PLATO

pleasure principle. See FREUD

plenitude, principle of. See ARISTOTLE; HIERARCHY OF BEING

Plotinus. See NEOPLATONISM; see also HIERARCHY OF BEING; IBN SINA

PLURALISM

Plutarch. See ARCHIMEDES

Pocomania. See box at AFRICAN RELIGIONS (New World)

pointillism. See IMPRESSIONISM

Pollock, Jackson. See box at ABSTRACTION

poltergeists. See PARAPSYCHOLOGY

Polybius. See MIXED REGIME

polymorphous perversity. See box at FREUD

polytheism. See GOD, CONCEPTS OF; see also ANIMISM; HINDUISM; PAGANISM

Popper, Karl. See VERIFIABILITY AND FALSIFIABILITY; see also box at BACON; HISTORICISM; LOGICAL POSITIVISM

popular sovereignty. See SOVEREIGNTY

POPULISM

POSITIVISM

POSTCOLONIAL THEORY

postimpressionism. See IMPRESSIONISM

POSTMODERNISM

post-painterly abstraction. See box at
ABSTRACTION

POSTSTRUCTURALISM

potentiality. See ARISTOTLE; HIERARCHY OF
BEING; VITALISM

Pound, Ezra. See CLASSICISM

power, political/social. See ABSOLUTISM;
ALIENATION; BALANCE OF POWER;
BEAUVOIR; BLACK POWER; CLASS; box at
CRITICAL THEORY; ELITE THEORY;
EQUALITY; FANON; FEDERALISM; FEMINISM;
FOUCAULT; FREIRE; GRAMSCI; HOBBES;
IMPERIALISM AND COLONIALISM;
INTERNATIONALISM; LENIN; LOCKE;
MACHIAVELLI; MILLETT; MONROE
DOCTRINE; NATIONALISM; NONVIOLENCE;
PLURALISM; REALISM, REPUBLICANISM;
RIGHTS; ROUSSEAU; SEPARATION OF
POWERS; SOCIAL CONTRACT; SOVEREIGNTY;
STATE; STATES' RIGHTS; TOTALITARIANISM;
WEBER; WILL TO POWER

power elite. See ELITE THEORY

powers, separation of. See SEPARATION OF
POWERS

pragmatics. See SEMIOTICS; see also box at
CRITICAL THEORY

PRAGMATISM

pranayama. See YOGA

pratyahara. See YOGA

praxis. See FREIRE; GRAMSCI; LUKÁCS; SARTRE

precedent. See COMMON LAW

precognition. See PARAPSYCHOLOGY

preconscious. See UNCONSCIOUS

PREDESTINATION

predeterminism. See DETERMINISM;
PREDESTINATION

preestablished harmony. See LEIBNIZ

Presbyterian Church. See box at
PROTESTANTISM

prescriptivism. See DESCRIPTIVISM AND
PRESCRIPTIVISM

Prime Mover. See ARISTOTLE; CAUSE; GOD,
ARGUMENTS FOR

Prisoners' Dilemma. See box at GAME
THEORY

PROBABILITY

PROCESS PHILOSOPHY/THEOLOGY

production, means/relations of. See
ALIENATION; CAPITALISM; COMMUNISM;
CULTURAL MATERIALISM; DIALECTIC;
DIALECTICAL MATERIALISM; MARX;
SOCIALISM

PROGRESS

PROGRESSIVISM

Prokofiev, Sergei. See SOCIALIST REALISM

proletariat. See ANARCHISM; CLASS;
CRITICAL THEORY; FASCISM; GRAMSCI;
IDEOLOGY; INTERNATIONALISM; LENIN;
LUKÁCS; LUXEMBURG; MAO; MARX;
MARXISM; MILL; RADICALISM; SOCIALISM;
TROTSKY

properties. See SET THEORY; SUBSTANCE;
UNIVERSALS

property, private. See ANARCHISM;
CAPITALISM; COMMUNISM; box at
DEMOCRACY; LIBERALISM;
LIBERTARIANISM; LOCKE; PLATO; RIGHTS;
SOCIALISM; STANTON

proportional representation. See box at
DEMOCRACY; MILL

proportionality. See JUST WAR

propositions, logical/mathematical. See
ANALYTIC PHILOSOPHY; ATOMISM;
DIALECTIC; LOGIC; LOGICAL POSITIVISM;
MEANING; RUSSELL; VERIFIABILITY AND
FALSIFIABILITY

Protagoras. See RELATIVISM; SOPHISTS

protectionism. See FREE TRADE AND
PROTECTIONISM; see also MERCANTILISM

Protestant denominations. See box at
PROTESTANTISM

Protestant ethic. See WEBER; see also
CAPITALISM

PROTESTANTISM

Proudhon, Pierre-Joseph. See ANARCHISM

Proust, Marcel. See STREAM OF
CONSCIOUSNESS

providence, divine. See AUGUSTINE;
DEISM; MANIFEST DESTINY; NATURAL
THEOLOGY; SPINOZA

proxy war. See BALANCE OF POWER

psi. See PARAPSYCHOLOGY
psyche. See PSYCHOANALYSIS; SOUL AND SPIRIT
psychic research. See PARAPSYCHOLOGY
PSYCHOANALYSIS
PSYCHODYNAMIC THEORY
psychokinesis. See PARAPSYCHOLOGY
psychosexual stages. See box at FREUD
psychosocial theory. See ERIKSON
psychosynthesis. See TRANSPERSONAL PSYCHOLOGY
Ptolemy, Ptolemaic system. See ASTROLOGY; COPERNICUS; GALILEO; KEPLER; PARADIGM
PUBLIC CHOICE
public goods. See MARKET
Pukkumina. See box at AFRICAN RELIGIONS (New World)
PUNCTUATED EQUILIBRIUM
Pure Land Buddhism. See box at BUDDHISM
PURITANISM
purpose. See TELEOLOGY; see also ARISTOTLE; CAUSE; EXISTENTIALISM; FUNCTIONALISM; GOD, ARGUMENTS FOR
Puvis de Chavannes, Pierre. See SYMBOLISM
Pyrrho. See SKEPTICISM

QED. See QUANTUM ELECTRODYNAMICS
Quakers. See box at PROTESTANTISM; see also NONVIOLENCE; NORTH AMERICAN NATIVE BELIEFS
qualities. See box at LOCKE; see also ABSTRACTION; ARISTOTLE; HIERARCHY OF BEING; box at KANT; OBJECTIVISM AND SUBJECTIVISM; SOPHISTS
quantifiers. See RUSSELL
quantity theory of money. See MONETARISM
quantum chromodynamics. See STANDARD MODEL
QUANTUM ELECTRODYNAMICS
quantum leap. See box at QUANTUM THEORY
QUANTUM THEORY
quarks. See STANDARD MODEL
QUEER THEORY
Quesnay, François. See LAISSEZ-FAIRE; SMITH

Quine, Willard van Orman. See A PRIORI/ A POSTERIORI; ANALYTIC PHILOSOPHY; BEING AND BECOMING; PRAGMATISM
Qur'an (Koran). See ISLAM; see also FUNDAMENTALISM; MUHAMMAD

RACE AND RACISM
Radcliffe-Brown, Alfred. See FUNCTIONALISM
Radha. See HINDUISM
RADICALISM
raja yoga. See YOGA
Rama. See HINDUISM
Ramakrishna. See HINDUISM
Ramanuja. See box at HINDUISM (schools)
Ramayana. See HINDUISM
Ramsey, Frank P. See TRUTH
Rand, Ayn. See LIBERTARIANISM
Rank, Otto. See PSYCHOANALYSIS
Ranke, Leopold von. See "GREAT MAN" THEORY
Ransom, John Crowe. See NEW CRITICISM
RASTAFARIANISM
rational choice. See SOCIAL CHOICE
rational egoism. See LIBERTARIANISM
RATIONAL EXPECTATIONS
RATIONALISM
rationality. See RATIONALISM; REASON
RAWLS, JOHN
reaction formation. See FREUD
Reaganomics. See SUPPLY-SIDE ECONOMICS
REALISM
reality. See METAPHYSICS; see also ABSOLUTE; ABSTRACTION; AESTHETICS; APPEARANCE VERSUS REALITY; AQUINAS; ATOMISM; BAUDRILLARD; CHRISTIAN SCIENCE; COGNITIVE DISSONANCE; CONSCIOUSNESS; DUALISM; EMPIRICISM; HOBBES; IDEALISM; IDEOLOGY; MATERIALISM; MONISM; NOMINALISM; PESSIMISM; PHENOMENALISM; PHENOMENOLOGY; PLURALISM; PROCESS PHILOSOPHY/THEOLOGY; REALISM; RORTY; SOCIAL CONSTRUCTIONISM; SUBSTANCE; SUNYATA; TRANSCENDEN-TALISM; UNIVERSALS; WITTGENSTEIN
reality principle. See FREUD
realpolitik. See IDEALISM; REALISM

REASON

Reconstructionist movement. See box at JUDAISM

recurrence, eternal. See ETERNAL RECURRENCE

Redi, Francesco. See SPONTANEOUS GENERATION AND BIOGENESIS

Redon, Odilon. See SYMBOLISM

redshift. See EXPANDING UNIVERSE

REDUCTIONISM

Reform Darwinism. See GILMAN

Reform Judaism. See box at JUDAISM

Reformation. See PROTESTANTISM; LUTHER; see also HUMANISM; INDIVIDUALISM; box at PROTESTANTISM

Reformed Churches. See box at PROTESTANTISM

regression. See FREUD

reification. See LUKÁCS

reincarnation. See KARMA; see also BUDDHISM; box at BUDDHISM; SCIENTOLOGY; THEOSOPHY

RELATIVISM

RELATIVITY

Religious Society of Friends. See box at PROTESTANTISM

Renaissance. See ENLIGHTENMENT; REASON; see also AQUINAS; BACON; CLASSICISM; HUMANISM; LEONARDO DA VINCI

Renoir, Auguste. See IMPRESSIONISM

renormalization. See QUANTUM ELECTRODYNAMICS

repression, repressed memory. See CATHARSIS; FREUD; box at FREUD; JUNG; KRISTEVA; PSYCHOANALYSIS; SCIENTOLOGY; SYMBOLISM; UNCONSCIOUS

REPUBLICANISM

res cogitans, res extensa. See DESCARTES; SUBSTANCE

resistance, nonviolent. See CIVIL DISOBEDIENCE; NONVIOLENCE

resurrection. See ESCHATOLOGY; JESUS

returns to scale. See DIMINISHING RETURNS

revealed preference. See UTILITY

revelation, revealed religion. See IBN RUSHD; ISLAM; JUDAISM; KIERKEGAARD; LOCKE; MAIMONIDES; MILLENARIANISM; MORMONISM; MUHAMMAD; NATURAL THEOLOGY; NEOPLATONISM; box at PROTESTANTISM; SCHOLASTICISM; TORAH

revivalism. See ADVENTISM; box at AFRICAN RELIGIONS (modern movements); NATIVISM; box at NORTH AMERICAN NATIVE BELIEFS; PENTE-COSTALISM; box at PROTESTANTISM

revolution. See ANARCHISM; ARENDT; BURKE; CLASS; COMMUNISM; CRITICAL THEORY; ELITE THEORY; EXPRESSIONISM; FANON; FASCISM; box at FEMINISM; FREIRE; GRAMSCI; JEFFERSON; LENIN; LUKÁCS; LUXEMBURG; MAO; MARX; MARXISM; PAINE; RADICALISM; SARTRE; SOCIALISM; TROTSKY; WOLLSTONECRAFT

Ricardo, David. See ADVANTAGE; DIMINISHING RETURNS

Richards, I. A. See NEW CRITICISM

Richardson, Dorothy. See STREAM OF CONSCIOUSNESS

RIGHTS

Rimbaud, Arthur. See SYMBOLISM

risk. See DECISION THEORY; GAME THEORY

Robeson, Paul. See BLACK POWER

Rockefeller, John D. See WASHINGTON

Rococo. See CLASSICISM

Rogers, Will. See quotation at EQUALITY

ROMAN CATHOLICISM

ROMANTICISM

Romero, Oscar. See LIBERATION THEOLOGY

Roosevelt, Franklin Delano. See EINSTEIN; LIBERALISM

Roosevelt, Theodore. See MONROE DOCTRINE; PROGRESSIVISM; WASHINGTON

RORTY, RICHARD

Roscelin. See NOMINALISM

Rosenberg, Harold. See box at ABSTRACTION; MODERNISM

Rothko, Mark. See box at ABSTRACTION

Rotter, Julian. See SOCIAL LEARNING THEORY

Rouault, Georges. See EXPRESSIONISM

ROUSSEAU, JEAN-JACQUES

Rowbotham, Sheila. See box at FEMINISM

Royce, Josiah. See ABSOLUTE

Rushdie, Salman. See POSTCOLONIAL THEORY

RUSSELL, BERTRAND
Russell, Charles Taze. See JEHOVAH'S
WITNESSES
Rutherford, Ernest. See QUANTUM
THEORY; box at QUANTUM THEORY
Rutherford, Joseph Franklin. See
JEHOVAH'S WITNESSES

Sabbatai Zevi. See KABBALAH
Sabbath, Sabbatarianism. See ADVENTISM;
JUDAISM; PURITANISM; TEN
COMMANDMENTS
Sacco, Nicola. See ANARCHISM
sacraments. See box at CHRISTIANITY; see
also box at AFRICAN RELIGIONS
(modern movements); AUGUSTINE;
MIND/BODY PROBLEM; NORTH AMERICAN
NATIVE BELIEFS; ORTHODOX CHURCH;
RASTAFARIANISM; ROMAN CATHOLICISM
Said, Edward. See POSTCOLONIAL THEORY
Saint-Simon, Claude-Henri. See CLASS;
MARX; POSITIVISM
saints. See box at AFRICAN RELIGIONS
(New World); MORMONISM; ORTHODOX
CHURCH; PURITANISM; ROMAN
CATHOLICISM; SUFISM; TEN
COMMANDMENTS
salvation. See box at BUDDHISM;
CHRISTIANITY; box at CHRISTIANITY;
DEISM; GNOSTICISM; HINDUISM; box at
HINDUISM (schools); INDIVIDUALISM;
JESUS; LIBERATION THEOLOGY; LUTHER;
PREDESTINATION; PROTESTANTISM; box
at PROTESTANTISM; PURITANISM; TORAH
samadhi. See YOGA
Samkhya. See box at HINDUISM (schools);
YOGA
samsara. See KARMA; see also BUDDHISM;
HINDUISM; JAINISM; NIRVANA; SIKHISM
sangha. See BUDDHA; BUDDHISM
Sankara (see Shankara)
Santería. See box at AFRICAN RELIGIONS
(New World)
Sapir, Edward. See DESCRIPTIVISM AND
PRESCRIPTIVISM; SAPIR-WHORF
HYPOTHESIS
SAPIR-WHORF HYPOTHESIS
SARTRE, JEAN-PAUL

Sat Nam. See SIKHISM
Satan; the Devil. See AUGUSTINE;
SPIRITUALISM; DUALISM; ESCHATOLOGY;
JEHOVAH'S WITNESSES; WITCHCRAFT
satisficing. See DECISION THEORY
satyagraha. See CIVIL DISOBEDIENCE;
GANDHI
Saussure, Ferdinand de. See box at
STRUCTURALISM; see also BAUDRILLARD;
GRAMMAR; MEANING; MERLEAU-PONTY;
SEMIOTICS; STRUCTURALISM
Say, Jean-Baptiste; Say's Law. See box at
SUPPLY AND DEMAND
Schelling, Wilhelm Joseph. See
UNCONSCIOUS
Schiele, Egon. See EXPRESSIONISM
Schiller, Friedrich von. See STURM UND
DRANG
Schlegel, Friedrich. See AESTHETICS;
ROMANTICISM
Schleiermacher, Friedrich. See
HERMENEUTICS
Schlick, Moritz. See LOGICAL POSITIVISM
Schnabel, Julian. See EXPRESSIONISM
Schneerson, Menachem. See HASIDISM
Schoenberg, Arnold. See MODERNISM
SCHOLASTICISM
Schopenhauer, Arthur. See PESSIMISM; see
also NIHILISM
Schumpeter, Joseph A. See box at SUPPLY
AND DEMAND
SCIENTIFIC METHOD
Scientific Revolution. See COPERNICUS;
GALILEO; HUMANISM; LOCKE;
MODERNISM; NEWTON; NOMINALISM;
SCIENTIFIC METHOD
scientism. See CRITICAL THEORY; POSITIVISM
SCIENTOLOGY
Scott, Dred. See STATES' RIGHTS
Searle, John R. See ORDINARY LANGUAGE
PHILOSOPHY
Second Coming. See ADVENTISM;
ESCHATOLOGY; MILLENARIANISM; see also
box at AFRICAN RELIGIONS (New World);
FUNDAMENTALISM; JEHOVAH'S WITNESSES
seduction theory. See FREUD
sefirot. See KABBALAH
segregation. See CIVIL DISOBEDIENCE; DU

BOIS; GARVEY; STATES' RIGHTS;
  WASHINGTON
self-actualization. See HUMANISM; NEW AGE
self-denial. See ASCETICISM
self-reliance. See BLACK NATIONALISM;
  EMERSON; INDIVIDUALISM; LIBERALISM;
  PURITANISM; RACE AND RACISM;
  STANTON; THOREAU; TRANSCENDENTAL-
  ISM; WASHINGTON; WEBER; WELFARE
self-similarity. See CHAOS THEORY; FRACTALS
selfish gene. See BIOLOGICAL DETERMINISM
semanalysis. See KRISTEVA
semantics. See MEANING; SEMIOTICS; TRUTH
SEMIOTICS
Seneca. See STOICISM
Senghor, Léopold. See NÉGRITUDE
separation of church and state. See
  JEFFERSON; LOCKE; MENDELSSOHN; box
  at PROTESTANTISM
SEPARATION OF POWERS
separatism. See box at AFRICAN RELIGIONS
  (modern movements); BLACK MUSLIMS;
  BLACK NATIONALISM; FEMINISM; MEN-
  DELSSOHN; box at PROTESTANTISM;
  PURITANISM; RACE AND RACISM;
  RADICALISM
Sephardim. See box at JUDAISM
SET THEORY
Seurat, Georges. See IMPRESSIONISM
Seventh-Day Adventists. See ADVENTISM
Sextus Empiricus. See SKEPTICISM
sexual politics. See box at FEMINISM;
  MILLETT
sexuality. See ERIKSON; FEMINISM; box at
  FEMINISM; FOUCAULT; FREUD; box at
  FREUD; JUNG; MILLETT; PSYCHOANALYSIS;
  QUEER THEORY; TANTRISM
Seymour, William J. See PENTECOSTALISM
sfumato. See LEONARDO DA VINCI
shahadah. See box at ISLAM (Five Pillars)
Shakers. See UTOPIANISM
Shakespeare, William. See STURM UND
  DRANG; UNITIES
shakti. See HINDUISM; TANTRISM
Shakyamuni. See BUDDHA
SHAMANISM
Shango. See box at AFRICAN RELIGIONS
  (New World)

Shankara. See ELEMENTS; box at HINDUISM
  (schools)
Shannon, Claude. See INFORMATION
  THEORY
shari'ah. See FUNDAMENTALISM; ISLAM
Shelley, Mary Wollstonecraft. See
  WOLLSTONECRAFT
Shelley, Percy Bysshe. See ROMANTICISM
Shi'ism. See box at ISLAM; see also BAHA'I;
  FUNDAMENTALISM
SHINTO
Shiva. See HINDUISM; TANTRISM
Sholokhov, Mikhail. See SOCIALIST REALISM
Shostakovitch, Dmitri. See SOCIALIST
  REALISM
shunyata. See SUNYATA
Shvetambara. See JAINISM
Siddhartha Gautama. See BUDDHA
Siger of Brabant. See IBN RUSHD
signifier, signified. See SEMIOTICS; box at
  STRUCTURALISM
sign. See SEMIOTICS; see also
  DECONSTRUCTION; STRUCTURALISM
SIKHISM
Simeon bar Yohai. See LUKÁCS
Simons, Menno. See box at
  PROTESTANTISM
simulation. See BAUDRILLARD
Sinclair, Upton. See PROGRESSIVISM
Singer, Peter. See ANIMAL RIGHTS
Sisley, Alfred. See IMPRESSIONISM
Sita. See HINDUISM
skandhas. See BUDDHISM
SKEPTICISM
Skinner, B. F. See BEHAVIORISM;
  CONDITIONING
slave morality. See NIETZSCHE; see also
  HEGEL
slavery. See box at AFRICAN RELIGIONS
  (New World); ARISTOTLE; BLACK
  MUSLIMS; CASTE; CIVIL DISOBEDIENCE;
  DEMOCRACY; DIALECTIC; DOUGLASS;
  EPICUREANISM; EQUALITY; HEGEL;
  JACKSONIAN DEMOCRACY; JEFFERSON;
  JUDAISM; MARX; NIETZSCHE; PLATO;
  RACE AND RACISM; RASTAFARIANISM;
  RIGHTS; SOVEREIGNTY; STATES' RIGHTS;
  WASHINGTON; WHIGS AND TORIES

SMITH, ADAM

Smith, Joseph. See MORMONISM

Smuts, Jan. See HOLISM

Smyth, John. See box at PROTESTANTISM

SOCIAL CHOICE

SOCIAL CONSTRUCTIONISM

social constructivism. See SOCIAL
    CONSTRUCTIONISM

SOCIAL CONTRACT

SOCIAL DARWINISM

social democracy. See box at DEMOCRACY

SOCIAL LEARNING THEORY

social welfare function. See SOCIAL CHOICE

SOCIALISM

SOCIALIST REALISM

Socianism. See box at PROTESTANTISM

Society of Jesus. See ROMAN CATHOLICISM

sociobiology. See BIOLOGICAL DETERMINISM

SOCRATES

SOLIPSISM

Solzhenitsyn, Aleksandr. See SOCIALIST
    REALISM

SOPHISTS

Sophocles. See ARISTOTLE

sorcery. See AFRICAN RELIGIONS;
    WITCHCRAFT

Sorel, Georges. See FASCISM

SOUL AND SPIRIT

SOVEREIGNTY

Soyinka, Wole. See NÉGRITUDE;
    POSTCOLONIAL THEORY

Sozzini, Fausto and Lelio. See box at
    PROTESTANTISM

space-time. See RELATIVITY; see also
    EINSTEIN; PARAPSYCHOLOGY

speech-act theory. See ORDINARY
    LANGUAGE PHILOSOPHY

Spencer, Herbert. See SOCIAL DARWINISM;
    see also FUNCTIONALISM; PROGRESS;
    UTILITARIANISM; VIRTUE

sphere of influence. See FIELD THEORY;
    INTERNATIONALISM; MANIFEST DESTINY;
    MONROE DOCTRINE

SPINOZA, BARUCH

spirit. See SOUL AND SPIRIT

spirit possession. See AFRICAN RELIGIONS;
    box at AFRICAN RELIGIONS (New World);
    SHAMANISM

spiritism. See SPIRITUALISM

spirits. See AFRICAN RELIGIONS; box at
    AFRICAN RELIGIONS (New World);
    ANIMISM; NORTH AMERICAN NATIVE
    BELIEFS; PARAPSYCHOLOGY; SHAMANISM;
    SHINTO; SOUL AND SPIRIT; SPIRITUALISM;
    TAOISM; TOTEMISM; WITCHCRAFT;
    ZOROASTRIANISM

Spiritual Science. See ANTHROPOSOPHY

SPIRITUALISM

spirituality. See AFRICAN RELIGIONS; boxes at
    AFRICAN RELIGIONS; ANTHROPOSOPHY;
    ASCETICISM; AUGUSTINE; BUDDHISM;
    CHRISTIANITY; CHRISTIAN SCIENCE;
    EMERSON; EXPRESSIONISM; GANDHI;
    GNOSTICISM; GODDESS WORSHIP;
    HASIDISM; HINDUISM; boxes at HINDUISM;
    ISLAM; JUDAISM; MYSTICISM; NEW AGE;
    ORTHODOX CHURCH; PAGANISM;
    PENTECOSTALISM; PROTESTANTISM;
    SCIENTOLOGY; SHAMANISM; SOUL AND
    SPIRIT; TANTRISM; TAOISM; THEOSOPHY;
    TOTEMISM; WITCHCRAFT; YOGA

spissitude. See MIND/BODY PROBLEM

Spivak, Gayatri Chakravorty. See
    POSTCOLONIAL THEORY

splitting. See OBJECT RELATIONS THEORY

SPONTANEOUS GENERATION AND BIOGENESIS

stages of human/historical development,
    theories of. See COMTE; ERIKSON; box
    at FREUD; HEGEL; KIERKEGAARD; MARX;
    PARADIGM; PIAGET

Stalin, Joseph; Stalinism. See ARENDT;
    COMMUNISM; LENIN; MAO; MERLEAU-
    PONTY; SOCIALIST REALISM; TROTSKY

STANDARD MODEL

Stanislavski, Constantin. See REALISM

STANTON, ELIZABETH CADY

Stanton, Henry Brewster. See STANTON

stare decisis. See COMMON LAW

Starhawk. See WITCHCRAFT

STATE

state of nature. See SOCIAL CONTRACT; see
    also FREEDOM; HOBBES; ROUSSEAU; STATE

state socialism. See COMMUNISM

STATES' RIGHTS

statism. See STATE

steady-state theory. See EXPANDING UNIVERSE

Steffens, Lincoln. See PROGRESSIVISM

Steiner, Rudolf. See ANTHROPOSOPHY

Stella, Frank. See box at ABSTRACTION

Stijl, de. See box at ABSTRACTION;
    CONSTRUCTIVISM

stimulus and response. See
    CONDITIONING; see also SOCIAL
    LEARNING THEORY

Stirner, Max. See HEGEL

STOICISM

Stoppard, Tom. See quotation at
    DEMOCRACY

strange attractors. See CHAOS THEORY

Stravinsky, Igor. See MODERNISM

Strawson, P. F. See TRUTH

STREAM OF CONSCIOUSNESS

Strindberg, August. See EXPRESSIONISM

structural-functionalism. See SYSTEMS
    THEORY; FUNCTIONALISM

STRUCTURALISM

STURM UND DRANG

sub specie aeternitatis. See SPINOZA

subconscious. See UNCONSCIOUS; see also
    GRAMMAR; SCIENTOLOGY; box at
    STRUCTURALISM; SURREALISM;
    SYMBOLISM

subject and object. See ALIENATION;
    BEAUVOIR; EPISTEMOLOGY; IDEALISM;
    MERLEAU-PONTY; OBJECTIVISM AND
    SUBJECTIVISM; PHENOMENOLOGY; RORTY;
    RUSSELL

subjectivism. See OBJECTIVISM AND
    SUBJECTIVISM

sublation. See HEGEL

sublimation. See FREUD

SUBSTANCE

sufficient reason, principle of. See
    LEIBNIZ; see also box at LOGIC

suffrage. See DEMOCRACY; DOUGLASS;
    EQUALITY; FEMINISM; JACKSONIAN
    DEMOCRACY; MILL; RADICALISM; STANTON

SUFISM

Sukarno. See box at DEMOCRACY

Sullivan, Arthur. See AESTHETICISM

Sullivan, Harry Stack. See FREUD;
    PSYCHOANALYSIS

Sullivan, Louis. See FUNCTIONALISM;
    MODERNISM

Sumner, William Graham. See
    ETHNOCENTRISM; SOCIAL DARWINISM

sunnah. See ISLAM

Sunnism. See box at ISLAM

SUNYATA

superego. See FREUD; PSYCHOANALYSIS

superman. See FASCISM; NIETZSCHE

superstring theory. See FIELD THEORY;
    STANDARD MODEL

superstructure. See GRAMSCI; IDEOLOGY;
    MARX; box at STRUCTURALISM

SUPPLY AND DEMAND

SUPPLY-SIDE ECONOMICS

suprematism. See box at ABSTRACTION

surplus value. See MARX

SURREALISM

survival of the fittest. See SOCIAL
    DARWINISM

suspension of disbelief. See AESTHETICS

SUSTAINABLE DEVELOPMENT

Suzuki, D. T. See box at BUDDHISM

swadeshi. See GANDHI

swaraj. See GANDHI

Swedenborg, Emmanuel. See
    SPIRITUALISM; SYMBOLISM

syllogism. See ARISTOTLE; DEDUCTION AND
    INDUCTION; LOGIC

symbol. See SYMBOLISM; see also SEMIOTICS

SYMBOLISM

symmetry. See CONSERVATION AND
    SYMMETRY

synchronicity. See PARAPSYCHOLOGY

syndicalism. See ANARCHISM; see also
    FASCISM

synesthesia. See SYMBOLISM

syntactics. See CHOMSKY; SEMIOTICS

synthesis. See DIALECTIC; DIALECTICAL
    MATERIALISM; HEGEL

SYSTEMS THEORY

Szasz, Thomas. See FOUCAULT

T'ien Ming. See CONFUCIANISM

taboo. See FREUD; TANTRISM; TOTEMISM

tabula rasa. See LOCKE

tachisme. See box at ABSTRACTION

Taft, William Howard. See PROGRESSIVISM

Talmud. See JUDAISM; see also KABBALAH;
    MAIMONIDES; TORAH

TANTRISM

Tao Te Ching. See TAOISM

TAOISM

Tarski, Alfred. See TRUTH

Tatlin, Vladimir. See CONSTRUCTIVISM

TAXATION

Taylor, Zachary. See WHIGS AND TORIES

TELEOLOGY

telepathy. See PARAPSYCHOLOGY

temperance. See ASCETICISM;
    EPICUREANISM; PLATO; box at
    PROTESTANTISM; PURITANISM; VIRTUE

TEN COMMANDMENTS, THE

Terra. See GODDESS WORSHIP

Tertullian. See ABSURD; GNOSTICISM;
    PAGANISM

Thales. See ELEMENTS

Thanatos. See FREUD

Thatcher, Margaret. See SUPPLY-SIDE
    ECONOMICS

theology, natural. See NATURAL THEOLOGY

THEOSOPHY

THERMODYNAMICS, LAWS OF

thesis, antithesis, synthesis. See DIALECTIC;
    DIALECTICAL MATERIALISM; HEGEL

Thetans. See SCIENTOLOGY

Thomas Aquinas. See AQUINAS

THOREAU, HENRY DAVID

Thrasymachus. See SOPHISTS

Thurmond, Strom. See STATES' RIGHTS

Tibetan Buddhism. See box at
    BUDDHISM

tirthankara. See JAINISM

TOCQUEVILLE, ALEXIS DE

Tolman, Edward Chase. See COGNITIVE
    PSYCHOLOGY

Tolstoy, Leo. See GANDHI

TORAH

Tore. See ANIMISM

Tories. See WHIGS AND TORIES

TOTALITARIANISM

TOTEMISM

Transcendental Meditation. See box at
    HINDUISM (modern movements)

TRANSCENDENTALISM

transference. See PSYCHOANALYSIS

transitivity. See SOCIAL CHOICE

TRANSPERSONAL PSYCHOLOGY

transubstantiation. See box at
    CHRISTIANITY; ROMAN CATHOLICISM

transvaluation of values. See NIETZSCHE

trickle-down theory. See SUPPLY-SIDE
    ECONOMICS

Trickster. See AFRICAN RELIGIONS

Trimurti. See HINDUISM

TRINITY, TRINITARIANISM

TROTSKY, LEON

Truman, Harry S. See PROGRESSIVISM

TRUTH

truth, contingent and necessary. See
    FOUCAULT; box at KANT; RATIONALISM

Tsongkhapa Lozang Dragpa. See box at
    BUDDHISM

Tsu Ssu. See MEAN

Tullock, Gordon. See PUBLIC CHOICE

Turgenev, Ivan. See NIHILISM

Turing, Alan. See ARTIFICIAL INTELLIGENCE

Twelvers. See box at ISLAM (Sunnis and
    Shi'ites)

twin paradox. See RELATIVITY

two truths doctrine. See SUNYATA

Tylor, Edward B. See ANIMISM

types, theory of. See box at RUSSELL

tyranny of the majority. See
    TOCQUEVILLE

Tzara, Tristan. See DADA

Übermensch. See FASCISM; NIETZSCHE

Umbanda. See box at AFRICAN RELIGIONS
    (New World)

Unamuno, Miguel de. See ORTEGA Y
    GASSET

UNCERTAINTY PRINCIPLE

UNCONSCIOUS, THE

underworld. See SHAMANISM; SHINTO

unified field theory. See FIELD THEORY;
    STANDARD MODEL

uniformitarianism. See CATASTROPHISM
    AND UNIFORMITARIANISM

UNINTENDED CONSEQUENCES

Unitarianism. See box at PROTESTANTISM;
    see also TRINITY

UNITIES, THE THREE

unity of opposites. See DIALECTIC;
    DIALECTICAL MATERIALISM; MAO; YIN AND
    YANG

universal pragmatics. See box at CRITICAL
    THEORY
Universal Church of the Master. See
    SPIRITUALISM
Universal Declaration of Human Rights.
    See RIGHTS
Universalism. See box at PROTESTANTISM
UNIVERSALS
Untouchables. See CASTE
Upanishads. See HINDUISM
UTILITARIANISM
UTILITY
UTOPIANISM

Vaiseshika. See box at HINDUISM (schools)
Vaishnavism. See HINDUISM
Vajrayana. See TANTRISM
Valéry, Paul. See SYMBOLISM
value-added tax. See TAXATION
value-freedom. See WEBER
values. See CYNICISM; DESCRIPTIVISM AND
    PRESCRIPTIVISM; ETHICS; IDEOLOGY;
    IS/OUGHT PROBLEM; NIETZSCHE;
    OBJECTIVISM AND SUBJECTIVISM; RELATIVISM
Vanzetti, Bartolomeo. See ANARCHISM
Vardhamana. See JAINISM
Vasarely, Victor. See box at ABSTRACTION
Vatican II. See box at ROMAN
    CATHOLICISM
Vauxcelles, Louis. See CUBISM; FAUVISM
Veblen, Thorsten. See box at CLASS
Vedanta, Vedas. See HINDUISM; box at
    HINDUISM (schools); see also ELEMENTS
VERIFIABILITY AND FALSIFIABILITY
    (verification and falsification)
Verlaine, Paul. See SYMBOLISM
Verstehen. See WEBER
Vesalius, Andreas. See HIPPOCRATES
Vienna Circle. See LOGICAL POSITIVISM
virtù. See MACHIAVELLI
VIRTUE
Vishnu. See HINDUISM
vision quest. See NORTH AMERICAN NATIVE
    BELIEFS
VITALISM
VOLTAIRE
vortex theory. See DESCARTES; MIND/BODY
    PROBLEM

Vygotsky, Lev. See SOCIAL
    CONSTRUCTIONISM

Wagner, Richard. See FASCISM; NIETZSCHE
Walcott, Derek. See NÉGRITUDE
Waldorf movement. See ANTHROPOSOPHY
Wallace, Alfred Russel. See EVOLUTION
Wallace, George. See STATES' RIGHTS
Wallace, Henry A. See PROGRESSIVISM
Wang Yang Ming. See CONFUCIANISM
Wanniski, Jude. See box at SUPPLY-SIDE
    ECONOMICS
war crimes. See JUST WAR
WASHINGTON, BOOKER T.
Washington, George. See FEDERALISM;
    FREEMASONRY; PAINE
Watson, James D. See CENTRAL DOGMA
Watson, John B. See BEHAVIORISM
Watts, Alan. See box at BUDDHISM
WAVE-PARTICLE DUALITY
wealth, distribution and redistribution
    of. See box at DEMOCRACY; EQUALITY;
    MARX; POPULISM; RAWLS; SOCIALISM;
    TAXATION; WELFARE
WEBER, MAX
Weber, Max. See EXPRESSIONISM
Webster, Daniel. See WHIGS AND
    TORIES
Wedekind, Frank. See EXPRESSIONISM
Weismann, August. See CENTRAL DOGMA;
    LAMARCKISM
Weizmann, Chaim. See ZIONISM
WELFARE
Wells, H. G. See box at UTOPIANISM
Wertheimer, Max. See GESTALT
Wesley, John. See box at PROTESTANTISM
West, Rebecca. See quotation at FEMINISM
Westminster Confession. See box at
    PROTESTANTISM
Wheeler, John. See RELATIVITY
WHIGS AND TORIES
White, Ellen Gould. See ADVENTISM
Whitehead, Alfred North. See BEING
    AND BECOMING; FORMALISM; LOGIC;
    PROCESS PHILOSOPHY/THEOLOGY;
    RATIONALISM; RUSSELL; SET
    THEORY; see also quotation
    at PLATO

Whorf, Benjamin Lee. See SAPIR-WHORF
   HYPOTHESIS
Wicca. See WITCHCRAFT; see also
   SPIRITUALISM
Wiener, Norbert. See CYBERNETICS
Wilde, Oscar. See AESTHETICISM
will, human. See AUGUSTINE; FREEDOM;
   KANT; LOCKE; NIETZSCHE; PESSIMISM;
   PHENOMENOLOGY; ROUSSEAU; SOCIAL
   CONTRACT
will, divine. See ABSOLUTISM; BAHA'I;
   CHRISTIANITY; ETHICS; FUNDAMENTALISM;
   ISLAM; JUDAISM; NATURAL LAW; PASCAL;
   PREDESTINATION; ROMAN CATHOLICISM;
   STOICISM; SUFISM; TORAH
will to believe. See JAMES
WILL TO POWER
William of Ockham. See NOMINALISM; box
   at NOMINALISM; SCHOLASTICISM; SOCIAL
   CONTRACT; UNIVERSALS
Williams, Raymond. See CULTURAL
   MATERIALISM
Wilson, Arno. See BIG BANG
Wilson, Edward O. See BIOLOGICAL
   DETERMINISM
Wilson, Woodrow. See PROGRESSIVISM
Wimsatt, W. K. See NEW CRITICISM
Winnicott, Donald W. See OBJECT
   RELATIONS THEORY
Winters, Yvor. See NEW CRITICISM
wisdom. See VIRTUE
WITCHCRAFT
WITTGENSTEIN, LUDWIG JOSEF JOHANN
Wöhler, Friedrich. See VITALISM
Wolff, Christian. See MONISM
WOLLSTONECRAFT, MARY
womanism. See FEMINISM
women's liberation movement. See
   FEMINISM
Woolf, Virginia. See MODERNISM; STREAM
   OF CONSCIOUSNESS
Wordsworth, William. See EMERSON;
   ROMANTICISM
working class (see proletariat)

World of Forms. See PLATO; see also
   IDEALISM; INNATE IDEAS; UNCONSCIOUS
world soul. See ANIMISM; NEOPLATONISM;
   SOUL AND SPIRIT; SPIRITUALISM
World Year. See ETERNAL RECURRENCE;
   STOICISM
Wovoka. See Ghost Dance
Wright, Frank Lloyd. See MODERNISM
wu-wei. See TAOISM

Xango. See box at AFRICAN RELIGIONS
   (New World)

Yama. See YOGA
yasna. See ZOROASTRIANISM
Yeats, William Butler. See SYMBOLISM
Yeltsin, Boris. See PERESTROIKA
YIN AND YANG
YOGA
Yoga Darshana. See box at HINDUISM
   (schools)
Young, Brigham. See MORMONISM
Young Hegelians. See HEGEL; MARX

Zamyatin, Yevgeny. See box at UTOPIANISM
Zarathushtra. See ZOROASTRIANISM
zeitgeist. See SOUL AND SPIRIT
Zemelo, Ernst. See SET THEORY
Zen Buddhism. See box at BUDDHISM
Zeno of Citium. See STOICISM
Zeno of Elea. See ZENO'S PARADOXES
ZENO'S PARADOXES
zero population growth. See MALTHUSIAN
   POPULATION THEORY
zero-sum game. See GAME THEORY
ZIONISM
zodiac. See ASTROLOGY
Zohar. See KABBALAH
Zola, Émile. See NATURALISM; REALISM
zombies. See box at AFRICAN RELIGIONS
   (New World)
Zoroaster. See ZOROASTRIANISM
ZOROASTRIANISM
Zwingli, Huldreich. See PROTESTANTISM

About the Author

CHRIS ROHMANN was raised in the college town of Yellow Springs, Ohio, and educated at Brandeis University, but became a student of ideas only after a fifteen-year musical career—first as composer for the social-activist New York Free Theater, then as a singer-songwriter based in London, England. Since the mid-1980s he has worked as a freelance author, drama critic, and editor of academic and trade books. He was co-compiler, with Jane Davidson Reid, of *The Oxford Guide to Classical Mythology in the Arts*. He lives in Northampton, Massachusetts, and is an officer in the National Writers Union.

WATERFORD CITY AND COUNTY
WITHDRAWN
LIBRARIES